Folk Art

Fish Decoys

With Values

Donald J. Petersen

Schiffer Publishing Ltd

77 Lower Valley Road, Atglen, PA 19310

Printed in China

ISBN: 0-7643-0053-9

Library of Congress Cataloging-in-Publication Data

Petersen, Donald J.
Folk art fish decoys with values/Donald J. Petersen.
p. cm.
Includes bibliographical references and index.
ISBN 0-7643-0053-9 (hard)
1. Fish decoys--Collectors and collecting. 2. Spear fishing--Equipment and supplies. I. Title.
SH451.3.P47 1996
745.593'6--dc20 96-28227
CIP

Published by Schiffer Publishing, Ltd.
77 Lower Valley Road
Atglen, PA 19310
Phone: (610) 593-1777
Fax: (610) 593-2002
Please write for a free catalog.
This book may be purchased from the publisher.
Please include $2.95 for shipping.
Try your bookstore first.

We are interested in hearing from authors
with book ideas on related subjects.

CONTENTS

DEDICATION

To my beautiful wife, Sandy, without whose love, patience, and encouragement this book would never have been completed.

DARK HOUSE

It was just ten years ago that my son Bob came home to catch the feeling of the Minnesota-Ontario border country in mid-winter. He wanted, above all, to sit in a "dark house" with me again and watch the circling decoy and the scene below the ice. He wanted time to think long thoughts and hear the whispering of the snow outside the thin, tarpaper walls. He wanted the good feeling he used to know at night after a long day on skis, and perhaps the taste of a fish fresh from the icy waters of the lakes of the north.

So, one morning in January, though it was twenty below, we took off for the old haunts. The ski harnesses creaked as we pushed across the lower reaches of Fall Lake. Smoke rose straight above the chimneys in the little town of Winton at the end of the road and golden sun dogs* blazed over the horizon. It was far too cold to travel slowly. We pushed hard on our sticks, and the skis hissed over the powder-dry snow. We were the only ones abroad, the only ones foolish enough to be outside when we did not have to be. Still, fresh deer tracks crossed the lake, and on the portage into Cedar there were signs of rabbits, weasels, and mice.

A tiny tarpaper shack off the end of a long point was our goal. A friend had set it up weeks ago, told us where the spear was cached and the wooden decoy. For its use, we were to bring him a fish. That meant we had to take two. We shoveled the snow away from the door, fanned a flame to life in the little stove, and dug the spear and the decoy out of a drift.

Six inches of ice had to be cut out of the hole. We filled the coffeepot, closed the door, and settled down to wait. Outside the wind howled, but the little shelter was cozy and warm. At first we could see nothing but the green translucent water, but gradually our vision cleared and we could see farther and farther into the depths, finally to the very bottom itself. Light streamed through the snow and ice, and the bottom all but glowed.

In our field of vision were several whitish rocks and bits of shell, important landmarks of the scene. Soon eel grass and feathery milfoil emerged in the half-light, weaving slowly in the slight current of the narrows. The rocks and shells became as familiar as though we had been watching them for weeks, the tufts of waving grass as outstanding as trees in a meadow. In one corner was a clam, its narrow furrow distinct and sharp in the sand. A shaft of light angled over our hunting ground, light reflected through flashing prisms of ice. The stage was set for action. This was worth the cold trek out, compensation for weeks of waiting; it was a scene of stark beauty and suspense such as the most elaborate stage setting has never attained.

The spear rested easily against the inside edge of the ice, its handle free and ready to grasp, a cord fastened to Bob's wrist. Occasionally he shifted the point of a tine before it became too firmly embedded in its notch, twisted it slightly so that when the great moment came there would be no resistance, no wrenching free, nothing to interfere with the thrust. When the time came, the strike must be made with lightning speed.

I played the decoy, a six inch model of a sucker minnow replete with fins and tail of shining tin. Whittled from a piece of cedar, it was weighted with lead and hung from the end of a string. Its tail was set so that with each motion of my hand it made wide and beautiful circles all around the hole.

As the coffee began to simmer, we shed outer jackets and mitts. Outside, it was still close to twenty below and the snow was whispering as Bob had hoped. After an hour of tension we began to relax, talked quietly about many things. A fish house is a fine place for visiting — not for arguments or weighty ideas, but rather for small talk, local politics and gossip, things we had seen coming in, ideas that required no effort, short simple thoughts that came as easily as breathing. Furthermore, our energies must be conserved for the moment when the flash of a silver side below would eclipse everything else in the world.

"A northern pike will taste pretty good tonight," I said.

"Would taste pretty good" was Bob's reply.

"We'll clean it before it freezes," I said. "Save us the job when we get home."

"See that clam?" said Bob. "It's moving toward the outside of the hole. Getting out of the way while there's time."

*Spots of color, sometimes resembling miniature suns, seen one on either side of the sun when, in very cold weather, it shines through ice crystals in the atmosphere.

"Those deer tracks this morning looked as though they'd been chased. Twenty feet at a jump for a while."

"Heading for the cedar on the south shore, really making time."

The small talk went on and on, and after a while there was nothing more to say and we lapsed into quiet, just sat and stared into the hole, watching the rhythmic turns of the little decoy, back and forth, around and around, its metal fins flashing in the light. After a time our vision blended with the bottom itself and we began to feel as though we were a part of the subterranean world below us, part of the clean sand, the white rocks, the waving eel grass. We became intimately familiar with each irregularity of the bottom, the ripple marks, the moving habits of each blade of grass, the air bubbles at the edge of the ice, even the shadows of clouds drifting by outside. Two hours went by and our senses all but fused with the blue-green environment below.

Then, when we had begun to feel as though nothing could ever change, as though we might have been sitting in that same position for years, a huge torpedolike shape slipped swiftly into the open and the static little world we had created exploded before our eyes. The grasses waved erratically, the white rocks disappeared, the water roiled.

The spear! screamed everything within us. Slowly - so slowly - cramped senses became aware, muscles began to move. As in a dream, fingers tightened around the cold, heavy steel; the point, withdrawn from its icy notch, hung poised, ready to strike. Directly below lay the long, dark form of a great northern pike, its fins and tail moving slowly, its gill covers opening and closing with barely perceptible motion.

"Now!" came the shout, and suddenly the spear plunged downward, and in a violent instant the water boiled and the fish, the rocks, and the weeds disappeared in a green-white turmoil of confusion.

The spear and the fish came out of the hole in a cascade of water. I pushed out the door and we stumbled outside into the brilliant dazzle of sunlight on the snow, shouting, laughing at our good fortune, pounding each other on the back. This was a pinnacle of experience, and during that instant it seemed that few triumphs in the world of men could compare with it.

The pike stopped its thrashing at last and began to stiffen in the cold. We stepped back through the little door into quiet and darkness once more.

Finally the water cleared, and we could now see fresh scales on the bottom. The eel grass and milfoil were waving once more, and there again were the identical rocks and the whitened bits of shell. Even the clam was in the same position, working its way slowly toward the outside perimeter of our field. It seemed impossible that things could be the same after the violent eruption of a short time ago. But nothing had changed at all - a few more air bubbles under the ice, the scattered scales on the sand. Again the rhythmic turns of the decoy, around and around and around, its silver fins flashing in the light. The spear point wore itself down into another icy notch.

"That's one," said Bob. "That one goes to the house."

"The next one is ours," I answered, "the one we'll clean for supper."

Again the scene became familiar, and soon we were finished talking, just sitting there watching and waiting as men have watched and waited since the beginning of time. The drifting snow whispered and swirled around our little house.

A shadow crossed one corner and the waving grasses trembled slightly, bowed gently toward the movement, came back to their old positions. The spear was loosened from its notch. At that moment the whole civilized world moved back to where it belonged, faded into a background that was nothing compared to the tremendous event taking place before our eyes. The grasses trembled as though expecting something to happen. The water itself seemed charged.

Then the shadow returned and another pike lay directly below us, so close and real our numbed senses could not grasp what had actually happened. Its fins were moving slowly, its gills opening and closing. It lay there quietly looking at the decoy quivering at the end of its string.

The spear was withdrawn and with a single movement plunged into the water. Again the white-and-green turmoil, the open door and the sunshine.

We had enough: one for the house and one for our supper. We cached the spear and decoy, closed the door, and started off for home. It was a little warmer now and the skis slid smoothly over the trail we had made that morning. The west was orange and mauve and apple green, and the birches shone silver in the last level rays of the sun. By the time we reached the portage it was dusk and the afterglow burned behind the black masses of pine and spruce.

When we reached Fall Lake we could see the lights of the village at the end of the bay. Smoke still rose straight above the chimneys. With the dark it would be twenty below again, and in the morning the sun dogs would be out. The ice would soon be thick over the hole we had cut, and the tarpaper shack would be cold and dark. The grasses tremble on the bottom, and the clam would plow its furrow unseen and undisturbed.

Sigurd F. Olson, *Sigurd F. Olson's Wilderness Days,* New York, Alfred A. Knoff, 1972, pp. 209-214.

FOREWORD

Sigurd Olson's wonderful description of a day of Minnesota spear fishing helps explain why the technique has survived the hundreds of years that it has been practiced. Not every fisherman has tried spear fishing, and not all who have attempted it, like it. However, for those who enjoy spearing, the fascination reaches almost cult proportions. Over the years a kind of tradition and lore of the sport has been passed down from father to son including the individual techniques (and tricks) of spearing, as well as the decoys and other equipment associated with it, such as ice augers, the spear, ice saws, etc., many of which were "homemade."

Briefly, spear fishing, for those who have not tried it before, involves selecting a suitable location on the ice covering a lake; cutting a hole in the ice; placing a dark house or shanty [without windows] over the hole so that the fisherman can see into the water by the light through the ice, but outside light is eliminated inside the shanty [just as a person in a dark room can see outside into the light, but an individual who is outside cannot see into the darkened room]; working a wooden decoy that has been leaded so that it sinks in the water, in order to attract a large fish; and then spearing the fish that comes into the water below the hole to peer at the decoy. Decoys may be painted or unpainted, but some have been known to have been decorated with bits of mirrors, bright tin, feathers, etc., in an attempt to attract a fish and draw the prey into the hole.

In the past 15 years particularly, spear fishing decoys have achieved popularity as folk art, perhaps the last truly American folk art, and have also emerged as highly desired collectibles. Yet, there have been few systematic attempts to study fishing decoys, and so collectors interested in them have been largely "left in the dark." In such a situation, not only is there a dearth of information, but what information is available sometimes is not accurate.

This book does not pretend to be encyclopedic. Much of what is discussed regarding the history and techniques of spear fishing [not to mention collecting considerations] apply to all spear fishing states and collectors; however, the focus here is on the spear fishing decoys of Minnesota. Accuracy became the watchword for this book. Information provided by others was always verified by interviews with the decoy maker, and in the case of deceased decoy makers, with members of the immediate family and/or with the Minnesota Department of Public Health, Vital Statistics Section. Nevertheless, interview data were compared to previously verified information. For example, I was told by one informant that a particular decoy was made by his "brother." Recognizing the decoy as one made by Harry Sandell, I asked the informant if his brother's name was Harry Sandell, but he replied that it was not.

One book that deals with fishing decoys provides names of decoy makers along with pictures of the makers' fish decoys. This information has frequently been recanted by the authors. They seem to have the notion that if their information is wrong, someone will correct it. However, information that is provided as authoritative and then recanted, can prove confusing and mischievous to collectors and dealers in decoys alike. Rather than chance offering a name of a decoy maker in the *hope* of being correct, I have opted to reduce the scope of this book to Minnesota makers who *actually* made the decoys. This book provides birth and death statistics in order to allow collectors the possibility of setting a time frame as to when the majority of a maker's decoys were completed [or at least a time after which they could not possibly have been made]. Also, some of the personal history of each maker is provided.

Moreover, this book does not attempt to include all Minnesota decoy makers and their decoys, even when attribution has been authoritatively established. Some makers have been excluded because their decoys were too crudely made and were lacking in any artistic value. While decoys [at least the old ones] were made and judged by their maker in utilitarian terms, i.e., did they attract fish or not, collectors and dealers pay special homage to a decoy's artistic qualities [among other criteria]. This, of course, is what makes folk art what it is—folk art. It is the decoration of a utilitarian or religious item that is no longer judged on the basis of its originally intended purpose, but rather on eye appeal.

I have further chosen to separate Minnesota contemporary makers of fish decoys from those of the "old time" makers. This division is, admittedly, sometimes arbitrary because the "old timers" may, in some cases, still be making decoys for their own use or for resale. Including contemporary makers with old time fish decoy makers would be confusing to the readers because it may be difficult to differentiate those decoys which are old from those which have been recently made. Another book dealing with spear fishing decoys indicates some decoy makers as "deceased," leaving the reader to wonder whether the makers who are not so indicated are still alive. I have, instead, indicated birth dates and death dates as appropriate. The absence of a maker's date of death indicates that he or she was alive at the time of the writing of this book.

Another feature of this book is the chapter dealing with Minnesota spear makers. Because virtually every town in earlier days sported at least one blacksmith, and because so many of these blacksmiths who made spears were dead long ago, background information regarding these makers was more difficult to obtain than that of decoy makers. I resisted the temptation, however, to simply tie a name to a spear until or unless the information could be verified. The chapter also includes examples of jigging sticks and fish decoy boxes, subject matter which is unique to this book.

It is the primary purpose of this book to review the known decoy makers from the state of Minnesota as an aid to collectors and/or dealers who wish to make proper identification of decoy examples. I also was concerned that if the history of the makers was not preserved now, the information might be lost forever. Much historical damage has already been done by "pickers" (individuals who buy decoys for resale from the individuals owning them) who failed to gather any data when buying fish decoys. Thus, in some cases, the name of the maker or even the town or area from which the decoys were purchased is not known. I have included pictures of fish decoys that have no maker-attribution at the present time, even though several examples of the decoys exist, in the hope that readers will be prompted to provide information regarding these "unknowns." This information can then be verified or refuted. Research is ongoing and my hope is that more data will be available in the future. Readers are encouraged to write the undersigned regarding information that they may possess relative to the decoys designated as "unknown." My address is given below.

It is hoped that this book will serve as a frequently consulted source for both new and established fish decoy enthusiasts.

Donald J. Petersen, Ph.D.
Loyola University Chicago
820 North Michigan
Chicago, IL 60611
(312) 915-6542

CHAPTER I

COLLECTING SPEAR FISHING DECOYS

Spear fishing is currently permitted in six states: Alaska, Michigan, Minnesota, Montana, South Dakota and Wisconsin.[1] Fishing decoys have emerged in the 1990's as one of the most desirable art form collectibles. Ironically, unlike some art objects, such as furniture, which was specifically made with beauty along with a utilitarian purpose in mind, fishing decoys were judged by their makers primarily on the basis of performance. Old informants would sometimes reach down into their decoy or tackle boxes, pick up an aesthetically "ugly" decoy, and then begin to extol the virtues of its powers of attraction. Thus, it must be constantly borne in mind that the vast majority of the fish decoy makers did not have the "art" or beauty of their craft as their foremost thought, only the results. Nevertheless, without any formal training, decoy makers created some beautifully carved and painted "works of art." Often, but not always, the maker who fashioned his decoys to sell to others (as well as for his own use) reached the highest art levels (see e.g., the decoys of the Faue brothers, Leroy Howell, Pearl Bethel, Harry Sandell, etc.).

This book focuses on the decoys and makers from Minnesota. It is currently the state which embraces the majority of spear fishing activity.

Interest in fish decoys and their prices[2] by collectors and antique dealers is reflected in the increasing number of articles regarding the subject, many of these in "popular" journals and not just fishing magazines.[3] In addition, one even notices fish decoys in advertisements for fine interior decoration as well as for country decoration.[4]

Collecting Fish Decoys

For the individual wishing to begin a collection of fish decoys at the present time, he or she is starting at a point which might be described as the "middle era." Fifteen to 20 years ago, one would have noticed raised eyebrows [at the minimum], and would probably have received a "what's a fish decoy?" response to an inquiry regarding spearing decoys, at least among the general public, and perhaps even with many antique dealers. Decoys were plentiful in the late 1970's and early 1980's, and could be found in rummage and garage sales in Minnesota and other northern Great Lakes states. Virtually no one placed any value on them and they could be obtained for a few dollars. Some individuals had the foresight to see the fish decoy as a piece of American folk art. They sought decoys by running ads in newspapers, "picked" them from old time spear fishermen who no longer used them, and bought them from others, such as lure collectors who had limited, if any, interest in them. Thus, great numbers of decoys are in the hands of the early ("first era") collectors.

Nevertheless, there still exists vast quantities of spearing decoys which remain stored in garages, basements, sheds, attics, dark houses, and elsewhere. It is also possible to obtain decoys from other collectors who have duplicates and surplus fish decoys that they wish to sell. Duck decoy collectors and fishing lure collectors are frequently willing to part with their spearing decoys in favor of cash or a duck decoy or lure that they prefer. Dealers also exist whose primary interest is to sell the fish decoys that they have amassed. The author is acquainted with individuals whose full time occupation is the collecting (picking) of fish decoys and their subsequent sale. It is wise, however, if you are going to buy from a dealer, that you know your dealer's reputation for honesty if you are unfamiliar with the fish decoys themselves.

If you are interested in "picking" fish decoys, you must be prepared to spend long hours searching, often without any luck at all. Unless you have a lead, picking is haphazard at best. The best picking is done around lakes that were favorites for spearing, or in towns in a lake region. Look for homes with fishing shacks behind them or where a fishing boat is parked outside. These will frequently indicate that a fisherman resides there. The task is made more difficult when one remembers that not all fishermen are ice fishermen and not all ice fishermen are spear fishermen, and not all spear fishermen use decoys! For instance, some spearing enthusiasts utilize live bait instead of decoys.

One of the best times to pick decoys is on a Friday or Saturday during the summer months, especially if it is a beautiful day. Then, many old-timers are outside of their house, mowing the lawn, tending the garden, and you can "pop the question," "Do you have any old spearing decoys that you want to sell?" It is easy, cruising in a car up and down the streets of a small town, to spot older people who might have the decoys with the age that you want. When you collect "fish," however, do not forget to secure the name of the individual from whom you purchased the decoy(s), the name of the maker (if different), when the maker was born, and if known, when he died; where he was born; what he did for a living; anything about his spearing techniques; construction of his decoys; etc. It is extremely important that such information be preserved.

Factors in Collecting Fishing Decoys

Telling someone which fish decoys to collect is similar to advising that person on whom to marry. The advice is sometimes not taken—and it is often not wanted. Nevertheless, I have attempted the (thankless?) task of doing just that! Various factors by which you may wish to judge an individual decoy must be weighed against your own personal taste. It is highly probable that various criteria will be taken in combination in making a final choice to buy or not to buy.

Price. Spearing decoys range in price from less than $5.00 each (if you collect them from a spear fisherman who no longer wants to keep them) to well over $5,000. The middle price range is between $50 to $350. Unless money is no object, collecting fish decoys at higher prices requires informed judgment. In general, however, one builds a collection based on quality and not quantity. It is better to have one great decoy which cost $250 than five average ones costing $50 each.

Painting. Decoys range in painting quality from the ubiquitous red heads and white bodies, to fish that are painted so realistically that the decoy appears as though it could "swim away" if placed in the water. Some collectors prefer decoys that successfully imitate the species they represent. Other decoys are abstractly painted and the species of fish is a moot point. Attention to detail and technique are also important considerations. Some fish were only carved and then varnished. They sometimes had details burned into them before varnishing and have an attractive appearance. These fish can also be abstractly done.

Carving. Naturally, the way that a fish was carved will be a major factor influencing its collectibility. Again, does the decoy closely resemble the species it represent? Are important details carved (or burned) into the fish such as a carved or opened mouth (some even had teeth carved in), gills, eyes or scales? These are some important considerations. Usually the fins were made of metal, but not always. The more detail, the higher the quality of the fish.

Eye Appeal. This is the question of your initial reaction to the fish, and may outweigh any other factor. There are no rights or wrongs here—only what strikes your fancy.

Named Carver. I was recently shown a decoy made by John Tax for sale at $400 at a flea market. The quality of the painting on the sun fish decoy was fair to poor, yet the seller was relying on the "name" value of the fish alone, because the decoy's quality did not begin to measure up to the price. There can be no doubt that name appeal will increasingly effect the value (but not the quality) of a fish. Adding to collecting confusion is the fact that some old decoys were carved and painted to resemble those made by their better known counterparts. In my opinion, it is better to have a high quality decoy by an unknown than either a poorly painted decoy or one in bad condition which was made by a "name" carver. Yet, it is likely that attributed decoys will far outstrip the others in price, given equality of condition. This latter fact reinforces the need to obtain all available information when picking decoys.

Rarity. In some cases, the decoys made by certain carvers were limited to a small number. For example, Ray Thompson carved only eight decoys. One of these recently sold to a private collector for $7,500. In other instances, rarity is understood in terms of the species that the decoy imitates. Frogs, crawdads, mice, tadpoles, and other similar "critter" decoys are scarce relative to the more usual fish decoys, and consequently may command a higher price. It is a fair estimate that for every 300 "regular" fish decoys, only one critter decoy was made. In some instances, collectors will forgive the condition of a "critter" decoy more readily than a run-of-the-mill fish. That is not to say, however, that these critter decoys do not reach great heights of artistic accomplishment.

Condition. In general, collectors prefer that the decoys be as close to original condition as possible. Practically speaking, this means no repainting—a very serious fault; no broken or missing fins or tail; no cracked or peeling paint; no cracked or broken wood bodies; and no missing eyes (if the carver used taxidermist imitation fish or bird eyes). All of these defects may drastically reduce, depending on the severity of the fault, the decoy's value.

Most carvers did not use a primer and thus frequently, paint chipping or flaking was a problem. Also, decoys were not often treated with special care, but were thrown in buckets and boxes where the fins of one decoy could chip the paint of others, etc. Adding to the condition problem is the fact that sometimes decoys were hit by the spear as the fisherman attempted to snag his prey. This unfortunate circumstance usually resulted in a good sized gouge left in the decoy. While undoubtedly adding to its realism, such a defect detracts from the decoy's value. Moreover, spear fishermen sometimes repainted decoys when the original paint was worn, or when the decoy failed to attract fish. Overpaint and repaint can be removed by acetone and/or scraping, but the results are not always pleasing. Repainted fish decoys result in a severely depressed price for them.

Age. It is safe to say that the older the fish (other things being equal), the more desirable the fish. Most available earlier decoys were made from the 1920's to the 1940's. Many more decoys have survived today from the 1950's to the 1960's. After 1970, decoys should be considered modern and were frequently made for the collectors' market.

Size. Generally, collectors will prefer a high quality large decoy to a high quality small one. Sad to say, many large decoys are of poor quality. There is no reason to shun high quality small decoys, however.

Hand made or commercially made. Most of the interest in fishing decoys centers around the hand made fish. This is strictly a matter of taste. Fishing lure (plug) collectors may prefer commercially manufactured decoys because of their interest in certain manufacturers and their predilections based on lure collecting itself.

Collecting Strategies

The above listed factors may suggest a variety of strategies that may be used in assembling a collection of fishing decoys. If financial resources are limited, it may be a worthwhile idea to specialize. For example, one could collect only those decoys made by a particular maker, or a particular species of fish such as sun fish, or only commercial decoys. On the other hand, in choosing such a plan, it is possible to overlook very good decoys that are available, while pursuing a narrow focus. Collecting fish from one state is also a way of limiting a collection, but it does not restrict one very much. Specializing in decoys from a certain area or even from a particular lake is another approach and may yield the collector important research information regarding regional influences of carvers, stylistic similarities or differences, techniques of carving, painting, etc.

Still another approach might be to collect contemporary carvers. Some of these people were carving in the 1930's and 1940's and retain much of their earlier style today. Such carvers as Gerhart Berens, Joe Leach, John Jensen, etc., have established reputations and their decoys are respected additions to any collection.

The Problem of Fakes

The bane for decoy collectors and dealers alike is the fake. Phony fish decoys may cause potential buyers of decoys to hesitate to buy or even cease collecting altogether. It is inexpensive to create a fish decoy—all one needs is some wood, metal for fins and tails, lead for weighting, some paint, and some carving or whittling ability. When someone pays hundreds of dollars for a fine fish decoy, it becomes imperative to possess the ability to identify a new fish made to look old. A good rule of thumb is: if there is doubt in your mind—pass on the decoy.[5]

There is no substitute for experience in spotting phony decoys. After one has handled hundreds of old and real fish decoys, a sense is developed as to whether or not they are genuine. Of course, not everyone has had the opportunity to inspect large numbers of old fish decoys. The following guidelines, while not infallible, may prove helpful to new (as well as seasoned) collectors for spotting the fakes.

1. Know your source. Naturally, the best sources for obtaining decoys are the original makers or their families. Then, it is possible to learn the exact or approximate age of the "fish" that are being purchased. Experience is also useful when buying decoys from a collector, dealer, or picker. It is possible that anyone can pass along a fake fish to another without being aware that the fish decoy is not old, but if it happens more than one time perhaps the wisest course of action is to refrain from purchasing from that individual in the future.

2. Fins. Metal fins on decoys sometimes were broken in normal use and replaced by their maker. Sometimes the repair was not as well done as the original. However, fins may be recently added to make decoys more saleable. Look at the edge of the fin. If it reveals shinning metal, the fin, of course, is not old. Also, it may be possible to discern the serrations made by a metal cutter on the fins. Old decoy fins are smooth to the touch and free from such serrations. Metal fins with a powdery red or orange colored rust indicate fins of recent vintage. Old, unpainted fins appear to have a black scale which is bonded tightly to the metal. Copper and aluminum fins darken with age and those which appear bright and lustrous are probably not old.

If the fins are painted, one should determine whether the paint *exactly* matches the color used on the wood body of the decoy. Also, if some of the paint on a fin has chipped off, it is important to note if the chipping occurs at a point on the fins that could have been bent by the fisherman, and/or at the outer edges.

Signs of glue on the wood body of the decoy where the fin is inserted is another tipoff that a fin has been added at a later date. Normally, fins were made to pass entirely through the body of the fish decoy including the cavity where the lead was poured [before it was poured, of course] and were never glued in place. Fins were also tacked by brads to the body of the decoy. Thus, signs of gluing clearly indicate the existence of a replacement fin.

Leading. If the lead weight in a fish decoy is not covered by paint, it is also possible to judge the age of a decoy by careful examination of the color of the lead. Old lead appears as a dark grey color, while newly poured lead possesses a light-silverish color.

Wood. One can examine the body of a decoy to see if there are holes or paint chips where the wood body of the fish decoy shows through. If the wood underneath appears to be a dark color or silver-grey color, the wood is probably old. On the other hand, a light (bright) colored exposed wood indicates that the wood is new, because wood, of course, darkens with age.

Paint. Paint on the decoy is often one of the most difficult characteristics from which to determine its age. Decoys that were well cared for and stored away from sunlight may not show the natural darkening and mellowing of color that other, more carelessly handled fish decoys, may exhibit. Some collectors/dealers are using ultraviolet lights to help spot later paint touch-ups or restorations.

However, touch-ups and even repainting could have taken place years ago by the user or original maker of the decoy, so that even this high tech method of fraud detection is not infallible. Of course, one can also smell the decoy to determine if it has the odor of fresh paint. Needless to say, if the decoy smelling of paint is not being sold as a contemporary one, do not buy it.

CHAPTER II

THE ORIGINS OF SPEAR FISHING

The notion of spearing fish is a simple one. It probably represents a step upward from attempting to catch fish by hand. William Radcliffe suggests that spear fishing dates to Paleolithic times.[1] Harpooning fish ceased to be a commercially profitable venture after the second prehistoric age, according to Radcliffe.[2] Evidence exists in the form of tomb drawings that spearing fish in Egypt was practiced, at least for sport, from the banks of rivers or in a papyrus punt from at least the 5th dynasty.[3]

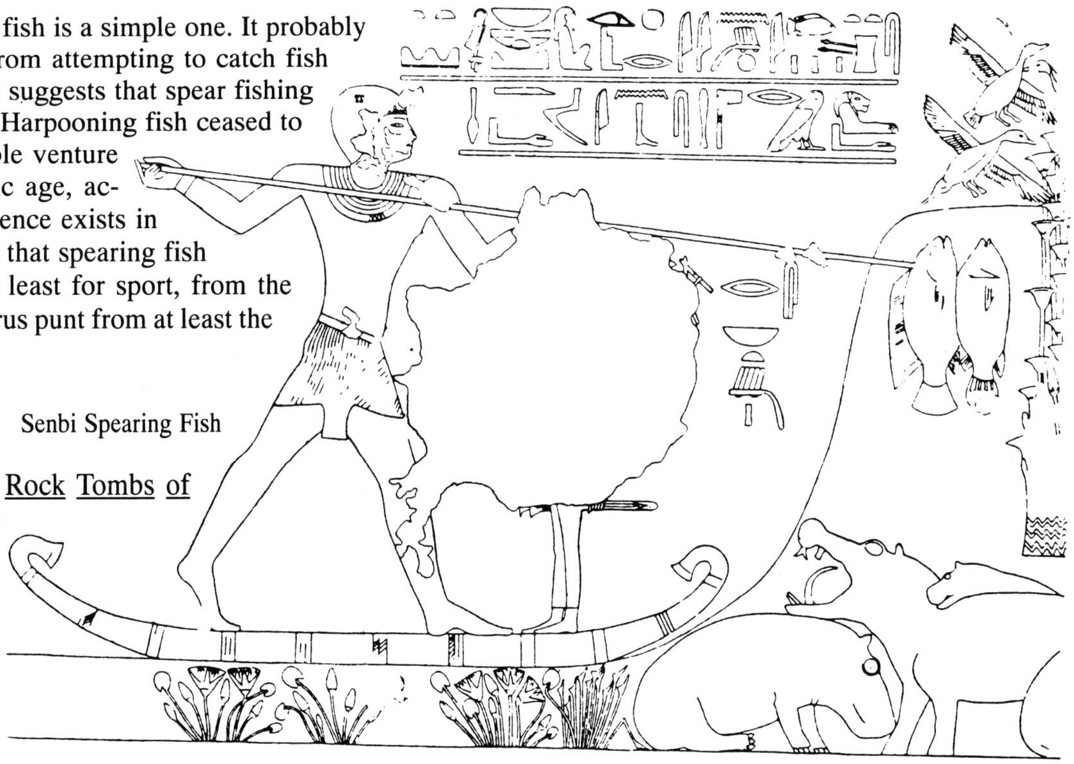

Senbi Spearing Fish

Source: A.M. Blackman, Rock Tombs of Meir, Vol. I, P1.II; in Radcliffe, op. cit., p. 310.

Angling was mentioned in Egypt over a thousand years before China, where the earliest referral to the practice occurred at about 900 B.C.[4] Spearing with a four-pronged weapon is mentioned in China in the ninth century A.D.[5] It is impossible to say with any certainty that the notion of spearing fish migrated to China or Japan from Egypt. Obviously, spearing of fish through the ice in Egypt did not exist. More likely, Asian development of spearing techniques came about independent of any Egyptian influence.

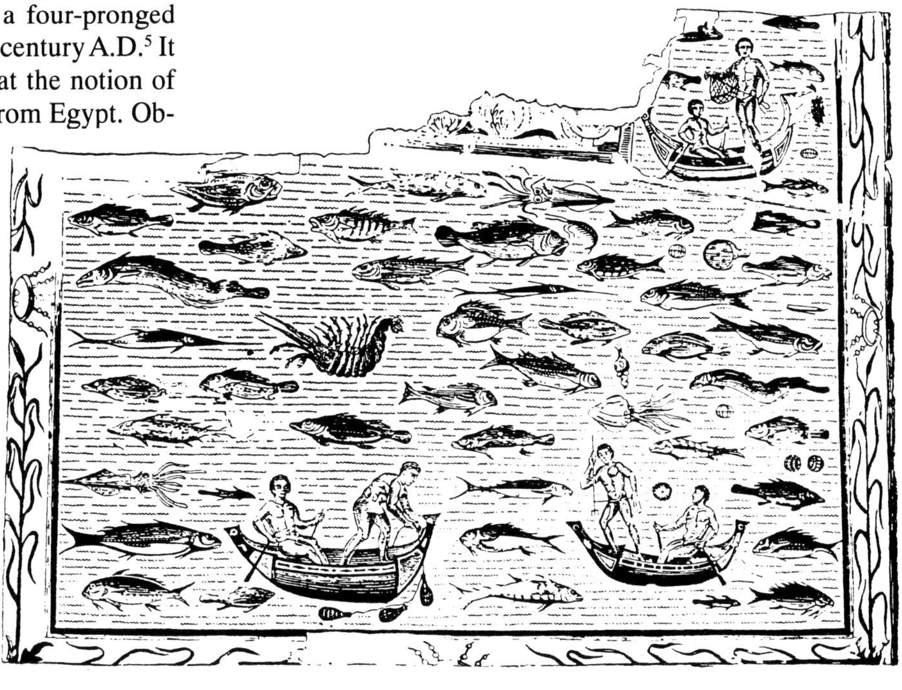

Methods of Fishing including Spearing in Roman Times

Source: From a Roman mosaic at Sousse in Radcliffe, op. cit. p. 75

Leitch points out that there are old Japanese silk paintings which depict Ainu spearing through the ice while sheltered under semiconical mat dark tents.[6] There is, however, additional evidence from other sources indicating that winter spear fishing originated in Asia. For example, Duane Esarey, who has been studying this topic, noted:

> "Stone fish decoys of Neolithic age, from 7,000 to 3,000 years ago, have been found in eastern Asia. Their presence in the Lake Baikal area (the deepest body of fresh water in the world) from 5,000 years ago into modern times is sufficient cause to assign Asia as the original source of decoy fishing."[7]

Obviously, the fact that stone decoys have survived over thousands of years does not automatically mean that wood decoys were also in use during these early times. Wood, of course, would not likely survive decomposition over thousands of years. Thus, it is not clear at the present that early Asian spear fishermen utilized weighted wood decoys. Nevertheless, what is crucial is that they were aware of the *notion* or *idea* of spearing, utilizing a fish decoy, whatever the material from which the decoy was constructed. It would not have been a quantum leap for human inventiveness to move from the use of a stone decoy for spear fishing to one made of wood, if proper weighting of such a wood decoy could have been achieved. Asians likely possessed knowledge of lead [to weight a decoy] at least by 1000 B.C.[8] Frankenberger has concluded that:

> "Until further archeological findings surface, it appears that fish decoy carving began in western Asia, simultaneously in Japan and China, and was brought to the North American continent over the Aleutian land bridge."[9]

No doubt the movements of these Asian people across northeastern Siberia into North America caused them to make many adaptations to their new homes including changes in hunting, herding and fishing practices.[10] Most of these changes had been effected by the time that they had contact with the first explorers to the "New World."

Eskimo Spearing Techniques

Ethnologists traced the migration of people in a southerly direction after their initial entry into Alaska. Among the Bering Sea and North Alaskan Eskimo, there was little ceremonial or ritual attention given to fishing, even in those areas where fish provided the bulk of the diet. Instead, the Eskimos reserved their ceremonies to more dangerous occupations such as sea mammal hunting or even fishing for large and powerful sea halibut that were taken at sea.[11] Eskimos used two types of spears for fishing. One type was a harpoon-type spear with a detachable point attached to a line. The head is barbed or shaped to pivot side-wise inside a fish [or other animal or mammal] to hold it on the line and to pull it in or play it in the water. Less common, but also put to considerable use, was a spear with two barbs and a center point glued and lashed together to contain a socket and a line attachment.[12]

Eskimos speared fish through the ice, using various types of decoys. This technique was probably known to them even before they crossed the Bering Strait. The historic Eskimos of the Bering Strait used a sinker carved out of ivory in the shape of a fish. Some of these early examples were carved in the shape of a fish. Some also had carved eyes, mouth, gills, fins and scales.[13]

Archeological information shows that sites along the Pacific coast line, in the Aleutians, near Point Barrow, contained fishing decoys. It is possible, therefore, that the spearing technique was known even before the Eskimos crossed the Bering Strait.[14]

It is likely, because the Eskimos may have lived in Asia at one time, that their knowledge of spear fishing originated from that continent. Eskimos do possess an Asian look, but are a physical type that is unique to themselves [average height, plump, massive-faced, narrow-nosed, long headed].[15] They are not, however, Indians.[16] There was a common knowledge of the fish figure as an imitation in Kamchatka and the islands connected with Japan.[17] Leitch, as previously noted, pointed out the existence of old Japanese silk paintings which show Ainu spearing through the ice in a manner commonly practiced by American Indians [i.e., spearing under conical tents], as well as by Eskimos.[18] Thus, the diffusion of spear fishing may have begun in ancient Japan, spread to the Eskimos who traveled across Asia, reaching North America after crossing the Bering Strait. From the Eskimos, it is believed that the technique of spear fishing was diffused downward to the northern Indian tribes that fished. Finally, the technique was observed and practiced by early fur traders, trappers, soldiers, and eventually the settlers in northern states.

Early Observations of Indian Spear Fishing Techniques

Seth Rosenbaum has stated that:

> "Prior to 1840, Eskimos were the only ones to use this decoying technique. Their fish decoys were made of ivory and are hundreds of years old."[19]

This observation by Rosenbaum is incorrect. In point of fact, Indians other than Eskimos, were well acquainted with spear fishing with decoys much before 1840. Alexander Henry, a fur trader, described in detail the technique of spearing in 1763 by Chippewa Indians in the Fort Mackinac [Michigan] area. Henry points out that the Indians he observed were using a lead weighted decoy while spear fishing. His account is worth quoting in its entirety.

> "The commandant, and all the rest, now lived in one small house, subsisting

only by hunting and fishing. The woods afforded us some hares and partridges, and we took large trout with the spear. In order to spear trout under the ice, holes being first cut, of two yards in circumference, cabins of about two feet in height, are built over them, of small branches of trees; and these are further covered with skins, so as wholly to exclude the light. The design and result of this contrivance is, to render it practicable to discern objects in the water, at a very considerable depth; for the reflection of light from the water gives that element an opaque appearance, and hides all objects from the eye, at a small distance beneath its surface. A spear head of iron is fastened on a pole, of about ten feet in length. This instrument is lowered into the water; and the fisherman, lying upon his belly, with his head under the cabin or cover, and therefore over the hole, lets down the figure of a fish, in wood, and filled with lead. Round the middle of the fish, is tied a small pack-thread; and, when at the depth of ten fathoms [about 60 feet], where it is intended to be employed, it is made, by drawing the string, and by the simultaneous pressure of the water, to move forward, after the manner of a real fish. Trout and other large fish, deceived by its resemblance, spring toward it, to seize it; but, by a dexterous jerk of the string, it is instantly taken out of their reach. The decoy is now drawn nearer to the surface; and the fish takes some time to renew the attack, during which the spear is raised, and held conveniently for striking. On the return of the fish, the spear is plunged into its back; and, the spear being barbed, it is easily drawn out of the water. So completely do the rays of the light pervade the element, that in three fathom water [about 18 feet], I have often seen the shadows of the fish, on the bottom, following them as they moved; and this, when the ice itself was two feet in thickness."[20]

The process described above by Henry is remarkably similar to modern day spearing (note the use of the decoy and even that of the barbed spear, although the account does not specifically mention multiple tined spears). The major difference between Henry's (Indian) technique and that of today's spear fisherman lies in the depth of water in which the former was fishing. Most spear fishermen currently spear in only five to twelve feet of water, not 60 feet, and do not draw the decoy to the surface. Dark houses are employed instead of the tepee-like structure preferred by the Indians.[21]

Writing in 1793, fur trader John MacDonell observed that in a large bay of Lake Nipising, the water was so shallow that..."they spear fish in winter in the middle of it under the Ice (sic) not exceeding three to four fathoms [18 to 24 feet] ..."[22] It is not certain that the "they" referred to by MacDonell were Indians or his white colleagues. In either case, spear fishing was certainly known and practiced by the year 1793 in the north shore of the Lake Superior region.

Gurdon Saltonstall Hubbard, a soldier, in 1811 was ordered to canoe up the Muskegon River in present Michigan, to trade with the Indians. Relying on information contained in a book, Hubbard decided to attempt winter spear fishing. He stated:

> "I thought that what an Indian could do in that line, I could, and set about making my preparations. I whittled out a stick into the shape of a fish, shaping it as artistically as I could, and colored it by searing with a hot iron. In an excavation made for the purpose I poured melted lead to sink it, and after having placed in the head beads for eyes I had quite a natural looking fish, handle (sic), I marched with them to the middle of Muskegon Lake, cut a hole in the ice, and erected a shelter by sticking poles in the ice and stretching a blanket over them. Everything being in readiness, I crawled into the hut, and lying flat on the ice dropped my 'little pet'—as I called my little fish—and anxiously awaited the result. I was soon gratified by the appearance of a large fish that made a dart at my decoy. I hurled my spear at him, and missed. And thus every few minutes for more than two hours I repeated the operation with the same results, when, mortified and angry, I returned cold and hungry, to my solitary home and made a dinner of corn."[23]

Modern-day spear fishermen could empathize with Hubbard, as many come home empty handed, perhaps settling for beans (or corn or McDonalds) for dinner. The spearing technique described by Hubbard is definitely an Indian one.

George Featherstonhaugh, an Englishman by birth and a geologist by profession, made extensive travels in the northern midwestern states in 1835 and 1837. He noted Indians spearing near Michilmackinac [Makinaw City, Michigan]:

> "In the winter season the Indians cut holes in the ice where it is transparent, and contrive to drag their nets beneath it. They also spear the trout, using upon such oc-

casions a painted fish as a decoy, which attracts the minnows. The veracious trout, perceiving that something is going on, now gets in motion, and the minnows, aware of his approach by the movements of the water, run off in a contrary direction; which apprizing [sic] the Indian of the quarter from whence he is making his approach, he adjusts his spear and transfixes him as he come up."[24]

It is interesting in Featherstonhaugh's account of the importance placed on the action of minnows under the ice. This is the only observations of spearfishing, either old or contemporary, that makes any mention of minnows as significant for spearing success. Featherstonhaugh also points out that the decoy or decoys he observed were painted. The decoy made by Hubbard was plain wood decorated with burned designs. Existing examples of American Indian spearing decoys made during the past 60 years, are both painted and unpainted.

Schoolcraft also documented the Indian approach to spearfishing in 1820.[25] His observation occurred somewhere between Michilimackinac and Detroit. He stated:

"they have a method for taking fish through the ice in the winter season, which is equally novel and ingenious. After a hole has been cut through the ice, they encompass it with a slender circular frame of rods, or a kind of open basket, over which a blanket is thrown to exclude the light. The savage now lays himself down upon the ice, with his head under the hood, and playing a decoy or artificial fish upon the surface of the water with one hand, holds a drawn spear in the other, and when the large trout suddenly darts up to seize their fancied prey, pierces the body of his victim with unerring certainty. The spear is short, and loosens itself from the handle the moment it is struck, but is attached to a string line, with which he plays the fish a while in the water below, and draws it out as soon as it becomes sufficiently enfeebled with the wound. This method of fishing was first noticed by Mr. Hudsen, a missionary among the Saganaws, to whose manuscript journal I am permitted to refer for the facts."[26]

Indian Method of Spearfishing

Source: Tim Pfaff, *Paths of the People The Ojibwe in the Chippewa Valley,* Eau Claire, Wisconsin, Chippewa Valley Museum Press, 1993, p. 23.

Modification to Indian Spear Fishing Techniques by Whites

Lewis Henry Morgan, an attorney by vocation, and an explorer by avocation, noted during his 1861 trip through Minnesota that:

"Some parts of Minnesota are full of lakes. I have been thus particular about these lakes for this reason, that their fish as a means of Indian subsistence is an important element in the history of this region, and made it a most desirable one to the Dakotas who held it at the discovery, and to the Chippewas, who by the recession of the Dakotas have now come into its possession. There are literally thousand of these lakes in Minnesota. In these lakes large and small are found the pike, pickerel, bass, sun fish and carp."[27]

Morgan stated many years ago a fact that is well known today—namely, that Minnesota is a state blessed with many fine lakes for fishing. Morgan also noted that a "Mr. Cook"...." last week took a pike weighing 16-1/2 pounds, in whom was another pike weighting 2-1/2 pounds, through the ice."[28] It is not clear, however, whether this large pike was caught by angling or spearing.

Probably the principal white modification to the traditional Indian technique of spearing, i.e., laying on the ice with a conical structure over the hole in the ice, has been the invention of the dark house or shanty. This change must have occurred in Minnesota roughly between 1840 and 1880. Dark houses were observed dotting the surface of Lake Chautauqua, New York in December of 1880.[29] Undoubtedly, the dark house was in use prior to that time in New York state. It is not unreasonable to assume that it was also being utilized in northern midwestern states by at least 1880, and probably before then.

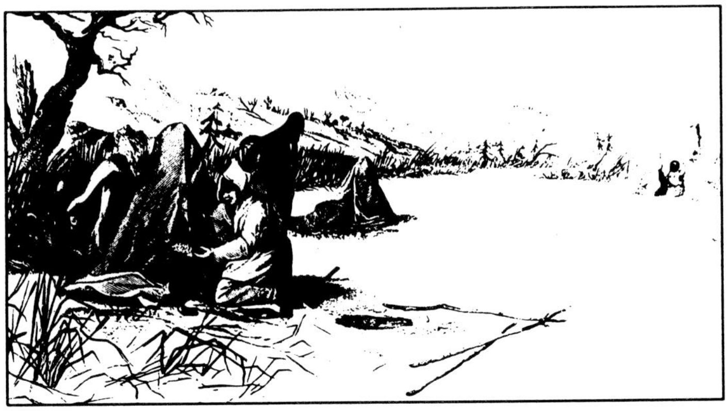

Spearing fish through the ice, c.1831-32. Drawing by Seth Eastman. State Historical Society of Wisconsin.

Chapter I Photographs

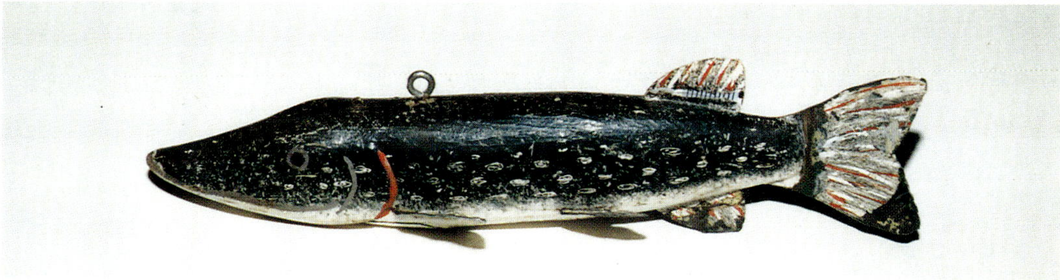

Realistically painted northern pike, length 8 1/2 inches, maker unknown, found in Park Rapids, Minnesota area.

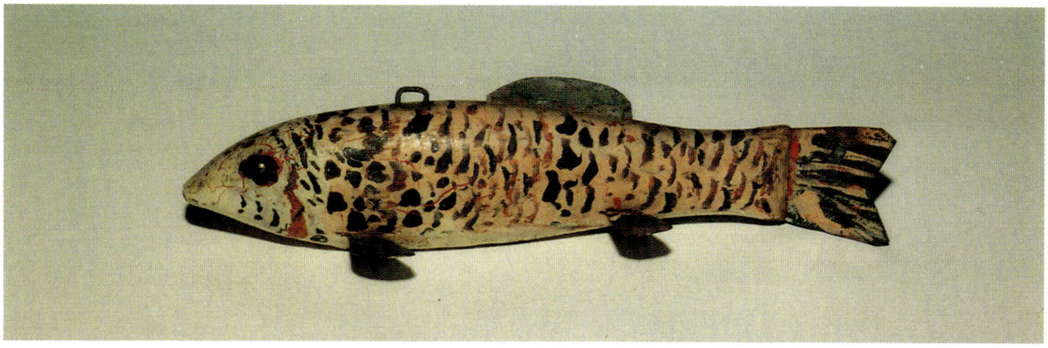

Abstractly painted fish decoy, ca. 1920's, 6 inches long, found near Lake Shetek, Minnesota. Maker unknown.

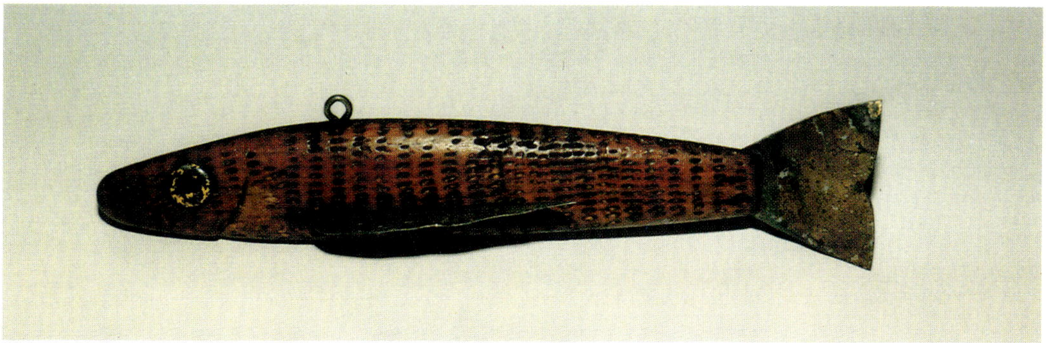

Decoy incised by burning, then varnished, length 7 inches, ca. 1930's, unknown maker.

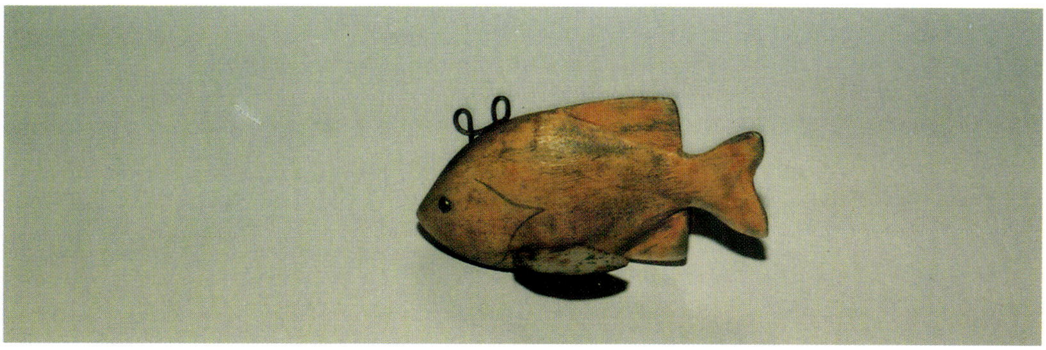

Highly stylized sunfish with wooden anal and dorsal fins, but with metal pectoral fins, maker unknown, length 3 inches.

Chapter II Photograph

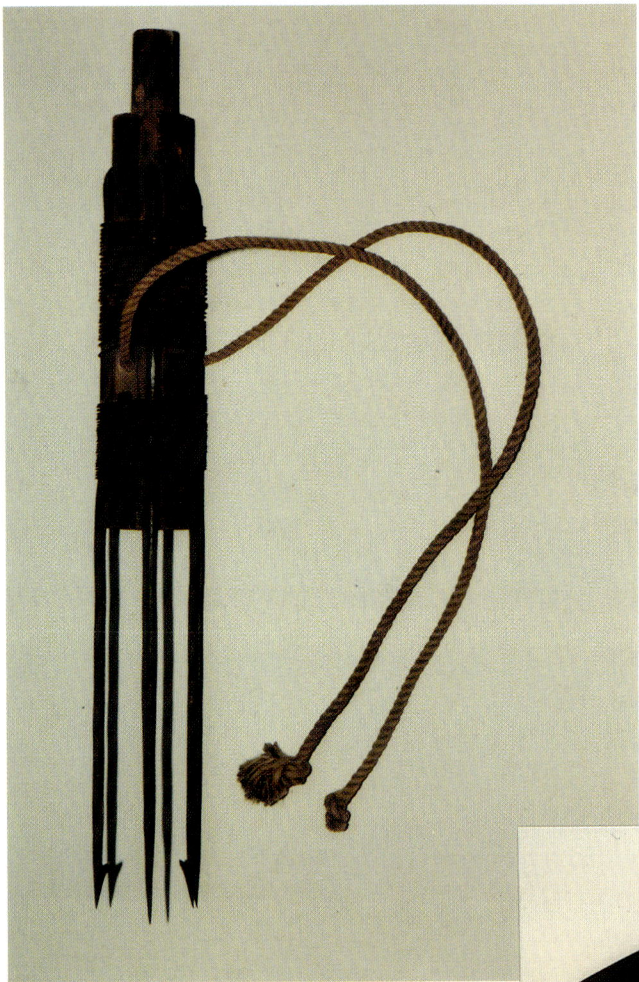

Figure 2-3. Typical Eskimo Four-Barb Spear.

Chapter III Photographs

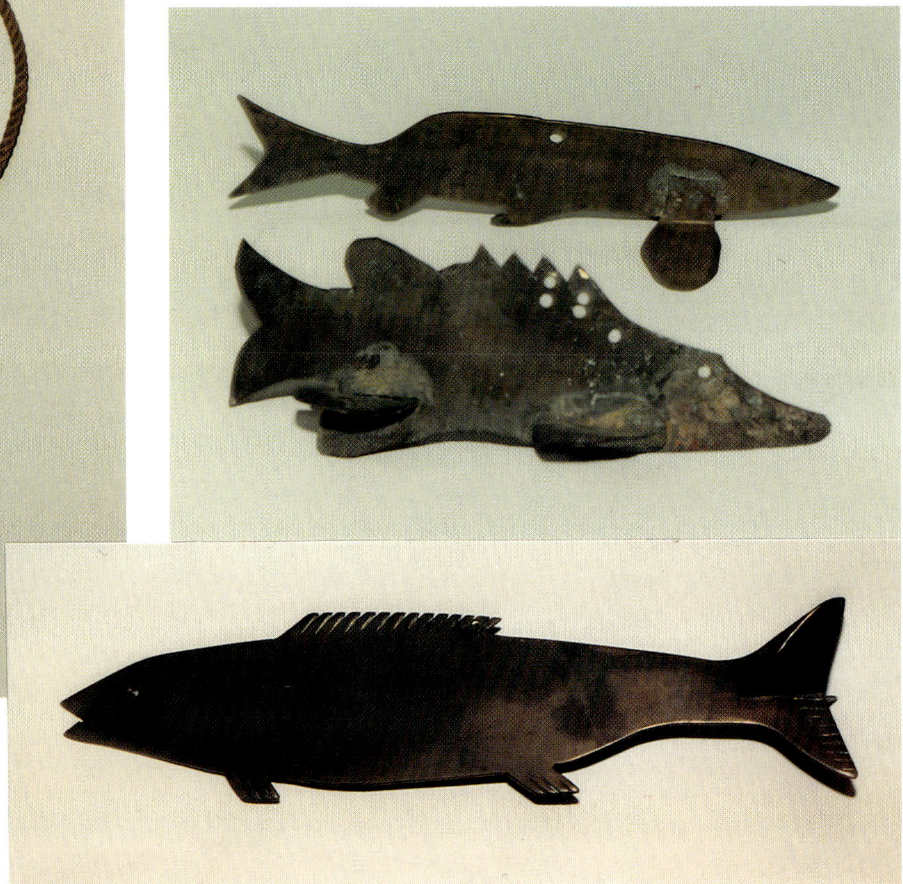

Figures 3-9 & 3-10. Silhouette Metal Decoys

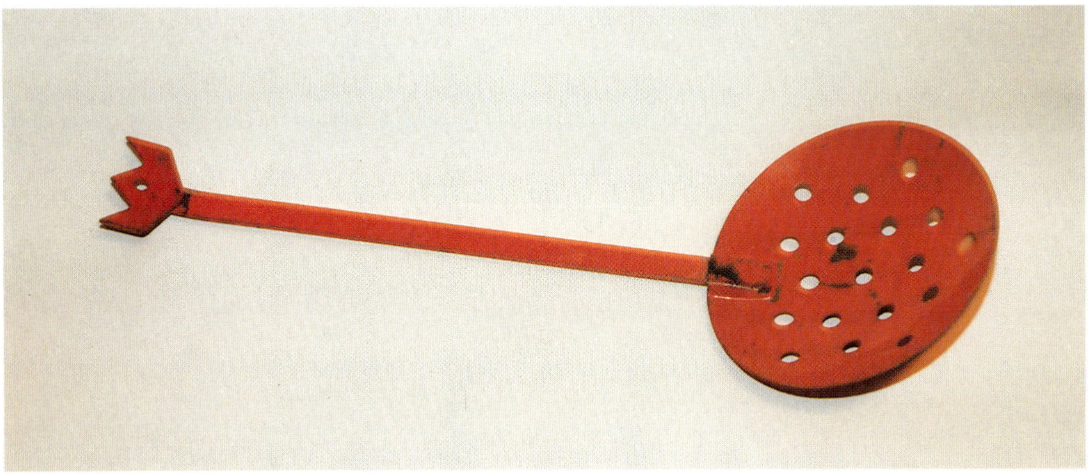

Figure 3-4. Typical Ice Scoop

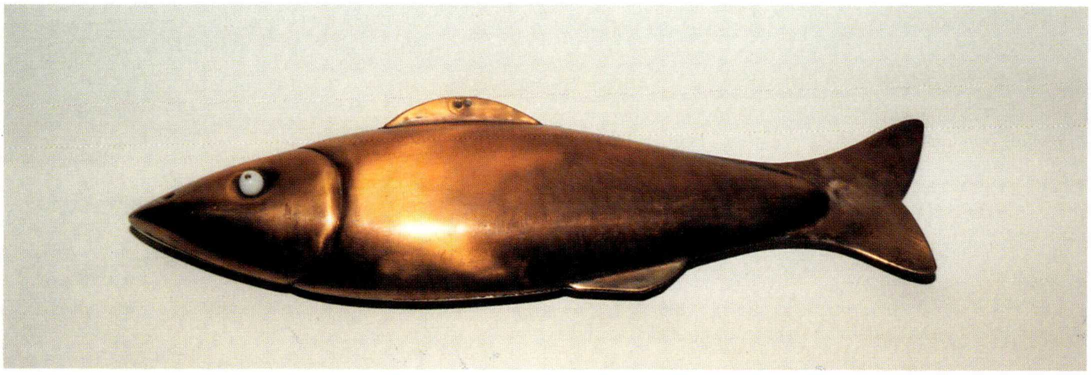

Figure 3-11. Northern Pump Decoy

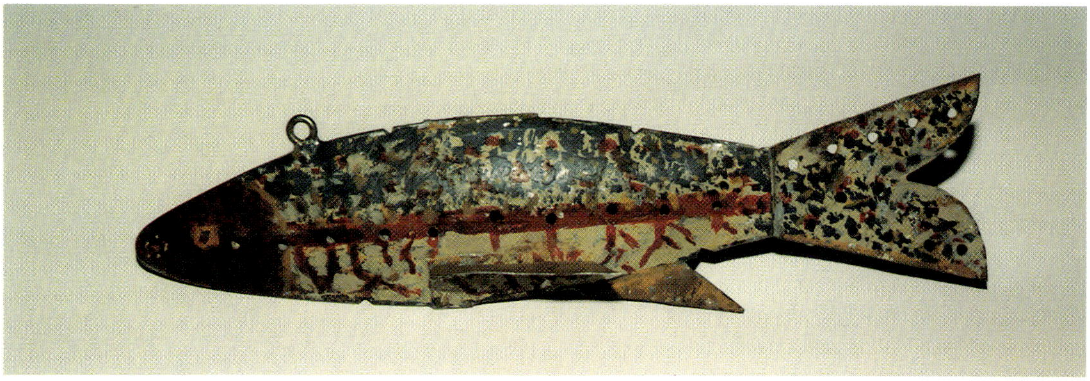

Figure 3-12. Painted Metal Decoy

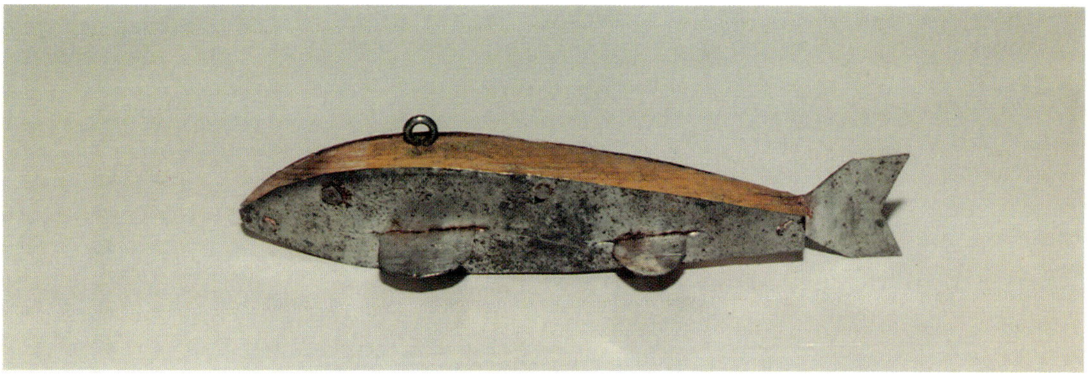

Figure 3-13. Decoy with Metal Sides

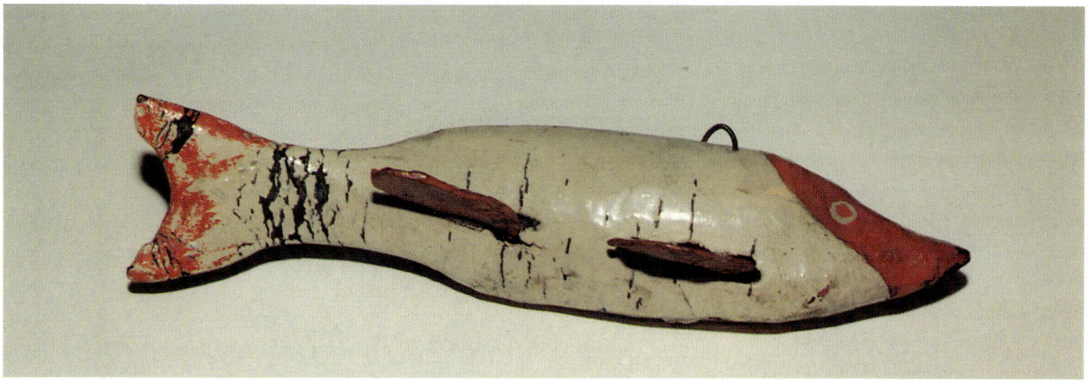

Figure 3-14. Decoy Made from Rubber

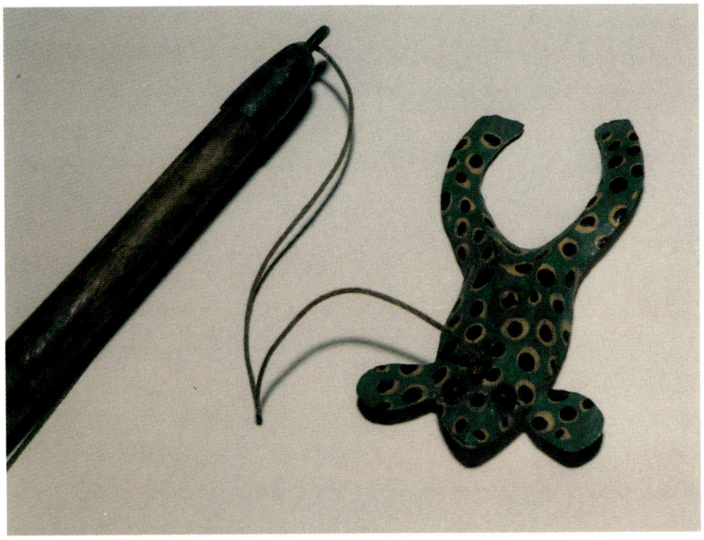

Figure 3-15. Frog Decoy Made From Bone

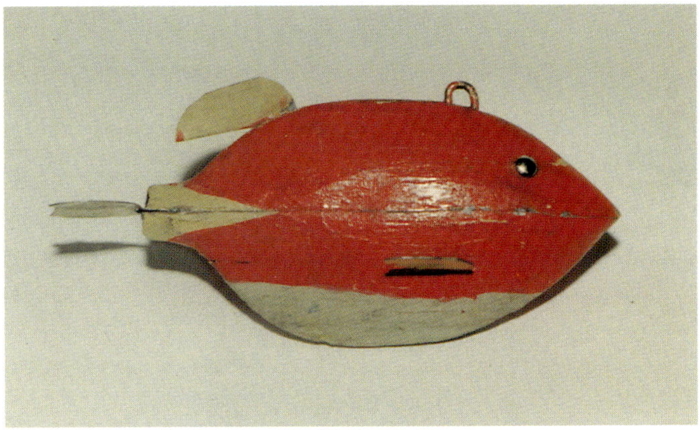

Figure 3-28. Fish Decoy Showing The Splitting Method

See Chapter III text for figures 3-16 to 3-23

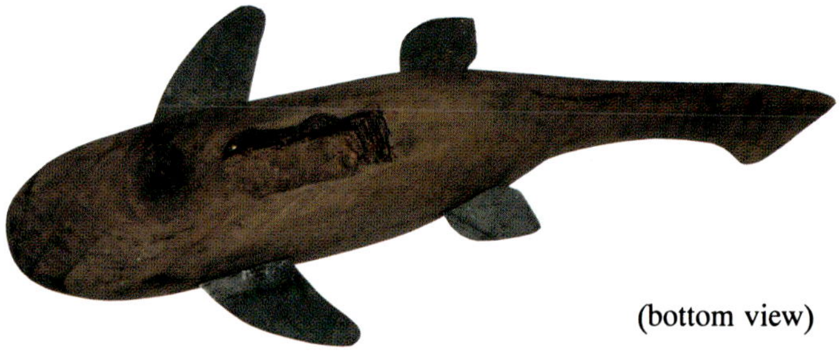

Figure 3-24. Bottom view of a decoy showing fin placement

(bottom view)

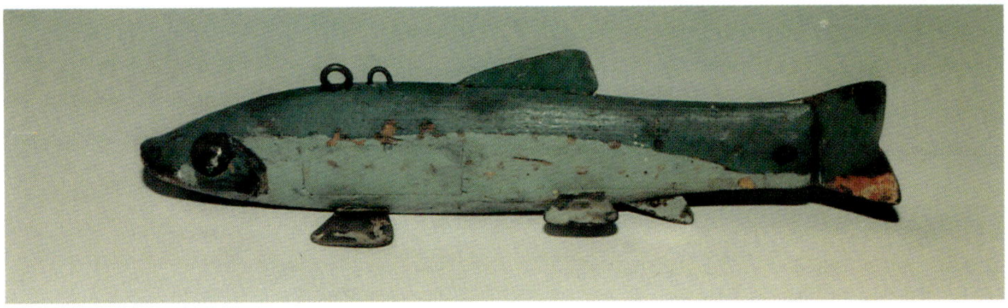

Figure 3-29. Minnesota Fish Decoy With Side Weights

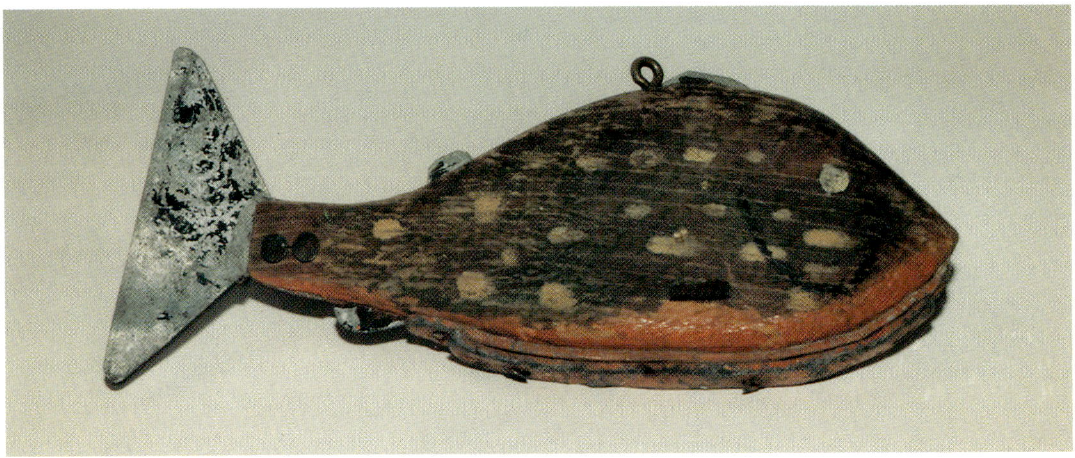

Figure 3-30. Sun Fish with Lead Bands for Weights

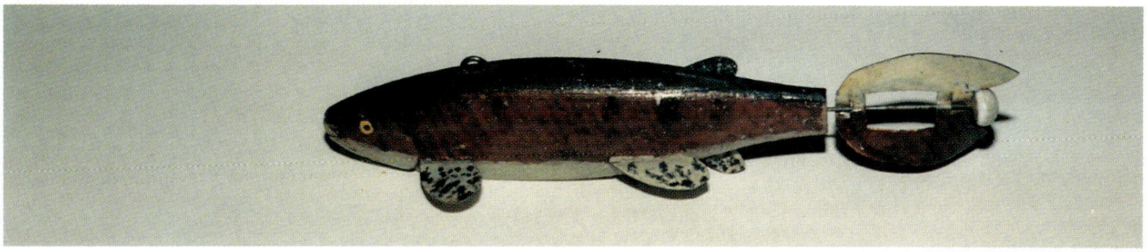

Figure 3-31. Minnesota Decoy with Stabilizer Tail Fin

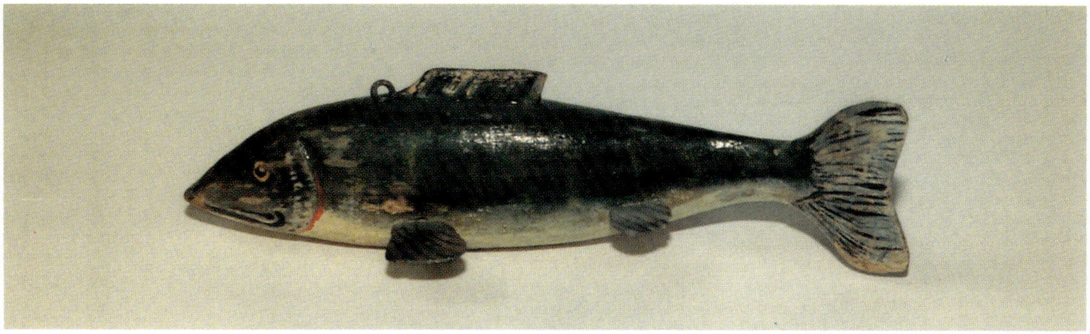

Figure 3-32. Minnesota Decoy With a Wood Tail

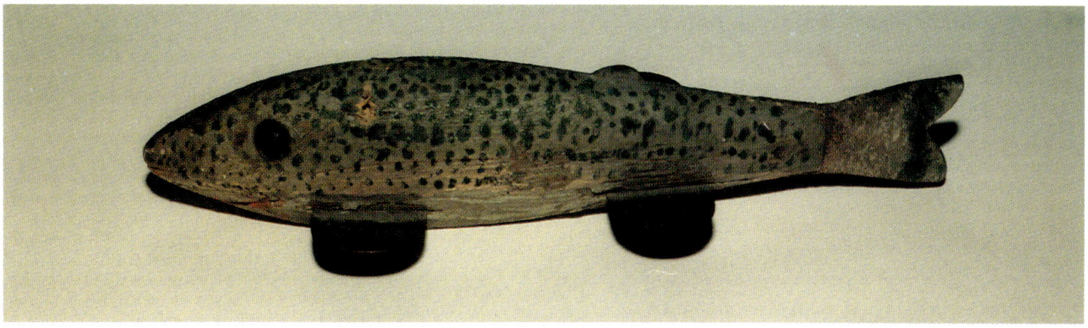

Figure 3-33. Fish Decoy With a Leather Tail

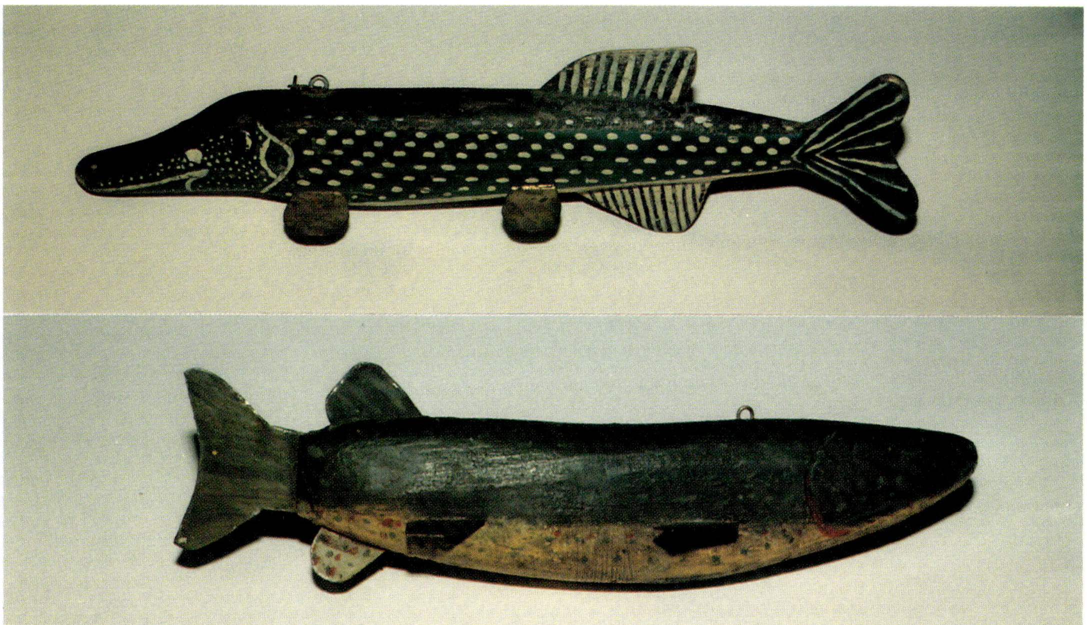

Figure 3-35 & 3-36. Northern Pike Decoys (Minnesota)

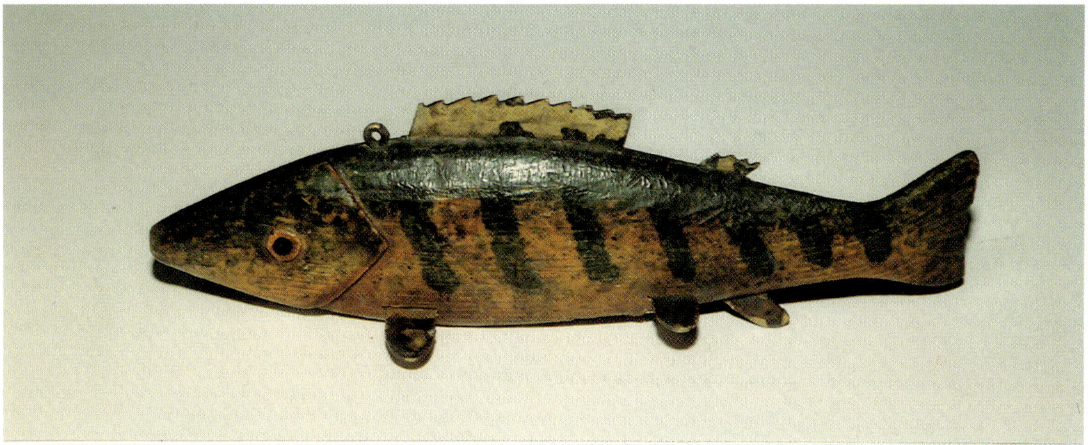

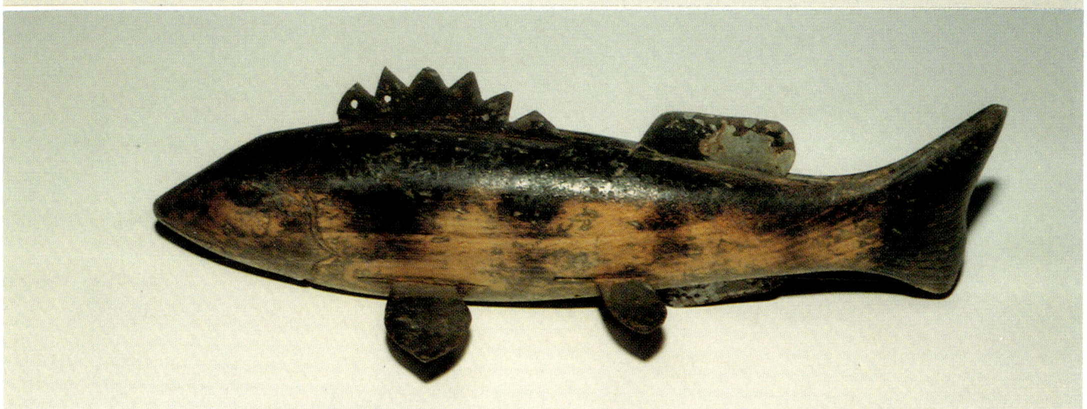

Figure 3-37 & 3-38. Perch Decoys

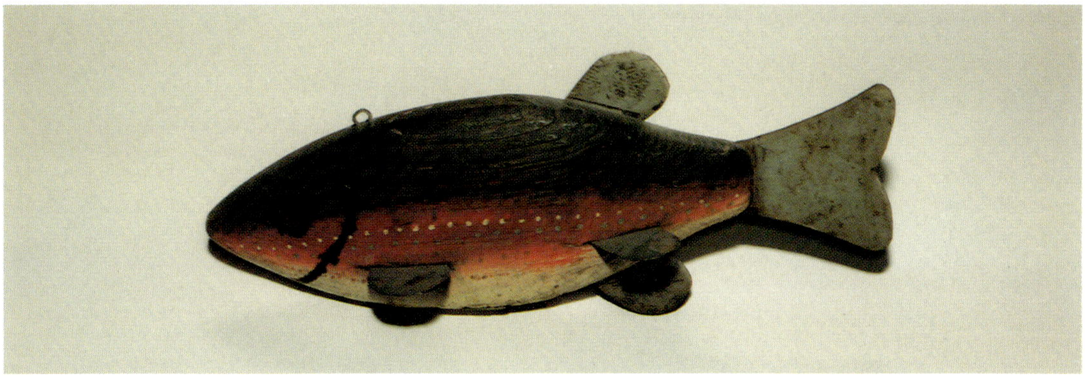

Figure 3-39. Trout Decoy

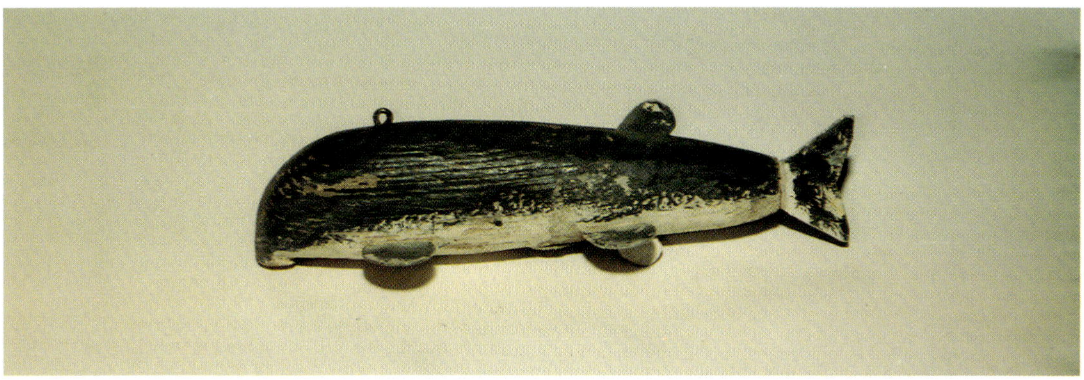

Figure 3-40. Sucker Decoy

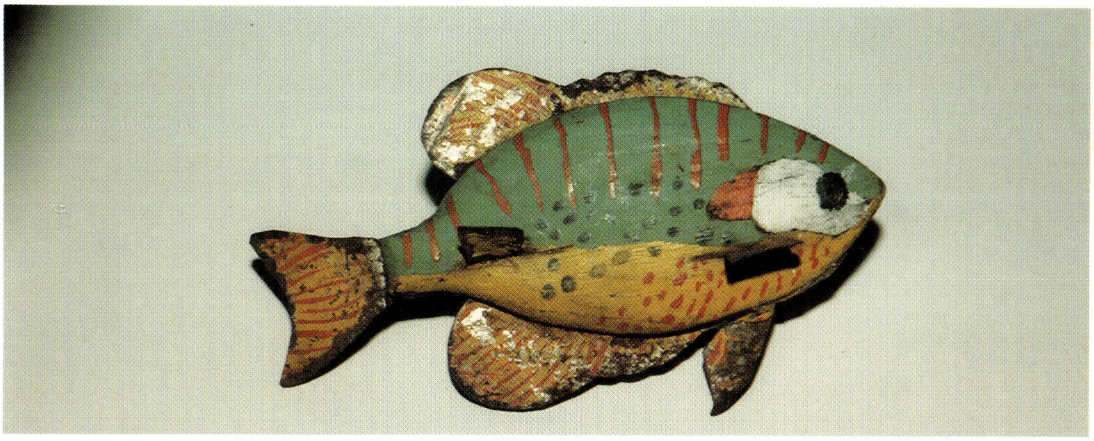

Figure 3-41. Sunfish

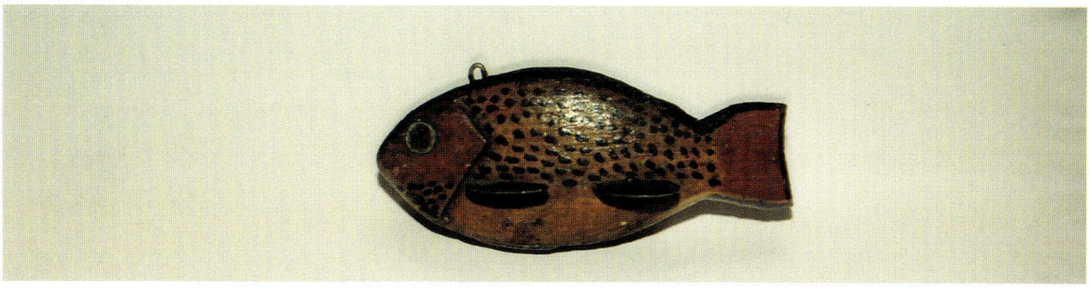

Figure 3-42. Sunfish

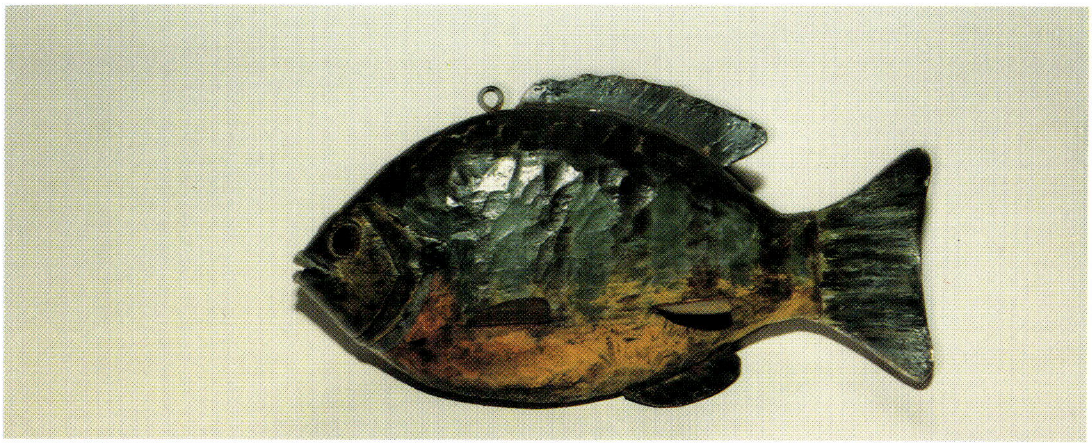

Figure 3-43. Sunfish

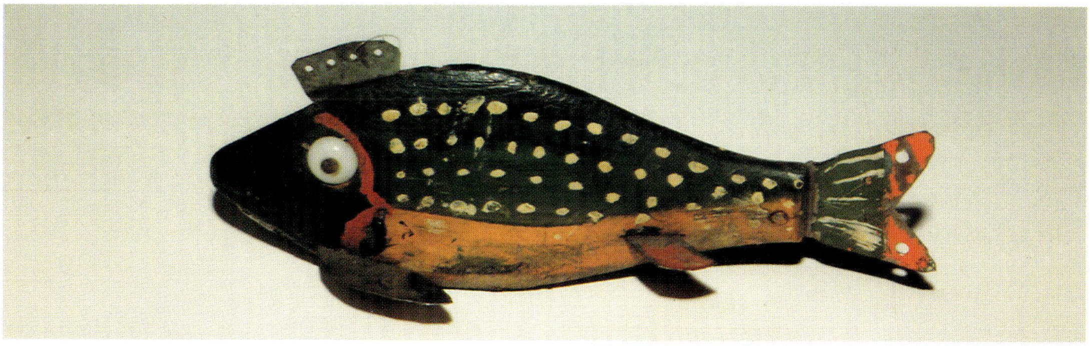

Figure 3-44. Sunfish

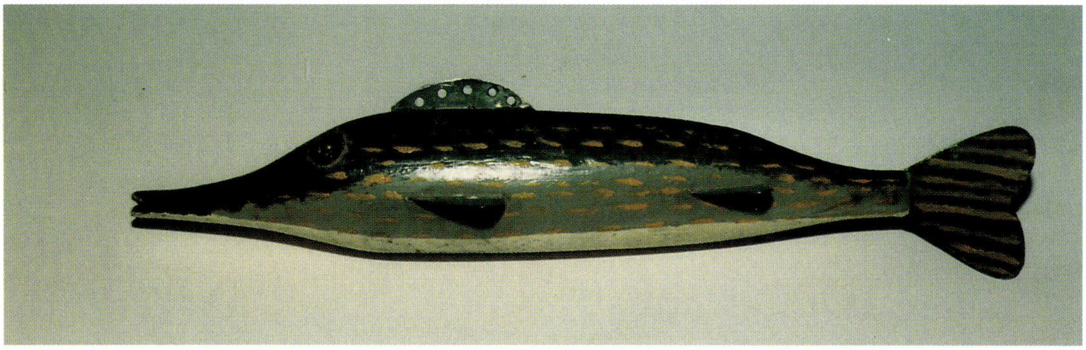

Figure 3-45. Gar Fish Decoy

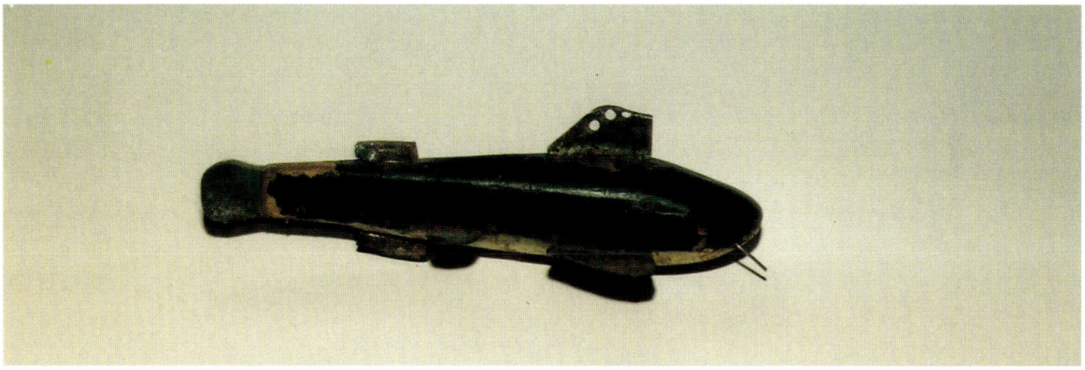

Figure 3-46. Bullhead

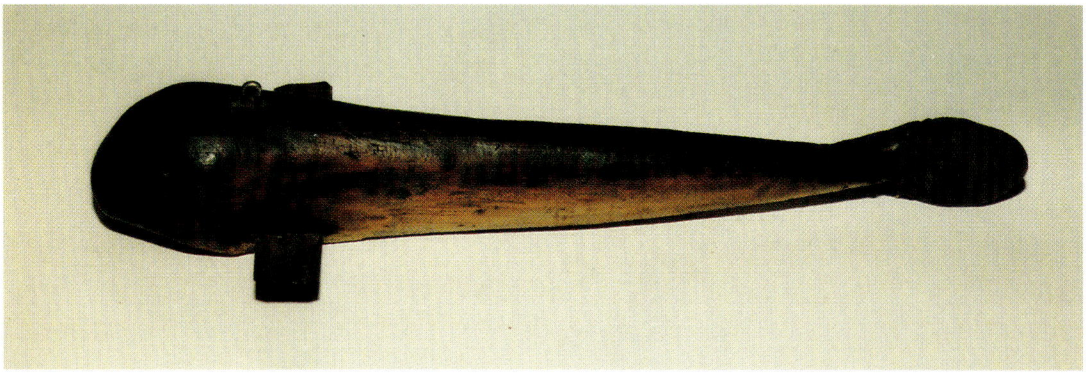

Figure 3-47. Bullhead

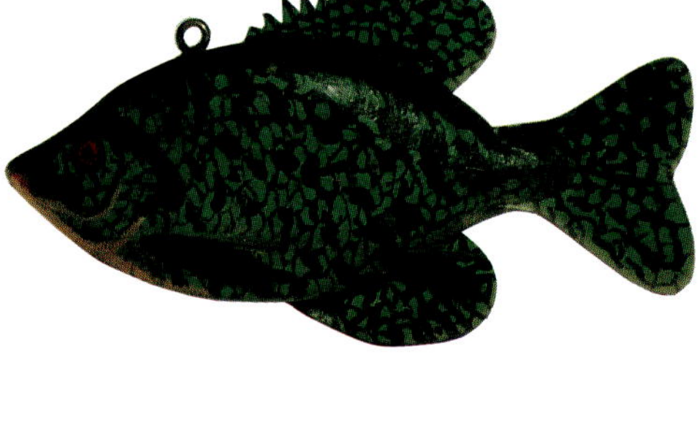

Figure 3-48. Crappie Decoy

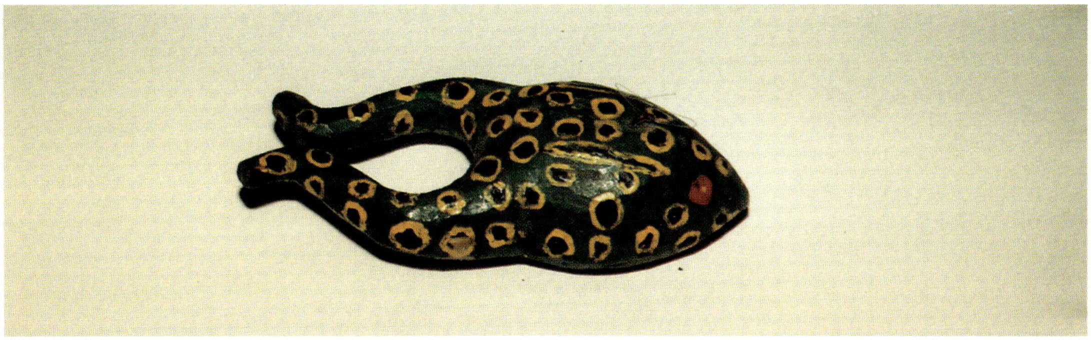

Figure 3-49. Frog Decoy without Fins

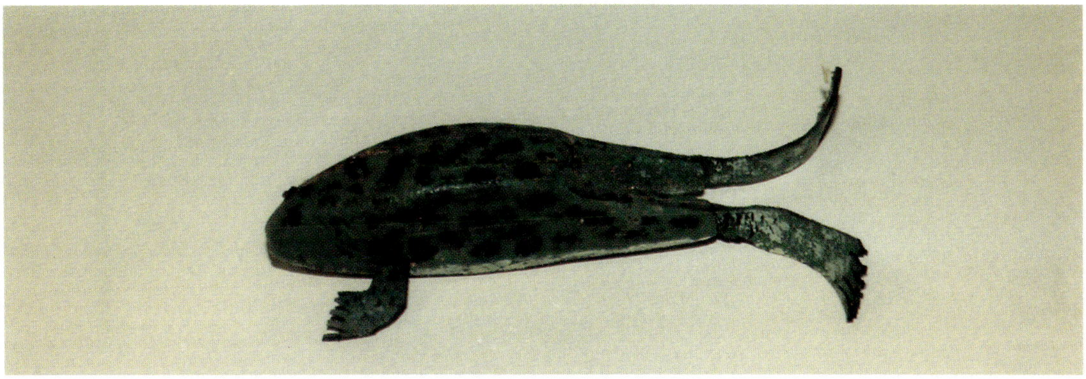

Figure 3-50. Frog Decoy with Rubber Feet

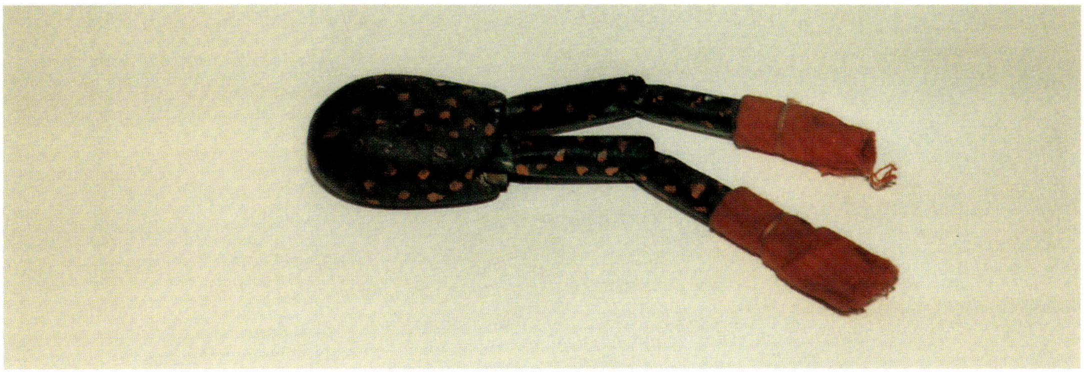

Figure 3-51. Frog with Long Articulated Legs

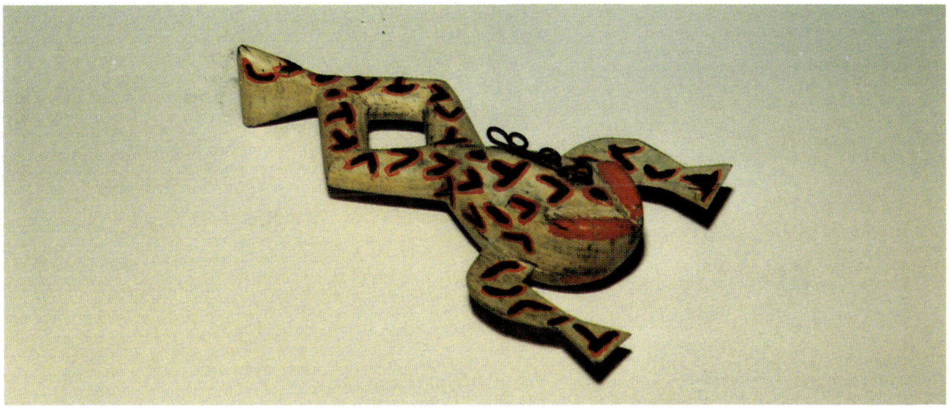

Figure 3-52. Crossed-Legged Frog

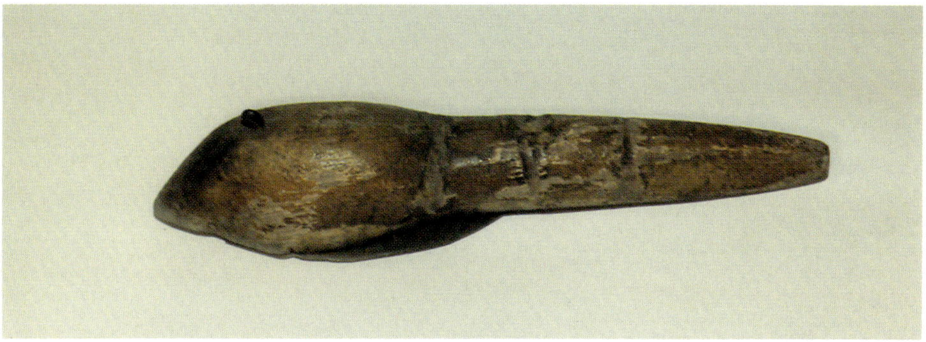

Figure 3-53. Tadpole Decoy

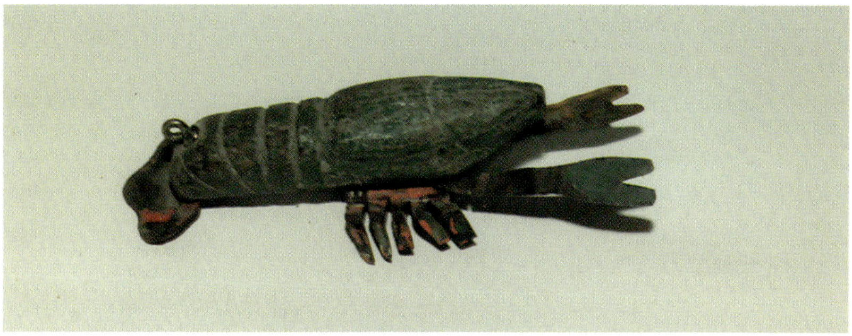

Figure 3-54. Crawdad with Metal Pincers

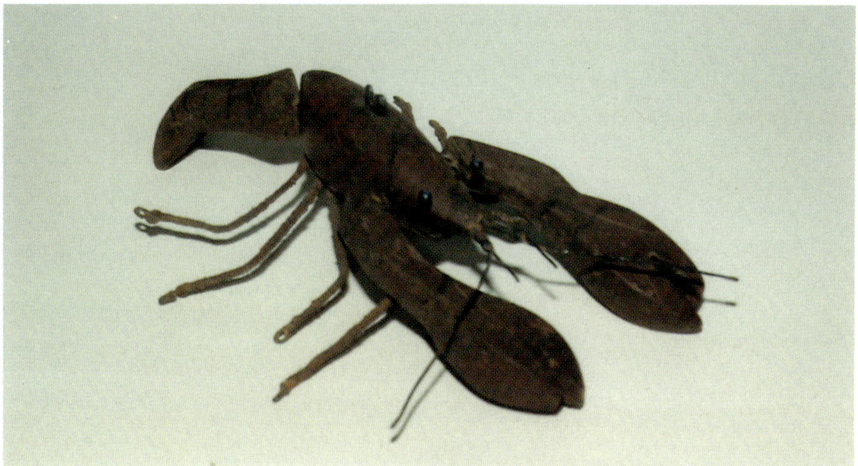

Figure 3-55. Crawdad with Movable Arms

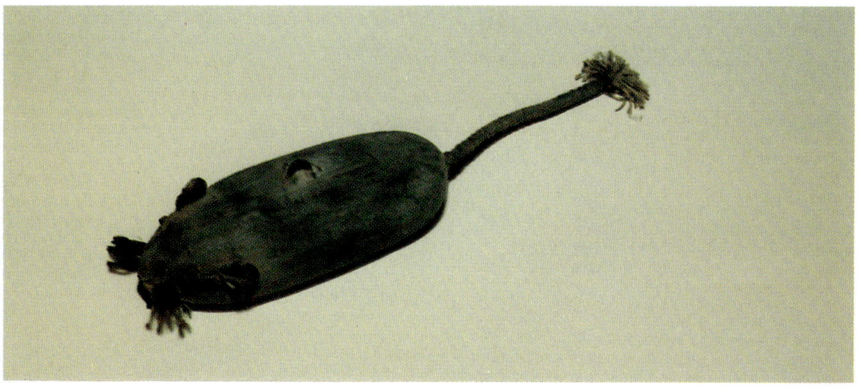

Figure 3-56. Mouse Decoy

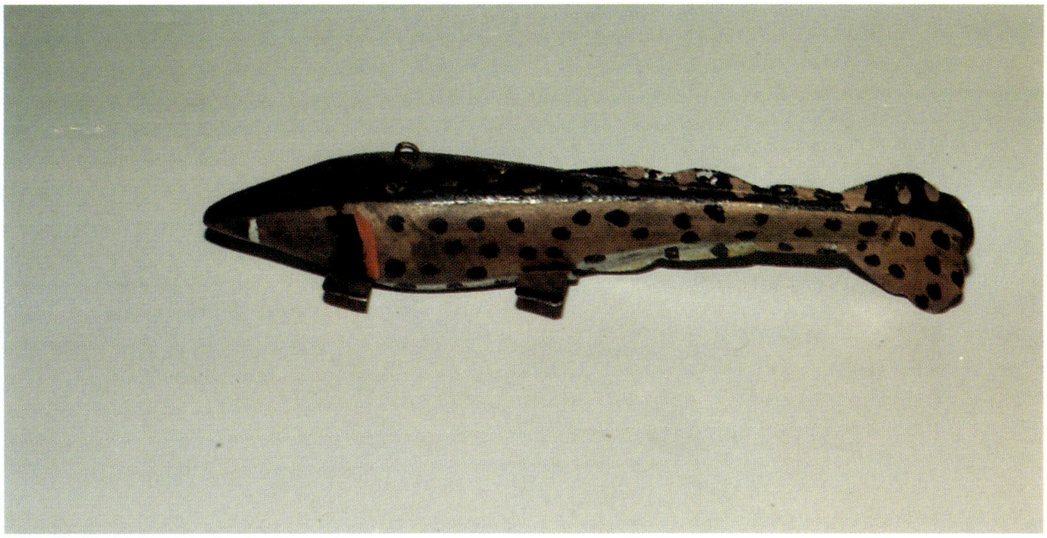

Figure 3-57. Eel Pout Decoy

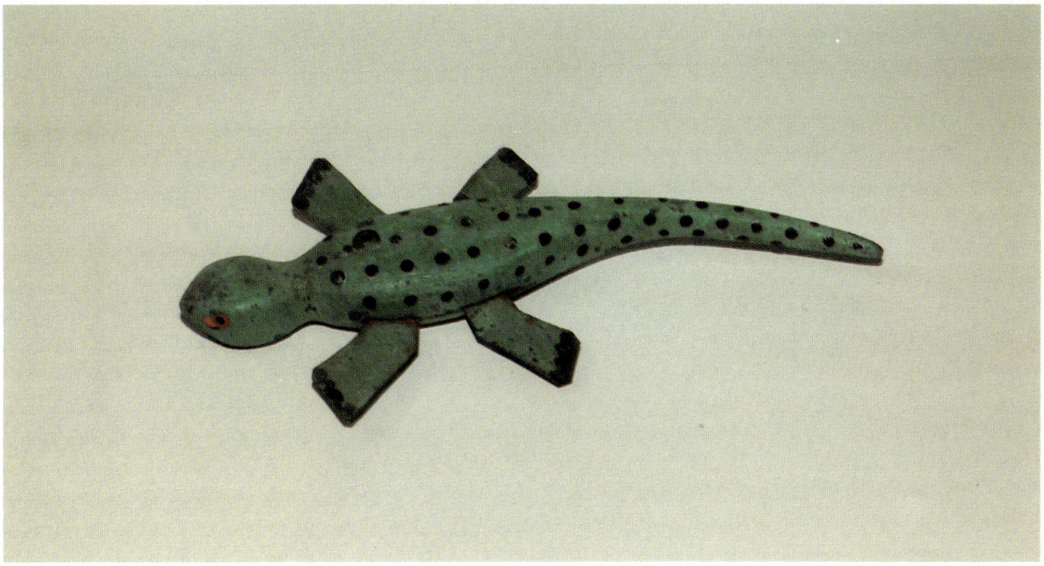

Figure 3-58. Salamander Decoy

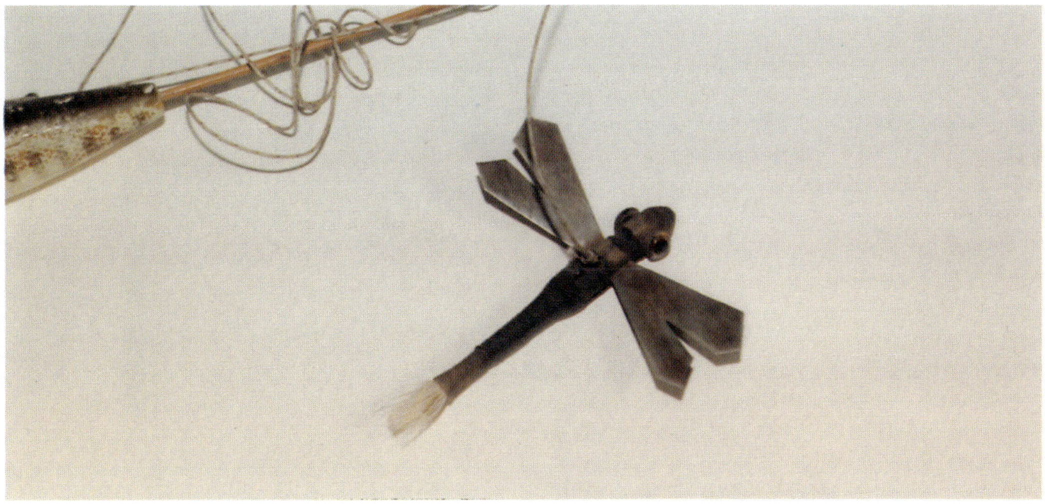

Figure 3-59. Dragon Fly Decoy with Jigging Stick

Chapter IV Photographs

Ernest Aamodt

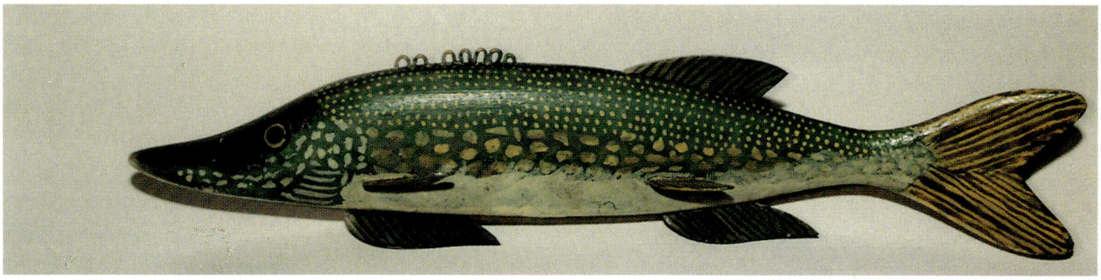

Northern pike by Ernest Aamodt, length 12 inches.

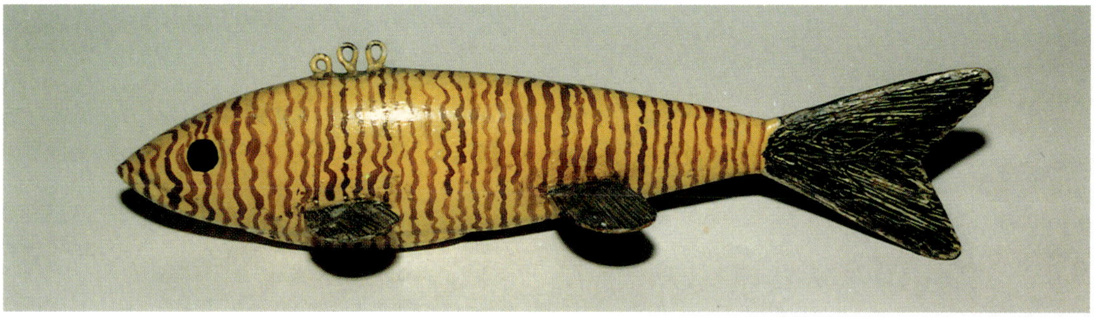

Aamodt perch with wooden tail, 7 1/4 inches long.

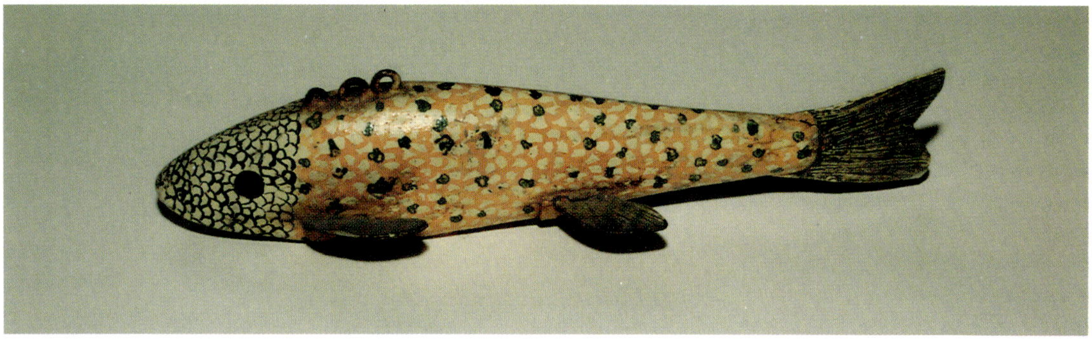

Aamodt decoy showing imitation of scales as well as scaled head, with metal tail, 7 1/2 inches in length.

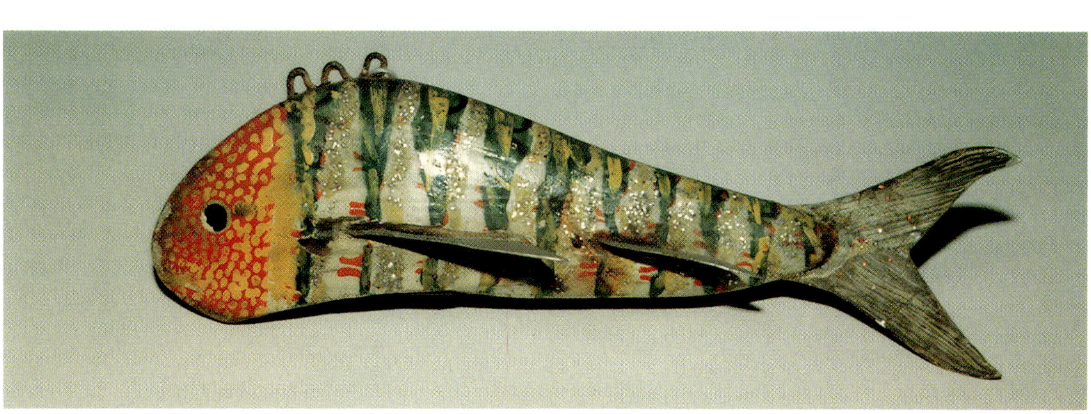

Decoy by Aamodt with scaled head and lined body covered with glitter, metal tail, 8 1/8 inches long.

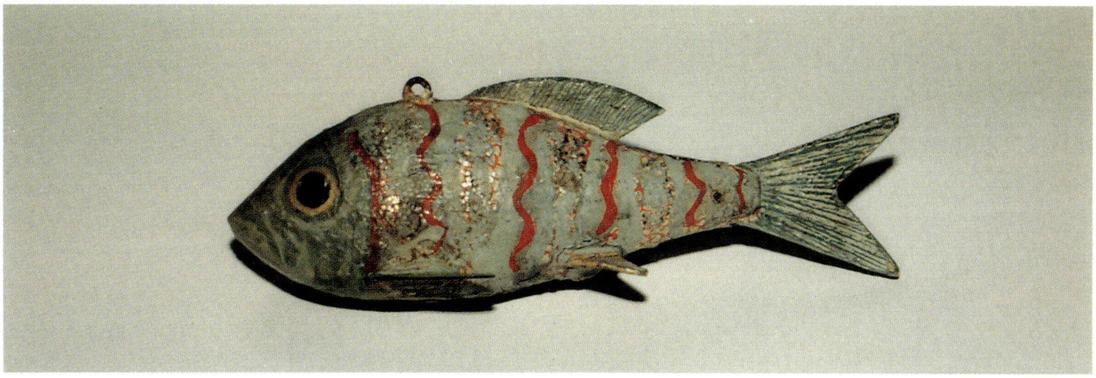

Sunfish by Ernest Aamodt with metal tail and wavy line decoration, decorated with glitter, 5 3/4 inches in length.

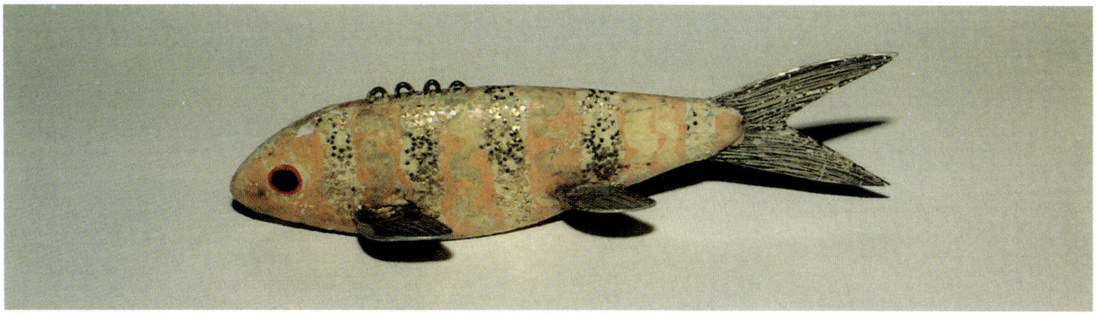

Minnow (?) by Mr. Aamodt with metal tail, glitter decorated, 5 1/2 inches long.

Arvid Arthur Alho

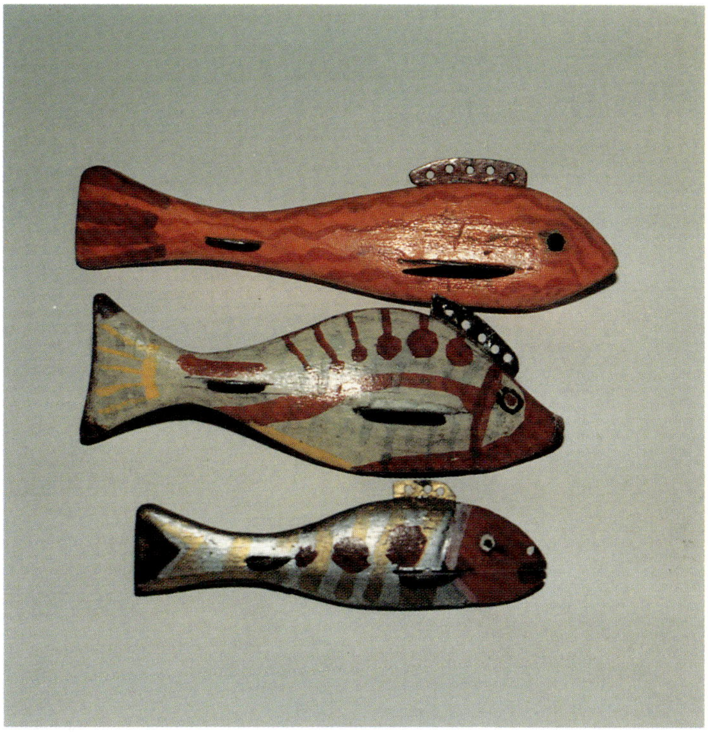

Arvid Alho decoys. Top: orange with red wavy lines, 7 inches; middle: sunfish, white and red, 5 1/2 inches; and bottom: minnow, silver with red spots, 4 1/2 inches.

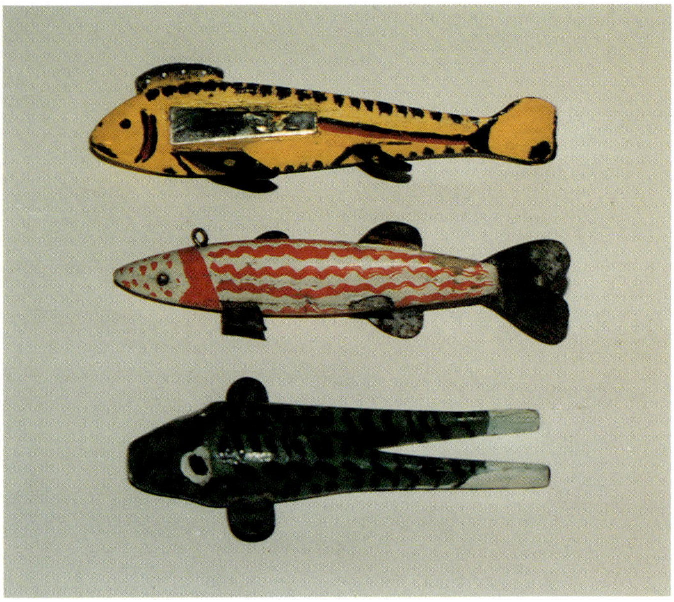

Three Arvid Alho decoys. Top: yellow painted with mirror inset into sides, 7 inches; middle: white minnow with red wavy lines, 6 1/2 inches; and bottom: frog painted green with black spots, 5 1/2 inches.

Lewis W. "Louie" Anderson

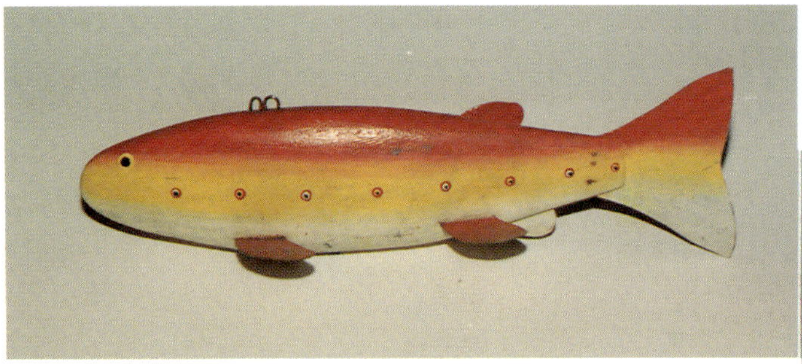

Red, yellow and white painted decoy by Louie Anderson (7 1/4 inches long, collection of Frank Pasiewicz).

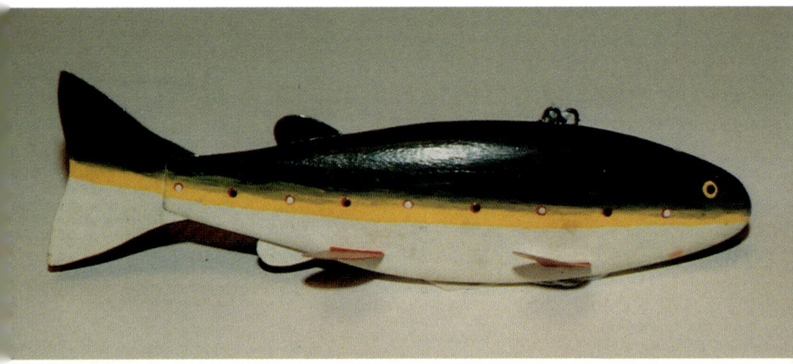

Louie Anderson decoy (7 1/4 inches long, Bill Nikoley collection).

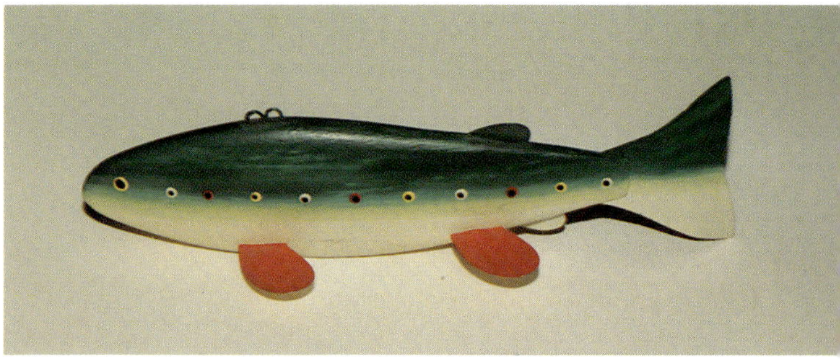

Dark blue, light blue and white painted decoy by Louie Anderson (Frank Pasiewicz collection).

Thomas J. Annis

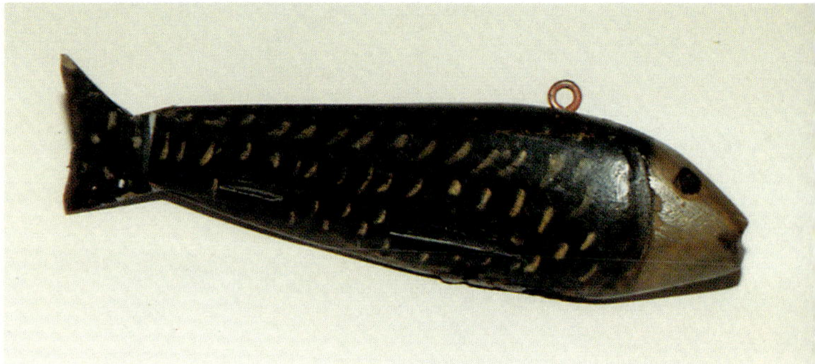

Tom Annis decoy with painted lines imitating scales, 6 3/4 inches long.

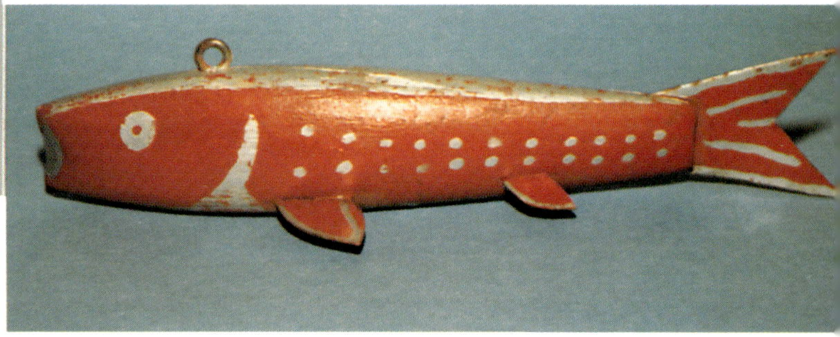

Red painted Annis decoy with circles to represent fish scales.

William "Slow" Batters

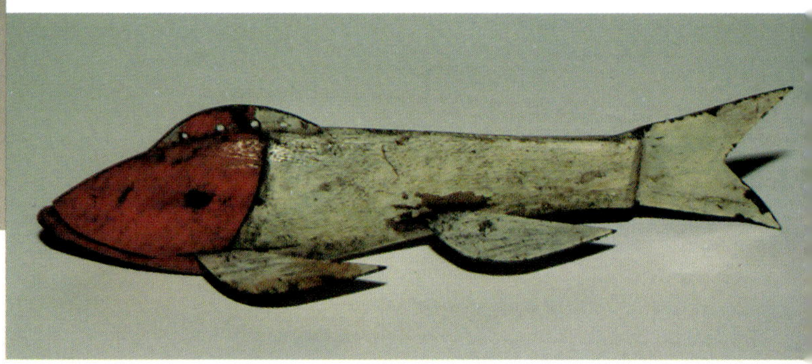

A Batters' red and white decoy in the "minnow" form, 6 1/4 inches long.

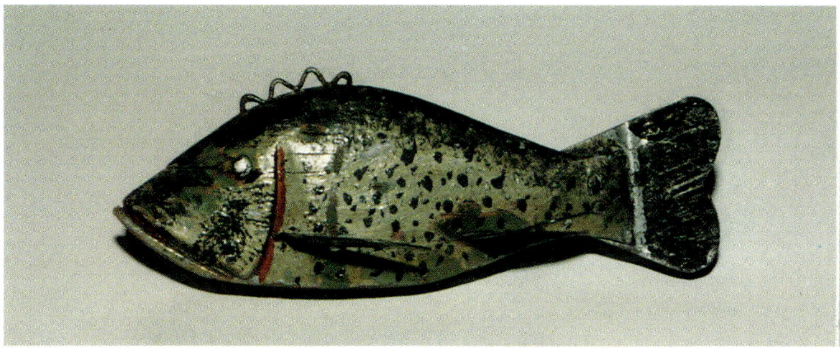

Crappie by Batters. Note loop line tie and rounded tail. 4 1/4 inches.

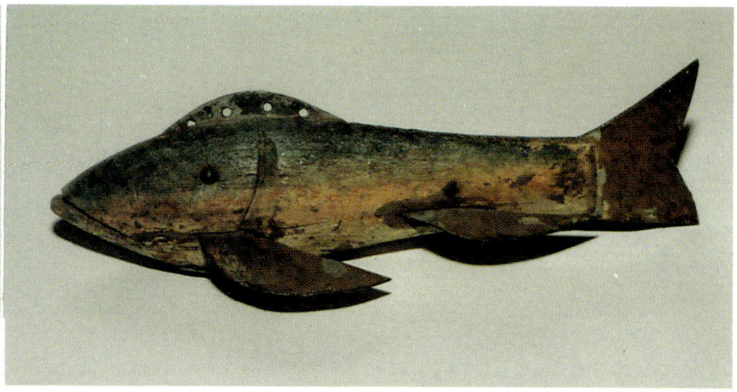

Minnow realistically painted, 5 1/4 inches in length.

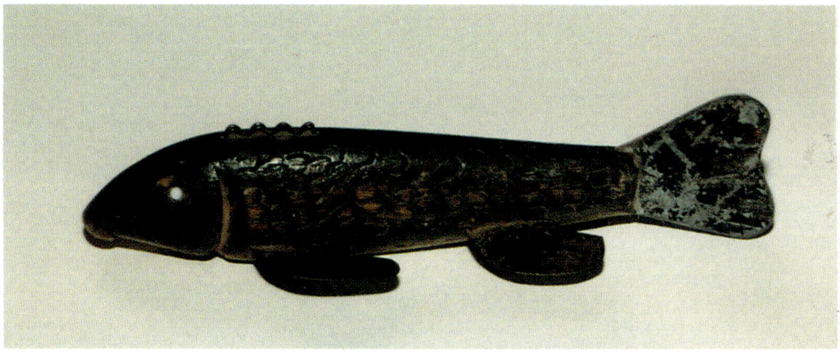

Sucker made by Batters. Note white eye and rounded tail; 5 inches long. This specimen also has carved scales in the sides.

Gerhart Berens

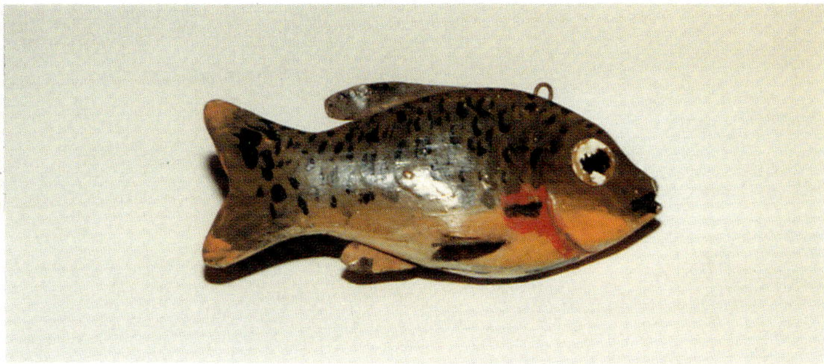

Early Berens' sunfish decoy with a wooden tail (many of his later decoys were made with a metal tail), ca. 1940's, 3 1/2 inches long.

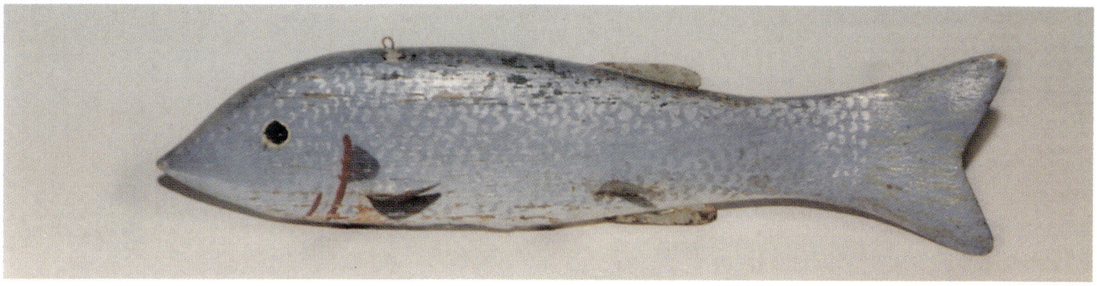

Berens' silver painted (bass?), 9 1/2 inches long, with wood tail, ca. 1940's.

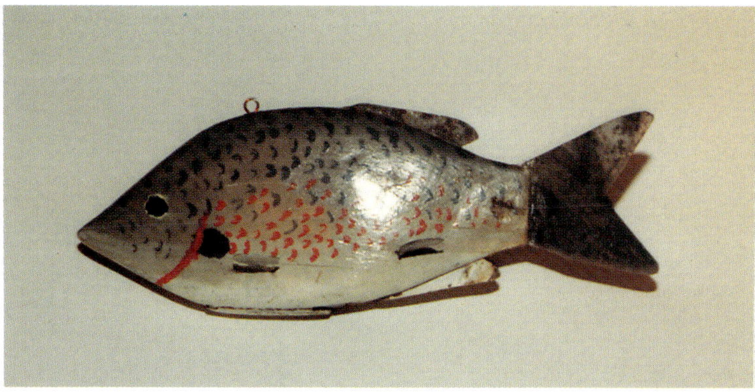

Crappie with metal tail by Berens, ca. 1950's, showing transition from earlier style, 6 1/2 inches in length.

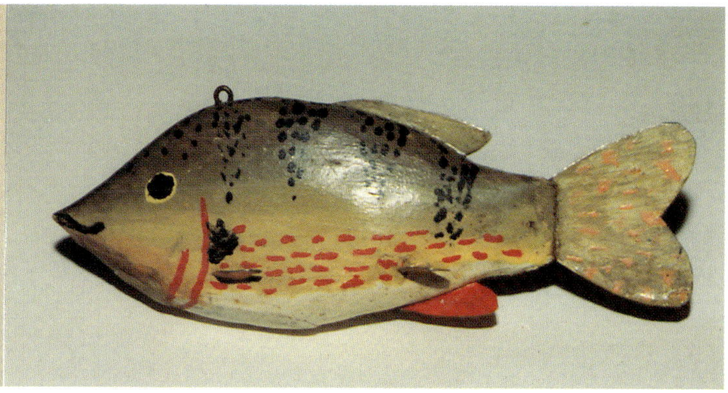

Berens' crappie, 1980's, showing most recent style of decoys, 6 1/4 inches long.

Pearl Bethel

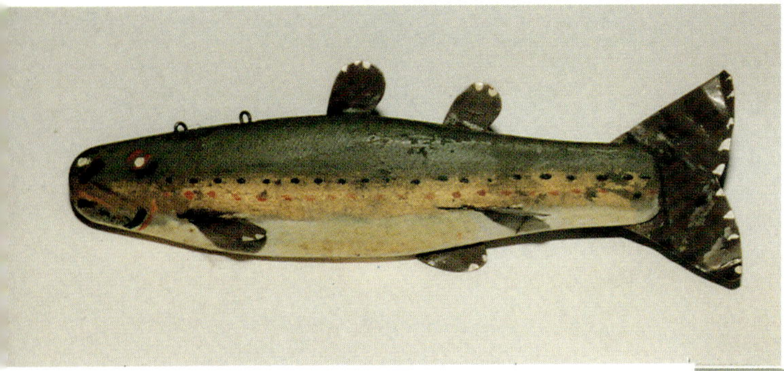

More recent Bethel decoy with strong green paint and tack eyes, 8 1/4 inches.

Pearl Bethel trout, 8 1/4 inches.

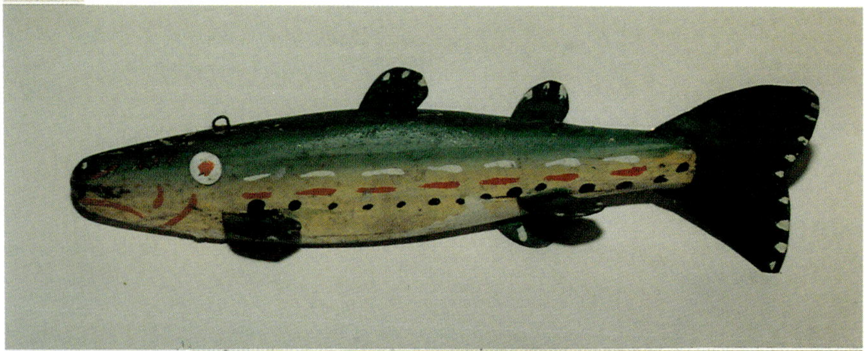

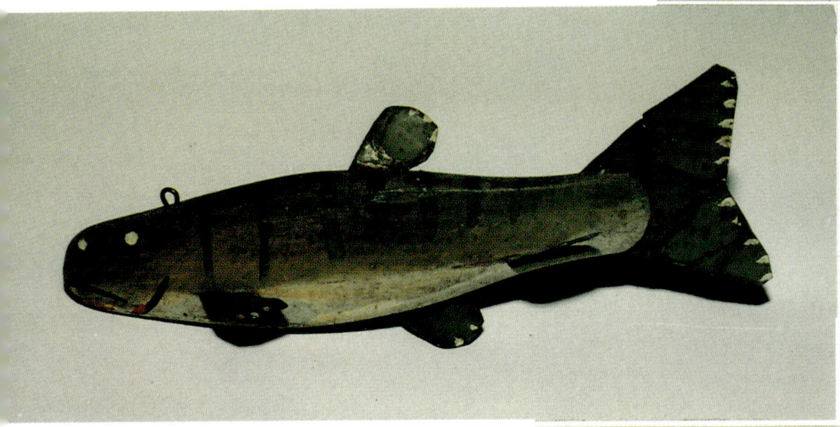

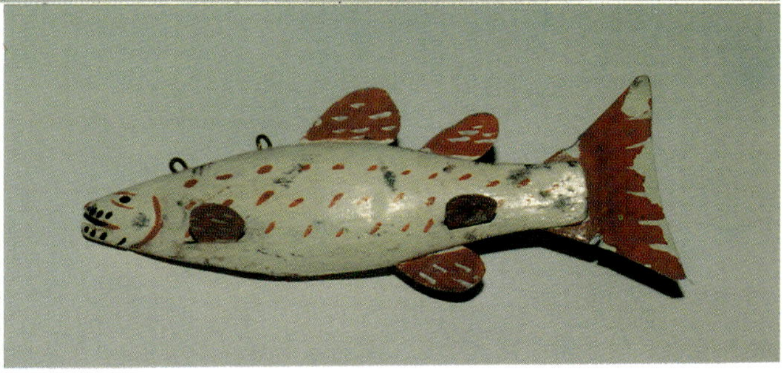

Rare Bethel decoy with open mouth, 6 1/2 inches.

Bethel perch, 6 inches.

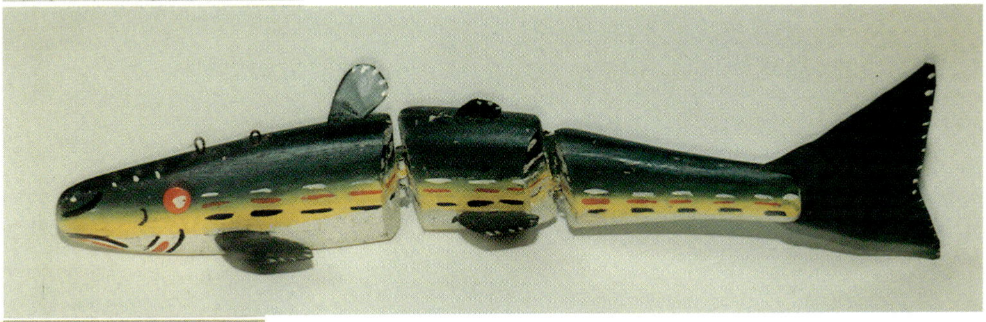

Bethel jointed decoy with tack eye, 12 1/2 inches.

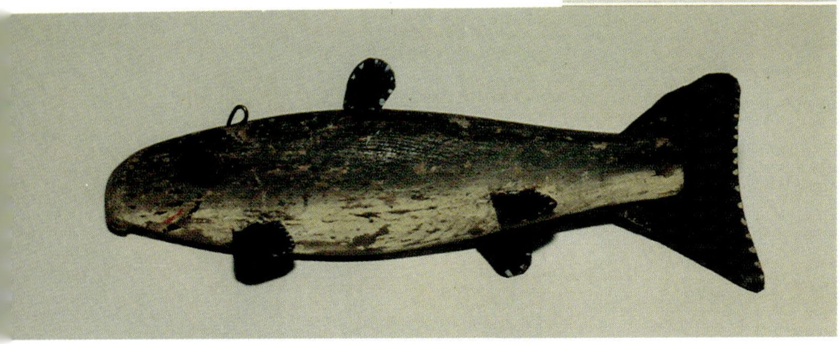

Rare Bethel sucker, 6 3/4 inches long.

Cyril Bethel

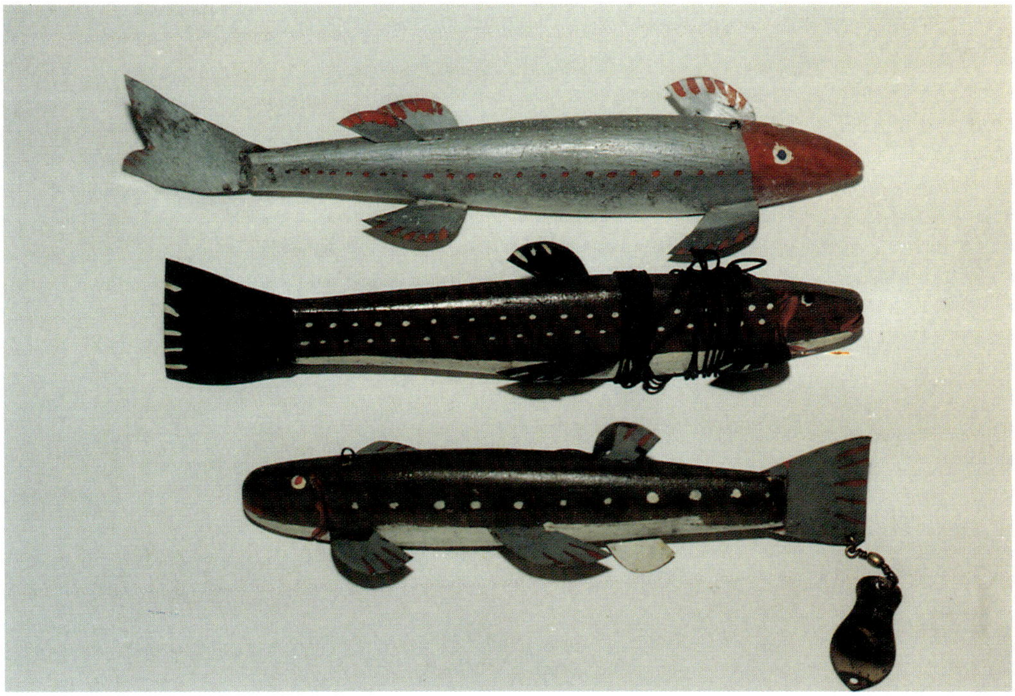

Top: silver bodied Cyril Bethel with red head and dots painted on sides, 10 inches. Middle: brown painted Cyril Bethel with white spot decoration, 9 1/4 inches. Bottom: Cyril Bethel decoy, 9 inches. Note sun-ray-like painted lines at the end of the fins, similar to Pearl Bethel's style.

Otto Bishop Sr.

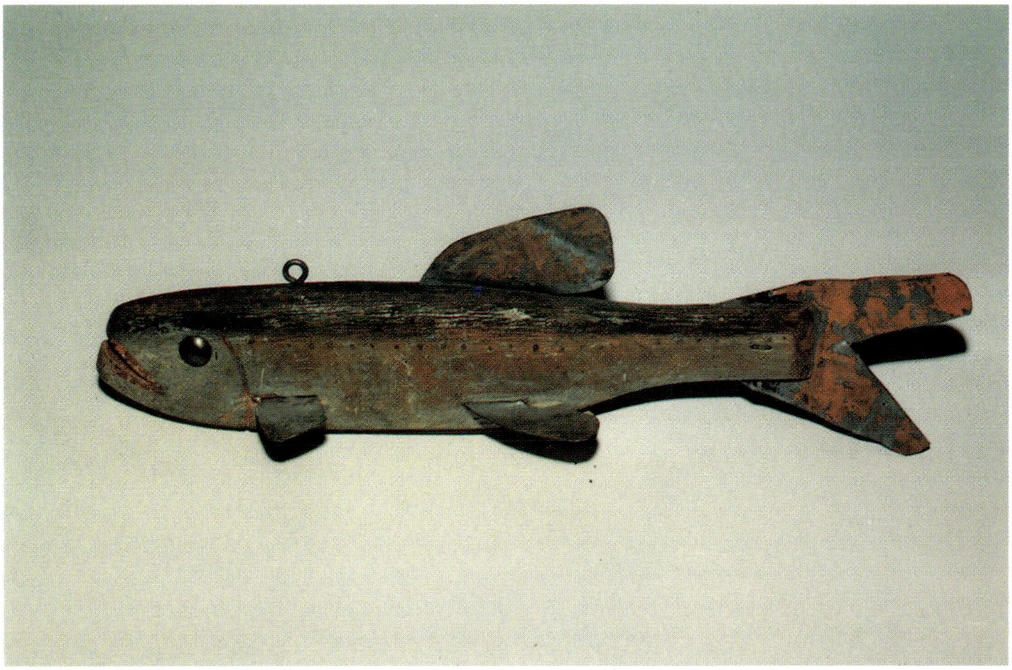

Fish decoy by Otto Bishop, Sr., 8 1/2 inches.

Cecil Blank

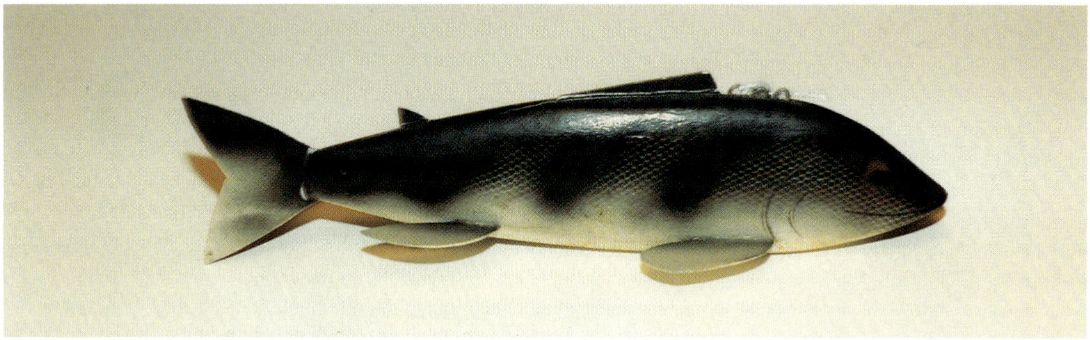

Cecil Blank decoy.

Art Boelter

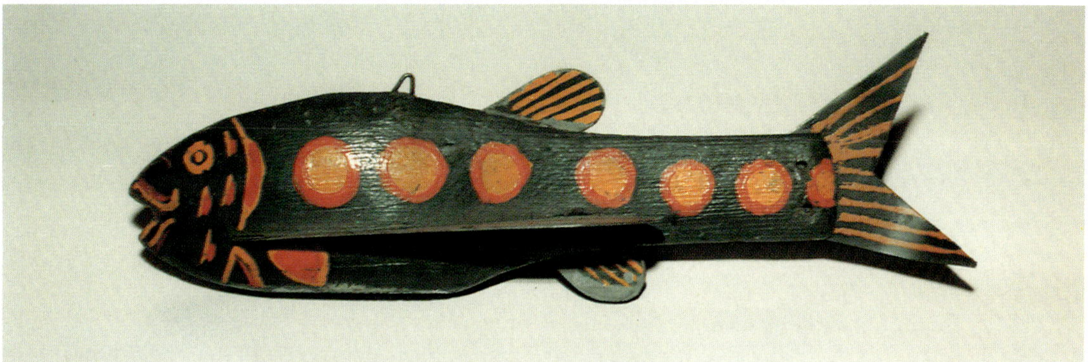

Rare Boelter green and orange painted decoy, 7 inches long.

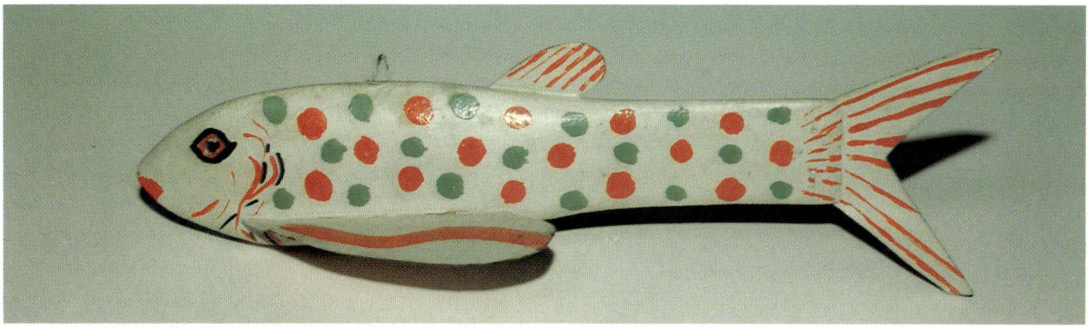

White and red Boelter decoy with polka dot decoration, 8 inches long.

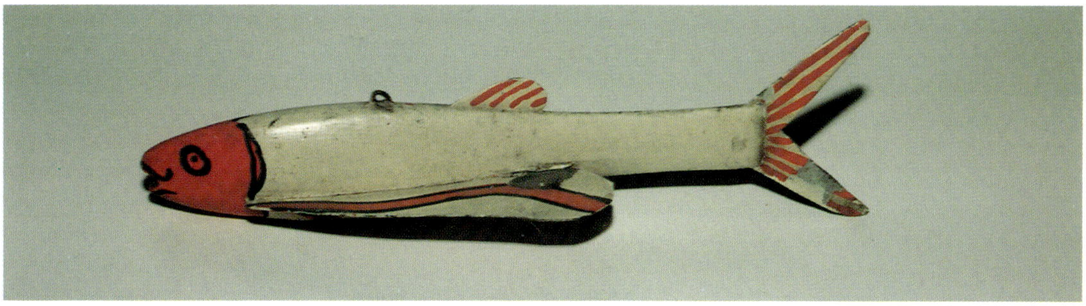

The smallest Boelter decoy known to the author, 6 inches in length.

Merrill Booth

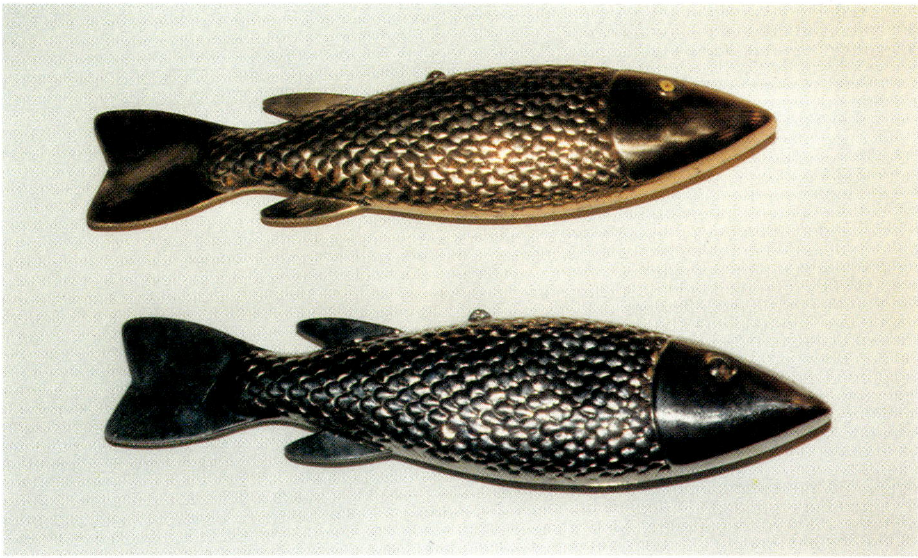

A Booth copper and nickel plated decoy (Frank Pasiewicz collection).

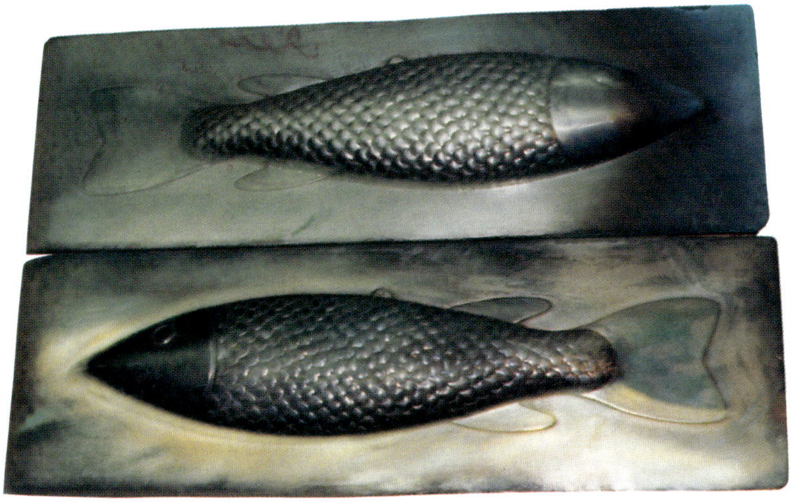

Closeup of Booth molds.

Leo Borash

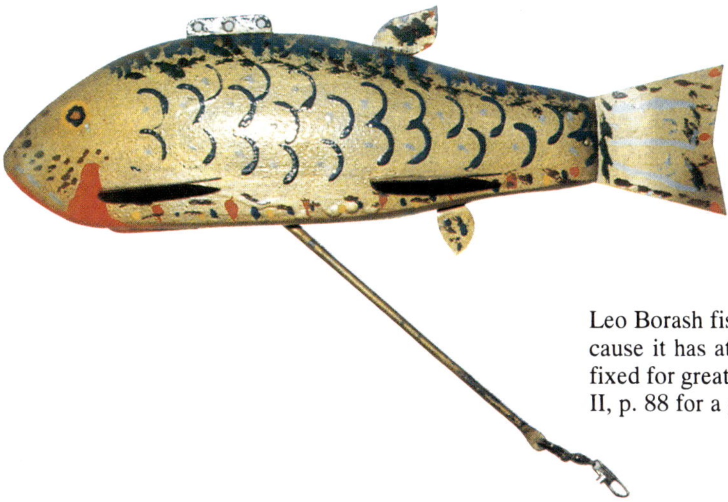

Leo Borash fish decoy showing scaling. This decoy is unusual because it has attached a wire to which a live minnow could be affixed for greater attraction. Length 8 1/2 inches. (see Kimball, Vol. II, p. 88 for a grouping of Borash decoys).

Lawrence J. "Slim" Brinkman

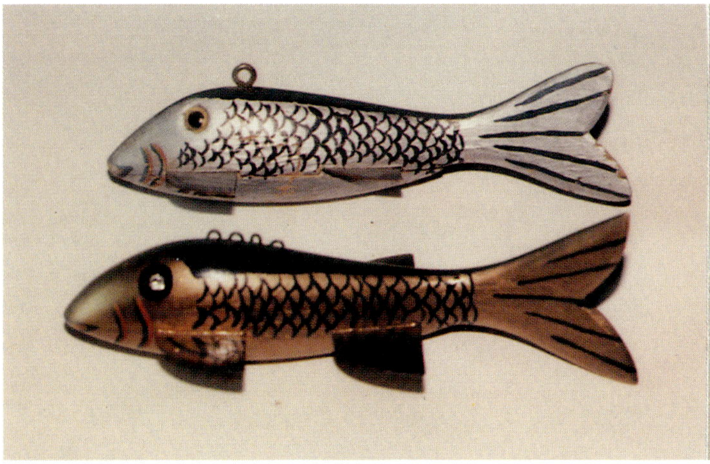

Brinkman quality decoys in silver and gold (Carter Stenberg collection).

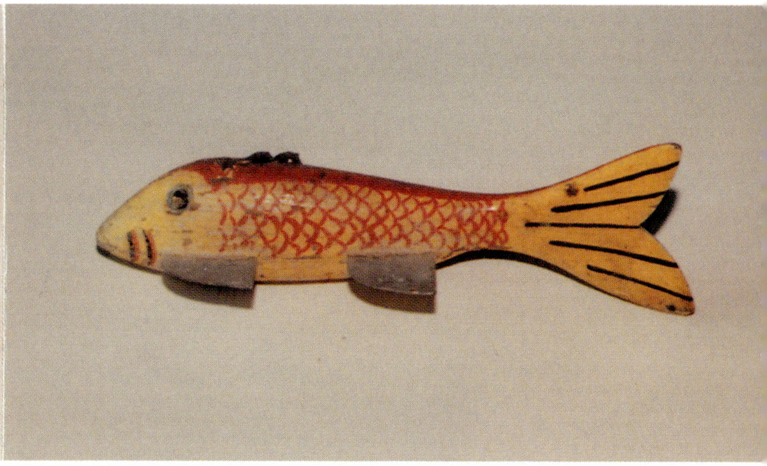

Brinkman yellow painted decoy with red painted scales (K. David Hirschey collection).

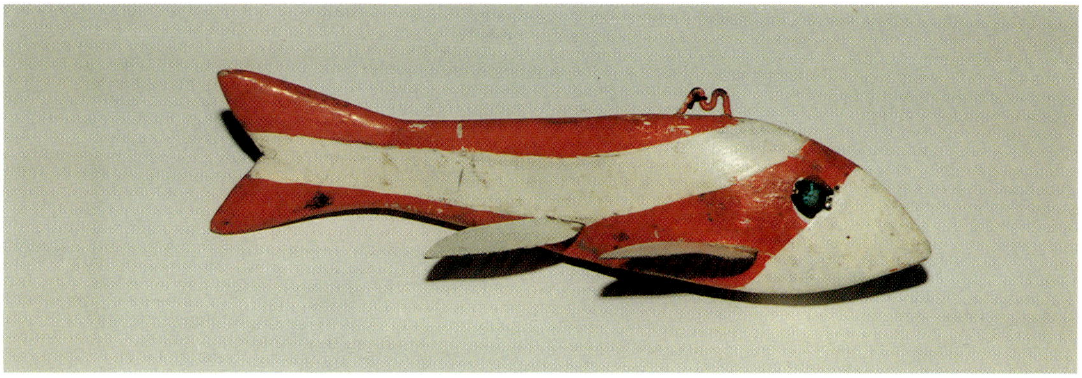

Peppermint painted Brinkman decoy. Contrast the shape of the Brinkman fins on the peppermint painted decoy above to the more detailed painted [quality] decoys.

Chester Buss

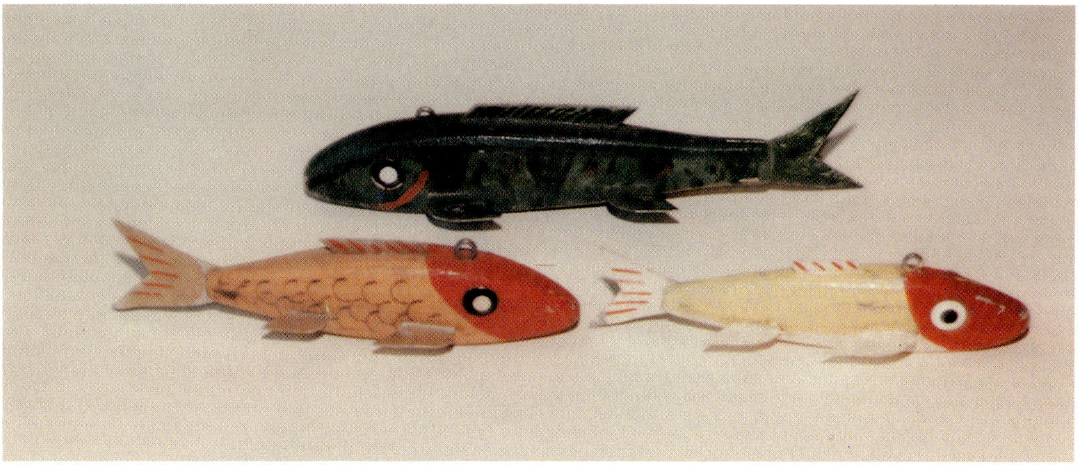

Three fish decoys made by Chester Buss. The top decoy (green) is painted as a perch, while the lower left decoy is adorned with scaling and the bottom right decoy is the ever-present red and white (collection of K. David Hirschey).

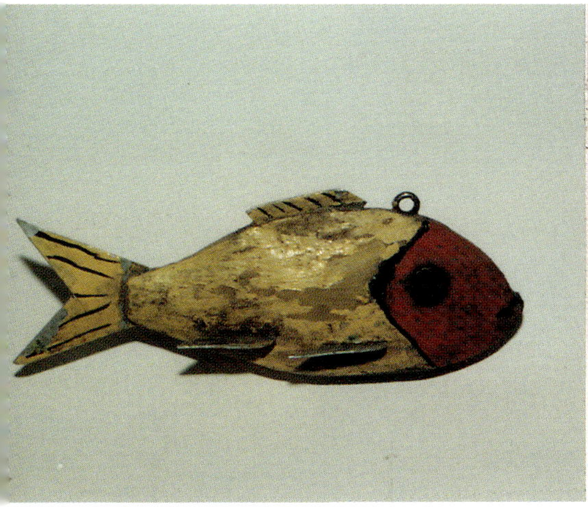

Buss sunfish decoy, 5 inches long.

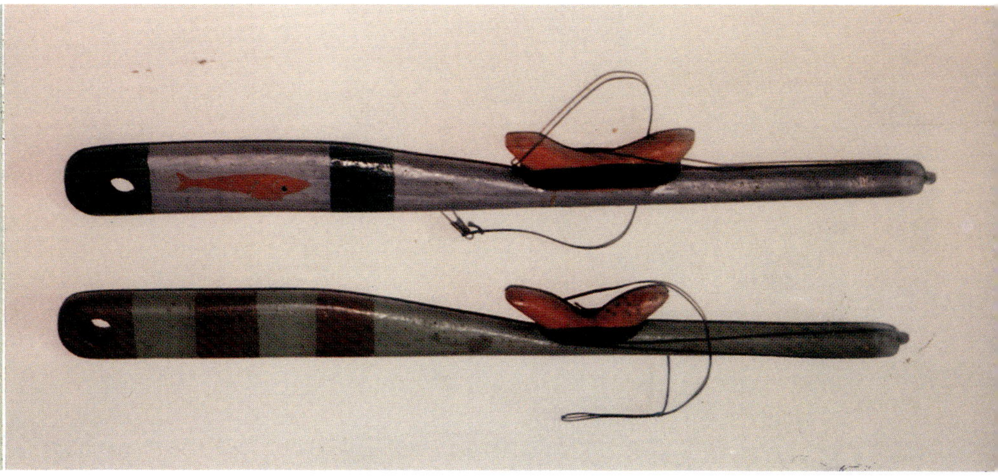

Two jigging sticks made by Chester Buss; one has a Buss decoy painted on it.

Marion W. Butcher

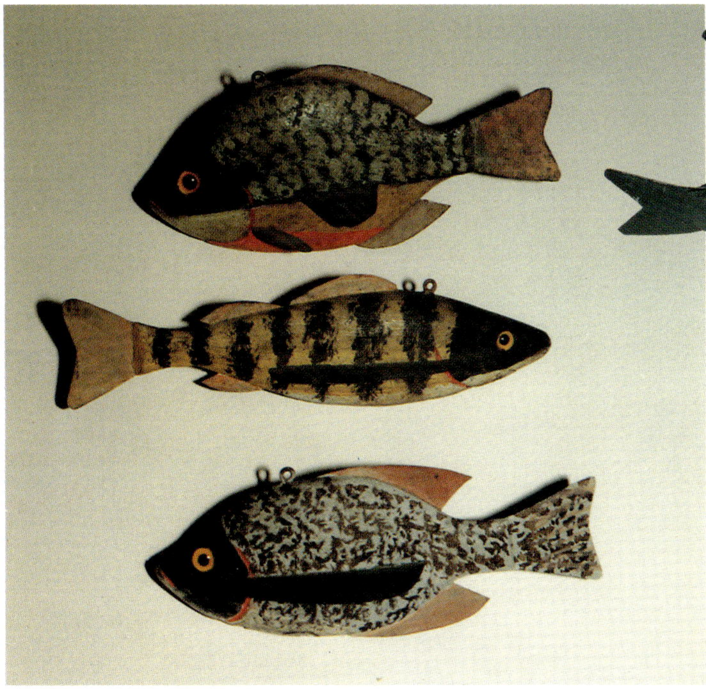

Three surviving Marion Butcher fish decoys. Top: a sunfish, 6 1/2 inches long; middle: a perch, 7 1/4 inches in length; and bottom: a crappie, 6 1/4 inches.

Harvey Case

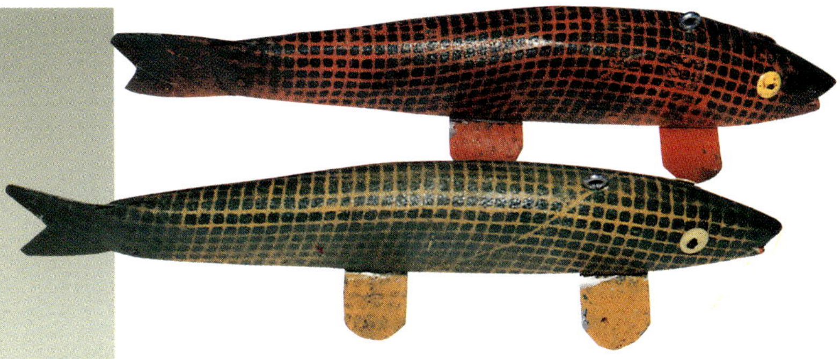

Two Harvey Case decoys, each 10 inches long.

Willis Clark

Willis Clark decoy, 11 inches in length, ca. 1930's. Decoy has painted gills and mouth, white bead eyes, and metal pectoral fins, tail fin and dorsal fin.

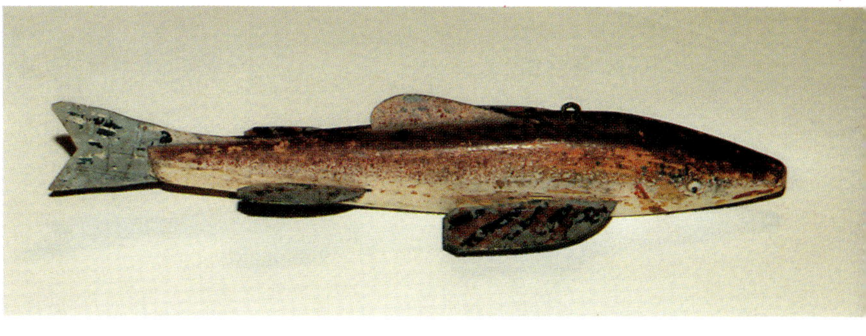

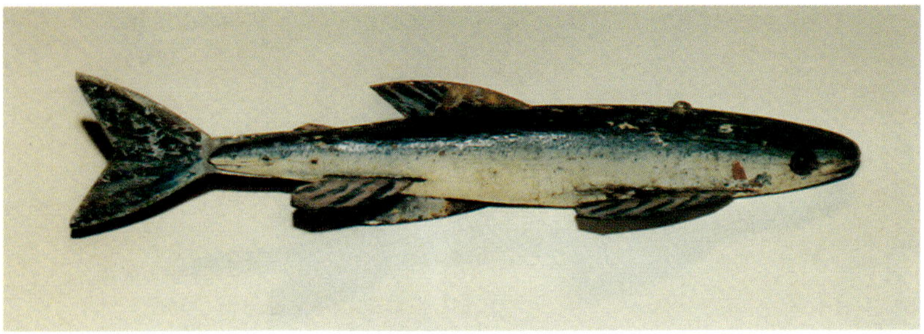

A 9 inch Willis Clark decoy with metal pectoral fins, tail fin and both a dorsal and anal fin, ca. 1930's.

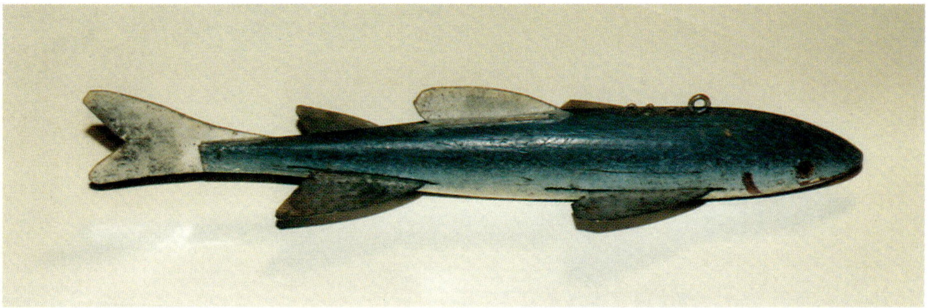

Blue painted Willis Clark decoy. Metal pectoral fins are flat on the back, giving them a distinctive shape, ca. 1930's. Courtesy of John Cook.

Jack Cooper

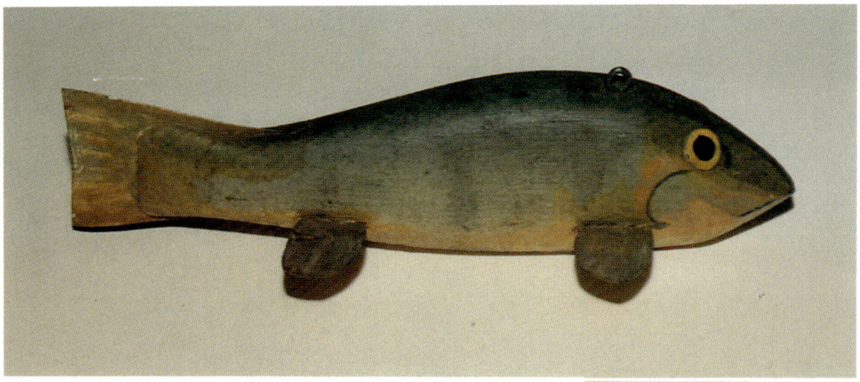

Jack Cooper sunfish, 9 inches long.

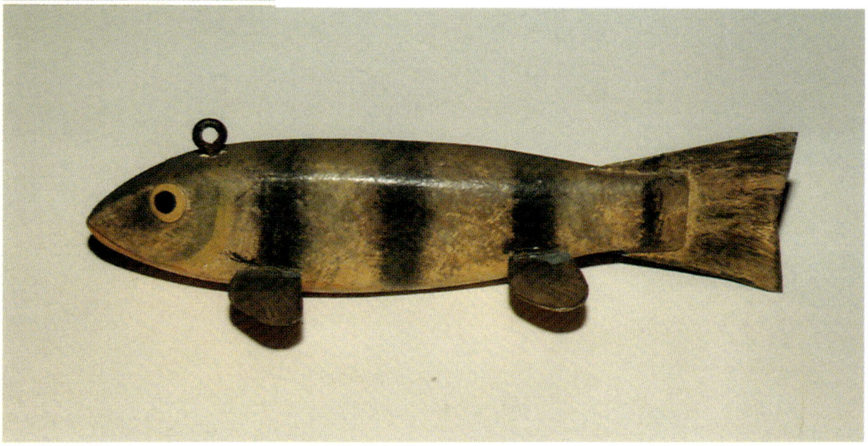

Perch made by Jack Cooper, 7 inches.

George G. Dahl

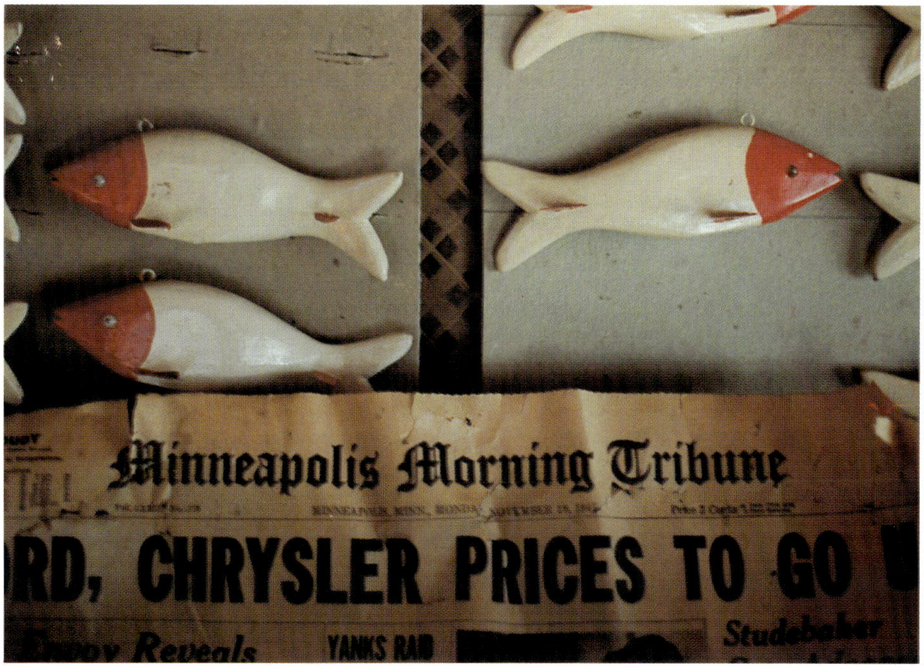

George Dahl decoys, length 4 3/4 inches. Photo courtesy Carter Stenberg.

Al Dincau

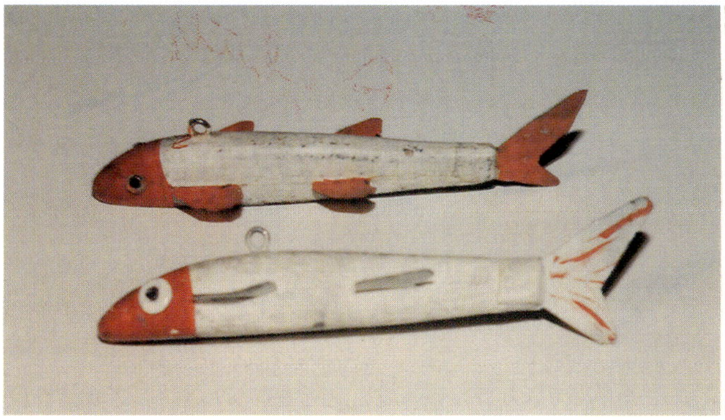

Two Al Dincau decoys.

Otis Doty

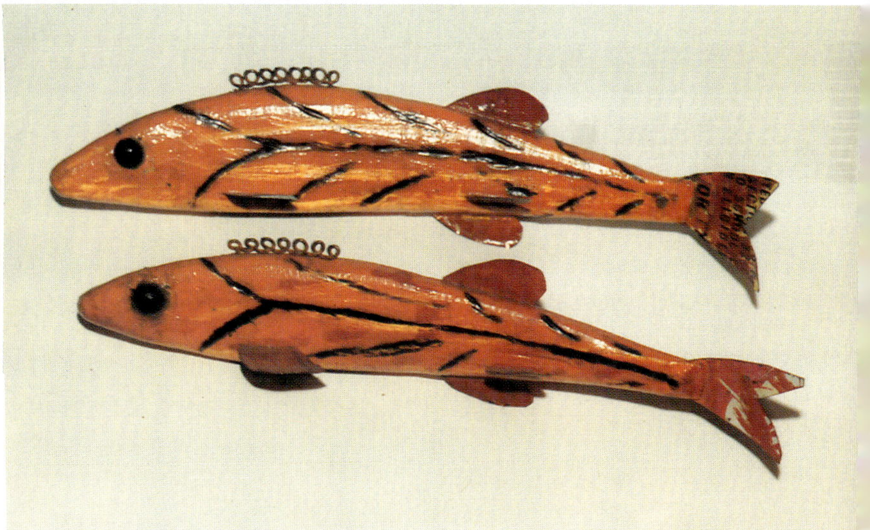

Otis Doty curved body decoys, painted orange and heavily varnished, ca. 1950's, 10 inches in length.

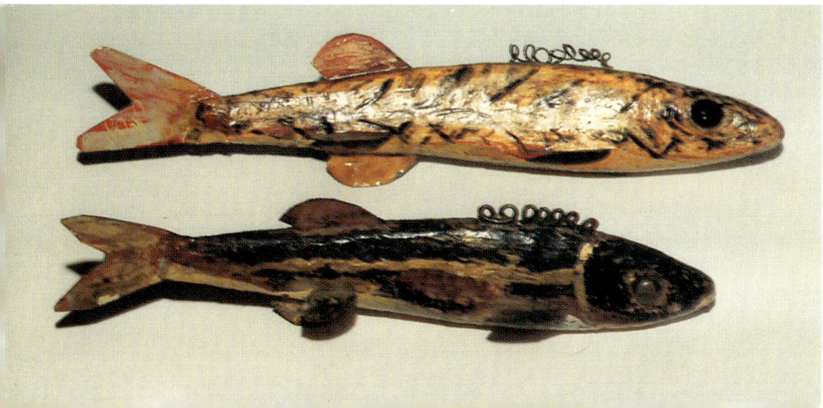

Painted and varnished Doty decoys, 7 1/2 and 8 inches long.

Carl "Gus" Dornquast

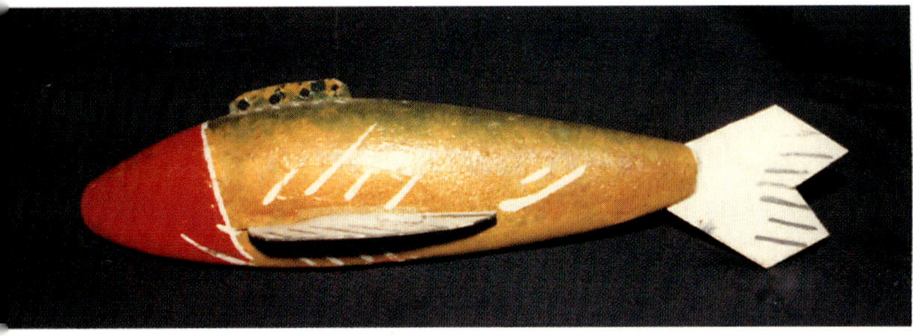

Two fin Gus Dornquast decoy. Photo courtesy of Bill Stoetzel.

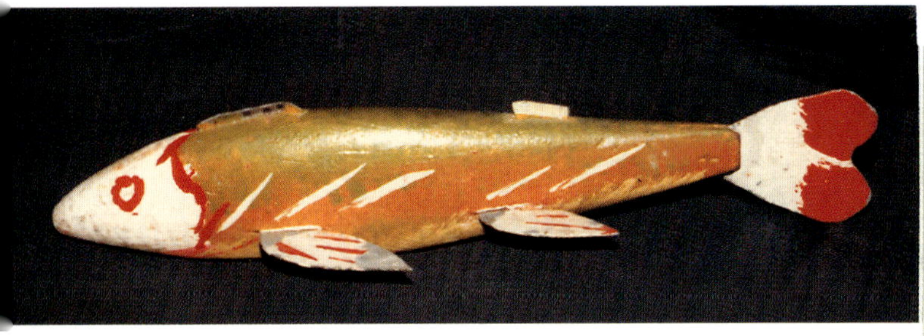

Gus Dornquast decoy with four fins. Photo courtesy of Bill Stoetzel.

Milton Ebinger

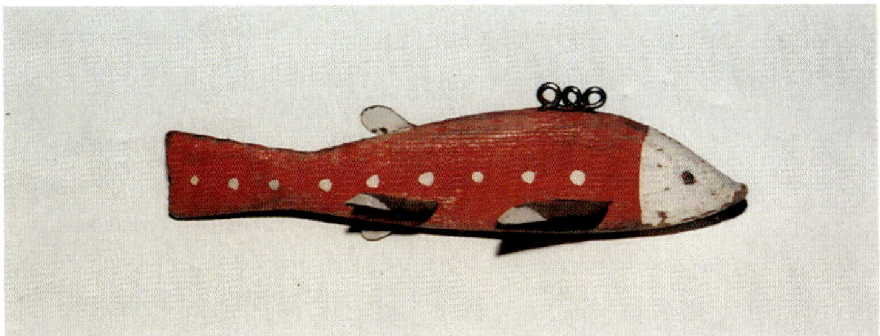

A typical Milton Ebinger decoy, painted red and white. Length, 4 inches.

Charles Engel

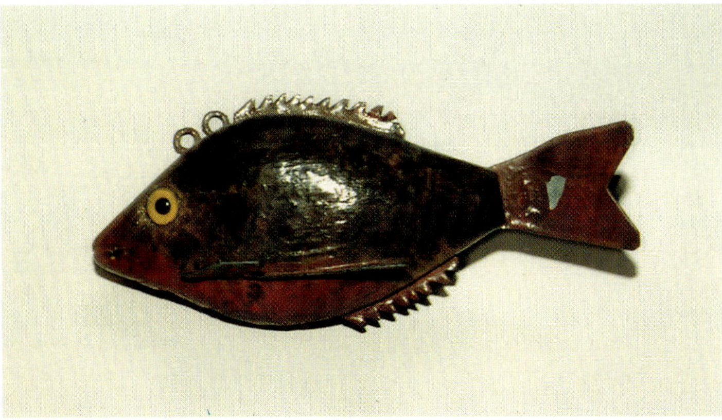

Sunfish by Charles Engel, 5 inches.

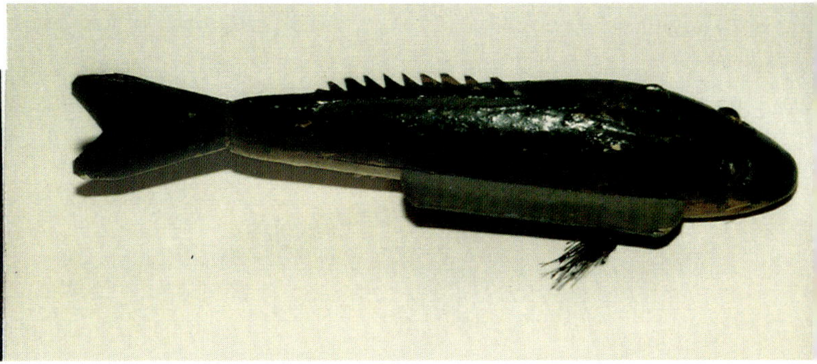

Charles Engel bullhead. This one had tufts of horse hair to imitate the bullhead whiskers, 5 1/2 inches.

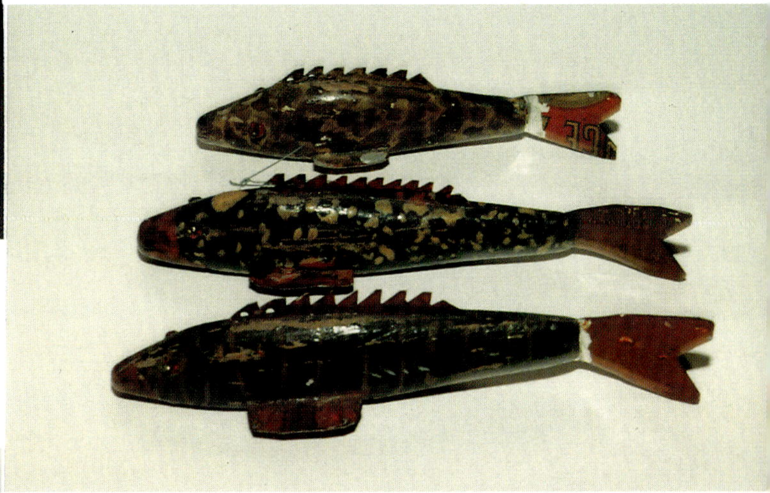

Three Engel minnows; top was 4 inches, middle 4 3/4 inches and bottom 5 inches.

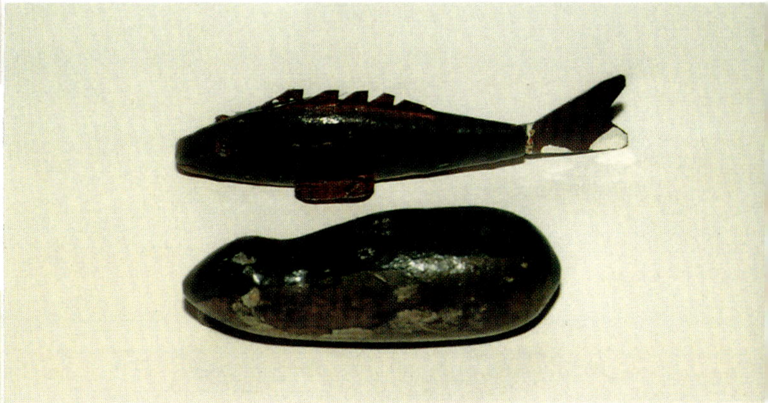

Engel minnow and mouse. The minnow measures 4 inches and the mouse is 3 inches in length.

Leo Eppel

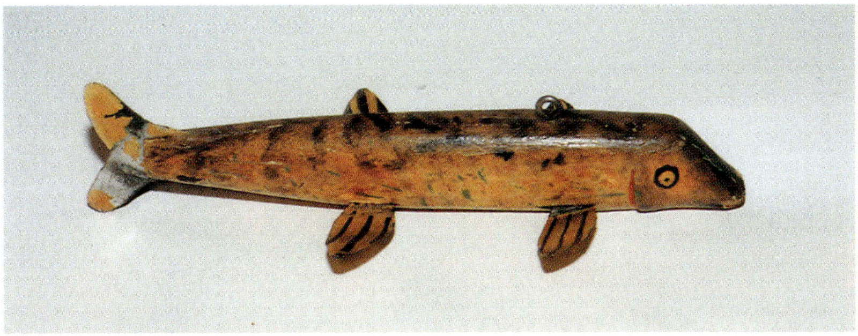

Leo Eppel decoy, ca. 1930's, about 7 inches in length. John McCormick collection.

Nels Fairbanks

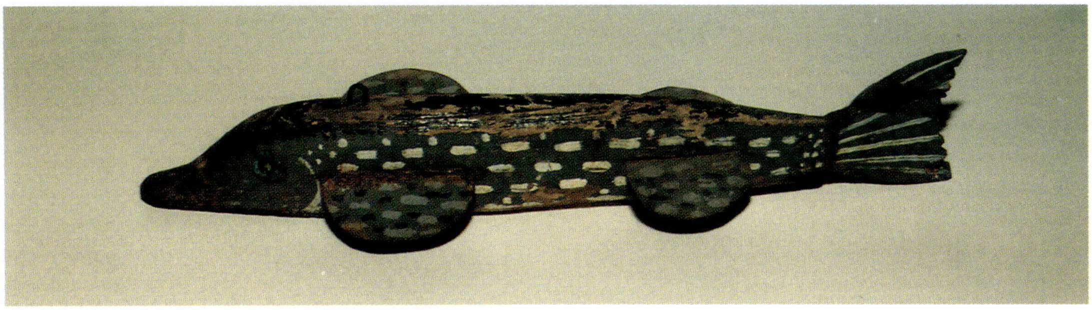

Fairbanks northern, painted grey with white dashes, ca. 1930's, 7 1/4 inches.

Otto Faue

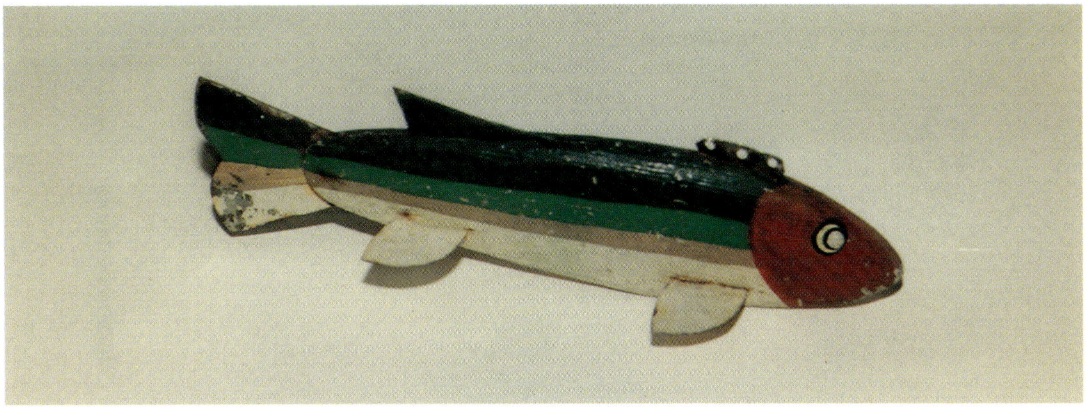

Otto Faue decoy, with white underside in shades of green with beige line for decoration, 6 3/4 inches.

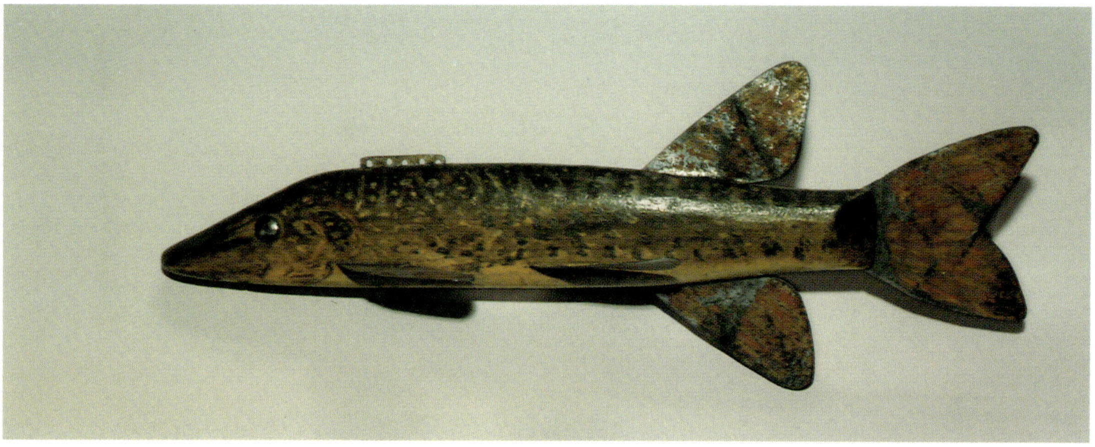

Northern Pike by Otto Faue, 11 inches long.

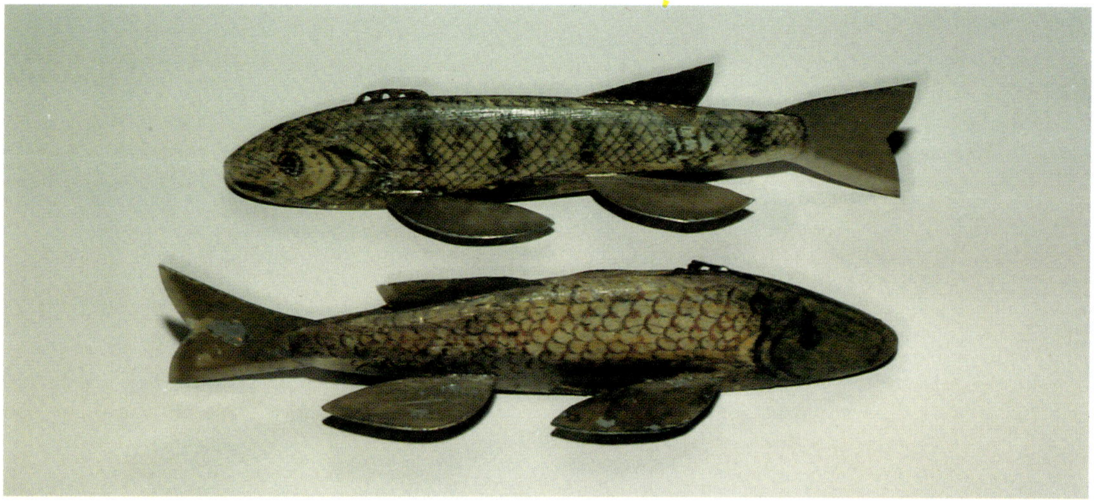

Two early decoys by Otto Faue, showing unusual decorative scales, both 6 3/4 inches.

William Faue

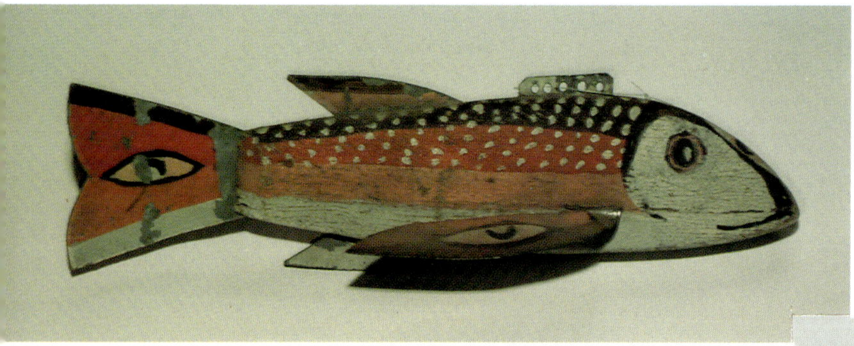

William Faue "angel eye" fish. Note eye on tail and fin of decoy, 6 3/4 inches.

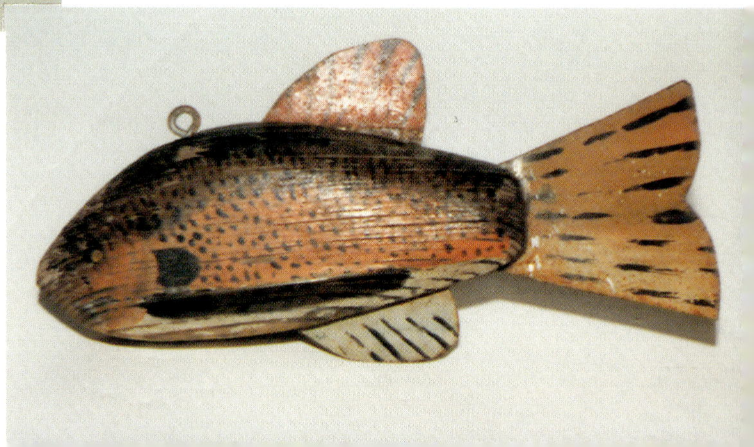

Beautifully painted William Faue sunfish, 6 3/4 inches.

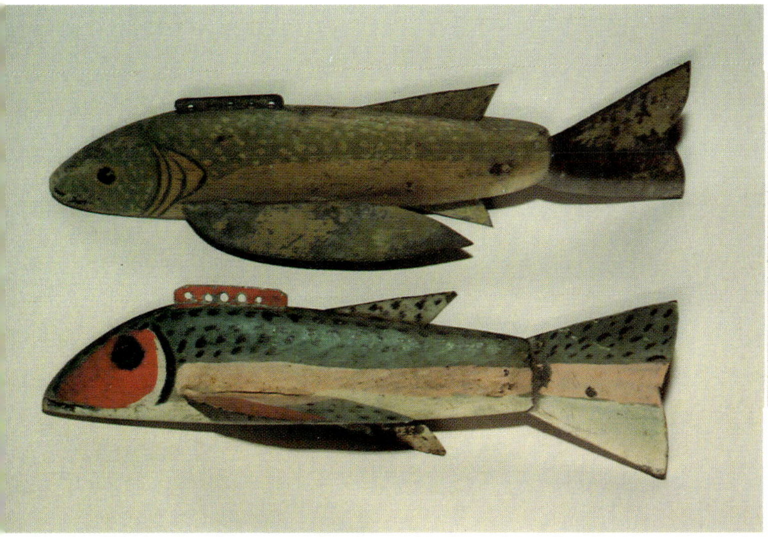

Frank Filipek

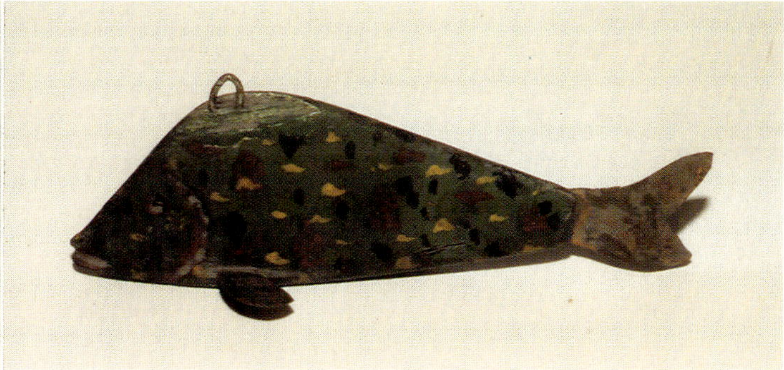

Frank Filipek crappie, 4 3/4 inches.

William Faue minnows. Top is 6 1/2 inches long and bottom is 5 3/4 inches.

William Flanagan

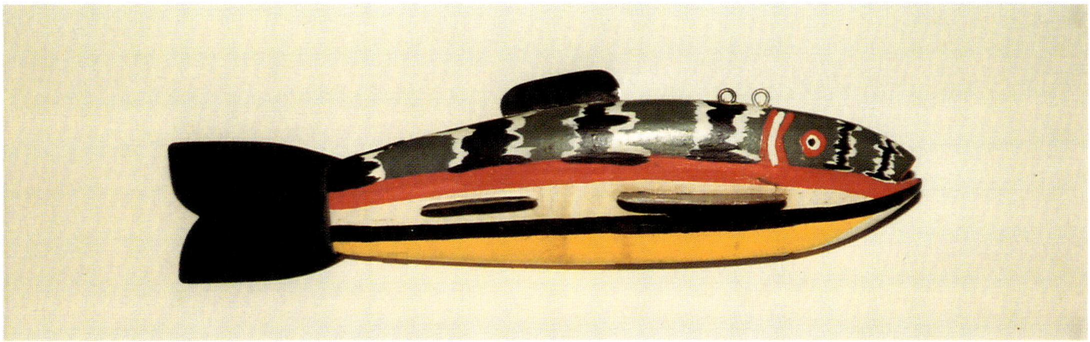

William Flanagan decoy, 9 1/2 inches.

Peter J. Fuchs

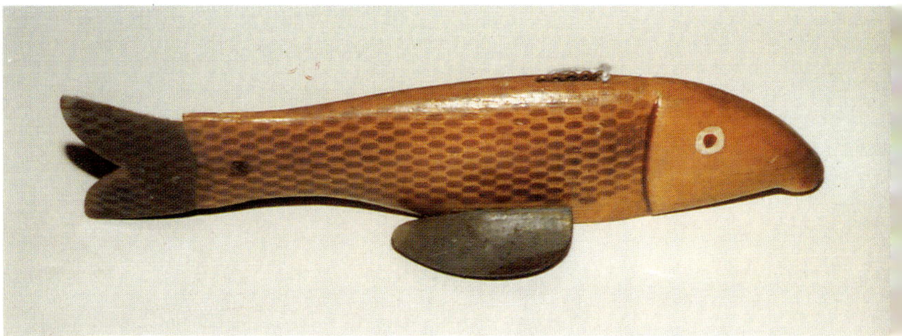

Peter Fuchs' sucker with metal tail, 7 3/4 inches.

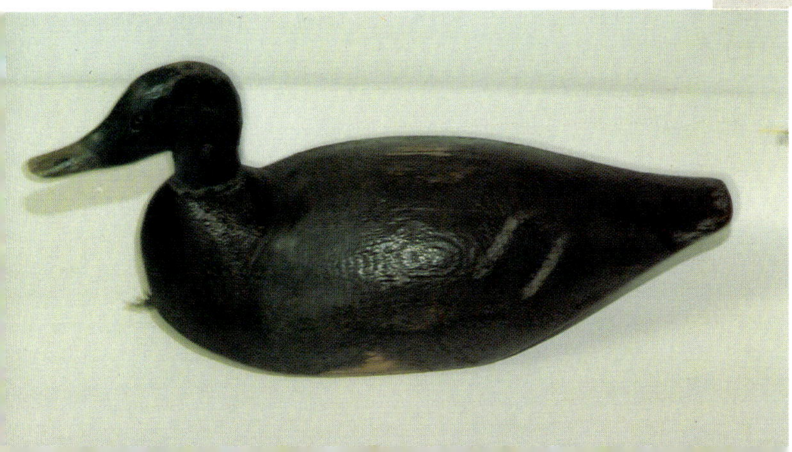

Duck decoy, ca. 1939, by Peter Fuchs. Collection of Tom Swentufske.

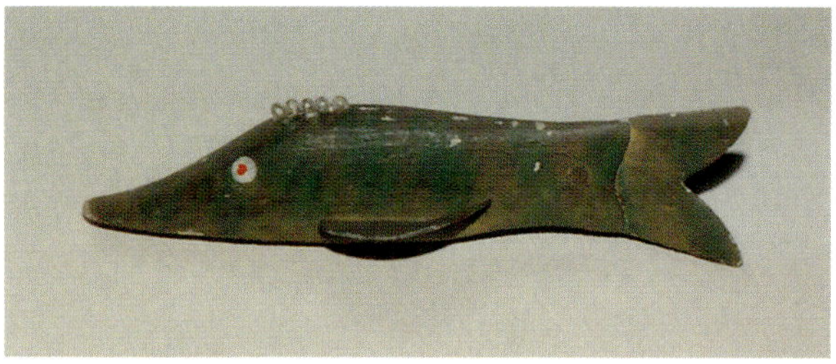

Northern pike with metal tail, 6 1/4 inches.

Clarence "Tarz" Geiselhart

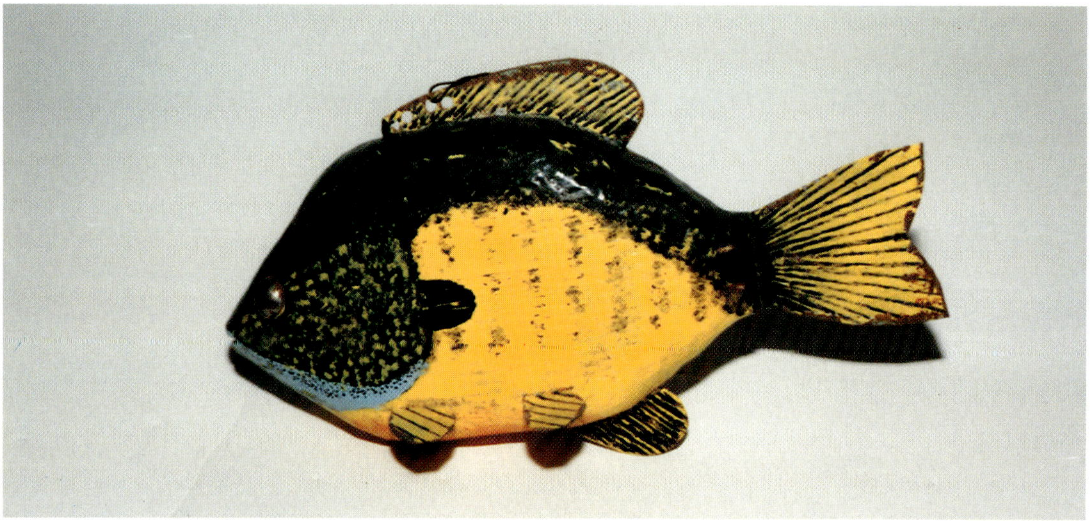

A "Tarz" Geiselhart decoy.

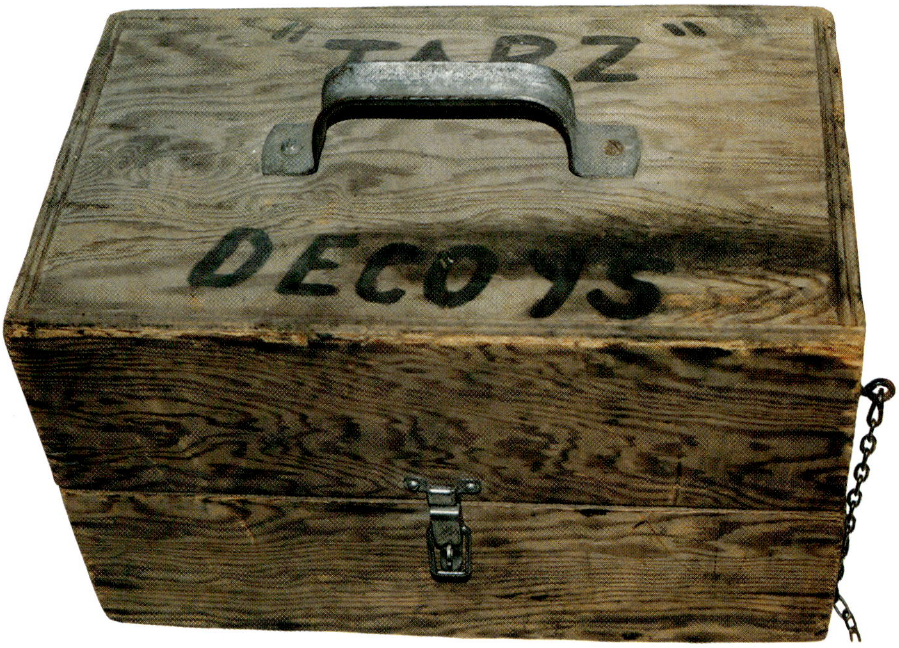

Mr. Geiselhart's personal decoy box.

William H. "Bill" Green

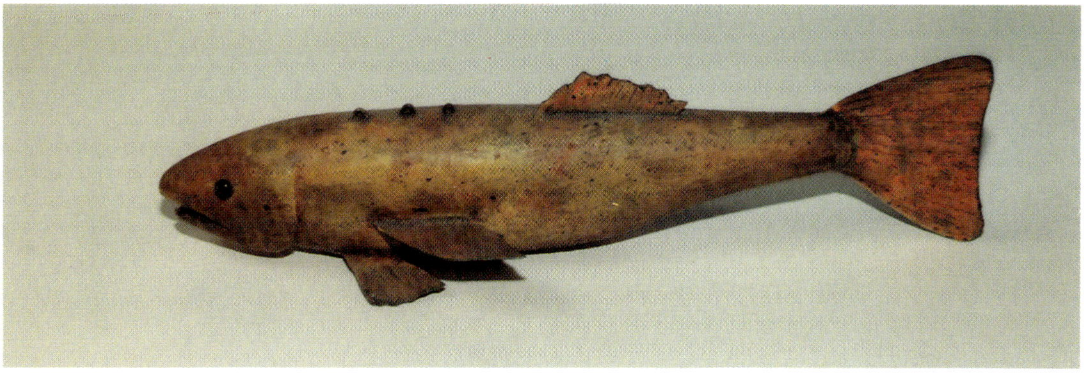

Only known surviving Bill Green decoy from the 1940's.

Joe Gustin

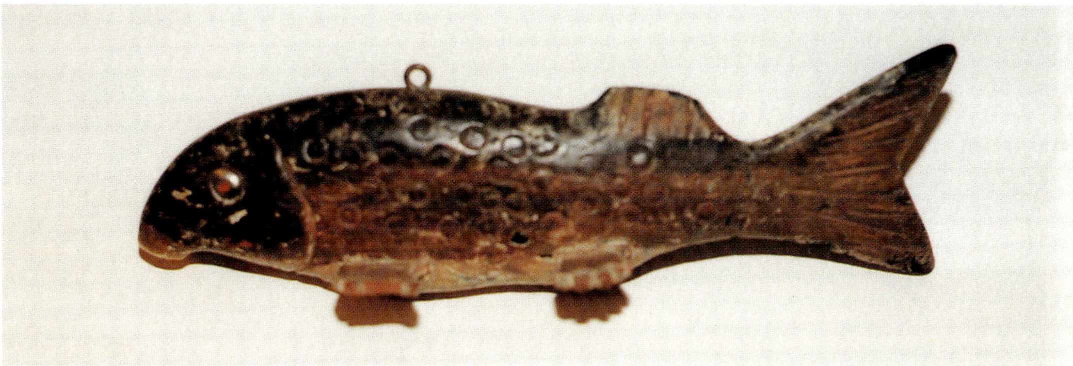

Sucker decoy by Joe Gustin, ca. 1930's, about 9 inches in length. Collection of John Banholzer.

Arnold G. Hafstad

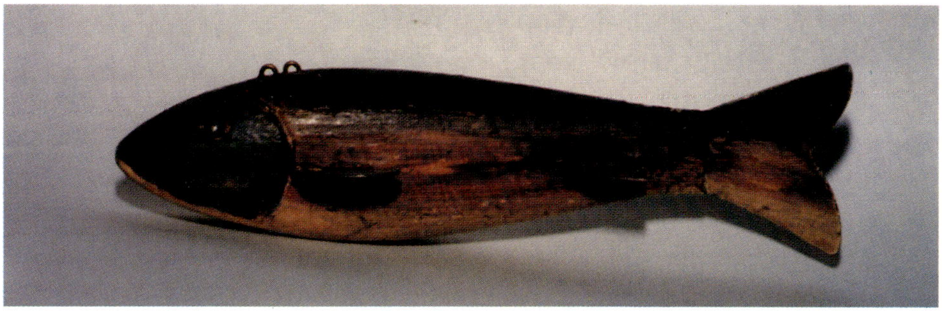

Arnold Hafstad decoy.

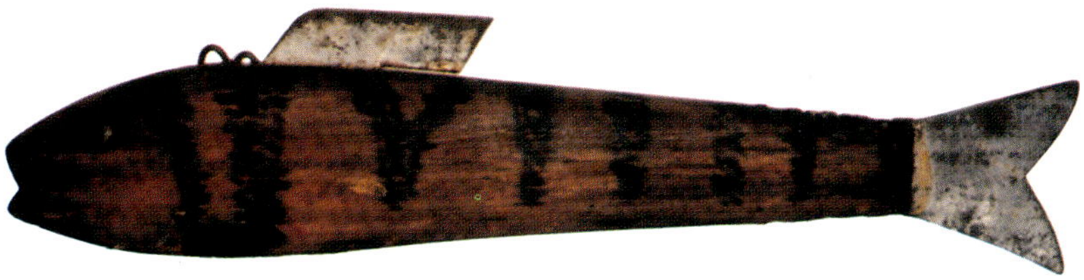

Arnold Hafstad decoy.

Charles "Chuck" Hall

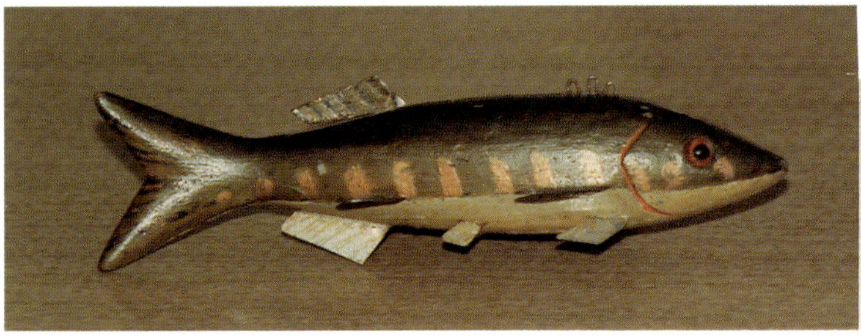

Chuck Hall perch, 8".

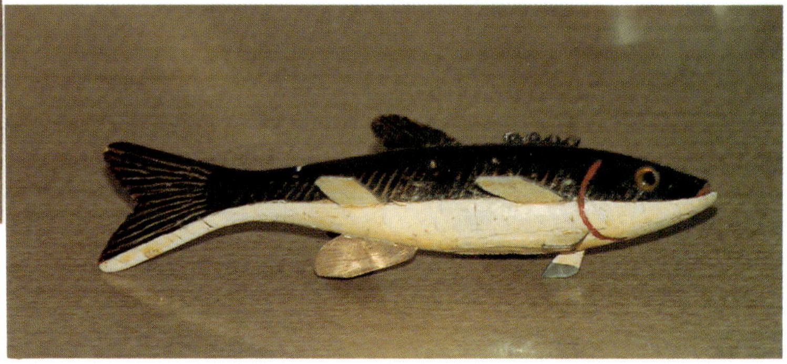

Walleye pike by Chuck Hall, 8 1/2 inches.

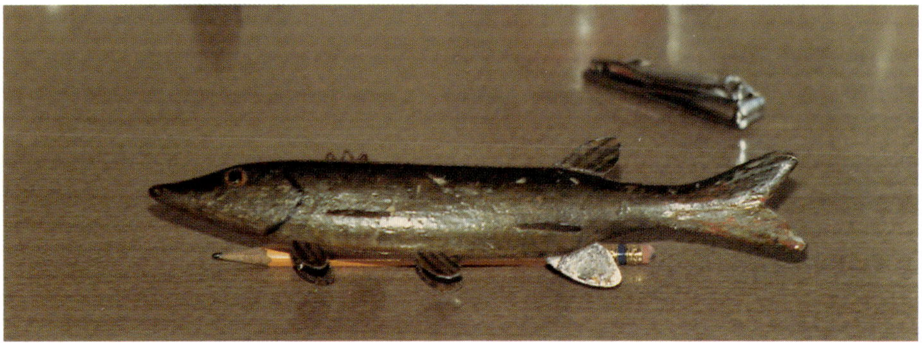

Hall northern pike, 9".

William D. Harrison

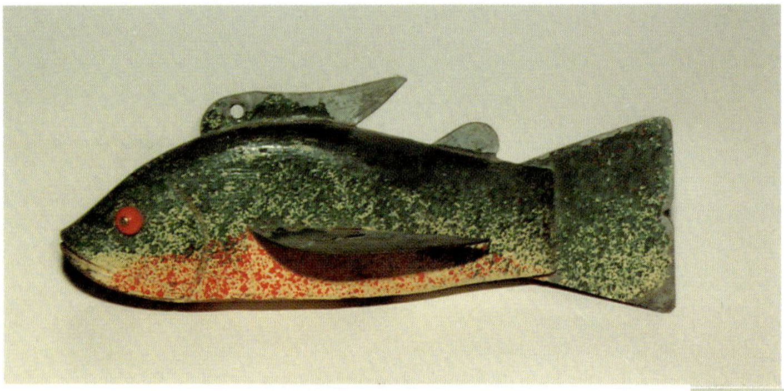

Harrison crappie with metal tail, characteristic line tie with a single hole. Eyes are red leader balls. Note speckling paint and carved mouth, 5 1/8 inches.

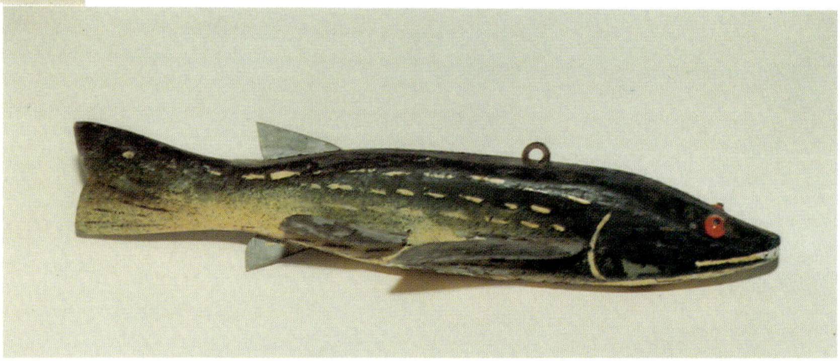

Northern Pike by Bill Harrison with wooden tail, red leader balls for eyes, and screw eye for line tie, 6 3/4 inches.

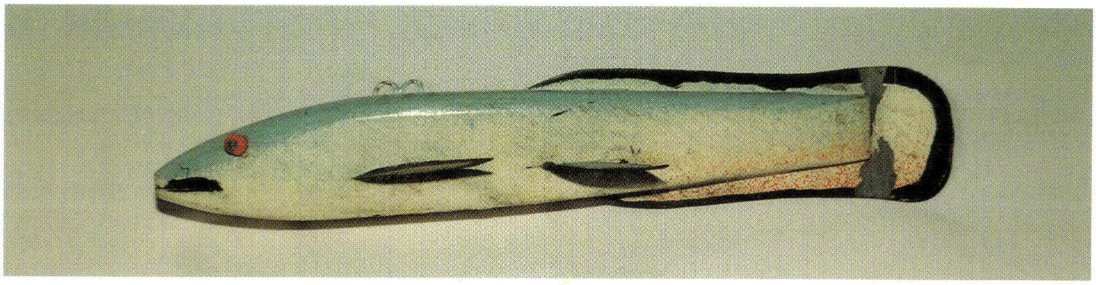

Eel pout (fresh water ling) by Harrison, with metal tail, unusual line tie [for Harrison], 7 1/4 inches.

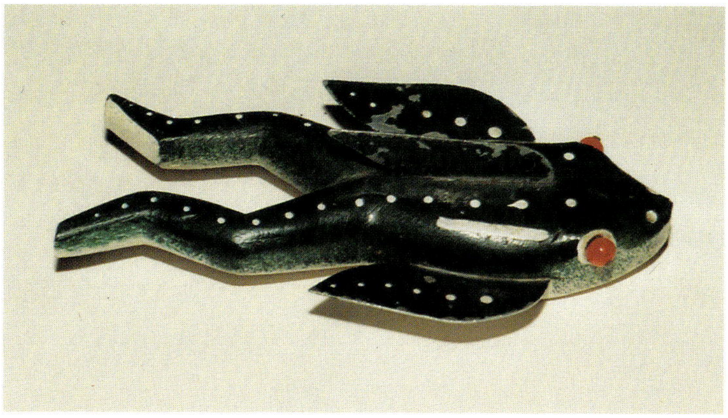

Harrison frog with speckled paint and dots for decoration, 3 1/4 inches.

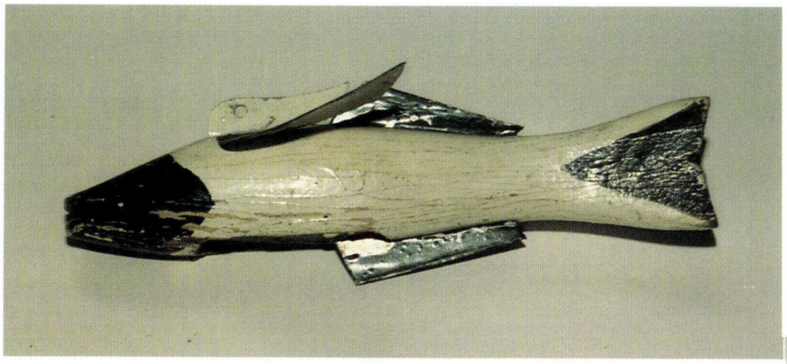

Black and white painted Harrison decoy with wooden tail and metal anal fin, 5 1/4 inches.

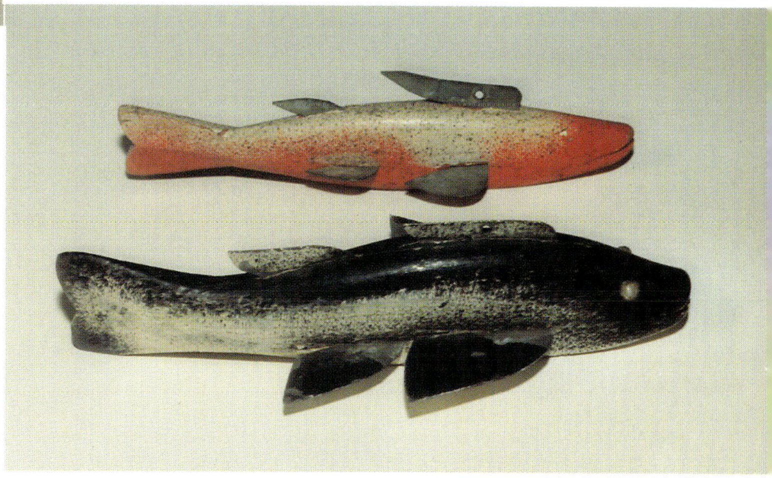

Two Harrison decoys with wooden tails. Note top decoy has no eyes, but bottom one has large white beads for eyes. Top decoy, 5 inches, and bottom decoy, 5 1/2 inches.

John Hesjedal

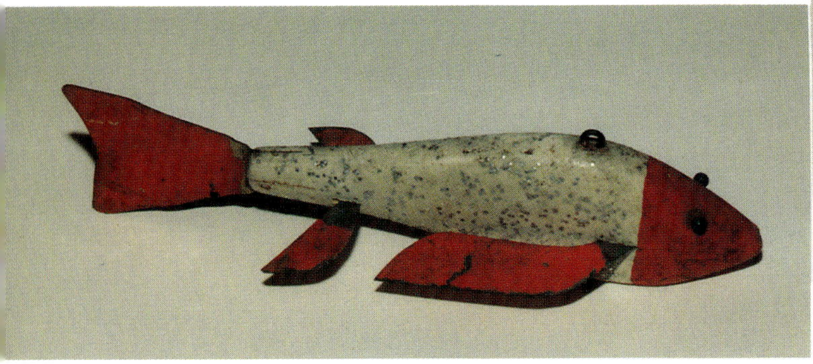

Typical Hesjedal red and white decoy showing glitter decoration and map pin eyes. Note swept back fins, 7 1/2 inches.

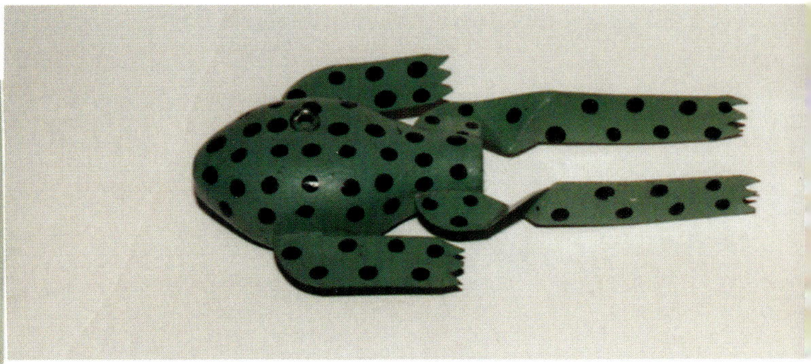

Rare Hesjedal frog. Mr. Hesjedal apparently made a few of these later in his carving career, 5 1/8 inches.

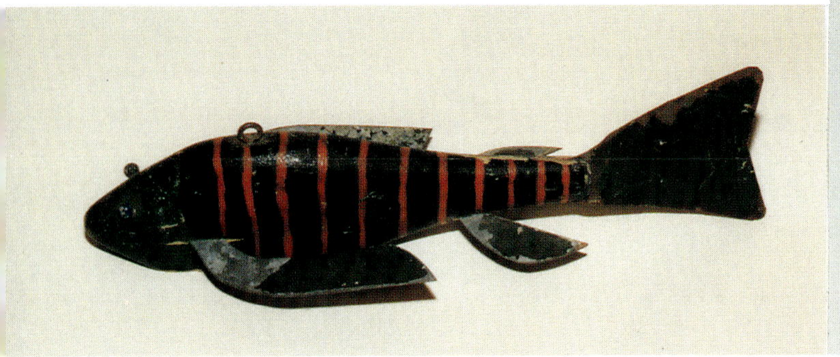

Nicely painted Hesjedal decoy. Russel Johnson collection.

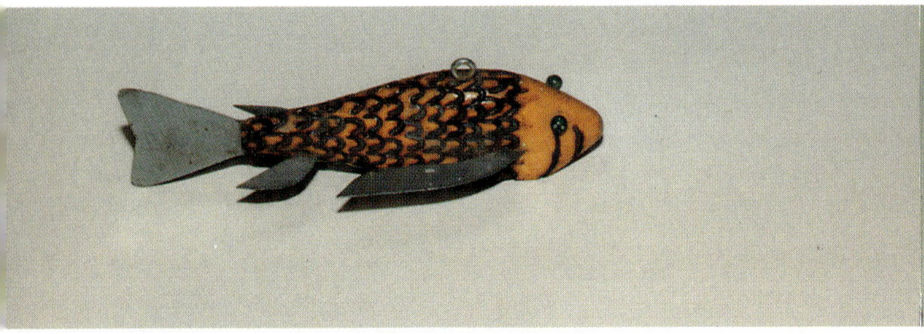

Unusual burned scale and gills decoy by Hesjedal. 5 inches long.

LeRoy Howell

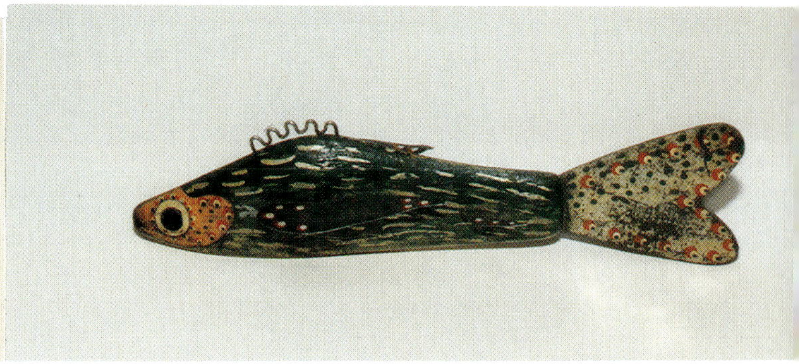

LeRoy Howell angel fish with unusual dash design, 6 1/4 inches.

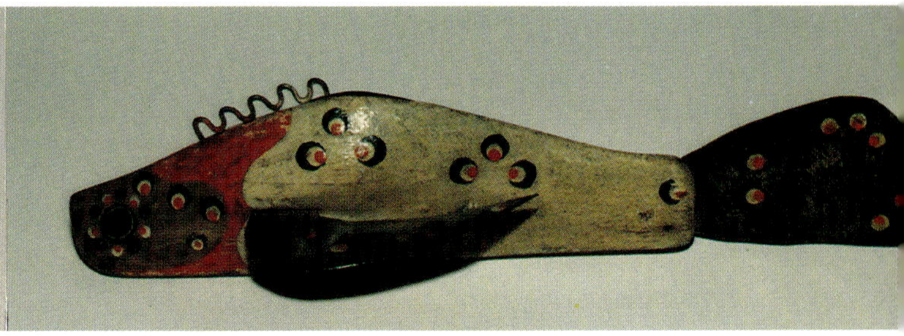

Middle period Howell "flowered" decoy. Note simpler tail fin design that marked Howell's middle and later period fish, 8 1/2 inches.

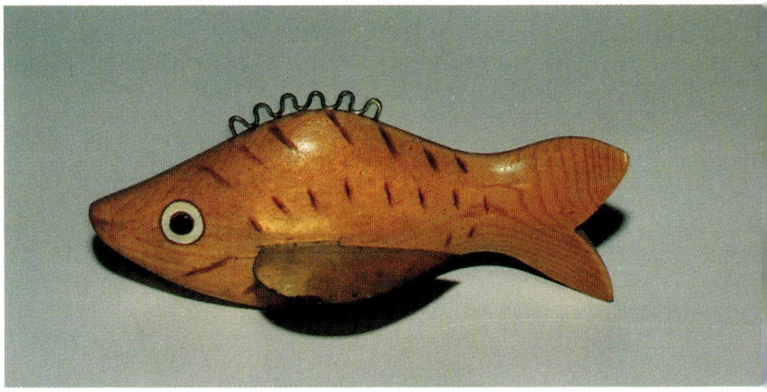

Varnished sunfish with wooden tail by Howell. Decoy is varnished with some decoration, 4 1/2 inches.

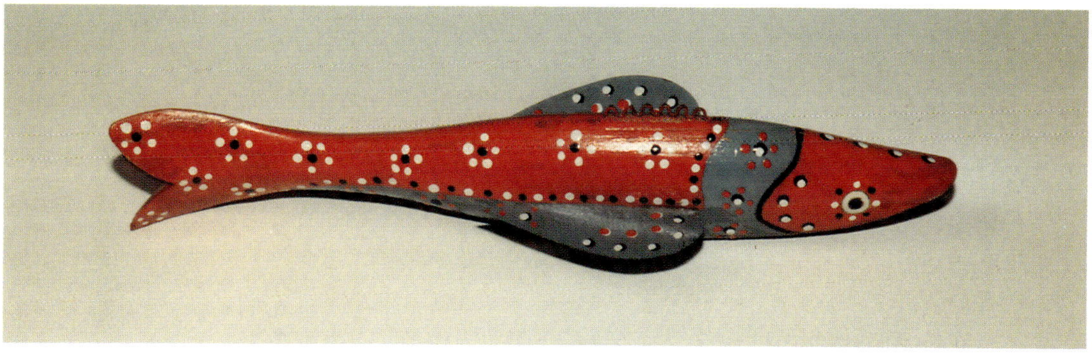

Large middle period pike by Howell with wooden tail. This decoy is highly stylized and retains the flower decoration, 10 1/2 inches.

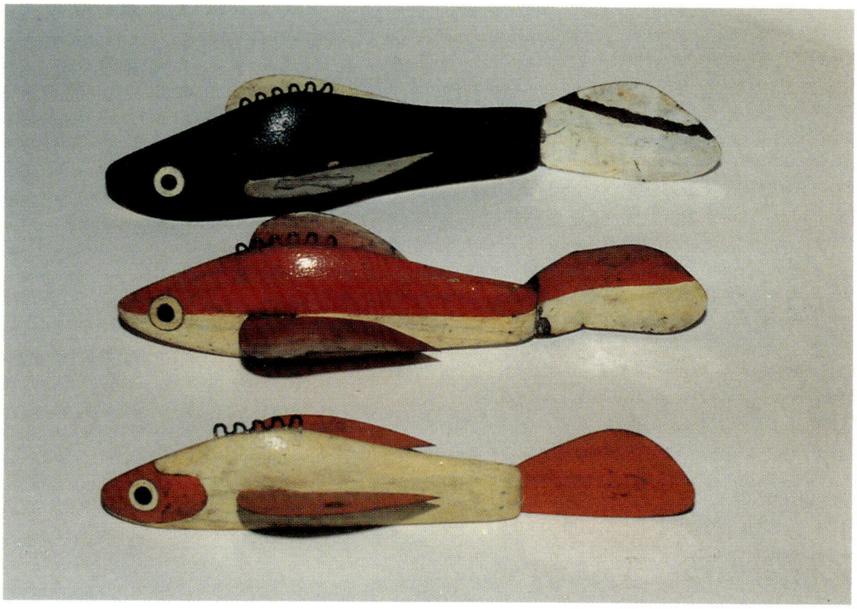

Group of three Howell later period decoys. Two of the decoys show solid body colors with fins of contrasting colors. Middle shows Howell penchant for the dual color pattern characteristics of later fish.

Andrew Huse

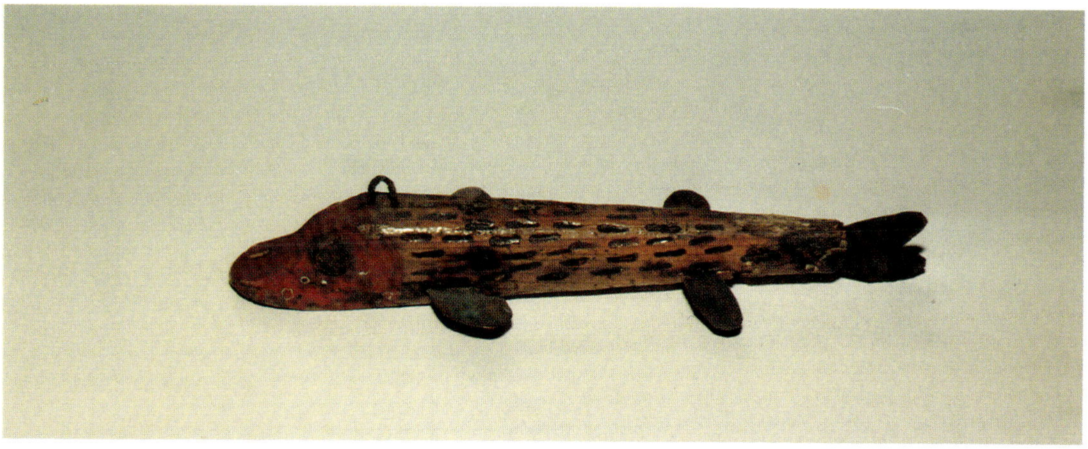

Andrew Huse decoy imitating a northern pike, with red painted head and burn decoration on the varnished body, 6 1/4 inches.

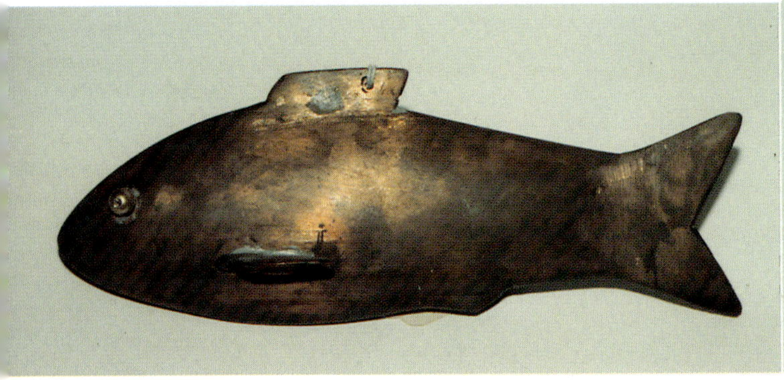

Copper decoy by Andrew Huse, 8 inches.

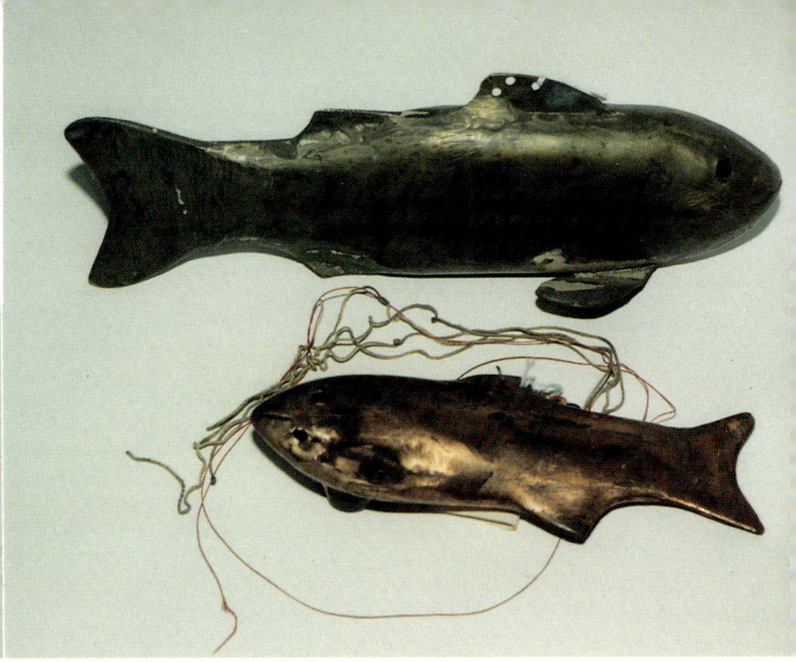

Two metal decoys by Andrew Huse. The top example is made from brass and is 10 inches long. The lower decoy is copper, measuring 6 inches in length.

Steve Jarnot

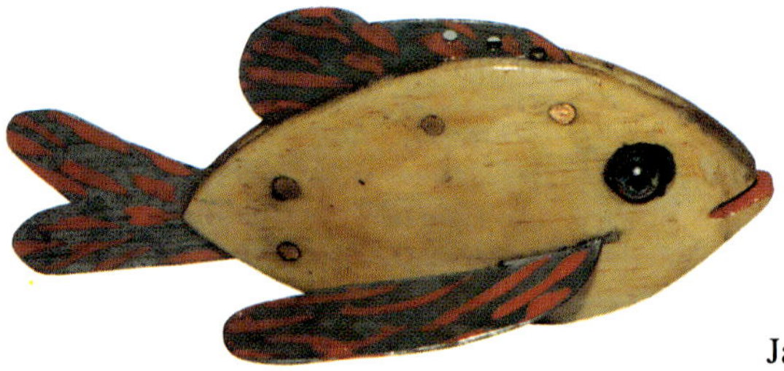

Jarnot sunfish with unpainted body and red lined metal fins, length 5 1/4 inches.

R. Edward Johnson

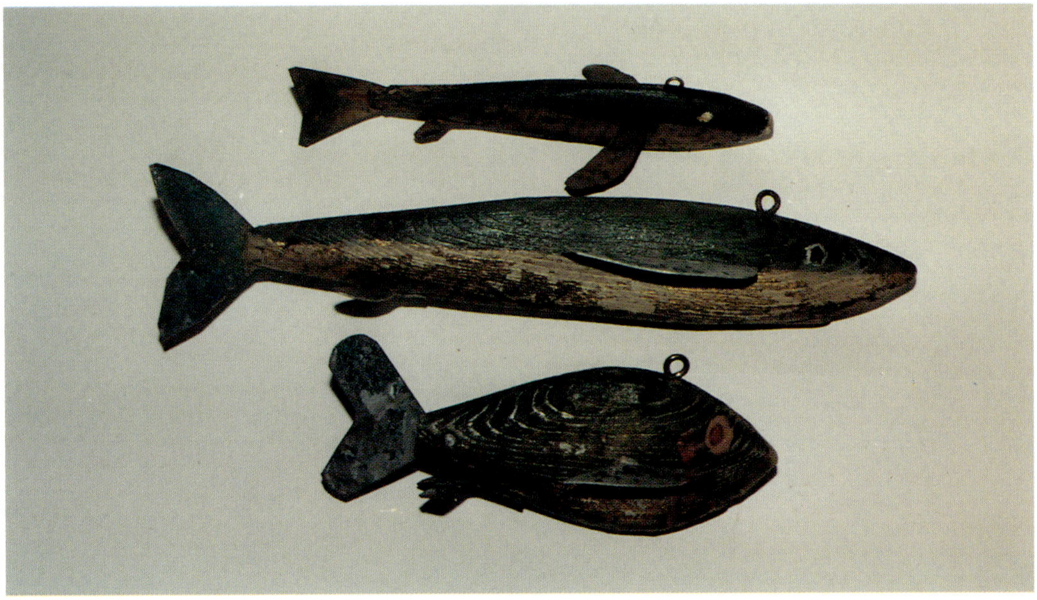

Three R. Edward Johnson decoys. Top: minnow 6 1/2 inches; middle: 10 inches; and bottom sunfish: 5 1/2 inches.

Dr. Lester Johnson

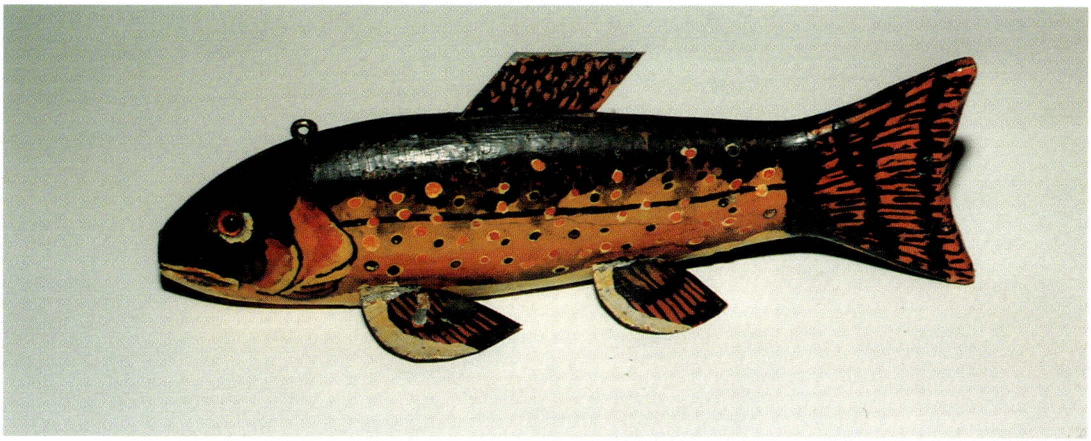

Trout by Dr. Lester Johnson, 8 inches.

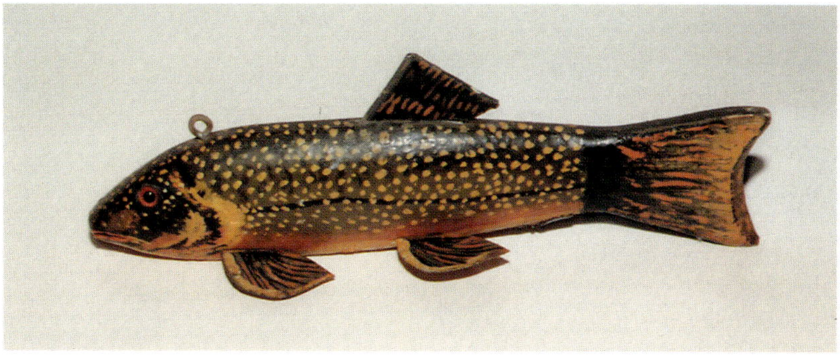

Dr. Johnson trout, 8 1/4 inches.

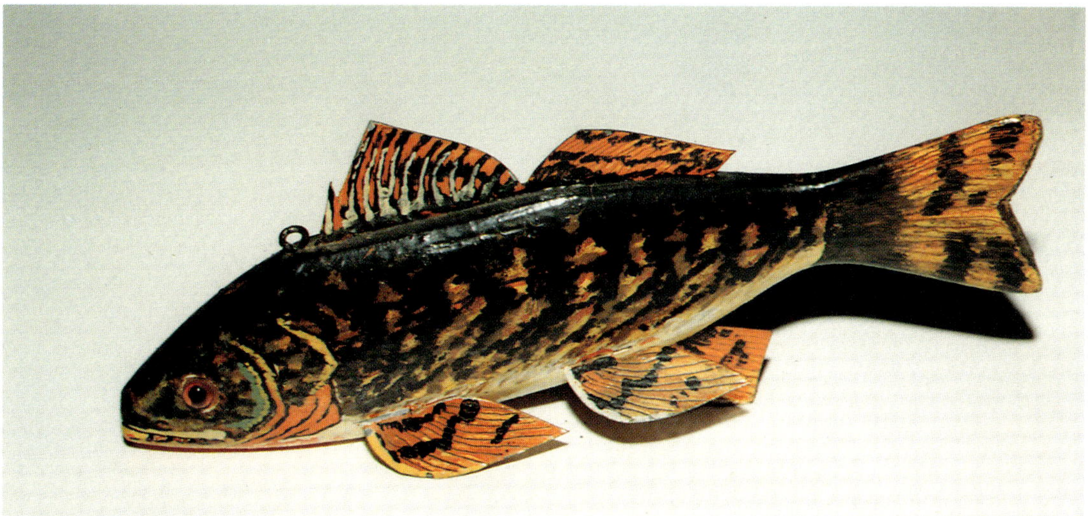

Trout, 8 1/2 inches by Dr. Lester Johnson.

Sheldon Iver Johnson

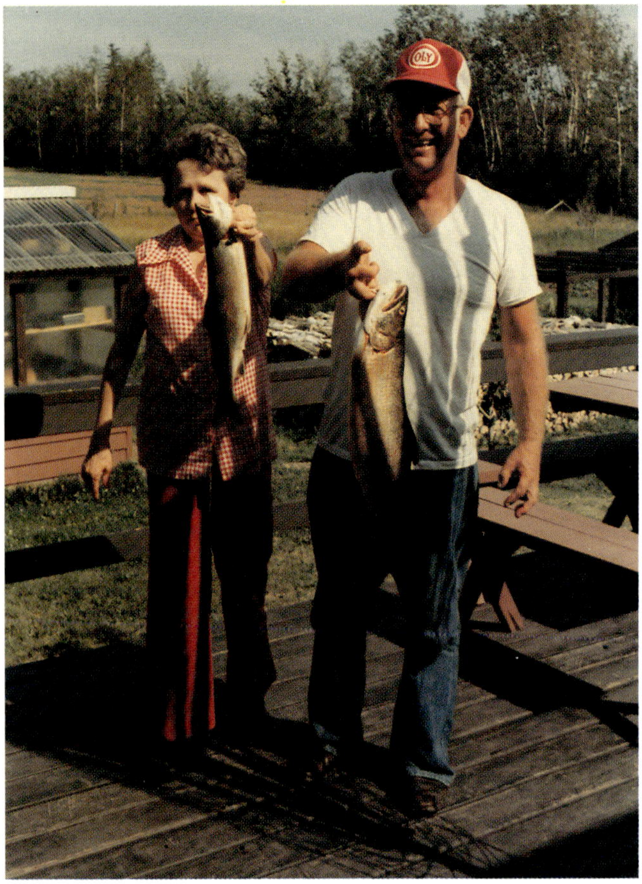

Mr. and Mrs. Sheldon Johnson with a good catch.

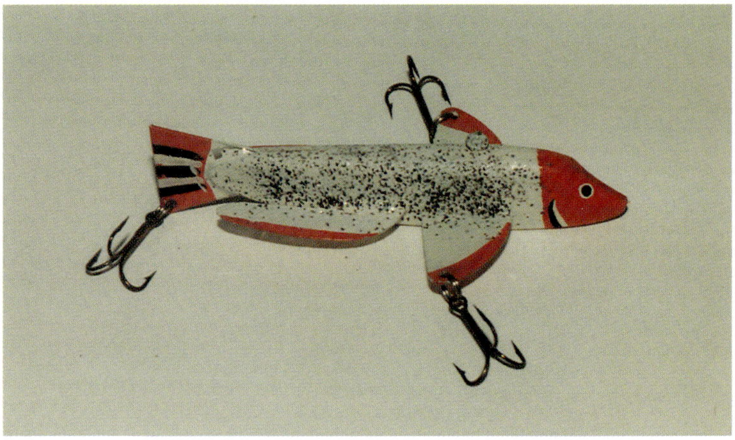

A red and white jig plane by Mr. Sheldon Johnson.

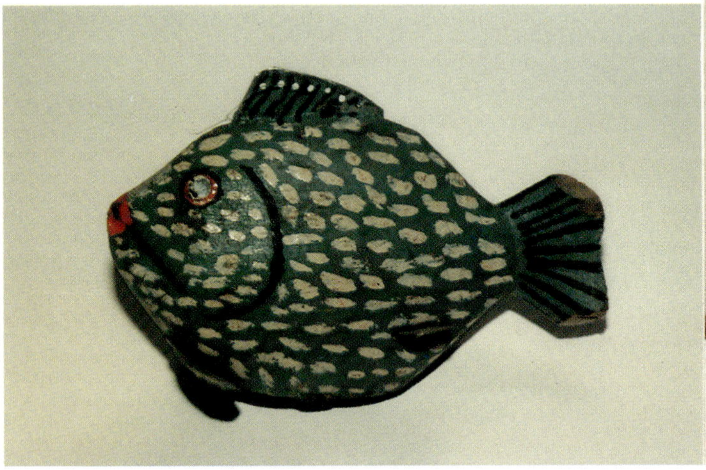

The earliest Sheldon Johnson sunfish with a wooden tail. He abandoned this model because it was too time consuming to produce.

Albert Jokela

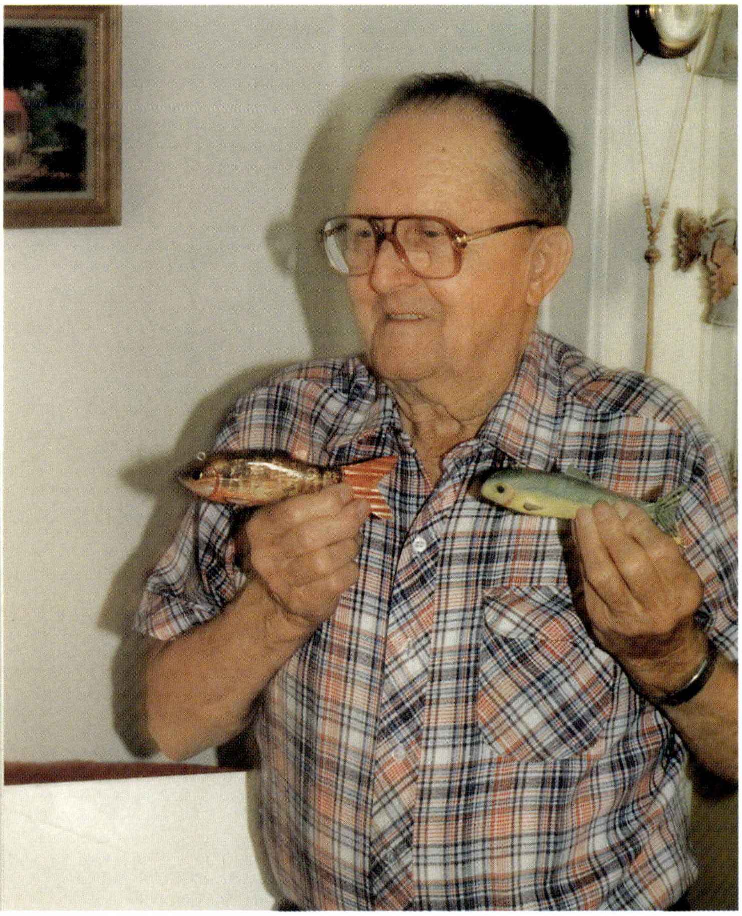

Albert Jokela holding two of his decoys.

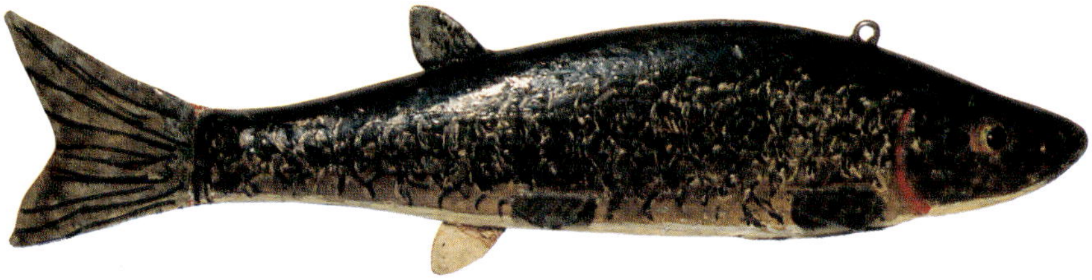

Jokela bass, 10 inches long.

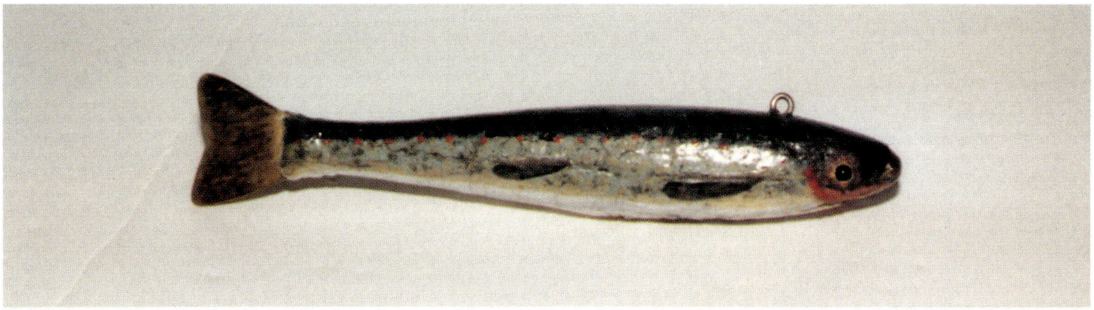

Smelt by Albert Jokela, 7 1/2 inches.

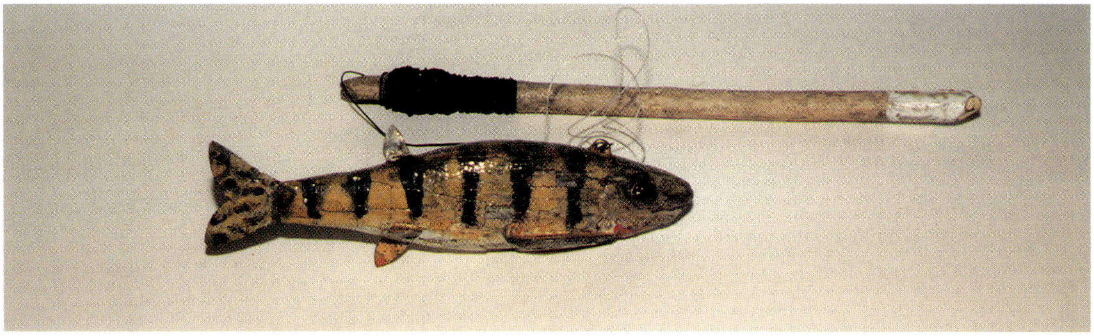

Perch made by Albert Jokela and his jigging stick.

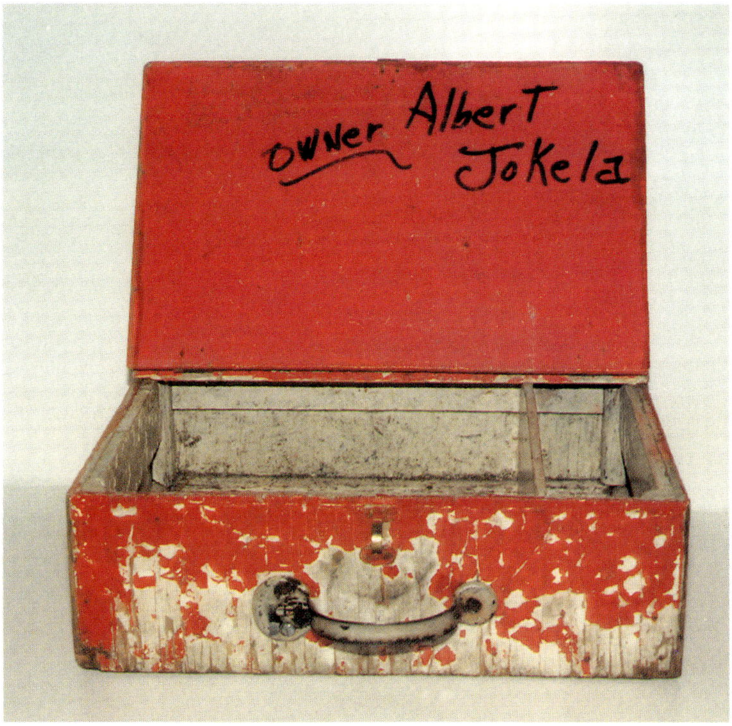

Albert Jokela's decoy box.

Vince S. Kampmann

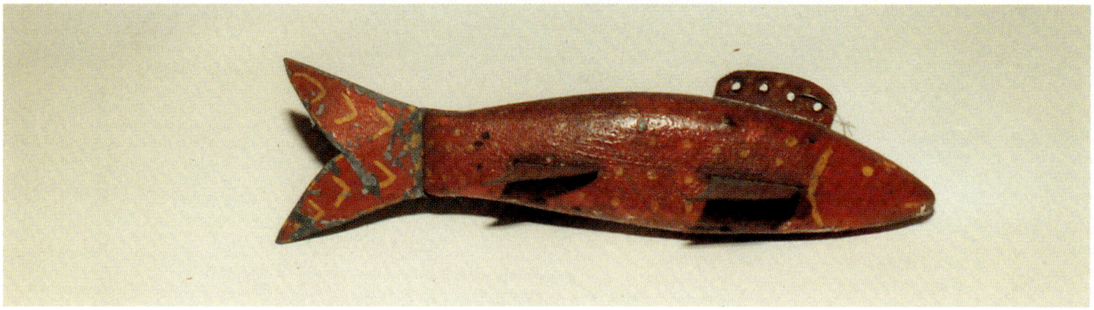

Vince Kampmann decoy with dot decoration, 5 3/4 inches.

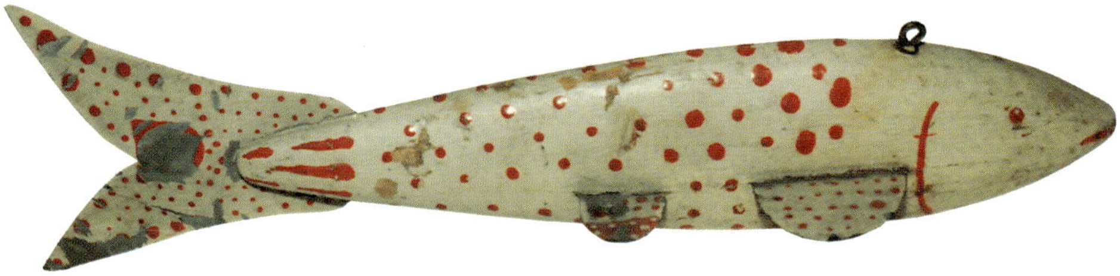

White painted decoy by Kampmann with red dot decoration, 8 3/4 inches.

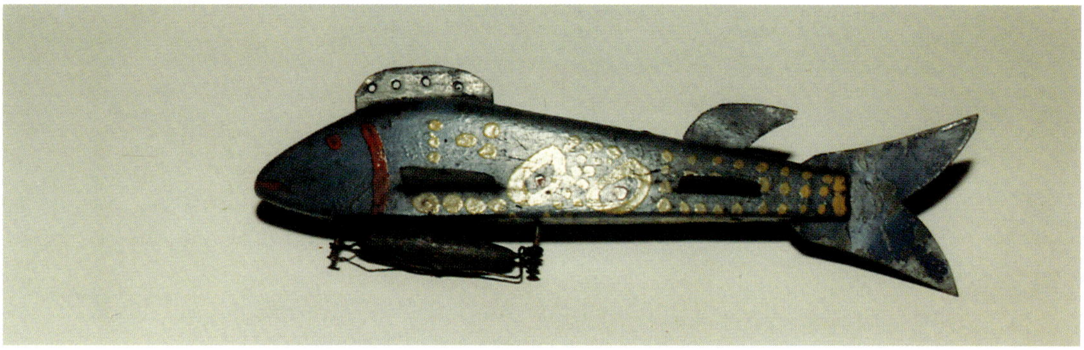

Kampmann blue painted decoy with yellow dot decoration. Note extra lead weight underneath to compensate for insufficient weighting, 6 inches.

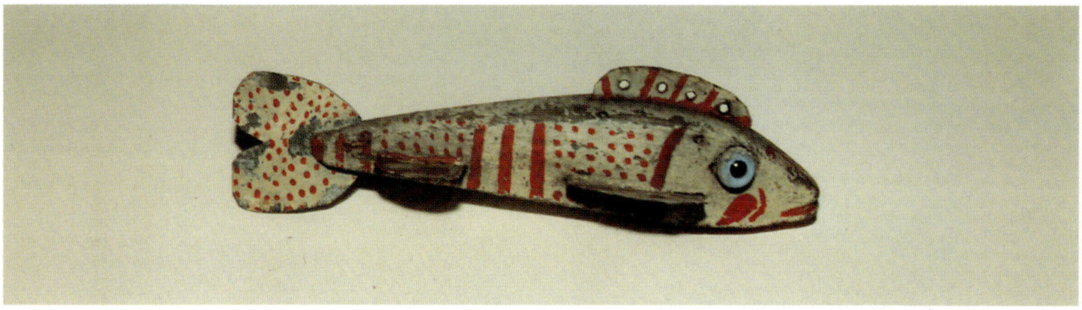

Kampmann decoy with dot and line decoration. This decoy has a glass eye, 6 inches in length.

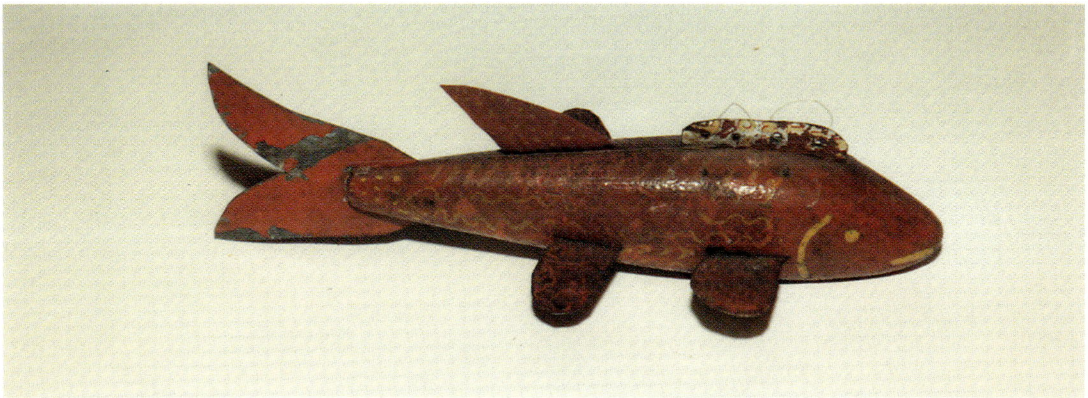

Red painted Kampmann decoy with yellow wavy line decoration, 6 1/4 inches.

Emil Keck

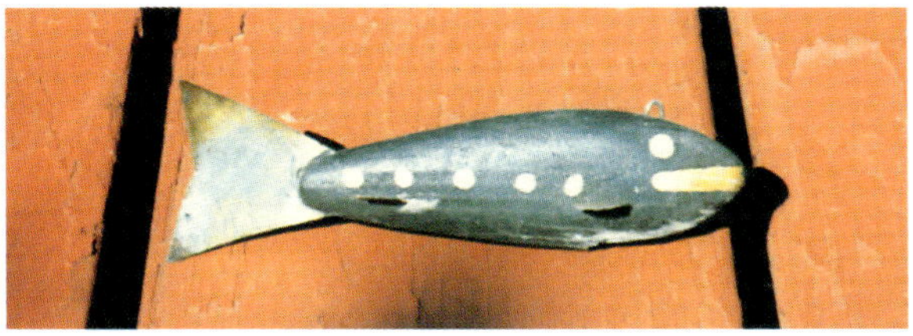

A "full faced" Emil Keck decoy. Photo courtesy of Bill Stoetzel.

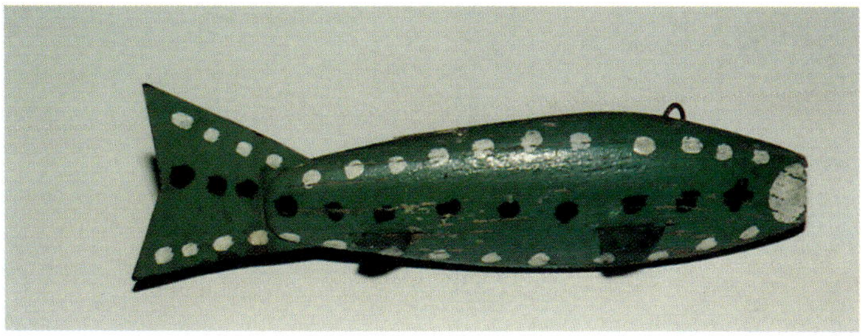

Green decoy by Emil Keck with cut out face and black and white spotted decoration, 5 1/2 inches.

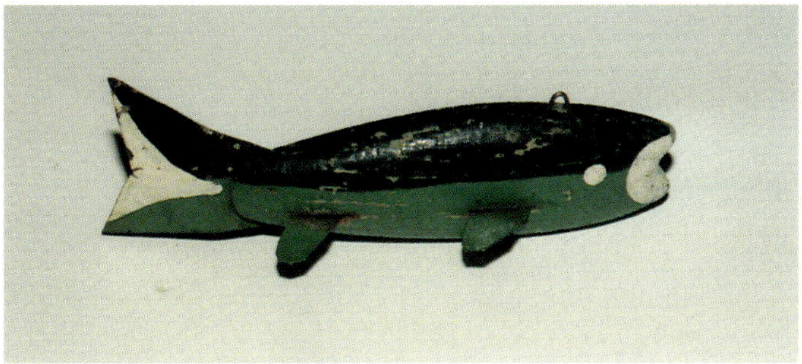

Emil Keck cut out face decoy in two tone, black and green decoration, 5 inches.

John L. Kent

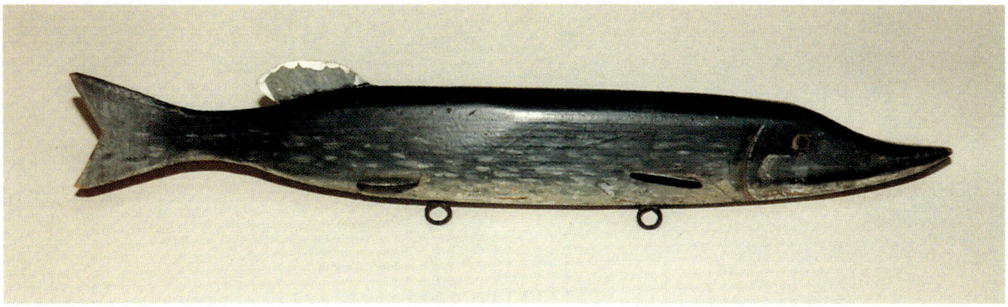

Northern pike floater decoy by John L. Kent. Note two eyelets on the bottom of the decoy to attach line and weights as floater decoys, of course, were not lead weighted. Length 20 inches.

Earl H. Kielmeyer

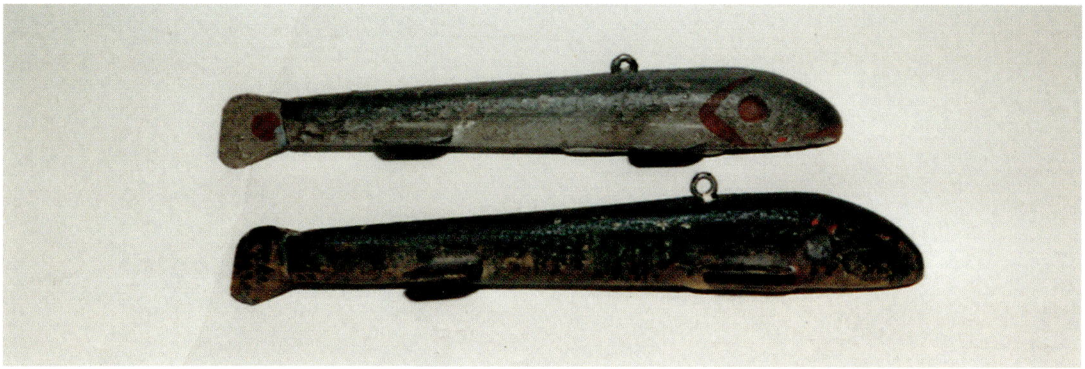

Two Earl Kielmeyer decoys ca. 1930's. These have realistic paint on them and show good craftsmanship. The eyes on these decoys are carved indentations and then were painted. Top is 6 1/2 inches long and bottom is 6 3/4 inches.

Russell C. Kolb

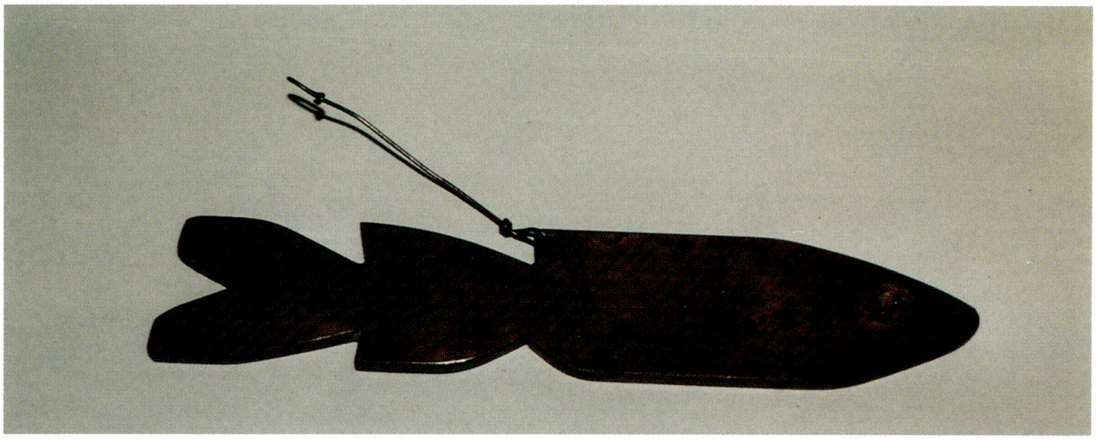

A copper fish decoy by Russell Kolb, 10 1/4 inches in length.

Nick Knaus

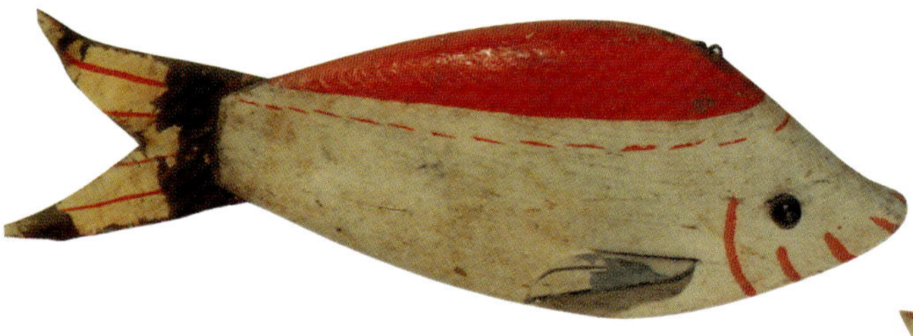

A bass (?) by Nick Knaus, 7 1/4 inches.

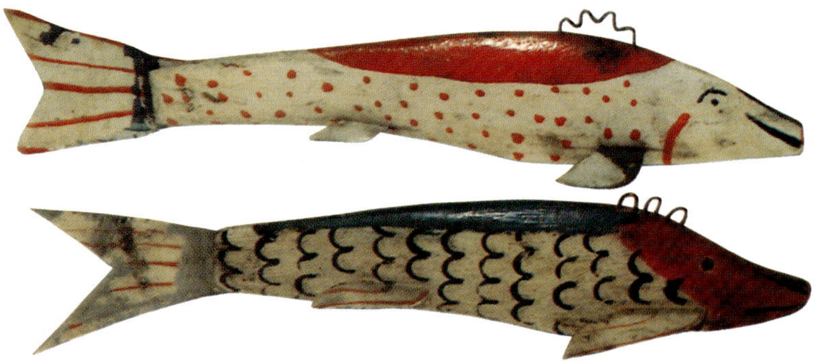

Two decoys by Nick Knaus in a minnow form. Top decoy is 8 inches in length while the one below is 7 inches.

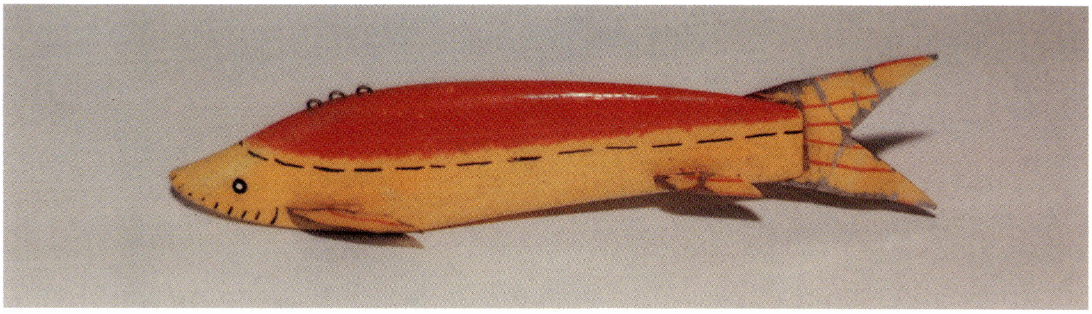

Nice yellow and red painted decoy by Knaus. K. David Hirschey collection.

Clarence Koehler

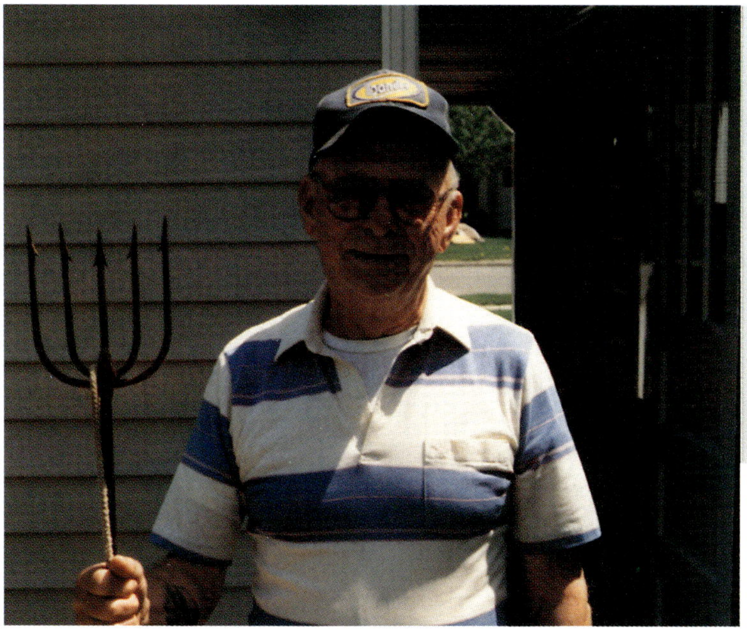

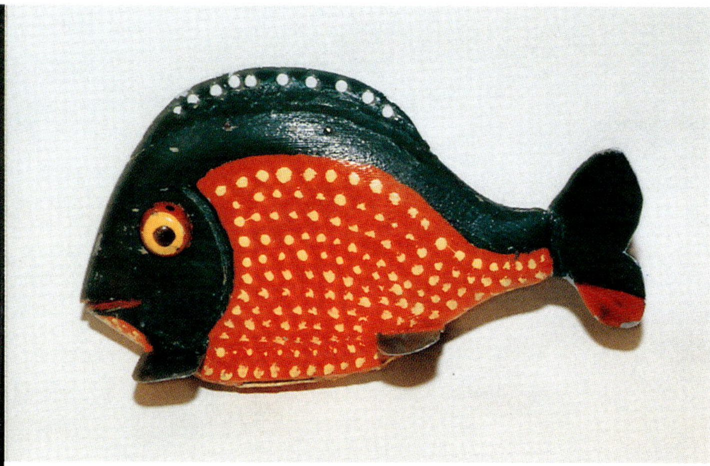

Clarence Koehler sunfish, 6 1/4 inches.

Mr. Koehler holding his favorite spear, made by Gideon Kauppi of New York Mills. (see Chapter 7).

Lambert Kolodji

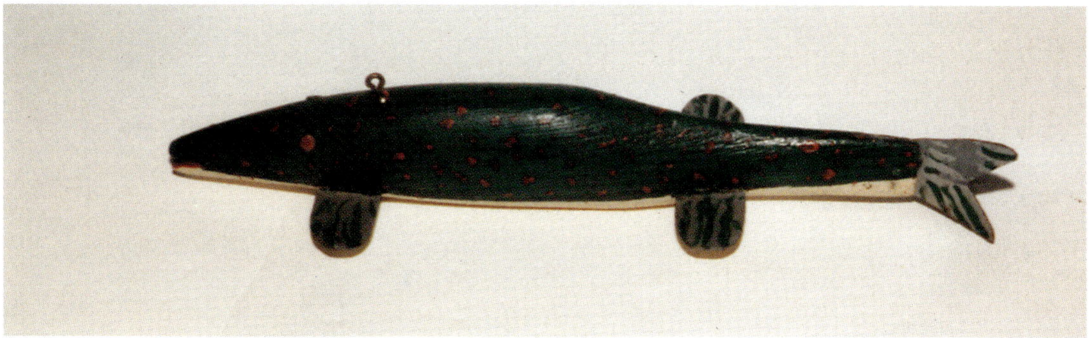

Dark green painted decoy with red spots and white underside by Lambert Kolodji, 10 3/4 inches.

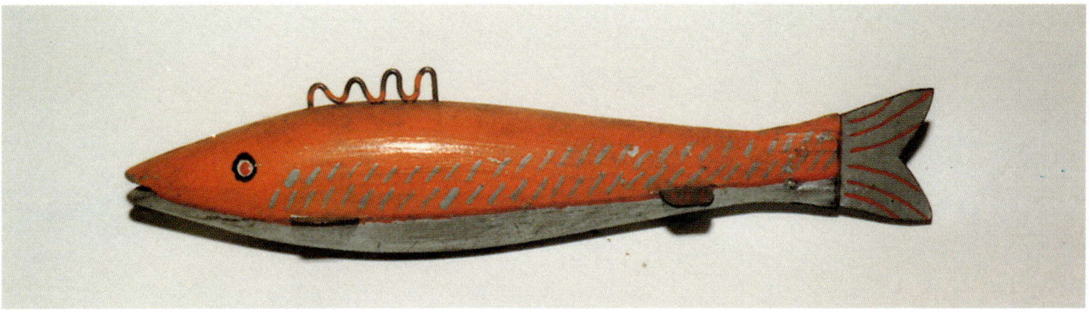

Orange top and silver-grey underside by Kolodji. Body has silver striping decoration, 8 inches.

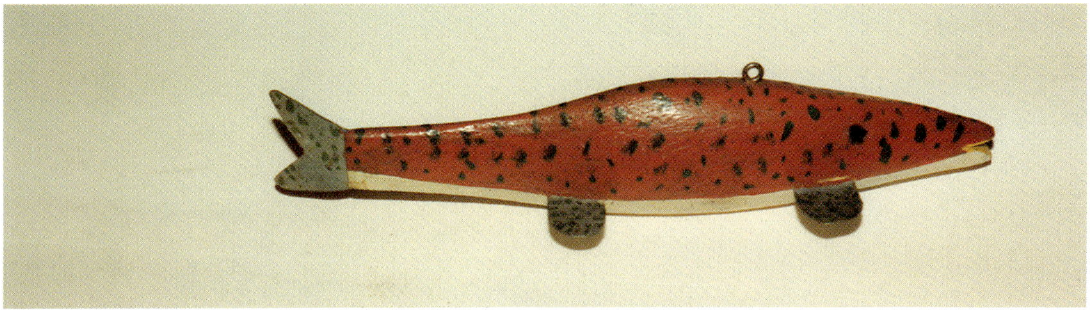

Red and white Kolodji decoy. Collection of Ron Adamson.

Toivo "Dave" Lahti

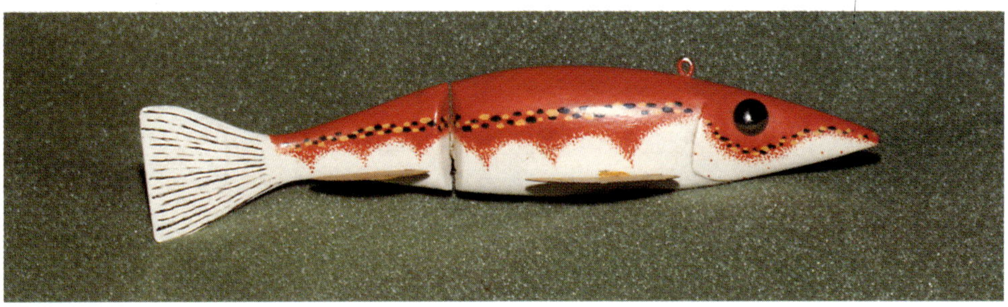

A red top with type 2 limiter, high-domed tack eyes, by Toivo Lahti. Photo courtesy of Bill Stoetzel.

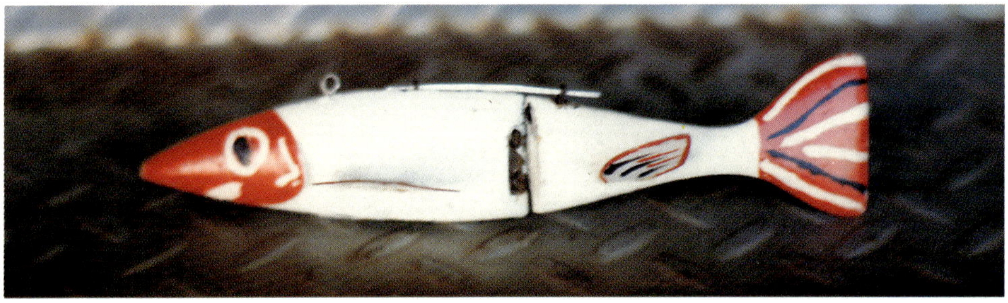

A red head Lahti decoy with type 2 limiter. Photo courtesy of Bill Stoetzel.

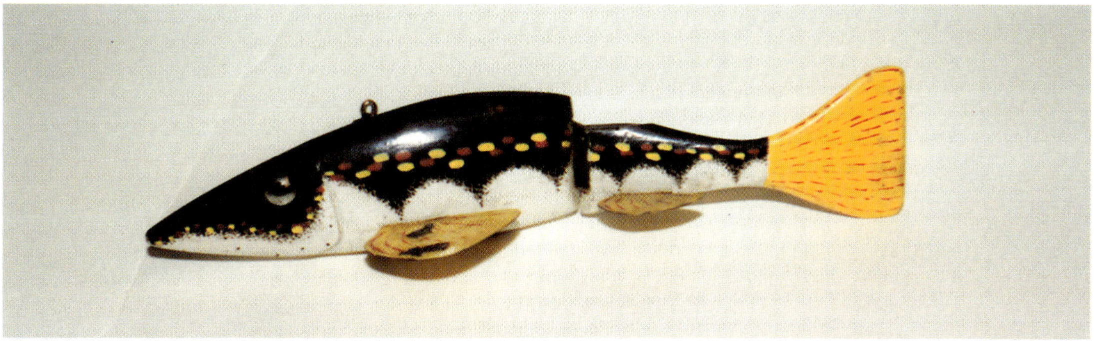

Black top, white belly, yellow tail decoy by Toivo Lahti, 8 1/2 inches.

Leonard E. LaPlante

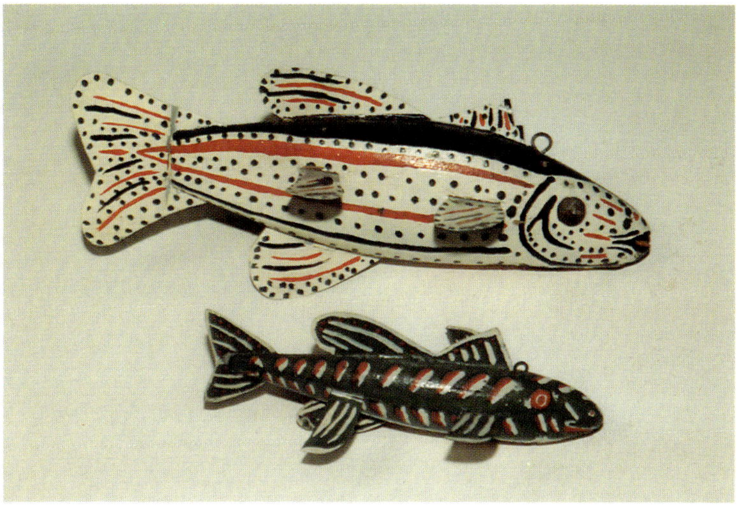

LaPlante decoys, top is 8 1/2 inches long and bottom is 5 inches in length.

Gus Larson

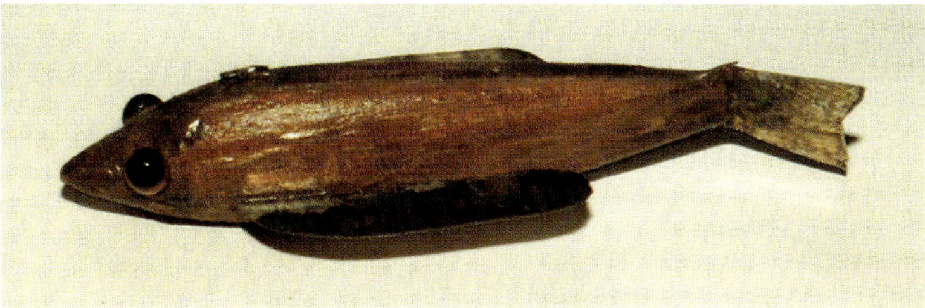

Unpainted but varnished decoy by Larson, 5 1/2 inches.

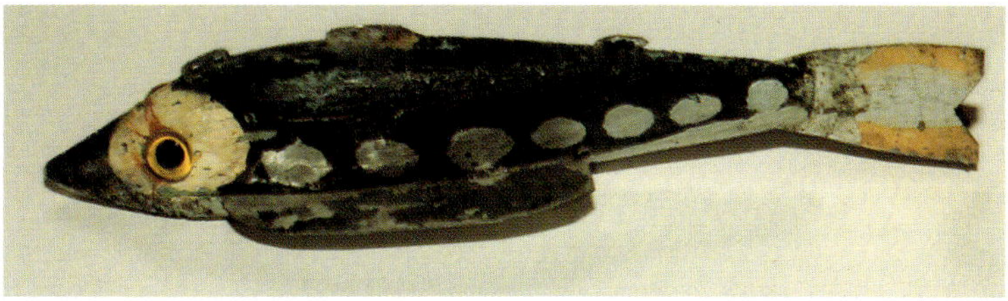

Gus Larson decoy with silver circle decoration, 6 1/2 inches.

Louie Leach

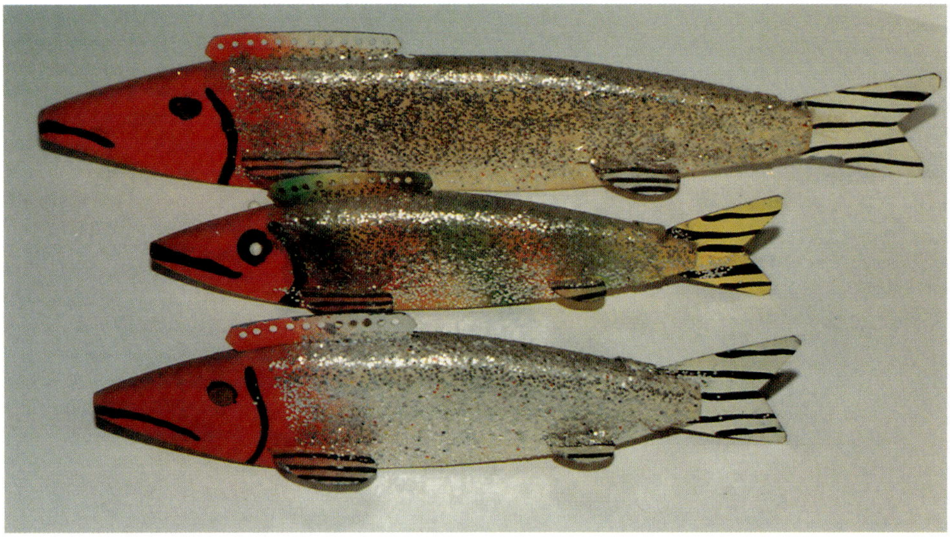

Three various sized Louie Leach decoys, top: 13 inches; middle: 8 inches, and bottom: 8 3/4 inches.

Fred Max Lexow

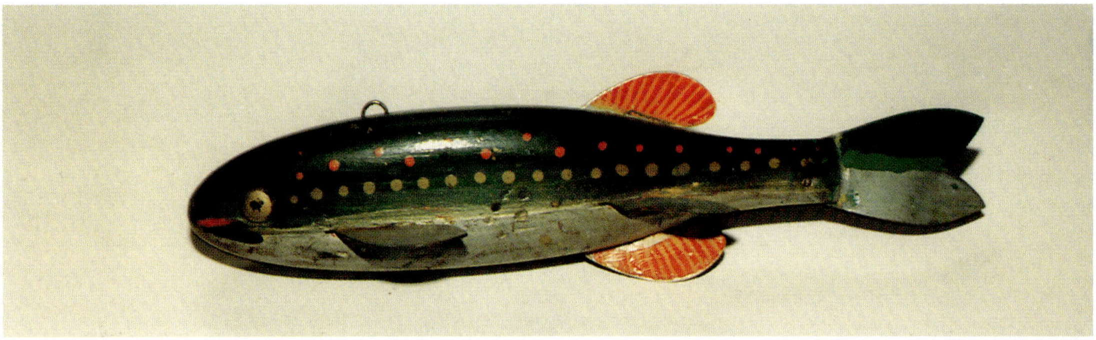

Fred Lexow decoy showing typical fin style and sun ray painting on dorsal and anal fins, 7 1/4 inches.

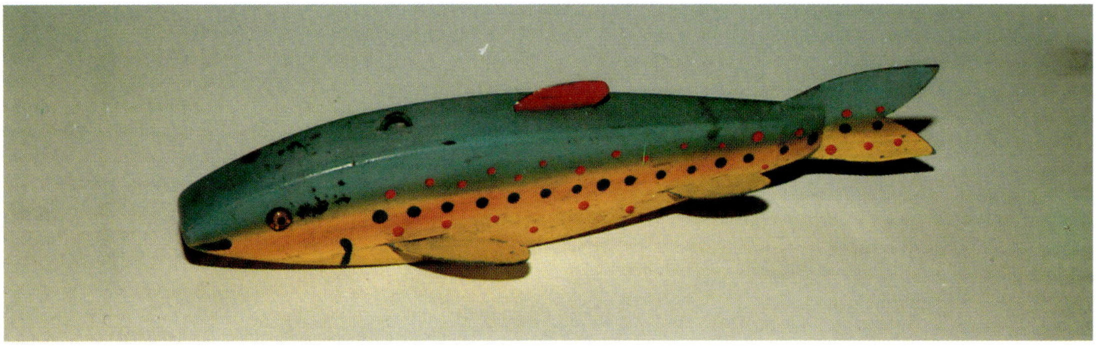

Square shape Lexow "commercial" decoy, 7 inches.

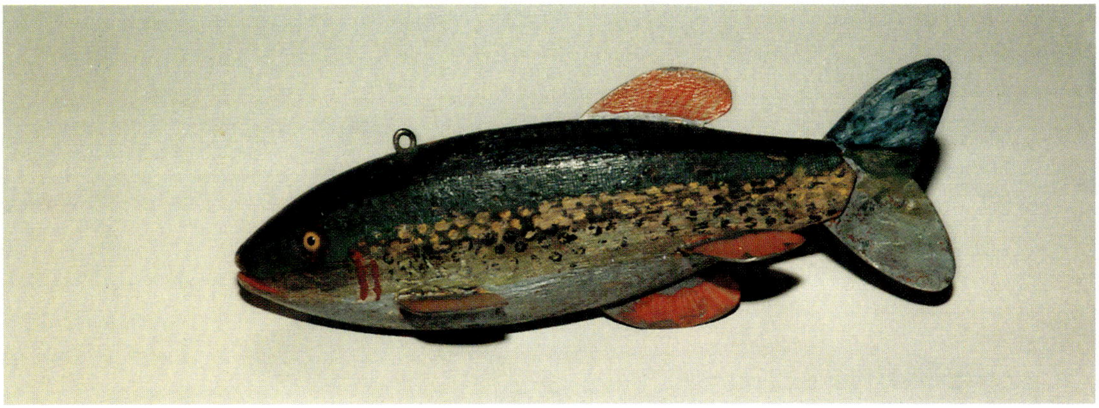

Rare Lexow bass with sun ray painting intact on fins, 6 3/4 inches.

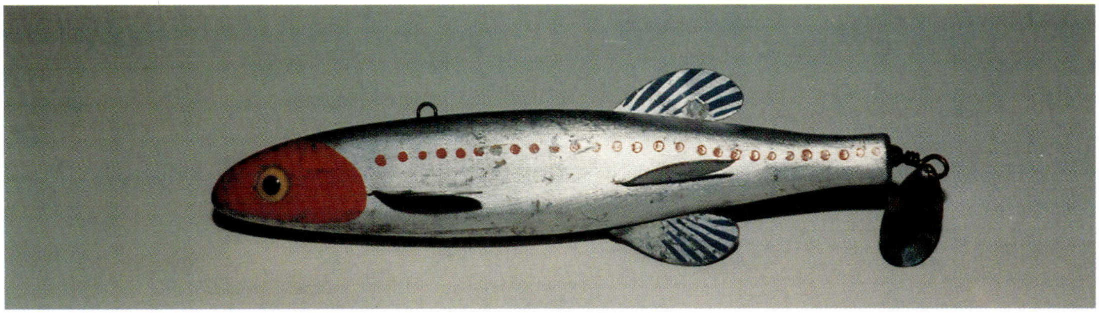

Silver decoy with dot decoration and a spinner for a tail, 6 1/4 inches.

Norman Lien

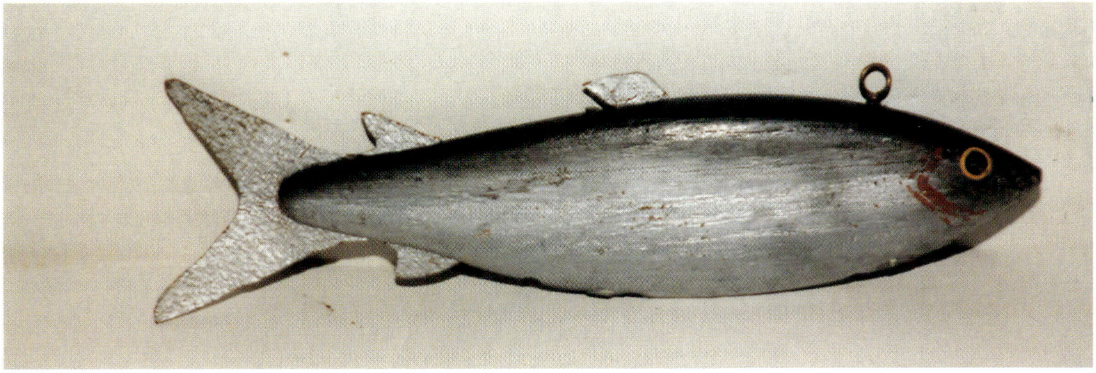

Norman Lien whitefish [?] with typical silver and black painting and with rubber tail, without pectoral fins, 10 inches.

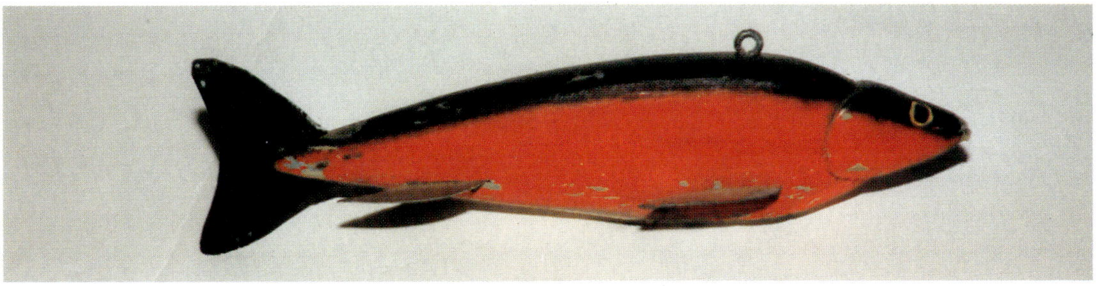

Metal tailed Lien decoy, 9 inches.

Emil Liers

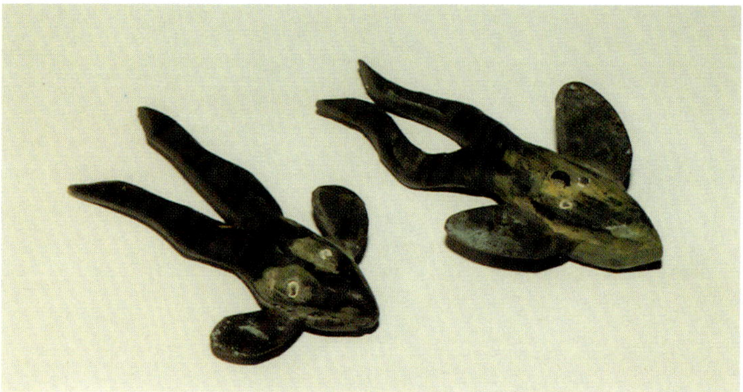

Two Emil Liers frog decoys, ca. 1920, discolored slightly from being in a damp cigar box. They were possibly used for catching otters, as well as for spear fishing, length 3 3/4 inches.

Harry Lillis

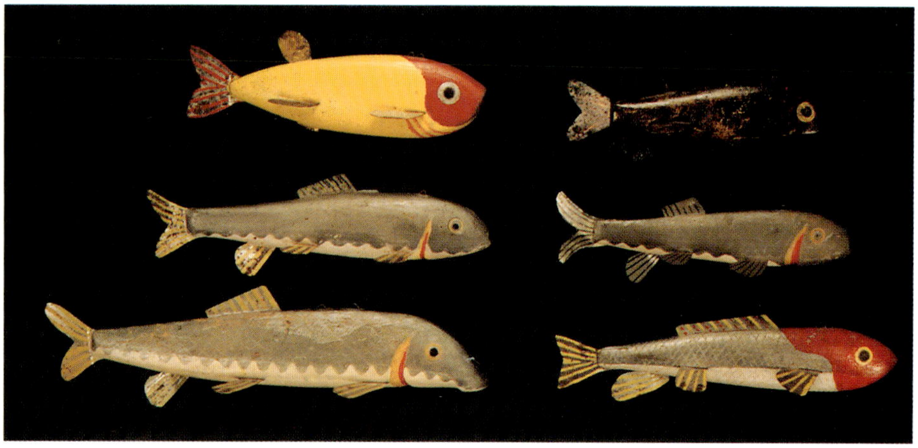

Harry Lillis decoys. (Photo courtesy of Russell Johnson)

Gust Lind

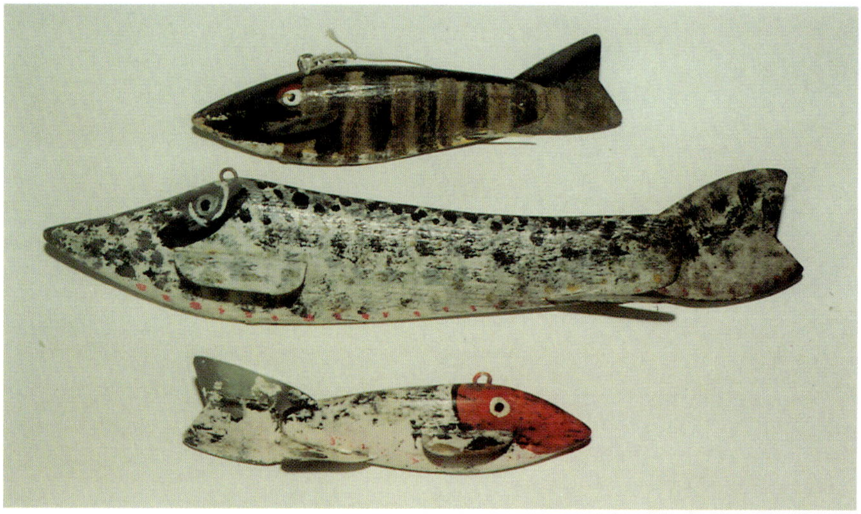

Three decoys by Gust Lind. Top: (a realistically painted perch), 6 inches long; middle: 10 inches long; and bottom: 5 inches.

Emil J. Loe

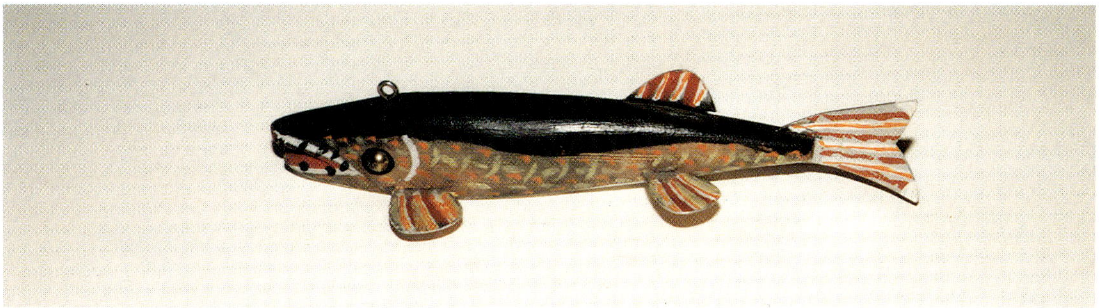

Emil Loe decoy with teeth painted on the outside of the mouth [black teeth painted on a white band]; length 7 1/2 inches.

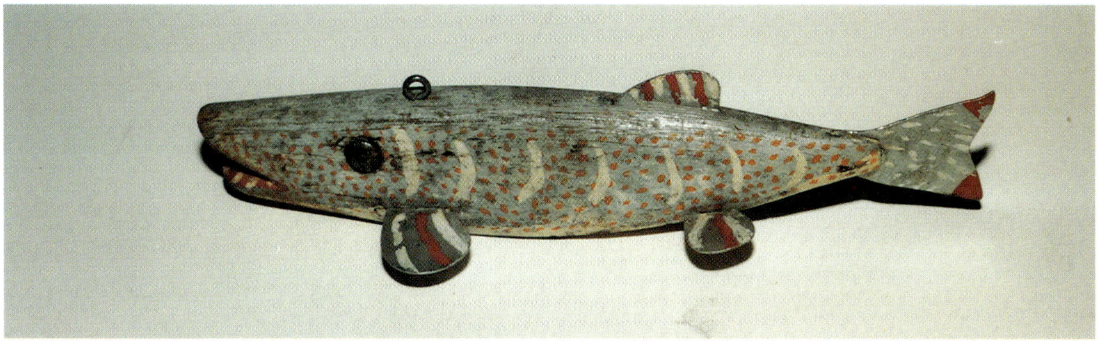

Early Loe decoy with dot and rib painted decoration, 7 1/2 inches in length.

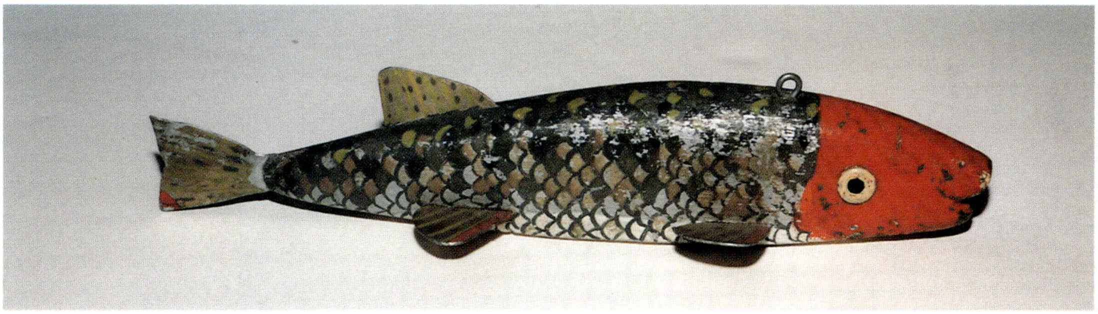

Loe decoy with painted scale decoration [Art Kimball collection].

Charles "Charlie" Lundgren

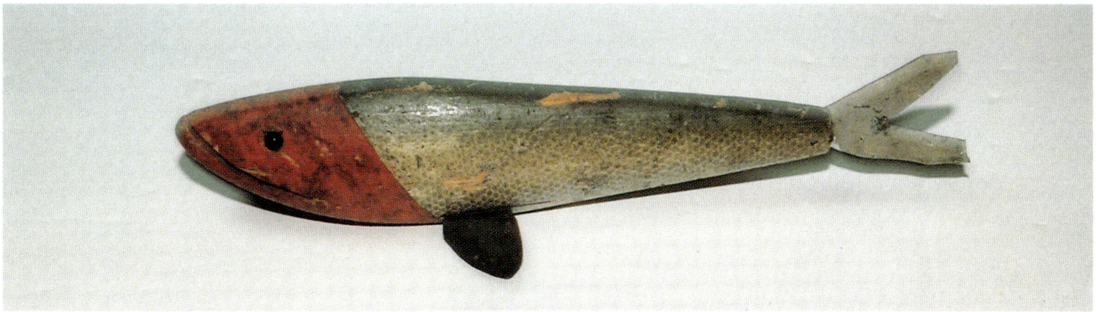

Shiner with red head, scaled effect on body, and pronounced "smile" on decoy's mouth, by Charlie Lundgren, ca. 1950's, length 7 3/4 inches.

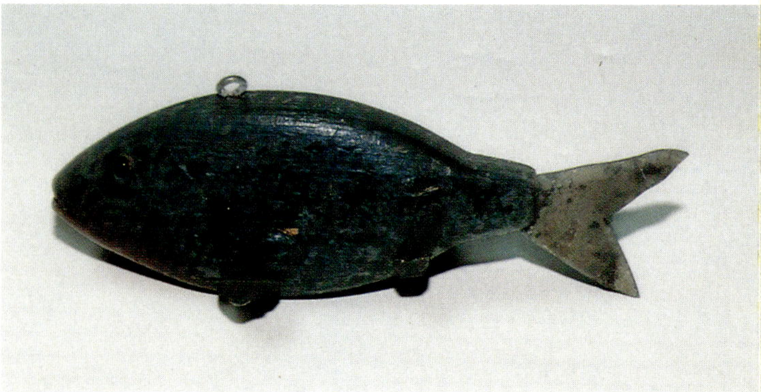

Blue painted and scaled sunfish (?) by Charlie Lundgren, ca. 1950's, length 5 1/2 inches.

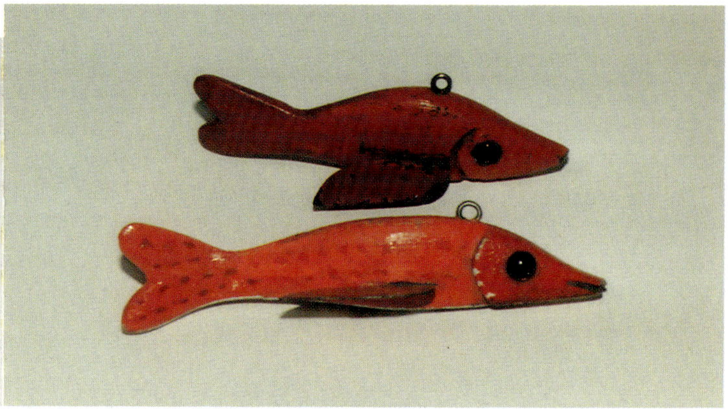

Two smaller size McGillis' decoys. Top: 4 1/2 inches long; bottom: 5 1/4 inches long.

John McGillis

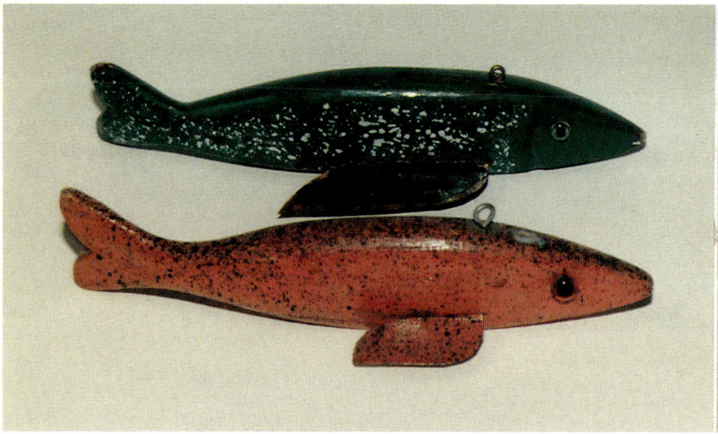

Two large size McGillis' decoys. Note distinctive pectoral fin shapes and wooden notched tails and glass eyes. Top: (green painted) 7 1/4 inches; bottom: (pink) 7 inches.

Henry G. Max

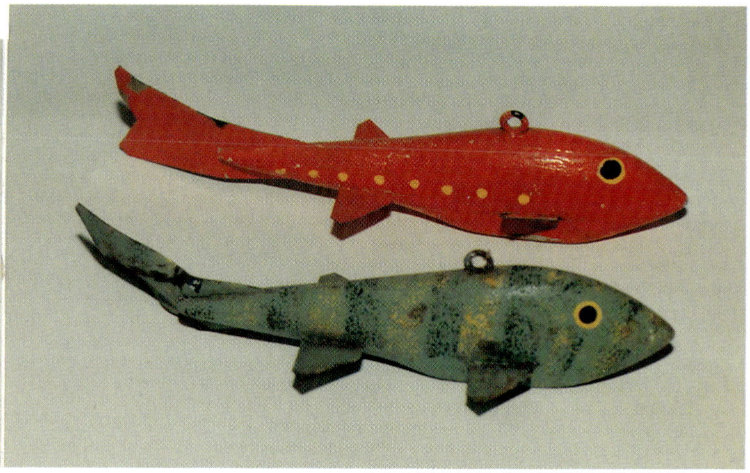

Two spearing decoys by Henry Max, 6 inches.

Mike Meholensky

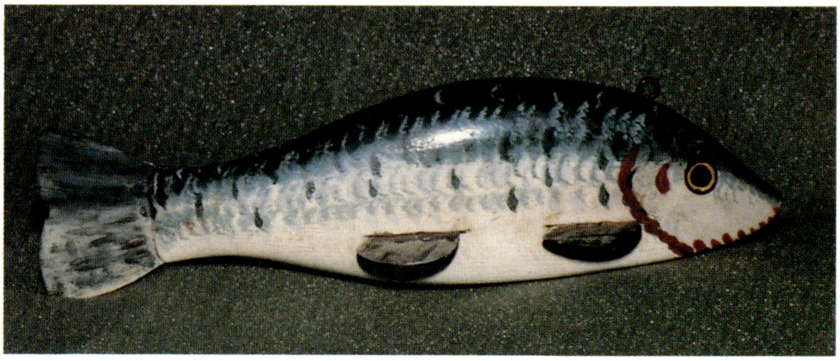

Meholensky crappie, 9 1/2 inches.

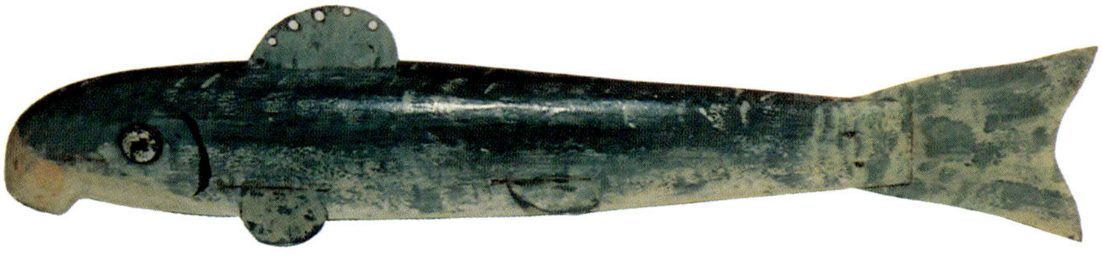

Typical Meholensky sucker, 12 1/2 inches.

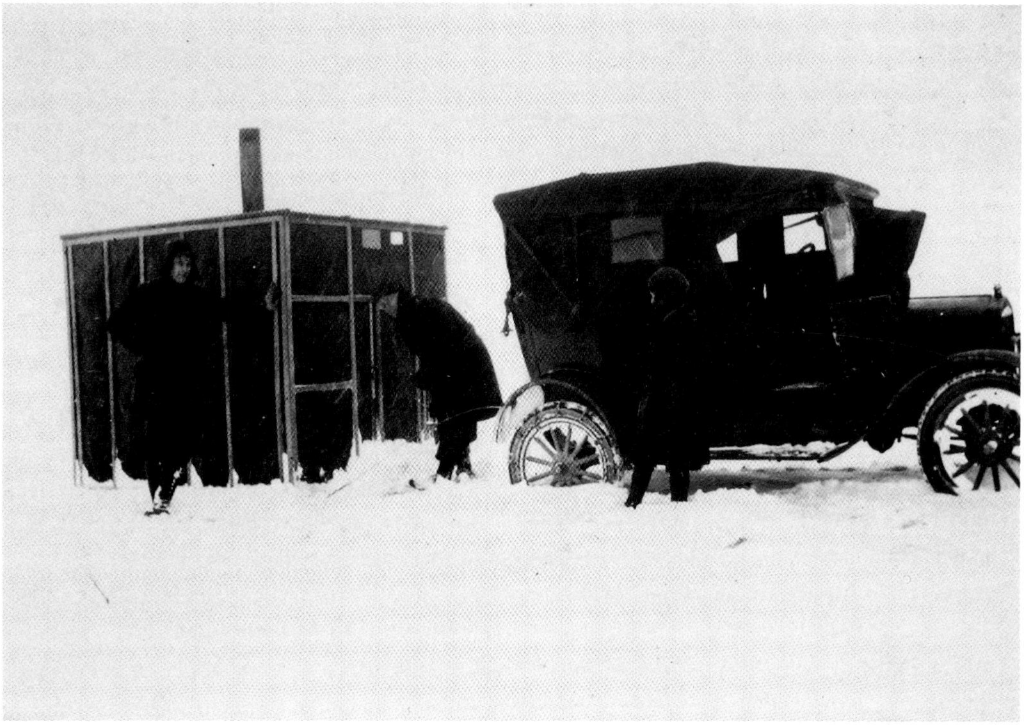

A Dark House Being Moved onto the ice in Minnesota in the early 1930's.

It is likely that the principal reason for white rejection of the Indian technique of spearing in favor of the dark house, was comfort. In a dark house, a person can sit down [instead of laying on the ice] on a bench or stool, in the comfort of a shelter heated by a small wood-burning stove. Moreover, a dark house permits the fisherman to stretch while still being able to view the fishing hole. Larger dark houses accommodating two persons allowed conversation, thus alleviating boredom while waiting for a pike to appear. All of these considerations emphasize the sporting, rather than the commercial, nature of spear fishing.

In addition, the dark house also offers the advantage for the spear fisherman of being able to tie a line to the spear and attach the other end to the ceiling of the dark house, so that the spear would not be lost when throwing it into the water after intended prey. A dark house can also be locked after use, permitting the fisherman to leave decoys and other equipment for another day.

Spear fishing was not the only winter fishing technique learned by white men from Indians. Netting fish through the ice was practiced by Indians [see the reference to netting made by George Featherstonhaugh, quoted earlier in this chapter], and also utilized by whites. For example, John Long, a native of England, who came to Canada in 1768 to become involved in the Indian trade, observed:

> "The ice was three feet thick, and the snow very deep; this we were obliged to clear away, before we could cut holes in which to put our nets. For the space of two months we had uncommon success, having caught about eighteen thousand weight of fish, which we hung up by the tails across sticks to freeze, and then laid them up for store. This was to us an important acquisition, as fishing in the middle of winter is precarious, and the return of the Indians to supply the wants of the trader very uncertain."[30]

Long was netting fish on Lac La Mort, north of Lake Superior in Canada.

Did European Immigrants Bring the Idea of Spear Fishing With Them?

Because the major spear fishing states, i.e., Minnesota, Michigan and Wisconsin, are heavily populated by Scandinavians and Germans, who immigrated from countries similar in terrain and climate to those states, it was thought possible that such immigrants might well have practiced spear fishing with decoys, even before they came to the United States. If that was true, then spearing would have been a natural past time for them and the American Indian would not have been the dominant influence regarding the diffusion of the technique among white settlers. Although this possibility seemed likely, the research showed that spear fishing with decoys must have been either unknown in the Scandinavian countries and Germany, or not used if known.

In Norway, a spear fishing technique was, however, utilized, called "lystring" [leistering in English]. It was practiced mainly in the rivers and lakes, but perhaps most in rivers when salmon, sea trout and fresh water trout were running. The spears ranged in quality from properly smithied ones, to crude affairs that youngsters might make by driving five or six nails through a wood piece attached perpendicular to a handle. It would thus resemble an industrial broom with only a few "bristles." Lystring provided a source of food for the rural poor. Sometimes a day was set aside, mostly in the fall, for the event. Lloyd Hustvedt reports that spear fishing through the ice was rarely, if ever, done.[31] Moreover, decoys were not employed for spearing. Lystring has been illegal for a long time in Norway.

Ted Rowberg, Archivist with the Swedish American Historical Society, located at North Park College in Chicago, also reported that to his knowledge, spear fishing through the ice, using decoys, was not done in Sweden. Nor was the Swedish American Institute in Minneapolis or the Naturhistoriska Riksmuseet (Natural History Museum) in Stockholm, Sweden able to confirm the use of a spear fishing technique similar to that used in the United States, employed in Sweden.

A review of Scandinavian books, which covered the history of fishing also failed to produce any documentation that an American-type spear fishing technique, using decoys, was practiced in Scandinavia.[32] Similar results were obtained by checking appropriate Finnish and German sources.

It seems clear, therefore, that at best, European immigrants might have been familiar with spearing as a fishing technique, but were either unacquainted with, or did not practice, spear fishing through the ice, using a fishing decoy.

CHAPTER III
SPEAR FISHING TECHNIQUES AND THE CONSTRUCTION OF SPEAR FISHING DECOYS

Dark house spear fishing has been practiced in Minnesota since at least 1880, and probably some years prior to that date, by whites.[1] Spear fishing as a sport reached its zenith in 1951 when nearly 65,000 Minnesotans purchased a spearing license, but this number fell to 35,000 such licenses in 1981.[2] By the year 1992, the number of spear fishing licenses purchased had shrunk to 21,182.[3] It would appear, therefore, that the long term trend for spear fishing is a declining one. This result may be due to increased state regulation of spearing, adverse media reaction to the sport, the work involved in setting up the equipment needed for spearing, etc.

The Dark House

As previously noted, the techniques, equipment, decoys and traditions of spear fishing have been passed down from father to son. In December, January and February, dark houses (also referred to as "shanties" or "coops") would be placed on favorite spearing lakes. Dark houses were built to be as light as possible, particularly in earlier days when it was necessary to haul them by horse or behind cars.[4] Sometimes they were constructed with sled-type runners beneath to facilitate transportation across snow or ice. A dark house being moved by a horse near Fergus Falls, Minnesota is shown in Figure 3-1.

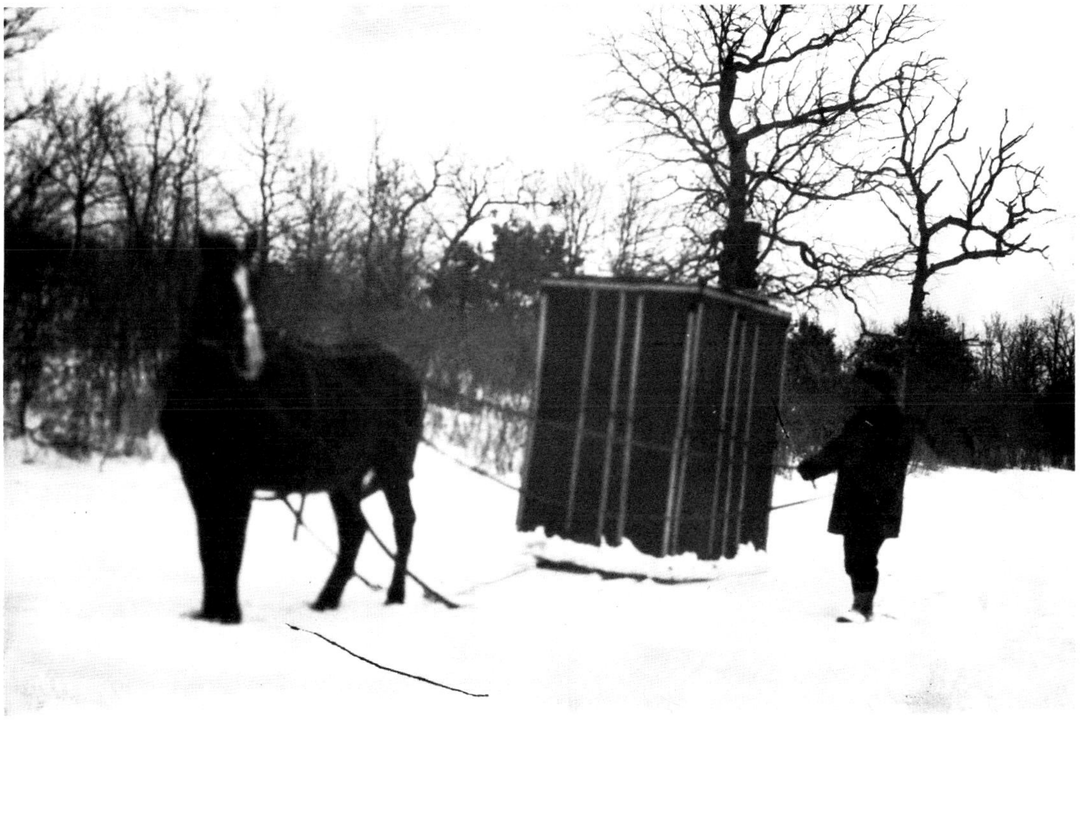

Figure 3-1. Horse Pulling Dark House in the 1930's. (Oxley Photo)

The inside of a typical dark house consisted of a floor with one or two areas of the floor cut out so as to be placed over the hole(s) in the ice, a small wood heater, a box to sit on (which sometimes also served as the container for the decoys) and very little else.[5] A typical floor plan of such a dark house is shown in Figure 3-2.

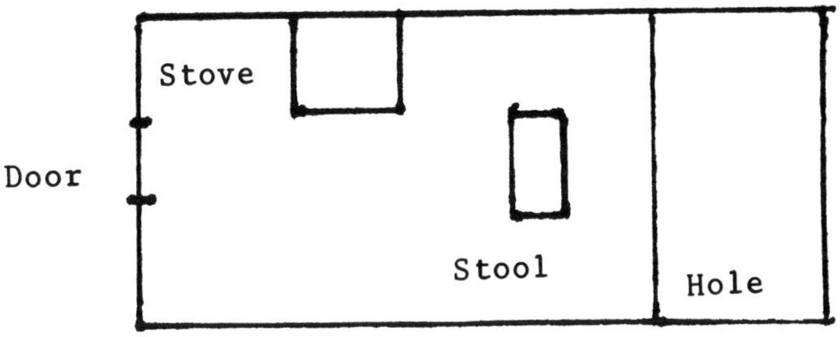

Figure 3-2. Floor Plan for a Typical Dark House.

Currently, the most usual sizes of Minnesota dark houses are four feet by six feet and four feet by eight feet.[6] Contemporary dark houses are constructed from plywood, chipwood, buffalo board, tin, or aluminum, sometimes insulated with styrofoam.[7]

After the dark house was hauled to its desired location on the ice, usually in a place where there was no more than five to twelve feet of water below, but before final place-

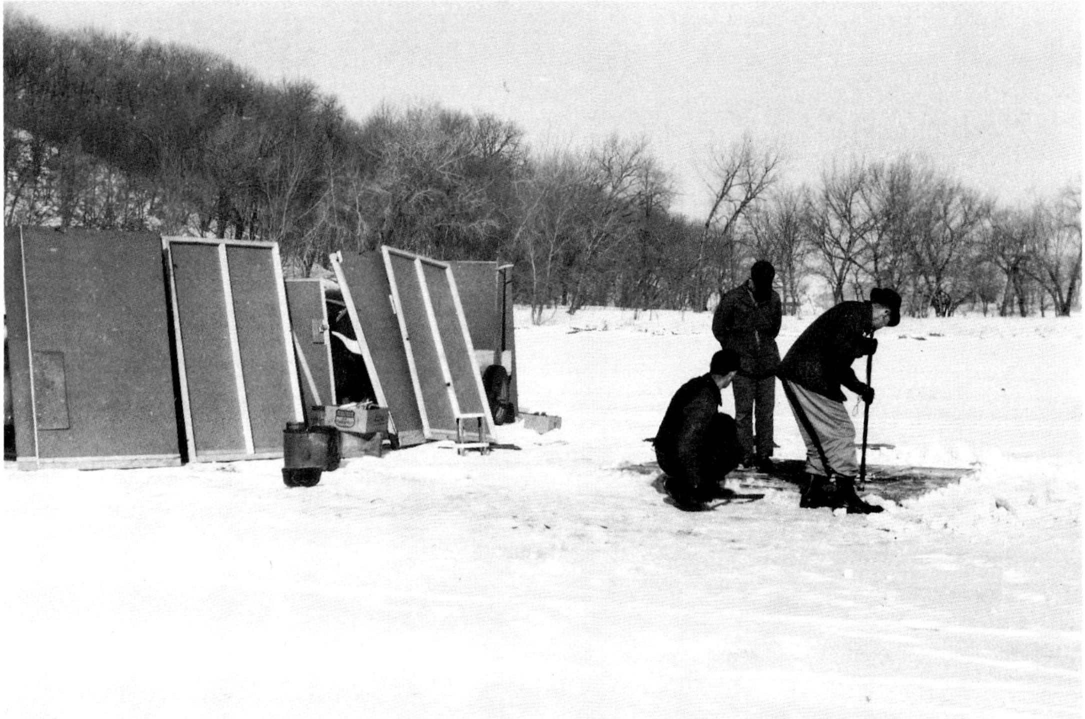

Figure 3-3. Chiseling a Hole in the Ice Before a Dark House is Placed Above It. (Oxley Photo)

ment was made, a hole in the ice had to be cut.[8] This was accomplished with the aide of an ice chisel, ice saw, or auger.[9] Figure 3-3 shows fishermen chiseling out a hole in the ice preparatory to placement of the dark house.

The heat from the stove in the dark house helped keep the hole from freezing over, but if an ice film began to form, the fisherman would use an ice scoop, such as the one show in Figure 3-4, to skim it off (see page 18).

After the dark house was moved over the hole(s), snow was banked up around the base of it to block out the light. In the absence of snow, tarpaper or pine branches were placed around the dark house's base for the same purpose. The ice was shoveled clear in a wide arc around the dark house, particularly on the south side, to permit the maximum amount of winter light to penetrate through the ice into the water below. Some spear fishermen would then toss egg shells, oatmeal, bottle caps, sliced potatoes, white pebbles, etc., down the hole to provide contrast when a fish passed over them.

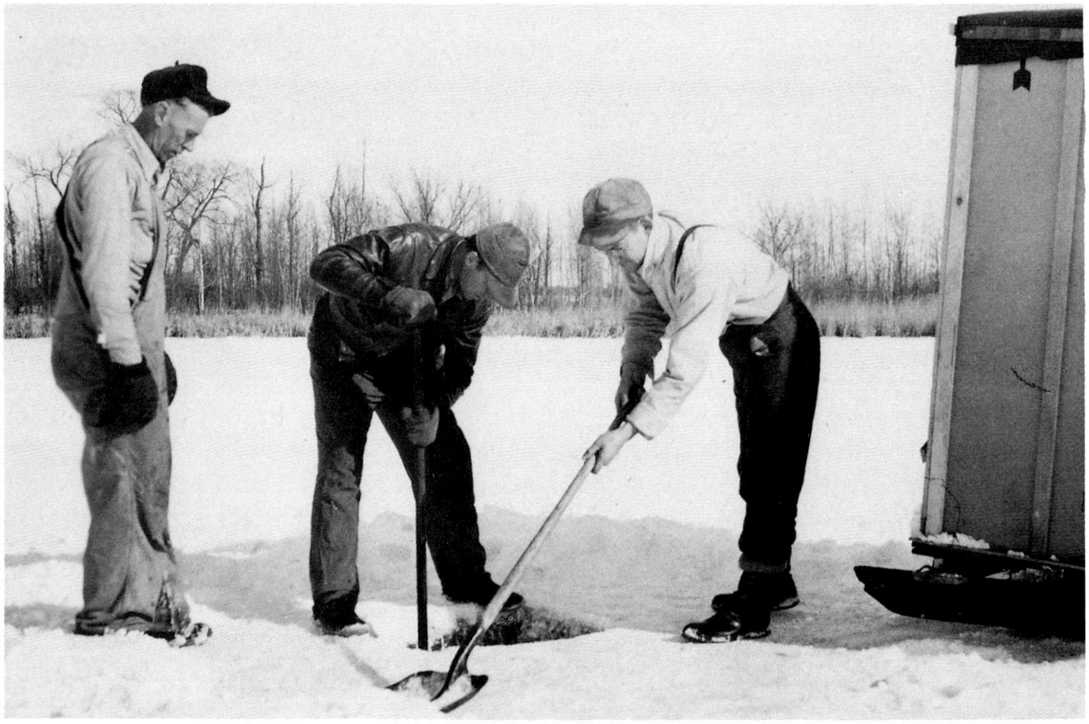

Figure 3-5. Shoveling Snow Off the Ice Around the Hole (Oxley Photo)

Then, the spear was attached to a strong cord and secured to an eye bolt in the ceiling of the dark house. This, of course, was done so that the spear could be retrieved after it was thrown at a fish. Spear fishermen will rest the spear in the water with one prong catching the lower edge of the ice at the bottom of the hole. This practice allowed the spearer to avoid breaking water with the spear when thrusting it, and thus, spooking the fish. When a fish was speared, it was removed from the hole and thrown on the ice outside the dark house.

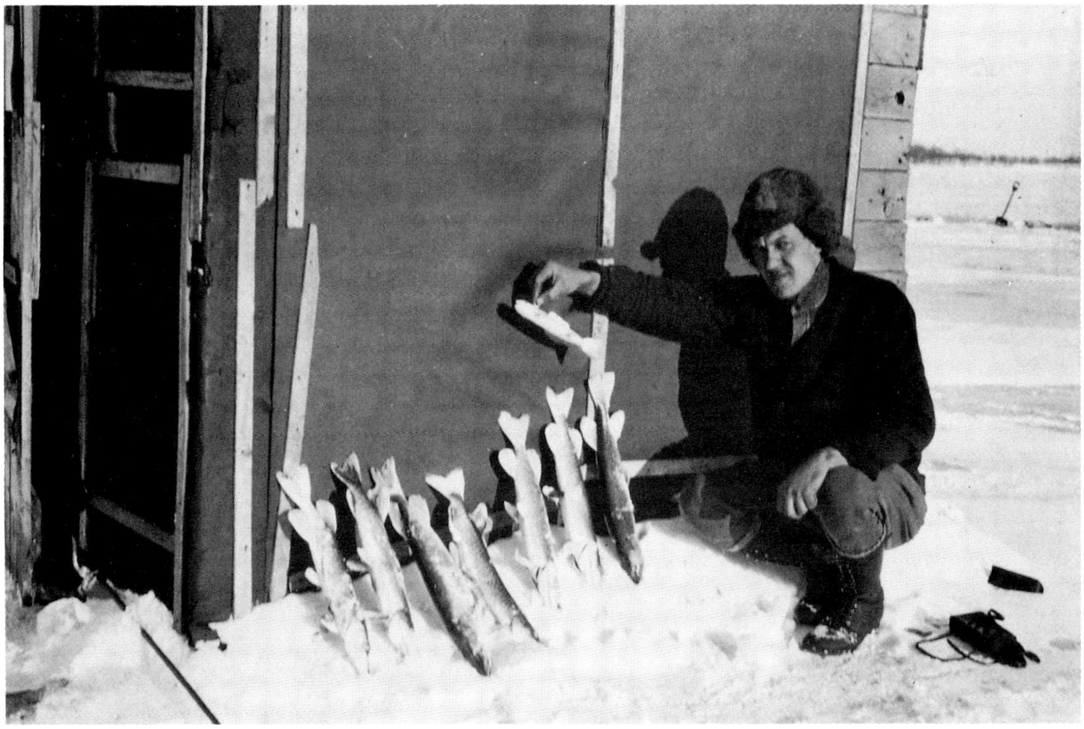

Figure 3-6. A Good Day's Catch (Oxley Photo)

Jigging Technique

At this point, the spear fisherman was ready for the decoy. One technique frequently employed was the jigging technique. Using this method, the decoy was attached to a short stick, called a "jigging stick," with heavy test fishing line (as much as 60 pound test). If the spearer was right handed, he would attempt to make the decoy appear as if it was swimming in tight circles by moving the jigging stick in his left hand in a slow circular motion (thus, leaving the right hand free for the spear). The slower the decoy was moved, usually the slower the fish would come into the hole. The fins and tail of the decoy were bent to a proper pitch in order to achieve the desired circle. If the decoy was swung in too wide of a radius, it would range under the ice and be lost to the spearer's view. Normally, the decoy "swims" in not more than two to three feet of water under the hole. While usually only one decoy was used, one informant stated that he would sometimes use two decoys, a large one and a small one to slow a fish's entry into the hole. He explained that with a small (three to four inch decoy) alone, the quarry would often charge the decoy, mouth it, let it go, and be off before there was time to have a real chance to spear it. In addition, Minnesota spear fishermen would occasionally use a "floater" decoy.[10] This was an unleaded wooden decoy with an eye screw on the bottom of it to which would be tied a string. At the end of the string a heavy weight was attached. Thus, the spearer could toss the floater into the hole, and the weight would prevent the buoyant wooden decoy from rising farther than the length of the string would allow (see Figure 3-7).

The floater decoy added "interest" to the action under the fishing hole.

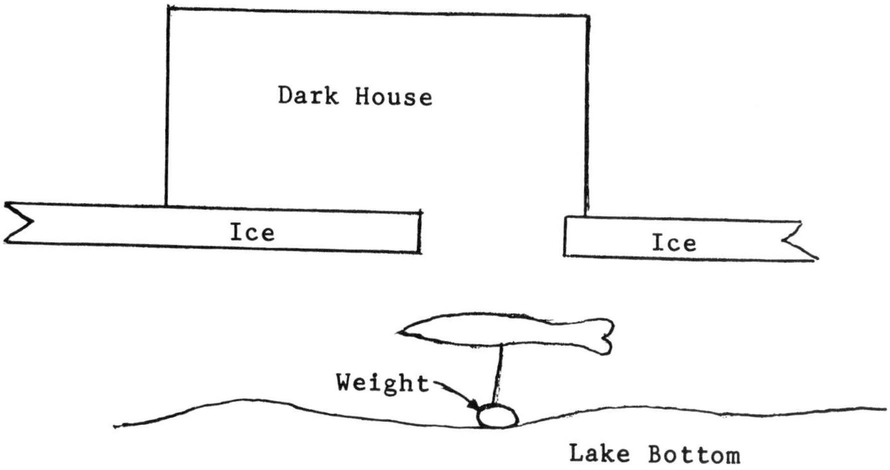

Figure 3-7. Use of a Floater Decoy

The Egg Beater Technique

To obtain a preferred slow moving decoy in the hole, some spear fishermen would weld to the bottom of a hand-held egg beater, a loop. To this loop, the line (or several lines) was [were] fastened with the decoy at the very end. After gauging the proper depth in the water for the decoy, the fisherman would then crank the egg beater so that the line would twist. When the desired tautness was achieved, he would cease cranking, and the line would begin to unwind, slowly turning the decoy in the water. As a substitute for an egg beater, an old hand cranked Victrola or other mechanical device that would turn the line by battery power, were also used.

Live Bait

Not all spearing is done with decoys, however. It is becoming more and more popular for spear fishermen to use live bait, such as minnows, to attract their prey.[11] The minnows do not have a hook through their back as in angling, but are rather placed in a harness which permits them to swim freely.

One old time informant explained that he took a very large light bulb, removed the end that screws into the socket, filled it with water, placed small minnows inside, and then capped the open end. He would then attach the capped end to a string and lower it into the hole. According to him, it worked well — truly an electrifying idea!

Plastics

Along with live bait as a substitute for the wooden decoys, plastic decoys are becoming a preferred way of spear fishing today. Plastic decoys are readily available and are relatively cheap in comparison to the time and effort required to make one by hand. One even finds the plastics in use by old time spear fisherman who have their own wooden decoys. An old time spear fisherman remarked to the author that: "Those wooden ones [decoys] are no good." It must be confessed that the author then quickly purchased the bucket full of hand-made decoys from the disgruntled fisherman!

With the growing acceptance of plastics, the number of hand made wooden decoys will continue to dwindle as the art and tradition of making them declines. It is likely that at some point in the future, homemade wooden decoys will become as common as making fire by rubbing two sticks together.[12]

American Indian Spear Fishing Technique

An excellent description of the American Indian method of spear fishing was given previously in Alexander Henry's account found on pages 14-15 of Chapter 2. Today, Indians still use tepee-shaped structures that are made of sticks about four feet long. These are covered by blankets (instead of skins in a bygone era). A number of pine branches or some boards are placed on the ice to give some insulation, as the spear fisherman lies on his stomach to peer over the hole. He also will spear from this prone position. Modern day Indians, like their white counterparts, do not spear fish in the deep water described by Henry.[13]

Densmore states that the Chippewa used a "... decoy fish ... made of wood with a tail of birch bark and body weighted with lead."[14] A jigging stick and decoy are shown in Plate 45 (d) of her book.

Figure 3-8. Scene of American Indians Spear Fishing.

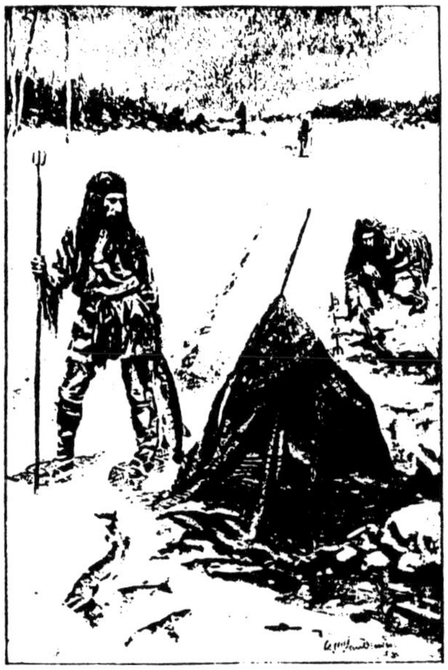

Source: Austin Hogan, op. cit. p. 18

The Anatomy of a Fish Decoy

The previous sections of this chapter have dealt with spear fishing techniques, but have not described, in detail, the fish decoy. This section discusses the many facets involved in decoy construction.

Wood. Examination of hundreds of decoys in private collections indicates that fish decoys were constructed from a variety of materials, but the most common one was, of course, wood. Pine is found in abundance in the Great Lakes region and is easy to carve. Therefore, it was the primary wood used for decoy making. Ponderosa pine was particularly sought after by carvers because it never swells or shrinks. Leroy Howell made all of his decoys from Ponderosa pine and the fine state of preservation of many of his used decoys are testimony to the effectiveness of that wood. Cedar was also a preferred construction material by many carvers because it does not easily split when the maker cut slots for fin insertion. Oak is a heavy wood and difficult to cut, but is nevertheless found as a base material in a few decoys as is ash and sumac. Basswood was also a frequently used source for the decoy's body. It has the advantage of being relatively light and does not gum sandpaper when the decoy is being finished. However, some carvers, such as Harry Sandell, picked up any type of wood they found along the road to make their decoys.

Metal. Decoys made of metal comprise the next most widely used body construction material. Copper was frequently used because it is soft, malleable, and could be shined to a high sheen. Decoys made from copper were believed to be particularly effective in lakes where the water was naturally dark or murky. They were made by either taking two thin sheets of copper, cutting them into the desired shape, rounding them into convex form and then welding the two pieces together to create a three dimensional fish, or by casting them in molds. Holes in the fish would allow water to enter the decoy's body and thus act as a natural sinker. Some hollow copper decoys were also leaded, however.[15]

Other metal decoys were made by cutting the outline of a fish from a piece of metal bar stock. These decoys, of course, lack three dimensional form. Sometimes metal fins were welded or soldered on for greater stability and realism (see Figure 3-9 and 3-10).

One category of copper decoy is the so-called "Northern Pump." Northern Pump decoys were given this name because some workers during World War II would fashion decoys from copper at the Northern Pump Company. One of these is depicted in Figure 3-11.

Brass decoys, although much less common than copper ones, were made using the same technique as described above. One interesting variation was found on a Minnesota decoy that was painted (see Figure 3-12).

Combination of wood and metal. A hybrid decoy combines both wood and metal together (see Figure 3-13). With this approach, the body of the decoy is fashioned from wood and usually left with flat sides to which a metal covering could be added. This gave the decoy greater powers of attraction in the water. Sometimes the decoy maker would also insert a mirror into the side of his decoy for greater attraction.

Rubber. Besides wood and metal decoys, one occasionally finds a decoy made entirely of rubber. Such a decoy is shown in Figure 3-14.

Another rubber decoy is shown in Chapter 4 and was made by Burt Thompson. It is a frog made from a rubber tire with felt to act as the frog's feet and to give the decoy greater action in the water.

Bone. Also, a one-of-a-kind decoy is a frog made from a bone — lead weighted and painted realistically. It is shown in Figure 3-15 with the jigging stick that it was attached to. Although Eskimos used bone and ivory for construction of decoys, it was not a preferred decoy construction material either among the American Indians or among white spear fishermen.

Clay. Simon Otto described clay fishing decoys made by the American Indians.[16] He stated that the decoy was made of fired clay, and fashioned in the shape of a fish. Otto claims that this technique was used in the early 1900's.

Line Tie Treatment

Screw eye. There are several commonly employed methods for attaching the line to a fishing decoy. A widely used one involves inserting a screw eye to the top of the decoy (see Figure 3-16). This, of course, represented an easy way to attach the line, but it was limited by the fact that if placement was not correctly made, the fisherman might not achieve the proper balance for his decoy, and also it might lack the desired action in the water.

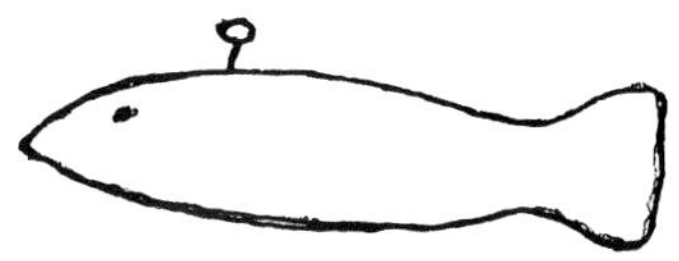

Figure 3-16. Decoy showing Screw Eye Line Attachment

Pig Tail Method. Another method of line tying is called the "pig tail method." It begins with taking a straight piece of small gauge wire and bending it at right angles at both ends so that it forms a flat bottomed, inverted, and elongated U. The flat bottomed U is then curled around a small round object to form loops. The remaining straight sections are then thrust into the top of the fish decoy where they extend into the cavity where the lead is poured. After pouring, the loops are held fast by the hardened lead. This technique permits the spear fisherman a choice of loops in which to attach his tie line so that he can best achieve the desired motion for his decoy. The steps of this technique are shown in Figure 3-17.

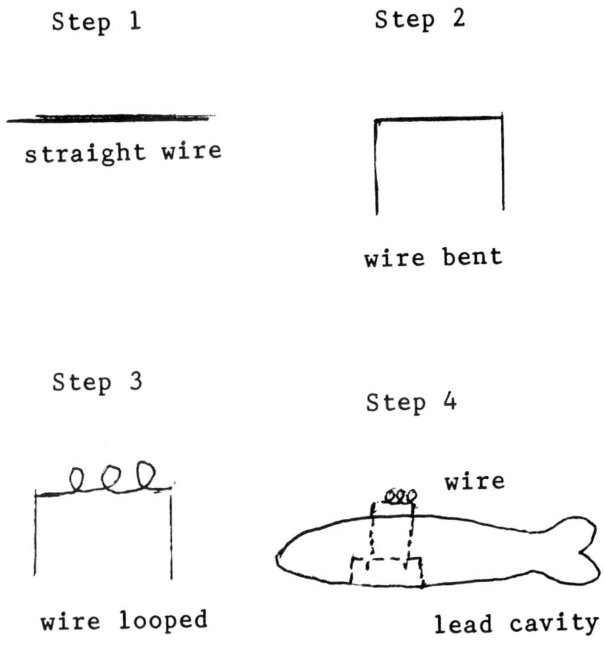

Figure 3-17. Steps in Constructing a Pig Tail Tie

A variation of the pig tail technique is found in decoys made by an unknown carver from the Brainerd, Minnesota area. He is one of a few makers (see also Harry Sandell) to use this method. His technique was to have one end of the wire inserted into the lead cavity of the decoy and the other end returned to the same hole (see Figure 3-18).

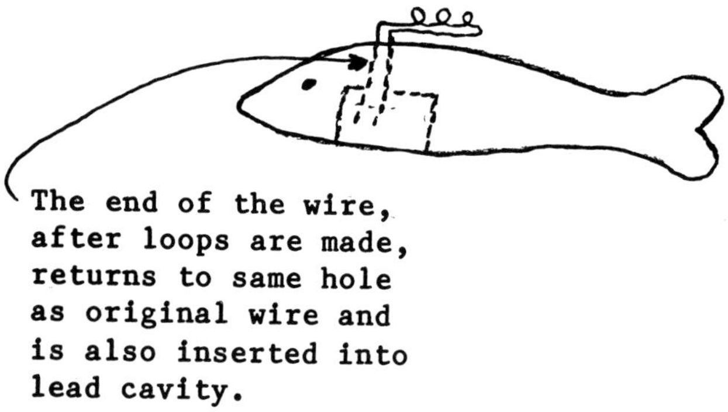

Figure 3-18. Variation on the Pig Tail Technique.

The end of the wire, after the loops are joined, returns to the same hole as the original wire and is also inserted into the lead cavity.

Loop technique. Another related line tie method is called the "loop technique." The decoy maker would take small lengths of straight, small gauge wire, bend them into the shape of an inverted U, and then push them through the body of the decoy into the lead cavity. After the lead was poured and hardened, the loops would be securely held. This technique differs from the pig tail by the fact that each individual loop is secured into the lead cavity instead of just the extreme ends of the wire. The loop technique is shown in Figure 3-19. Sometimes "bobby" pins were used for the same purpose.

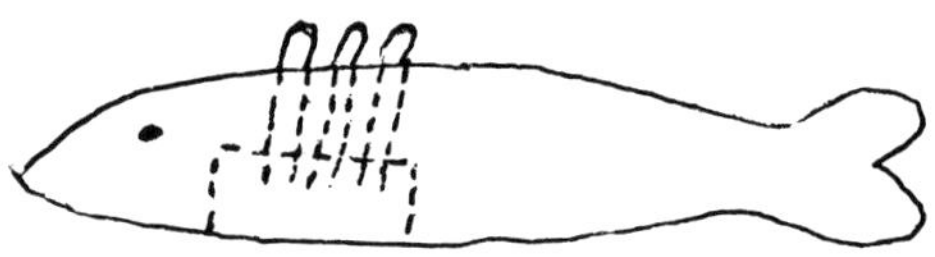

Figure 3-19. Decoy Showing the Loop Technique for Line Tying

Modified Loop Technique. In the modified loop technique, the decoy maker would begin with a length of straight wire. This was bent at right angles at a place so that the ends of the wire would be left long enough to penetrate the lead cavity of the decoy, but permitting enough wire outside (and on the top) of the fish, to make the necessary loops. Once the wire was firmly embedded in the decoy, the maker would use a screw driver (or other suitable instrument) to push down on the straight wire left exposed on the top of the decoy, at various strategic points, to form loops. Unlike the loop method, however, the tie line ridges formed by this technique, remained outside the decoy instead of each loop being individually inserted into the lead cavity. The Modified Loop Technique is shown in Figure 3-20.

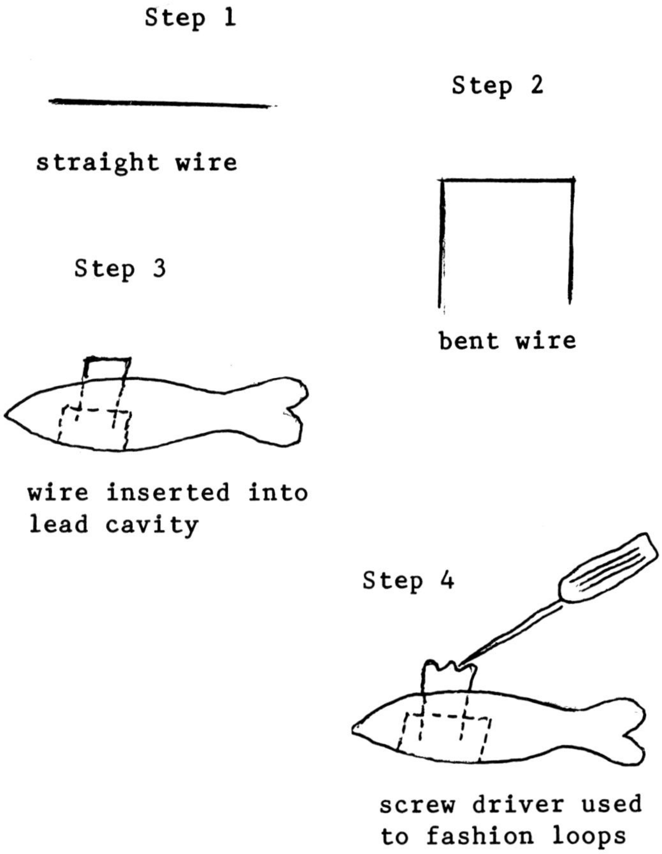

Figure 3-20. Steps in Line Attachment Using Modified Loop Technique

Dorsal fin ties. Still another line tie technique involved a hole, or several holes, punched into the dorsal fin of the fish decoy. Some variations of the technique are shown in Figure 3-21.

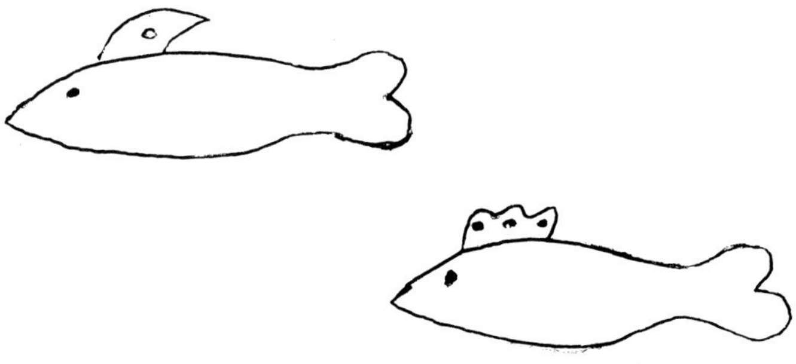

Figure 3-21. Types of Dorsal Fin Ties

Band Method. Some decoy makers would make their tie line attachments by drilling or punching holes in various shaped metal bands which were then inserted into the decoy, right behind its head. The band of metal was usually cut so that it would extend through the decoy's body into the lead cavity for stability purposes. This technique is illustrated in Figure 3-22.

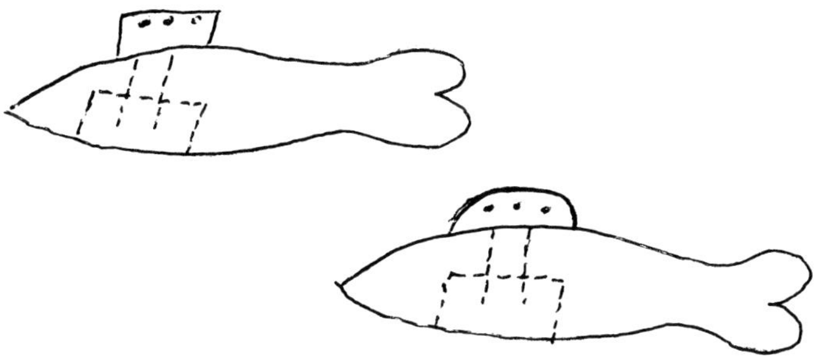

Figure 3-22. Band Method of Tie Line Attachment (Two common styles of bands)

Fin Treatment

The construction and placement of fins was extremely important for determining the action the decoy would give while in the water. Fins were normally made from thin gauge tin so that they could be readily bent in various ways to dive or rise. Old Prince Albert pipe tobacco tins were very popular for this purpose, but sheet metal or aluminum are found in a number of existing examples. Copper and brass fins are also found in some decoys but these materials seem to be associated with earlier crafted fish. It is possible that the rising price of copper and brass might have made these metals less attractive for decoy makers.

Fishing decoys had as many fins as were necessary to achieve the maker's purposes or as many fins as are found on the species of fish that the decoy imitated. Virtually all wood decoys had pectoral fins and some have dorsal as well as anal fins. The design (shape) of the decoy maker's fins for his models can give a collector a strong clue as to attribution. Decoy carvers virtually always shaped the fins of their decoys the same way and that shape is retained whether they were making small or large decoys. For example, Dave Mertens made his fins in the following distinctive form (see Figure 23).

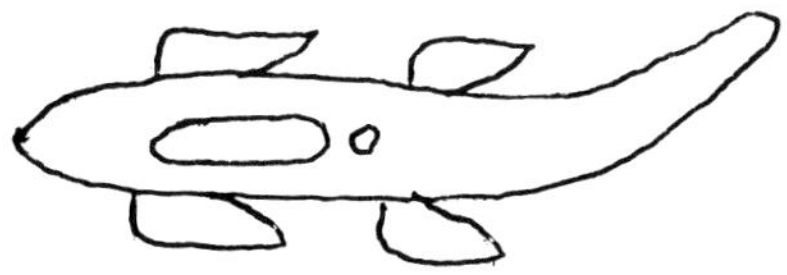

(bottom view)

Figure 3-23. Shape of Fins on Decoy Made by Dave Mertens

On the other hand Leroy Howell and the Faue brothers made their decoys' fins in a sweeping, graceful angel shape.

The fins, particularly the pectoral ones, were cut in one piece as to fit completely through the sides of the decoy, including the cavity for the lead. After the lead was poured and hardened, the fins were rigidly held in place (see Figure 3-24). Rear pectoral fins were also normally made in one piece and fitted through the side of the decoy (see Figure 3-24). Because the rear pectoral fins did not pass through the lead cavity, they were ordinarily nailed into place from the bottom of the decoy. The tail fin, if metal (rather than wood), was inserted into a slot made for that purpose in the rear of the decoy. Nails held the tail fin in place, but the fin still could be bent to achieve a desired motion for the decoy.

Fins, particularly dorsal fins, were rarely carved from wood. However, there are a few surviving examples of them. They were either made separately from the fish decoy's body and attached, or they were carved from the same piece of wood as the body.

Eye Treatment

Judging from examples existing in private collections, the most frequently used method for depicting eyes on fishing decoys was to paint them. Sometimes eyes were painted as a black circle, or as a black circle with white (or another contrasting color) outlining the eye.

Another common method for making eyes for decoys was to push thumb tacks into the decoy's head at appropriate locations. Sometimes the tacks were painted with a dot in the middle to represent a fish's iris. Regular carpentry nail heads were also used for this purpose, as were brass brads, and screw heads. Some very old fishing decoys even have square headed nails as eyes.

A more realistic approach to decoy eye treatment was the use of glass taxidermy eyes. Using this technique, the decoy maker would usually carve a depression in the decoy's head large enough to accommodate the eyes, so that they were flush or almost flush with the fish's head. Then, they were glued or more commonly pushed into the decoy's head by a pin attached to the reverse side of the taxidermy eye. Sometimes a hole was drilled through the eye socket of the decoy to connect with the eye socket on the other side of the decoy's head. A wire was then attached to one of the glass eyes and the wire pushed through the hole. Then, the end of the wire was attached to the other glass eye and the wire was twisted (by rotating the glass eyes in opposite directions) until the eyes were snugly in place (see Figure 3-25).

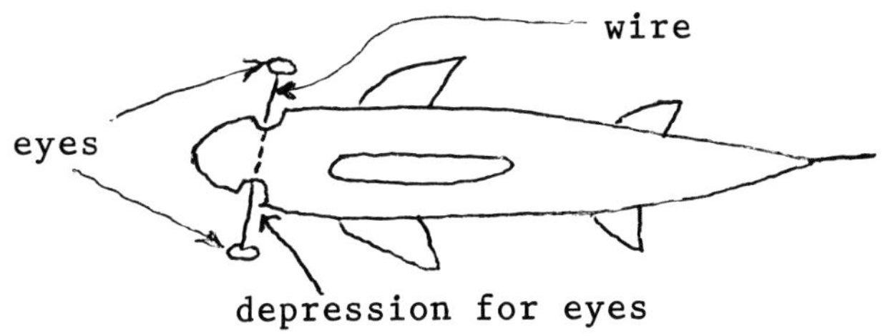

Figure 3-25. Method of Attaching Glass Eyes to a Fish Decoy

Occasionally, one finds costume jewelry (particularly rhinestones) used to give the decoy's eyes life in the water (a wife's discarded jewelry did not always go to waste). Sometimes decoy makers used the red balls found on leaders as eyes.

Mouth Treatment

Fish decoys often imitated a fish's mouth by painting it. Collectors prize those decoys where the mouth was carved into it or where the decoy's mouth was carved into an open position, sometimes even with such detail as teeth showing (see Ray Thompson decoy, Chapter 4).

Weighting Schemes

Weighting a wooden fishing decoy was normally accomplished by carving a rectangular cavity into the lower belly of the decoy and then filling it with lead. However, the shape of the lead cavity and the quality of the lead poured, i.e., no large bumps or overflows, can be as effective as fingerprints in the identification of a particular maker. Some of the lead cavities were long, narrow, and rectangular in shape, while others were almost square. Some decoy makers would also cut out the lead cavity on a bias (somewhat "V" shaped) so that the lead would be less likely to fall out (see Figure 3-26).

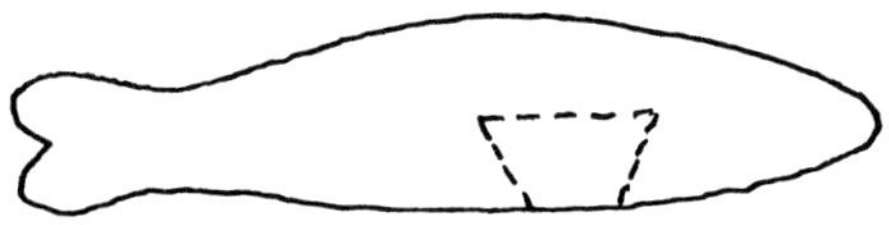

Figure 3-26. Fish Decoy Showing A Lead Cavity Cut on a Bias

Many beginning collectors fail to check the leading technique employed when purchasing a "name" maker's decoy. This can be a serious mistake.

Fishing decoys were also weighted by drilling a series of holes in the bottom of them into which lead could be poured.

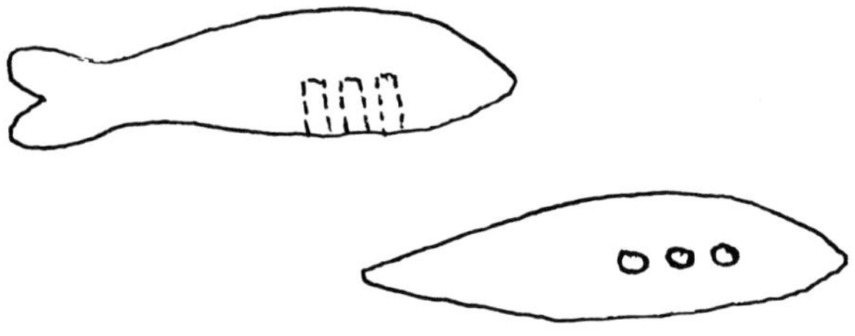

Figure 3-27. Side and Bottom View of Decoy With Drilled Hole Weighting

A rarely used approach to weighting involved splitting the fish decoy's body longitudinally and then hollowing out the body. After that, the cavity was filled with lead, and the maker glued the two halves of the fish back together (See Figure 3-28 in the color photo section for an example of such a decoy. Figures 3-28 through 3-59 are all located in the color photo section of this book.).

Another unusual weighting scheme was to insert lead weights into the sides of the fish decoy. This was accomplished by hollowing out the sides of the wood decoy in the shape of a rectangle and then pouring the lead into the cavity. Only one Minnesota decoy using this weighting scheme is known to the author and it is shown in Figure 3-29.

Sometimes a decoy maker would weight his decoys by nailing or screwing bands of lead to the bottom of the decoy (see Figure 3-30).

An old-time informant told me that he built a funnel made of clay around the top edge of the lead cavity so that, when pouring, he would not accidentally spill lead on the finished sides of his decoy. Others stated that they cut the lead cavity while the decoy was in block form, i.e., before they had finished final shaping of the fish, to reduce the chance of cracking the decoy's body.

Most old time decoys will, if permitted to be suspended freely from their tie line, not hang straight, but rather will be on an angle with the decoy's head well above the tail. When placed in water, the decoy would assume a more horizontal (realistic) position. Some fakes and modern decoys hang horizontally when suspended.

Tail Treatment

Examinations of various collections of fishing decoys reveal that the preferred materials for making a tail fin were tin, sheet metal, or aluminum. Tin tails were frequently used because they could be easily bent and they controlled the radius of the circle the decoy would make in the water. Normally, fish decoys were made with a single tail fin, but occasionally a stabilizer fin was also placed on it as shown in Figure 3-31. These were very rare, however.

Tails carved out of wood ("wood tails") seemed to be associated with older decoys (although this is an imperfect generalization). When the decoy's tail was carved as part of the decoy's body, it was frequently curved to better achieve a circular motion when it was jigged in the water. Figure 3-32 shows a good example of a wooden tail decoy.

Original leather tails are found on only a few surviving examples today. The constant exposure to the water and the cold, plus the wetting and then drying, soon cracked leather tails so that they had to be frequently replaced. Apparently leather tailed decoys were more frequently used for spear fishing in New York state than in the Great Lakes states. An example of a decoy with a leather tail is shown in Figure 3-33.

Rarely does a collector find an example of a jointed fish decoy. Most of the known examples were made by Pearl Bethel of Park Rapids, Minnesota (see Chapter 4).

found on a door, inserted between the sections so that the decoy in the water would exhibit a strong swimming action. The sides of each section were angled to a "V" shape to permit the fish to have a free swinging motion. A top view of such a jointed fish is shown in Figure 3-34 and a Bethel jointed fish is illustrated in Chapter 4 (see also Toivo Lahti).

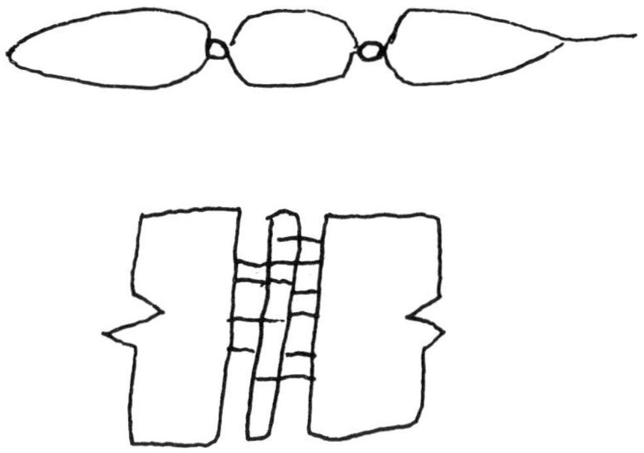

Figure 3-34. Top View of Jointed Decoy Showing Shape of Sections

Rubber and plastic were also utilized as materials for tail fins, but only rarely, judging by the examples of fish decoys in private collections.

Size of Decoys

Fishing decoys range in size from one inch to almost three feet in length. Most surviving specimens are between five to eight inches in length (at least for the non-critter decoys). Some old time informants told the author that very large decoys were ineffective in luring fish into the ice hole. On the other hand, occasionally large decoys were used as a gauge as to the length of a legal-sized fish, in order to avoid spearing an undersized one.

Color Schemes

An analysis of hundreds of decoys in private collections has shown that the most widely used color combination for fishing decoys was white and red. Success with red and white plugs for catching northerns probably accounts for this particular scheme. Much to the consternation of collectors, otherwise beautifully (and detailed) fish decoys have been repainted red and white to achieve a greater attraction power for northerns.

After red and white, silver paint was widely employed. Surprisingly, there are a large number of dark brown and some pure black decoys. In between, the color schemes for fish decoys run the gamut of the rainbow and their combinations on old decoys ran the limit of their makers' imaginations.

Decoys as Imitators of Various Fish Species

Fish decoys may be divided into two major categories: (1) those resembling fish or minnows, and (2) those which imitate "critters" such as frogs, mice, tadpoles, etc. In addition, there are decoys which were not made with any particular species of fish (or critters) in mind, but were designed only to attract fish into the hole to be speared. This section concentrates on those decoys which imitate various species of fish and critters. No attempt is made to assess the relative merits of these decoys with regard to their effectiveness as lures for fish, but only to give the collector/reader an appreciation of the wide variety of decoys that were used.

Northern Pike (Esox lucius). This fish exists both in the northern parts of Eurasia and North America. They, of course, are voracious predators, feeding on other fish, not to mention an occasional small muskrat, mouse, duckling, crawdad, or frog. This probably accounts for the number of "critter" decoys made by old time carvers, as northerns will chase almost anything (even a beer can, one informant told me) when they are in the mood. Perhaps the majority of known decoys which are identifiable as to species are northerns. Examples of northern-styled decoys are shown in Figures 3-35 and 3-36

Perch (Percidae). Next to northerns in frequency of decoys made, come the yellow perch (Percinae). In North America, they inhabit the Great Lakes and inland lakes as well as being found in large streams. Perch are also found in Europe. They serve as an important source food for northerns, which may account for spear fishermen's imitation of this species for their decoys. Figures 3-37 and 3-38 show perch decoys.

Trout (Salmo clarkit lewisi). Various species of trout are found in Europe, in the Great Lakes drainage area, and in the Great Lakes proper. They are abundant in a few cool inland lakes and in many trout streams. Trout belong of the salmon family. Trout are fine scaled fish having more than 100 scales in a lateral line. An example of a trout decoy is depicted in Figure 3-39.

Suckers (Catostomus commersonnii commersennii). The common white sucker is found all over North America from Canada to Georgia, and as far west as northeastern Oklahoma. They are a common food for predators such as northerns and walleye pike, bass, and muskies. Decoy makers usually depicted suckers by accentuating the hog nose of that fish (see Figure 3-40).

Sunfish (Lepomis humilia). The orange spotted sunfish (Lepomis humilis) has a distinctive black mark on the top of the gill and an orange-yellow lower body. It is difficult to discern decoys that are supposed to imitate that fish from a bluegill (Lepomis macrochirus macrochirus), which also has a black mark near the upper part of the gill, and the pumpkin seed (Lepomis gibbosus). Examples of these classes of fish are found in Figure 3-41 to Figure 3-44.

Gar fish (Lepisosteidae). Gars are distinguished by the more or less diamond-shaped, thick ganoid scales that cover its body and jaws and face extended forward into a beak. Their teeth are exceptionally strong, sharp, and conical. Fewer than ten species are found, all freshwater, and they are sometimes referred to as "living fossils" because nearly all their relatives are extinct.

Two species inhabit the Great Lakes area, the long nose gar and the spotted gar. They prefer quiet, warm waters in lakes and larger streams, and are sluggish except when feeding. Gars like to bask near the surface on warm days or nights.

It is doubtful that gars are a preferred food of northerns. Rather it is more likely that carvers made gar-shaped decoys to suit their own fancy along with a belief that a northern in likely to be lured by almost any object of curiosity. A gar decoy is pictured in Figure 3-45. They are very rare decoys and so are prized by collectors.

Bullhead (Ameirus melas melas). Bullheads are in the catfish family and are scaleless fish with a spinous ray in the dorsal fin and in each pectoral fin. They possess prominent whisker-like barbs which are sensory in function. Bullheads are further characterized by the presence of an adipose dorsal fin. An example of a bullhead decoy is shown in both Figures 3-46 and 3-47

Crappies. Crappies fall into two categories: (1) the white crappie (Pomoxi's) and (2) the black crappie (Pomoxis nigeo-maculatus). Both types inhabit the Great Lakes states and prefer clear, weedy lakes. It is relatively rare to find a decoy that was meant to imitate a crappie. One is, however, shown in Figure 3-48. Crappies are a source food for northerns and could serve as an appropriate lure for them.

Critter Decoys

As previously noted, the critter decoys were certainly not made as frequently by carvers as their fish counterparts, and their relative rarity enhances their desirability. Critters run a gamut of species from imitation frogs to bats and even bumblebees. Some of these may have been made solely from whimsy, but many were constructed because the carver believed that they would work, or that they were a preferred food for northerns in a particular lake.

Frogs. Frogs are by-far-and-away the most common type of critter spearing decoy. They range in size from small two to five inches long frogs to a very large bullfrog size. Some frog decoys are finless (see Figure 3-49) and some were made with rubber feet (see Figure 3-50). Most typically, frog decoys had two long extended legs (Figure 3-51), but others (much rarer types) had crossed legs (Figure 3-52). A few examples exist where frog decoys had movable legs to simulate a swimming motion.

Tadpoles. Tadpoles, of course, are frogs not yet fully developed. Decoys imitating tadpoles are very rare. One such decoy made by an unknown Minnesota maker is depicted in Figure 3-53.

Crawdads. Judging from the holdings in private collections, crawdads are very rare. Some were made with metal pincers and some were constructed entirely of wood. More exotic crawdad decoys even had movable arms (Figure 3-55).

Mice. There are a few legitimate old mice decoys in existence. The bodies are carved from wood and tails were made of strings or leather. One of these is pictured in Figure 3-56.

Eel pouts. Eel pouts, properly termed madtoms (schilbeodes marginatus marginatus), are in the catfish family and are found in the Great Lakes region. They have a characteristic dorsal fin right behind the head and the back part of their body appears to be surrounded by a fin, which gives them their peculiar shape. An example of an eel pout decoy is shown in Figure 3-57.

Salamanders. The author is aware of only two legitimate old salamanders. One is pictured in Figure 3-58.

Dragon fly. Two dragon fly decoys, apparently made by the same person in Minnesota, exist in two different collectors' holdings. The larger decoy's wings were made of brass and the body appears to be wrapped in a piece of an old brown rug. The smaller one has a wood body, taxidermy eyes, and metal wings. It has been wrapped by what appears to be fishing string. One is pictured in Figure 3-59.

Turtles and Muskrats. I have examined a large number of muskrat and turtle decoys, and I am unconvinced that these were made for any purpose other than to sell to collectors. Caveat emptor should be the watchword for anyone purchasing such decoys as old, used decoys.

CHAPTER IV

MINNESOTA DECOY MAKERS AND THEIR DECOYS

It is sometimes said that the fishing decoys from Minnesota lack the artistic quality of those found in Michigan. A review of the examples in various private collections does not bear out that conclusion, however. Michigan is a state that was settled before Minnesota and so some of the decoys found there are older. Michigan is also a state with a rich tradition of famous duck decoy carvers, some of whom carved fishing decoys. Their influence may have spilled over to fish decoy carvers, establishing a kind of standard of carving in Michigan.

What Minnesota carvers lacked in tradition, they more than compensated for by their willingness to innovate in the design, painting and construction of their fishing decoys as well as in their creativity in producing "critters" in large numbers. One finds more examples of frogs, crawdads, mice, etc. in Minnesota than in Michigan. Thus, lacking the traditions of Michigan carvers, Minnesota decoy makers may have been more innovative.

However, in the following pages, the reader will discover the richness and diversity of Minnesota decoys. Along with the many decoys attributed to individual carvers, there are also examples of fish decoys that were made by "unknown" carvers. Their works may be found at the conclusion of this chapter. It is hoped that the readers of this book will be able to furnish the names of these unknown carvers, along with any information readers might have concerning them.[1]

Perhaps more is known about the "commercial" carvers (see Chapter 6) — i.e., those carvers who made decoys not only for themselves but also to sell — than has come to light concerning those who made decoys solely for their own use. Because many more of the former decoys have survived, information concerning their makers has been preserved and more examples of their work are available to be studied. This does not diminish in any way the importance of other decoy makers, however.

Decoys were often traded (or sold) among spear fishermen, or borrowed and never returned. Thus, when decoys are collected, one may find decoys which do not seem to belong. It would be a mistake for the collector to assume that the person from whom the decoys were purchased was necessarily the maker.[2] Questioning may clarify which, if any, were made by the seller, and which were not. This situation, plus the fact that many dealers "pick" fish without any attempt at identification of their makers, makes proper attribution of decoys a very hazardous task.

The number of decoy makers presented in this chapter has been arbitrarily limited. I chose not to include individuals for whom only a name attribution exists, instead of proper identification. It is believed that this course of action is the wiser alternative, rather than presenting a name and being forced to recant that improper identification when additional information becomes available.

ERNEST AAMODT*

Ernest Aamodt was born in 1915 in Rose County, Minnesota. In 1929, he moved to Crosby, Minnesota where he has lived ever since. He has farmed, served as a guide and worked underground in the mines.

His spearing decoys were made of cedar because he claimed that it was an easy wood with which to work. Ernest has made a wide variety of decoys including northerns, perch, dog fish and sunfish. His decoys have the characteristic of being abstractly, rather than realistically, painted. The eyes of his decoys were always round in shape and painted black, usually with a yellow outline. He made both wooden and metal tails for his fish, and the fins for his decoys, always four in number, were made from metal from an old Chevrolet. Aamodt was fond of using glitter and a number of his surviving decoys bear that substance. His tie lines are interesting because he employed a number of tie techniques. In some examples he used the "loop method" but in others the screw eye method was utilized. He even used three screw eyes in a row as a line tie method. His painting was detailed and he attempted to imitate scales by painting pebble-like blotches or wavy lines around his fish decoys. Sometimes he would paint the head of his decoys white and then to show scales he would paint black markings over the white head of the decoy. These black markings resembled dried mud. He also used a wide variety of colors for decoys.

Mr. Aamodt is properly considered one of the finest decoy makers and painters in Minnesota.

*Information provided by Mr. Aamodt. The Kimball's erroneously spell his name as "Aamot" (see Kimball's, op. cit., Volumes I, II, and III.

ARVID ARTHUR ALHO*

Arvid Alho was born on November 9, 1907, in Eveleth, Minnesota. He came to Brainerd, Minnesota with his family at a very early age, and has resided there ever since. Arvid first worked in a paper mill in the pulp and grinder rooms. He was a common laborer at age 16 and then became an apprentice carpenter. Kampmann Sash and Door Company was his employer for 35 years where he worked as a shipping clerk, assembled windows, and then became a frame maker. During his tenure at Kampmann he also was a journeyman glazier and a first class machine operator.

He made his spearing decoys in 1932. Arvid remembered this date clearly because it was three years after he purchased his 1929 Ford. His decoys were fashioned from pine and have tin fins and tails. They were made for his use only. Mr. Alho was apparently fond of bright colors, as his decoys demonstrate, and he used an abstract rather than a realistic painting technique.

*Information provided by Mr. Alho.

LEWIS W. "LOUIE" ANDERSON*

Louie Anderson was born in Park Rapids, Minnesota in 1905. He resided there all of his life, passing away in 1986. Mr. Anderson worked on a farm and also performed carpentry.

He began making decoys as a young man. Over the years he produced hundreds of decoys which he sold to local people. The general shape of his decoys and their fins demonstrate that he was influenced by Pearl Bethel (see this chapter) who lived in the Park Rapids area. All Anderson decoys had two side fins as well as a pectoral and anal fin made of metal. The tail fin also was made of metal. Decoy bodies were made from white pine. His painting scheme was to use three colors with one color band on the top of the decoy, a contrasting color band across the middle of the fish and, typically, a band of white at the bottom of the decoy. A series of painted circles across the middle of the decoy usually completed the decoration.

*Information supplied by Mr. John Anderson.

THOMAS J. ANNIS*

Thomas Annis was born in Parkers Prairie, Minnesota on February 15, 1939. He was residing in Kensignton, Minnesota when he died on March 4, 1991. Mr. Annis did carpentry work and had his own construction business during the last few years of his life.

He began making decoys as a youngster. His decoys were produced for his own use only. Annis decoys are distinctive in that they have a carved open mouth, a copper loop line tie, relatively small side fins and a metal tail. Mr. Annis would paint lines or circles to imitate scales on his decoys.

Mr. Annis was married but had no children.

*Information provided by Mrs. Tom Annis.

WILLIAM "SLOW" BATTERS*

William Batters was born in Little Falls, Minnesota on January 19, 1882. He lived in the Little Falls area for his entire life. As a professional fireman, he rose through the ranks, eventually becoming fire chief. Mr. Batters was with the Little Falls fire department for 48 years, retiring in 1952. He died in 1957.

An enthusiastic spear fisherman, Mr. Batters began making decoys for his own use in the 1930's. Long shifts in the firehouse apparently gave him the time to whittle and paint his decoys. His decoys became popular and it was not long before he began selling them in bait shops and sporting goods stores in towns surrounding Little Falls.

Mr. Batters' decoys are very distinctive in form and construction, but they were not all necessarily made in exactly the same way. Some of his decoys had "band" line ties, while others had "loop" line ties. All, however, had a carved gill and smiling carved mouth with a protruding lower lip. Most of his decoys had small brass brads for eyes, although he preferred a tiny, white, marble-like piece for eyes in his sucker decoys. He made three primary types of decoys: a minnow-type decoy typically painted red and white, although occasionally painted with a more realistic pattern; a sucker decoy usually painted dark brown or black; and a crappie decoy painted green with black spots or with a red head and green body. Mr. Batters normally utilized a more rounded tail for his sucker and crappie decoys and a more sharply pointed tail for his minnow decoys. His decoys varied in size from three inches in length to about 12 inches, although longer specimens have been noted in some collections.

Mr. Batters was married and had four children.

*See "William `Slow' Batters Minnesota's Real `Harry Blancherd'" by Donna Tonelli, *Decoy Magazine,* September/October 1991, pp. 33-35, for a more complete biography of Mr. Batters' life.

GERHART BERENS*

Gerhart Berens was born in 1905 east of Grey Eagle, Minnesota. He resided in Burtrum, Minnesota. Before retiring, Mr. Berens had farmed for 15 years, did carpentry work for ten years, and worked for the State and County's highway department as a grader.

As a decoy maker, Mr. Berens could easily have been classified as contemporary in the sense that he continued to produce fish decoys until his death in 1994. However, his early decoys are so beautiful in construction and painting that he deserves a place as a premier old-time decoy carver.

He began making decoys in the 1930's for his own use. However, he soon discovered a ready market for his fish, and was able to sell them for the princely sum of $3.00 each. His decoys were carved from white pine and basswood. He made primarily three types of decoys: crappies, sunfish and perch.

Mr. Berens was married and had three daughters. He passed away in 1994.[3]

*Information from an interview with Mr. Berens.

PEARL BETHEL*

Pearl Bethel was born in March of 1894 in Souther, Iowa, and died in April of 1960. He came to Park Rapids, Minnesota in 1915. Pearl served in World War I. After his release from the service, he returned to Park Rapids. There, he worked as a stone mason, building fireplaces, and he also performed some carpentry work.

In the winter, Pearl would carve decoys in quantities, to be sold to the Earl Fuller Tackle Shop in Park Rapids. He also encouraged his children to sell his decoys to various bait shops whenever they took trips. His price was $1.00 to $1.50 per dozen in the 1940's. Pearl continued to make decoys until the time he died, but his carving production actually increased in his later years.

Pearl Bethel decoys are very distinctive. Most are slender in width and painted as rainbow trout; however, he also produced perch and suckers. The rounded nose, particular facial markings and dots or dashes on the decoy's body were his trademarks. His decoys varied in size from about three inches in length to almost one foot long. Most of his earlier decoys had a light brown color as the dominant hue, but in later years he began using bright greens, purple, mauve, etc. as well as substituting tack eyes for painted ones.

White pine was his preferred material for construction of decoy bodies, which (after whittling to size) he would smooth with a broken piece of glass. He used a cheap oil based paint to decorate his fish. Most of the Pearl Bethel decoys had fins made from old oil cans that he had burned to remove the paint and oil residue. Some of his earlier fish, however, had copper fins, along with a carved mouth and carved gills.

For weighting, he drilled out the bottom of the decoy with a band brace and bit and then smoothed the lead cavity. Often, drilling would commence before the decoy was finally shaped in order to avoid splitting.

Pearl Bethel also made jointed fish. Informants said that his jointed decoys had a tendency to either make too tight of a circle or went out under the ice and were lost to sight. Hinges for the jointed fish were made from tin with a pin inserted.

Two known hollow copper decoys were also made by Pearl Bethel.

*Information provided by Lawrence Bethel.

CYRIL BETHEL*

Cyril Bethel was born in Iowa in March of 1900 and died in July of 1980. He was Pearl Bethel's brother and came to Park Rapids, Minnesota at the same time as Pearl. While he did some carpentry work, his main vocation was trapping and serving as a fishing guide. He would brag that no one ever came back without a fish when he performed the guiding. His services cost $20 per day.

Like his brother Pearl, Cyril Bethel made fishing decoys which he sold. He received $14 for a dozen of them in later years.[4] Cyril's decoys differ greatly from those made by Pearl. One of their distinguishing characteristics is the blockiness of the decoy's body, as contrasted to the slender bodies on Pearl's decoys. Cyril always painted the eyes of his decoys on the very top of their head, while Pearl placed his in their more natural position. While the fins on Pearl's decoys are rounded in shape, Cyril's had cut his in a straight line on the back side of the fin.

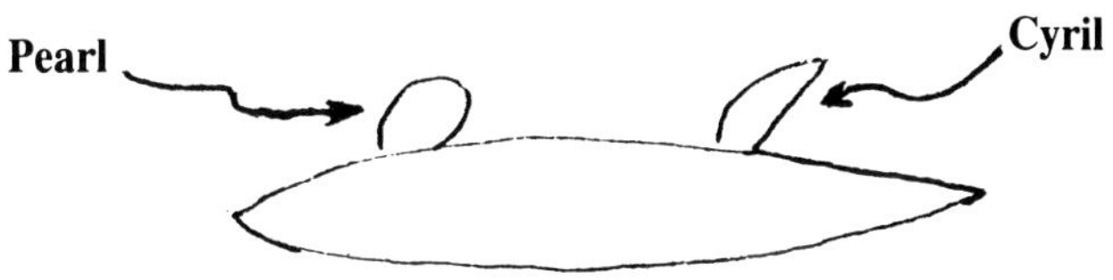

Comparison of fin shapes in Pearl and Cyril Bethel Fish Decoys

Cyril Bethel's painting technique was much more plain when contrasted to Pearl's. The former preferred silver, white and black or brown as major body colors with little, if any, detail painting, except for the use of dots.

The tail fins on Cyril's fish were also straight, lacking the wide fan-shape used by Pearl Bethel.

*Information provided in part by Lawrence Bethel.

OTTO BISHOP SR.*

Otto Bishop Sr. was born on February 28, 1915 in Clarks, Nebraska. In 1924, his family came to Minnesota. Mr. Bishop currently resides in Osage, Minnesota. He has been a mechanic and performed construction work for 28 years.

In 1949, he began making fishing decoys. He made about 40 decoys over the years. Most of these were left in a dark house when he stopped spearing in 1970. He early decoys were constructed from pine.

Mr. Bishop returned to making decoys in 1980. The later ones were made from butternut or basswood, which is easy to carve and does not split. He made walleyes, bass, crappies, and blue gills from 1980 until he stopped producing decoys again in 1990. Both he and his wife painted the fish. He placed the outline of the decoy on a piece of paper and from the paper, traced the outline on a board.

Mr. Bishop is married and has seven children, four girls and three boys.

*Information provided by Mr. Bishop.

CECIL BLANK*

Cecil Blank was born in 1911 in Iowa and died in 1991. He resided in Bemidji, Minnesota at the time of his death. Mr. Blank worked in a box factory for 22 years and was a lumberjack for five years.

He began making decoys in 1947. His decoys were constructed from basswood and he used car enamel to paint them. According to his son, making decoys was a sideline with Cecil and he did not sell decoys, but crafted them only for his own use. It was estimated that he made ten to 100 decoys over the years.

Mr. Blank was an avid spear fisherman, spearing from Lake Bemidji to Lake Marquette. He was married and had six children, all of whom are grown.

*Information courtesy of Robert Blank, one of Cecil's sons.

ART BOELTER*

Art Boelter was born June 9, 1896 in LeSueur, Minnesota and died November 18, 1989. Employed as a head mechanic, he maintained a fleet of Allied Moving Vans, retiring after 65 years of service.

He began carving fish decoys as a hobby in the early 1940's. When his decoys were found to work well in the water, his friends requested that he make some for them. Later, the success of his decoys prompted him to make 100 to 150 decoys which were sold exclusively in Small's Bait Store in Minneapolis.

Unfortunately, Art quit carving decoys after only two or three years so as to have more time to assist his mother.

Boelter's fish decoys have been erroneously attributed to Marion Butcher.[5] The former decoys were abstractly painted. A distinctive feature of a Boelter decoy is the wavy line painted on the large side fin. A favorite decoration was a series of circles painted on the sides of his decoys. Most of his known decoys were painted white and red, but a few were painted mostly green with orange trim or orange with green trim. Dorsal and tail fins were striped with paint.

Boelter's preferred wood for his decoys was pine, and he used tin from sheets of tin that he obtained for fins. His favorite spearing lake was Twin Lake in Robbinsdale, Minnesota.

*Information supplied by Lloyd Boelter.

MERRILL BOOTH*

Merrill Booth was born on September 24, 1892 in Mitchell, South Dakota. He died on January 16, 1966 in Minneapolis, Minnesota. Mr. Booth was employed at the Ford Motor Company in Minneapolis. There he met Charlie Slechta. The latter had been making copper spear fishing decoys that were all hand done on maple molds. Merrill Booth made one style of decoy which had a smooth tail and always had a scaled body. He began making his metal decoys in 1940 and likely stopped production in 1950-52.

Mr. Booth made his decoys in the basement of his house located on Abbott Street in Minneapolis. His decoys were formed in molds and were plated by electro-casting. He would keep plating until he achieved a certain thickness. The vast majority of his decoys were plated with copper (Mr. Booth purchased junk yard copper wire). Some of his decoys were nickel plated, however.

Merrill sold his decoys through a management co-worker at Ford, a man named Al Finberg. Finberg arranged to sell Booth's decoys on his (Finberg's) son's paper route. The decoys were sold for a $5.00 retail price through Finberg. Finished decoys were also placed in white socks or in a sock bag with Booth's name and address. The socks and sock bags protected the decoys against scratching.

Mr. Booth retired in October 1955 from Ford. He was married and had two sons.

*Information courtesy of Russell Booth, one of Merrill's sons.

Chapter IV Photographs (cont.)

John Melquist

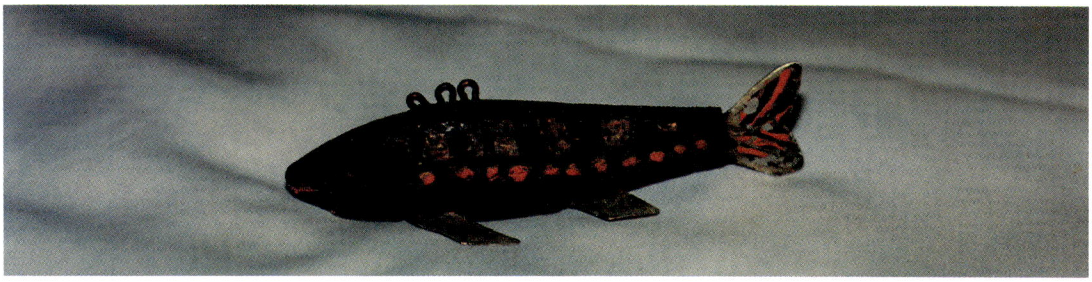

Black painted wooden decoy by John Melquist, 5 inches.

Dave Mertens

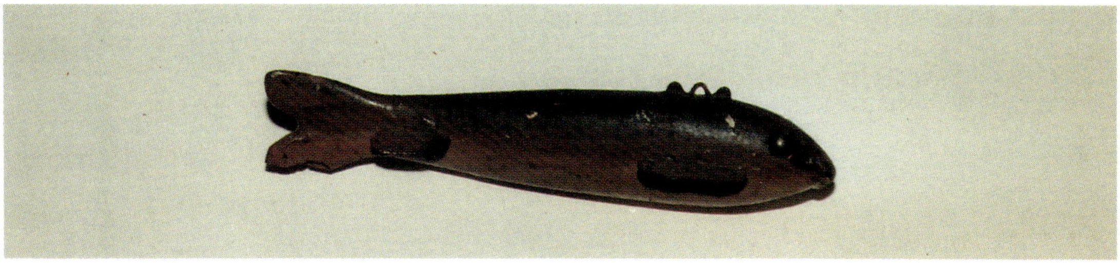

Sucker in muted brown tones by Dave Mertens. Note notched wooden tail. His suckers were not carved to show scales, 7 inches.

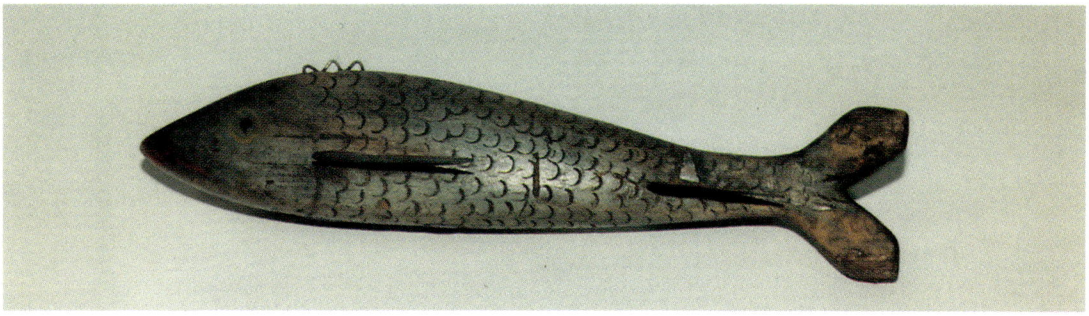

Northern pike by Mertens with scaled finish and painted red mouth, length 9 inches.

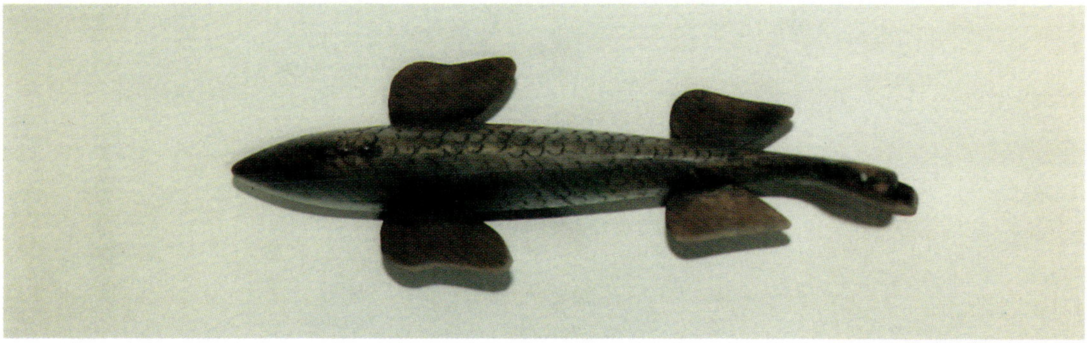

Bottom view of Mertens' northern showing distinctive pectoral fin shape.

Albert Meyer

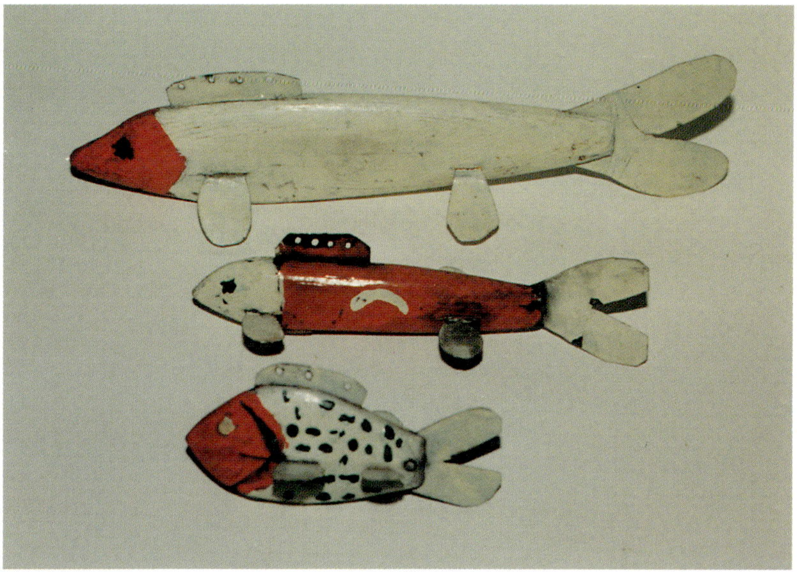

Three Albert Meyer's decoys. Top: 9 inches; Middle: 6 inches; and Bottom: sunfish, 4 inches.

Leo Miller

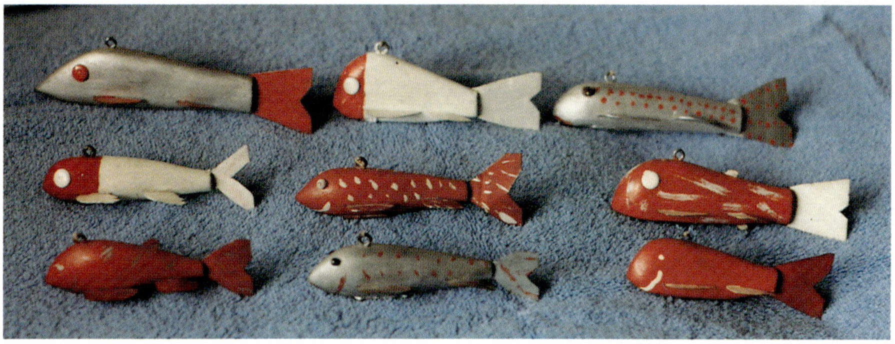

Group of 9 Leo Miller decoys.

Frank Mizera

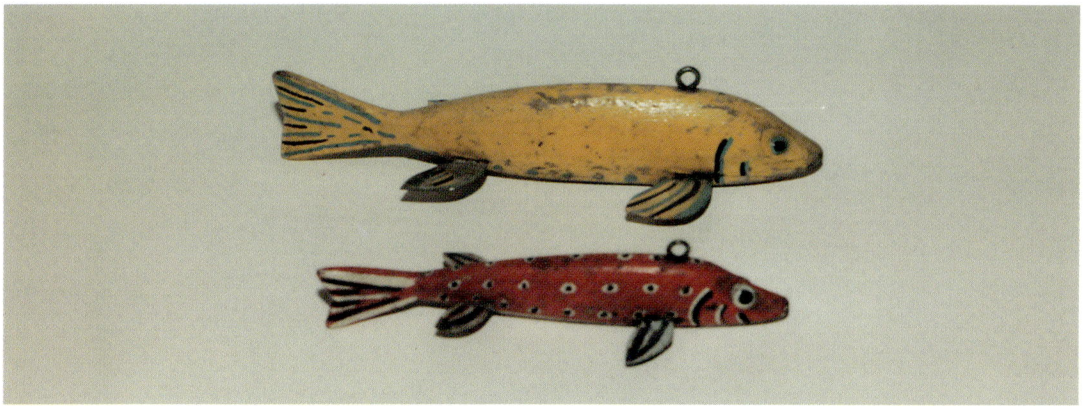

Two early Mizera decoys. Note lack of slope to yellow painted fish decoy. Top is 6 inches long. Bottom red colored decoy is one of the smallest Mizera decoys, 4 1/2 inches.

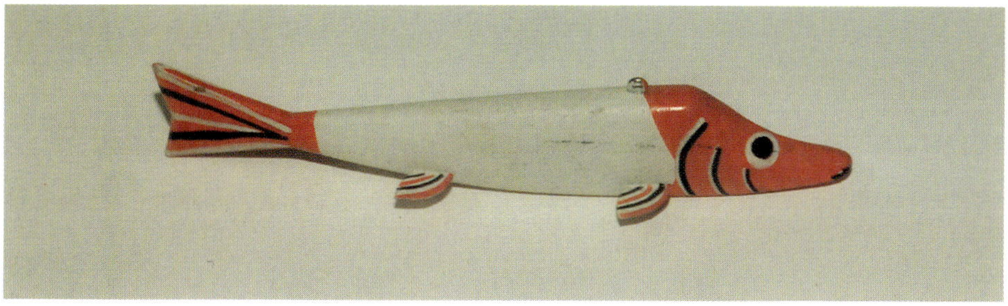

A more recent Mizera red and white decoy with pronounced nose slope, 7 1/2 inches.

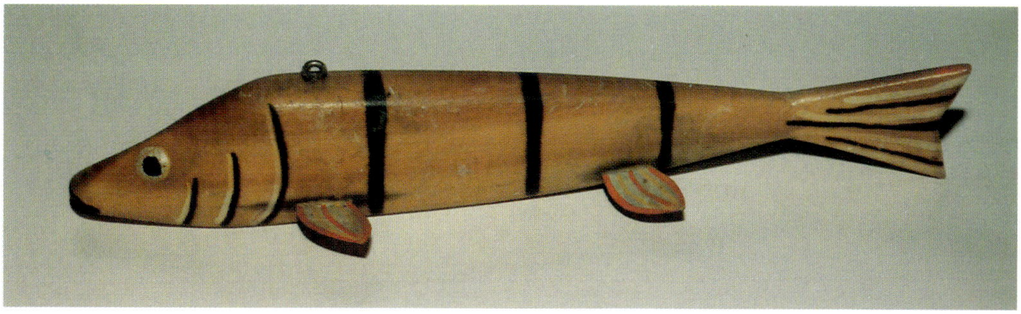

Natural wood Mizera decoy, 8 1/2 inches.

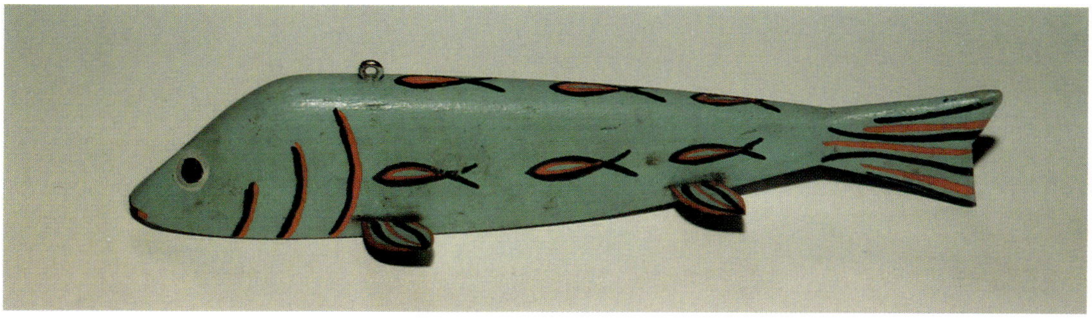

Turquoise painted Mizera decoy with fish designs, 8 1/2 inches.

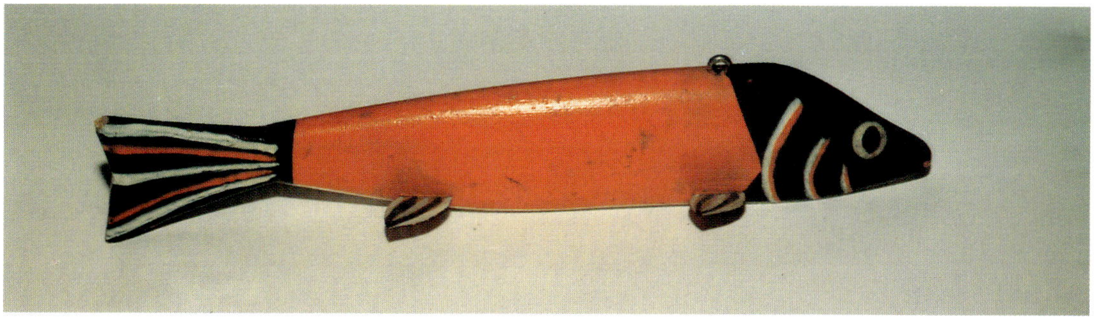

Rare Mizera orange painted decoy, 7 1/2 inches.

Black painted Mizera decoy with fish designs, 9 1/2 inches.

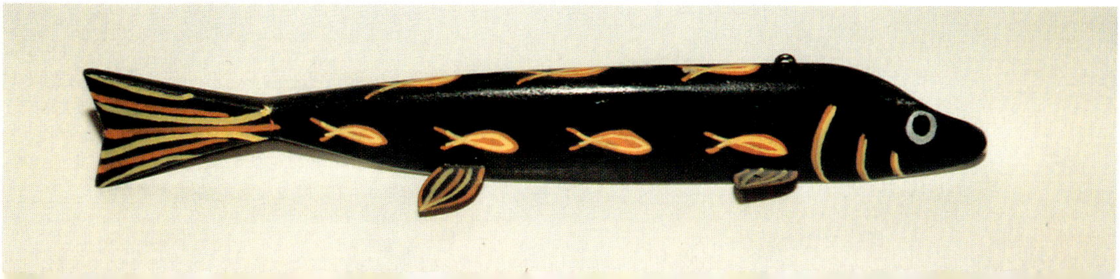

Nick Moes

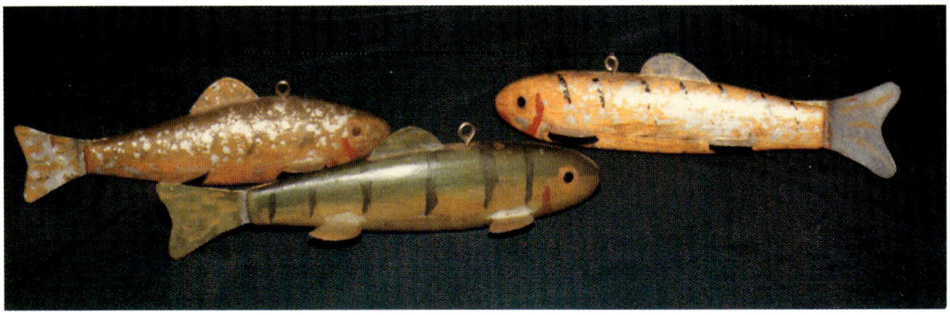

Grouping of three Nick Moes decoys. Photo courtesy of Bill Stoetzel.

E.W. Mooers

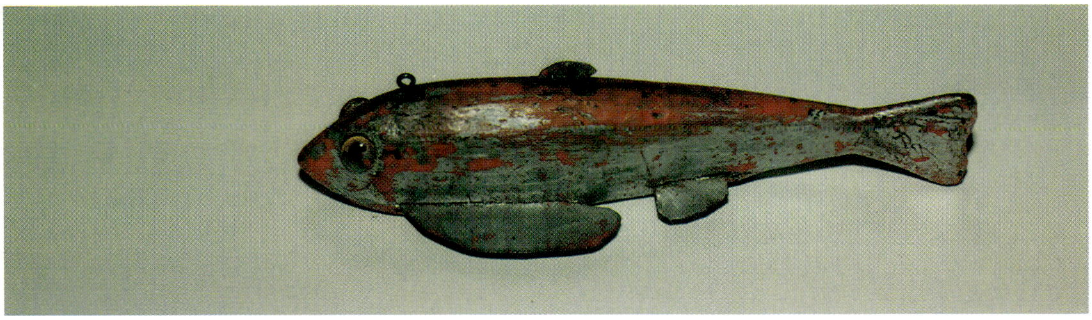

Red and silver, wood tail decoy by E. W. Mooers, 6 inches.

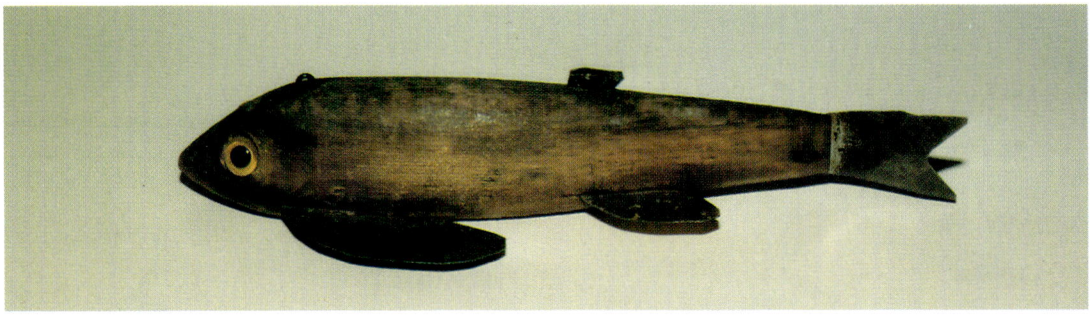

Metal tail decoy by E. W. Mooers, 6 3/4 inches.

Math "Matty" Muellner

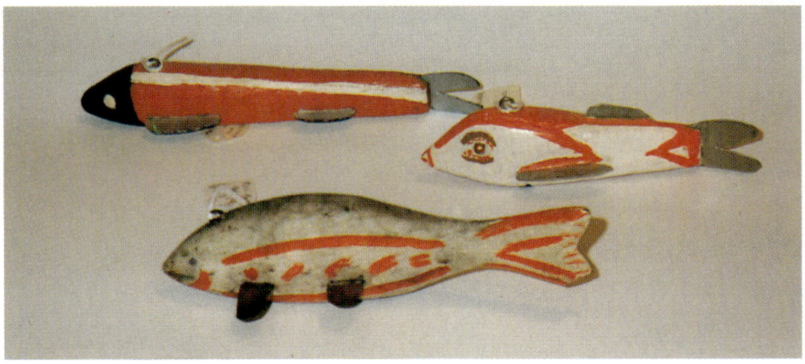

Three Math Muellner decoys. Photo courtesy of Joe Leach.

Melvin Nesset

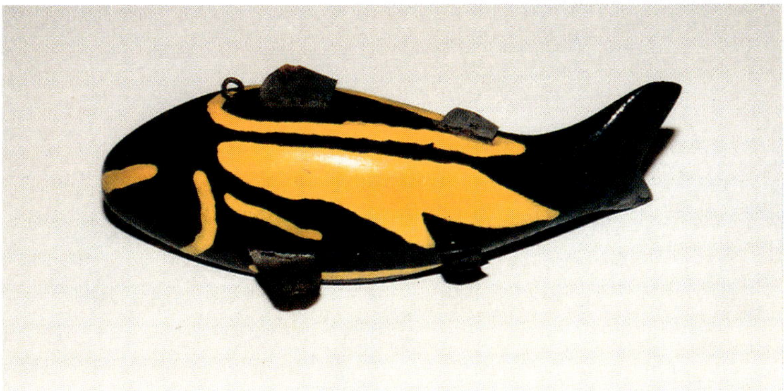

Yellow and black painted Nesset decoy, ca. 1950's, approximately 6 inches in length.

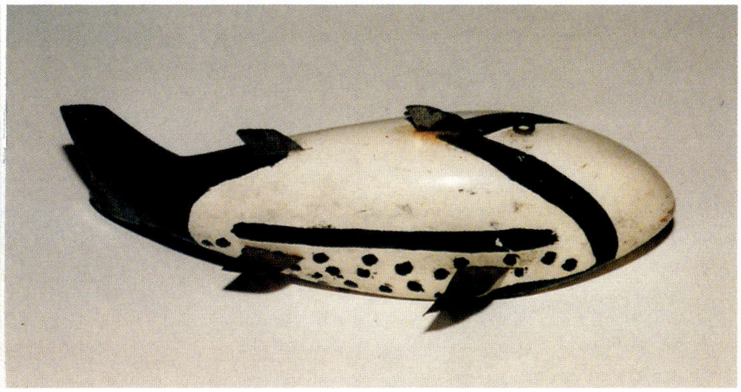

White and black decorated Nesset "whale" decoy, 6 1/2 inches in length, c. 1950's.

Ernest "Ernie" Newman

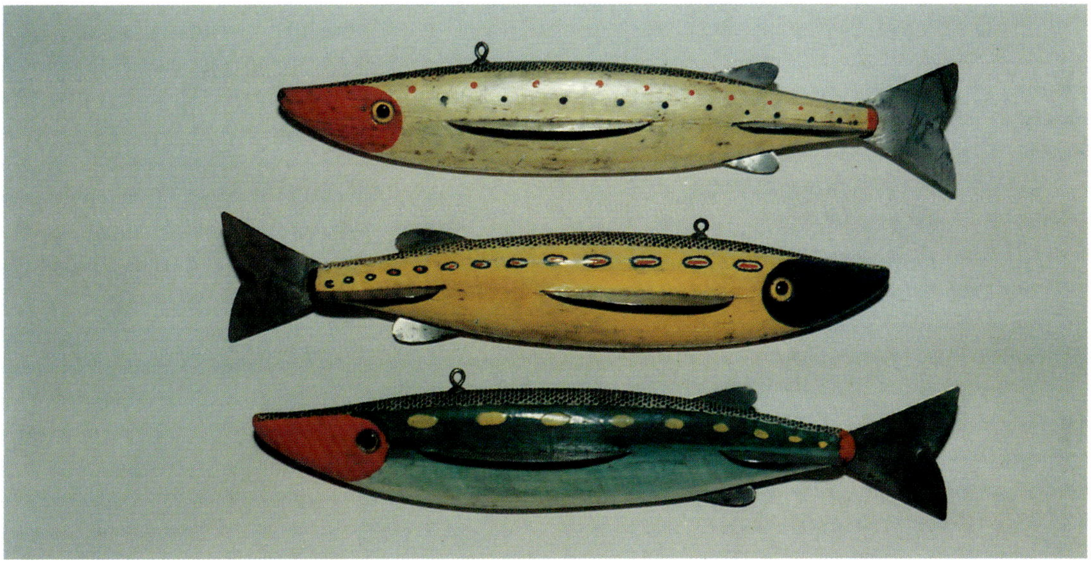

Three Newman decoys showing a variety of decorative patterns. Note scaling effect on the backs of each of these decoys. All are 9 inches in length.

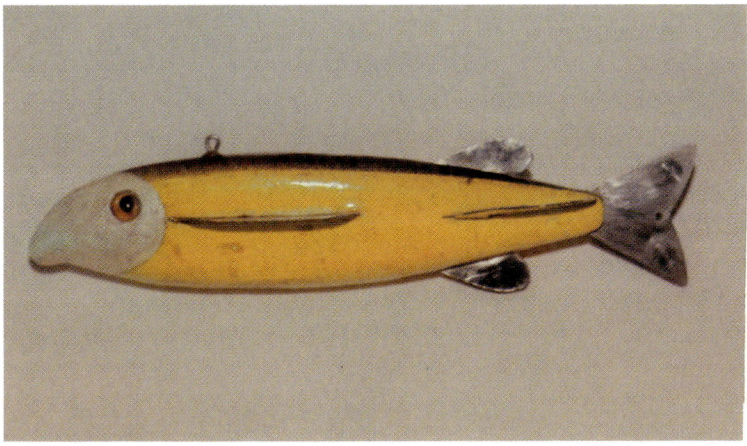

Newman sucker. K. David Hirschey collection.

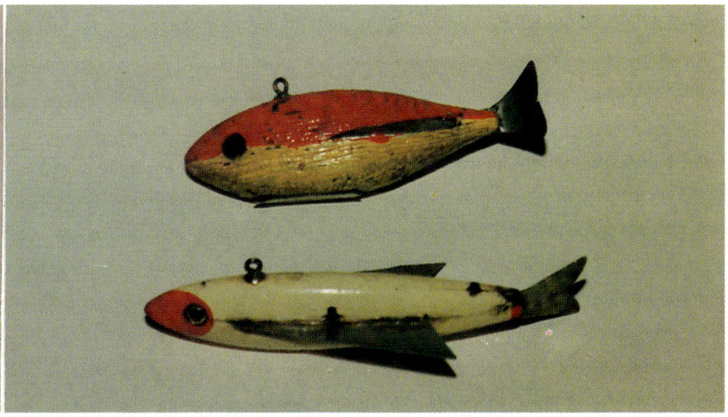

Two small Newman fish. Top is 4 inches and bottom is a Newman jig-plane. The hook is missing from the tail.

James F. Newman

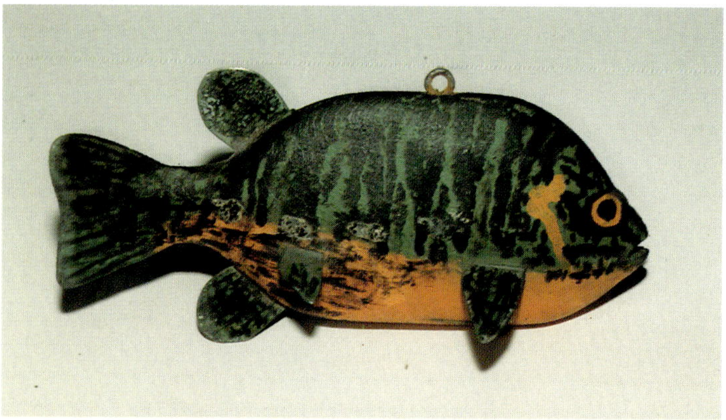

Sunfish by James Newman, 5 1/4 inches.

Albert Niehaus

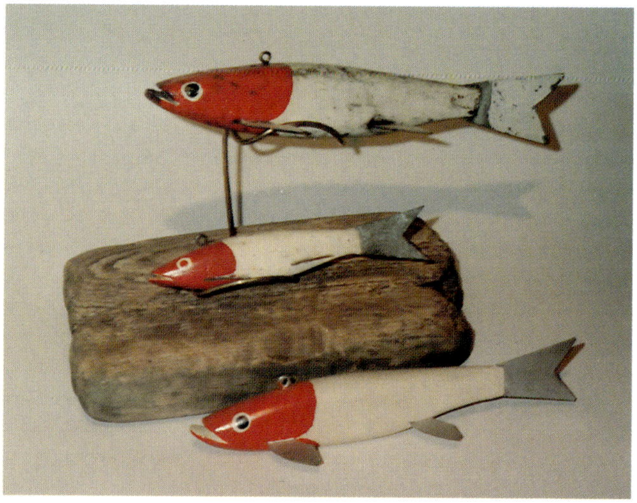

Three typical Niehaus red and white decoys. Joe Leach collection.

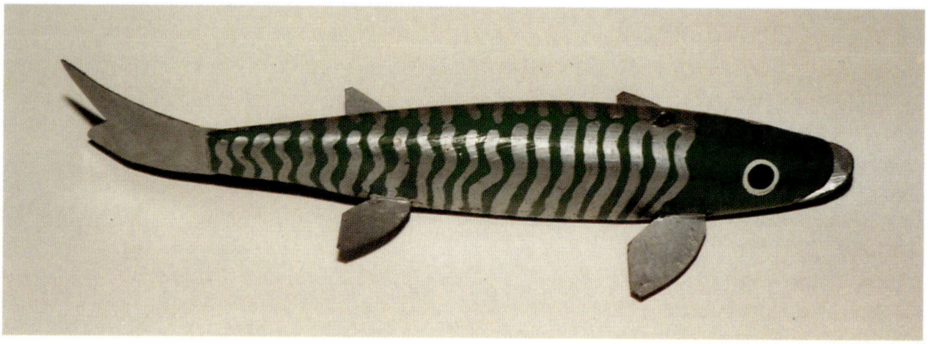

Nicely painted Niehaus decoy showing distinctive shape of the pectoral fins. John Banholzer collection.

Francis Northburg

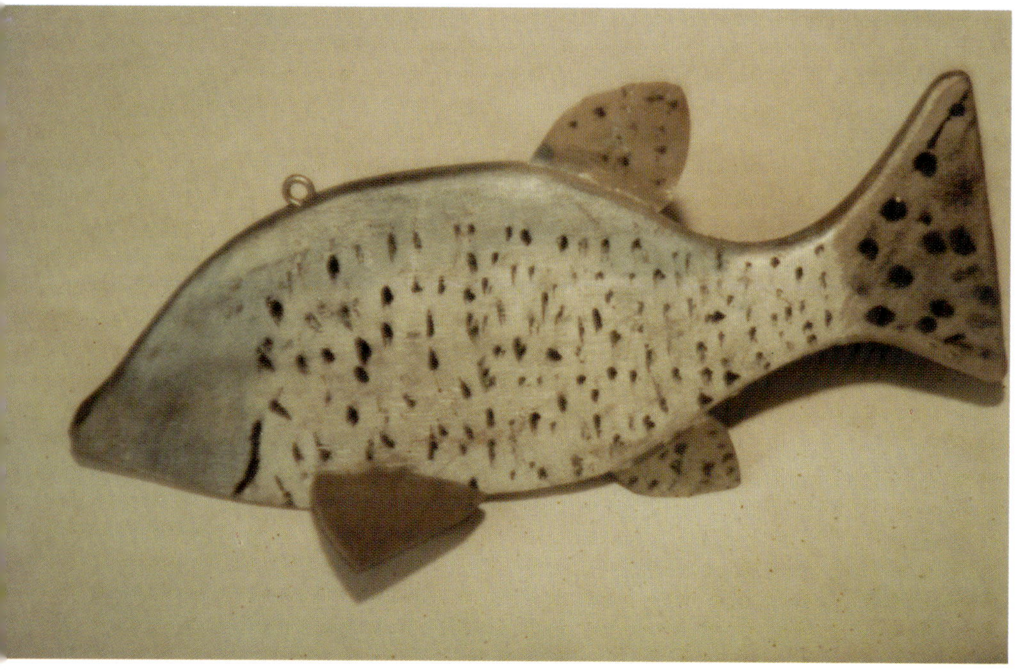

Francis Northburg crappie.

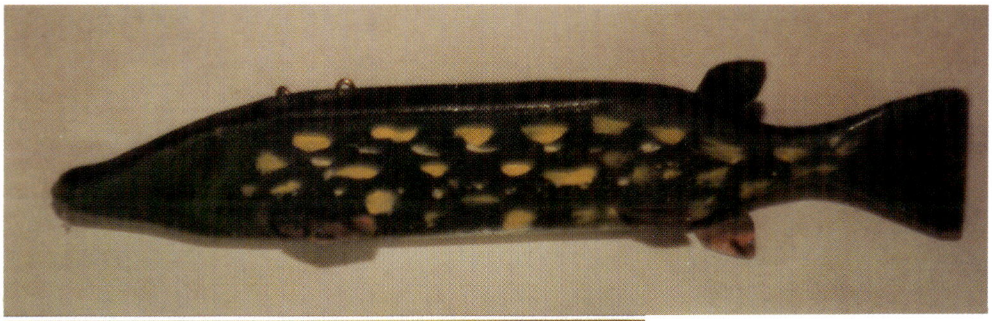

Northern by Francis Northburg.

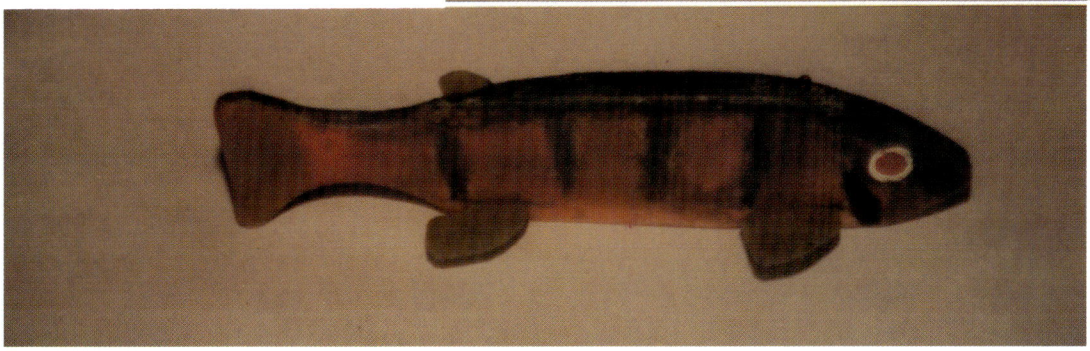

Perch by Francis Northburg.

John P. Novak

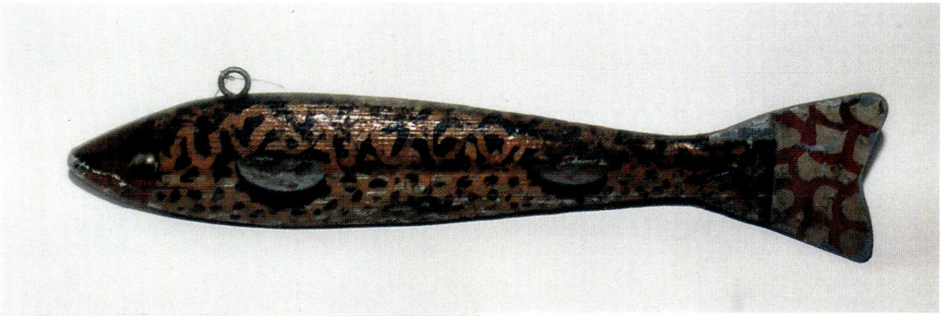

Novak decoy, 9 1/4 inches, ca. 1930's.

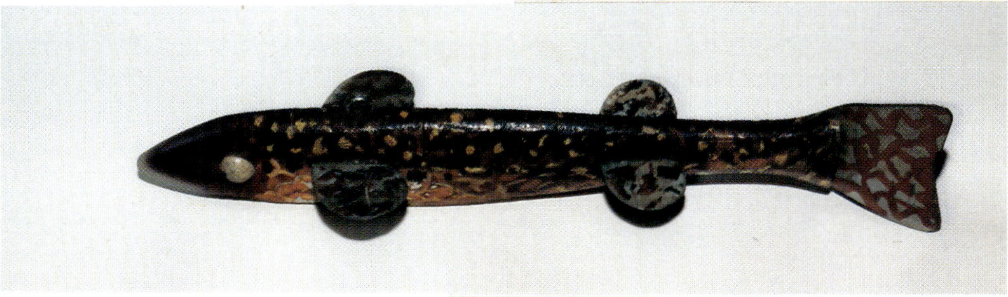

Decoy by Novak, 9 inches, ca. 1930's.

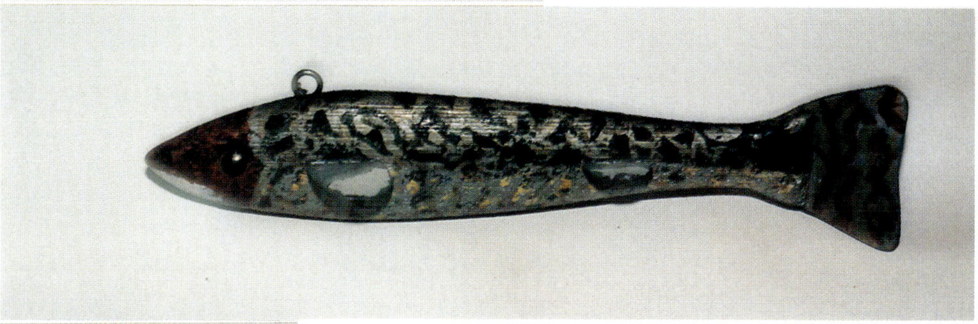

Novak decoy, 9 inches, ca. 1930's.

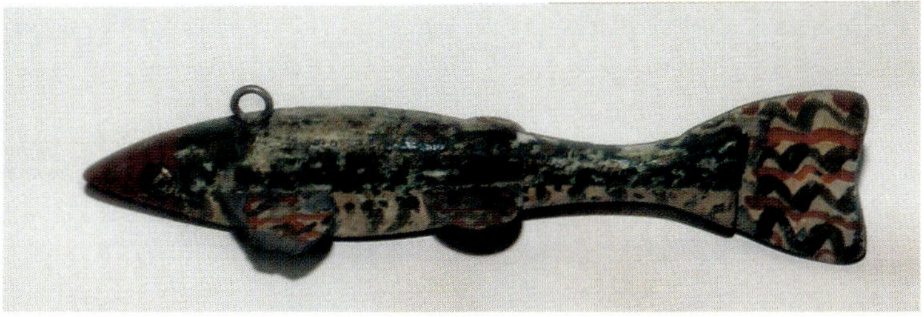

Novak decoy, 7 inches in length, ca. 1930's.

Reino Nurmi

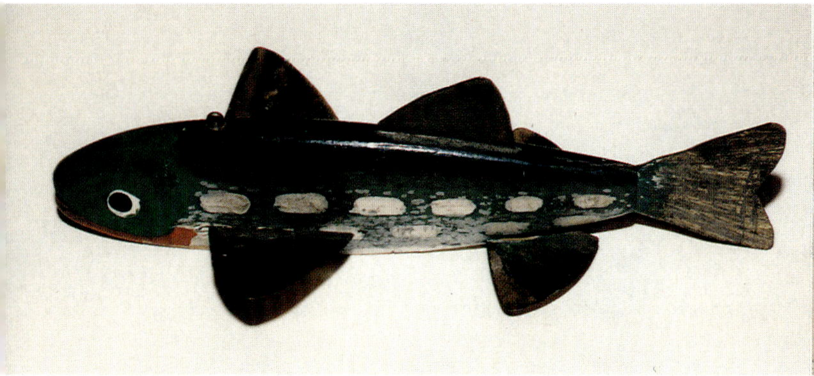

Green painted Nurmi decoy with white scale decoration and black painted back. Ca. 1960's, 7 1/2 inches in length.

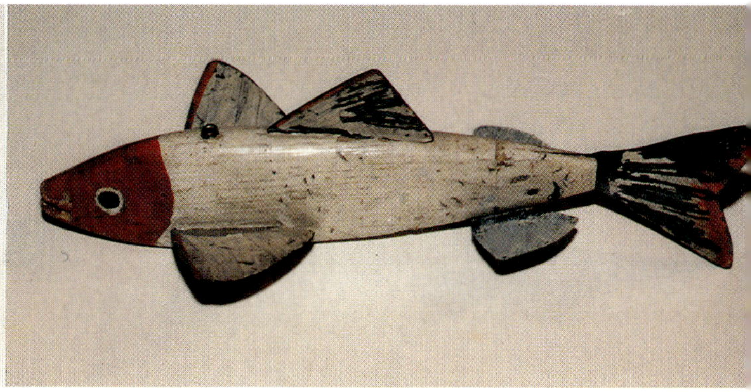

Red and white Nurmi decoy, 7 1/2 inches long, ca. 1960's.

Harold Nygaard

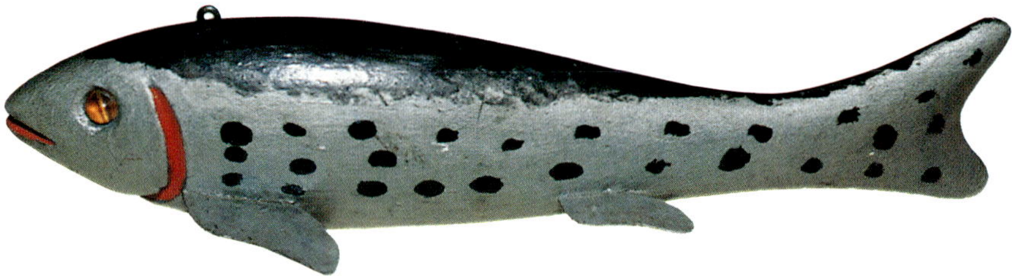

Harold Nygaard trout. Larry Hochmayr collection.

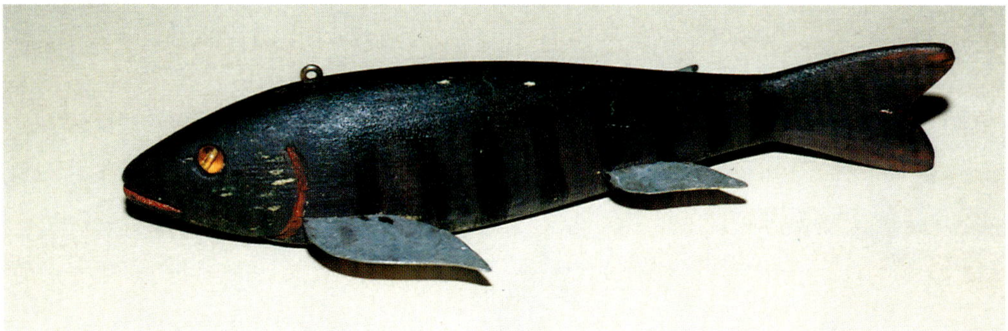

Nygaard perch with wooden tail. Larry Hochmayr collection.

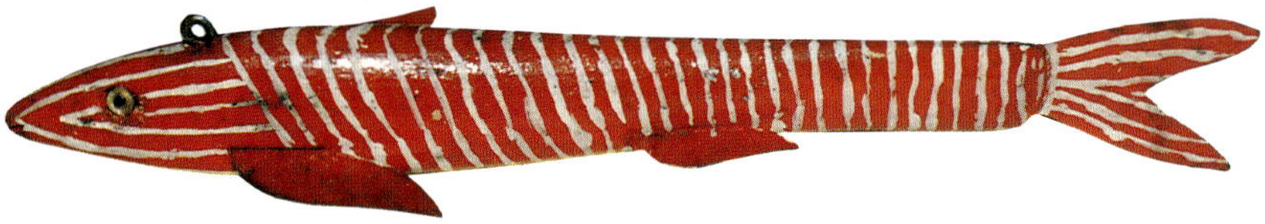

Red and white decoy by Harold Nygaard. Larry Hochmayr collection.

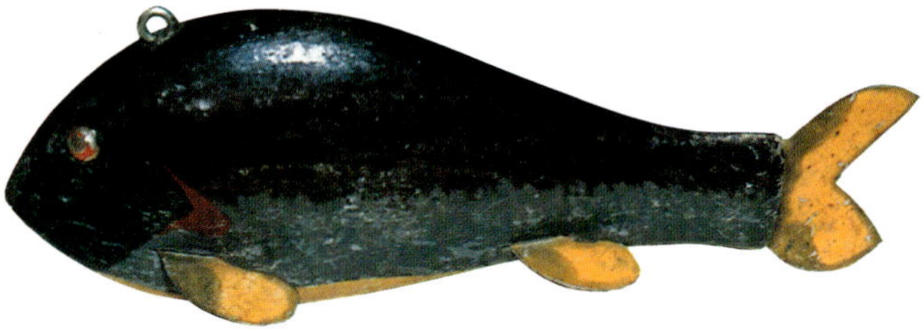

Sunfish by Harold Nygaard. Larry Hochmayr collection.

Oliver Olmschenk

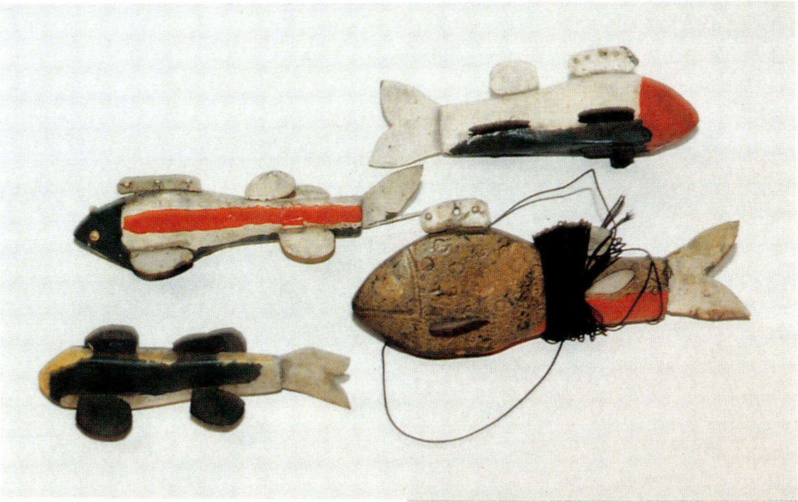

Four Olmschenk fish decoys.

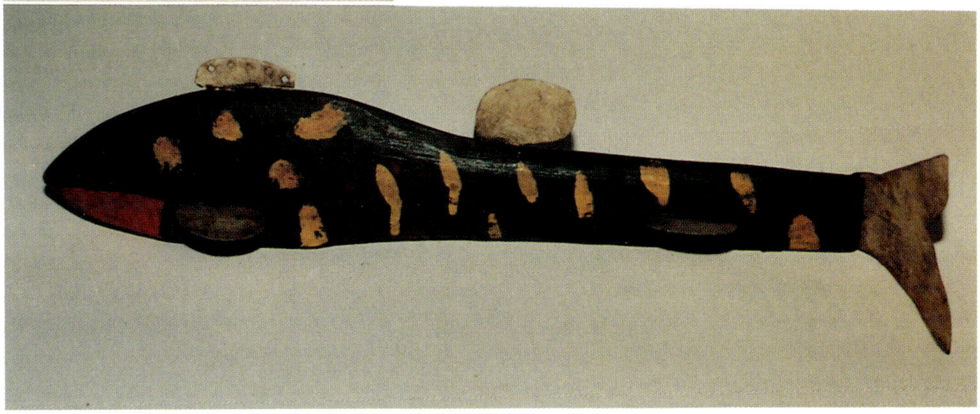

Large Olmschenk decoy.

Elmer Oxley

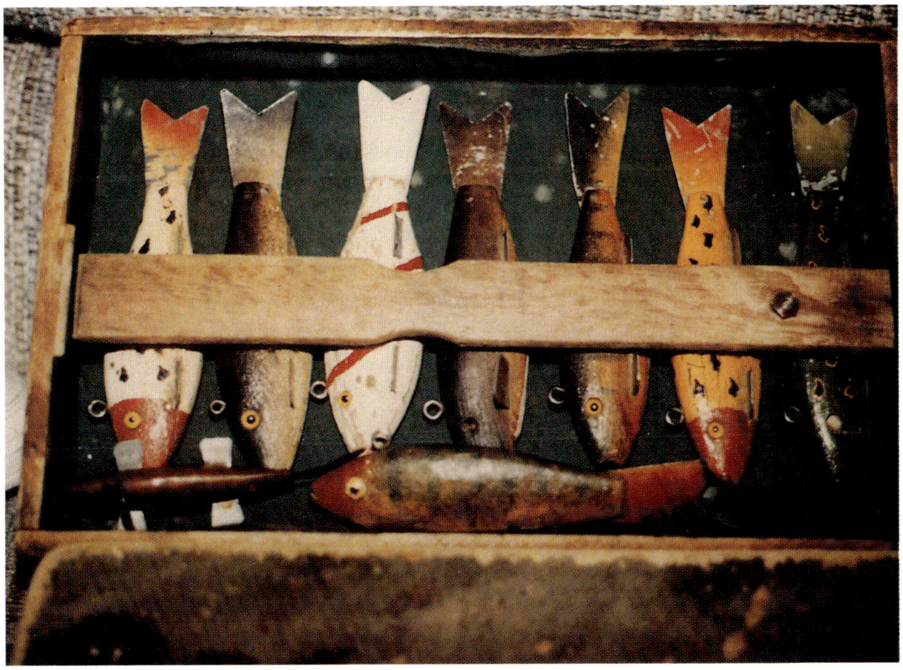

Uncovered carrying case for Oxley decoys.

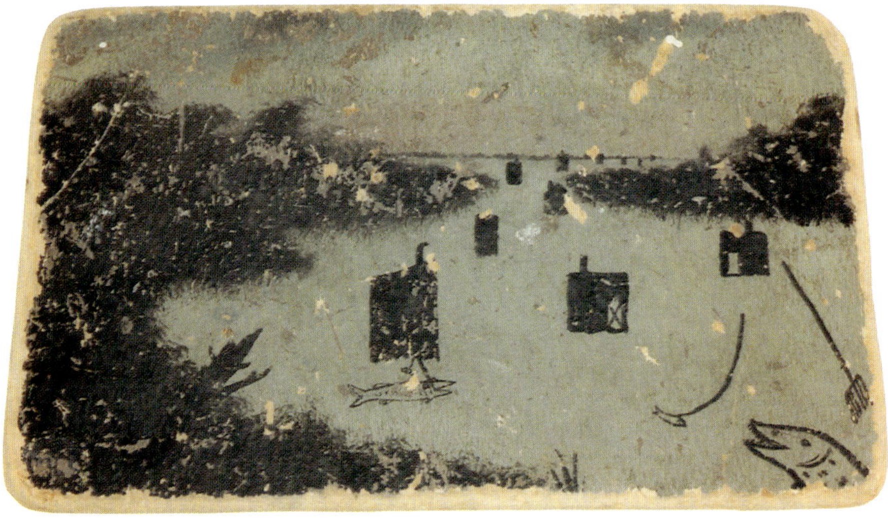

Cover of Oxley carrying case with ink drawing of a spear fishing scene.

Wilbur "Willie" Peterson

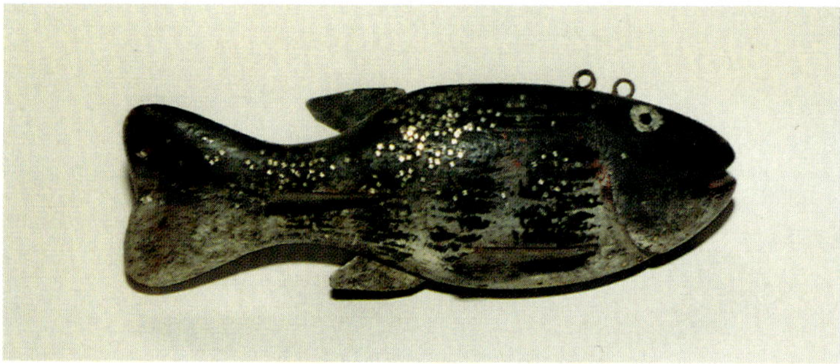

Early Wilbur Peterson decoy, painted black with glitter decoration, 5 inches. Note, Peterson decoys had carved open mouths painted red.

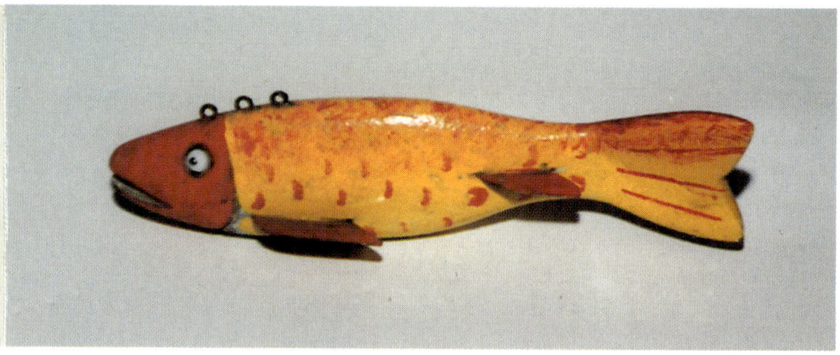

Peterson minnow with glass eye, 5 3/4 inches.

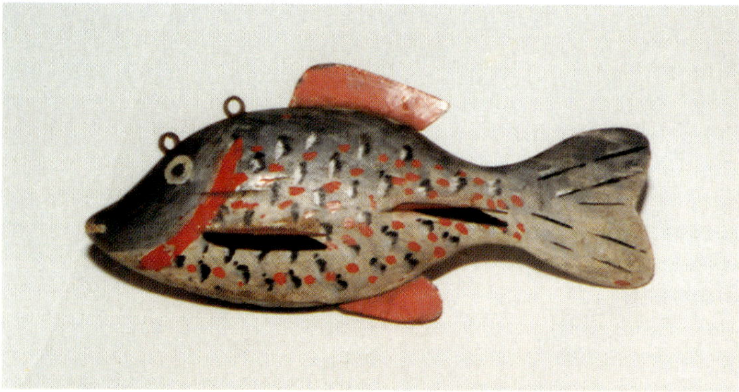

Wilbur Peterson sunfish. Note that the back pectoral fin on a Peterson decoy is always more elevated than the front pectoral fin, 4 1/2 inches.

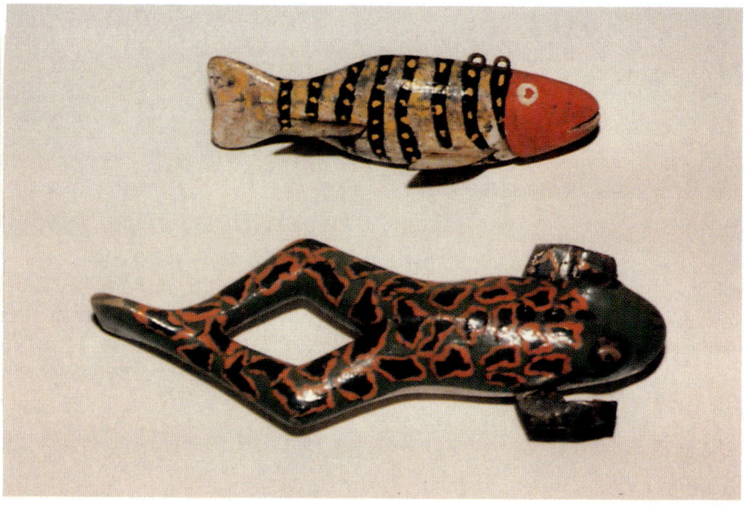

Two Wilbur Peterson decoys. Top is a minnow and bottom is a Peterson frog. Larry Hochmayr collection.

Clemen Place

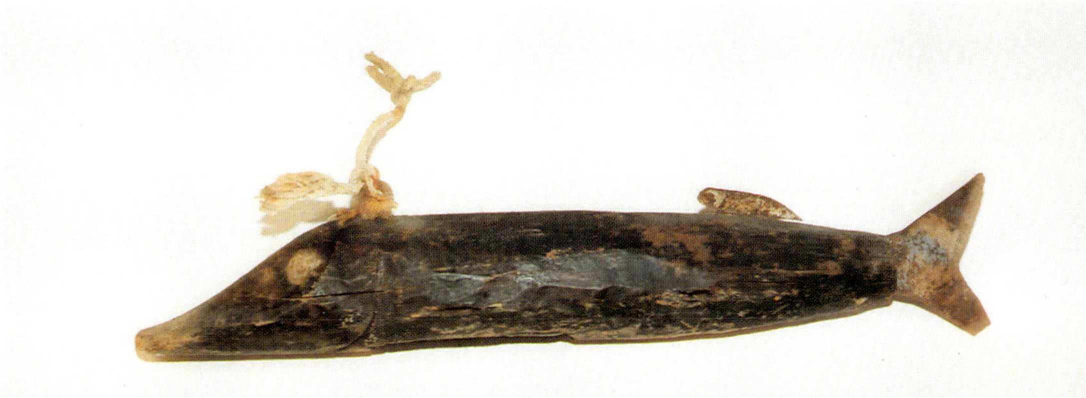

Northern pike by Clemen Place, 12 1/4 inches.

John Herman Plackner

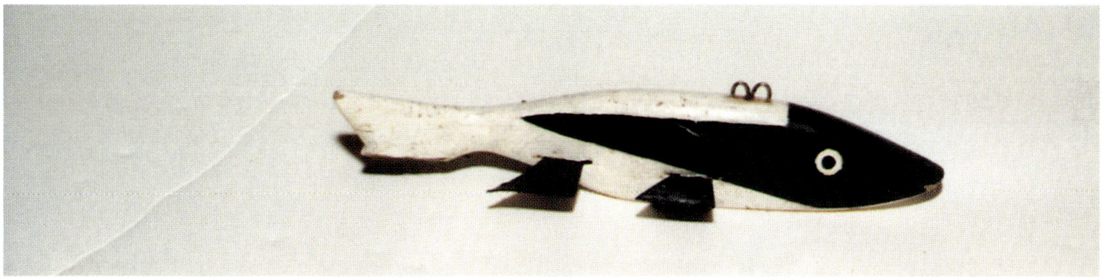

Black and white early Plackner decoy, 5 inches.

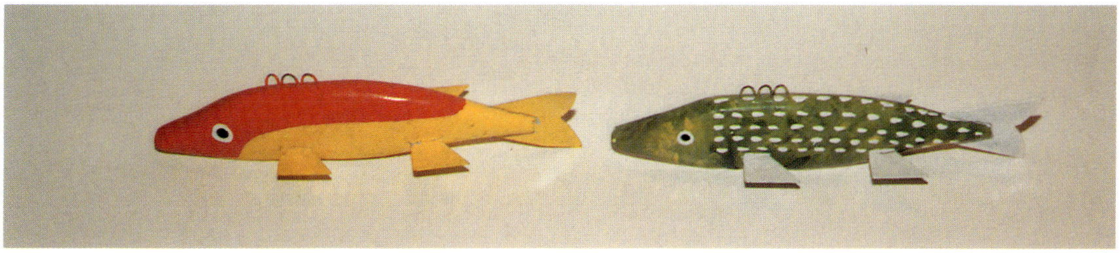

Metal tail Plackner decoys showing pectoral and tail fin shape. These decoys have three loop ties. Russel Johnson collection.

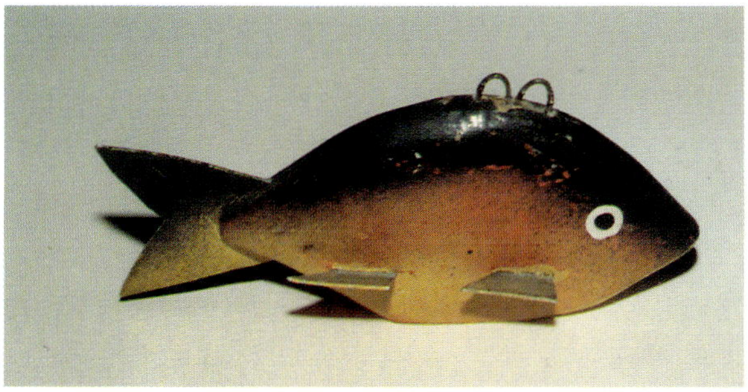

Plackner sunfish showing screen painting style.

Henry J. Ramthun

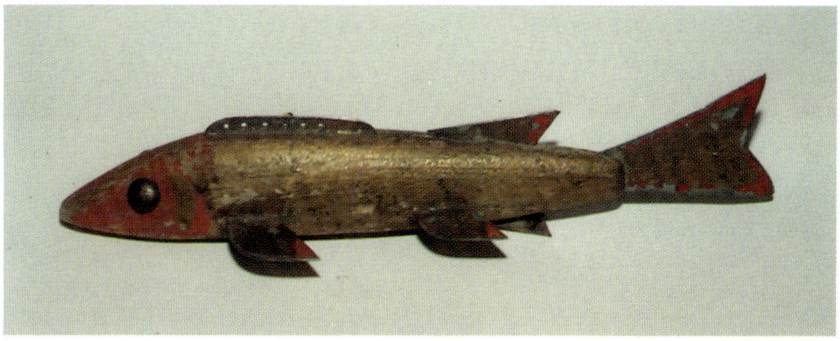

Typical Ramthun decoy in shape, but painted gold and red instead of his usual red and white, 8 inches.

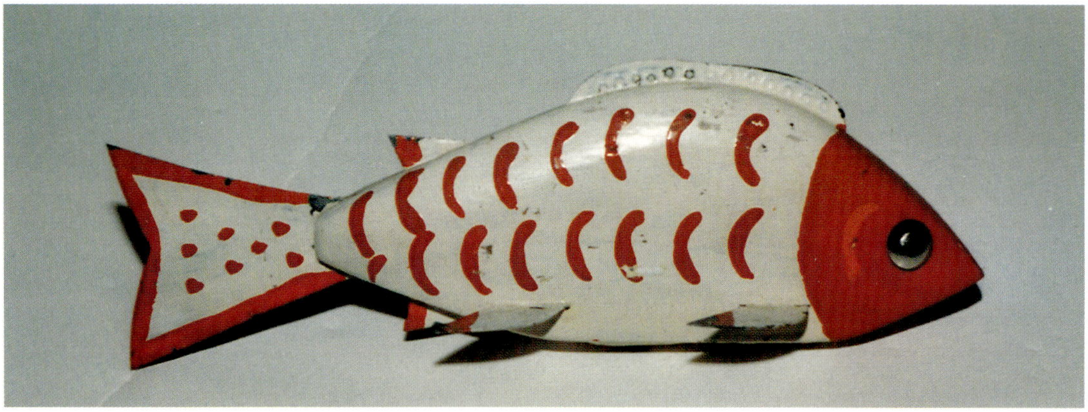

Rare Ramthun sunfish decoy with tack eye, 7 3/4 inches.

George Randall

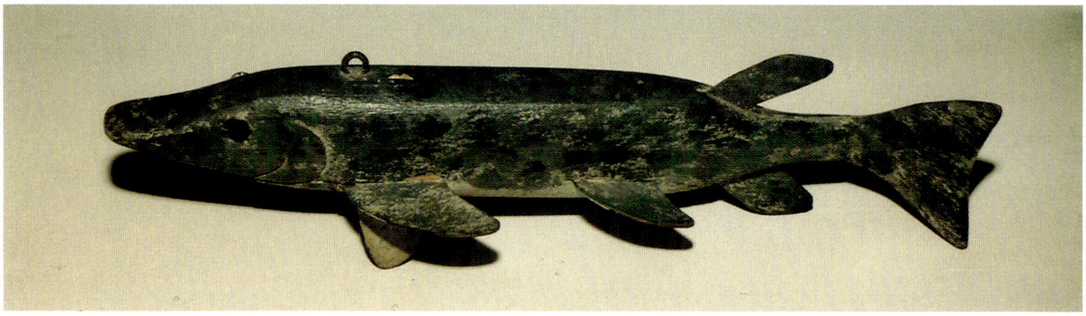

Northern pike by George Randall, 8 1/2 inches.

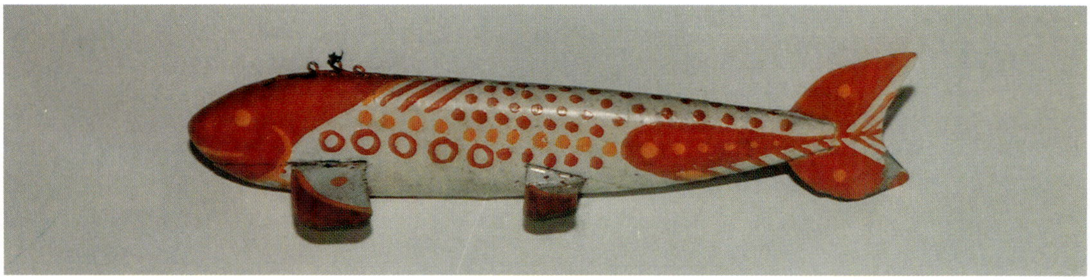

George Randall decoy with abstract paint decoration, 9 inches.

Myron Roberts

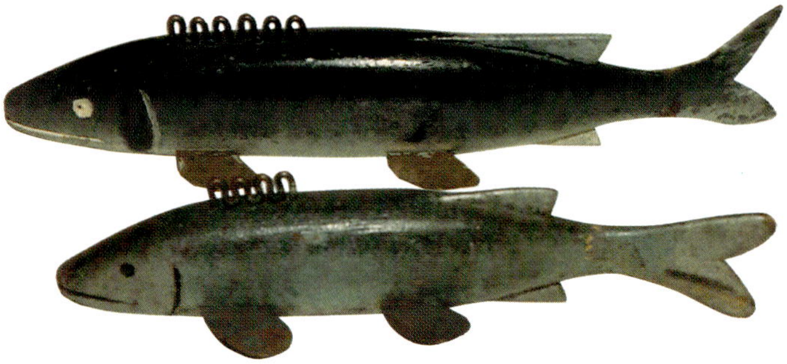

Myron Roberts decoys. Top has a metal tail and is 7 3/4 inches in length; bottom is 6 1/4 inches and has a carved wooden tail.

George Robideau

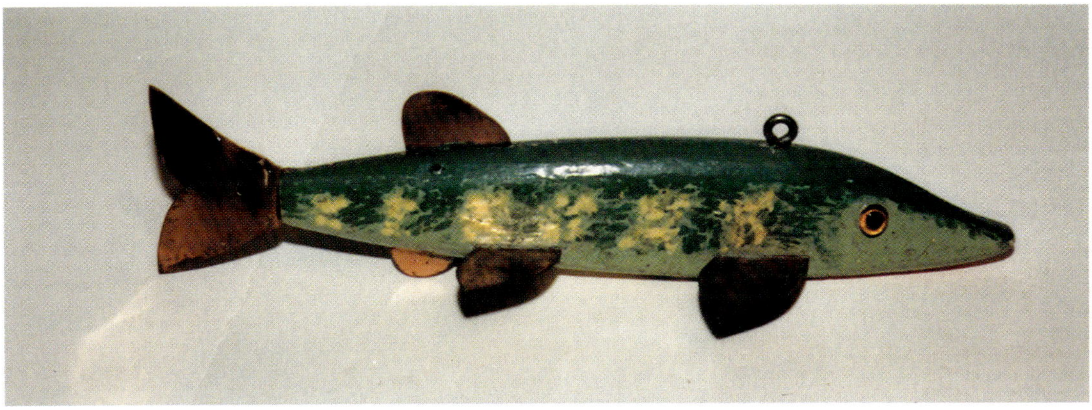

Northern pike with copper fins by George Robideau, 10 inches.

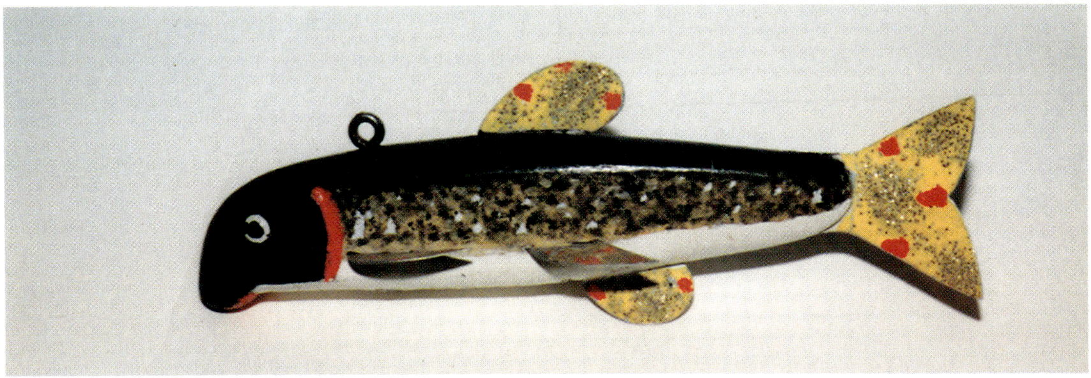

Sucker by George Robideau, 8 1/4 inches.

Ray Rosengren

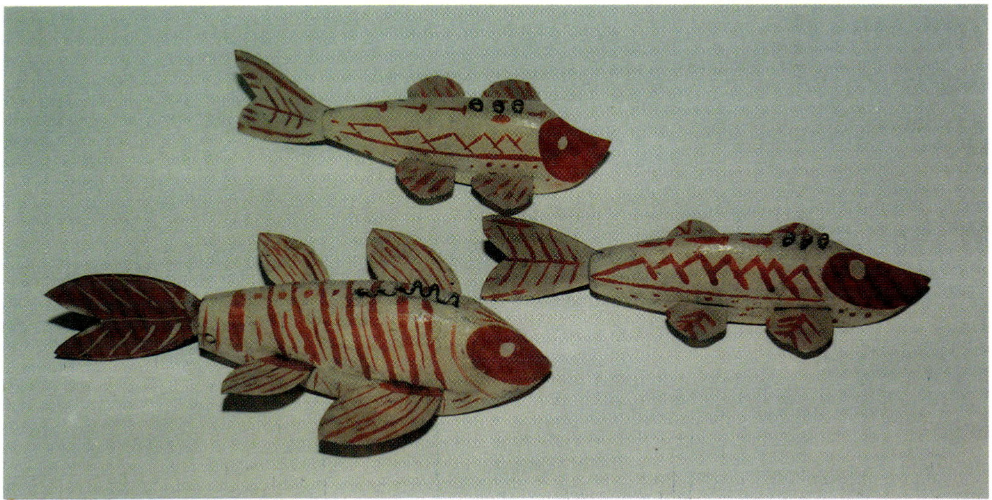

Three red and white Rosengren decoys, ranging in length from 6 1/2 to 5 1/2 inches.

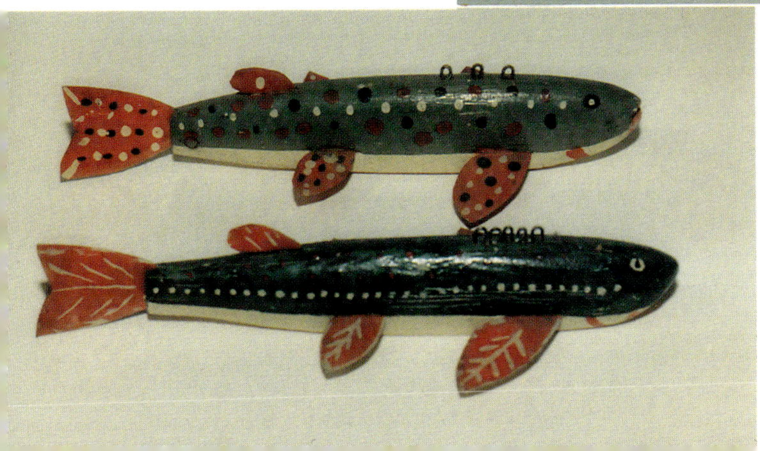

Two Rosengren minnow-style decoys; top is 5 1/2 inches; bottom is 6 inches.

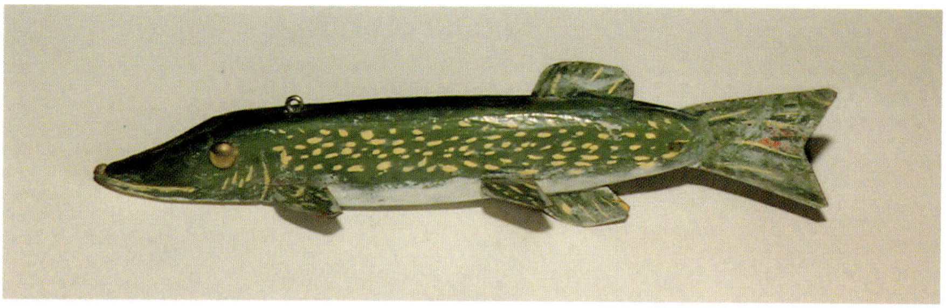

Only known northern pike by Ray Rosengren, 8 1/4 inches in length.

Harry Sandell

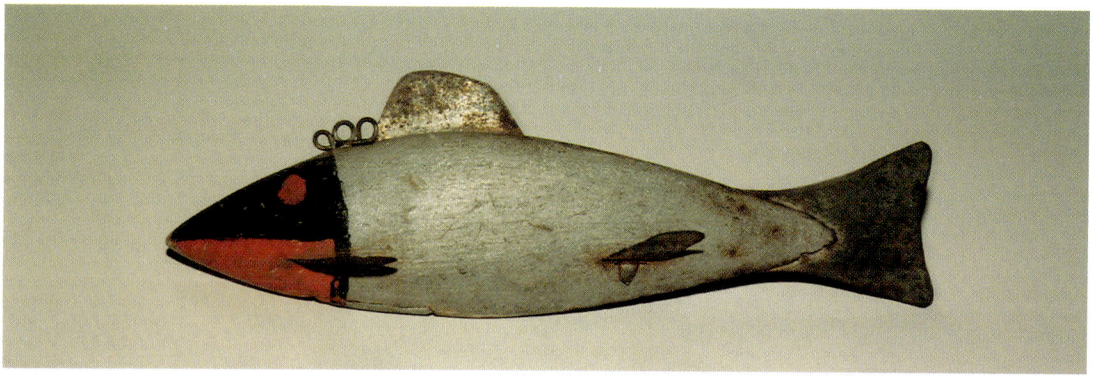

Sandell decoy with black and red paint decoration, 8 inches.

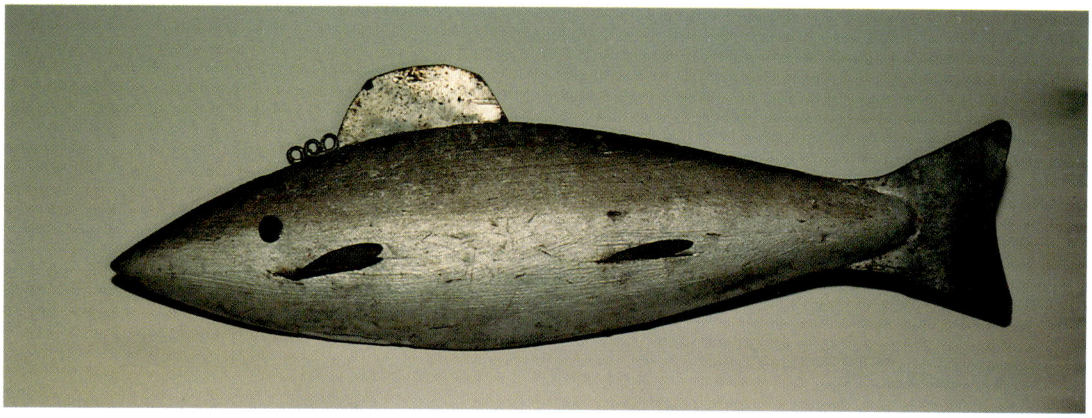

All silver painted Sandell decoy, 11 inches.

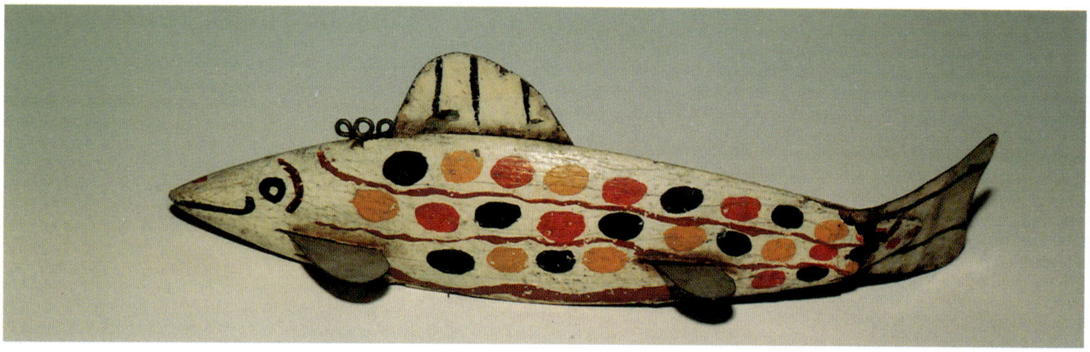

Unusually decorated Sandell decoy with white underpaint and multicolored dot decoration 8 inches.

Chester "Chet" Sawyer

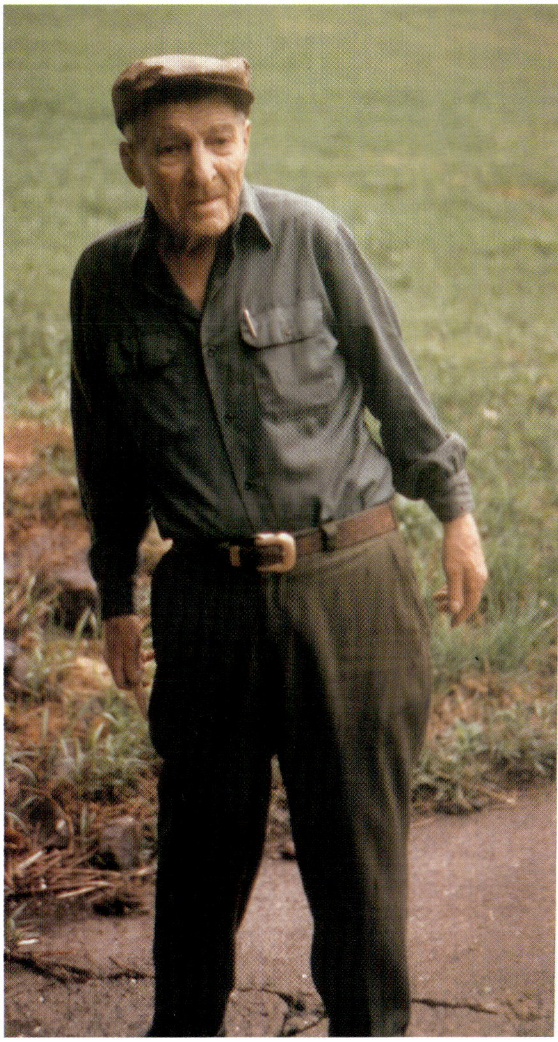

Chet Sawyer in 1992.

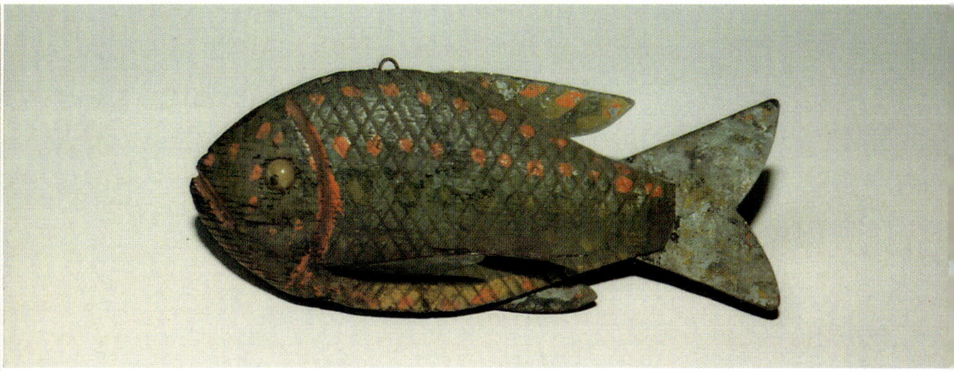

Superb Sawyer with glass eyes and carved scales, 6 inches.

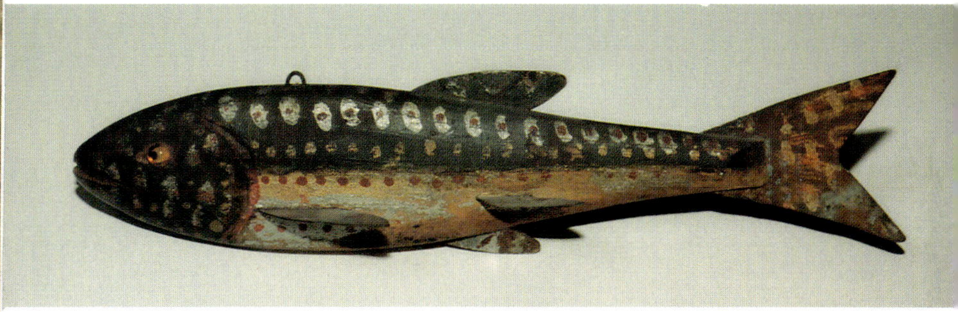

Nicely painted and unusually large Sawyer decoy, 9 inches.

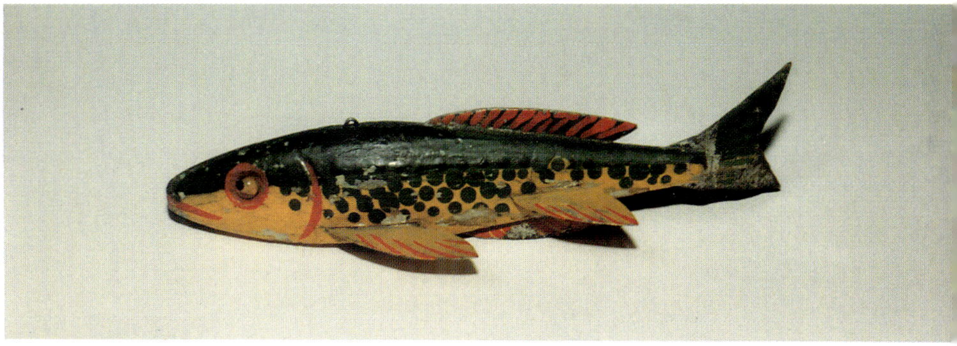

Sawyer decoy painted by Fred Lexow, 5 3/4 inches.

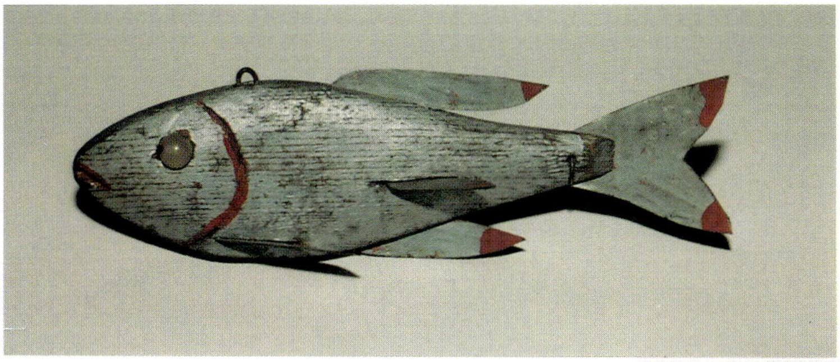

Silver painted Sawyer decoy, 4 3/4 inches.

Edward Herman Schultz

Brightly painted, slope nose Schultz decoy, 9 inches.

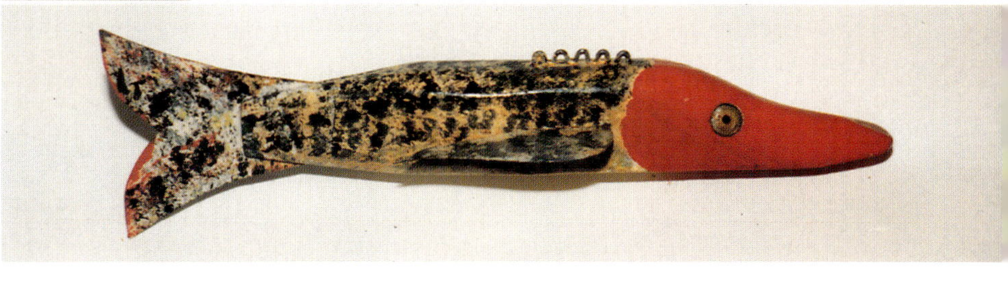

William A. Schultz

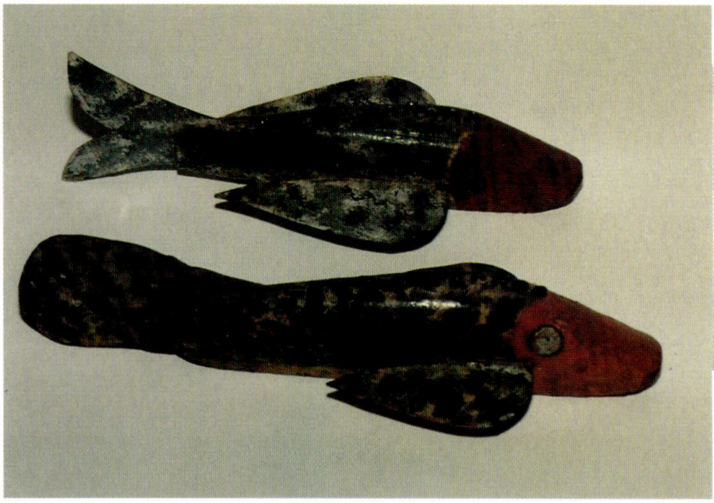

Two dark painted Schultz decoys. Note, the decoy on the bottom has a rounded tin tail. Top: 6 inches; bottom: 7 inches.

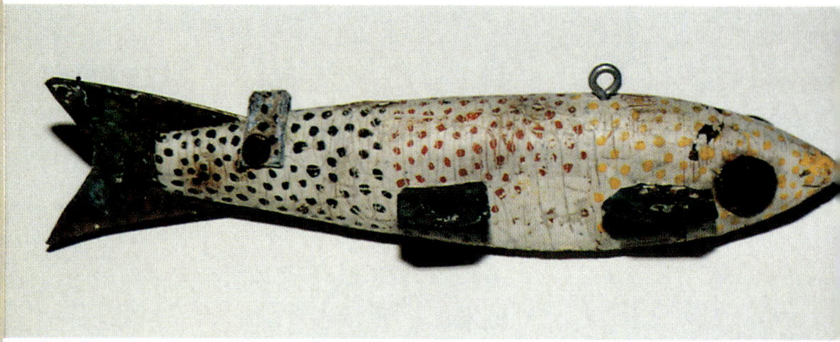

William Schultz decoy, painted with bands of black, red, and yellow dots, length 7 1/4 inches.

Art Seguin

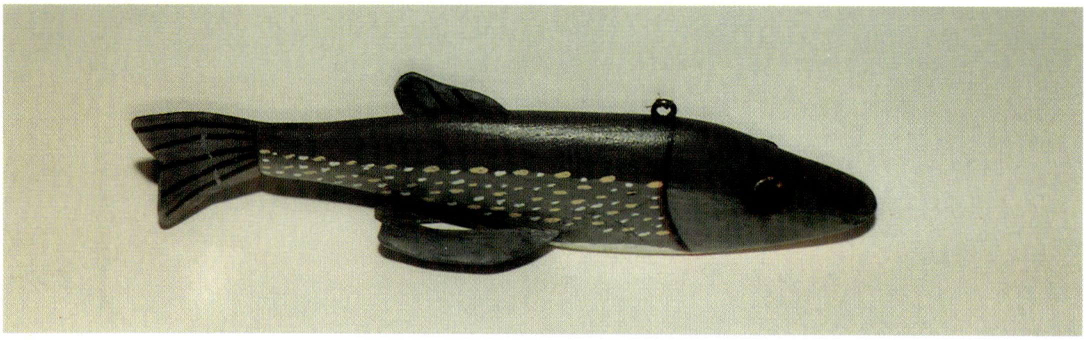

Art Seguin northern. Note shape of pectoral fin, 8 1/2 inches.

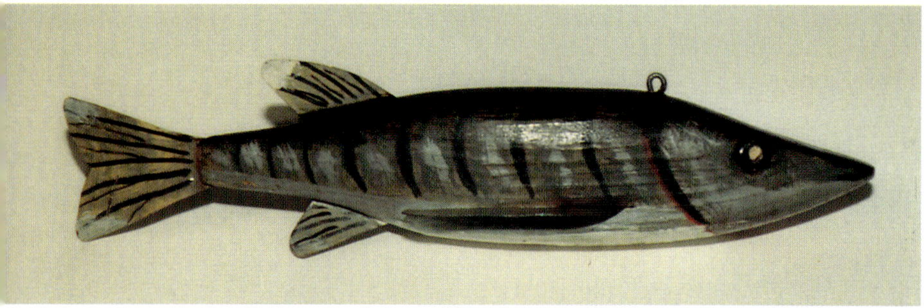

Art Seguin perch, tack eye, 9 inches.

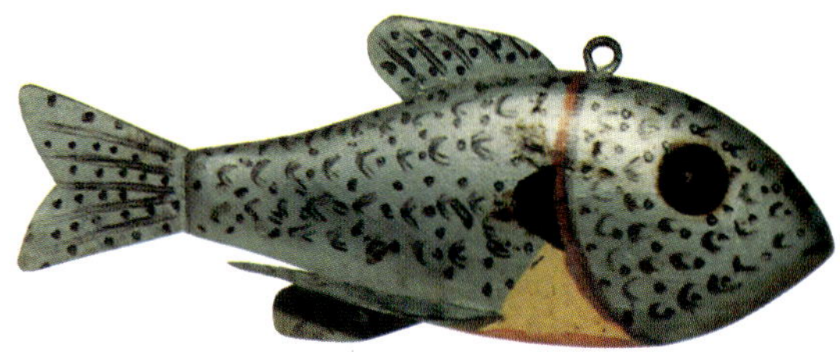

Sunfish by Art Seguin, 5 1/2 inches.

Art Seguin northern with two pectoral fins, 9 1/2 inches.

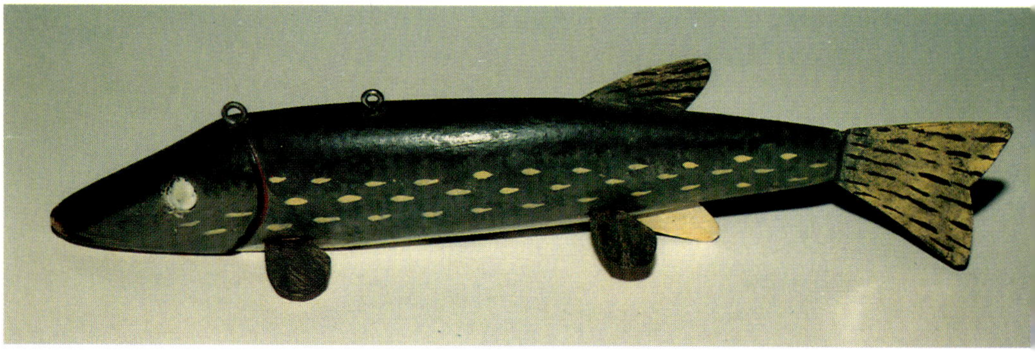

Louis & Ed Setka

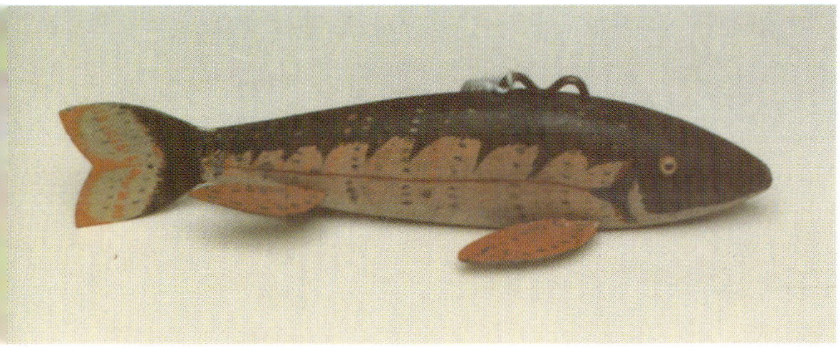

Nicely painted Setka decoy.

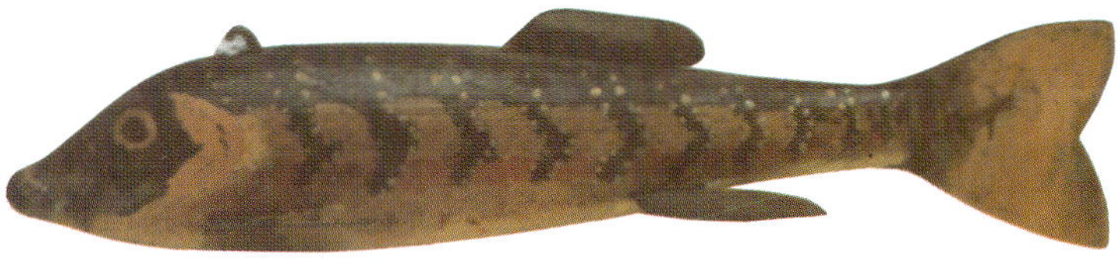

Louis Setka decoy with ribbed pattern. Private collection.

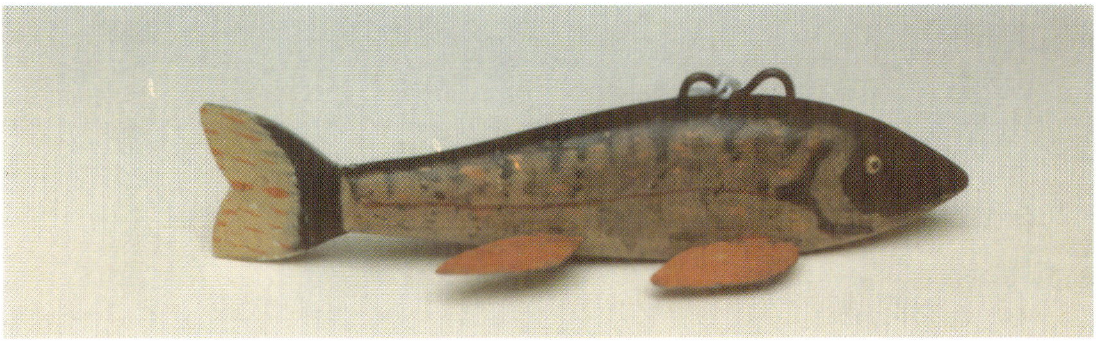

Louis Setka decoy with an interesting paint pattern. Private collection.

Harry Simonsen

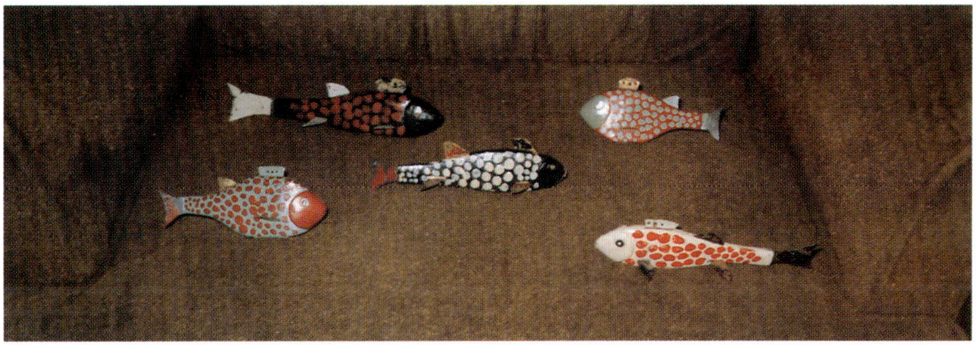

Five Harry Simonsen decoys in his personal rig. Collection of Ron Adamson.

Charles "Charlie" Slechta

Charlie Slechta copper decoy with diamond scales. Frank Pasiewicz collection.

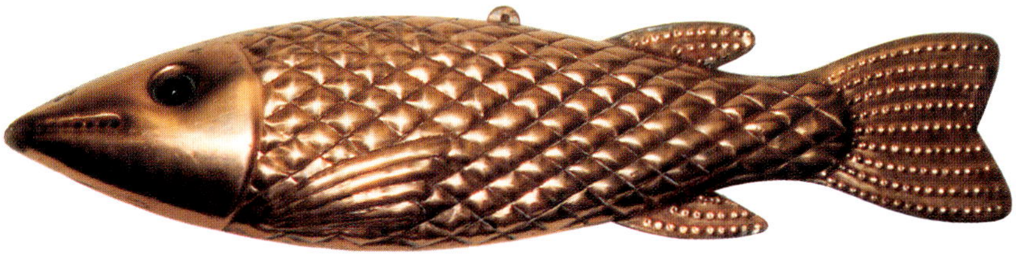

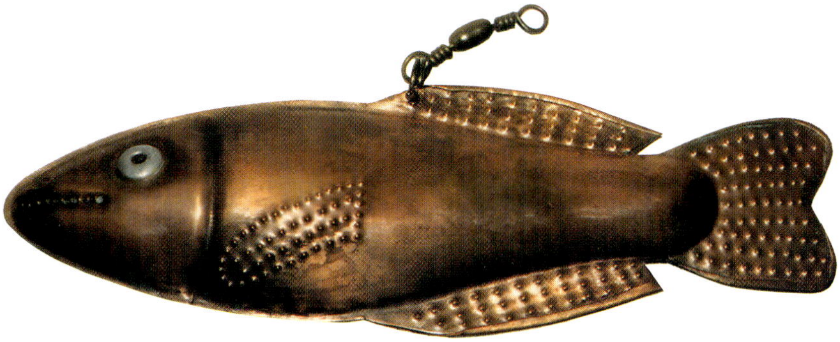

Very early Charlie Slechta decoy. Frank Pasiewicz collection.

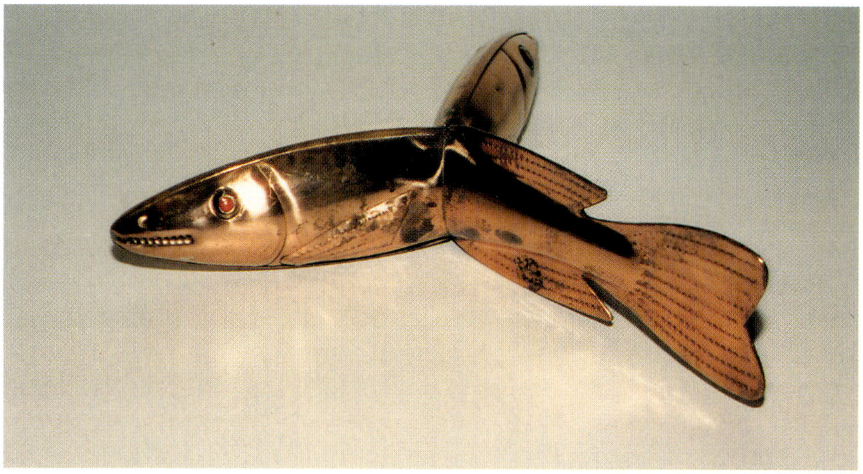

Two headed copper decoy by Slechta. Note the red eye. Frank Pasiewicz collection.

Ted Snell

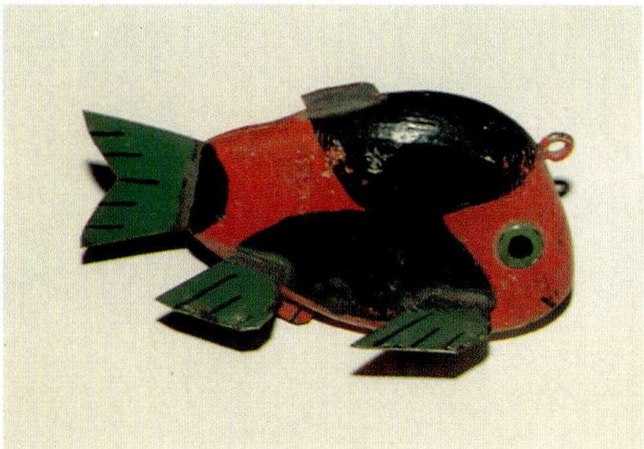

A Ted Snell sunfish, 4 1/2 inches.

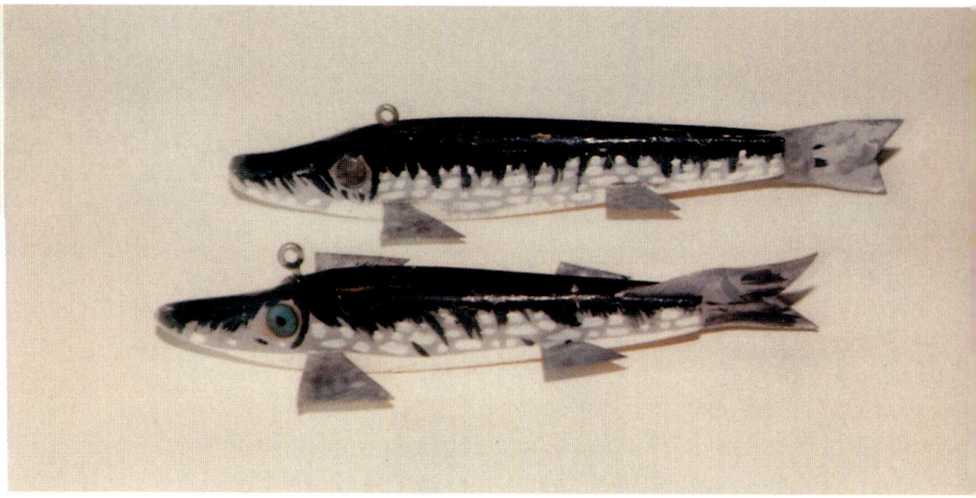

Two Ted Snell northern pike. Top: 8 1/2 inches long. Bottom: this decoy is in the collection of K. David Hirschey.

Hember Charles Steele

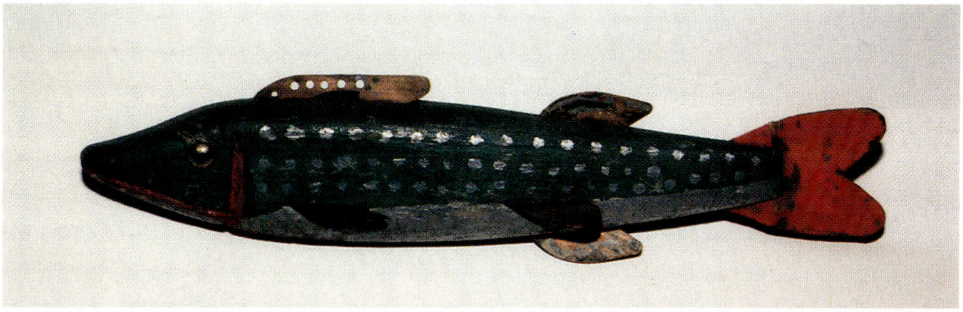

Northern pike decoy by Hember Steele, 12 1/2 inches long.

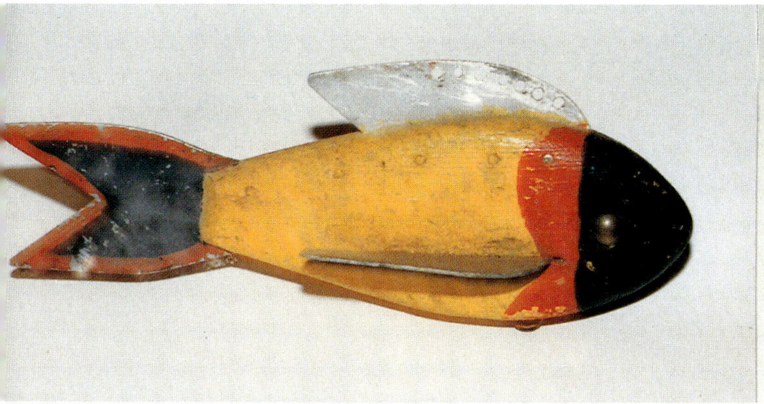

Hember Steele sunfish decoy, 7 1/2 inches.

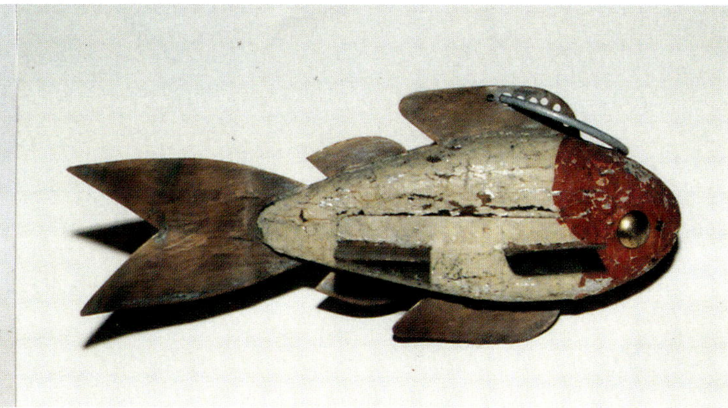

Red and white painted decoy with copper fins, 9 1/2 inches, by Hember Steele.

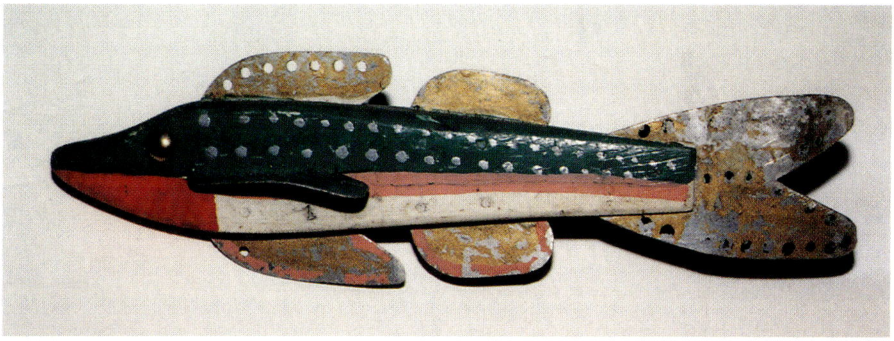

Northern pike? decoy, 9 1/2 inches, by Hember Steele.

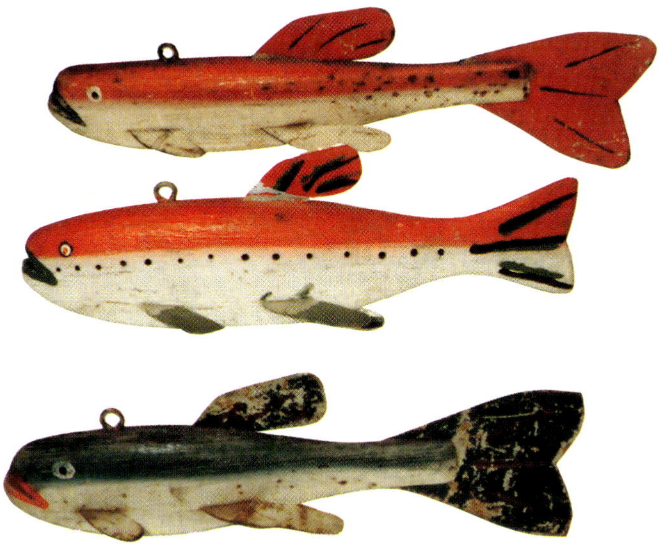

Jerome C. Steele

Three Jerome Steele decoys. Top and bottom decoys have metal tails, while the middle, later one, has a wooden tail. Note carved mouths on each decoy. Photo courtesy of Mike Meyers.

Leon "Ed" Stein

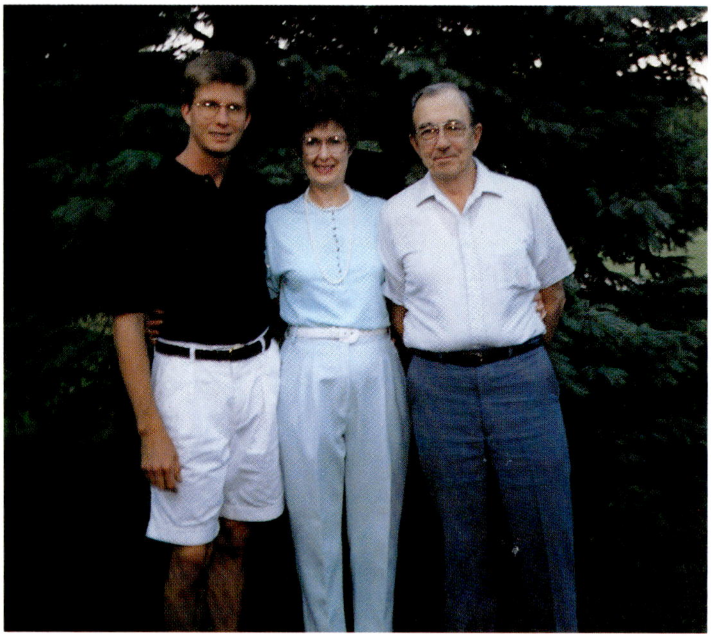

Leon and Betty Stein.

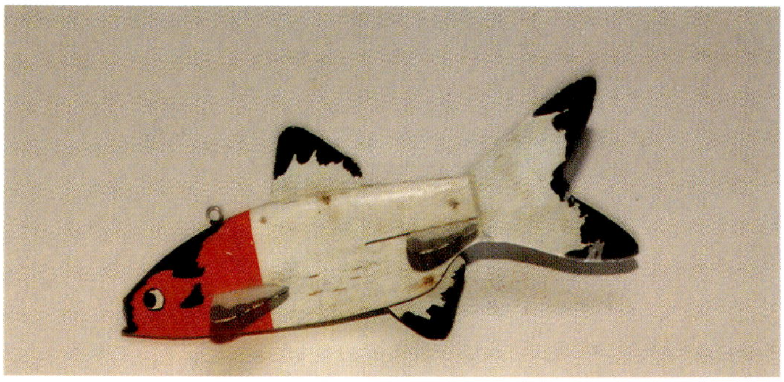

Typical Stein decoy, length 8 1/2 inches.

Homer Stinar

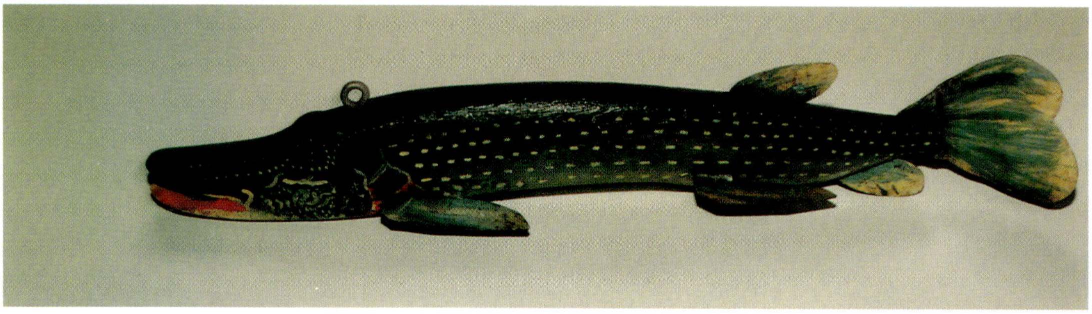

Northern pike by Homer Stinar, ca. 1950's, 12 inches.

Raymond Stotz

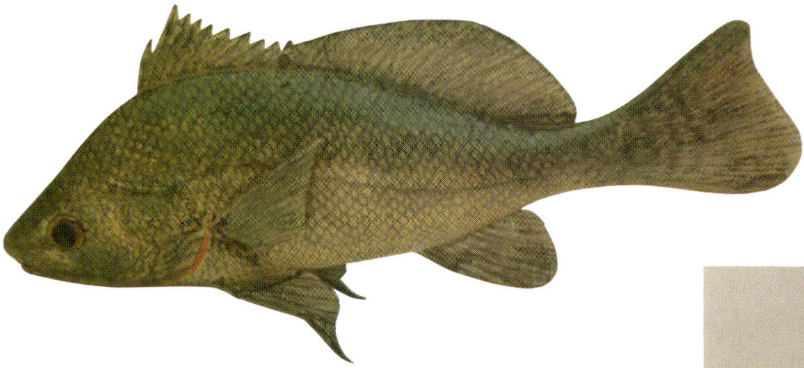

Very fine Stotz decoy. Private collection.

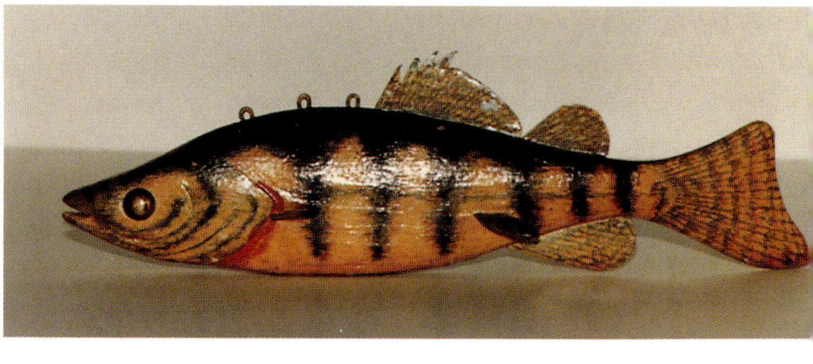

Raymond Stotz perch.

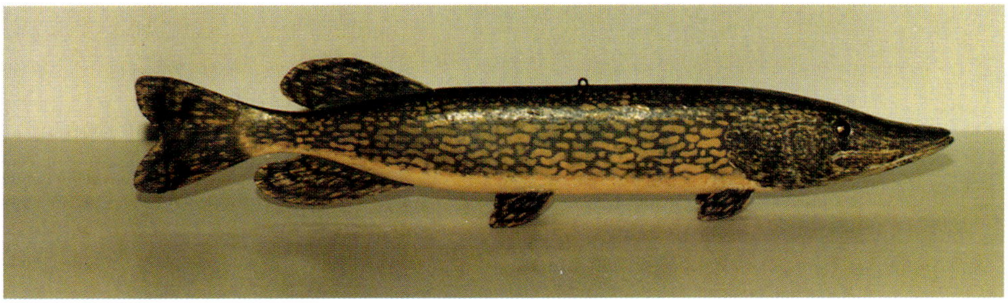

Raymond Stotz northern pike.

Clifford Jason Stubbs

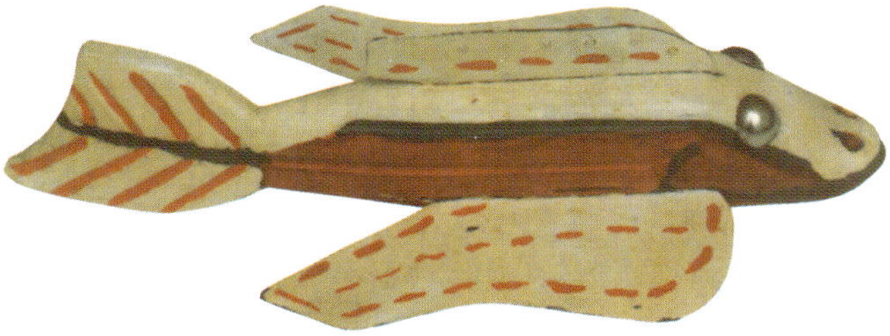

Fancifully decorated Clifford Stubbs' decoy done in red and white. Private collection.

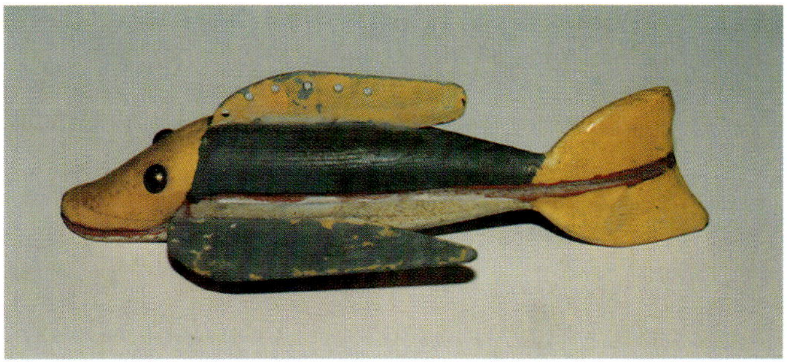

Stubbs' decoy, 5 1/2 inches.

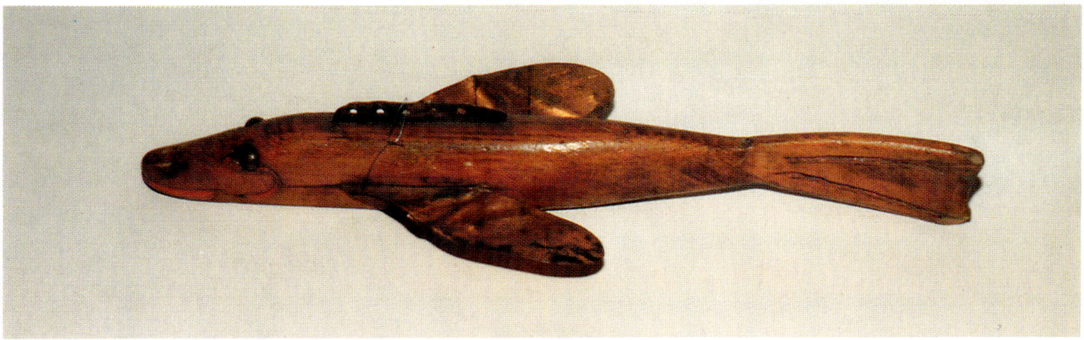

Early unpainted [but varnished] Stubbs' decoy. Note shape of pectoral fins and carving on the wood tail. Line tie is of the band type and not part of a more elegant dorsal fin, 9 1/2 inches.

John F. Tax

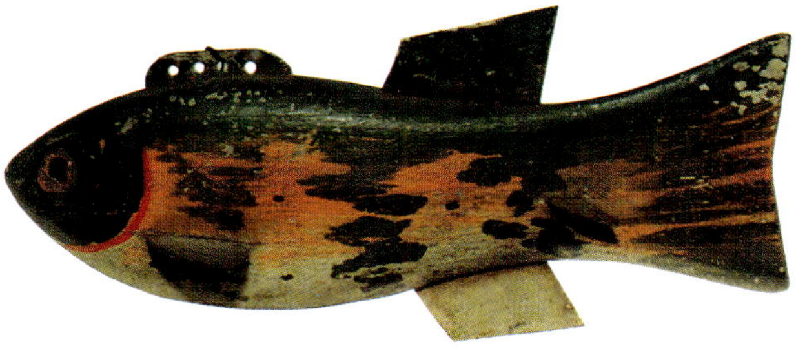

Typical John Tax decoy, nicely painted and in excellent condition, 5 inches.

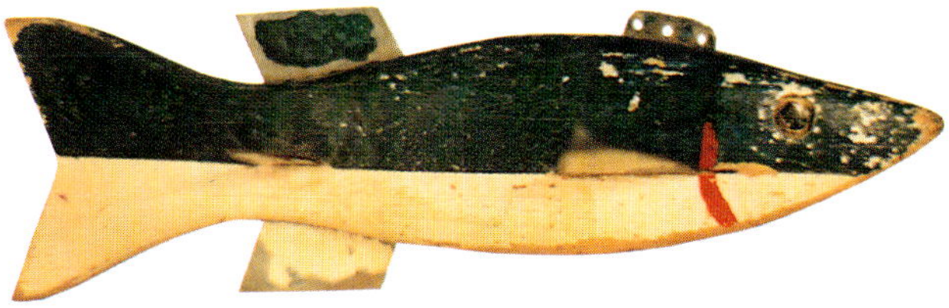

Northern pike by John Tax. Carter Stenberg collection.

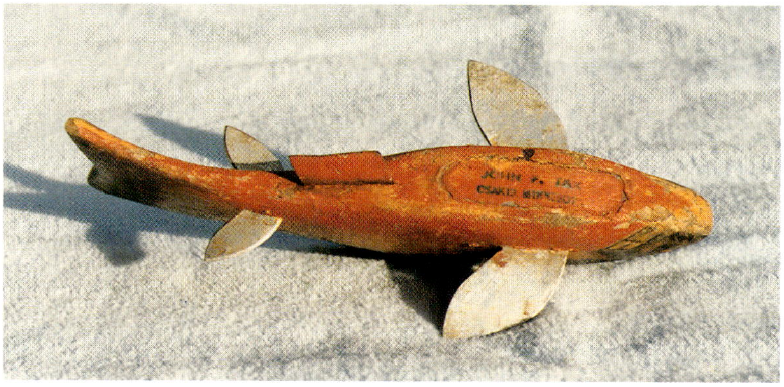

John Tax decoy showing his name marked on the bottom. Courtesy Terry Jacobson.

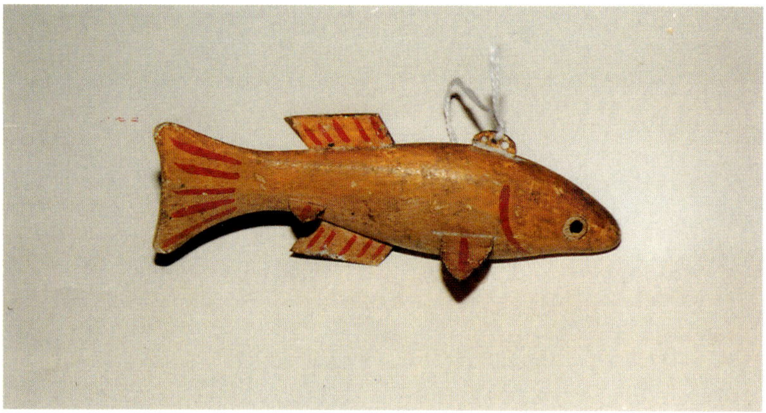

Sucker by John Tax's student Snook Barrett, 5 1/2 inches.

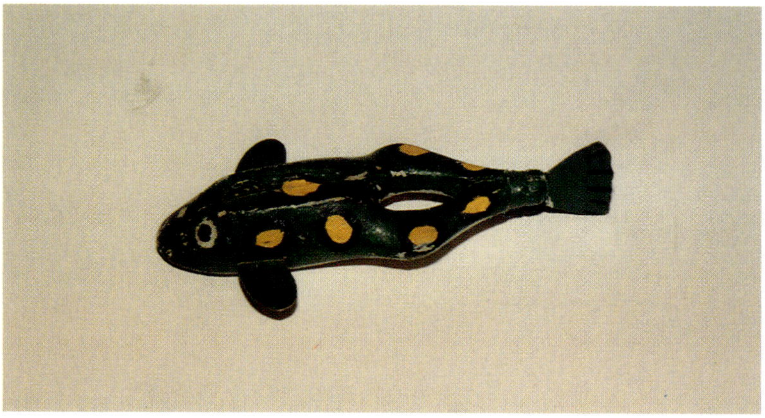

Frog by John Tax. John Banholzer collection.

Clarence Thomas

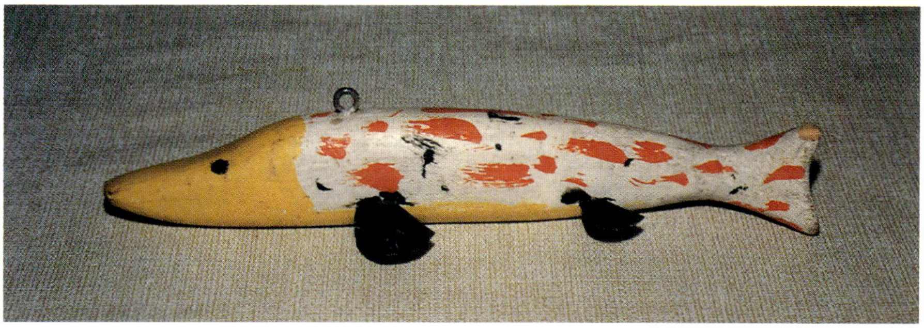

Clarence Thomas northern pike. Photo courtesy of Bill Stoetzel.

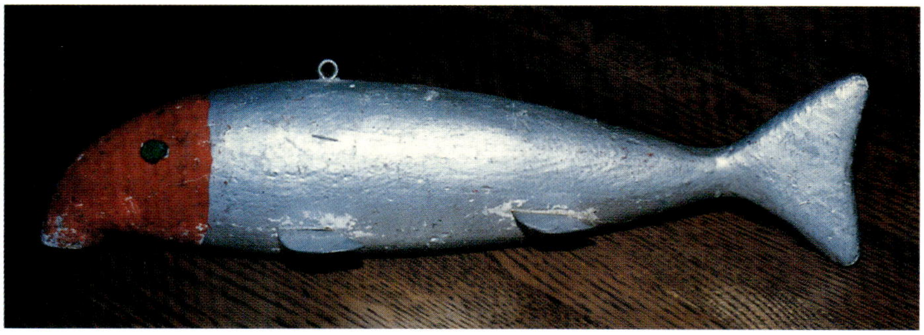

Sucker by Clarence Thomas. Photo courtesy of Bill Stoetzel.

Burt E. Thompson

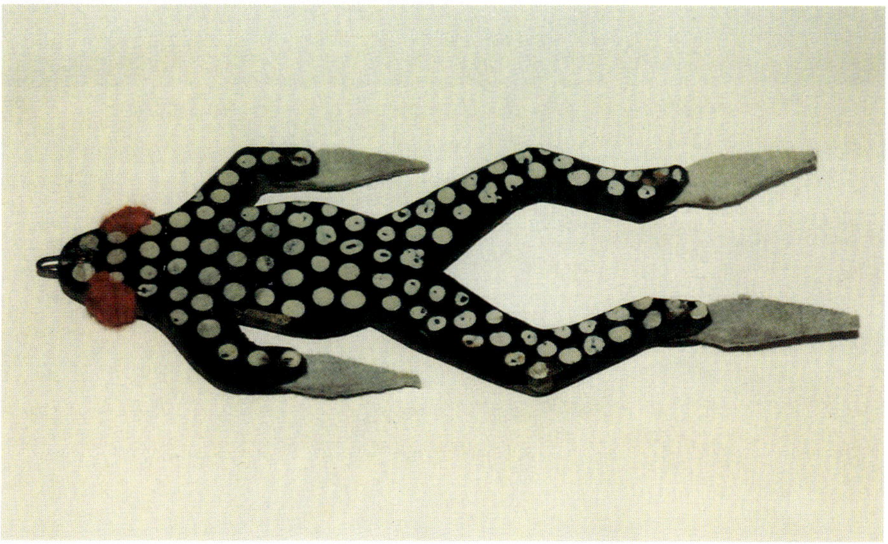

Rubber frog with felt decoration and painted spots, by Burt Thompson, 9 inches.

Raymond Albert Thompson

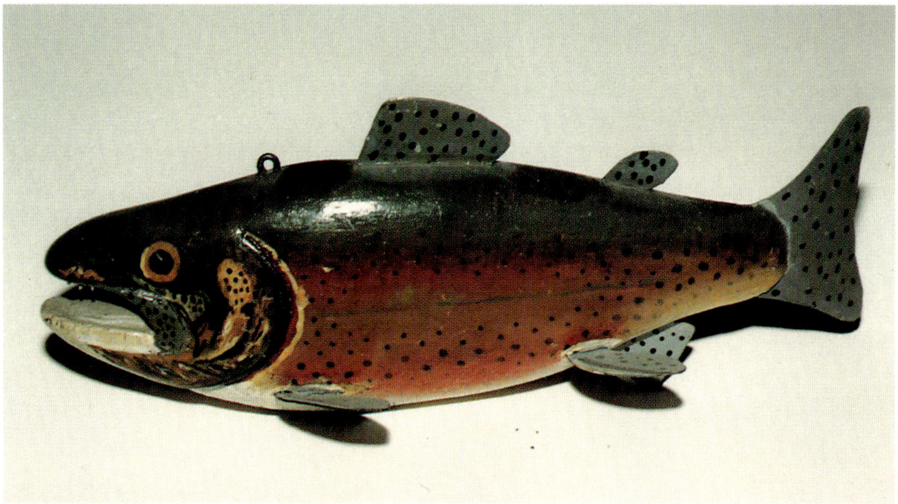

Ray Thompson trout, 8 inches

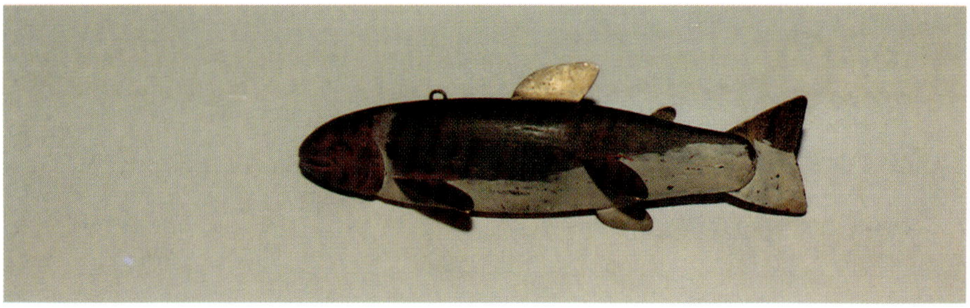

Working decoy by Ray Thompson, 5 3/4 inches.

George Tombarge

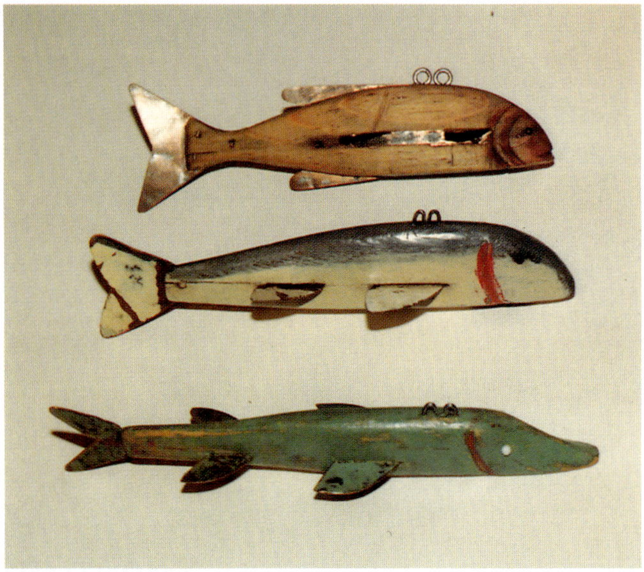

Three Tombarge decoys. Top resembles a walleye in shape, while the middle is a sucker and the bottom one is a northern. Collection of Ron Adamson.

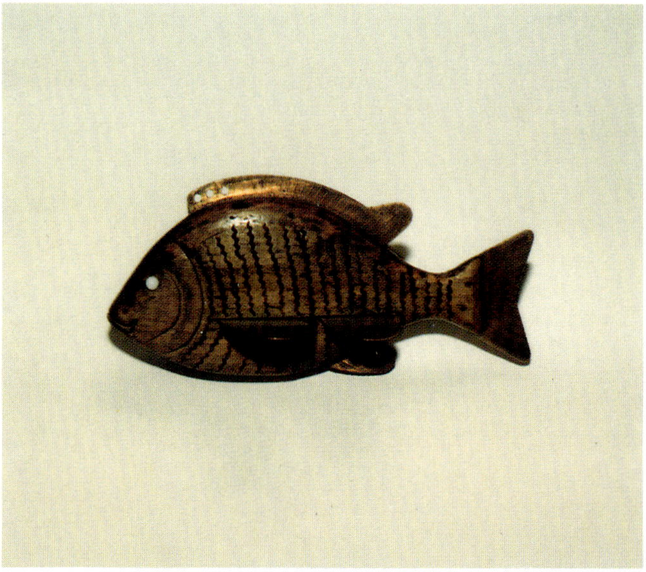

George Tombarge sunfish with burned scale decoration and copper fins, 3 1/2 inches.

John Vavra

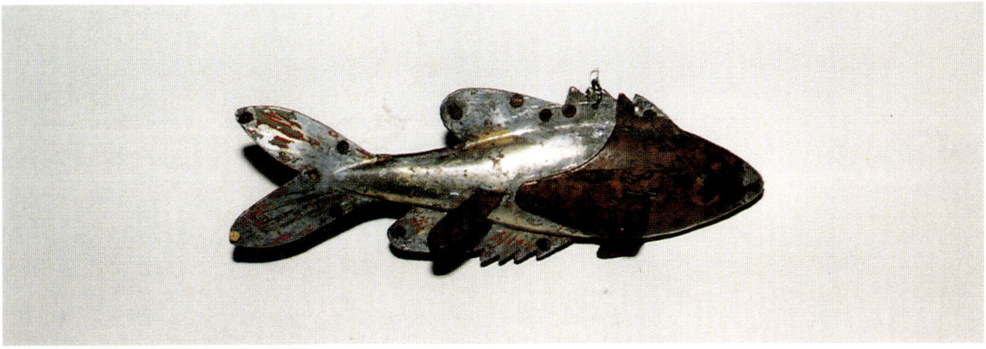

Small metal John Vavra decoy, 5 3/4 inches in length, ca. 1930's. The eye on the smaller decoy was part of the mold and slightly upraised and rounded, of course.

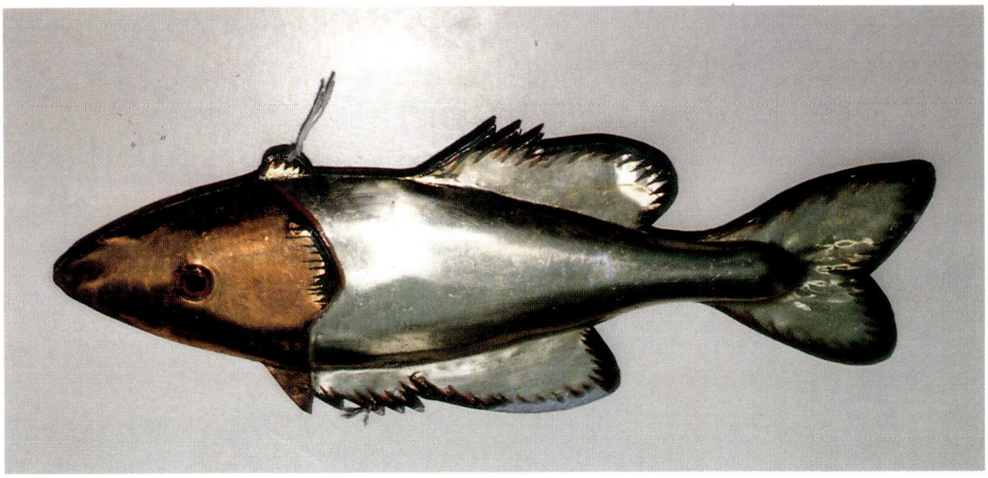

Larger Vavra molded metal decoy. Note on the larger decoy, the special two hole line tie, while the smaller version had a hole in the dorsal fin. The eyes of the larger decoy were glass. Length, 9-10 inches, ca. 1930's. Private collection.

Raymond N. "Pike" Weis

Ray Weis in 1952, holding a large northern.

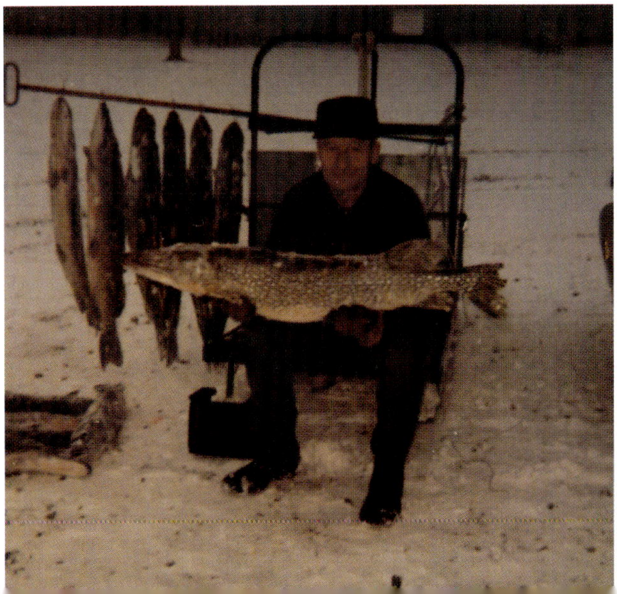

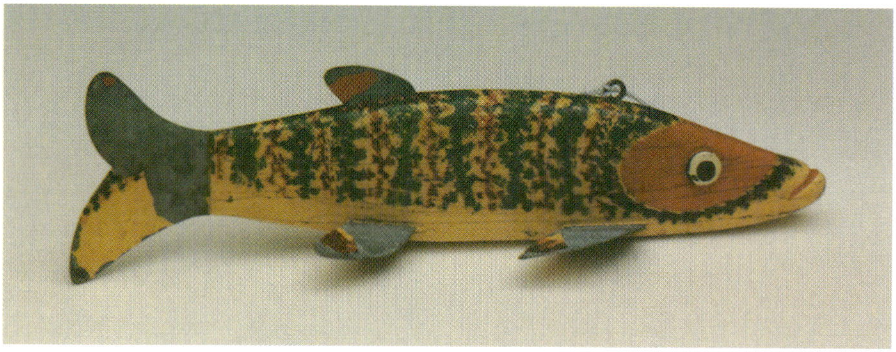

Second period Pike Weis decoy with "Christmas Tree" painting. Private collection.

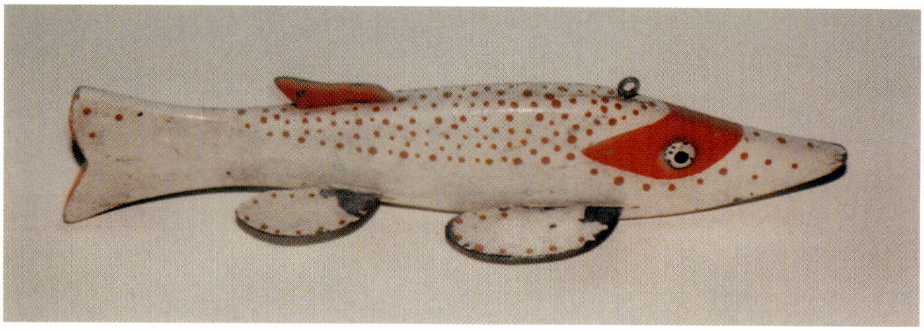

Third period Ray Weiss decoy with glass with "raccoon" eye patch and dot decoration. Private collection.

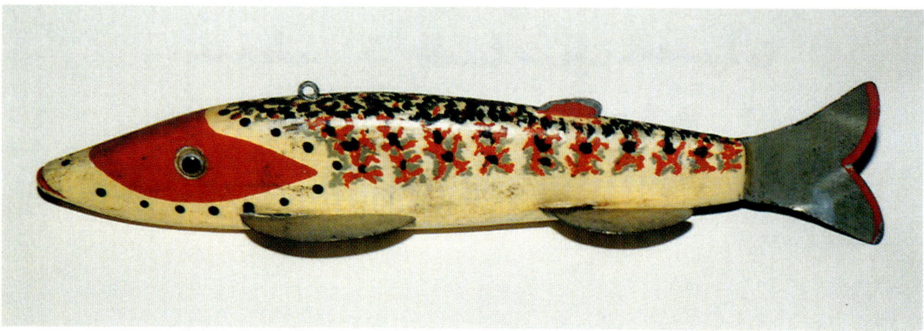

Hybrid Weis decoy with both vertical and dot decoration. Private collection.

Carl Woren

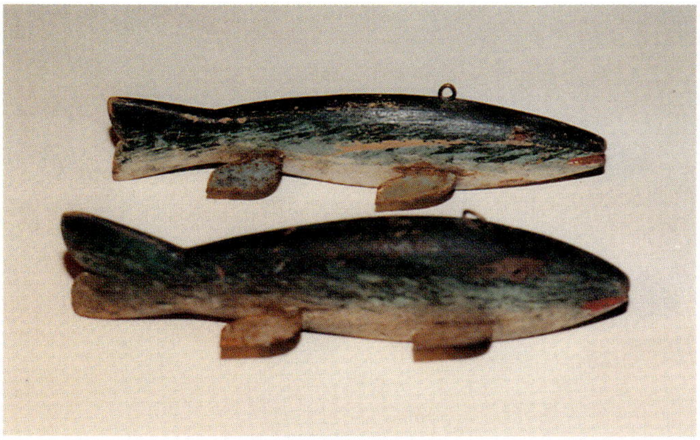

Two Carl Woren decoys. Collection of Carter Stenberg.

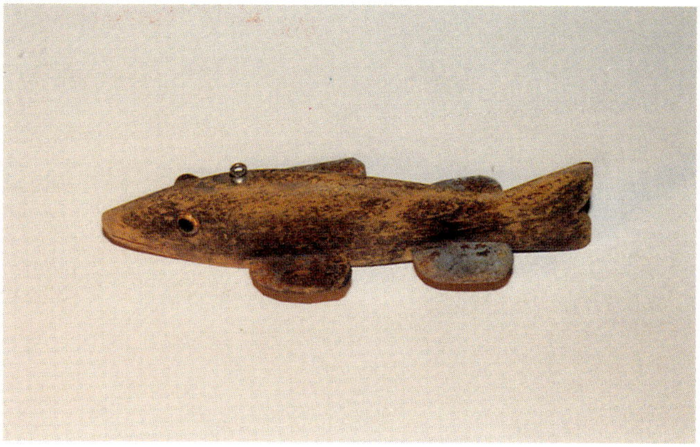

Woren decoy with glass eyes, 6 1/2 inches.

Francis C. "Frank" Wotring

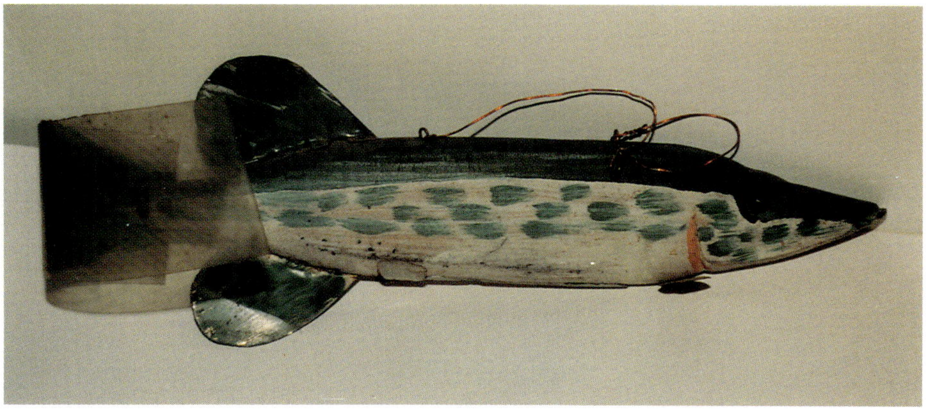

Northern pike decoy by Frank Wotring, 13 inches exclusive of plastic tail.

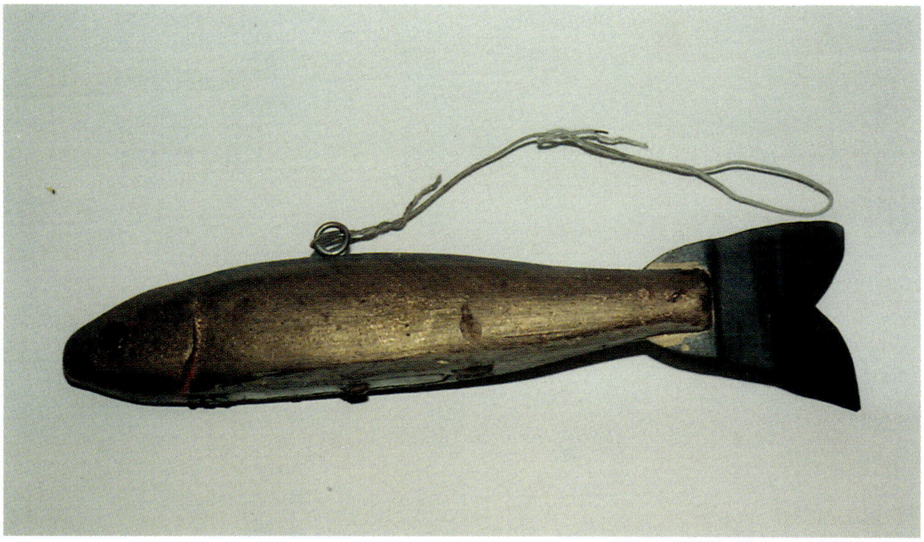

Metal tail Wotring decoy, 9 inches.

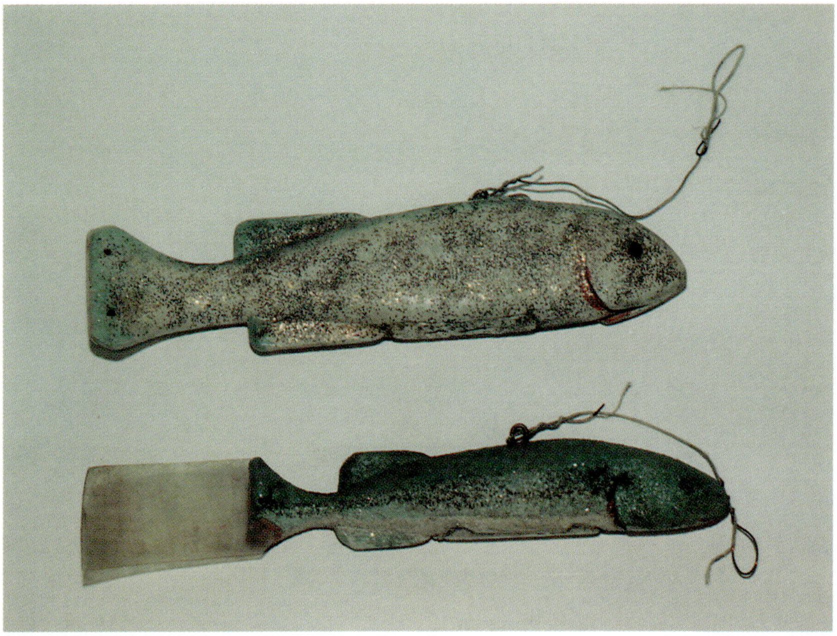

Two plastic tail Wotring decoys, top one has the tail missing, 10 1/2 inches. Bottom is 9 inches.

Joseph A. Zurn

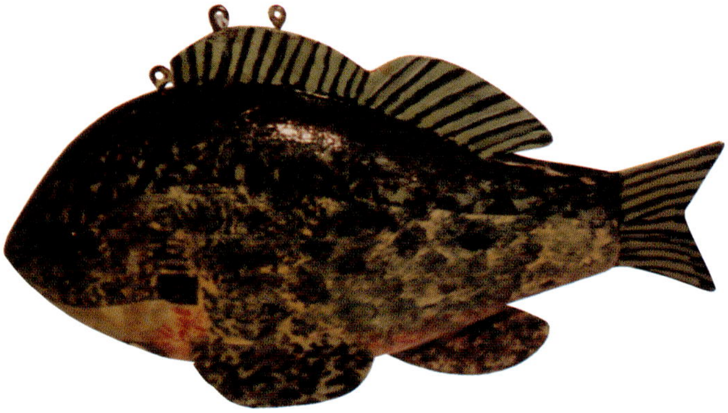

Zurn sunfish.

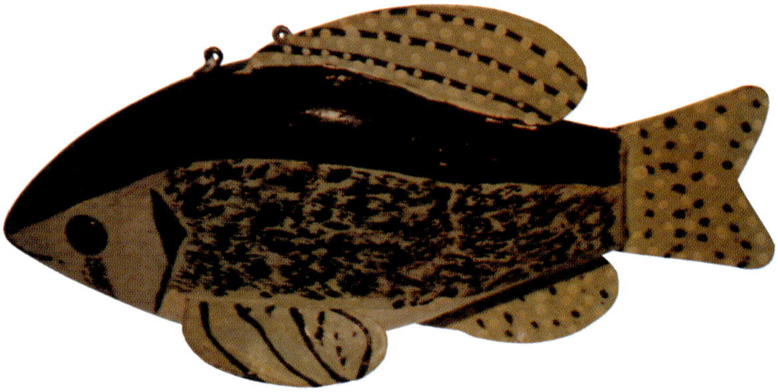

Joseph Zurn crappie.

Zurn pike with burned scale decoration.

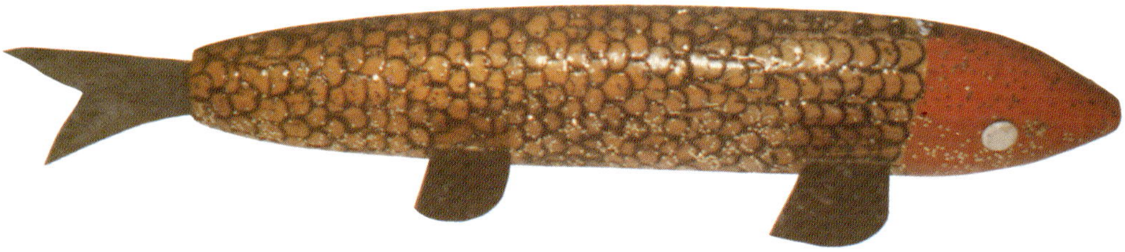

Rudolph Zwieg

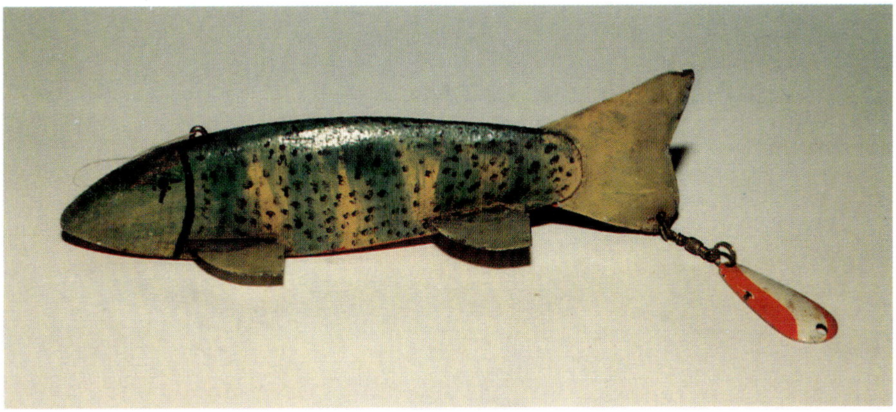

Rudy Zwieg perch with metal spinner attached to tail fin [this spinner was the work of a fisherman, not Rudy Zwieg], 5 1/4 inches.

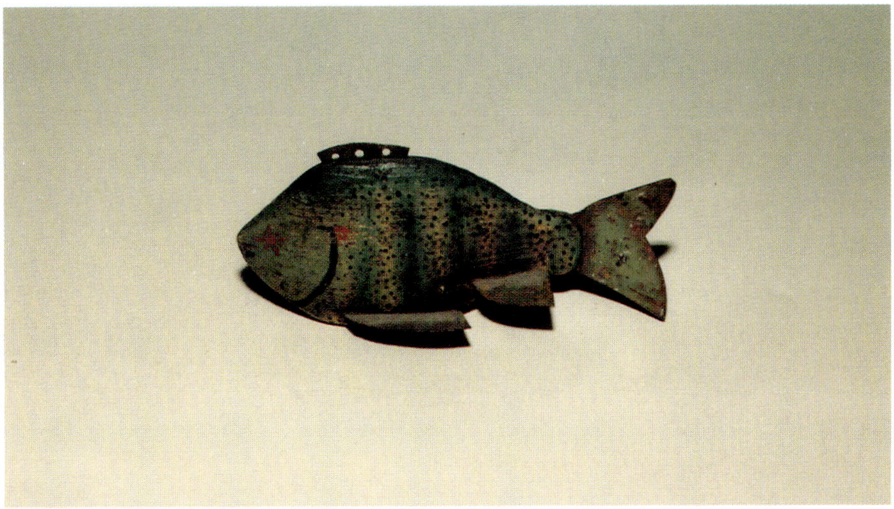

Zwieg sunfish decoy, ca. 1940's. Note band line tie and star eye treatment, 3 1/2 inches.

Rudolph Zwieg inspecting some of his recently made decoys. Photo courtesy of Joe Leach.

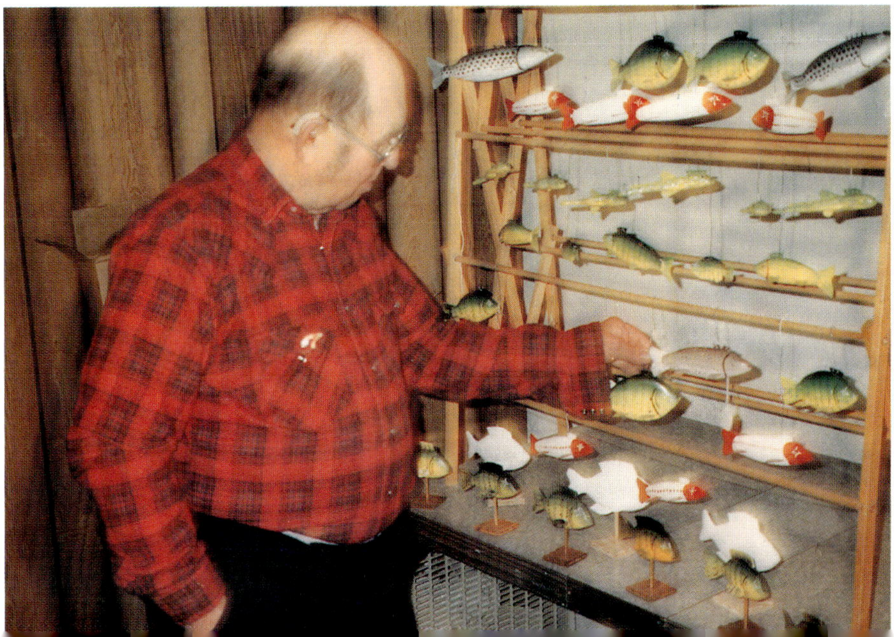

Unknown Makers

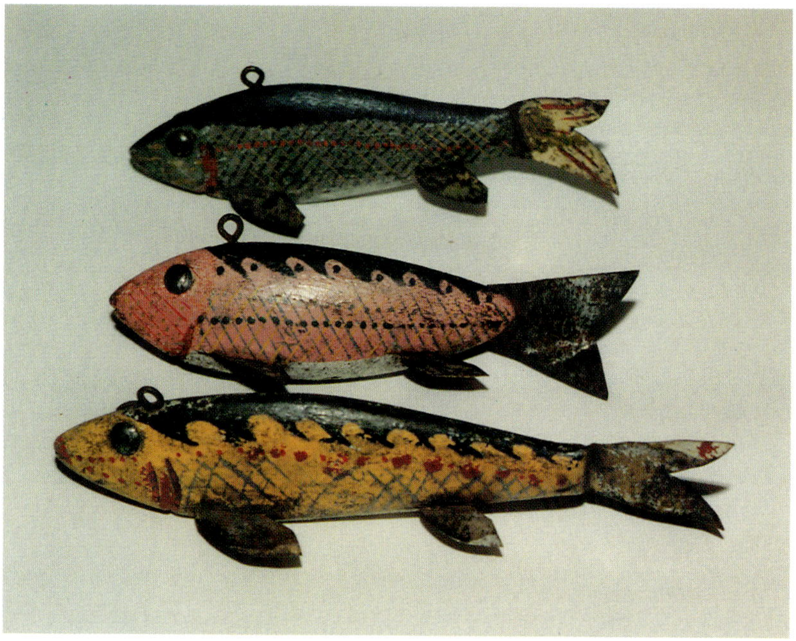

Three decoys found in the Alexandria, Minnesota area.

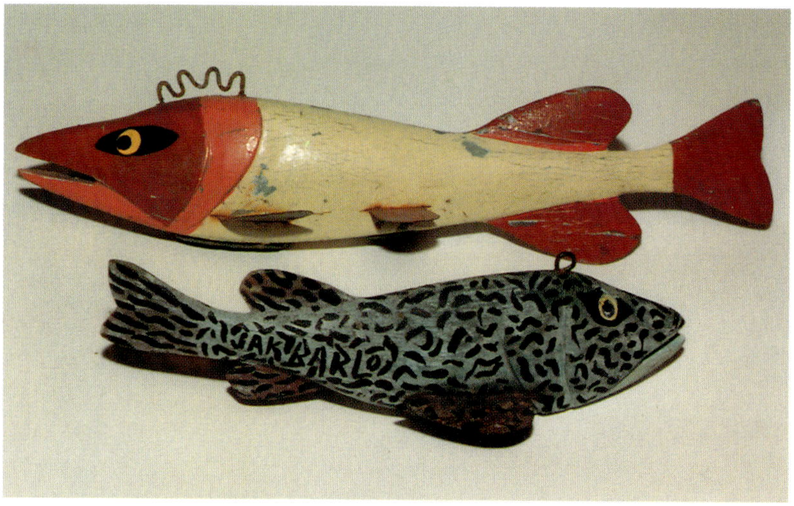

Two decoys by Jake or Jack Barlo. Bottom decoy bears the maker's signature, "Jak Barlo."

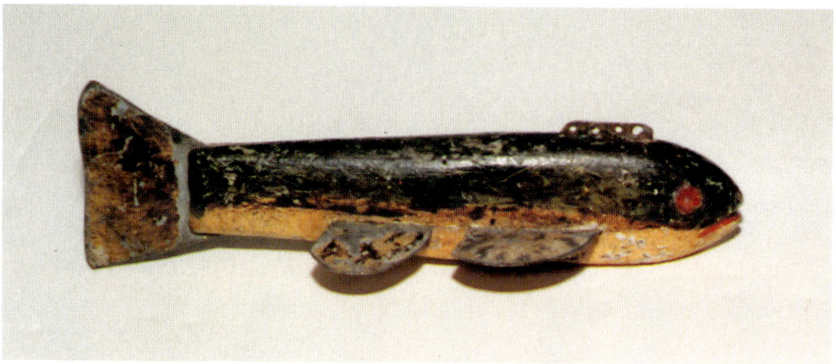

This decoy or one like it has been found in several collections and appears to have been made in the 1920's or early 1930's.

These two decoys were part of a rig of ten decoys found on Big Sandy Lake near McGregor, Minnesota. The owner disclaimed having made them and stated that they could be the work of the Fillipek's.

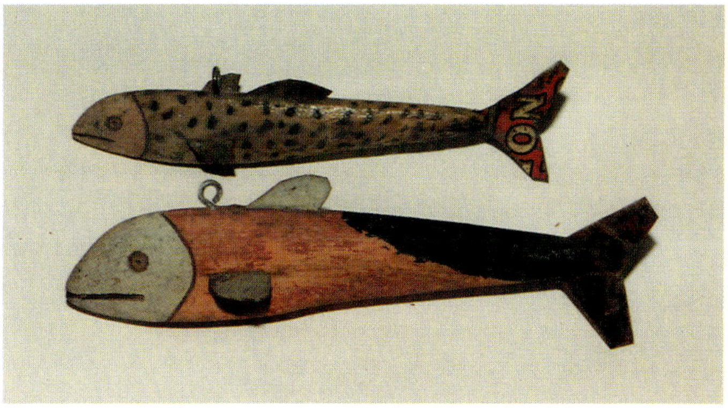

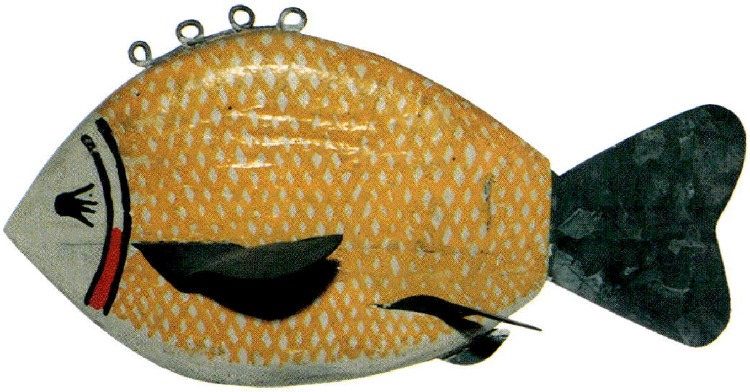

Sunfish made by the maker referred to frequently as "Renner." They appear in the Brainerd, Minnesota area with some frequency, but no "Renner" could be found in the records of the Crow Wing County Historical Society.

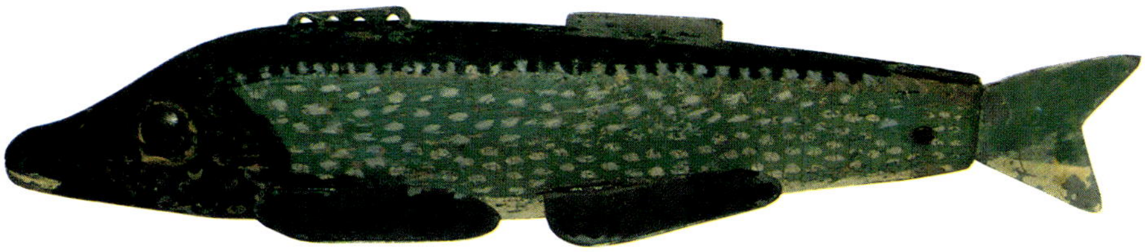

Several of the decoys by this maker have appeared in the Deerwood, Minnesota area, but no attribution, to date, has been documented.

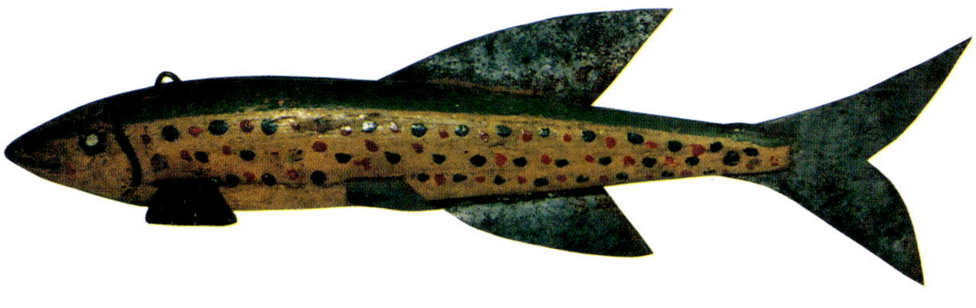

A number of these decoys have been found in the Brainerd, Minnesota area. They are nicely made, with an oversized metal tail and oversized dorsal and anal fins.

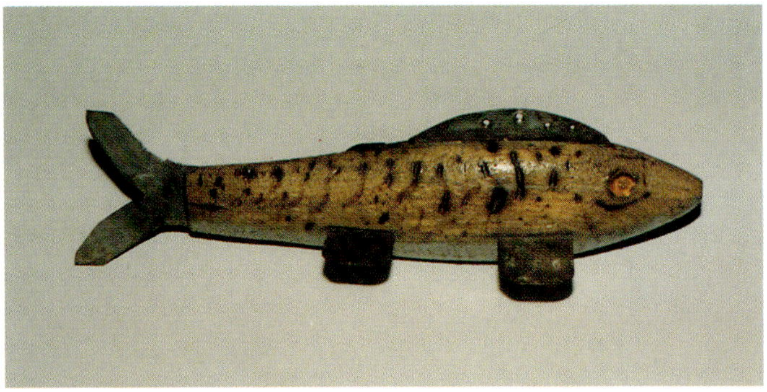

A group of five decoys similar to the one above have been found in the Range Cities area (i.e., Chisholm, Hibbing, and Virginia, Minnesota).

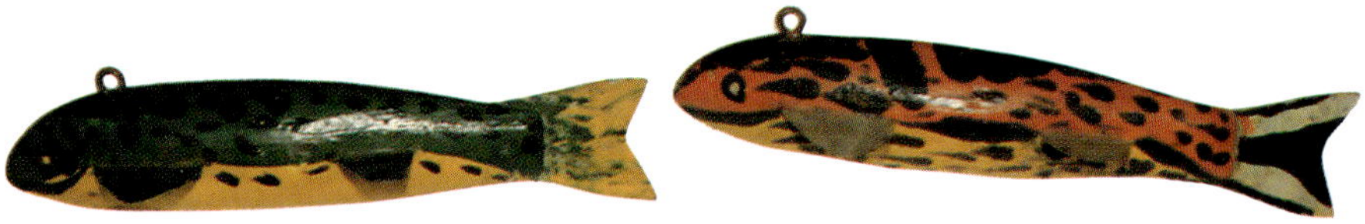

A group of six of these decoys have been discovered in the Hibbing, Minnesota area. Two are pictured above.

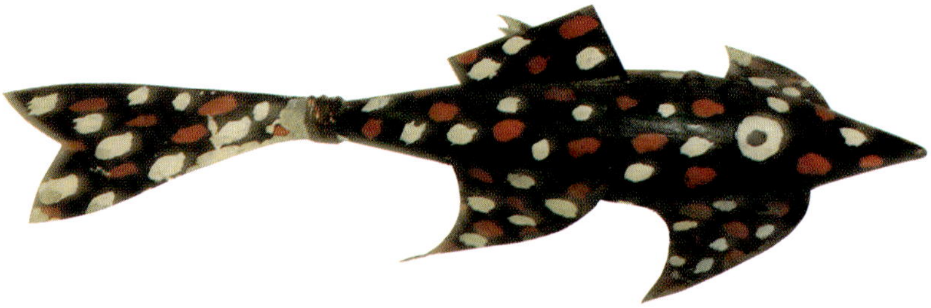

Bat wing decoy attributed to a Charles Dahlstrom located near Mille Lacs Lake.

These small unique decoys were found near Alexandria, Minnesota. Some have hinged tails and/or hinged pectoral fins.

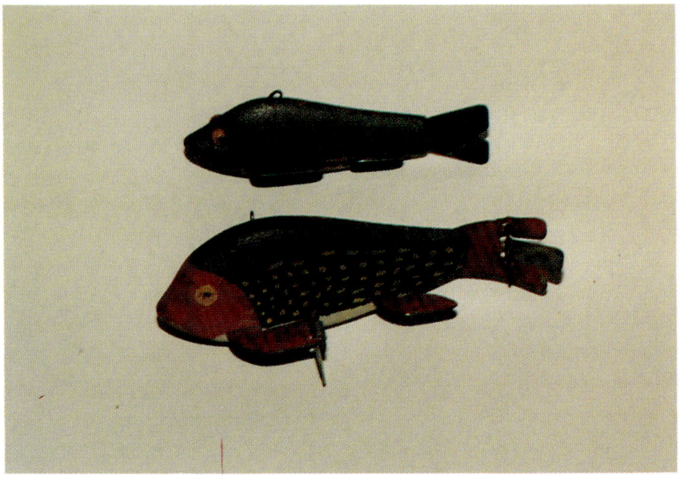

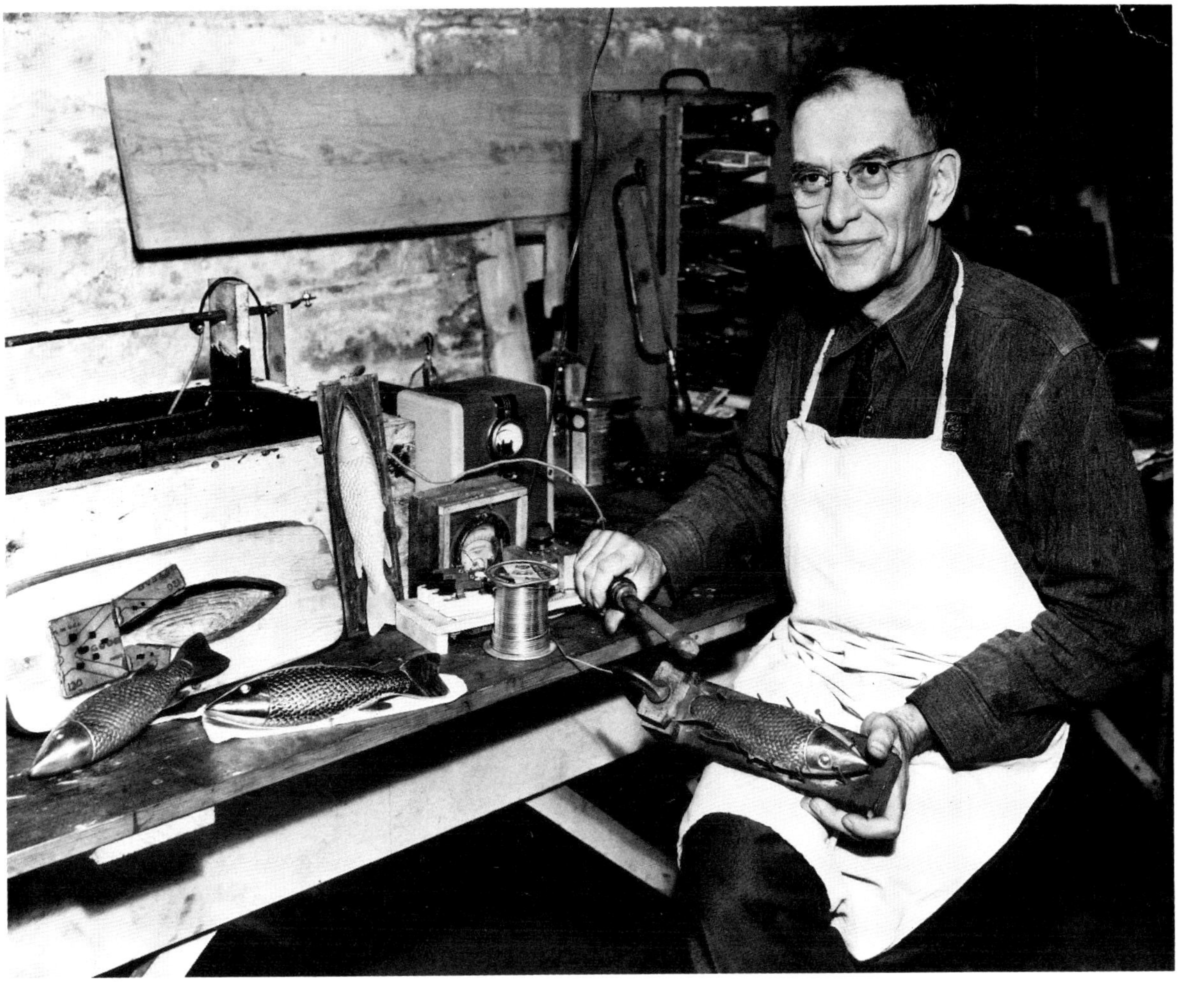

Mr. Booth in 1947 in his basement work shop on Abbott Street.
Note molds and electro-plating equipment on table.

LEO BORASH*

Leo Borash was born on April 5, 1921 in Minnesota and has resided for nearly all of his life in Duluth. A civil engineer by profession, Mr. Borash is married and has one grown daughter.

Influenced by an older brother and his father, both of whom made decoys, Mr. Borash began crafting his own decoys in about 1946. He utilized all types of wood for his decoys, especially pine and basswood. However, Leo also fashioned some curved body decoys using the hardwood in a captain's chair. His decoys were painted in a variety of colors and he would often paint scales on his fish. Over the years, Mr. Borash estimates that he made about 1,200 decoys, most of which he gave away to fishing and hunting friends. He used beads for the eyes in his decoys. Mr. Borash ceased making decoys in 1987.

He still spears and has made his own spears and ice chisels. Leo has speared on Big Rice, Thunder and Pike Lakes

*Information supplied by Mr. Borash in an interview.

LAWRENCE J. "SLIM" BRINKMAN

Slim Brinkman was born in 1905 near Kimball, Minnesota. He died in March of 1976 at the age of 70. Most of his spear decoy making time was spent in St. Cloud, Minnesota.

Mr. Brinkman's decoys apparently run a wide gamut of design and quality. As far as can be determined by surviving examples, all of his decoys had wooden tails. Some of his cruder fish were painted in a peppermint fashion in colors of red and white or yellow and red. His fancier decoys were painted gold, silver, or yellow and he painted detailed scaling on these decoys. The shape of fins was also changed over time (see pictures).

CHESTER BUSS*

Chester Buss was born April 23, 1896 in Illinois. Later, his family moved to Park Rapids, Minnesota. Mr. Buss served in World War I in France and returned to Park Rapids in 1919. He worked as a mechanic in a Ford garage in

Park Rapids. Because the air ventilation system was not effective in cleaning the air, Mr. Buss became ill from the persistent fumes. In 1929, he moved to Morris, Minnesota ostensibly to live and work on a farm. However, in that same year, he again toiled as a mechanic, this time for the State Highway Department in Morris.

It was about this time [i.e., the early 1930's] that he began making fish decoys. Initially, he made decoys only for his own use, but soon he was producing them to sell. His decoys are distinctive, with their flat-topped pectoral fins and sharply pointed tails. Most of his decoys were shaped like minnows, but a few were in the form of sunfish. His decoys were made from pine and the pectoral and dorsal fins were anchored into the lead cavity of the fish. He made approximately 3,000 decoys per year and sold them to Fuller Bait Shop in Park Rapids and to various hardware stores, even as far away as Duluth.

Mr. Buss also made spears and chisels from discarded Highway Department materials. He produced jigging sticks as well, some of which were decorated with likenesses of his fish decoys.

Chester Buss was married and had five children. He ceased producing decoys only upon his death on August 17, 1960.

*Information supplied by Clifford Buss. The latter also produced decoys which closely resembled his father's fish. However, most of the Buss decoys were produced by Chester and not Clifford.

MARION W. BUTCHER

Marion W. Butcher was born on July 24, 1903 in Ohio and died October 28, 1982 at New Hope, Minnesota. His occupation was a foreman for the railroad.

Only three Butcher decoys are known. They represent some of the finest workmanship in Minnesota. All three of the decoys have glass eyes and are realistically painted to imitate either a sunfish, crappie or perch.

HARVEY CASE

Harvey Hayward Case was born August 22, 1901 in Hayward, Wisconsin. He spent his boyhood in Wisconsin and Minnesota. In the 1920's, he moved with his family to the Whipholt, Walker, Akeley, Minnesota area where he resided until his death on July 22, 1994. Mr. Case was married and was survived by three sons and eight daughters.

Over the years that he made decoys, he produced thousands of them. His decoys are distinctive because of their torpedo-like shapes, metal fins and tails, and tack eyes. He always carved an open mouth on his fish. Mr. Case attached two sets of pectoral fins to the bottom of his decoys by means of a metal band which was nailed into the body of the decoys. He first painted his decoys a solid color. Then, by spraying a different (contrasting) color through a screen wrapped around the top of the decoy, he achieved a small, checker-like effect on the outward surface of his decoys. Mr. Case made decoys as small as 4 to 5 inches in length and others up to 18 inches long.

WILLIS CLARK*

Willis Clark was born near Dassel, Minnesota in 1878. He was a carpenter in his adult life and worked in and around Paynesville, Minnesota. Willis was married and had eight children. His wife, however, died in 1935.

In the 1920's, the Paynesville area was a "hot bed" for spear fishing. It was said that in the winter a new town of dark houses sprung up on the lakes. During this time [1920's], Mr. Clark began constructing fish decoys both for himself and to sell. Most of these were made in the winter time when he was not very busy with his carpentry work. Some of his decoys were constructed of cedar and had wooden tails, two pectoral fins on each side, and a flat dorsal fin. The metal pectoral fins were flat on the back.

Willis Clark's brother, Frank, made five prong spears.

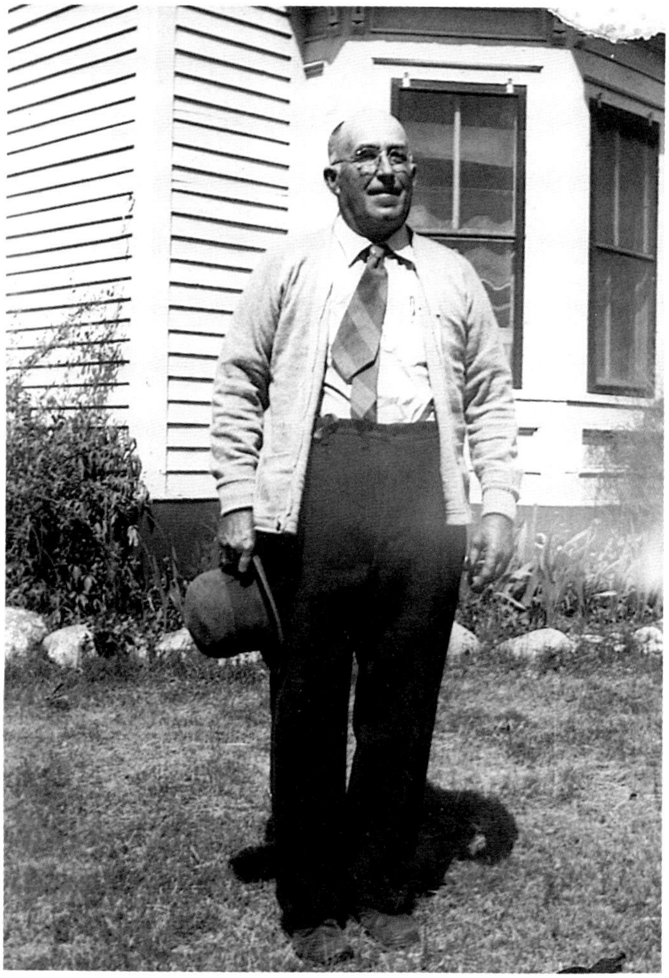

Willis Clark in 1950. Photo courtesy of Mrs. Lillian Clark.

Willis Clark passed away in 1957. His decoy construction work ceased three to four years prior to his death, when Mr. Clark moved to Wisconsin.

*Information provided by Mrs. Lillian Clark, one of Willis' daughters-in-law.

JACK COOPER*

Jack Cooper was born in 1922 in St. Paul, Minnesota. He entered the Navy in 1938 as a Seebee. In 1946, he left the service and worked as an electrician until his retirement in 1964. Mr. Cooper is married and has six grown children.

Upon his return from the Navy to civilian life in 1946, Jack began to fashion spear fishing decoys for his own use. These were made from basswood and were given a primer coat of paint. Mr. Cooper would then paint them as perch and sunfish. An ardent spear fisherman, Cooper speared on White Bear Lake, Pequot and Gull Lakes. He ceased making decoys in the 1950's and only four of his fish are known to the author, three perch and one sunfish. Mr. Cooper currently resides in Bock, Minnesota.

*Information provided in an interview with Mr. Cooper.

GEORGE G. DAHL*

George G. Dahl was born on March 22, 1890. He was married and had three daughters by his first marriage. Mr. Dahl was a steam fitter by trade and worked for the Caswell Well Company in Minneapolis. He subsequently was employed at an arms plant in New Brighton.

An avid spear fisherman, Mr. Dahl made decoys for himself and for friends beginning in the 1920's. He speared on Mille Lacs Lake. Most of his surviving decoys were painted red and white with wooden tails, but a few decoys with other color combinations have also been noted. Mr. Dahl also made some frog decoys.

Following the death of his first wife, George remarried in 1947. After that year he ceased spear fishing as well as making decoys. Instead, he turned his attention to building furniture and gardening.

Ironically, he predicted that he would die on his 72nd birthday. This prophecy came true as he passed away on March 22, 1962. His remaining decoys were found in an old suitcase wrapped in newspaper dated 1945, after relatives were cleaning the attic of his second wife's home upon her death at age 90.

*Information courtesy of Carter Stenberg and relatives of George Dahl.

AL DINCAU

Al Dincau was born in 1909 in Nashwauk, Minnesota. He worked in the steel mills in Duluth for 42 years. Mr. Dincau was married and had seven children. His large family prompted Mr. Dincau to pursue hunting and fishing as more than just sport. He made fishing decoys from the 1950's through the 1970's for himself and for friends. Over the years, he made about 40 decoys. Mr. Dincau also made spears and some duck decoys. His spear fishing decoys are distinctive in that the metal tail has a pronounced upper section relative to the lower section. His decoys are painted red and white with a red head and white body, and sometimes with red painted fins. Mr. Dincau died en route to his dark house in 1986.

OTIS DOTY

Otis Doty was born on September 23, 1897 in Adell, Iowa. He joined the army during World War I and, following his service, he returned to Iowa. Around 1920, he moved to Redwood Falls, Minnesota, where he became a farmer. He was married in 1922 and the union produced two sons. Otis continued farming in Redwood Falls until the 1940's, when he was diagnosed as having diabetes. His economic survival was aided by a pension from his service in World War I. After his diagnosis, Otis decided to buy a small farm in Palisade, Minnesota, in Aitkin County. There he became interested in spear fishing and he made several decoys for his own use. His decoys were made from pine or basswood, which he would carve and paint. Most were in the shape of perch and they had curved bodies.

Otis preferred spearing in nearby lakes such as Waukenabo, Round and Big Sandy. He also speared in the Mississippi River, which bordered his property in Palisade.

Mr. Doty also made spoons for fishing, which he beat from copper. He has also crafted decoys from coffee can lids.

Otis passed away on Easter Sunday in 1965.

CARL "GUS" DORNQUAST*

Carl Dornquast, best know as "Gus" Dornquast, was born July 27, 1883 in Germany. After coming to the United States, he settled in Owatonna, Minnesota where he worked as a farmer.

He carved a variety of fish decoys which had two or four dorsal fins. Many of his decoys had white heads and a rounded tail fin. His line tie was a band of metal with holes punched into it. Mr. Dornquast's best fish resembles a perch, with the majority of the body painted green withadded yellow or orange highlights.

He died on November 3, 1955.

*Some information courtesy of Bill Stoetzel.

MILTON EBINGER*

Milton Ebinger was born in 1918 and resides in Brainerd, Minnesota. He worked in the paper mills there and is now retired.

A spearing enthusiast, Mr. Ebinger made decoys from cedar. He sold a few, but mainly made decoys for his own use. His decoys were characteristically small, about four inches in length. He used the pig tail line tie method and stated that he achieved the pig tail effect by wrapping wire around a nail. Despite the relative diminutive size of his decoys, he placed two pectoral fins on each side of his fish, made from tin or brass, and also utilized a dorsal as well as an anal fin. Mr. Ebinger's tails for his fish were always made of wood. His painting technique was a simple one. He preferred a two color combination, white and red or yellow and white, and painted dots horizontally on the sides of his decoys in a contrasting color to the body paint.

*Information courtesy of Milton Ebinger.

CHARLES ENGEL

Charles Engel was born in Germany in 1876. After coming to the United States, he homesteaded in Montana. Subsequently, Mr. Engel owned and operated a hotel in Sanborn, Minnesota. In 1924, he moved to Frazee, Minnesota. It was about this time that he first began to make spear fishing decoys. His decoys were fashioned from basswood and/or poplar. The decoys produced were for his own use only.

Mr. Engel believed that small decoys worked best for attracting fish. He made a sunfish decoy, a bullhead, a mouse, and several sizes of minnows.

An avid spear fisherman, his favorite spearing lake was Hungry Lake. Mr. Engel was married and had ten children, five boys and five girls. He died in 1939.

LEO EPPEL*

Leo Eppel was born on July 22, 1875, in Delano, Minnesota. He owned a restaurant in Delano and later, one in Minneapolis. His establishments were called "Leo's Cafe" and his business cards contained advertisements such as "eat like Helen be happy" and "If you don't eat here we both starve." Babe Ruth once ate at Mr. Eppel's restaurant and it became a haven for sports figures to dine. During the last eight years in Minneapolis, his restaurant was called "Bud's Good Eats." Mr. Eppel was married and had seven children, four boys and three girls.

He began making decoys in the early 1920's. Most of these were made for his own use, but he may have sold a few to one of his brothers who owned Elm Beach Resort on Lake Sarah, located 20 miles west of Minneapolis. These decoys may have been distributed to resort guests. His decoys are characterized by a marked slope to the nose, carved and painted gills and nicely painted bodies. It is not known how many decoys he produced, but he continued making them until his death on October 7, 1939, in Minneapolis.

Mr. Eppel also constructed wooden lures with distinctive metal lips as well as miniature carvings of fish which could be used for a lapel pin. He held a patent (received in April of 1939, just six months before his death) for his "Eppel Frog Saver." Metal lilly pads for use in fish aquariums and frog boxes were also made by him.

*Information courtesy of Jerald Eppel.

NELS FAIRBANKS

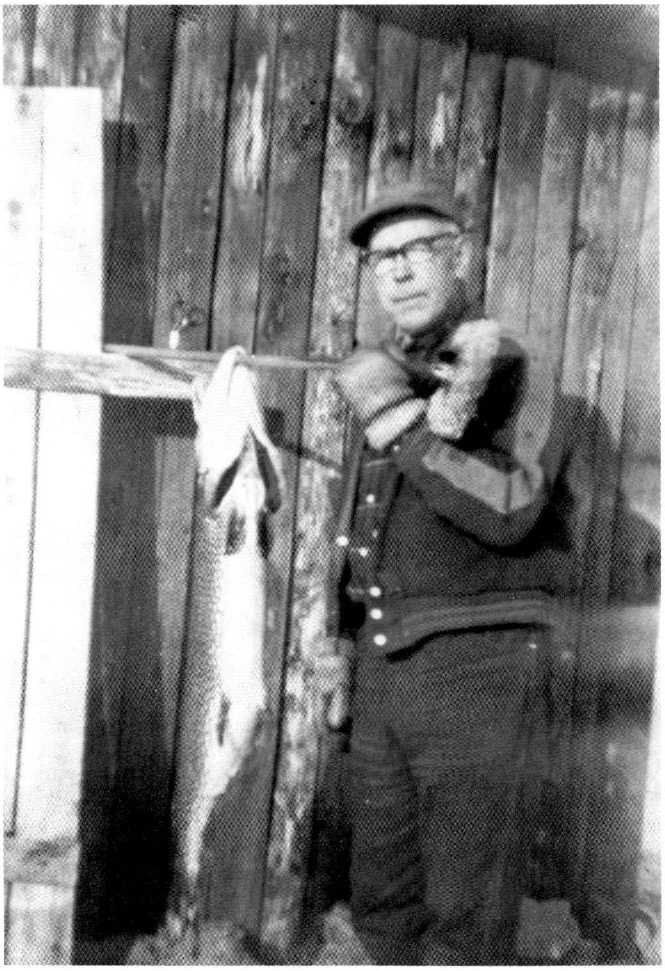

Nels Fairbanks with a fine catch.

Nels Fairbanks was born on October 12, 1884 in DeMet, South Dakota. He died in April of 1964. Mr. Fairbanks came to Minnesota with his family in 1892, settling in Dodge Center. In 1904, he became interested in spear fishing and began carving decoys. His brother, Charles, was also a decoy carver. They made their own fishing lures as well.

Nels Fairbanks was married and worked for the Milwaukee Railroad in St. Paul, Minnesota as a stationary engineer.

OTTO FAUE*

Otto Faue was born August 8, 1881 in Minneapolis, Minnesota. He worked as a carpenter and local handyman, building barns, sharpening saws, and working on saw rigs around Hanover, Minnesota. Single, he lived in shacks on Beebe Lake and Lake Charlotte, but later moved to a shack on a local farm, the John Dixon farm.

He began carving decoys in the late 1920's. Otto carved duck decoy as well as perhaps 50 spearing decoys a year. He did his carving for beer money, selling his decoys to local bars, and to friends.

He died on April 15, 1954.

Otto made his decoys with two fins on each side. In general, Otto Faue decoys lack the detail, color and imagination of those of his brother, William. Otto preferred red and white decoys, or shades of brown, as colors for his fish. Frequently, one finds that Otto used tacks to depict eyes for his fish, while William more often painted the eyes on his fish as having a black iris with a yellow outline. Both Otto and William placed both dorsal and anal fins on their decoys. These were similar in shape to each other, as were the metal tails on their fish decoys.

*Information courtesy of Peter Meyers.

WILLIAM FAUE*

William Faue was born on January 2, 1878 in Minneapolis, Minnesota. He was married and lived in Hanover, Minnesota, where he worked at the Hanover Milling Company. He also did carpentry work as well as house painting, wood working and carving.

William Faue began carving in the middle 1930's. He had a fine work shop where he carved fishing sticks, bobbers, duck calls, ax handles, canes, and toys, not to mention his spearing decoys. William carved about 100 such

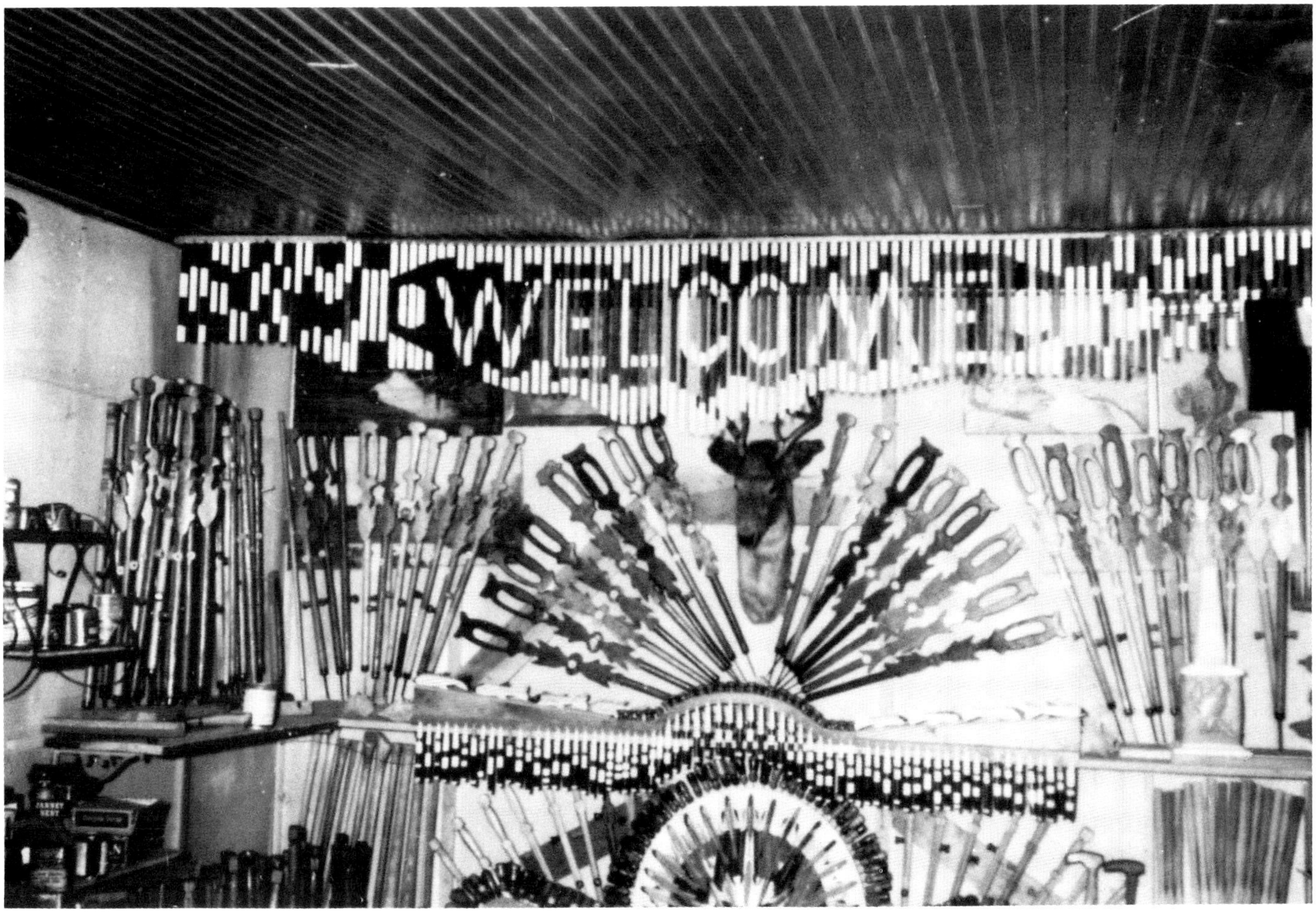

Large grouping of Otto and William Faue fishing sticks.

decoys each year, working on ten to twenty at a time, using different designs. His spearing decoys sold for 50¢ to local bars and hardware stores. He continued carving up until his death in 1950.

William was interviewed by *Sports Afield* magazine.[6] The resulting article, "The Lucky Stick," referred to his hand carved fishing sticks. Unfortunately, the article appeared in 1951 after his death.

William used only one pectoral fin on each side of his fish decoys.

*Information courtesy of Peter Meyers.

FRANK FILIPEK

Frank Filipek was born in 1900 and lived just south of Montgomery, Minnesota. He was a builder-contractor by profession. Mr. Filipek began making decoys in the 1920's for his own use. Most of his decoys were constructed from pine and/or basswood, and had tin fins. His favorite spear fishing lakes were General Shield Lake and Hunts Lake.

WILLIAM FLANAGAN*

William Flanagan was born in Staples, Minnesota in 1917. He began carving and selling his fish decoys door-to-door in 1935 and continued to do so up to 1960. Mr. Flanagan became ill in late 1960 and subsequently moved to the state of Washington. He was bedridden the last years of his life, but still continued to carve fish decoys. William would instruct his wife to purchase pine wood at lumber yards that was top grade with no knots. During his lifetime he was a writer, writing a book concerning honey bees. He was also an inventor, inventing automobile curb finders as well as a soldering gun. Mr. Flanagan passed away in 1970.

His decoys are noteworthy because of the wild paint jobs on them. He was known to paint decoys with as many as ten different colors with over 125 separate paint applications.

*Information courtesy of Frank R. Baron.

PETER J. FUCHS*

Peter J. "Pete" Fuchs was born in 1918 in Albany, Minnesota. As a youngster, he would carve 14 to 15 spearing decoys over the winter [when his father's blacksmithing business was slow]. He sold these for the grand price of 35¢ each. Pete was also interested in duck hunting and, in 1939, made some duck decoys. He continued to make fish decoys, which he sold in a bait shop that he opened in Avon, Minnesota in 1946. Hundreds of decoys have been sold there, the last ones fetching $1.50 each [collectors today will beat that price by a wide margin].

His decoys are made from pine or basswood—soft woods that are easy to carve. He has made wood tail spearing decoys, but his later fish have copper or galvanized metal for the fins and tails. Pete uses wire loops for his line ties. Most of his decoys were styled as northerns or suckers, and he made some sunfish.

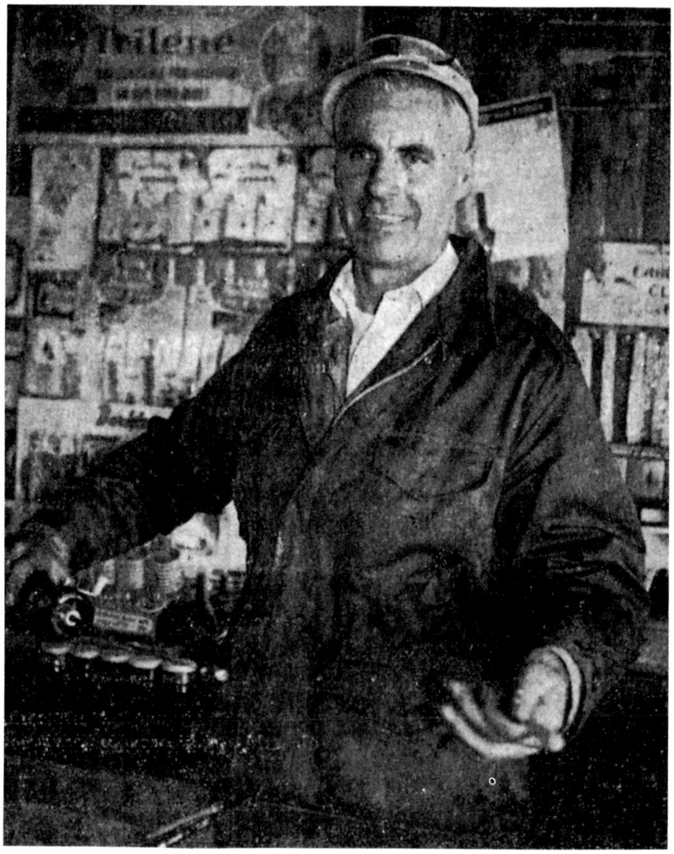

Mr. Fuchs in 1961 in his Bait Store.

*Information provided by Peter Fuchs. See Chapter 7 for another write up on Mr. Fuchs, as a spear-maker.

CLARENCE "TARZ" GEISELHART*

Mr. Geiselhart was born on May 7, 1919 in North Dakota. He is now living in a nursing home in Long Prairie, Minnesota. For more than 25 years he was in the lumber business, making deliveries.

He began making decoys in the 1930's while still in his teens. His decoys were made for resale. Geiselhart's decoys were quite artistic in his early days, but later ones were quite crude.

*Information courtesy of Mr. Geiselhart. His nickname was "Tarz," short for "Tarzan."

WILLIAM H. "BILL" GREEN*

Bill Green was born in 1922 in Grand Rapids, Minnesota. He worked for U.S. Steel for 42 years.

Mr. Green began making spearing decoys when he was seven years old. An avid spear fisherman, Bill speared Trout Lake, Lake Winnibigosh and Pokegama Lake. His decoys were made for his own use during the 1930's and 1940's. In 1981, someone stole his decoy rig and he began making decoys again, this time for resale. Bill's decoys were fashioned from basswood.

Mr. Green is married and has seven children.

*Information provided by Mr. Green.

JOE GUSTIN*

Joe Gustin was born in 1912 in Aurora, Minnesota and died June 18, 1995 in Keewatin, Minnesota. Keewatin is located in the Iron Range country of Minnesota, so it is not unusual that Mr. Gustin worked as a welder (class 1) for the mines. Later, he became a staff representative for the United Steelworkers of America, retiring from that position in 1980.

An avid outdoorsman, Mr. Gustin enjoyed hunting and fishing. He especially liked to spear on Lake Winnibigosh and Leech Lake. In 1937-38, he began constructing spearing decoys. Two distinct types of decoys were made: (1) red and white painted wooden decoys, and (2) decoys fashioned from rubber. The latter were made from discarded conveyor belt material used for carrying rock to the crusher machine. After burning the surface of the rubber material, Mr. Gustin would carve the desired form of his decoys. Three of these decoys are known to have survived: a sucker, a pike, and a minnow about 3 to 4 inches in length. His sucker had two pectoral fins on each side (made of vulcanized rubber), and a dorsal fin (one piece with the body). He used a tack for the eye with a red painted iris. Circles were stamped into the sucker's body to add a kind of scale effect (although suckers do not have scales). Mr. Gustin also made five-tine spears.

He was married and had two sons.

*Information courtesy of Edward Gustin, one of Joe Gustin's sons.

ARNOLD G. HAFSTAD

Arnold G. Hafstad, of Sedan, Minnesota, was born on December 16, 1901. He was involved in farming in his early years. During the 1930's, he operated a trucking business. As part of the business he drove a Model "A" truck with his name, address, and phone number painted on the doors. Mr. Hafstad was interested in swimming, roller skating, ice skating, hunting, fishing, boxing, and trapping. He was also an active member of the Chippewa Falls Lutheran Church and he held various church offices.

Mr. Hafstad was married and had one son. He passed away on January 25, 1989.

CHARLES "CHUCK" HALL

Born in LeSueur County in the spring of 1908, Charles "Chuck" Hall was the son of an avid outdoorsman. Chuck began fishing at an early age. His father had previously lived in northern New York state, where he learned the fishing skills that he would teach his son.

At the age of nine, Chuck and his family moved to a small farm in Carlton County a few miles outside the small town of Barnum, Minnesota. He began to carve his own spearing decoys in his early teens. Mr. Hall stated that he did not learn his carving skills from his father, but rather was self-taught. His father did make fish decoys, but they were crudely done.

During the period between 1930 and 1942, Chuck made approximately 400 decoys. Some were sold in two hardware stores, one in Barnum and the other in Moose lake. He also custom-made decoys for friends and others he just gave away.

Hall fish were one-of-a-kind. He mainly used pine to carve his fish and preferred wooden tail decoys. If a wooden tail was broken, he would repair it or replace it with a new tail. He did, however, construct some decoys with metal tails.

When he could get them, he would use glass eyes for his fish. Sometimes the glass eyes were removed from old duck decoys. A few of his fish have been found with red eyes, probably taken from a canvass-back duck decoy.

Most any sheet metal was used for the decoy's side fins, although he seemed to favor copper or galvanized metal. Chuck often inserted small fins in the decoy's belly near the gills. Although useless in the performance of the decoy, Hall put these fins in some of his decoys because "a fish has those little fins there."

Unlike his wood or metal supplies, Chuck bought his paints. He used a painting "kit." Hall would mix and blend the paints to obtain just the tone that he wanted. Most of his decoys were realistically painted.

Charles "Chuck" Hall passed away December 12, 1995.

See also "Chuck Hall Carving out the good life," by Donna Tonelli, *Decoy Magazine,* January-February, 1993, pp. 36-38.

WILLIAM D. HARRISON

William D. Harrison was born on July 15, 1896 in Little Falls, Minnesota and he died on October 2, 1962. His immediate family were pioneer residents of the Ross Lake (Minnesota) area. He lived in Crosby, Minnesota most of his life. Employed for many years in the mines as a security guard, William was also a carpenter.

Mr. Harrison made decoys for resale as well as for his own use. His decoys were highly stylized and a few were identifiable as to species. He made northerns, crappies, suckers, frogs and eel pouts. Most of his fish were painted using a screening method which produced a very fine speckling on his fish. He used white, green, blue, black, and red as predominant colors, often contrasted with some other color. On many of his decoys he utilized the small red balls found on leaders as eyes, but in some of his decoys he neither painted nor put in any eyes at all. A few of his decoys had screw eyes as a line tie, but the more classic Harrison technique was to place a hole in a very distinctive dorsal fin (see pictures). Some Harrison decoys have wooden tails and others utilize a tail made from tin; some have anal fins and others do not. The lead cavity in his decoys is long and rectangular in shape. In most of Harrison's decoys, the mouth is carved. He was also fond of a swept-wing pectoral fin (see pictures).

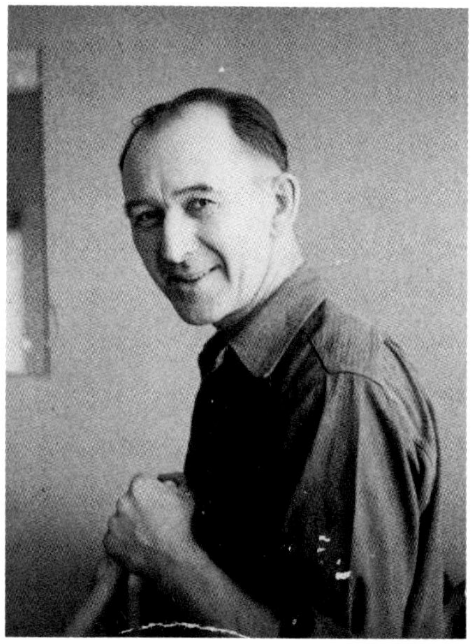

John Hesjedal.

JOHN HESJEDAL*

John Hesjedal[7] [pronounced "Hesh-ah-dawl"] was born August 5, 1896 in Sundahl, Minnesota. In his youth, John helped his father farm. He served in World War I. After his stint in the service, John became a custodian with the Moorhead Independent School District. Subsequently, he performed similar work at Concordia College in Moorhead. Toward the end of his career, he worked for the U.S. Postal Service. Mr. Hesjedal was married and had one daughter who still resides in Moorhead.

An ardent spear fisherman and angler, John began making decoys for himself and for resale in the late 1930's. His decoys are distinctive primarily for their long, swept back fins (see Figure 4-1).

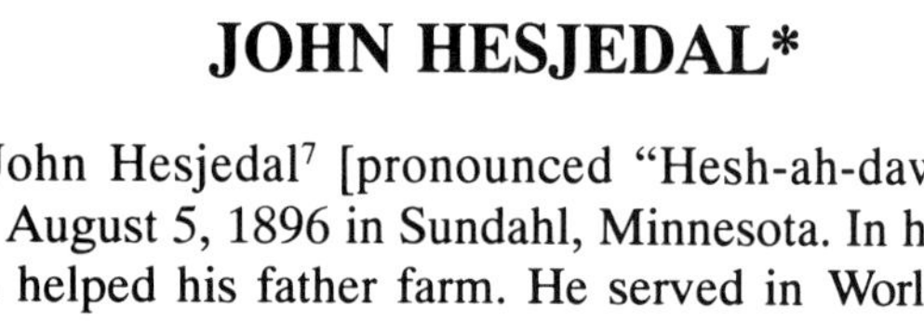

Top View of Hesjedal Decoy

The majority of Hesjedal decoys are painted red and white, with a red tail. Decoy bodies were painted and covered with glitter while the paint was wet. However, Mr. Hesjedal also used other paint schemes on some of his decoys. One surviving example has scales and gills burned into the body and the fins are painted silver instead of red. The decoy is varnished rather than painted.

The eyes of his decoys were map pins, usually dark green in color. Pine was his preferred medium for the decoy body and fins were frequently a light gauge sheet metal.

Mr. Hesjedal made decoys year around, but most frequently during the winter. He continued to make and paint decoys until he suffered a stroke in 1962. Then, his wife began painting the additional decoys produced after his stroke. John died on March 1, 1962.

*Information courtesy of Mr. Hesjedal's daughter.

LEROY HOWELL*

LeRoy Howell, one of Minnesota's best known decoy carvers, was born in Guthrie, Oklahoma on June 19, 1894. He was raised in Hinkley, Minnesota and was a house painter by trade.

Mr. Howell began carving fish decoys for his own use in the 1920's, then later for friends and relatives. He started marketing them in 1929 and continued to do so until the early 1950's. Howell ceased his business when it was no longer economical to compete with the plastic decoy models.

His earliest decoys were the so-called "angel fish." Most of these fish were painted with a fancy dot pattern and had tail fins with a swept pattern (see picture). After his angel fish period, Howell modified the design of his decoys, incorporating a simple tail fin and one large swept back pectoral fin on each side of his fish. During this time he continued to paint some decoys with dots in a flower pattern and also constructed some decoys with wooden tails. His bass, sunfish, pike, crappie and suckers all had wood carved tails.

Howell's most recent decoys showed a much simpler design, because of the public acceptance of his decoys. By this time, his preferred decoy color scheme involved two color combinations, such as red and white, green and white, etc. His fancy flowered paint jobs disappeared altogether. Howell's decoy eyes are his trade mark. They are perfectly round. The eyes were made by using a spent rifle cartridge as a cutting tool. All of his decoys were sealed and then painted. This probably accounts for the relatively good condition of his surviving decoys. Another unique Howell characteristic involves the tie line method that he employed, which might be referred to as a "modified loop."

He preferred making his decoys from Ponderosa pine — once it is cured, Ponderosa pine does not shrink or swell.

Mr. Howell would travel Minnesota state-wide, taking orders. Then he would carve and deliver them in time for the spearing season.

He carved only 36 decoys with glass eyes. There are several one-of-a-kind decoys made by Howell. He also made two prototype metal decoys, both were sunfish. Mr. Howell fabricated these when he thought of attempting to compete with the plastic models that were being produced.

*Thanks is extended to Ron Adamson for some of the material used in the Howell biography. See also, Donna Tonelli, "One of Minnesota's Finest LeRoy Howell," *Decoy Magazine,* November/December 1990, pp. 32-34.

ANDREW HUSE*

Andrew Huse was born north of Oslo, Norway on June 30, 1891 and died December 1, 1973. He came to the United States when he was about 17 years old. Prior to his arrival, Andrew Huse had already developed some skills with blacksmithing. One of his earliest jobs was in the logging camps around Bemidji, Minnesota. In 1917, he served in World War I and was in command of a company responsible for shoeing horses. After his return from the War, he moved to Minneapolis, but later went to Henriette, Minnesota, when he began blacksmithing as a business. Because of the depression, in 1929 he again relocated, this time to McGregor, Minnesota, where he began his own blacksmith business. Mr. Huse remained in McGregor until his death.

His surviving decoys date from the 1940's. He made copper, brass and wooden decoys. For the metal ones, he used taxidermist eyes or imitation pearls. Andrew would also forge spears. His interest in spearing was more than just monetary as he could often be found in winter on Lake Minnewawa north of McGregor spear fishing.

*Information courtesy of Ed Huse.

STEVE JARNOT*

Steve Jarnot was born in 1904 in Holdingford, Minnesota. In his younger days he worked in factories. Later, he opened a blacksmith's shop in Annandale, Minnesota. In 1955, he moved to Brainerd, Minnesota where he maintained a blacksmith shop on a hobby farm of about 80 acres. Mr. Jarnot made spears and ice chisels.

He began making decoys shortly after coming to Brainerd. Jarnot made two sizes of sunfish and a northern pike decoy. Most of these were left unpainted, but were varnished. The decoy fins were, however, decorated with painted red lines. Decoys were made in the winter, and he probably made hundreds of them. Steve enjoyed spearing on Bay Lake near Brainerd. He stopped making decoys in 1985 when he became ill. Mr. Jarnot died in 1991.

*Information supplied by Gertrude Jarnot, his wife.

R. EDWARD JOHNSON

R. Edward Johnson was born in 1918 in Crosby, Minnesota, where he lived all of his life. He started as a blacksmith's apprentice at the age of 17 and remained in that occupation until he retired.

Mr. Johnson made spears and ice chisels as well as fishing decoys. His decoys were constructed of pine. All of them were made in the early 1940's. An avid spear fisherman, his favorite spearing lakes were Big Rabbit, Clinker, and Serpent. His painting style was plain, preferring two colors, green and gold.

*Information supplied by Mr. Johnson.

LESTER JOHNSON*

Dr. Lester Johnson was born on October 5, 1900 in Lakefield, Minnesota. He resided there until he was 17. His father was a farmer, but desiring that his five children become university educated, he sold the farm and purchased a boarding-house in Sherburne, Minnesota.

Lester wanted to become a dentist and enrolled at the University of Minnesota in Minneapolis. After graduation, because of the depression and difficulties in building a practice, Dr. Johnson performed dental work in Dunnel and Thailand for several years. He returned to Sherburne to begin his practice in the mid-1930's. His practice continued for at least 40 years.

Dr. Johnson was married and had two sons—one became a dentist and currently resides in Shelby, Montanta; the other studied to be an attorney and currently practices in Sherburne, Minnesota.

During the late 1930's, Lester's brother-in-law (and an avid fisherman), Frank Bettenhausen, taught Dr. Johnson and one of his sons, Robert, how to make spear fishing decoys. Robert was only seven or eight years old when he assisted his father and "uncle" Frank. They could make about ten decoys between the three of them. Most of these decoys were red and white painted and had tin fins and tails. They continued making decoys together until about 1948. Artistically, the decoys left much to be desired, but they were apparently popular and easily sold. Despite the work making decoys, Dr. Johnson only speared once a year in the Whitefish Chain of Lakes in Minnesota.

Sometime between 1943 and 1946, Dr. Johnson made several decoys for recreational purposes. He took great care and effort in producing these decoys. According to his son Robert, Dr. Johnson made two perch, a crappie, a bass and a bluegill. Nevertheless, there are five known [hobby] fish that were made by Dr. Johnson—three trout, a perch, and a sunfish. All of these decoys were carefully painted and lead weighted. They were constructed from balsam or cedar and had tin fins and wooden tails. However, it is unlikely that the decoys ever saw water because they sat in a medical doctor's office [which was part of the family home in Sherburne] until they were sold at auction in 1990.

Dr. Lester Johnson died on October 27, 1977.

*Information courtesy of Robert Johnson.

SHELDON IVER JOHNSON*

Sheldon Johnson was born on July 9, 1935 in Duluth, Minnesota. He is married and has four children—two of whom are natural and two adopted. Mr. Johnson also has three grandchildren.

He holds a degree in education from the University of Minnesota-Duluth. After he graduated, Sheldon Johnson taught art education for seven years at Woodland Junior High School. He was then appointed to the post of Supervisor of Art Education for the entire Duluth School District and stayed in that post for 15 years. Mr. Johnson retired in June of 1990, following an eight year stint in the classroom.

His interest in spear fishing came about because his father spear fished. However, it was not until the 1950's that he began making fish decoys on a commercial basis. Able to complete about two dozen decoys in an evening, Sheldon Johnson sold his decoys for 75¢ to bait stores around Duluth. He stopped selling his decoys in the late 1960's, although he still makes them for friends.

Mr. Johnson made two types of fishing tackle: (1) the jig plane, a lure designed mainly for taking lake trout; and (2) his spear fishing decoys. The preferred material for his decoys was local cedar. Metal for the fins came mainly from gas station cans and he only used enamel for the paint. His earliest decoys were sunfish with wooden tails and metal fins. These early decoys bear no resemblance to his later works. He abandoned the sunfish decoys because they were too time consuming to construct.

Mr. Johnson came upon the design for his decoys through experimentation. Once he decided upon the pattern, he went to work producing decoys in quantity. Nevertheless, over the years, there were subtle changes. His earlier decoys had a straighter slope to the head of the fish, while the later ones have a much more pronounced slope. In addition, Mr. Johnson used a flat metal for the fins on his earlier fish, but used rippled metal for the fins on his most recent decoys. His earlier fish were hand painted and he would use glitter as a decoration. The more recent ones were spray painted with an atomizer.

Sheldon's decoy color schemes included paint combinations of: red and white; black and white; dark green and light green; orange and black; and some red and white "barber pole" design. His most recent fish were sometimes painted with phosphorescent paint.

It would be easy to mistake Mr. Johnson's fish decoys for those attributed to Frank Mizera of Ely, Minnesota (see this chapter), particularly when one views just the head of the decoy. Like Johnson, Mizera's earlier decoys had a sharply angled head which became more elongated and sloped over time. The painting of the respective decoys' heads is identical. Also, a comparison of the tails on the Mizera and Johnson decoys show a remarkable similarity. Of course, both used wooded tails and both are virtually identical in shape — not to mention the painted striping design. The main distinguishing characteristic between the two carvers is the shape of the pectoral fins on their decoys (see Figure 1 below).

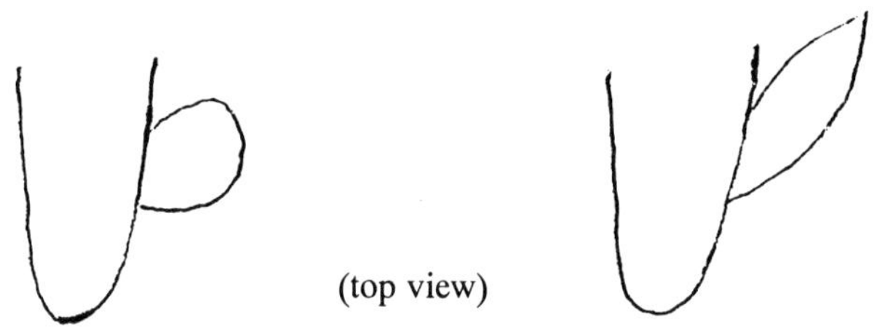

S. Johnson **Mizera**

Comparison in pectoral fin shapes in Mizera and Johnson decoys

Mr. Johnson enjoys spear fishing in the lakes around Duluth and prefers spearing just beyond a weed bed in eight to nine feet of water. He believes that red and white decoys were most attractive in clear water, while low contrast decoys (black and orange) were more effective in murkier waters.

ALBERT JOKELA*

Albert Jokela was born August 5, 1913 in Osage Minnesota. He currently resides in Hibbing, Minnesota. As a young man, Mr. Jokela worked on the family farm and did some logging. Subsequently, he moved to Montana and was employed in the copper mines in Butte and also worked on a ranch. In 1950, he began working for Arrowhead Steel in Duluth, Minnesota as an iron worker and remained there for 35 years.

Mr. Jokela started making decoys at the age of 12 or 13. He used whatever wood was available for the decoys' bodies, such as jack pine, poplar, white oak, spruce, basswood, and even apple boxes. His decoys show a high degree of craftsmanship and artistic accomplishment. Among others, he has made northern pike, smelt, bass, perch, sunfish, and rainbow trout. His painting is realistic and careful. Decoy bodies are sanded and polished.

Mr. Jokela is married and has one grown daughter. He has speared on Big Sturgeon, Swan and Deer Lakes.

*Information from an interview with Mr. Jokela. His name was erroneously spelled as "Jokala" by the Kimballs, op. cit.

VINCE S. KAMPMANN*

Vince Kampmann was born on April 7, 1909 in Dubuque, Iowa. When he was eight years old, Vince's family moved to Brainerd, Minnesota, where he has lived ever since. After completing high school, he began working in his father's millwork, sash and door business. Vince remained with the company until he and his brother sold the business some years ago.

All of his decoys were made in the early 1920's from white pine that came from the mill. He made the decoys for his use only. The lead cavities of his decoys were cut out on an angle so that the lead would stay in place (see Chapter 3). Vince related that he melted his lead in a Prince Albert can and heated it with sterno. His decoys show a marked preference for red and white painting, but with a diversity of fin shapes. Kampmann's painting demonstrates a great attention for detail in that he meticulously painted dots, bars or wavy lines on most of them. Vince's favorite lakes to spear were Cross, Pelican and Gull, all in the Brainerd area.

Mr. Kampmann passed away in 1995.

*Information from an interview with Mr. Kampmann.

EMIL KECK

Emil Carl Keck was born on June 11, 1900 in Alexandria, Minnesota. His parents came to the United States from Germany in 1882 and settled on what is now known as "Keck's Point" on Lake Carlos. Eventually they divided their time between farming this land and their home in Alexandria.

Emil was in the meat market business for a number of years in Garfield, Alexandria and in North Dakota. He was employed at the Alexandria Light and Power Company for 22 years until his retirement in 1965. An active member of Zion Lutheran Church, Emil Keck was a member of the Zion Men's Club. He was also a member of the Gem and Mineral Club. During World War II, Emil was a member of the Minnesota State Guard. He was well known for his long time interest in collecting Indian relics and cutting and polishing gem stones. Mr. Keck was married and had three daughters and one son. He passed away on January 7, 1986.

Mr. Keck was also a spear fisherman who made decoys for himself and for sale. He made one standard style of decoy—a minnow with two pectoral fins on each side and a metal tail. For paint, he showed a marked preference for green, but some of his decoys were painted red and white. Many of his decoys were made with a full face, but for others he would carve only a cavity in the face area (see pictures).

JOHN L. KENT*

John L. Kent was born on July 14, 1897 in Rudd, Iowa. He was a farmer and also worked on the railroad in his earlier days. In the 1930's, he resided in the Isle, Minnesota area. In Isle, John Kent began making decoys for his own use. Only one of his decoys has survived, a floater in the form of a northern pike (pictured). Mr. Kent stopped making decoys in the 1950's.

He was married and had ten children. He died in 1961.

*Information supplied by John Banholzer.

EARL H. KIELMEYER

Earl Kielmeyer was born on November 24, 1902. He resided in Fairbault, Minnesota and was employed as a police officer for the City of Fairbault. Mr. Kielmeyer was married. He died on September 29, 1984.

A prolific carver, Mr. Kielmeyer produced literally thousands of spear fishing decoys in his life-time. Although he made decoys of various sizes and shapes, his decoys are most identifiable by the shape of the tail fin (see picture). Many, if not most, of his decoys had the shape of a sucker. His preferred color combination was red and white, but he painted many decoys in other colors and even produced many wild, decorative patterns. Two more subdued and almost realistically painted decoys are shown. He also produced some decoys that, while unpainted, were varnished.

RUSSELL C. KOLB*

Russell C. Kolb was born November 17, 1905 in Hillsboro, Wisconsin. He lived there until he was 16 years old. He left Hillsboro to go to Milwaukee, working in a hotel. Russell later returned to Hillsboro to begin work at the family restaurant. Civil engineers would sometimes eat there and they invited Russell to join them. He proceeded to work with them for an entire summer, mapping and surveying Vernon County, Wisconsin. His fondness for the work led him eventually to apply for and obtain a full time job with the Corps of Engineers. One of his first jobs involved dredging channels, but in 1940 he was placed in charge of the Big Sandy Lake Dam in Minnesota. He remained in the position until his retirement in 1970.

It was only after his transfer to Big Sandy Lake in 1940 that Russell began spear fishing. All of his fishing decoys were cut from heavy gauge (about 1/4 inch) copper bar stock. An example is pictured.

*Information supplied in an interview with Mr. Kolb.

NICK KNAUS*

Nick Knaus lived in Cold Spring, Minnesota and was the actual carver of the fish decoys erroneously attributed to Joe Rausch. Nick was a barber for many years and carved from at least the 1940's to the 1970's. He made about 100 decoys per year during a peak period of approximately 15 years in the 1950's and 1960's. Most were sold at Svihel's Hardware in Cold Spring with lesser numbers sold at other local hardware and sporting goods stores. A number were also sold at Hohnen's Resort, located somewhere in northern Minnesota (this resort was remembered by Nick's widow, although she could not recall the exact location).

Nick was born in 1903 and passed away in 1980.

Nick's decoys are distinctive for their dramatically sloping noses and sharply pointed tail fins. He used a variety of line tie methods. Also, he used two or four pectoral fins.

*Information supplied by Bill Stoetzel, based on information supplied by Mrs. Knaus and Joe Svihel, owner of Svihel's Hardware.

CLARENCE KOEHLER*

Clarence Koehler was born on February 7, 1921. His father owned and operated a resort on Big Pine Lake for over 20 years. Clarence took over the operation of the resort in the 1940's. He ran it for 41 years, retiring in 1989.

Clarence speared on Big Pine Lake and made decoys for his own use. His best known decoys are the spectacular sunfishes that he made.

Upon retirement, Mr. Koehler moved to New York Mills, Minnesota.

*Information from an interview with Mr. Koehler.

LAMBERT KOLODJI*

Lambert Kolodji was born in 1926 in Chisholm, Minnesota and has been a resident of that city all of his life. He worked for the National Steel Company for 22 years and retired in 1988. Mr. Kolodji is married and has four grown children, three boys and a girl.

An avid spear fisherman for a time, Lambert preferred spearing on Pelican Lake. He began making decoys for his own use in 1955 or 1956 and made six to eight decoys each year. Lambert stopped making decoys in 1959. He states that his decoys produced a fast action in the water. Judging by their torpedo-like shape, it is easy to imagine why this was true. His decoys are distinctive for their humped backs, carved mouths and their aforementioned torpedo-like shape.

*Information supplied by Mr. Kolodji.

TOIVO "DAVE" LAHTI*

Toivo Lahti, or Dave — as he was known to his friends, was one of eight children born to Finnish immigrants in the Virginia, Minnesota area. Born in 1905, Dave was stricken with the crippling disease of rheumatoid arthritis while still in his early twenties. This affliction had an effect on Dave for the rest of his life. It prevented him from handling the usual occupations at that time for men of his age—lumbering or mining.

Lahti was unable to lift his arms above his waist and had to fashion devices to assist in his movements and care. As the progressive nature of his illness forced further handicaps upon him, affecting one of his legs, his doctors gave no hope of any rehabilitation. Instead of accepting the advice of his doctor, he decided to make a pulley device to straighten his leg. His strength and fortitude won out over the disease. In less than a year, Dave Lahti was able to hunt with his friends. This courage and commitment was the key to helping Dave regain limited movement in all his limbs, and was also instrumental in his becoming as productive as possible.

Not being able to perform rigorous physical labor, Dave Lahti began woodworking with small items. At the request of friends and relatives, he made some spearing decoys which worked quite well. This became the avenue through which he could support himself in the 1940's and 1950's. Although jointed decoys were sometimes made by other carvers of the period, Dave improved on the design by using a movement limiter—a flexible, springy piece of metal spanning the joint between the two decoy sections.

This limiter allowed the tail section to move relative to the body when the decoy was worked, but then it returned to an in-line position.

There were two types of limiters on Dave Lahti's decoys:

1. a metal strap firmly imbedded in the top of the body section, passing back through a screw eye in the tail section; and
2. a small diameter wire, one end inserted into the back of the body section, the other into a hole in the front of the tail section (this is a difficult feature to see).

A third type of joint was also made on Lahti's decoys—featuring two sections joined by a piece of rubber. It is probable that this rubber hinge preceded the metal hinge on Lahti's decoys.

In general, the shape of Dave Lahti's decoys approximate the northern pike, measuring 8 inches to 9 inches in length. They are thin-bodied, having been carved from apple crate ends. The body of the decoys are carved in behind the head to simulate the gill covers and their construction features a wood tail and four metal fins of distinctive shape. The colors of Lahti decoys found to date are:

1. red head;
2. red top, white belly with black and yellow dashes for lateral lines;
3. black top, white belly, yellow tail with red and yellow dashes for lateral lines; and
4. orange top, white belly with black and yellow dashes for lateral lines.

The shading of the solid colored top to the white belly is accomplished by small dots of a dark color. The metal fins of Lahti decoys are white or yellow with red and/or black striping. The eyes of his decoys are either painted or are nickel-plated, high domed tacks with black painted pupils.

In addition to decoys, Dave Lahti made metal spoons and wood plugs for his own use and for friends and relatives. He is also reported to have carved plaques and made cranberry pickers that attached to the picker's legs.

Dave Lahti was able, in large part, to successfully overcome his arthritis, but he lost a battle to cancer in 1962 at the age of 57. The number of decoys carved by Dave Lahti is unknown, but probably is in the area of several hundred.

*Information from "Minnesota Style: The Decoys of Dave Lahti," by William Stoetzel, *The NFLCC Gazette,* Vol. 12, No. 39, December 1988, p. 10.

LEONARD E. LAPLANTE

Leonard LaPlante was born on March 9, 1912 in White Bear Lake Minnesota. He lived most of his life in Cohasset, Minnesota near Grand Rapids. Mr. LaPlante was engaged in construction as a mason. He served in World War II and was married. Mr. LaPlante passed away on March 15, 1992.

He produced a number of decoys for his own use. These are distinguishable because of the almost wild paint jobs (see picture).

GUS LARSON*

Gus Larson was born in 1898 in Sweden. He was 16 or 17 years old when his family came to the United States. Mr. Larson worked as a plasterer in Crosby, Minnesota. He passed away in 1974.

In the 1920's, he became interested in spear fishing and made decoys for his own use. His decoys had glass eyes and a single pectoral fin on each side.

*Information supplied by Mr. Mooers, who was the son-in-law of Gus Larson.

LOUIE LEACH*

Louie Leach was born in Atwater, Illinois on July 30, 1905. As a small boy, he moved to Heron Lake, Minnesota with his family. Heron Lake, at that time, was known for its abundance of ducks and geese. At an early age, Louie became interested in hunting and fishing.

He moved to the Fairmont, Minnesota area and worked for the Fairmont Canning Company most of his life. During the winter months, Louis and his friends would spend time ice fishing on the local lakes. Occasionally they would decide to take a trip to northern Minnesota for spearing.

Subsequently, Louie began making decoys for both himself and his fishing friends. He experimented with various sizes, shapes and colors. They would then take these decoys along on their trips to northern Minnesota and, almost always, they managed to spear their limit. Other spearers wondered what their "secret" was, and when Louie would show them the decoys, there were usually offers to buy them. These experiences prompted Louie to begin making them for sale. Louie soon discovered he could finance his fishing trips to northern Minnesota by selling his decoys. He began making decoys sometime in 1950 and continued to do so until his death in 1982.

No one knows the actual number of decoys that Mr. Leach made, but his widow estimates that number to be around 2,000. He made his decoys in various sizes ranging from approximately five inches, seven inches, and nine inches, to a few 13 inch or longer models.

The most important feature of the Leach decoy is its lead balancing. When it was suspended and moved in the water by the tie line, it had a natural gliding motion. The predominant colors that Louie used were red and white. While the paint was wet, it was covered with glitter. Some of Louie's early experimental decoys lacked the glitter effect.

A colored or copper tack was used for the eyes, and some of his decoys are stamped with "LL"—his initials.

Leach also made four inch decoys with two hooks attached on the bottom with a screw eye. These, however, are illegal to use for spearing in Minnesota.

*Information supplied by Ron Dickenson, an old friend of the Leach family.

FRED MAX LEXOW*

Fred Lexow was born October 15, 1888 in Shakopee, Minnesota. His parents had come to the United States from Germany. Subsequently, Fred moved to the Bovey, Minnesota area. He worked for the mines for awhile as a timekeeper. Later, Lexow and his wife, Ida, purchased a sweet shop in Bovey which they operated for a number of years. After his wife died, Fred sold the sweet shop and became something of a recluse, living in a cabin by Balsam Lake, outside of Bovey.

Although he had begun making decoys at an early age, Lexow turned his attention to making decoys for resale after selling his sweet shop. He would make three or four decoys and, reportedly, would make a pilgrimage to town to sell them and then engage in a drinking spree. After his money was gone, he would return to his cabin and the process was repeated. Despite his life-style, Lexow did not pass away until September 6, 1971.

His decoys imitated northerns, trout, bullhead, bass, suckers, etc. One of the characteristics of his decoys is the use of taxidermy glass eyes. He also used either a single or double loop method for his line tie attachment. Decoys normally had two sheet metal pectoral fins, plus a dorsal and anal fin. Usually, Lexow painted these fins in a bright red color with orange "sun rays." Often, this paint is missing (i.e., chipped) from his surviving decoys.

Another Lexow characteristic was the distinctive shape of the metal tail fins that he made (see pictures). He sometimes, however, used a metal spinner for a tail.

Lexow made two types of body shapes for his decoys. One was almost square in form, but the other was rounded and more graceful. It is not known whether these body shapes were made contemporaneously, or if one shape represents an earlier style. The squared form has been referred to as Lexow's "commercial" decoy because he reportedly was offered financial backing to produce decoys on a large scale basis.[8] This enterprise did not seem to develop to any great degree as there are many more surviving rounded-shaped decoys than those with a square shape.

The Lexow painting style is distinctive. He frequently utilized a dark green upper body paint, a light blue-green paint in the middle of his fish, and a silver under belly. However, his trout was often much brighter by comparison, with a yellow body color and colorful use of dot decoration. Other paint combinations were less frequently used.

Mr. Lexow carved duck decoys, painted pictures in different colored inks, and made lures.

*See also Donna Tonelli, "Fred Lexow: One of Minnesota's Fine Folk Artists," *Decoy Magazine,* July/August 1989, pp. 32-35.

NORMAN LIEN*

Norman Lien was born in 1927 in Downer, Minnesota. He currently resides in Sabin, Minnesota. A veteran of World War II, he recently retired from an excavating business that he owned. Mr. Lien is married and has 7 children, all of whom are grown.

He is an avid spear fisherman who began making spear fishing decoys following his return from the service (in about 1947). Over the years he has made approximately 1,000 decoys. His preferred wood is pine because it is easy to work. Often his decoys are painted silver on the body with a black back. The eyes of his decoys are black, with a yellow circle around each iris. He fashioned some of his decoys with rubber tails. The gills are normally carved and painted red.

Mr. Lien still spears on Big McDonald and West McDonald Lakes near his home.

*Information supplied in an interview with Mr. Lien.

EMIL LIERS

Emil Liers was born July 2, 1890 in Clayton, Iowa. He was graduated from the State Normal School (now the University of Wisconsin-LaCrosse) in 1920. Mr. Liers was married and had one daughter. He resided in Homer, Minnesota until his death in 1975.

Liers operated an otter sanctuary near Homer, Minnesota for more than 50 years. He was an ardent naturalist, a professional trapper, and the author of several children's books such as *An Otter's Story, A Beaver's Story,* and *A Black Bear's Story* (for the latter he received the Aurianne Award from the American Library Association in 1964). Mr. Liers also served as a teacher and was the technical advisor to Walt Disney Studios for the film, "Beaver Valley."

He also carved spearing decoys and sold them between LaCrosse, Wisconsin and Winona, Minnesota in the 1920's and 1930's. After his death, his sister recalled that Mr. Liers had carved some frog decoys that were in an old cigar box. The box was warped and the decoys were discolored from dampness. Under the frog decoys, in the bottom of the cigar box, was a folded piece of newspaper containing an ad that stated: "Come to the Dodge Auto Company Garage and listen to the Louis-Schmelling prizefight on the radio."

HARRY LILLIS

Harry Lillis was born in 1900 and resided in Butler, Minnesota. He farmed for a living. It is not known how many decoys he made during his lifetime. However, following his death in 1990, six surviving decoys were displayed in a cafe in Perham. The decoys were then sold by Lillis' granddaughter to a collector.

GUST LIND

Gust Lind was born on March 27, 1887. He came to the Brainerd, Minnesota area as a child and lived there all of his life. Mr. Lind worked for the Northern Pacific Railroad as a machinist for 55 years. He was married to Margie. His date of death was April 26, 1957.

Mr. Lind was apparently a prolific maker of spear fishing decoys, judging from the number of surviving specimens. His decoys are very distinctive and easy to recognize. They have two pectoral fins on each side of the decoy with the back fins placed in a slot at the end of the decoy. His metal tail fin is also very distinctive in shape. Many of his decoys were painted with mottled grey over a white or cream colored body. Occasionally, one finds a realistically painted one, such as the perch pictured in this book.

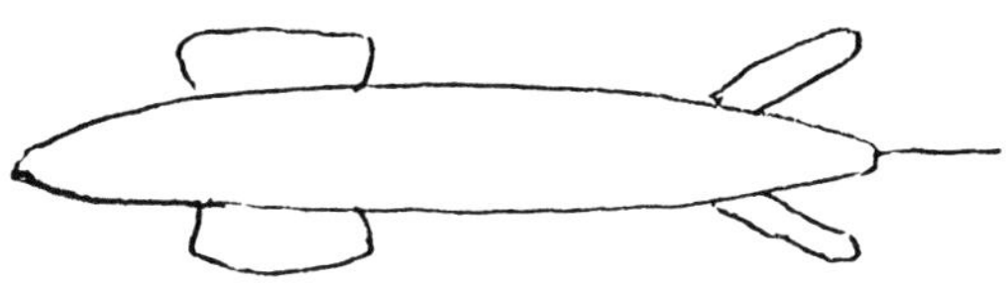

Top View of a Lind Decoy Showing Fin Shapes

EMIL J. LOE*

Emil J. Loe was born on March 2, 1902, in Akeley, Minnesota, and died February 11, 1981. He lived much of his life in Hibbing, Minnesota where he was employed by the Minnesota Division of Land and Minerals, and also worked as a crusher house man in the mines around the Range Cities. Mr. Loe was married and had seven children, five sons and two daughters.

An avid outdoorsman, Emil hunted and fished at any opportunity despite being handicapped — he was blind in one eye, had two hearing aids and a wooden leg. These handicaps did not prevent him from guiding friends to the best fishing and hunting locations. He angled in the summer and spear fished in winter. His favorite lake to spear was Pelican Lake near Orr, Minnesota.

He began constructing decoys in the 1940's for his own use and to sell. His decoys were sold to the V-Store [a sporting goods store in Hibbing] for 50¢ each, as well as to resorts, gas stations, hardware and other sporting goods stores throughout the Range. Sometimes he would barter his decoys for wool trousers or for other items that he needed. Mr. Loe ceased constructing decoys two or three years before his death in 1981. From the 1940's until the end of his period of active decoy making, it is estimated that he fashioned hundreds of decoys.

Mr. Loe's preferred wood for the body of his decoys was balsam as it was easy to carve. His decoys all were made with open mouths. Teeth were frequently painted in the lower part of the mouth. The upper portion of the decoy's mouth protruded beyond the lower part of the open mouth, giving his fish a kind of shark-like appearance. Fins were often cut from aluminum. He used two pectoral fins on each side of the decoy, a dorsal fin and a tail fin. Thumb or other types of tacks were used for eyes, often decorated with a painted iris. His paint designs were pleasing, ranging from plain [e.g., red head and grey body] to rather elaborate dot and/or dash decoration. One surviving example even had detailed scales painted on it [see photo]. Fins were typically painted with stripes. Mr. Loe tested each of the decoys that he sold for proper weighting and balance.

*Information courtesy of Mike Meyers and interviews with Dale Timmerman and Bill Loe, the latter, one of Emil's sons.

CHARLES "CHARLIE" LUNDGREN*

Charlie Lundgren was born on February 3, 1914, in Ironton, Minnesota. He was the youngest in a family of ten children. When he was seven years old he contracted double pneumonia and lived on a farm with an uncle in South Dakota. Charlie returned to Minnesota while in his late teens to care for his ailing mother. At that time, he was employed as a hunting and fishing guide, along with his brother, Bill. It was during this time [1930's] that Charlie began constructing spear fishing decoys. He also was a musician and played guitar with a group.

In 1934, Charlie moved to the Pontiac, Michigan area because he had heard that the Detroit area offered steady employment for a musician. He stated that he played seven nights and two afternoons a week in the city's dance halls, despite the depression. A year after Charlie moved to Pontiac, he married his wife, Loretta. They had four children, 17 grandchildren and eight great-grandchildren.

After dancing was prohibited in Pontiac, Mr. Lundgren went to work on the assembly line at a General Motor's plant in 1940. He later became a pressman at G.M.

and subsequently was employed at Slade's Printing. Charlie also owned his own print shop, which he sold in 1967.

Mr. Lundgren moved back to Minnesota in 1951, but remained there only for a year and a half. The prospect of higher pay caused him to return to Michigan.

Over the years, Charlie estimates that he made about 50-60 spear fishing decoys for his own use. Among others, he constructed a black sucker, perch, crappie, and a shinner. His perch and shinner decoys were painted with a scaled effect. To obtain this effect, he wrapped a wedding veil lightly around the decoy body, and spray-painted over the veil and allowed it to dry for 15-20 seconds to achieve the scaled effect. Charlie preferred using cedar wood for his decoys as it did not burn easily when pouring the molten lead for weighting. By the 1980's, he ceased making decoys and has not resumed this avocation.

Charlie Lundgren is a true Minnesota fish decoy maker because he made a pilgrimage back to Minnesota every year, where he made many of his decoys. When spear fishing in Minnesota, Charlie and his brother, Bill, used spears constructed by their father, a blacksmith in Ironton, Minnesota.

*Information obtained in an interview with Mr. Charles Lundren. See also, "Musician strums fishing tune," by Don Vogel, *The Oakland Press,* Sunday, July 20, 1986, p. E-6.

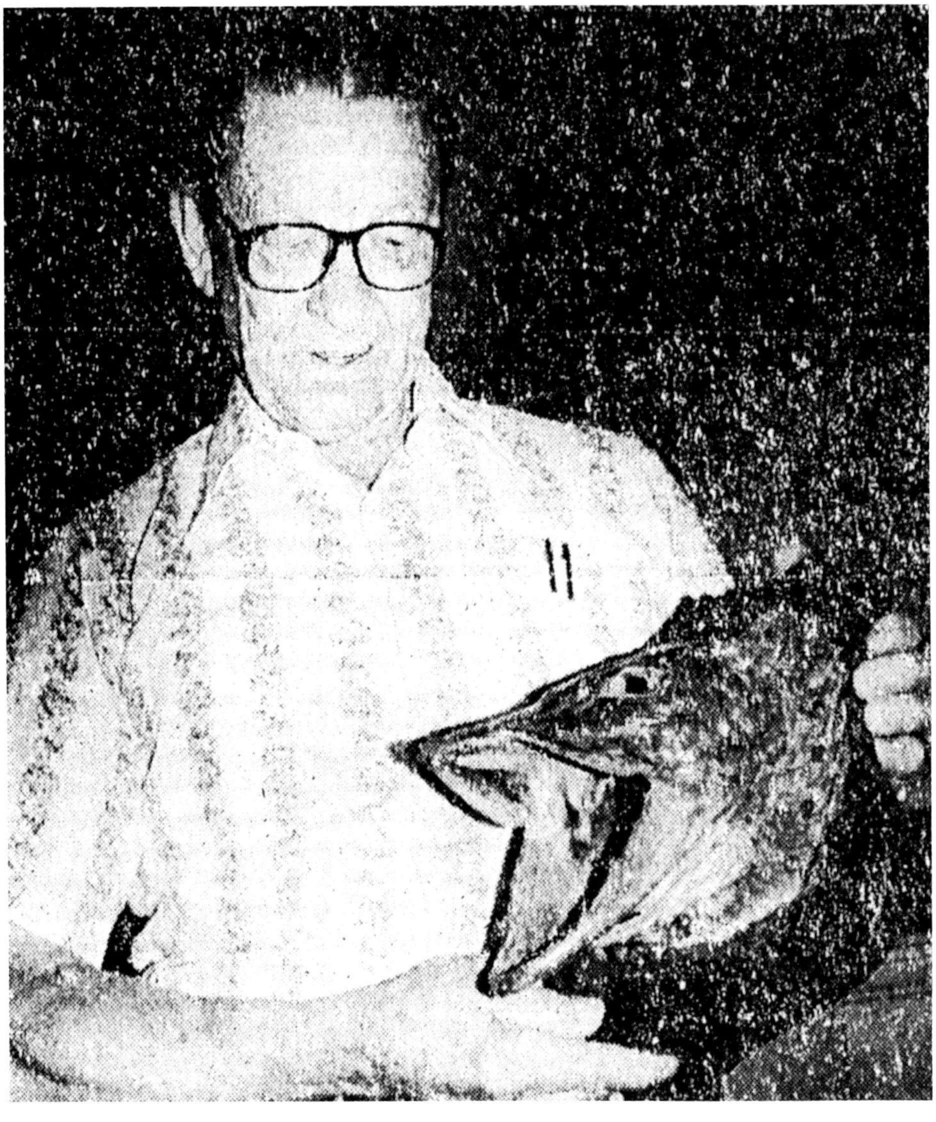

Charlie Lundgren in 1986, holding the head of his largest pike. Photo courtesy Don Vogel.

Unknown Makers (cont.)

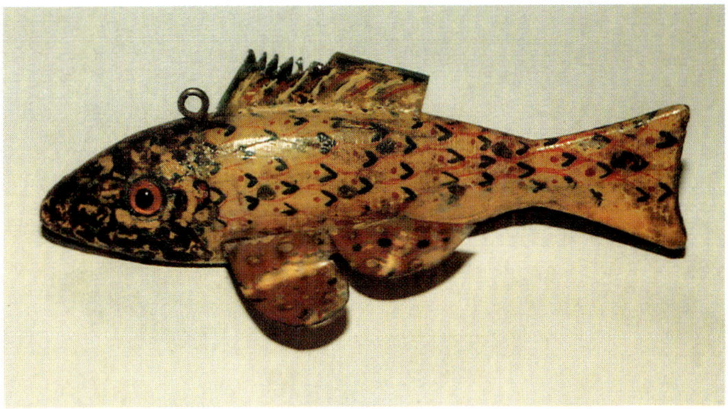

Several of these interesting and well painted decoys have been found in collections. All have the dorsal fin serrated in part and the remainder left straight.

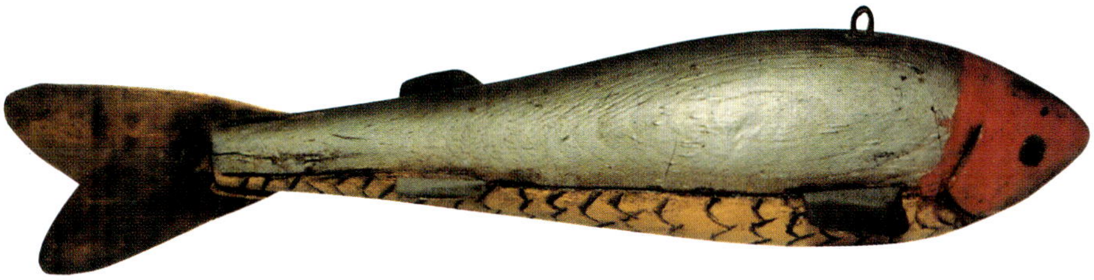

Several of these decoys were found at an auction near Aitken, Minnesota.

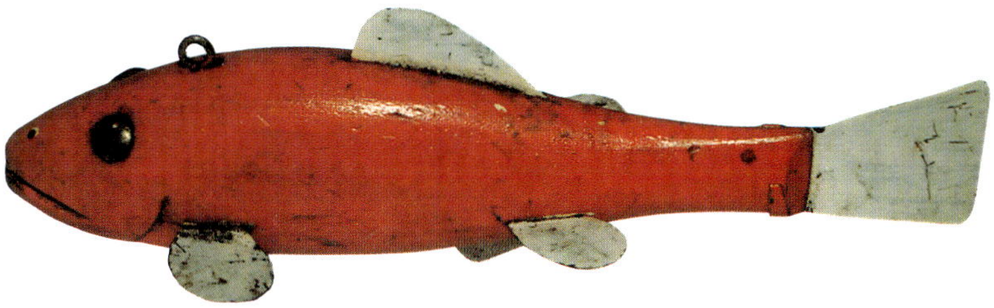

Decoy attributed to "Joe Peterson." No other information is available.

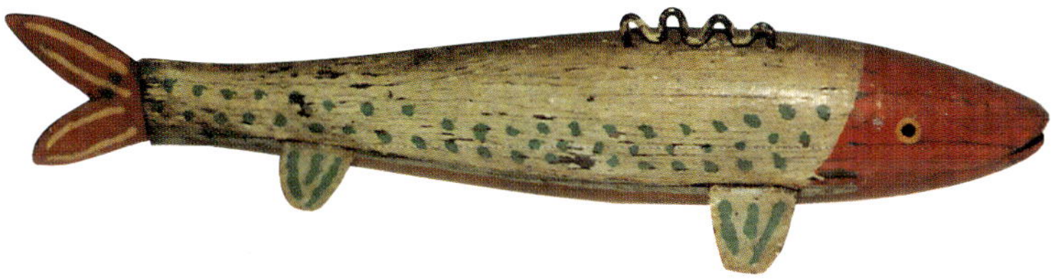

Many of these decoys are found in Minnesota collections.

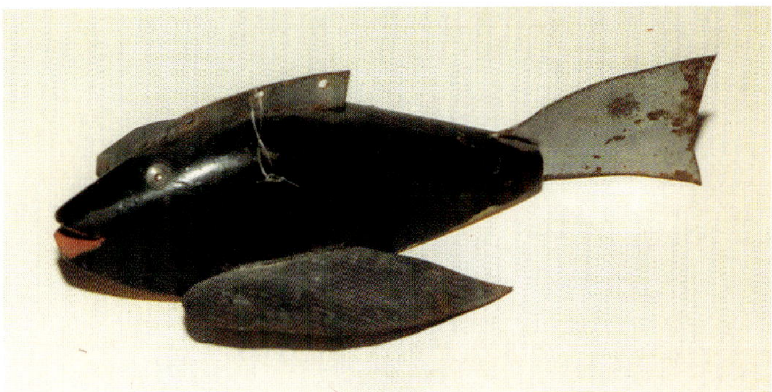

Another bat wing decoy found in numbers in northern Minnesota.

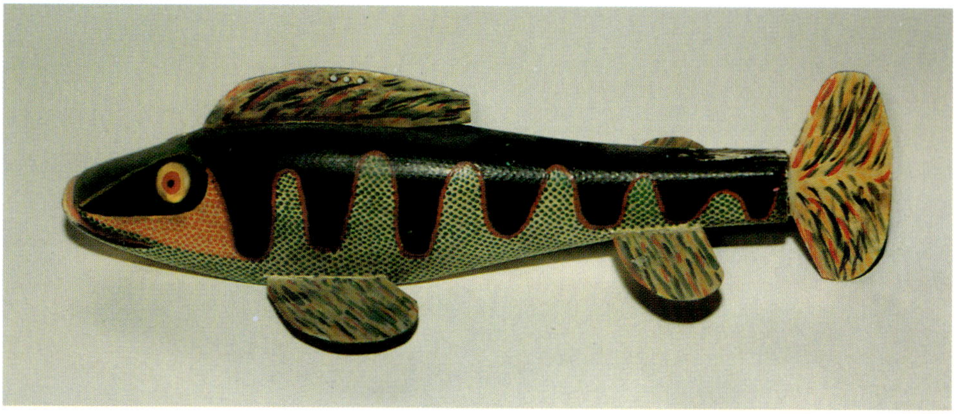

Decoy attributed to "Fred Gibbon" of Sauk Rapids, Minnesota. No such person was found to exist by this name who made decoys.

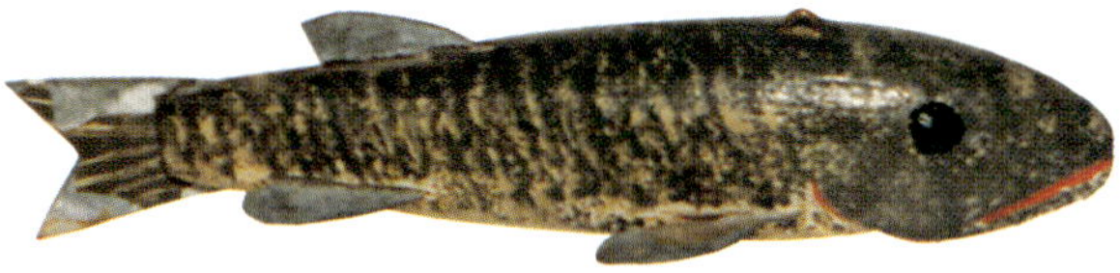

Nice Lexow-like decoy found in the Range Cities area.

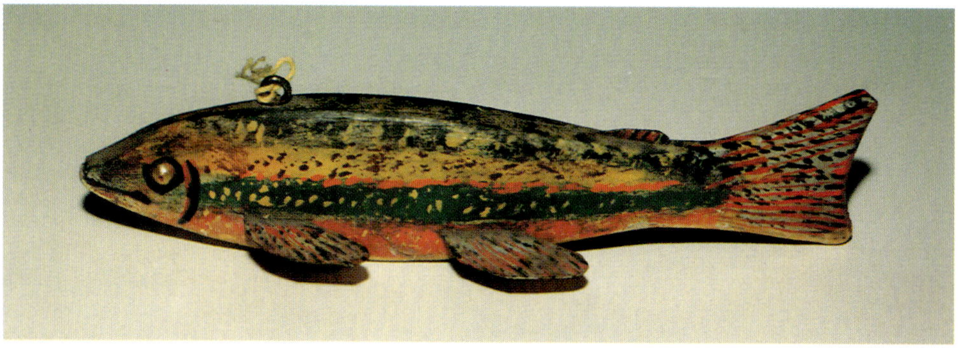

The maker of this decoy also made a companion fish that was painted dark green and had the same shape and size.

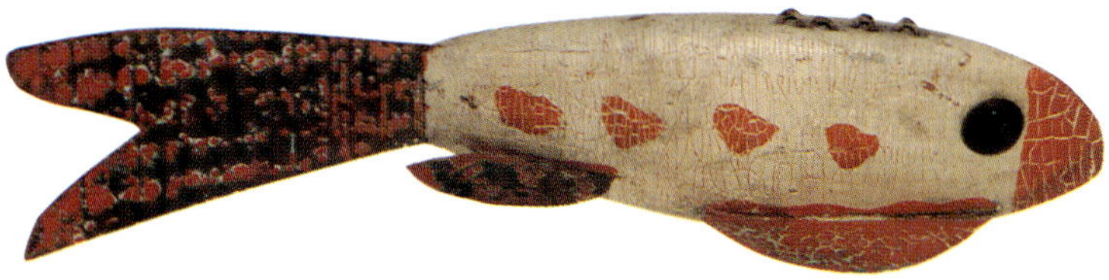

Elongated tail decoy found in some numbers in Minnesota.

Chapter V Photographs

Mel Asserude

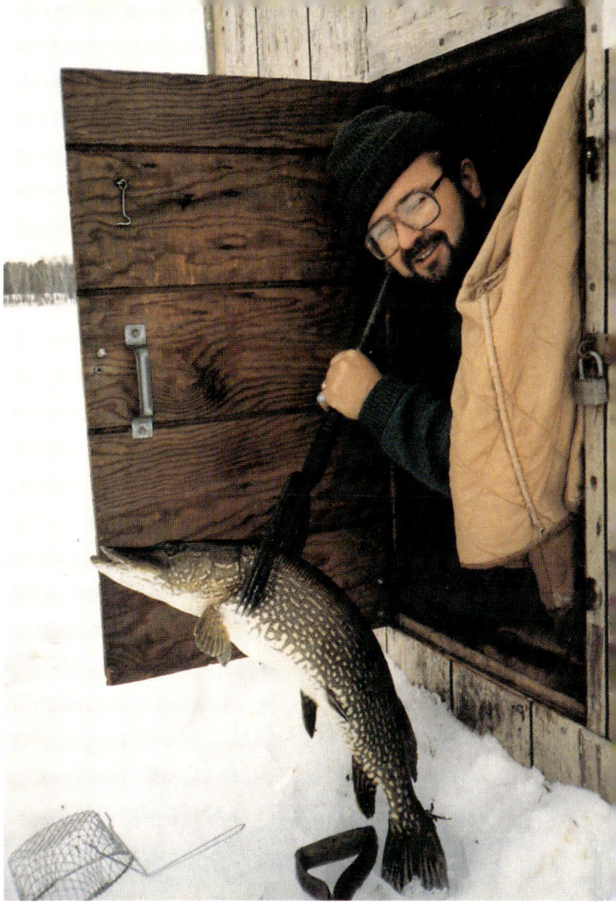

Mel Asserude peering out of his dark house after spearing a nice northern. Photo courtesy of Mel Asserude.

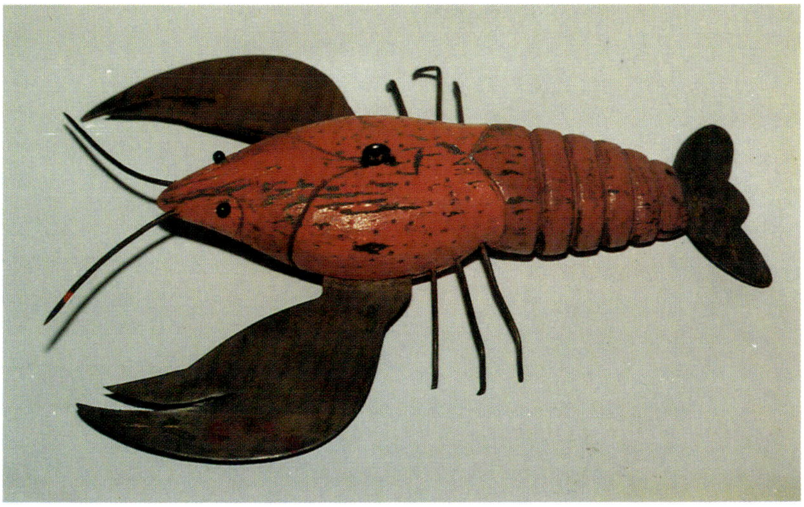

Early Asserude crawdad with copper pincers, tail, and antennae.

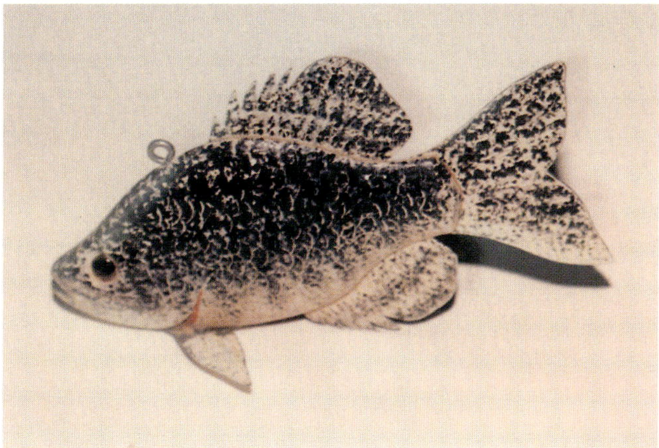

A Mel Asserude crappie. Collection of Carter Stenberg.

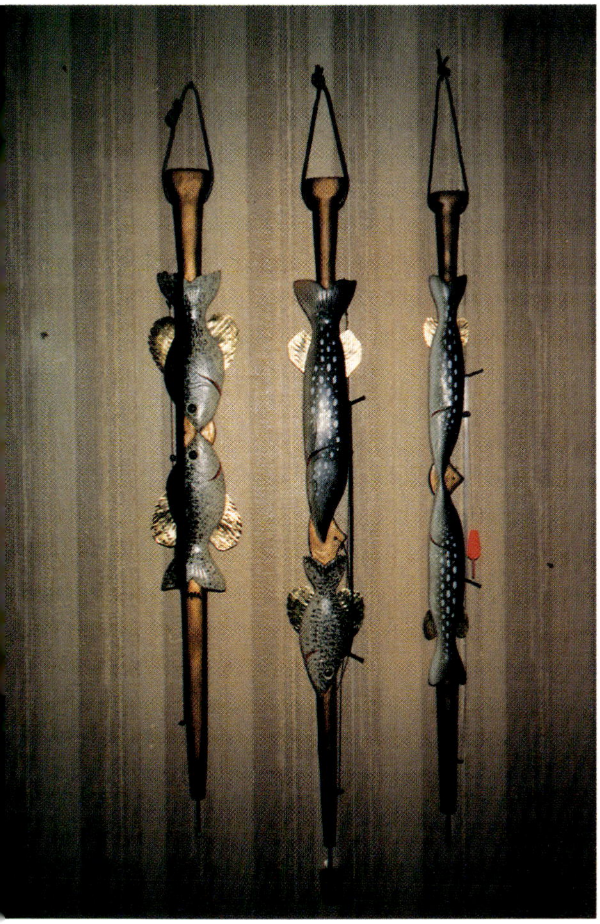

Fishing sticks by Mel Asserude. Photo courtesy of Mel Asserude.

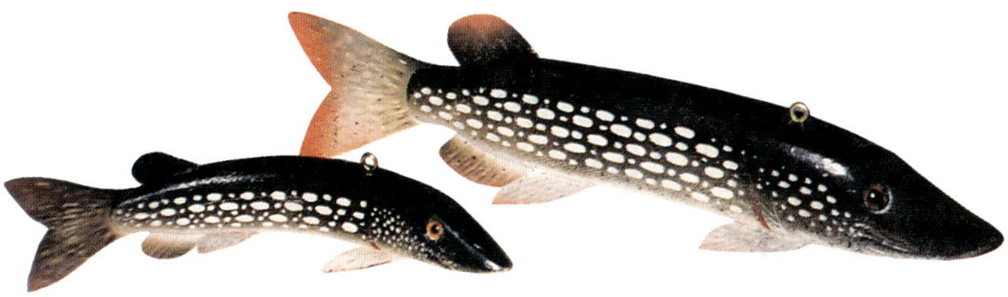

The northern pike has the curved body. Photo by Mel Asserude.

Lawrence Bethel

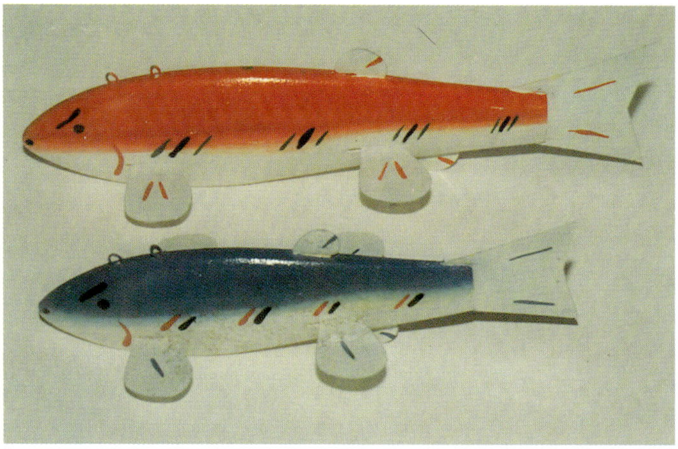

Two Lawrence Bethel decoys, 8 3/4 inches and 7 inches long.

Vern "Bub" Coss

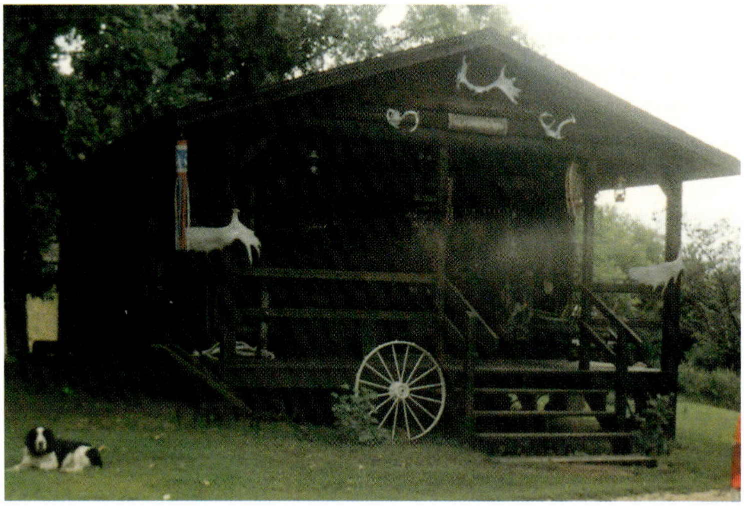

Bub's Gun Store in Spicer, Minnesota.

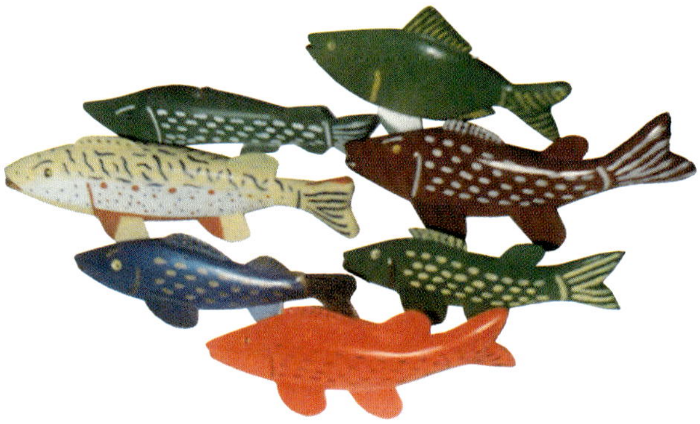

Group of painted Coss decoys.

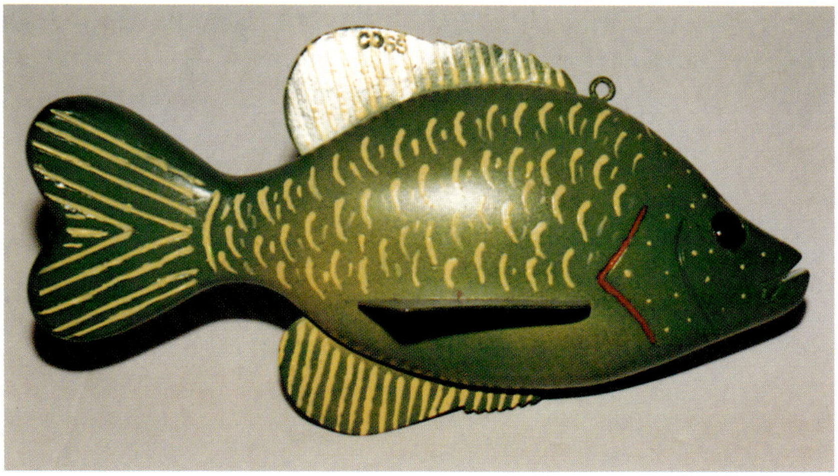

Sunfish, 7 1/2 inches long, by Coss.

Bruce Dixon

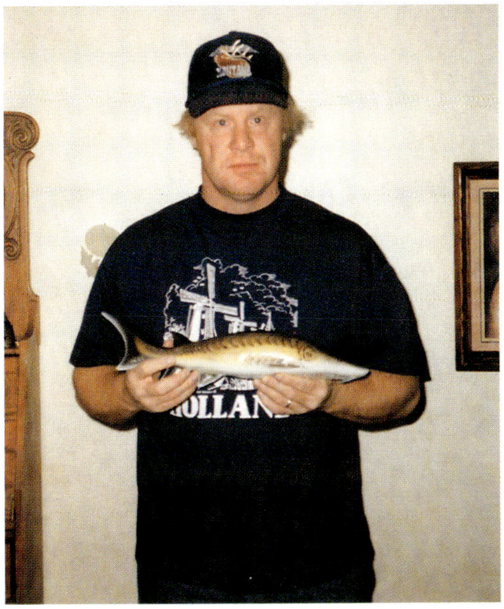

Bruce Dixon holding his sturgeon decoy. Photo courtesy of Bruce Dixon.

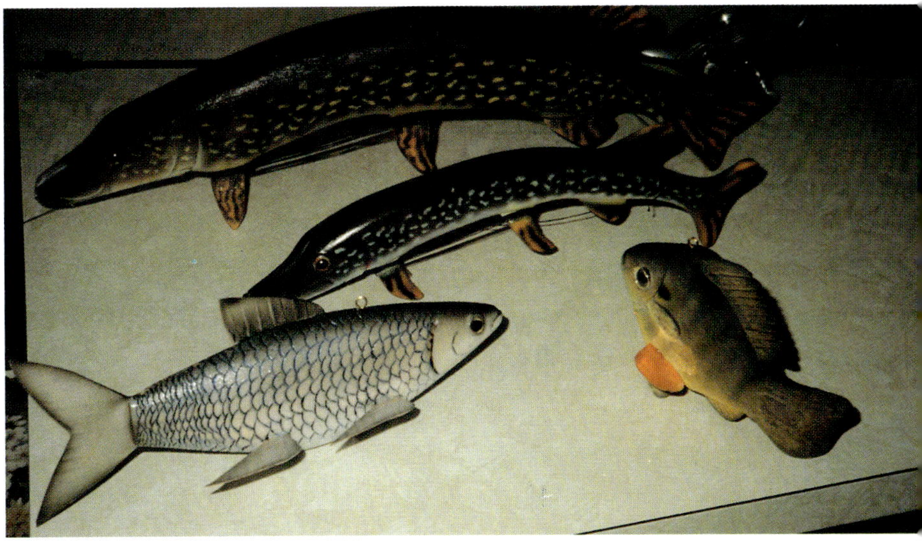

Two sizes of northern pikes, tullipee [also known as a "cisco"] and a sunfish. Photo courtesy Bruce Dixon.

Willard Leroy "King" Henson

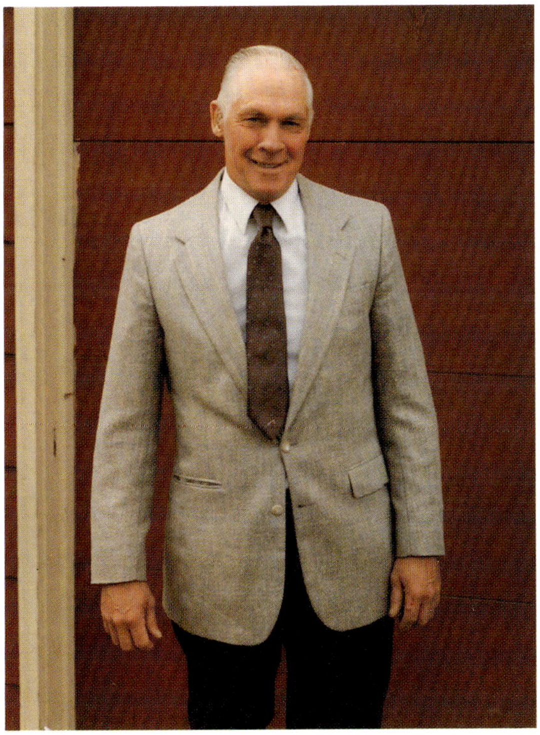

Willard "King" Henson.

Henson sunfish.

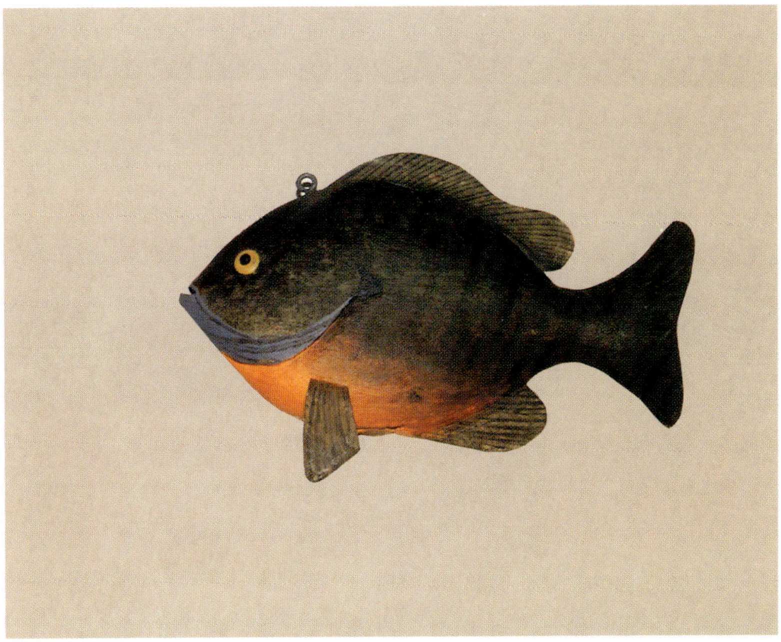

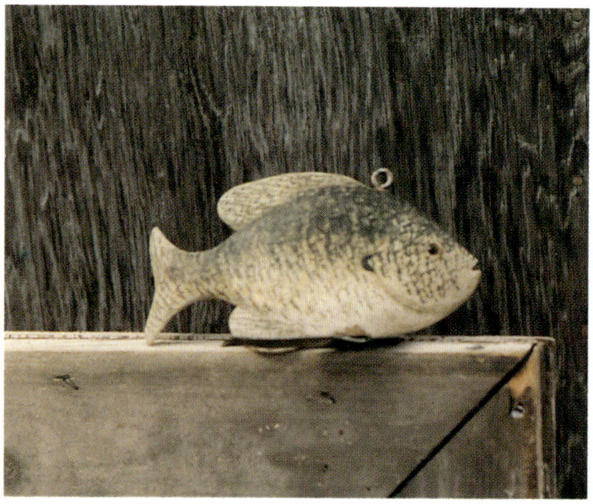

Crappie used for spear fishing by Henson's brother.

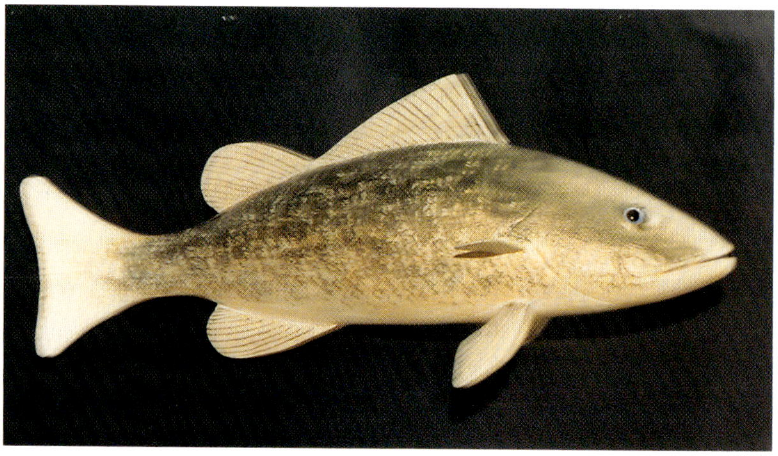

Henson walleye.

Burt Hyatt

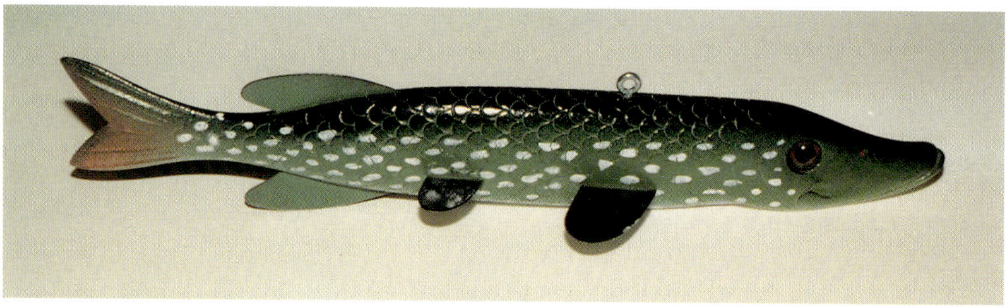

Northern pike by Burt Hyatt, 11 inches long.

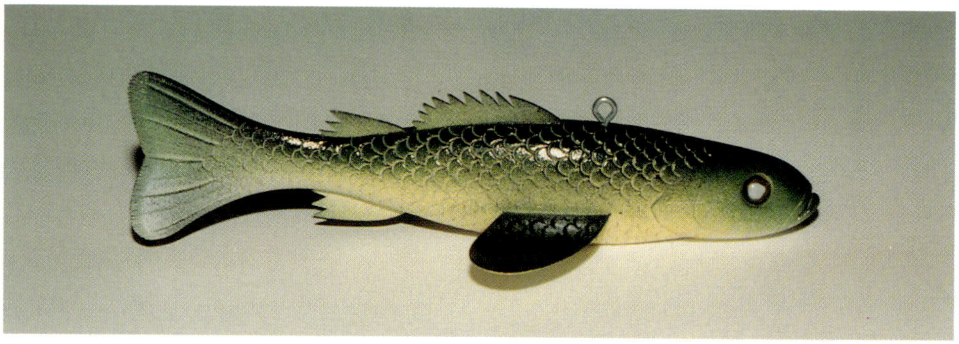

Hyatt walleye pike, 7 1/2 inches long.

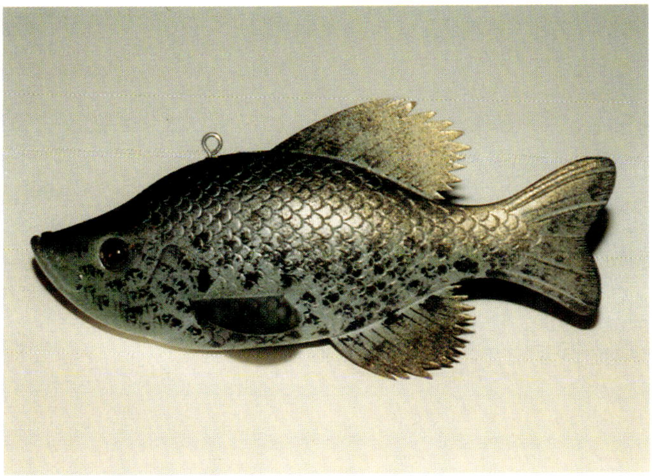

Crappie done by Burt Hyatt, 7 3/4 inches long.

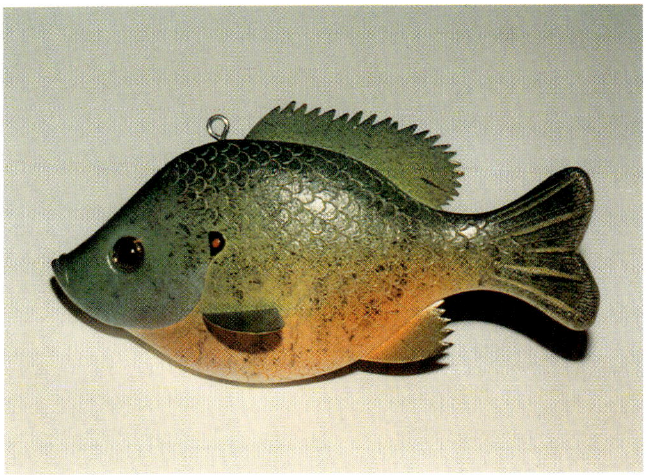

Sunfish made by Mr. Hyatt, 6 1/2 inches in length.

John Jensen

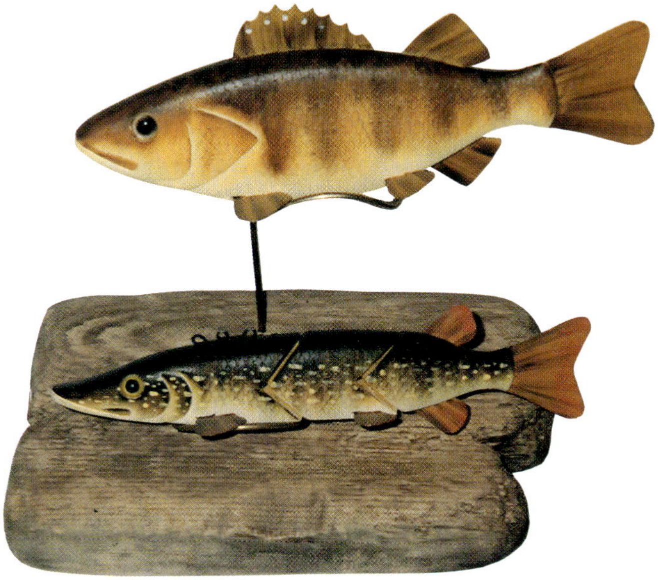

Jensen 9 1/2 inch bass and 9 inch articulated northern pike.

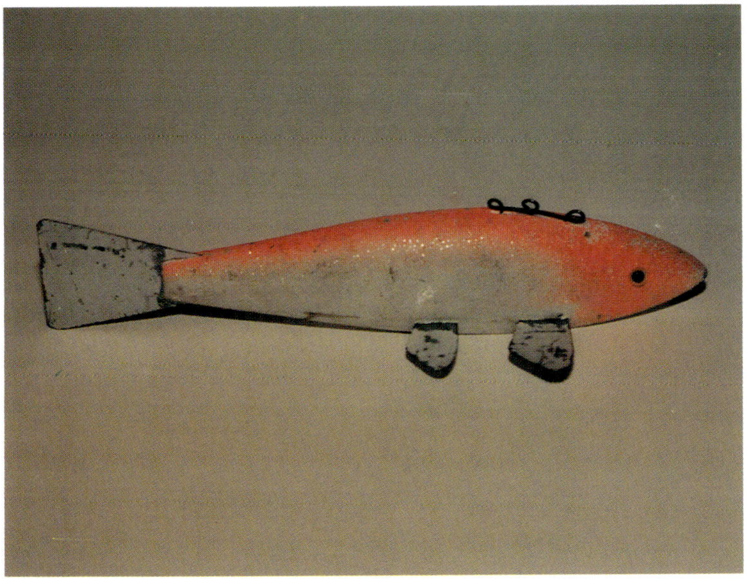

A Jensen working decoy from the 1960's, 8 inches long.

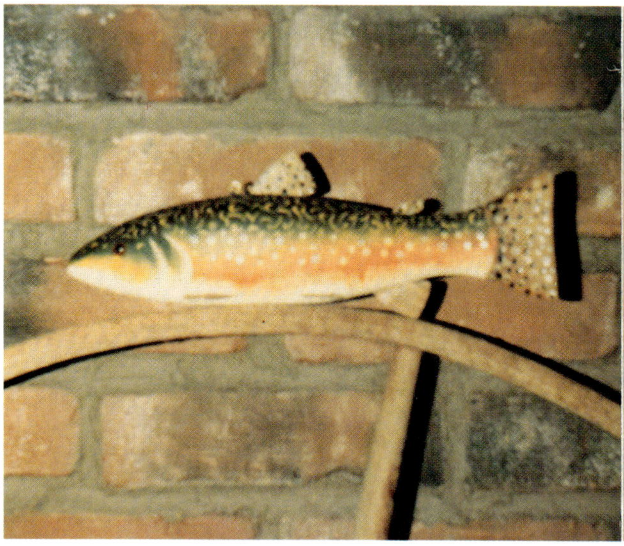

Rainbow trout, 10 1/2 inches in length, by John Jensen.

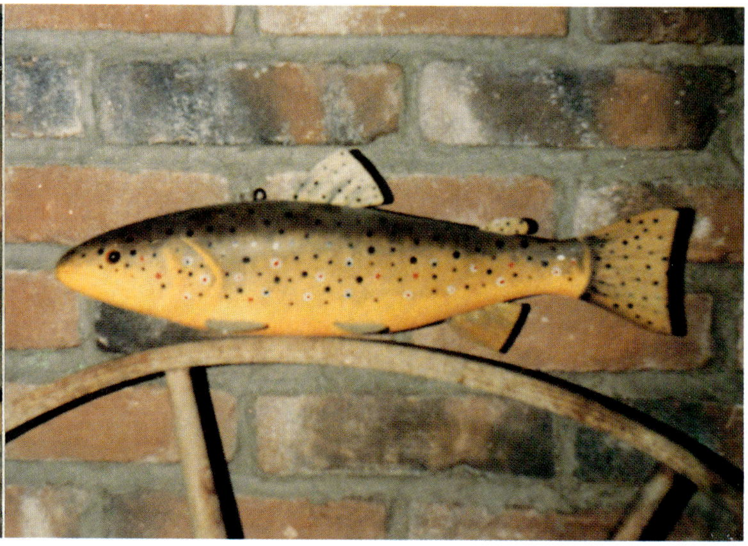

Brown trout, 15 1/2 inches long, by Jensen.

Laurence Kasper

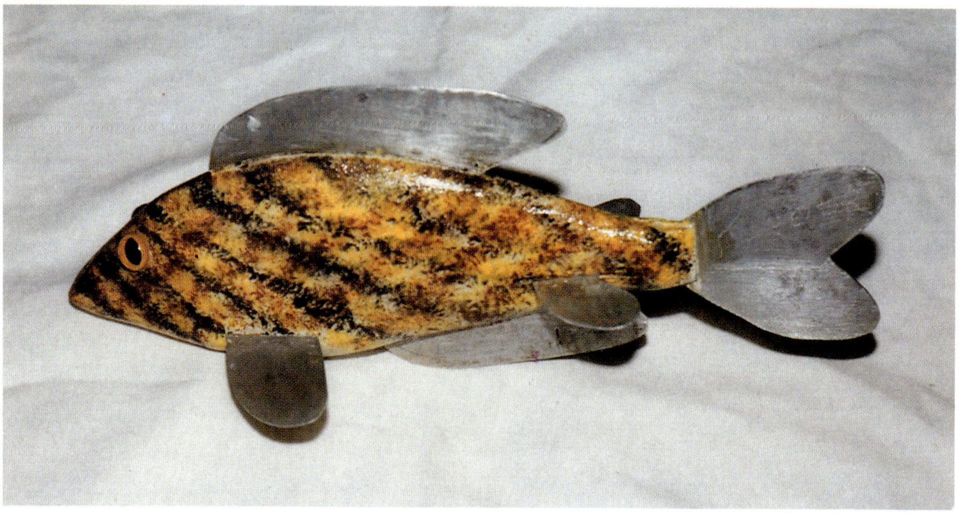

Laurence Kasper "bass," 10 1/2 inches.

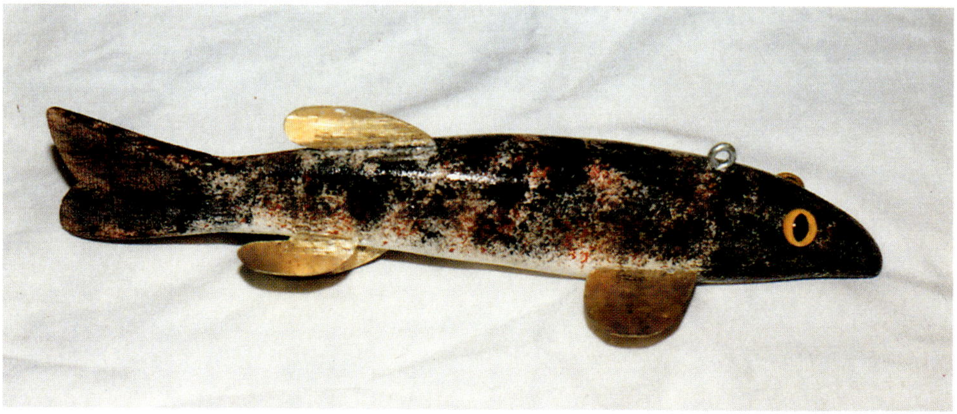

Kasper sucker with wooden tail, 11 inches.

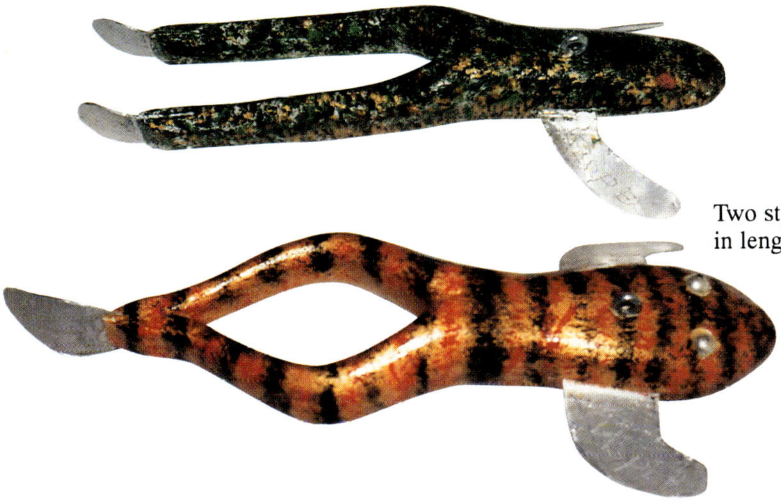

Two styles of Kasper frogs; top: 9 inches; bottom: frog, 10 inches in length.

Kasper "alligator," 11 inches.

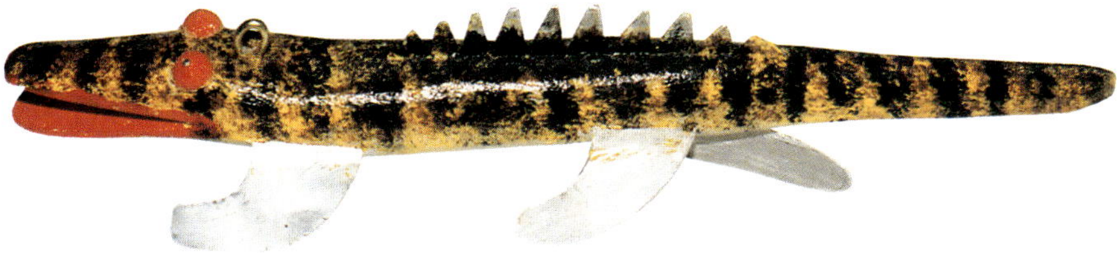

Richard Larsen

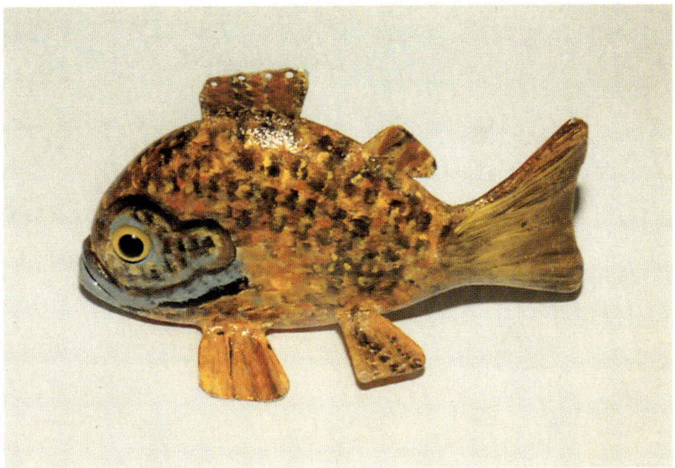

Richard Larsen sunfish. Collection of John Banholzer, 6 inches.

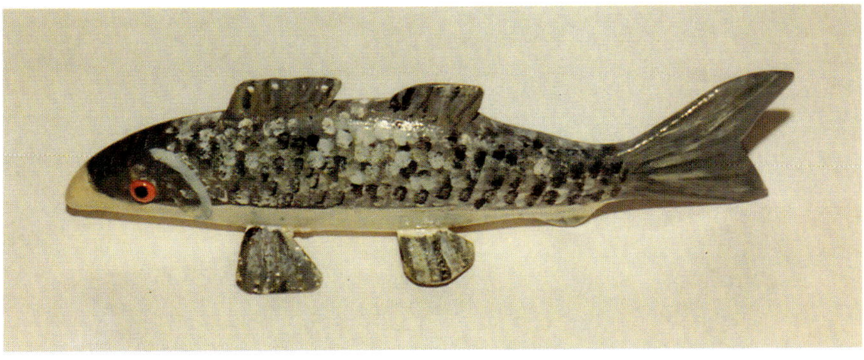

Larsen sucker. Collection of John Banholzer, 9 inches in length.

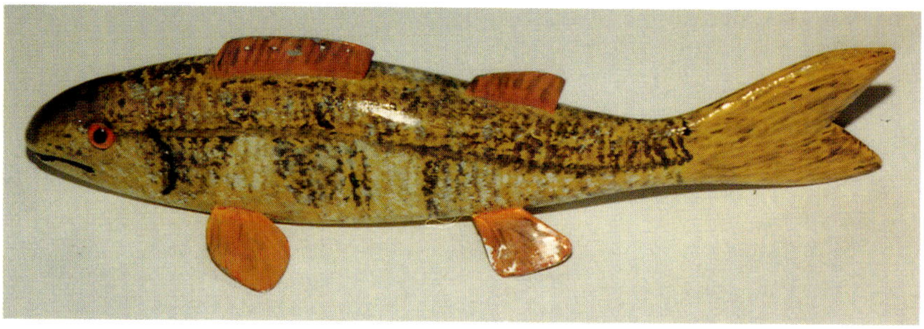

Perch by Richard Larsen. Collection of John Banholzer, 10 inches long.

Clifford Larson

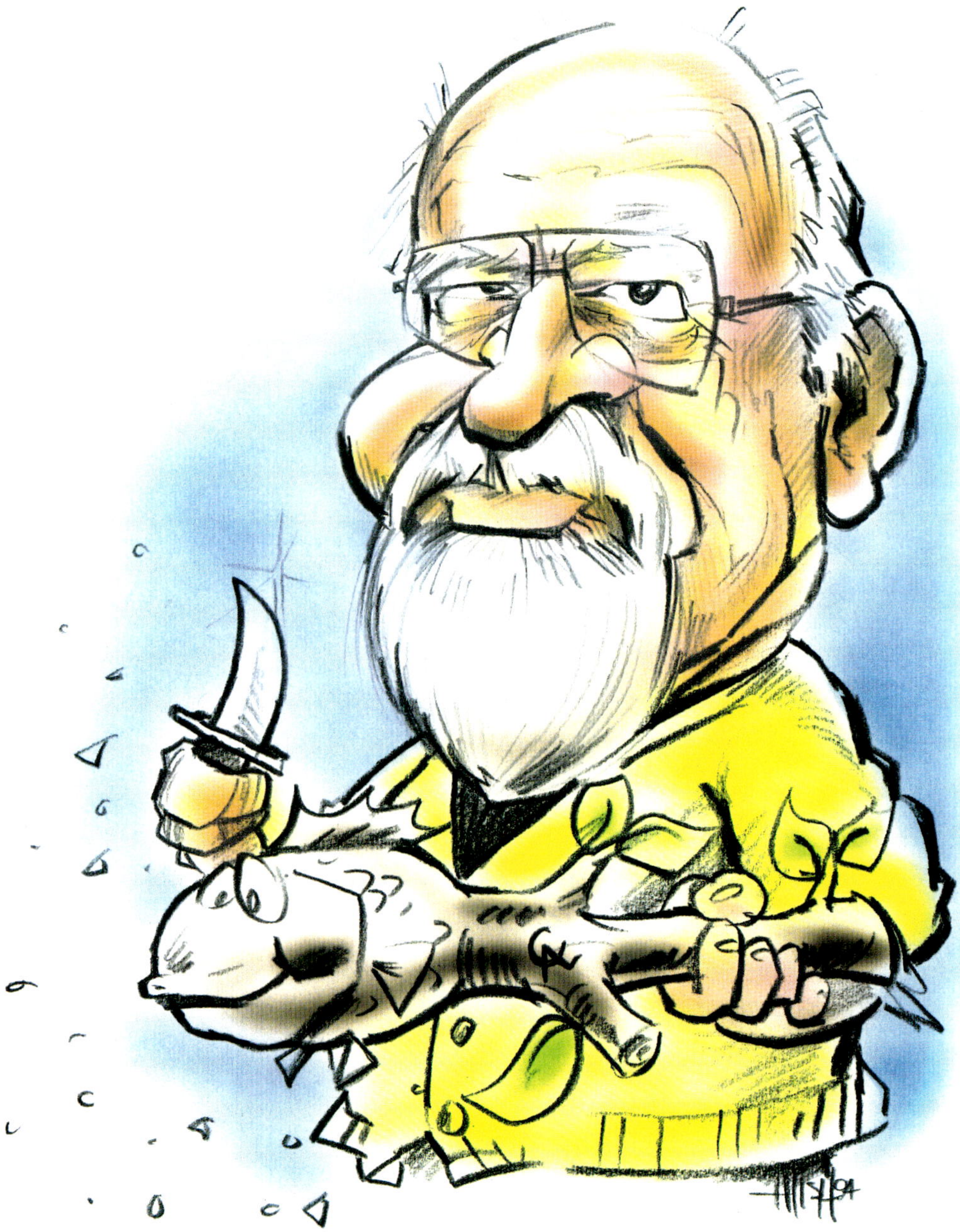

Cliff Larson caricature. Courtesy of Clifford Larson.

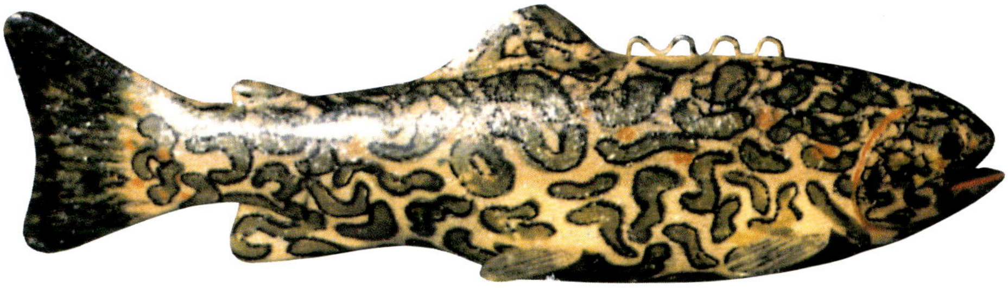

Larson "tiger" trout.

Larson turtle.

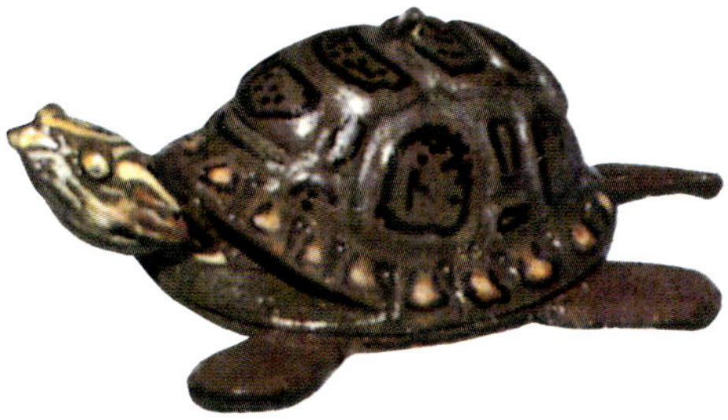

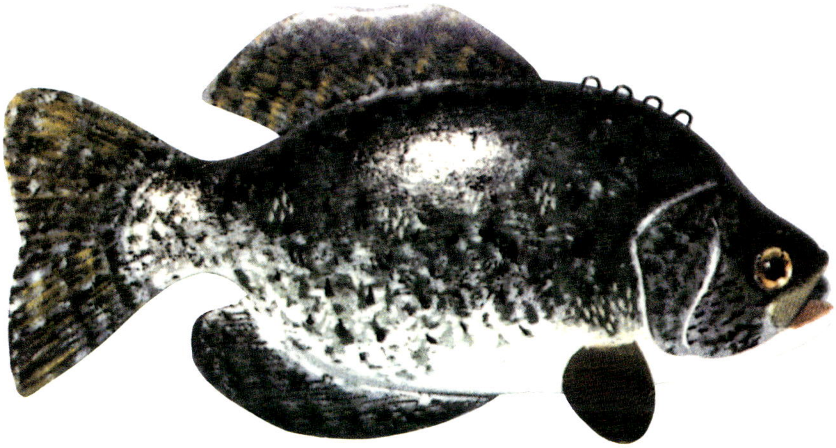

Crappie by Cliff Larson.

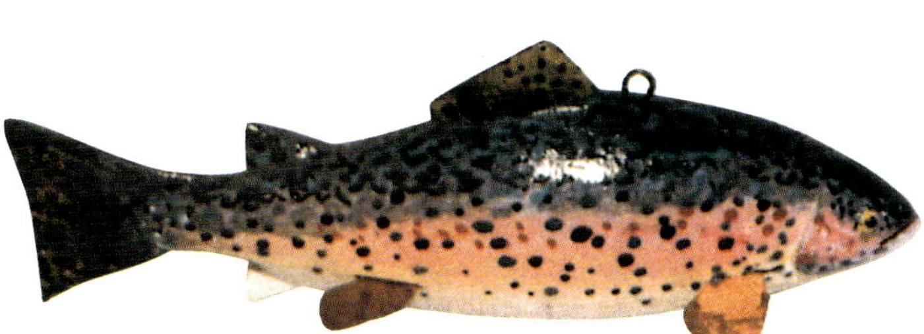

Rainbow trout by Cliff Larson.

Roger Lashua

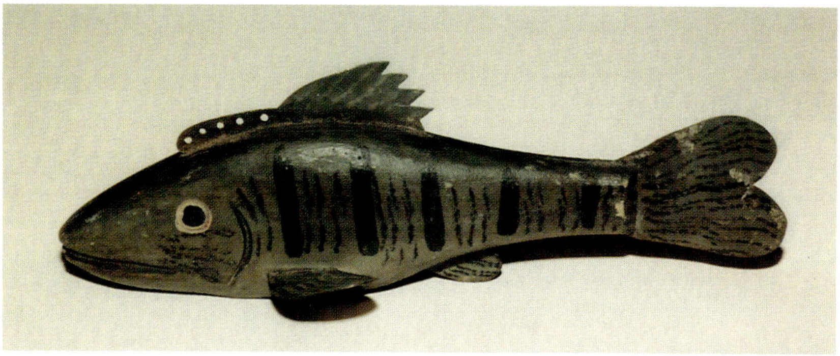

Perch done by Roger Lashua, 6 inches long.

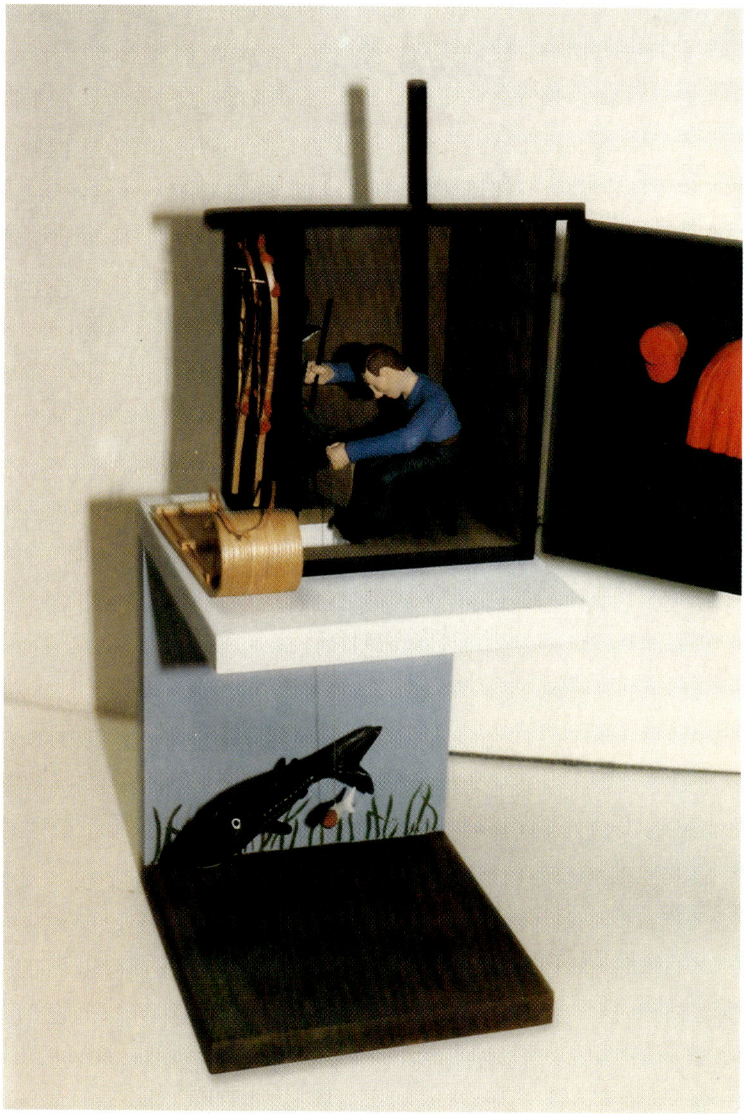

Spear fishing shanty made for the author by Roger Lashua.

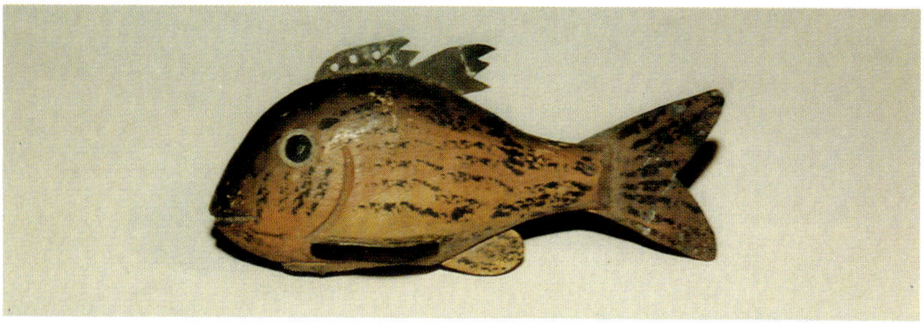

Lashua sunfish, 4 inches long.

Joe Leach

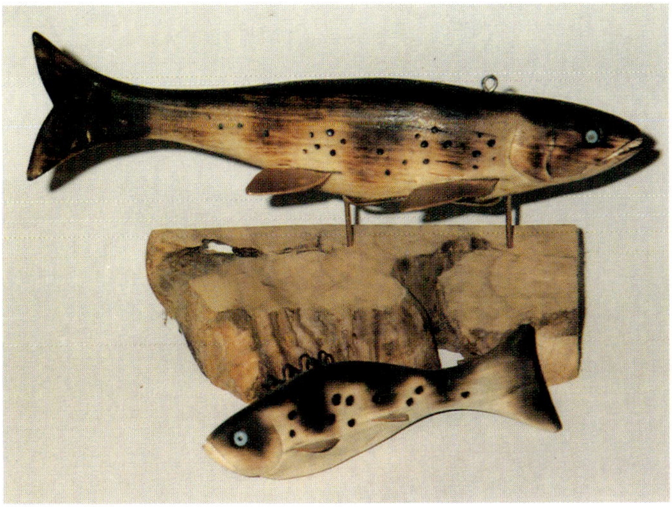

Joe Leach walleye, 8 inches long and "fish," 4 inches. Photo courtesy Joe Leach.

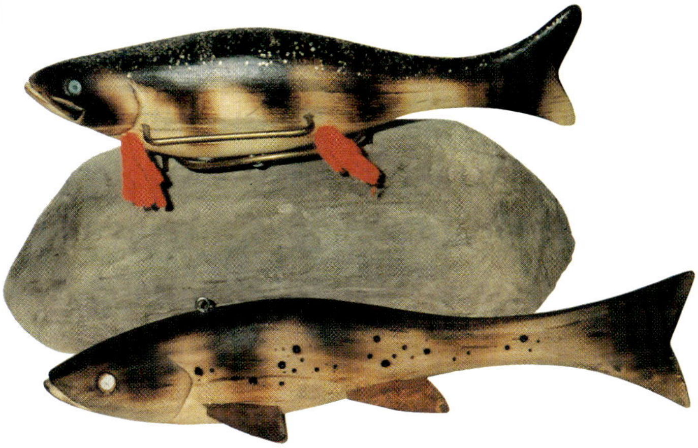

Leach floater decoy. The bottom fish is one of Joe's favorite, 10 inches. Photo courtesy of Joe Leach.

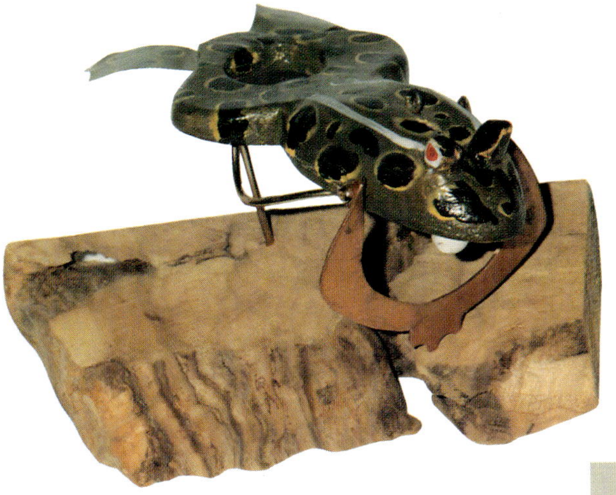

Frog with swinging front legs, ca. 1991. Photo courtesy of Joe Leach.

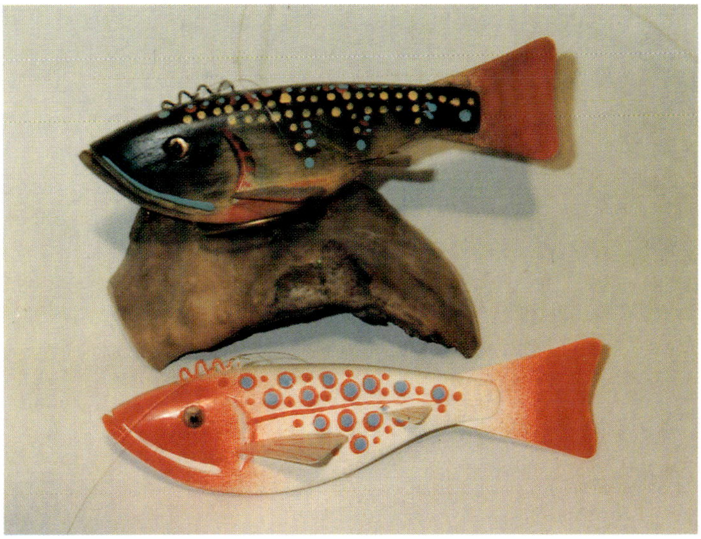

Joe Leach painted fish, 7 inches. Photo courtesy of Joe Leach.

Murray J. Marlette

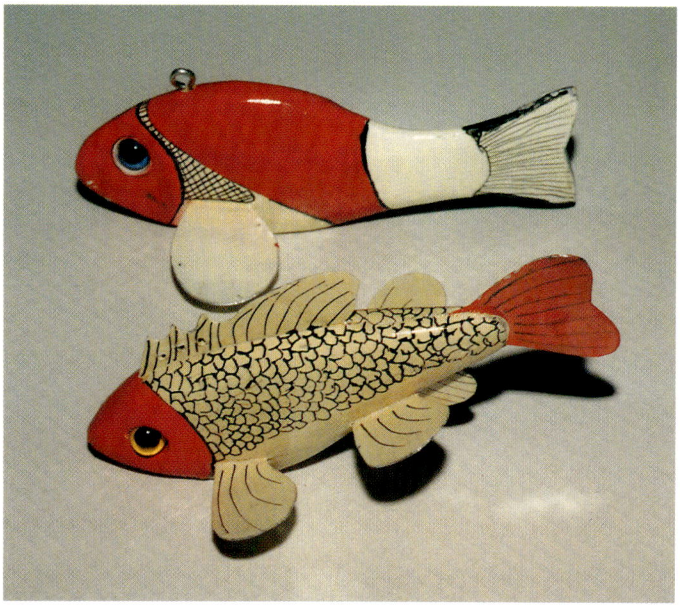

Two so-called "generic" fish by Murray Marlette.

David E. Perkins

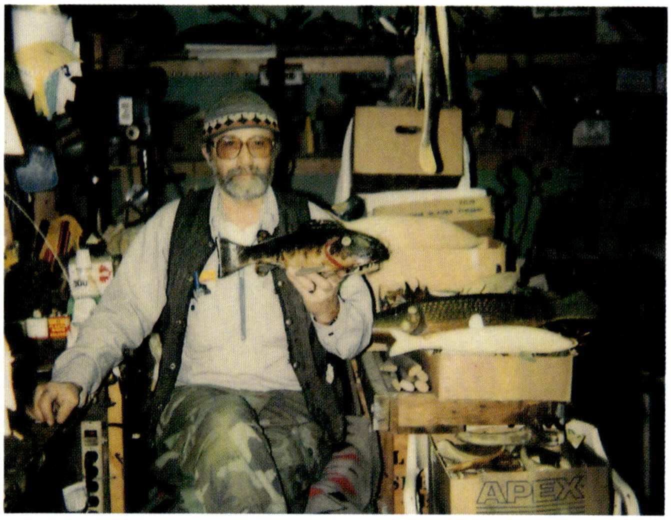

David Perkins, holding one of his decoys.

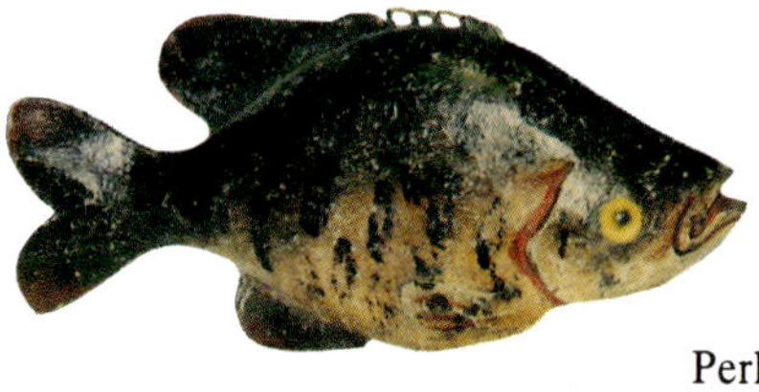

Perkins' crappie and trout.

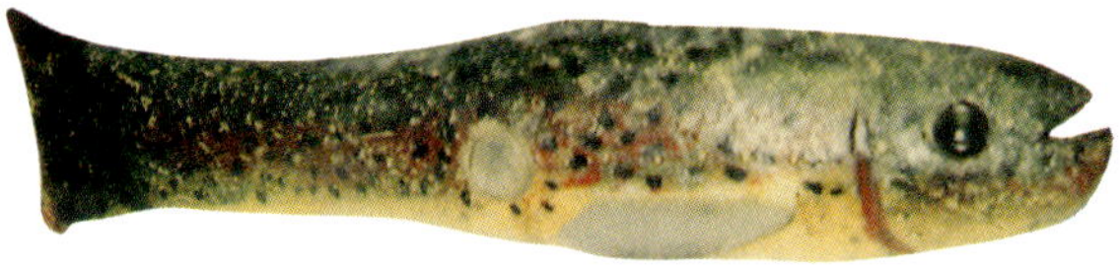

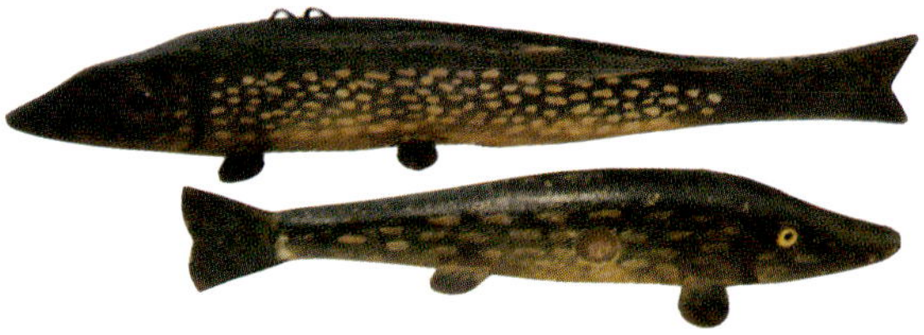

Northern pikes are the decoys for which Perkins is best known.

Larry Peterson

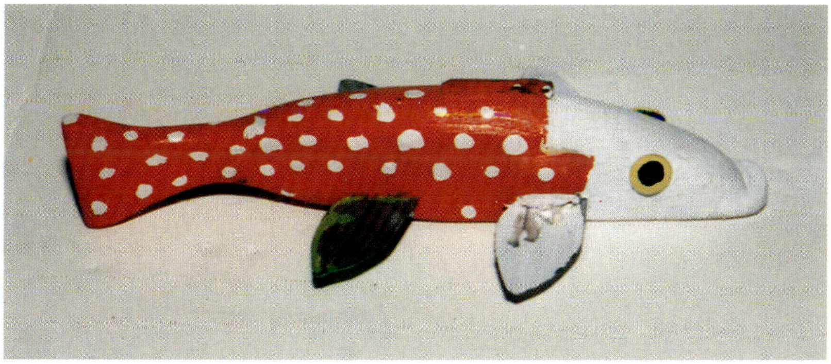

Bullhead by Larry Peterson, 5 inches long. The protruding lower lip on the decoy is a Walter and Herbert Peterson characteristic.

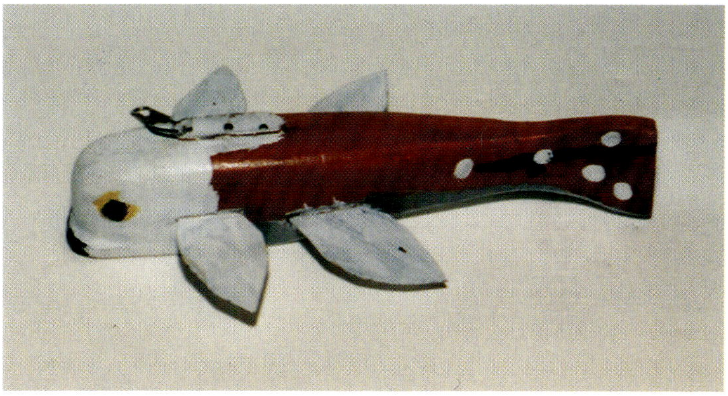

Minnow by Larry Peterson, 6 3/4 inches long, with copper fins.

Carl L. Silver

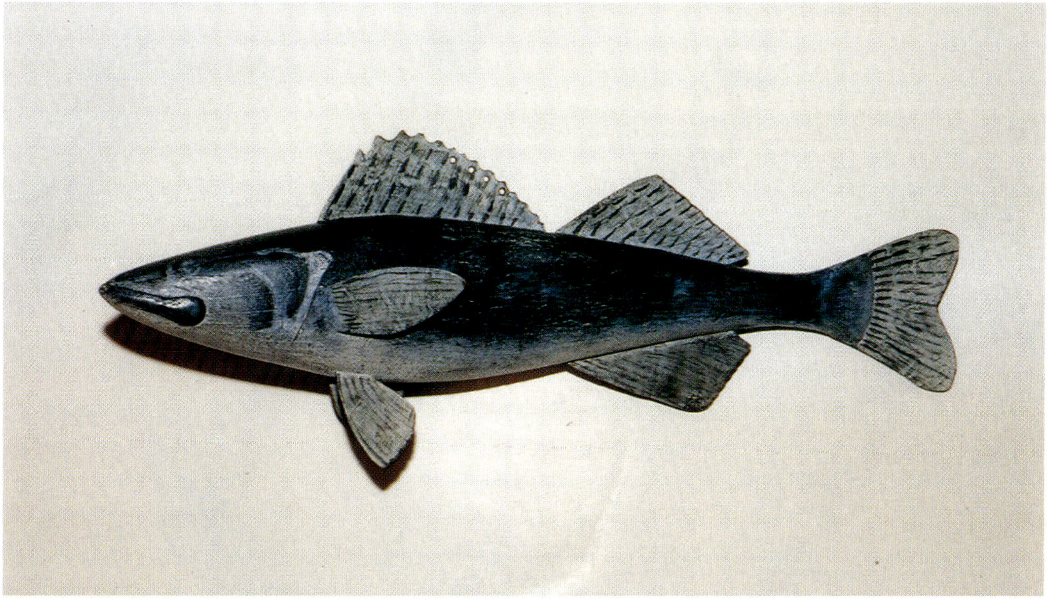

Carl Silver walleye decoy, ca. 1980's, length 12 inches. Collection of Frank Pasiewicz.

John & Evelyn Swenson

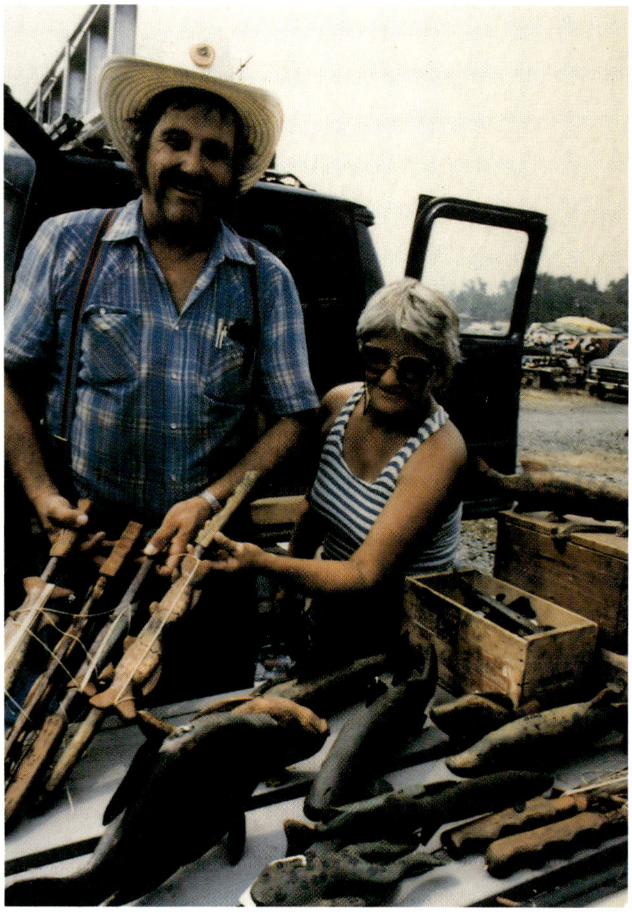

The Swensons preparing to display their decoys at a show. Photo courtesy of the Swensons.

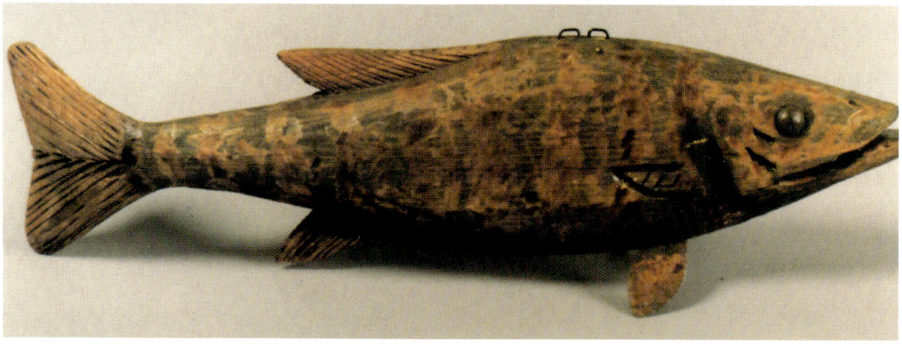

John Swenson's yellow perch. Photo courtesy of the Swensons.

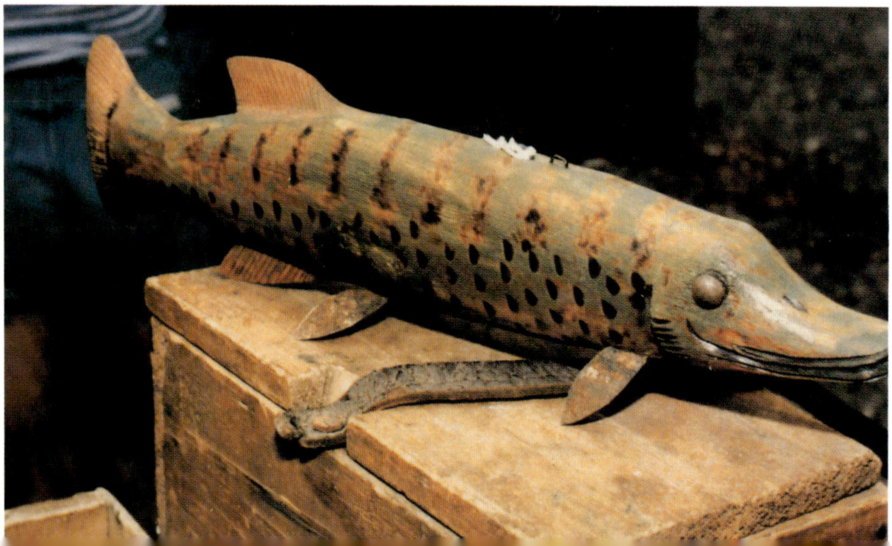

Swenson musky reclining on a decoy box. Photo courtesy of the Swensons.

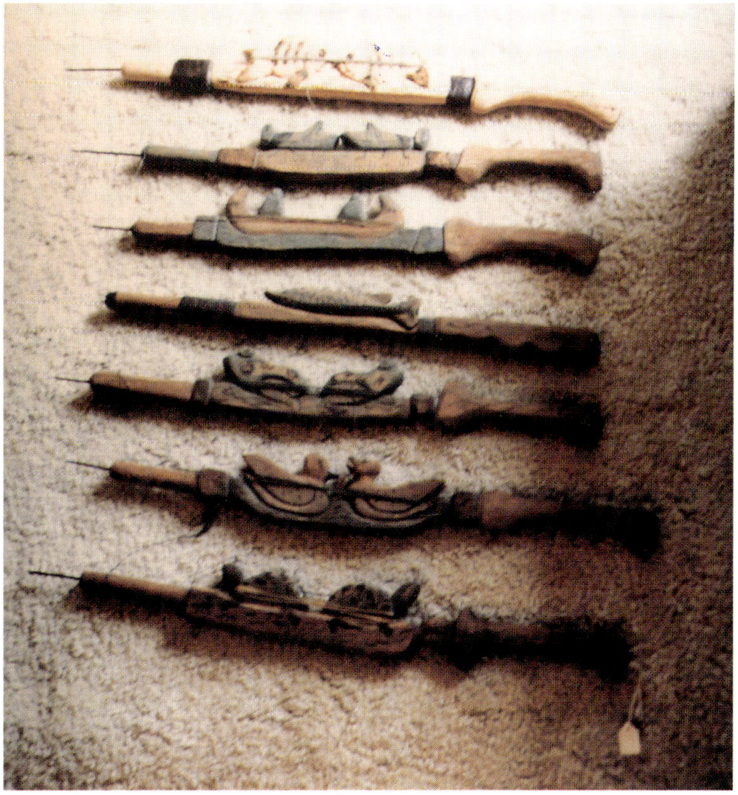

Swenson fishing sticks. Photo courtesy of the Swensons.

John Unger

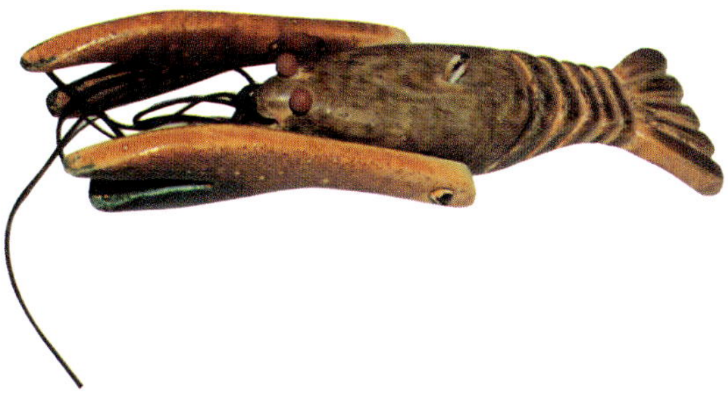

John Unger crawdad decoy, c. 1960, 5 inches long.

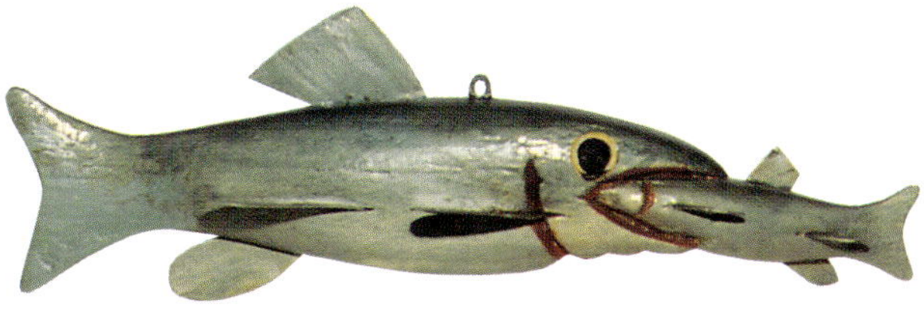

Smelt-like decoy by John Unger, holding a minnow in its mouth, ca. 1980's, 6 inches.

Chapter VI Photographs

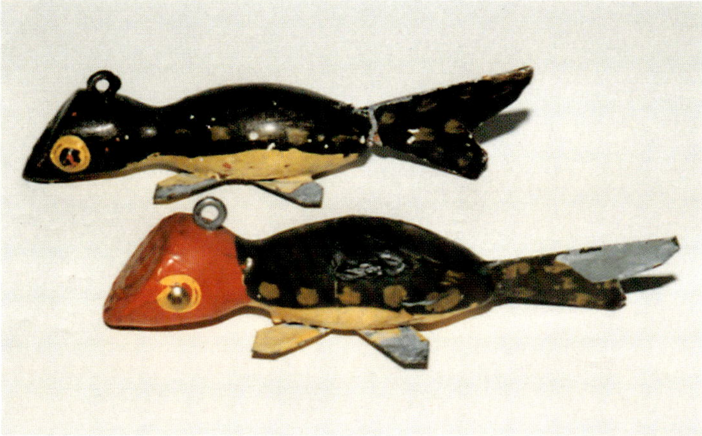

Brown Brothers' "Fisheretto"

Two Brown Bros. "Fisheretto" decoys, 5 inches long.

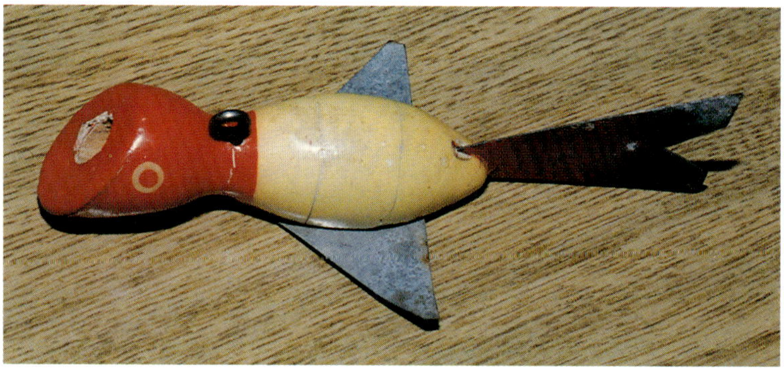

Rare Brown Bros. decoy, third style "wing" with hole through its head. Terry Jacobson collection.

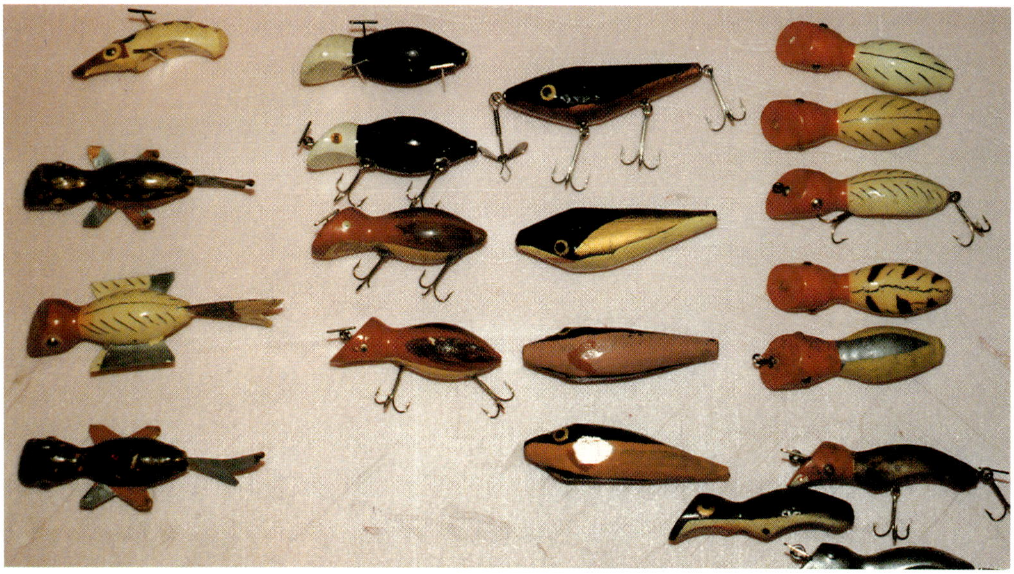

Brown Bros. lures on right, decoys on left.

Bru-ell Decoys

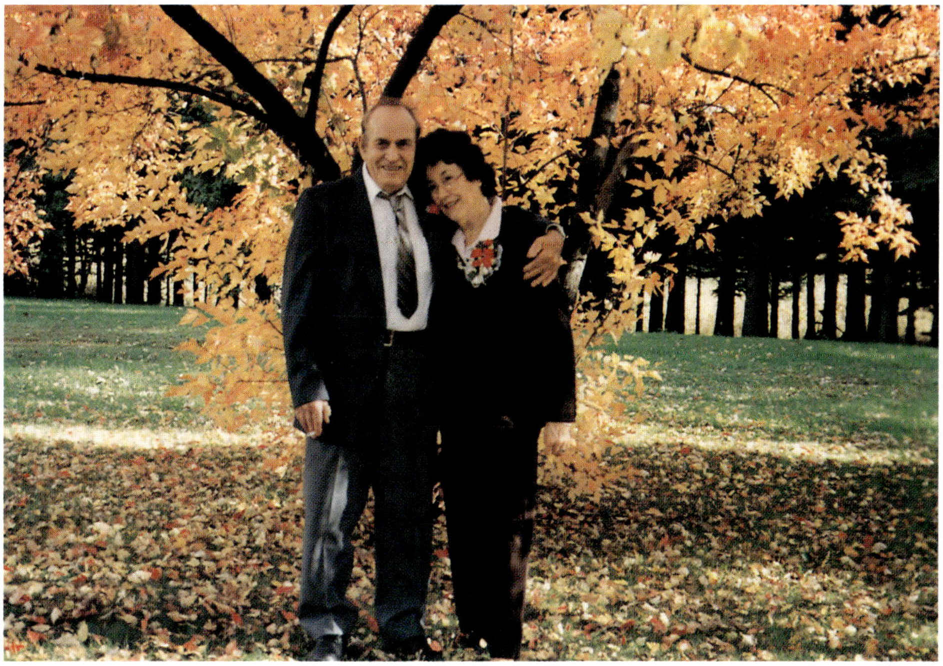

The "Bru-ells," Bruce and Helen Wakefield.

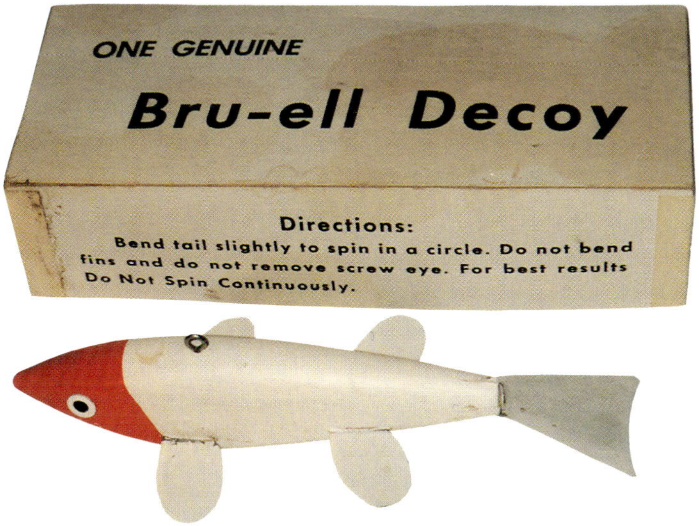

Tack eye Bru-ell decoy 7 1/2 inches in length, with box. Photo courtesy of Frank Baron.

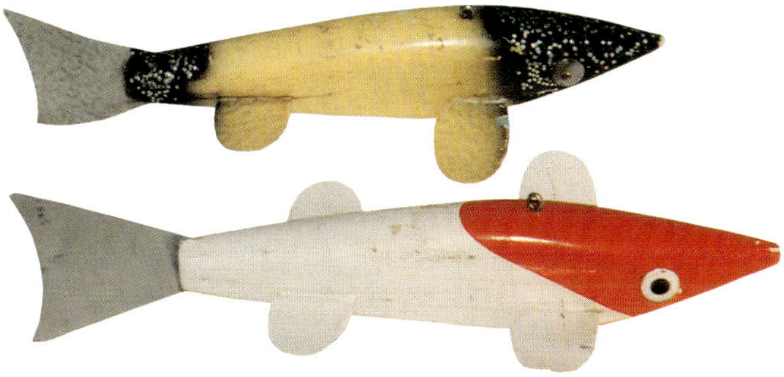

Two Bru-ell decoys. Red and white one is 7 1/2 inches in length, while the yellow and black one has glitter decoration and is 7 inches long.

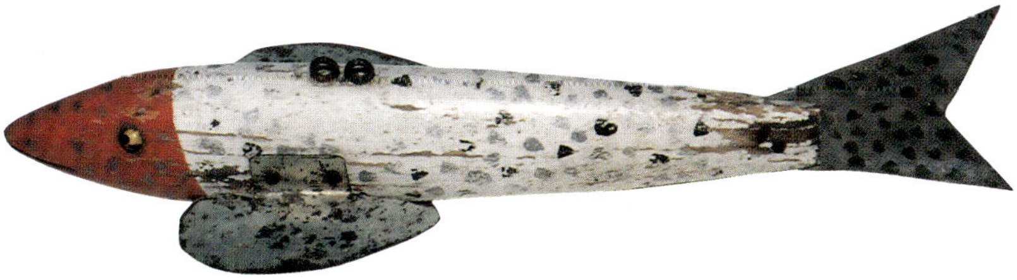

Early Bru-ell decoy, ca. 1950's, taxidermy eyes; carved mouth and spotted paint decoration. Length 9 inches.

Cy's Decoys

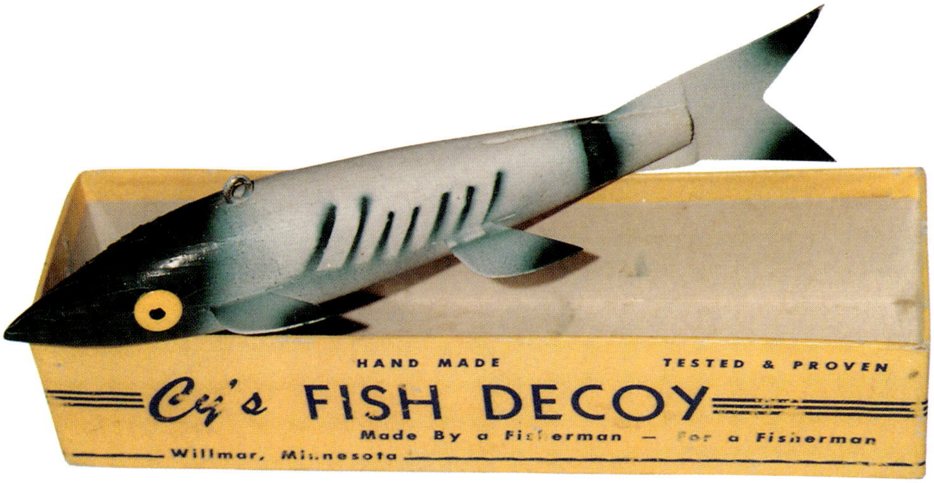

An unusual blue and white Cy's decoy, 7 1/2 inches. Collection of Frank Baron.

Fish Bust'r

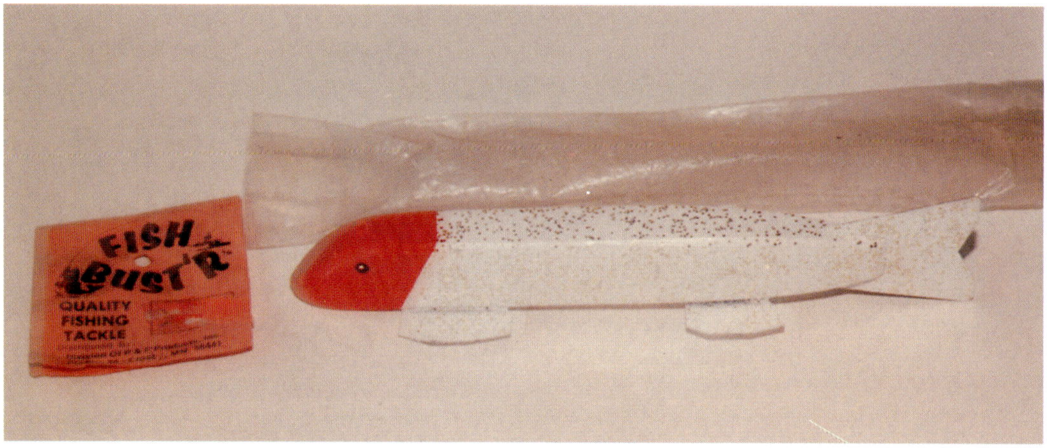

"Fish Bust'r" decoy with its original wrappings. Collection of K. David Hirschey.

Herter's, Inc.

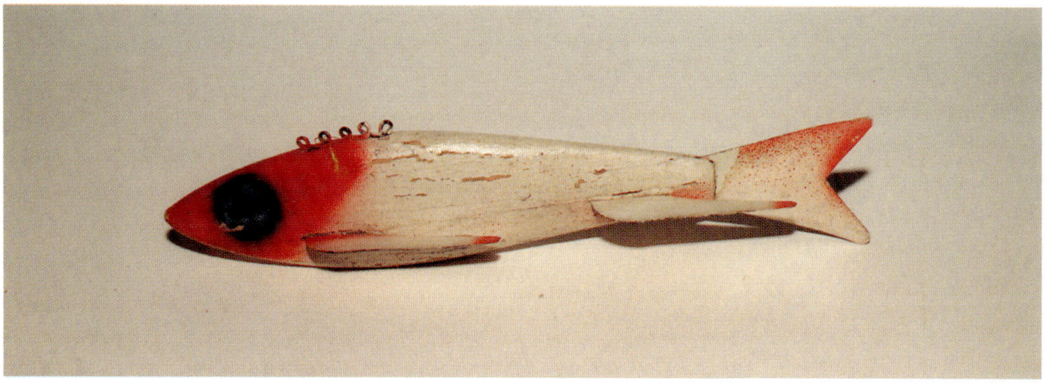

Red and white catalog decoy, 7 inches actual length.

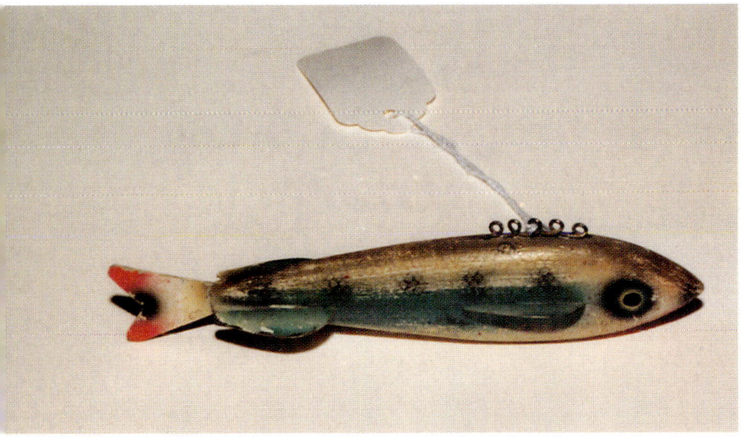

Herter's non-catalog decoy.

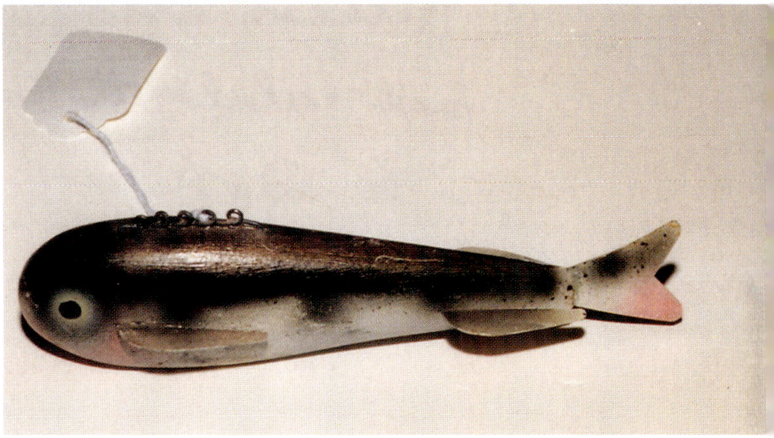

Herter's non-catalog decoy.

Lee's Decoys

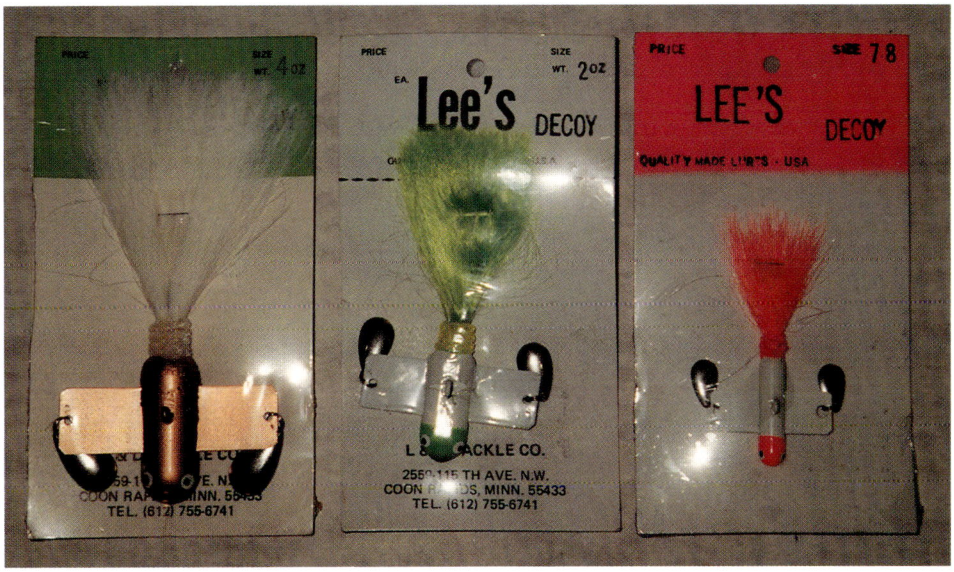

Three styles of Lee's decoys on cards. One is copper colored, one is green and white and one is pink and white. Mr. Carlson's Tackle Company was located at 2550 - 115th Avenue, N.W., Coon Rapids, Minnesota. Photo courtesy of Frank Baron.

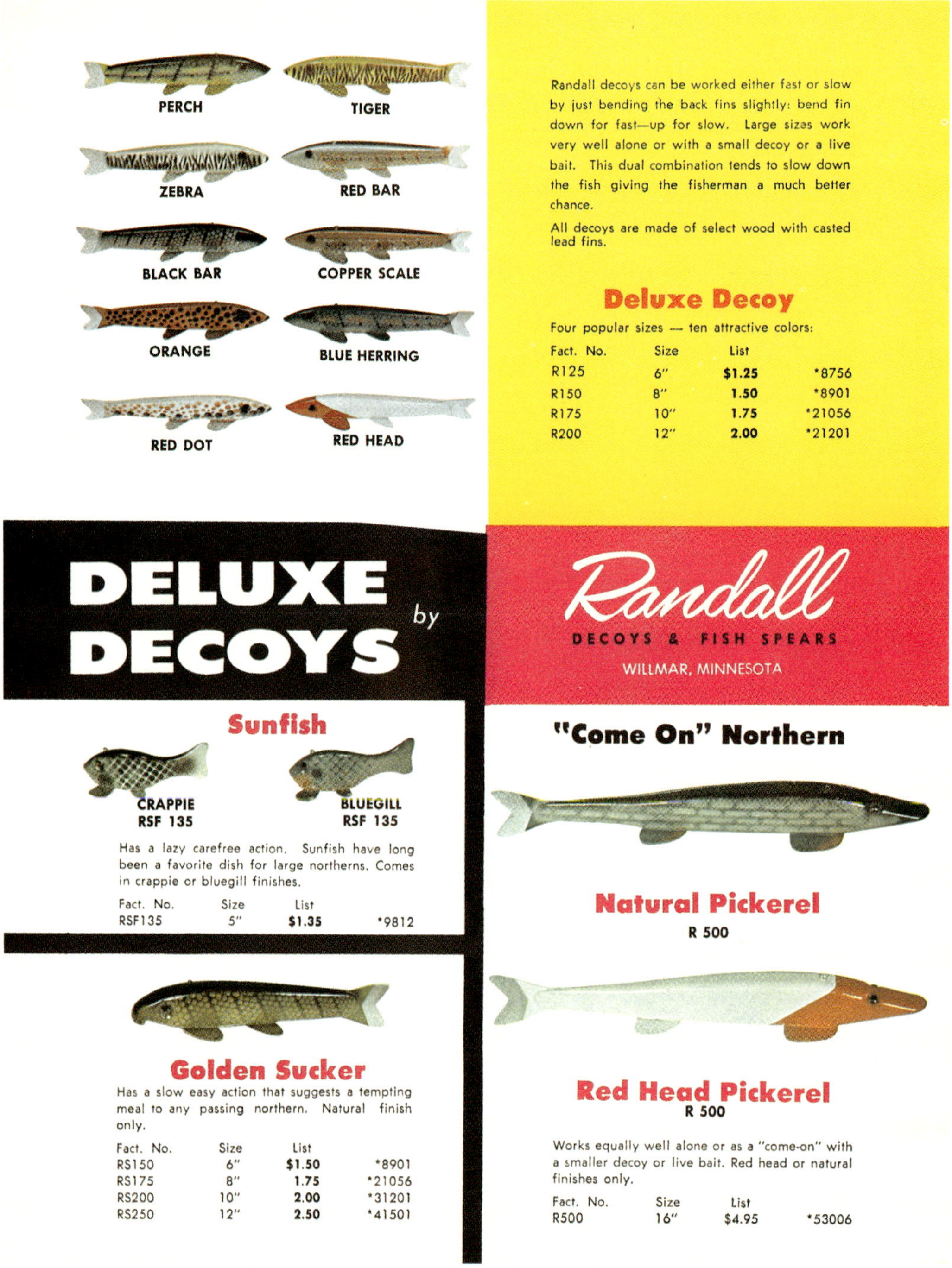

Advertisement showing a variety of Randall spear fishing decoys and their prices.

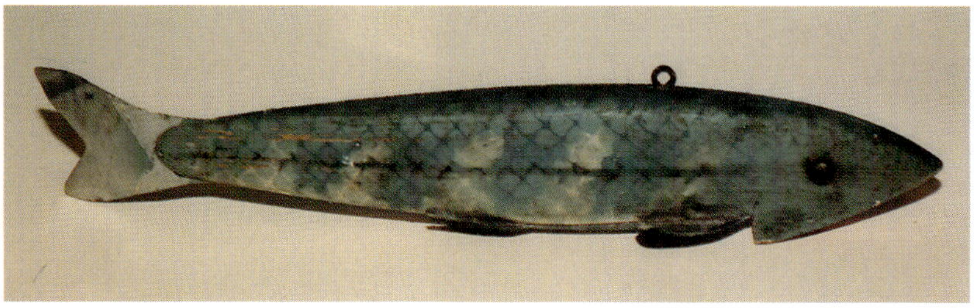

Early 16 inch Pickerel decoy by Randall.

Reigstad Decoys

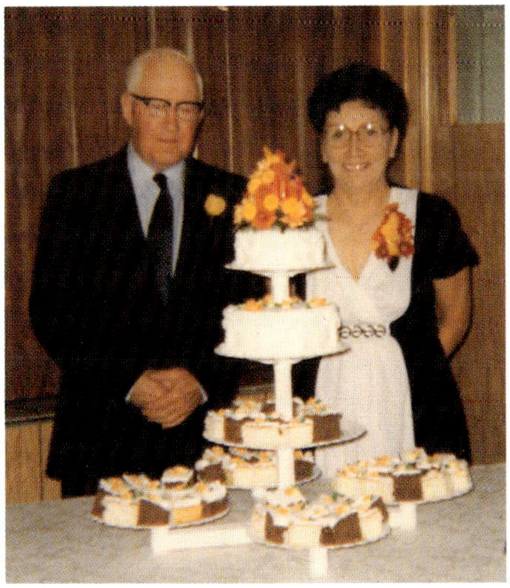

Oliver and Olga Reigstad at an anniversary celebration.

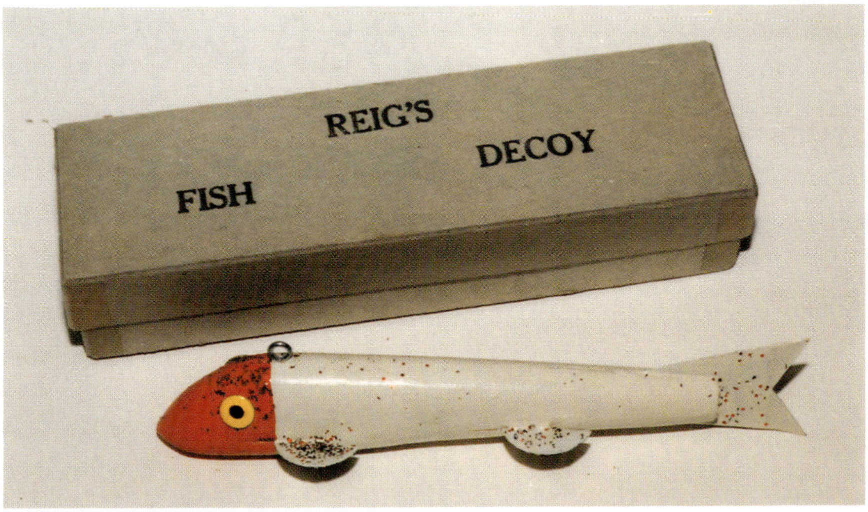

Reigstad decoy with box.

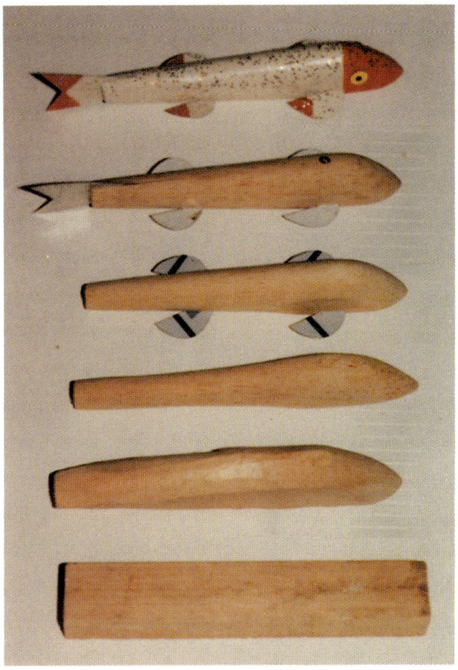

Steps in the production of a Reigstad decoy, from a blank of wood to a finished decoy.

Ripley's "Decoy Minnow"

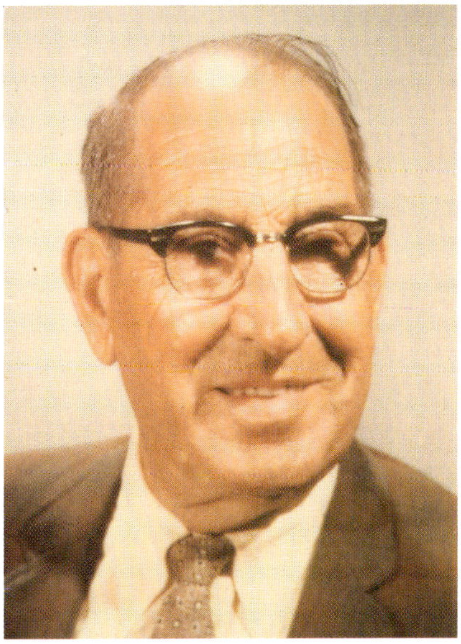

Horace E. "Slim" Ripley. Photo courtesy of Mrs. Mary Hibbard.

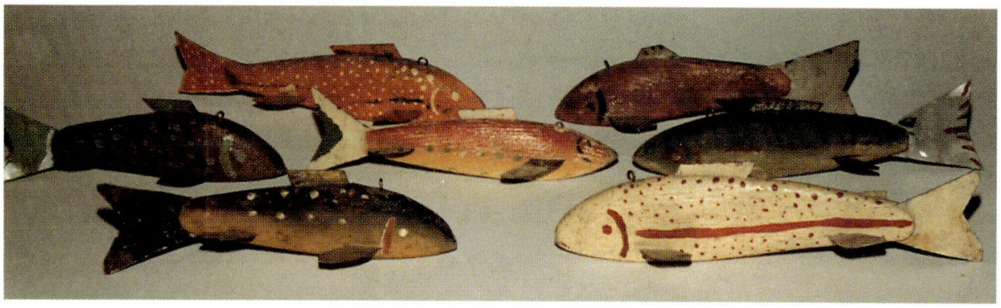

Grouping of seven Ripley decoys showing the variety of decoration patterns.

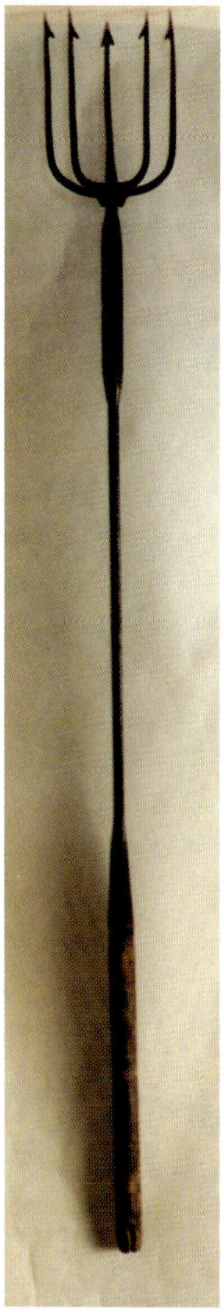

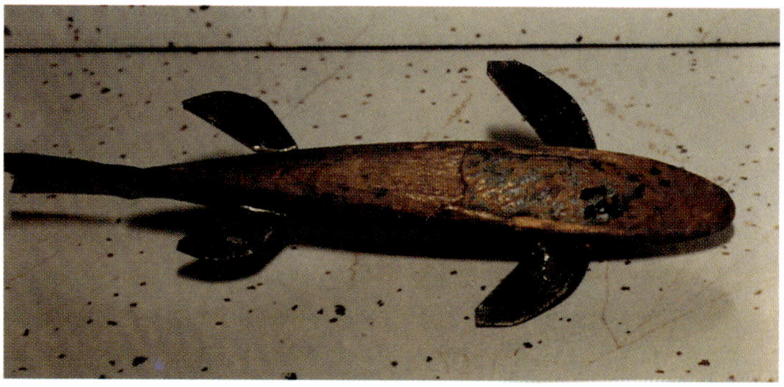

Bottom view of a Ripley decoy. The "R" is not visible, but fin shapes are apparent.

Slim Ripley's personal spear.

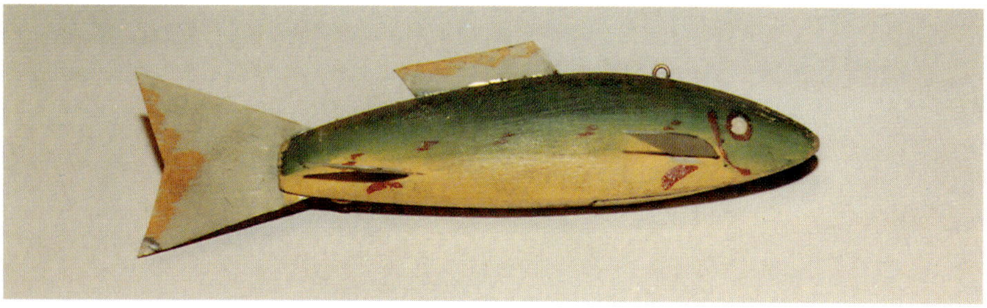

Green and yellow painted Ripley decoy with dash decoration.

Sletten Mfg. Company

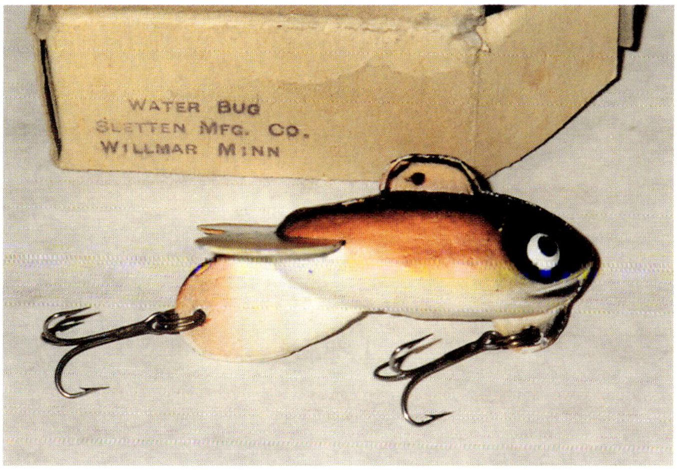

Sletten Manufacturing Company "Water Bug" with box. Decoy 3 inches in length. Photo courtesy of Frank Baron.

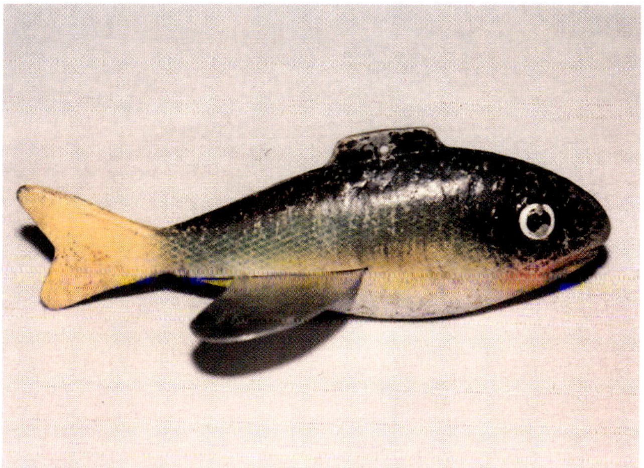

Green and yellow Sletten decoy. Courtesy of Carter Stenberg.

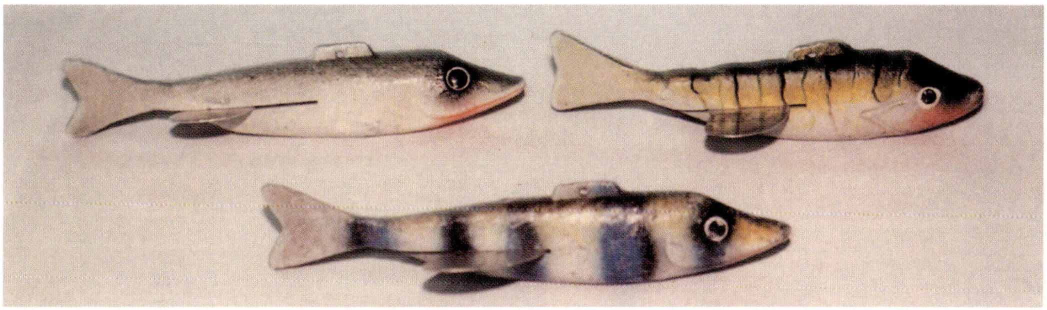

Grouping of three Sletten decoys. Courtesy of Carter Strenberg.

Titloe Heights Bait Mfg.

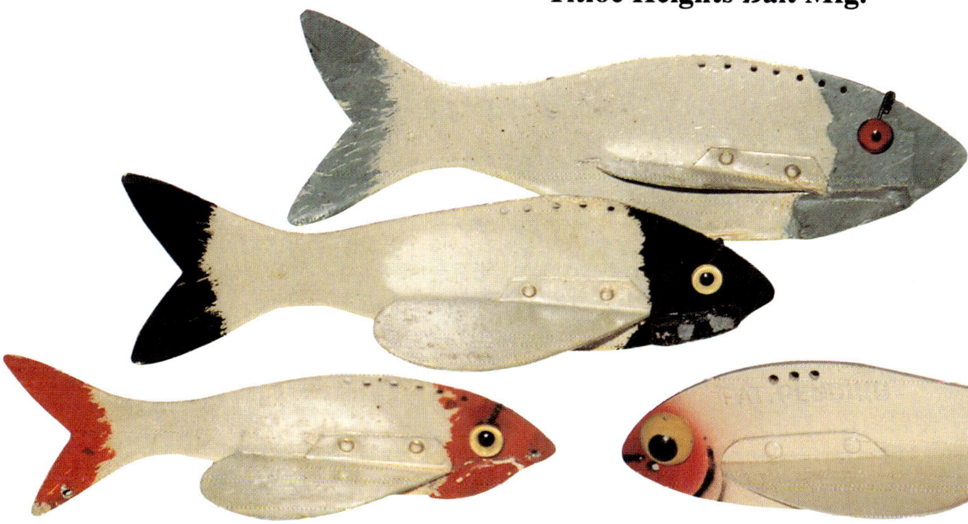

Grouping of three early Ole fish decoys with six line tie holes. They measure (top to bottom) 6 3/4, 6, and 4 inches in length. Photo courtesy of Frank Baron.

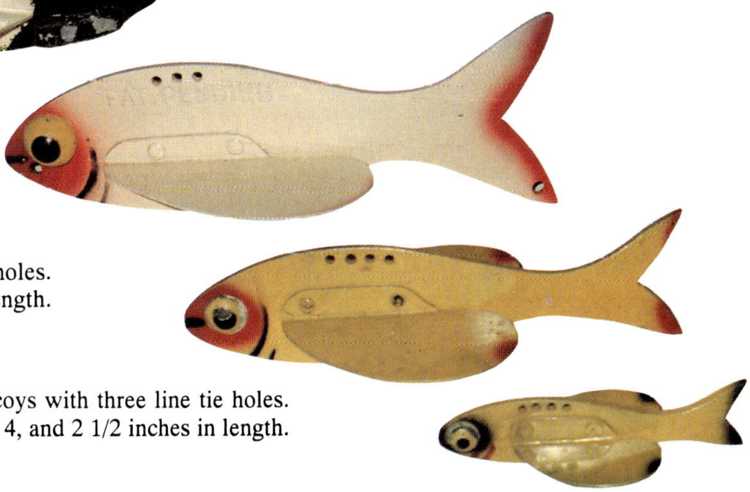

Grouping of three later Ole fish decoys with three line tie holes. They measure (top to bottom) 4 3/4, 4, and 2 1/2 inches in length. Photo courtesy of Frank Baron.

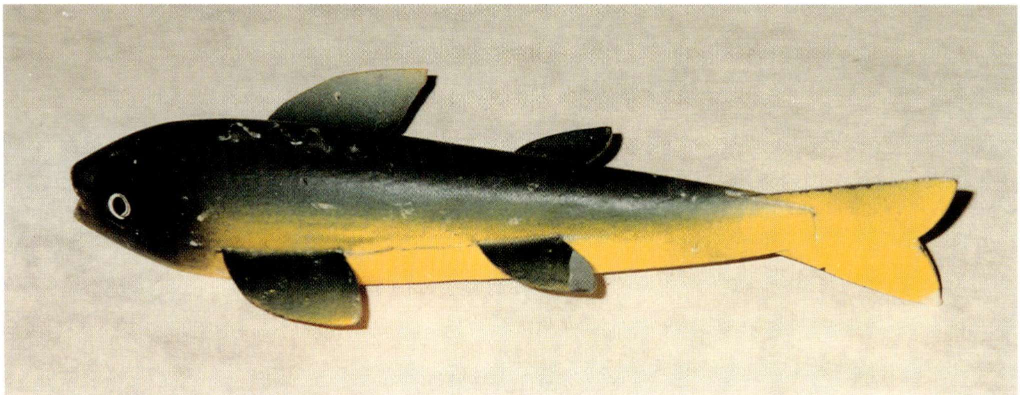

"Large" Schipper decoy, green and yellow color combination. Photo courtesy of Frank Baron.

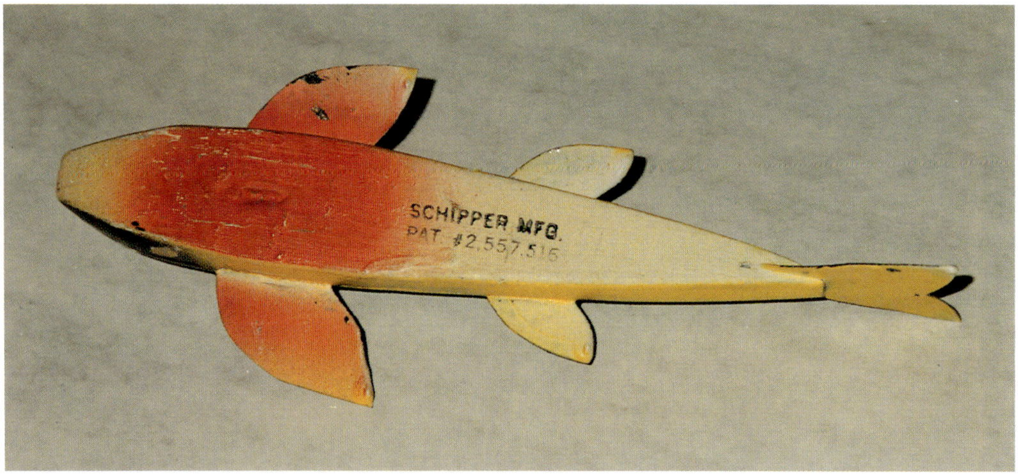

Bottom view of above decoy showing Schipper Mfg. and the patent number.

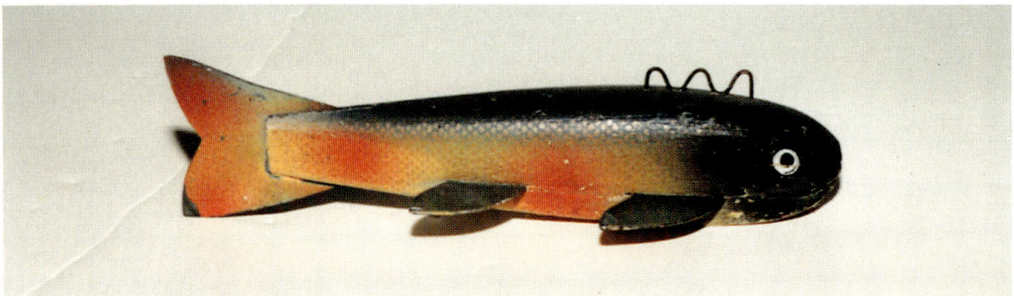

Schipper Mfg. perch decoy, 5 1/2 inches long.

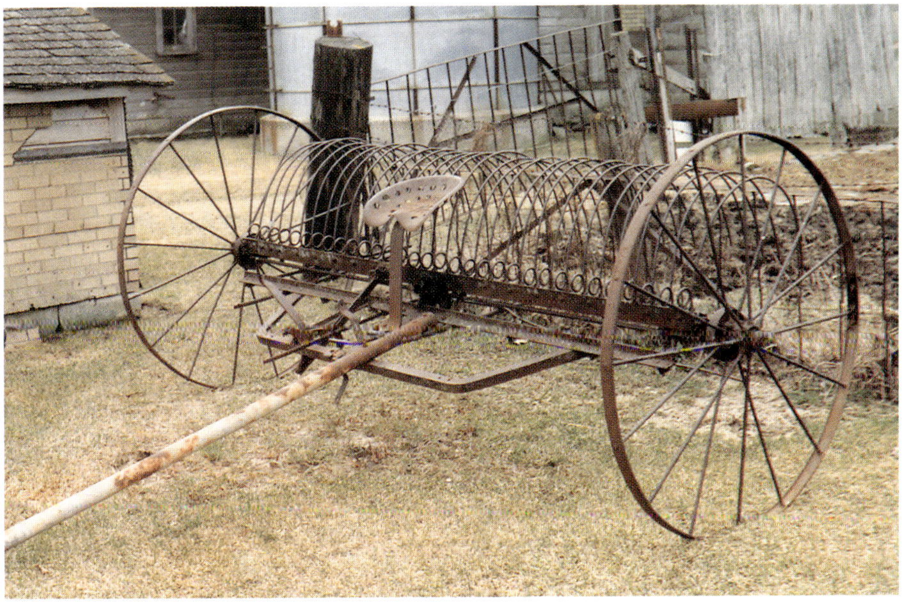

Hay rake from which some blacksmiths made spear tines.

Milton Betts

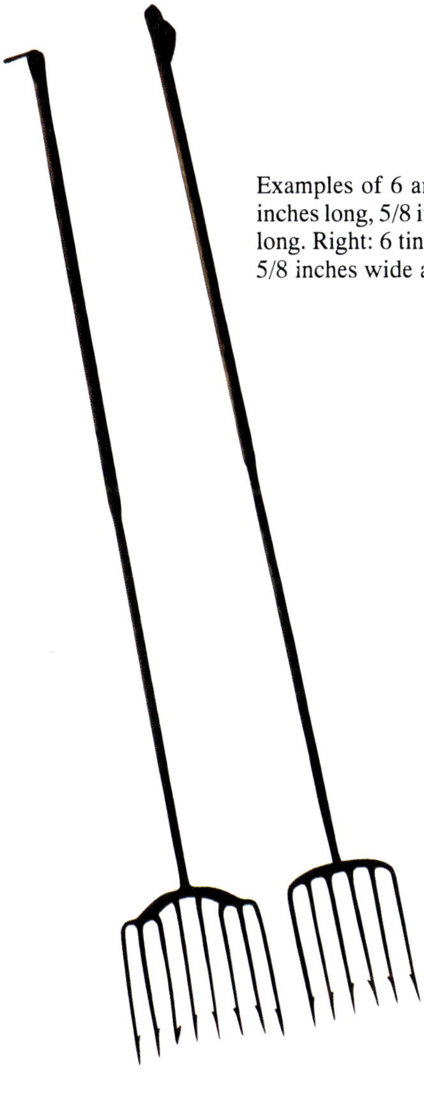

Examples of 6 and 9 tine Betts' spears. Left: 9 tine spear, 59 1/2 inches long, 5/8 inch stock; tines 8 3/4 inches wide and 9 1/2 inches long. Right: 6 tine spear, 60 1/2 inches long, 5/8 inch stock; tines 6 5/8 inches wide and 9 1/2 inches long.

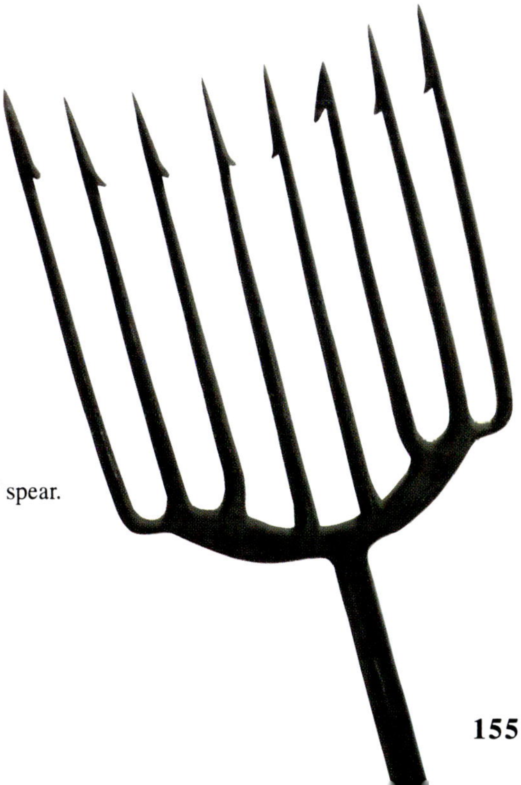

Closeup of 9 tine Betts' spear.

Frank Clark

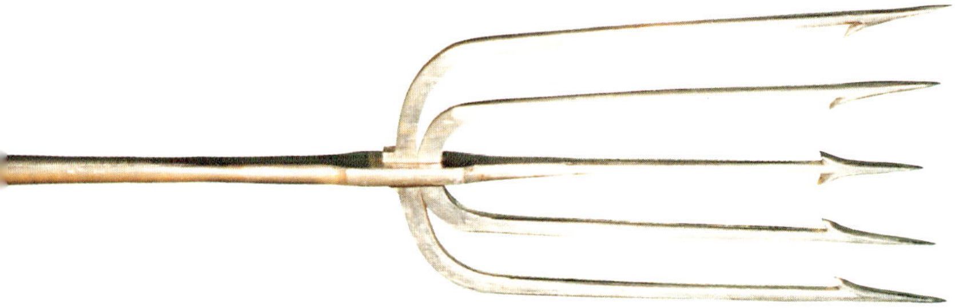

Closeup of tines of Frank Clark spear.

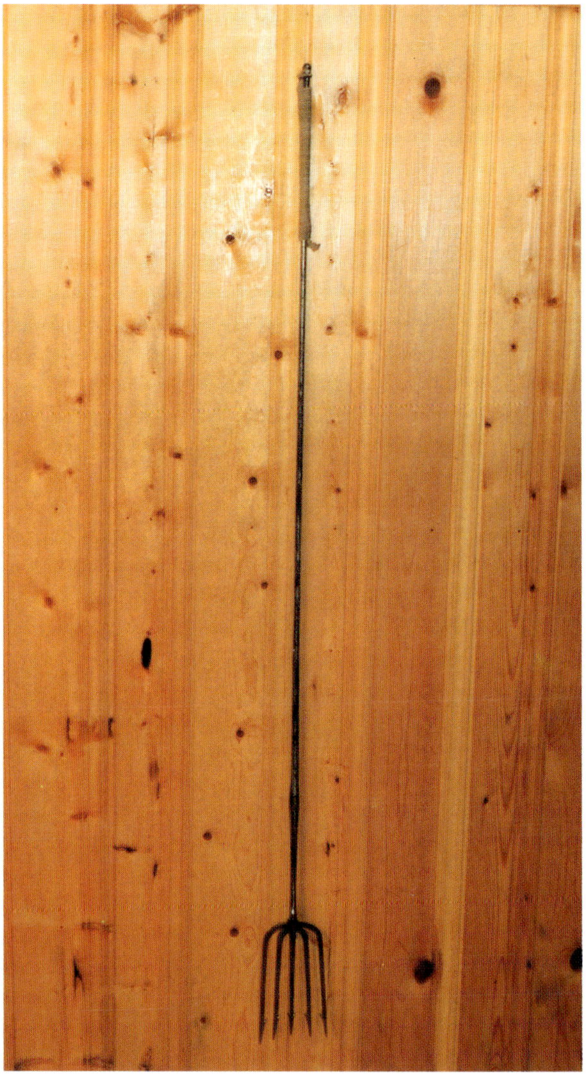

Frank Clark stainless steel spear; overall length 61 1/4 inches, 3/8 inch shaft width, 8 1/8 inch length of longest tine, width of head of spear, 4 5/8 inches at the widest point.

Fred Drexler

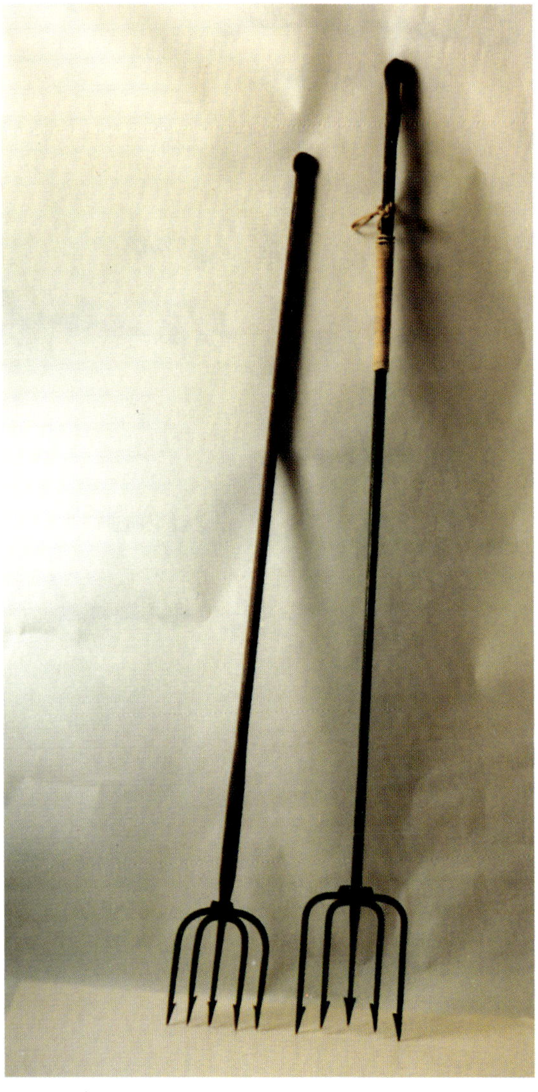

Two Drexler spears, about 4 feet in length. Left: 5 tine spear, 46 3/4 inches long, 5/8 inch stock; tines, 5 3/4 inches wide and 6 3/8 inches long. Right: 5 tine, 52 1/4 inches long, 1/4 inch stock; tines, 5 3/4 inches wide, 7 3/4 inches long.

Spear head, marked "F. Drexler," 18 5/8 inches in length-with a 1/2 inch rod. Collection of Larry Hochmayr.

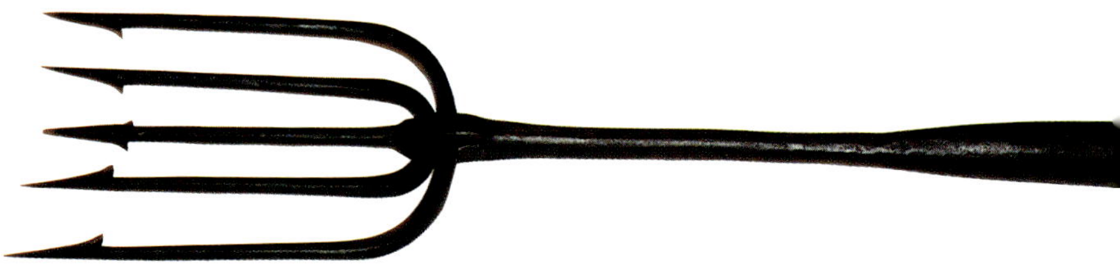

William Elmor

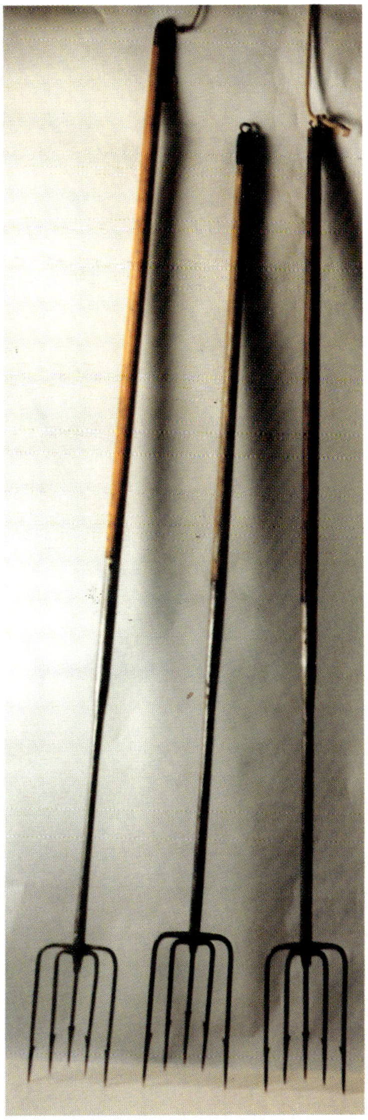

Elmor spears. All Elmor spears were 5 tine. Left: 66 3/4 inches long, 5/8 inch stock; tines, 9 inches long and 5 1/4 inches wide. Middle: 60 1/2 inches long, 5/8 inch stock; tines 9 3/4 inches long, 5 1/4 inches wide. Right: 61 1/2 inches long, 5/8 inch stock; tines 9 inches long, 5 3/8 inches wide.

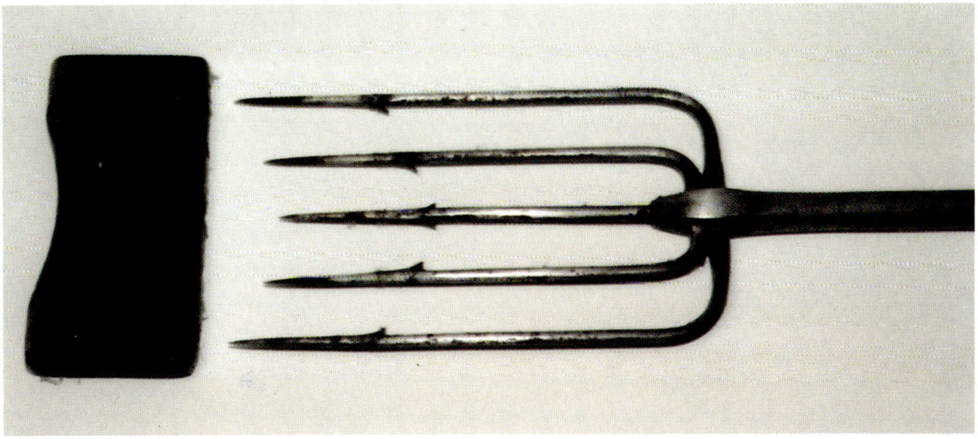

Closeup of tines on Elmor spear.

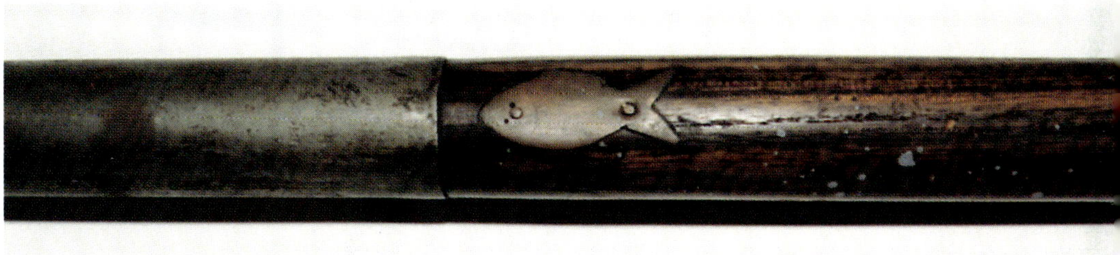

Closeup of copper fish inserted into wooden handle of an Elmor spear [this was not, however, a common characteristic for Elmor spears].

Lloyd Fredericks

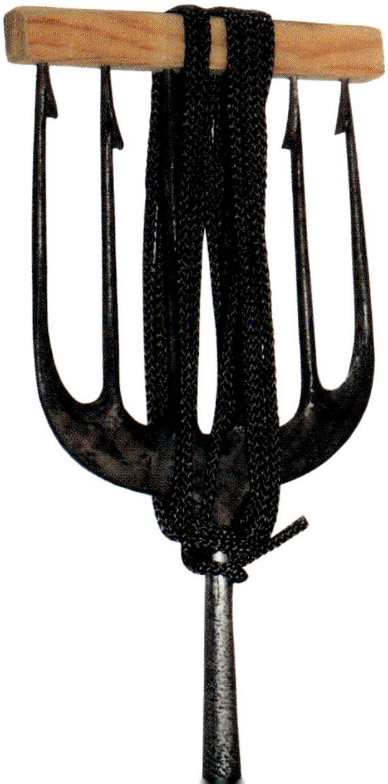

Closeup of Fredericks' spear. Larry Hochmayr collection.

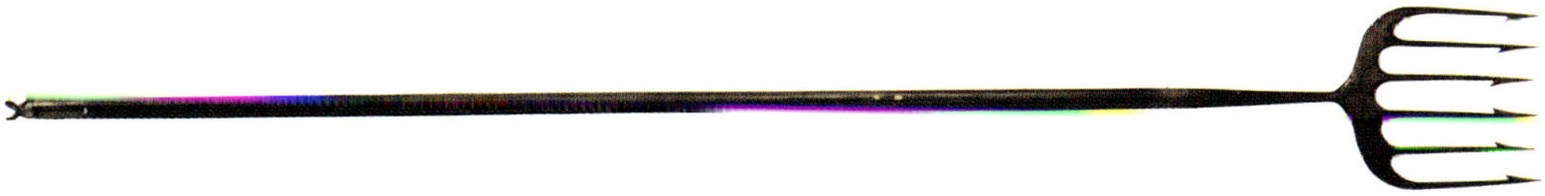

Lloyd Fredericks' spear; 57 3/4 inches long with a tapered stock; tines are 6 3/4 inches wide and 6 5/8 inches long. Larry Hochmayr collection.

Peter Fuchs

Fuchs' spear, ca. 1960, 58 1/4 inches long, 1/2 inch stock; tines are 9 inches long and 5 1/2 inches wide.

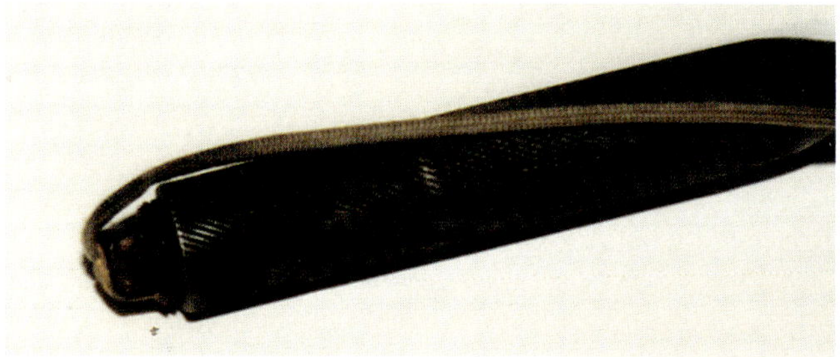

Closeup of line tie on a Fuchs' spear.

Ben George

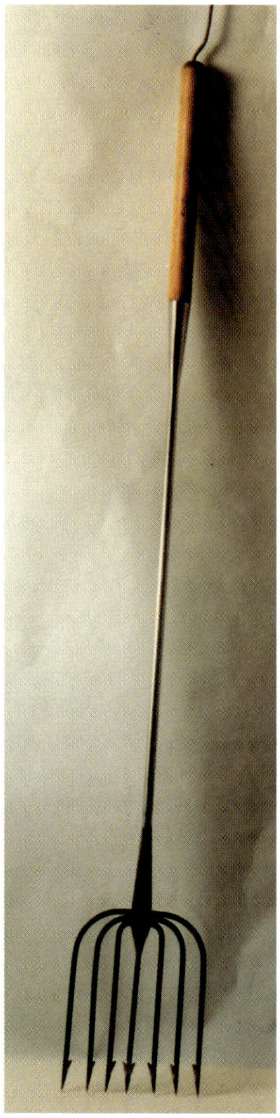

Ben George spear, 7 tines; 52 1/4 inches long, 1/2 inch stock; tines were 9 1/2 inches long and 7 inches wide.

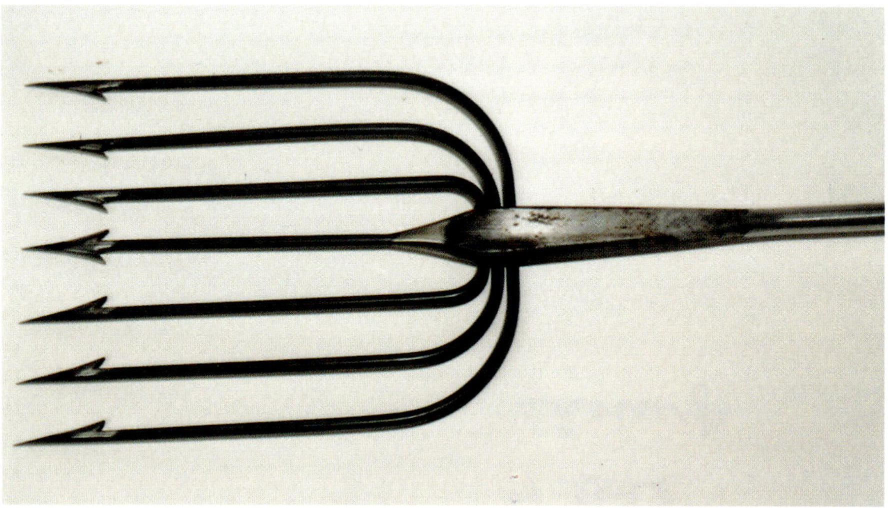

Closeup of a 7 tine Ben George spear.

Louis A. Gustis

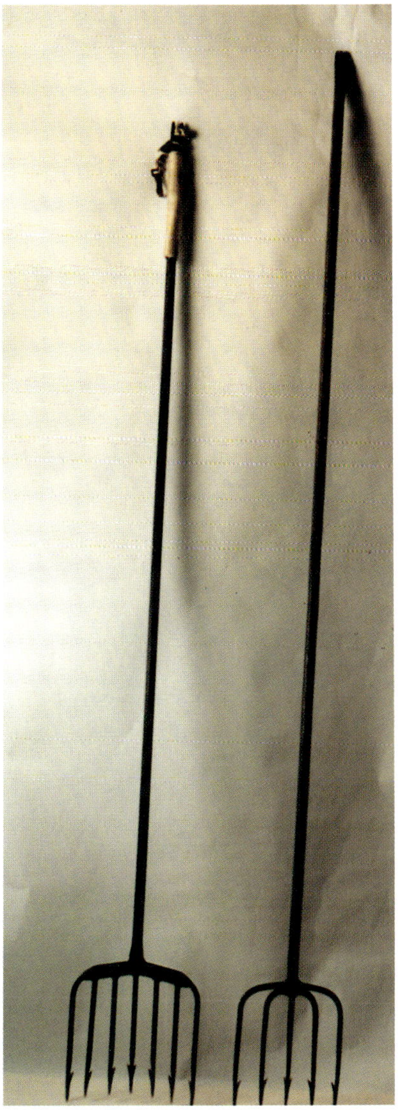

Two Brainerd spears by Louis Gustis. Left: 7 tine spear, 57 1/2 inches long, 1/2 inch stock; tines are 7 1/2 inches wide and 8 1/2 inches long. Right: is a 5 tine spear, 61 3/4 inches long, 5/8 inch stock; tines are 6 1/2 inches wide, and 7 1/2 inches long.

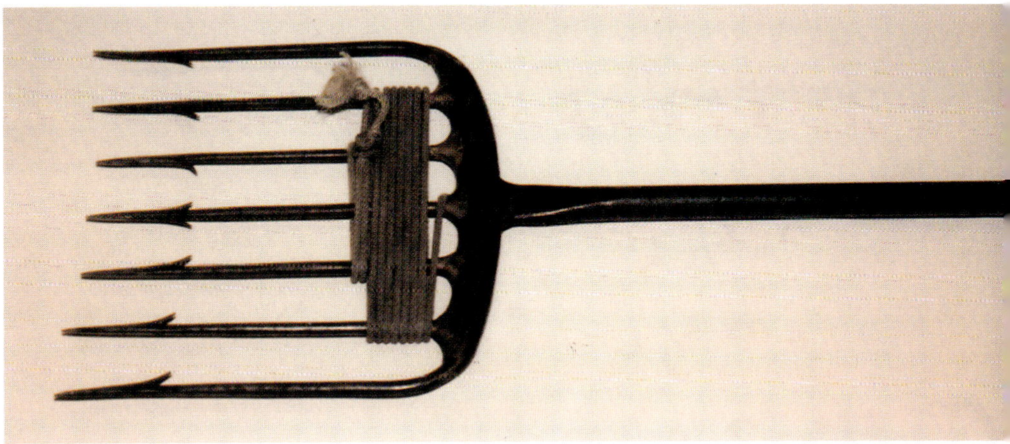

Closeup of tines on a Brainerd spear. The tines measure 7 5/8 inches in length and they are 7 1/2 inches in width. Collection of Larry Hockmayr.

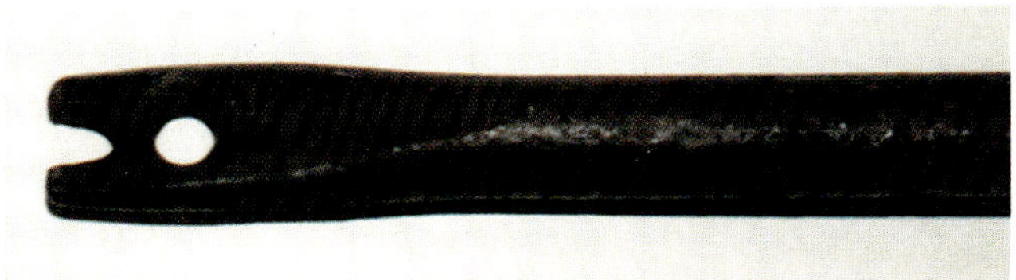

Closeup of U shaped cord holder on a Brainerd spear.

William O. "Bill" Hein

Two Bill Hein spears. Left is a 5 tine spear, 54 1/4 inches long, 5/8 inch stock; tines are 5 1/4 inches wide and 7 3/4 inches long. Right is a 7 tine Hein spear, 60 inches long, 5/8 inch stock; tines are 7 1/2 wide and 9 1/4 inches long.

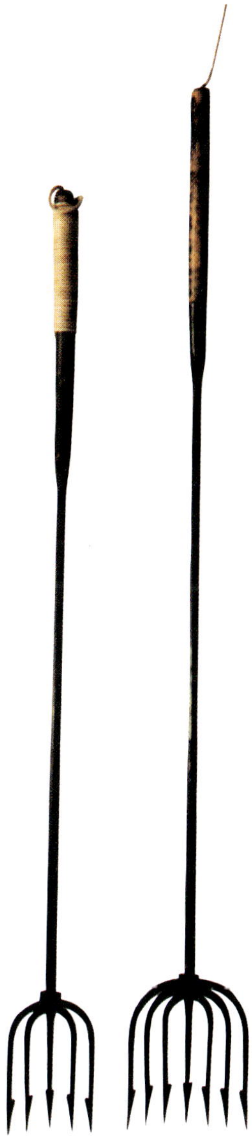

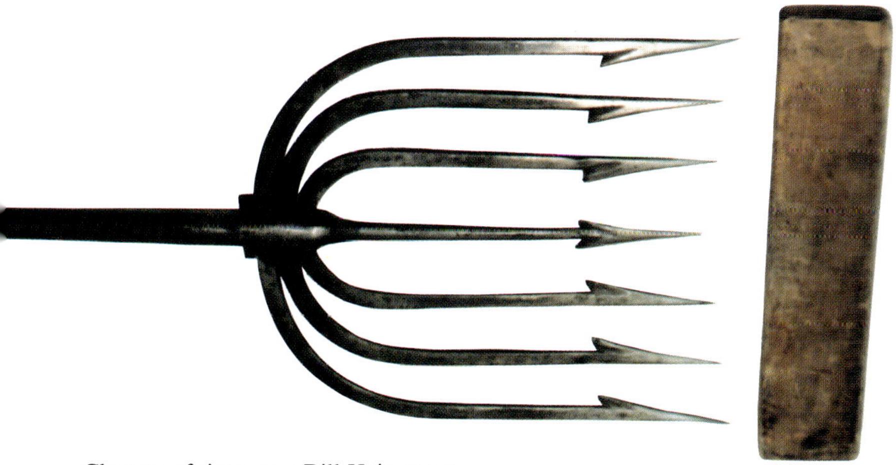

Closeup of tines on a Bill Hein spear.

Dillo Hinnenkamp

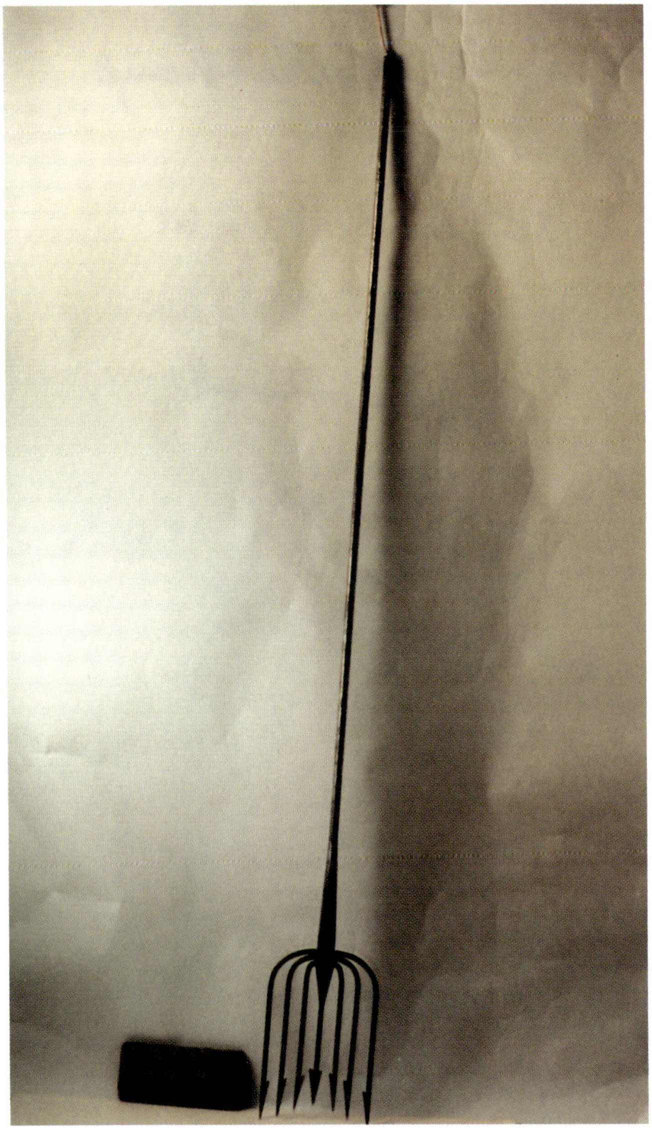

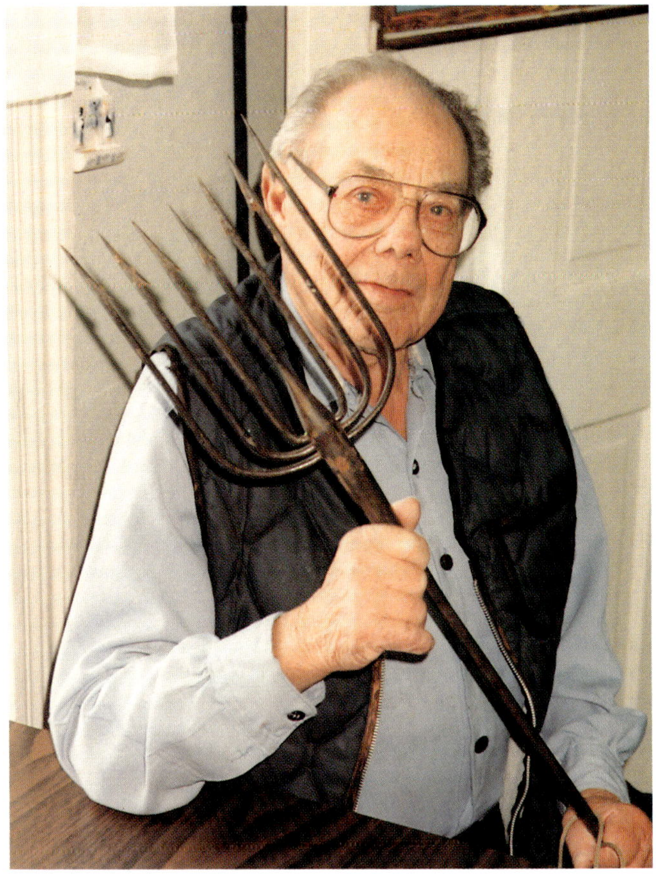

Dillo Hinnenkamp in his home, holding one of his spears. Photo courtesy of Joe Leach.

Dillo Hinnenkamp spear, 7 tines, length 59 1/2 inches, 1/2 inch stock; tines 6 1/2 inches long.

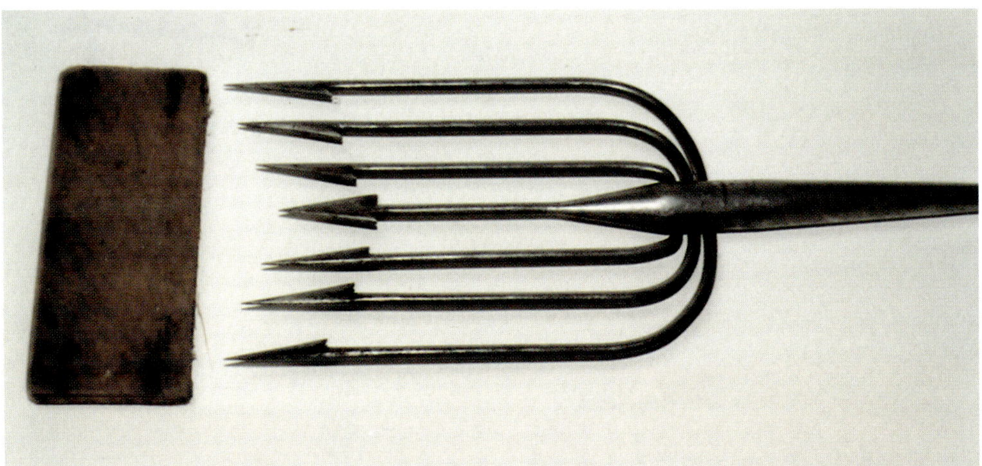

Closeup of a Hinnenkamp spear. Tines pass through the end of the all metal shaft. Hinnenkamp spears usually had 7 tines, but he also made some 5 tine models. The line was attached to a screw at the end of the shaft to minimize splash in the water when the spear was thrust.

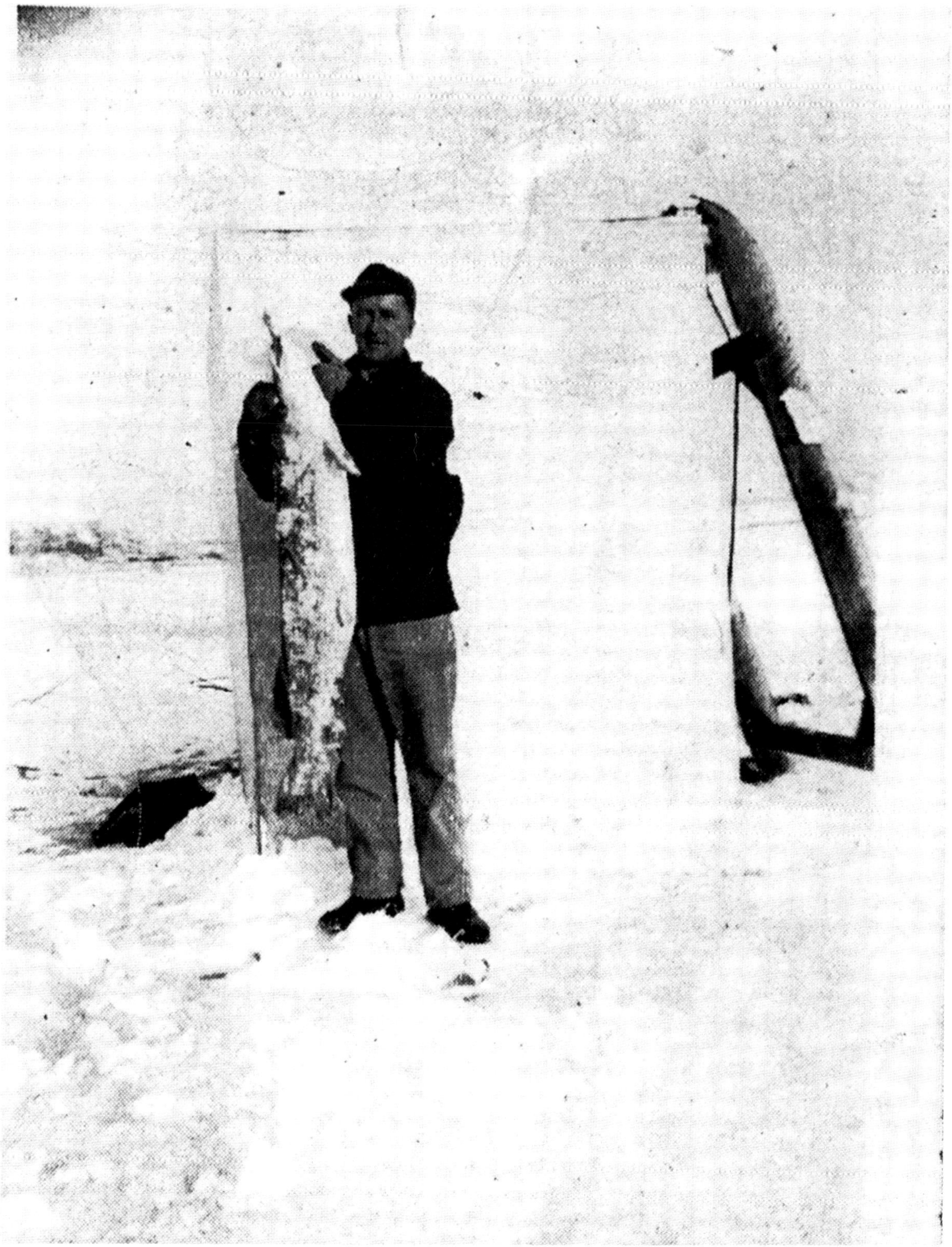

Charlie Lundgren in 1986, holding the head of his largest pike. Photo courtesy Don Vogel.

JOHN MCGILLIS*

John McGillis was born in 1912 in Aitkin, Minnesota. He drove a truck for the mines and also tended bar. Later, he joined Woodland Container Company in the 1950's and worked there until his retirement.

When he was eleven or twelve years old, he suffered a serious cut on one leg. He was in the hospital for a long convalescence. After his release, and with limited mobility, he asked to be carried to the family dark house on Blind Lake where he would remain from the early morning until sunset. Despite these long hours spear fishing, he never lost his enthusiasm for the sport.

John began making his own decoys in the 1950's and continued making them for himself or for friends until his death in 1978. His decoys were constructed from one piece of sugar pine and had wooden tails. John's son sold some of his decoys in Blegin's Bait Shop in Aitkin for $5.00 each in the early 1950's.

A style change occurred in the McGillis' decoys in the 1970's. John began to make his decoys thinner in width, but retained the same general shape. He crafted a northern pike, sunfish and two types of minnows. One decoy viewed by the author (but not pictured) had a natural wood finish with burned designs. McGillis decoys range in size from 5 inches to 9 inches in length. In some of his decoys he inserted glass eyes.

John's favorite spearing areas included the Mississippi River and Cedar Lake.

*Information supplied by John McGillis' son.

HENRY G. MAX*

Henry Max was born on August 28, 1903 in Minnesota. His parents were both from Germany. He lived most of his life in Fergus Falls, Minnesota. Henry was employed as a garage mechanic when he was first married and continued in that occupation until 1938. Thereafter, for 32 years, Henry and his wife, Hazel, owned and operated a grocery store. He died on May 26, 1978.

In 1935 or 1936, Henry was stricken with arthritis which became progressively more debilitating. Forced to spend many hours in bed, Henry started to whittle to pass the time. Neighbors requested that he make some decoys and when these were found to be effective, he began marketing them in stores. After awhile, Henry was able to walk with a cane and he marketed his decoys with a greater fervor. It took him about an hour and a half to make one decoy. Max produced about 1,500 to 2,000 decoys per year. His decoys came primarily in two sizes, five inches and six inches in length, but some larger decoys have been found. Although he employed several color patterns, the predominant one was red and white.

*Information provided by Hazel Max and in an unsigned article in *Forum,* No. 5, by the American Fish Decoy Association.

MIKE MEHOLENSKY*

Mike Meholensky was born September 17, 1913 in Chisholm, Minnesota. He worked his entire adult life in the mines in the Hibbing, Minnesota area, retiring in 1978. Mike now resides in Buhl, Minnesota. He was a mechanic in the processing and taconite sections of the mines. He and his wife had three girls and a son, Michael. Mike Meholensky is now a widower.

During the 1930's, he first began to make spear fishing decoys. These were made mainly for his own use and were never intended to become a business. Nevertheless, some Meholensky decoys were sold to friends or acquaintances. These latter were sold for $1.50 or $2.00, small recompense considering a decoy was two or three hours in construction. Over the years, he might have made as many as 500 decoys.

Mr. Meholensky never made a single decoy, but used a batch process, tracing his tail and fin configurations onto metal. A Meholensky decoy can be distinguished from other makers on the basis of the decoys' eyes. Each eye has a black outer ring and a yellow band surrounding a black pupil.

Meholensky decoys are also notable because their paint is often in a good state of preservation. This may be attributed to the fact that the decoys were constructed from native cedar. This wood does not shrink or expand as much as other wood when it gets cold, or when it is removed from icy water into a warm dark house. Meholensky fish were also painted three times with good quality oil based paint, adding to their exterior preservation.

The typical, or general, outside shape of his decoy was that of a sucker. However, he also made crappies, blue gills and northerns. A red and white decoy with no particular fish species in mind was also made.

Mr. Meholensky lost interest in spear fishing, and consequently in making decoys, in the 1950's. About this time, his son Michael [the elder Meholensky is known as "Mike" and the son as "Michael"], began to spear and also started making decoys, using his father's fin patterns and techniques. Thus, fish decoys from the 1950's or 1960's may very well have been made by Michael instead of Mike Meholensky. In the past few years, however, the elder Meholensky has again begun constructing decoys, although he still does not spear fish.

*Information supplied by Mike Meholensky and Bill Stoetzel.

JOHN MELQUIST

John Melquist was born November 19, 1892 in Ebro, Minnesota. He was a section foreman for the Great Northern Railroad in Minnesota and North Dakota. Most of his life, John resided in Warba, Minnesota.

John began spear fishing in 1932. He made several decoys for his own use. Some were fashioned from cedar and others he made out of rubber. All of John's decoys were painted. His favorite spear fishing lake was Shallow Lake near Warba.

Mr. Melquist died on March 5, 1986.

DAVE MERTENS*

Dave Mertens was born April 8, 1919 in Staples, Minnesota, where he has lived all of his life. He worked as a train engineer for the Northern Pacific Railroad from October of 1943 until his retirement in January of 1983. Married in 1950, Mr. Mertens had two grown children, a boy and a girl.

He began carving fish decoys in the 1940's after becoming a spear fishing enthusiast. He preferred working with cedar; cedar does not rot and it is difficult to split. Dave's earliest decoys had fins made of copper that he obtained from an old copper boiler. He made suckers, perch, northern pike and sunfish. All of his decoys have notched wooden tails and distinctive fin shapes. He placed two pectoral fins on each side of his fish. His decoys are also distinctive because he meticulously carved scales into all of them, except for the suckers. Dave's preferred colors were browns and silver tones. He stated that he used a good grade of exterior paint and applied clear lacquer to his decoys after the paint had dried. His decoys had eyes painted with a contrasting circle around each of them. He used the modified loop method for his line ties. The mouths on his decoys were painted red.

Dave still carves decoys but his contemporary fish utilize brighter colors, have tack eyes, and their mouths are carved open and painted red. His later fins also are made from aluminum instead of copper.

*Information supplied in an interview with Mr. Mertens. His name is erroneously given as "Mertins" in Kimballs, op. cit., Vol. II, p. 108.

ALBERT MEYER*

Albert Meyer was born in 1897 in Aitkin County, Minnesota. He died in 1981 after living in Crosby, Minnesota most of his life. He was employed as an underground miner until his retirement.

Mr. Meyer spear fished in the 1930's and 1940's on Serpent Lake, Placid Lake and Cedar Lake. He made his spear decoys at this time, some of which are pictured.

*Information courtesy of Mrs. Albert Meyer.

LEO MILLER

Born in 1909 in Sauk Center, Minnesota, Mr. Miller worked for the railroad. Leo carved fish decoys from the 1930's until the early 1980's. He began carving when he and his wife, Pearl, lived in Westport, Minnesota. Leo would make decoys when his wife was watching a program on T.V. which he did not enjoy. He would go into the basement and carve decoys with a jack knife and sand the decoys by hand.

Twelve years before his death in 1993 [February 2], he suffered a stroke and stopped making decoys.

FRANK MIZERA*

Frank Mizera was born in Ely, Minnesota on December 4, 1898. As a teenager, he worked on iron ore boats which operated from Duluth. This job ended in 1925 when his parents were drowned in a boating accident. In 1929, he married; he and his wife, Josephine, lived in his parents' home on Lake Shigawa near Ely.

With a great knowledge of the Boundary Waters area and a quiet and congenial nature, Frank Mizera soon became a popular guide. Mizera began making decoys to supplement his income in the 1930's. Over the years he probably produced thousands of them, working during slow times and in the evenings. A barber in town acted as the distributor for his decoys. Mizera decoys are found, even today, in virtually every part of Minnesota. Due to a stroke suffered in the mid-1960's, Mizera had to move to town. He nevertheless continued making decoys until his death on June 12, 1969.

Mizera decoys [he also made lures which were painted in much the same manner as his decoys] are very distinctive in shape and paint design. Over the years, his decoys changed little, although his later decoys had more of a pronounced slope to the nose. In addition, his more recent decoys also became thinner. Mizera decoys had two pectoral fins on each side and wooden tails with painted strips. The fins also had painted lines for decoration. Three double-line gill lines were painted on as well. For the eyes of his decoys, Mizera painted a black iris with a white circle surrounding it.

Most Mizera decoys were painted the ubiquitous red and white, although he left some natural wood (varnished) with paint or burned designs. Others basic Mizera colors were black, orange and turquoise. His most scarce decoys are the ones painted turquoise or black with whimsical fish painted on the sides.

*See also Donna Tonelli, "Frank Mizera Minnesota Fish Decoy Maker," *Decoy Magazine,* July/August 1991, pp. 33-35.

NICK MOES

Nicholas Moes was born in Germany on September 11, 1859. He came to the United States when he was 16 years old. In 1888, he married his wife, Anna. Nick and his wife lived in Lakeville, Minnesota. They had five children — three boys and two girls. Nick was a carpenter and cabinet maker. He died on January 5, 1953 at the age of 93.

It is uncertain when Nick began making fishing decoys. He probably made only about twelve. They were nicely constructed with a distinctive rounded dorsal fin and metal tails. Most were made to resemble minnows.

E.W. MOOERS*

E.W. Mooers was born in 1896 and died in 1971. He was a beautician in the Crosby, Minnesota area. Part Chippewa Indian from the White Earth Reservation, he was related to Chief Hole-in-the-Day.

Mr. Mooers made decoys for his own use in the 1920's. His decoys had both wooden and metal tails, glass eyes, and a small dorsal fin.

*Information supplied by Mr. Mooers of Crosby, Minnesota — E.W. Mooers' son.

MATH "MATTY" MUELLNER*

Math Muellner was born on June 30, 1917. In 1936, he married his wife, Sally. At this time he was employed at the creamery in New Munich, Minnesota. Matty went into business for himself in 1945, purchasing a bar in New Munich, selling beer with a 3.2% alcohol content.

An avid fisherman, Mr. Muellner made his own decoys. At first, some were given to friends, but later he began selling them. Because his decoys worked so well, there were individuals who copied his design. It is estimated that over the years Math made hundreds of decoys.

Mr. Muellner passed away on December 1, 1982.

* Information courtesy of Joe Leach.

MELVIN NESSET*

Melvin Nesset was born in 1897 in Iowa. While Melvin was still quite young, his family moved to Minnesota. In the 1920's and 1930's he was employed in logging. However, by the early 1940's Mr. Nesset became a farmer in the Blackduck, Minnesota area. Melvin was married and had three daughters and one son.

His decoy making began in the 1940's. As Mr. Nesset was a farmer, he would whittle decoys during the winter when his work load had slacked. He made two distinct types of decoys. One model was his "whale" decoy. These were blocky fish, almost 1 3/4 inches wide at their widest point, and about 6 1/2 inches long with wooden tails. The whales sported two dorsal fins. Two metal pectoral fins, small in size relative to the body, were located on each side. Mr. Nesset painted these with enamel paint in abstract decoration. The "whale" decoys were heavily weighted with lead.

His second decoy type more realistically resembled a fish. He made a perch, small northern and a sucker. Unfortunately, no specimens were available to be photographed.

Mr. Nesset stopped his production of decoys in the early 1970's. Over the years, he might have made 200 decoys, most for his own use, but he also gave them away to friends and neighbors. He passed away in 1987.

*Information courtesy of Dean Nesset, Melvin's son.

ERNEST "ERNIE" NEWMAN*

Ernie Newman was born in Washburn, Wisconsin on July 26, 1908. In 1940, he moved to Minnesota and settled in Carlton. Shortly thereafter, he went to work for the U.S. Steel plant in Morgan Park. Ernie retired from that plant 32 years later in 1973. Unfortunately, he did not enjoy a long retirement; he died on November 4, 1976.

Newman began whittling lures at the age of 15. Later, as an adult, he began making fish decoys, both to supplement his income and as a hobby. Ernie used a fine grain redwood for the body of his decoys because it would not rot in water. He claimed that it took him about ten minutes to whittle and sand a decoy. Holes were drilled for the lead weighing. He used a white base coat and painting was done by brush, followed by two to four coats of marine sealer. Some of the eyes for his decoys were made by using the squared off end of a brush. This marking was then dotted with a smaller brush. However, many Newman decoys have survived adorned with glass eyes. Ernie achieved a scale effect on his decoys by rubbing thin cooking foils over the wet paint, or he would paint over a scale cloth. Most of

Newman's designs were abstract with strong contrasting colors. Newman stated that his smaller sized decoys were made only after 1963.

*See Jim Blubaugh, "Whittling Fish Lures a Delicate Procedure," *Duluth News-Tribune,* February 4, 1973; and Donna Tonelli, "Ernest Newman Minnesota's master tackle maker," *Decoy Magazine,* March/April 1991, pp. 16-18.

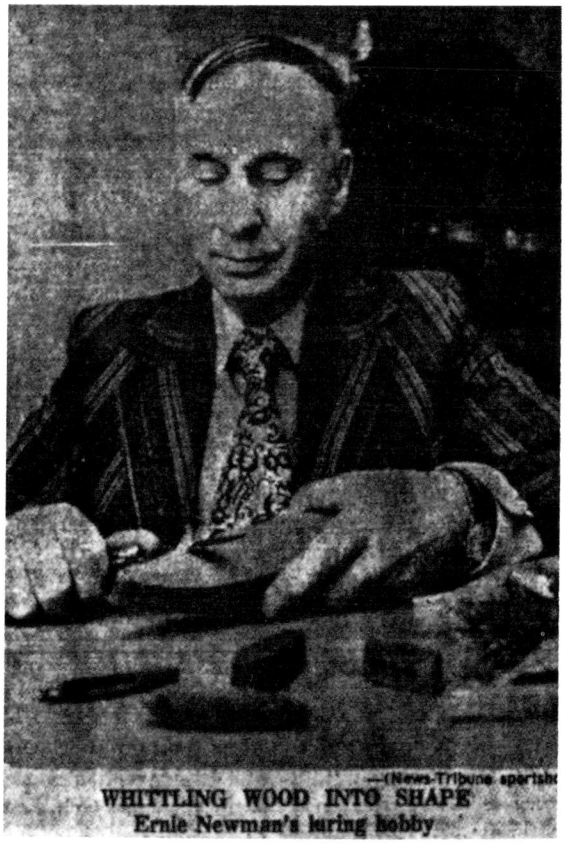

Ernie Newman in 1973.

JAMES F. NEWMAN

James F. Newman was born at Cohato, Minnesota in 1919. As a youth he went to a Civilian Conservation Corps camp. He served in World War II and was a tank driver during the Battle of the Bulge in Germany.

After returning from the War, Newman became a jeweler in Cohato, and later moved to Milaca, Minnesota where he started a jewelry store. He operated this store for about 30 years until his death in August of 1982.

Mr. Newman was an avid spear fisherman and speared Shakopee Lake, Mille Lacs Lake, Onamia Lake as well as the Rum River around Milaca. He was the president of the Whittler's Club. Newman carved pickerel, bass and sunfish.

ALBERT NIEHAUS

Albert Niehaus was born on October 22, 1912 in Richmond, Minnesota. Never married, he was a former employee of Heying and Torborg Chevrolet Garage, and Brinkly's Service Station. Mr. Niehaus was also the city assessor of Richmond. For the twelve years prior to his death he was employed as a maintenance man at Richmond Disposal Plant. Mr. Niehaus passed away on April 25, 1987. His obituary described him as a "manufacturer of winter spear fishing decoys."

Niehaus was a prolific decoy maker, as he produced 500 to 600 decoys per year. He sold them through various Twin Cities sporting goods stores from the 1940's through the 1970's. Most of his decoys had eyes painted black with a contrasting color around them. His decoys were carved with an open mouth and he had two distinctive pectoral fins on each side of his fish.

FRANCIS NORTHBURG*

Francis Northburg was born in 1915 in North Dakota. At an early age he moved to Crosby, Minnesota. Later, he began working in the mines around the Crosby-Ironton area. He also worked in construction and as a carpenter. His last employment was with the Scorpion Company where he worked on engines. Francis was married and had three children.

He became interested in spear fishing in the 1930's. Mr. Northburg made decoys for his own use from butternut wood. His surviving decoys were crafted in the 1970's. He made wood tail decoys with one or two pectoral fins and a dorsal and anal fin.

Francis ceased spear fishing in the 1960's. He continued, however, to make decoys almost to the time of his death in November of 1985.

*Information supplied by Mr. Northburg's son Darrell. The Kimballs, op. cit., erroneously picture an Art Seguin decoy for that of Francis Northburg in Volumes II and III.

JOHN P. NOVAK*

John P. Novak was born on June 8, 1922 in Ely, Minnesota. He began working as a "minnow boy" at age 14, seining minnow and doing boat repairs at a resort near Ely. Later, John was a fishing guide. Service in the military during World War II interrupted this business. After the War, Mr. Novak went back to guiding fishermen and hunters to over 500 lakes in Minnesota and Canada. After 14 years of guiding, he went to work for School District

696 in Ely, where he did maintenance work and was a fireman for the school boilers. He retired after 31 years of service for the School District.

His spear fishing decoy production began in 1938. Mr. Novak constructed his earliest decoys from cedar because it was a light wood and was easy to work. Later, he began using birch wood as it was stronger and more durable. Over the years, Mr. Novak estimated that he made about 1,000 spear fishing decoys. He painted them red and white, silver, and with a scaled effect (see pictured decoys). He sold his decoys for 50¢ initially and over the years, raised the price to $3.00.

Mr. Novak also made jigs for summer fishing. These were initially made of wood, then lead, and later he used rifle shells with bucktail. He claimed that these worked well for walleyes, lake trout and pike. Jigs sold for $1.50 each to fishermen and resort owners who ordered them. Mr. Novak stated that he made approximately 20,000 jigs. He also constructed dark houses on demand. These were first made of wood, but later he used aluminum.

He is married and has one step son, six grandchildren and six great-grandchildren. Mr. Novak still enjoys spear fishing, especially on Lake Shagawa and Basswood Lake.

*Information courtesy of Mr. John Novak.

REINO NURMI*

Reino Nurmi was born on August 12, 1914 in Finland, Minnesota. Since 1934, he has resided in Two Harbors. Mr. Nurmi began working for the railroad in 1940 and continued in this line until 1975, when he retired. Beginning as a laborer, he worked with various types of machines and ultimately became a foreman. Mr. Nurmi is married and has two sons, three daughters and 14 grandchildren.

When he returned from military duty in 1950, he began constructing fish decoys for his own use. Mr. Nurmi estimated that he made 12 to 24 decoys over the years. His preferred medium was cedar wood and he utilized tin cans for fins. He had two pectoral fins on each side of his decoys, a tail fin and a pronounced dorsal fin. The back pectoral fins were affixed to a notched out area at the bottom of the decoy's body. Decoy eyes had a black painted iris with a white outline encircling the iris. He carved an open mouth in his decoys. He used hobby enamel paint to decorate his decoys because "it dried quickly." Mr. Nurmi ceased making decoys at about the time of his last spearing license in 1972.

An avid spear fisherman, Reino speared on Stump Lake, Stone Lake and Bear Lake.

*Information courtesy of Reino Nurmi.

HAROLD NYGAARD*

Harold Nygaard was born in 1909 in Crookston, Minnesota. After his family had moved to Walker and then to Akeley, Minnesota, they eventually came to Brainerd in 1919. Mr. Nygaard worked for awhile in the paper mills in Brainerd, but spent most of his working life in the Northern Pacific Railroad shops. He was first employed as a stockman, was subsequently promoted to a foreman, and retired from the railroad in 1974.

An avid spear fisherman, he preferred to spear on Gull Lake, Mission Lake, and Lake Mille Lacs. He began constructing decoys for himself and for friends in the late 1920's. Over the years, he made about 24 decoys, but only seven or eight have survived. His decoys were fashioned from white pine. His decoys typically had glass eyes and, among his species-specific fish, he made trout, sunfish, perch, and minnows. Nygaard decoys had metal or wooden tails.

*Information courtesy of Mr. Nygaard.

OLIVER OLMSCHENK*

Oliver Olmschenk was born in 1913 at Elrosa, Minnesota. In 1916 his family moved to Stapleton, Minnesota and in 1936 he came to settle in Crosby, where he has resided ever since. His first occupation was carpentry; he next went to work in the mines. He later returned to carpentry work. In 1941 he returned to the mines until his retirement in 1970.

Oliver constructed his decoys from pine. All of them were made in the 1930's. His decoys ranged in length from approximately 4 1/2 inches to 14 inches. The decoys are characterized as being wide near the head of the decoy and then tapering down to a straight length of uniform size in the rear of the fish. He utilized one dorsal fin and two pectoral fins which were rounded in shape. His fins were always made of metal. The metal tail fin of the decoy was rather straight cut instead of round in form. Tie lines were of the band type. His painting was somewhat crude and his predominant colors were green, yellow, red and white. To represent the decoys' eyes, he used screw and nail heads. Sometimes Mr. Olmschenk's decoys had no eyes at all.

*Information from an interview with Mr. Olmschenk.

ELMER OXLEY*

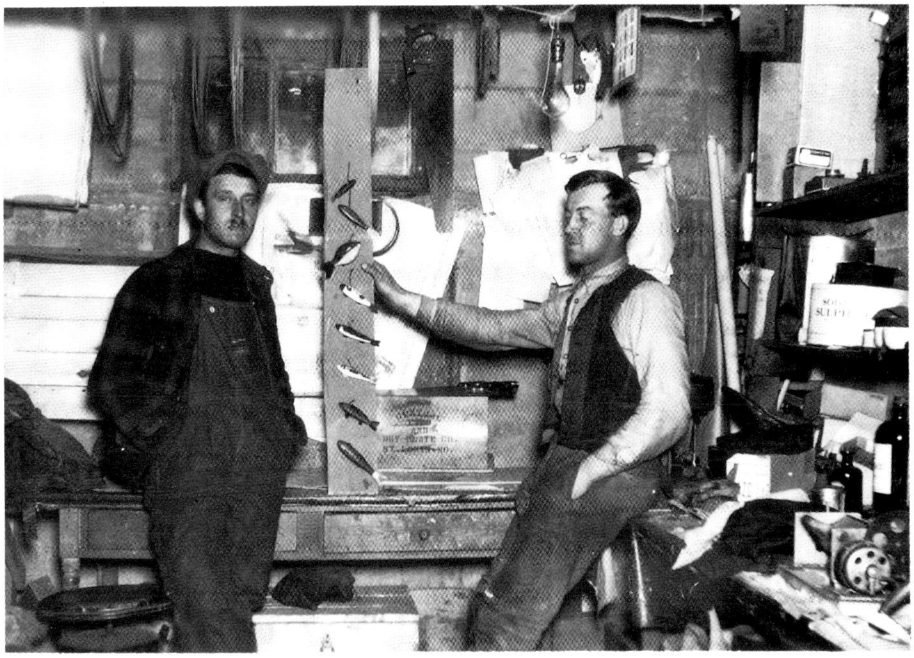

Elmer Oxley was born in 1902 in Foxhome, Minnesota but lived most of his life in the Fergus Falls area. Never married, Mr. Oxley was a taxidermist for 60 years. In his youth, he helped his father in the latter's photo finishing business. Elmer later made classic films showing spear fishing, hunting and other events around Fergus Falls.

Mr. Oxley began making decoys in his late teens. His decoys were for his own use only. His decoys were all approximately the same size, five inches. All had glass eyes and were painted abstractly. He stopped making decoys in the 1940's.

Mr. Oxley passed away in 1991.

*Information supplied by Rich Oxley, Elmer's nephew.

Mr. Oxley (right) showing some of his decoys to a friend.

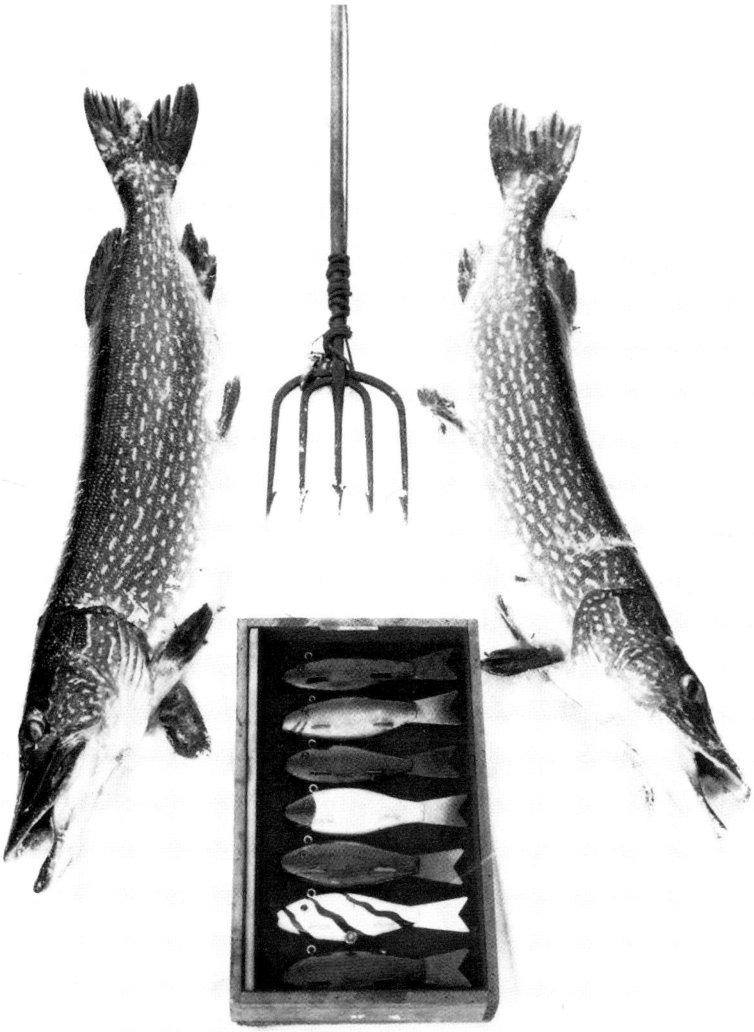

Two large northern pike speared by Elmer Oxley, with his spear and decoys displayed.

WILBUR "WILLIE" PETERSON*

Willie Peterson was born on December 8, 1921 in Brainerd, Minnesota. One of his first jobs was as a blacksmith's helper for the Northern Pacific Railroad [now the Burlington Northern] in 1941. However, by December of 1942, Willie was serving in the army in Greenland. He came home on furlough in July of 1944, and in August, was married. The Army then sent him to Germany and he was mustered out in November of 1945.

Upon his return to civilian life, Willie went back to the Northern Pacific as an apprentice blacksmith [later he became a journeyman blacksmith]. Although he had speared from childhood, Peterson began making decoys only after his Army service had ended [i.e., 1945]. At work, he had an hour for lunch and would whittle decoys there, or at home, during this time. Decoys were made for his own use and he also sold them to people with whom he worked. Peterson decoys were also sold to Martin Sports Shop in Brainerd [now located in Nisswa, Minnesota] with about twelve fastened to a card for $6.00 or $7.00.

Willie's preferred decoy body material was butternut or white pine because it was easy to carve. All Peterson decoys have a white undercoat [his paint was leaded and came from the railroad]. Decoys were hung to dry on a coat hanger. Because Willie was partially color blind, he would ask his wife's advice regarding the proper color on the finish coat. Often, Peterson would sprinkle glitter on the wet finish paint on his fish. The lead in his decoys extends almost to the top of each for proper balance, and the front fins are locked into the lead. The back fin was not nailed, but pulled into position in the slot made for it. It [the back fin] was all one piece.

The eyes on his decoys were either painted on or were glass beads nailed into the body. His decoys all have wooden tails and his line ties were wire attached into the lead. Peterson made a variety of species of decoys including northerns, sunfish, sucker, bullhead, minnows and frogs.

Willie retired in 1977. In 1981 he had surgery on an eye. This ended his decoy making. He died in January of 1986.

*Information courtesy of Mr. Peterson's son, daughters and wife.

CLEMEN PLACE

Clemen Place was born in 1887 in Independence, Iowa, but lived most of his life in Mango, Minnesota. He was a farmer. Mr. Place died in 1970.

One surviving decoy is a northern, said to be carved between 1930 and 1932. It, however, appears to be much older.

JOHN HERMAN PLACKNER*

John Plackner was born on September 27, 1899 in Frazee, Minnesota. He lived in Frazee all of his life. He was married and had four daughters. Mr. Plackner was a road grader, working for Becker County, and retired at age 65. He died on October 27, 1981.

John began making decoys in the 1950's and probably made thousands over the years [he stopped making them in the late 1970's]. Most of his decoys were given away to friends. His earliest decoys had wooden tails, but at some point he abandoned this style in favor of metal tail fish. His decoys had two to three wire line ties and two pectoral fins on each side of his decoy bodies. The eyes on his decoys were painted with a black iris and contrasting white paint encircling the iris. His earlier decoys were painted with enamel paint, but for his later ones he seemed to use a screening process for his paint.

*Information courtesy of Mrs. Mary Plackner.

HENRY J. RAMTHUN*

Henry J. Ramthun was born on October 21, 1874 in Buffalo, Minnesota. He was a farmer. He was married and had nine children.

When he retired from farming in 1942, he moved to Buffalo and began carving decoys for his own use and to sell. Henry would make his decoys in a fish house on his property in the summertime.

Undoubtedly influenced by the Faue brothers who lived in the area, Ramthun decoys closely resemble those made by Otto Faue. The tail fin, dorsal and anal fins on his decoys are virtually identical to Faue's. Ramthun also used the band-style tie line.

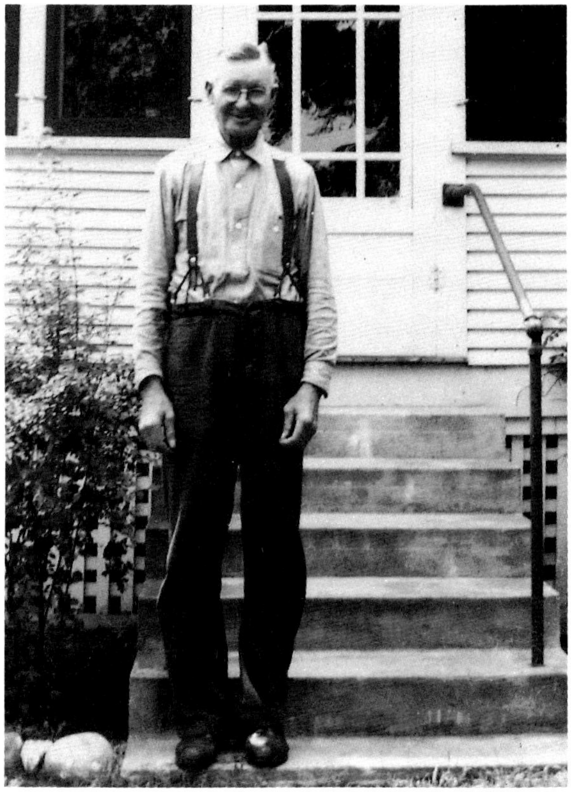

Henry J. Ramthun.

However, Henry did not use the colorful and imaginative paint schemes for which the Faues were noted. Instead, most of his decoys were painted red and white. His largest decoys were eight to twelve inches in length.

Over the years he crafted hundreds of decoys. Mr. Ramthun continued making decoys until his death on December 30, 1957.

*Information provided by Mrs. Ferne Bruhn, one of Mr. Ramthun's daughters.

GEORGE RANDALL*

George Randall was born August 19, 1921 in Morris, Minnesota. He began making decoys for his own use in the 1940's. Naturally, he is best known for the large number of decoys he fabricated for sale. However, Mr. Randall was an avid spear fisherman and a number of decoys have survived from his personal rig. He passed away on February 12, 1979.

*See Chapter 6 for a more detailed biography of Mr. Randall.

MYRON ROBERTS*

Myron Roberts was born in 1914 in Chisholm, Minnesota. He has resided there all of his life. Never married, he worked for U.S. Steel, performing a variety of duties including tractor operator and working in the plumbing department.

An avid spear fisherman, Mr. Roberts crafted decoys for his own use. These were made from pine. He made decoys with both wood and metal tails. Unusual characteristics of his decoys are the streamlined anal and dorsal fins which were carved from wood. His line ties were made of heavy gauge wire, using the modified loop method. The gills were carved and eye cavities were carved out and painted.

*Information provided in an interview with Mr. Roberts.

GEORGE ROBIDEAU*

George Robideau was born July 7, 1917 in Virginia, Minnesota. He was married and had three daughters who are all grown. George worked in the mines on the track gang, and in the sampling department. He also worked in factories in Milwaukee and as a carpenter. He retired from Jones and Laughlin where he worked as a mine mechanic. Mr. Robideau resided in Hibbing, Minnesota.

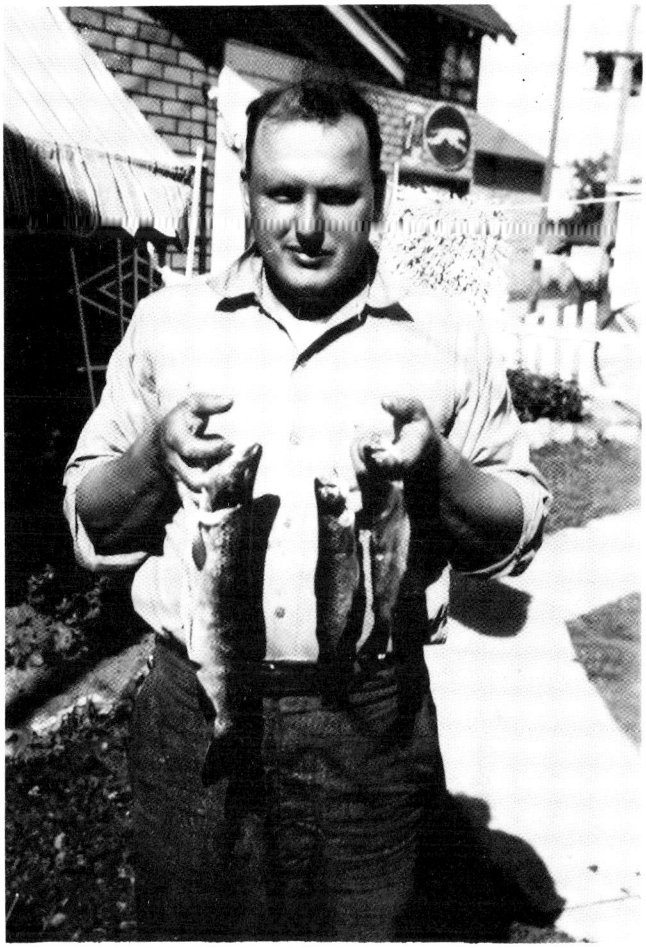

George Robideau with a good catch.

Mr. and Mrs. Robideau owned a cabin on Swan Lake and George enjoyed spearing there. He began making decoys in 1946 and over the years made about 15 of them. They were diverse in size and shape. All were made from pine.

Mr. Robideau died on January 7, 1994.

*Information supplied by Mrs. Robideau.

RAY ROSENGREN*

Ray Rosengren was born on August 13, 1916 in Farwell, Minnesota. Ray was married but had no children. He served in World War II in the Army Air Force. Employed as an accountant, Mr. Rosengren moved to Elbow Lake, Minnesota in 1940 and he resided there until his death in 1992.

Ray made fish decoys for his use only. His craftsmanship was not limited to one type of decoy, but rather he made three distinct types. He made three red and white painted decoys with sloped noses and a leaf-type painted motif on the tail. He also made minnow-type decoys with a dorsal fin that was absent from his red and white models.

In addition, Mr. Rosengren made a northern decoy which was his favorite. It has both a dorsal and anal fin and is realistically painted as opposed to the more abstract or geometric styles utilized on his other decoys. Judging from the quality of his decoys, Mr. Rosengren was one of Minnesota's top decoy makers.

*Information supplied in an interview with Mr. Rosengren.

HARRY SANDELL*

Harry Sandell was born on January 22, 1923 in St. Paul, Minnesota. He lived in the Pine River/Pequot lakes area for most of his life, prior to his placement in a nursing home in 1973.

He began making decoys with his father in 1938. Although his father did not sell his decoys, Harry would hitch a ride to various towns to sell them. He charged from 25¢ to 75¢ for one. Harry used to pick up wood and scrap pieces of metal from which he would craft his decoys. His decoys are very distinctive, having graceful, flowing lines. The eyes for his decoys were usually painted as solid black circles. Silver was the preferred color for the fish that he made and the bodies of his decoys were very slender in width. He made two metal pectoral fins on each side of the decoy and also used a metal tail fin. His decoys' line ties were of the pig tail type, and the metal dorsal fin would be placed immediately after the line tie loops. He sometimes would paint his fish with geometric designs of red and black.

Sandell's decoys have to rate among the best in Minnesota in consideration of the craftsmanship, design, and overall eye appeal.

*Information from an interview with Mr. Sandell.

CHESTER "CHET" SAWYER*

Chet Sawyer was born on March 20, 1904 in Grand Rapids, Minnesota. His father was a trapper and hunter who had homesteaded on Sawyer Lake, north of Grand Rapids. Chet would perform a number of duties for his father, including driving deer. His father would take individuals deer hunting or fishing. Word of mouth recommendations brought outdoorsmen to the Sawyers, as they did not advertise.

Already at age eight or nine, Chet was carving decoys while in trapping shacks and/or in the evenings. Always enterprising, young Chet knocked on dark house doors, and to an amazement of the inhabitant, demonstrated the efficiency of his decoys over whatever the spear fisherman was using. His sales pitch was often successful and he would receive 25¢ to 50¢ for one of his decoys.

As a teenager, Chet worked for the old Pokegama Hotel in Grand Rapids. He also found time to carve decoys. These were sold to the Powers Hardware Store in Grand Rapids for 25¢ each. Powers, in turn, marked his decoys for sale at 50¢.

At age 15, Chet was under contract to produce 10,000 decoys for the Marshall Wells Wholesale Company in Duluth. According to Mr. Sawyer, these decoys were sold mainly to buyers located in Canada and Alaska. This latter fact may account for the relatively few Sawyer decoys found in Minnesota.

Chet subsequently worked as a locomotive tender on a steam engine for the Danube Taconite Mine located between Taconite and Bovey, Minnesota. Danube was a strip mining operation. After three months, Chet was transferred to another strip mine in Calumet, Minnesota. Despite being kept busy during daylight hours, he would carve decoys at night and sell them to coworkers or other fishermen.

Chet later went to work for A. Guthrie and Company. He had previously learned to be a locomotive engineer, but could not "officially" pilot a train until he reached the age of 21. He also learned to operate the heavy steam driven mining equipment known as "muckers."

At one point, Chet was discharged from the Guthrie Company while working in northern Michigan because he had talked to an I.W.W. delegate [Industrial Workers of the World, a radical, class conscious, labor organization which recruited members from the men who worked in the mines]. He was reinstated after the general superintendent of operations interceded in his behalf.

Later, Chet became proficient in iron working and was involved in the construction of radio towers.

No slacker, he worked until he was 73 years old. However, Mr. Sawyer maintained that he has not made decoys for sale in 30 years. Presumably, he could have made a career of producing decoys. Chet claimed that sometime after the end of World War II [but before 1950], Fred Lexow, the famous Bovey, Minnesota decoy carver and artist [see this chapter], wanted to go into business with Sawyer, producing spear fishing decoys. Lexow proposed that Sawyer construct the decoys, and that he [Lexow, an artist in his own right] would paint them. Sawyer boasted that Lexow's decoys could not begin to operate in the water as well as his. He claimed that he would sell his [Sawyer's] decoys for $5.00 each.

Mr. Sawyer stated that the type of fish he carved most often was a small [four by five inches] shiner or smelt. His wood of choice for the body of the decoy was green cedar. He also made northern pikes, sunfish, crappies, blue gills and walleyes. His preferred paint style was silver on the bottom of the decoy, followed by grey sides, and black on the top. These colors were blended. Other decoys were painted solid colors. Some were decorated with red heads. A few of Sawyer's decoys were painted by Fred Lexow and others by his daughter. Chet would also sometimes carve scales into the sides of his decoys.

Fins and tails for the decoys were made from tobacco tins, and later from coffee cans, before the days when coffee cans had ridged bodies. Sawyer's back fins were always smaller than the front fins and placed higher in the fish's body than the front fins. His fins were made in one piece to slide through the body of the fish. The front fins were leaded into the fish, but the back fins slid into a slot made for them and were then tacked into position.

After he had obtained a drill, Sawyer would drill several holes in the bottom of the decoy and then take a knife to carve the cavity in a rectangular shape. Once the cavity was carved, he inserted the front fins and the tie line, and poured the lead to secure them.

Chet claimed that the largest fish that he has ever speared was a 48 pound northern or muskie. He said that he has never met a lake where he did not like to go spear fishing. His decoys reflect the love that he had for the sport and his pride in his craftsmanship.

Mr. Sawyer passed away in 1994.

*Information supplied in an interview with Mr. Sawyer in 1992. See also Donna Tonelli, "Chet Sawyer Folk Artist of the North Woods," *Decoy Magazine,* July/August 1992, pp. 32-34.

EDWARD HERMAN SCHULTZ*

Ed Schultz was born on August 12, 1880 in Fairhaven, Minnesota. He was married to Carrie Barrett in 1918 at Clearwater, Minnesota. They lived together in St. Cloud, Minnesota. She preceded him in death on December 28, 1946. Mr. Schultz was the head gardener at the St. Cloud Reformatory for 33 years, prior to his retirement in 1945. He remarried in 1952 and his second wife passed away in 1962. Mr. Schultz died on January 15, 1966.

In his spare time, Schultz operated a small fix-it shop in the garage of his home in St. Cloud. He repaired broken toys and furniture, sharpened saws and lawn mowers, etc. Ed began making his fish decoys in 1945. In a three year period [1945-48] he manufactured more than 3,000 decoys. His decoys ranged in length from four to nine inches and were painted in various colors. Mr. Schultz sold his decoys to sports, hardware and novelty shops in both Wisconsin and Minnesota.

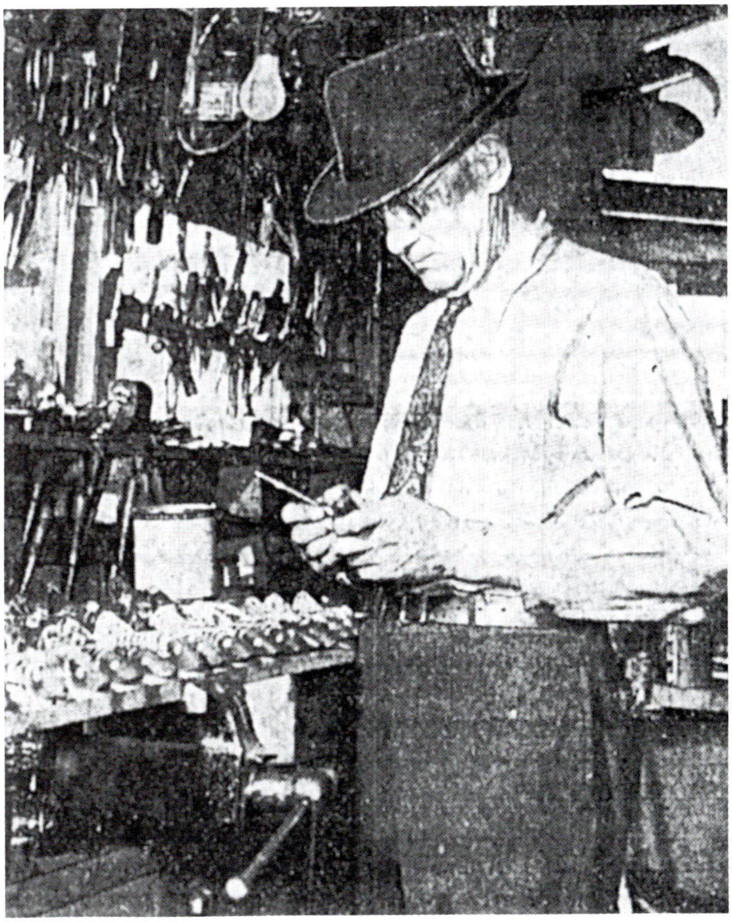

Ed Schultz in 1948 in his garage. Note several of his decoys are sitting on his work bench.

His decoys are easy to spot. They have one swept-wing pectoral fin on each side and carved and painted eyes. Some of his decoys had long sloped noses and he made other decoy noses more abrupt. He painted most of decoys with a red head, and with a kind of mottled pattern on the body. Some of the tail fins were sharply divided while some were rounded, almost like a Howell.

*Some of the information was obtained from an article entitled "Fish Decoy Manufacturer Talks a Cold Language," *St. Cloud Daily Times,* 1948.

WILLIAM A. SCHULTZ*

William Schultz was born on December 22, 1895 in Minnesota. He was a farmer. After his marriage, he and his wife, Hedwig, moved to a house in Hector, Minnesota. Then, William farmed only on a part time basis.

He enjoyed hunting and fishing. It was not until the mid-1930's, however, that William began carving decoys for his own use. There is no accurate information as to how many decoys he produced over the years in his spare time. Most surviving examples of his work suggest that he made decoys of a uniform length (about 7 1/4 inches) with tack eyes and brass or copper fins. He showed a marked preference for painting his decoys with tiny dots, sometimes all in the same color and at other times with dots of various colors.

Mr. Schultz passed away on September 6, 1953.

*Information courtesy of Mrs. Hedwig Schultz.

ART SEGUIN*

Art Seguin [pronounced "Seegun"] was born in 1901 in Cloquet, Minnesota, but came to Crosby, Minnesota in 1918. For many years he worked with electric motors underground in the mines around Crosby. He died in 1991.

An avid spear fisherman and outdoorsman, Art made fishing decoys both for himself and for sale. It is estimated that he may have made as many as 500 to 1,000 decoys. His decoys typically imitate perch, sunfish, crappies, and northern pike. Surviving examples of his work suggest that he had a preference for painting his fish grey with yellow and white dots imitating scales on the sides of his decoys' bodies. The decoy fins were made of tin. He normally used one pectoral fin on each side of his fish, as well as an anal and dorsal fin. The pectoral fins on his decoys, viewed from the top or the bottom, would appear like an inverted horseshoe. Nevertheless, he would sometimes utilized two small pectoral fins on each of his decoys. Sequin would carve gills into his decoys as well as carve the mouth and eyes. He would paint dashes or lines on the tail fin of his decoys and red lines on the underside of the head of the fish.

*Interview with Art Seguin in 1990. His name is erroneously spelled as "Segun" in Kimball, op. cit., Vol. II, p. 118.

LOUIS & ED SETKA*

The world lost two very talented men when Louis and Ed Setka of Montgomery, Minnesota passed away. Ed died from diabetes complications in 1981, while his brother Louis tragically perished from a fire in their home.

Louis and Ed Setka, of Czechoslovakian descent, never married. They shared each other's company on their farm in Montgomery. Most of their farm machinery they made themselves. Tractors, wagons, building boxes, and tools were all constructed from junk yard scrap and milled hardwoods. Their garden tractor motor had two cylinders, cut from a Model T four cylinder engine.

Emil Filipek, a mutual friend, was employed at a nearby power plant and supplied the Setkas with steam pipes and pressure information. This led Louis and Ed to begin to construct their locally renown steam engines. These engines ranged in size from full sized to miniature. They also became proficient with gear drives and developed talent in the area of applied electricity. They made their own clocks and electric motors and their workmanship was worthy of note. Ed was known as a metal and pipe fitter, while Louis possessed a flair for artistic endeavor.

It could have been their friend, Emil Filipek, who first introduced the Setkas to spear fishing. In any event, Louis was the brother who crafted duck and fish decoys. Unfortunately, he produced decoys in very limited quantities; however, their quality was excellent. Louis' fish decoys were small, ranging in length from four to six inches, but more were made in the four inch size. He also made two distinct styles of decoys which could be mistaken as having been made by a different individual. However, the similarity of the painting on the fins as well as the line ties on the two styles confirm that the decoys had one maker. Louis' painting shows exceptional precision and fine detail. His fish were painted with pleasing color combinations of blue, orange, and green — paint colors not often seen together in Minnesota.

Louis also made a few copper decoys, as these were found with his hardwood molds in the Setkas' shop. The shape of these copper decoys is very similar to those of Charlie Slechta [see this chapter].

*Information courtesy of Jerry Wintheiser.

HARRY SIMONSEN

Harry Simonsen was born on May 27, 1892 in Lake Ripley, Minnesota. He passed away on March 4, 1980.

CHARLES "CHARLIE" SLECHTA*

Charlie Slechta was born in 1872. He was married and fathered five boys and one girl. Mr. Slechta passed away in 1965.

In his youth he was a coach and carriage maker. In 1914, Charlie was hired by the Ford Motor Company, where he held various positions over the years, such as mechanic, body repairman and body assembly. He became a body foreman in 1919, a job that he held until 1937. Then he retired and moved to Spring Park, Minnesota.

It is uncertain when he began making copper spear fishing decoys, although it is likely that it was in the 1930's. At Ford he was acquainted with Merrill Booth, a maker of copper decoys. Slechta's brother Tom made such decoys in the 1920's, and he may have used his brother's idea. In any event, it was only after Mr. Slechta retired to Spring Park, Minnesota that he made the majority of his decoys. His molds for the copper decoys were fashioned from fiber and wood. He used a vice to press and make the eyes. He had a tool to scale the side of the copper fish. This was done before the two sides were placed together. His earliest coppers were sweated together, so they took a long time to fabricate. These early, sweated, copper decoys were glass eyed. His later decoy eyes were made from red colored aluminum drinking cups that were given as premiums at Erickson Gas Stations in the early 1950's. He would cut out the eyes from these cups, so later Slechta decoys have red eyes. These later copper fish were also rolled and seamed instead of sweated. This process permitted him to increase his production of copper decoys. The mouth of a Slechta decoy was punched out with an awl. Although the Slechta decoy resembles that of Merrill Booth, the latter used a slit for the mouth. Moreover, Slechta decoys have diamond shaped scales while Booth preferred semicircles as scale decorations.

*Information courtesy of John Banholzer.

TED SNELL*

Ted Snell was born in Eden Valley, Minnesota in March of 1899. He lived there all of his life. Mr. Snell was married and had one daughter. He was employed as a rural mail carrier. Mr. Snell died on August 9, 1968.

He began making decoys for his own use and for sale in the 1940's. Mr. Snell would make the decoys and his wife, Opel, did the painting. They would make 25 to 50 at one time and they were sold in his brother's bait shop [Snell Bait Shop]. Snell would charge $1.75 to $2.00 for one of his decoys. He made crappies, sunfish, northern pike and walleye pike. Over the years his decoys changed little. They were constructed of pine. The decoys' eyes were usually thumb tacks and were painted.

*Information courtesy of Mrs. Snell.

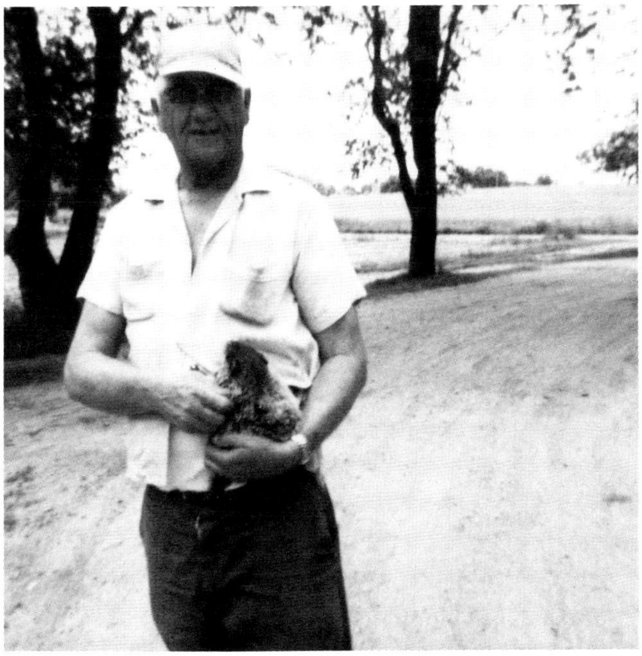

Ted Snell.

HEMBER CHARLES STEELE*

Hember Steele was born on October 17, 1889 in Berlin Township, Minnesota. He married Ruth Johnson in 1925. They had no children. He served in World War I as a private, but was not sent overseas.

Mr. Steele was a very handy individual who held a variety of jobs. As a mason, he did brick work and constructed fireplaces. He also was a skilled carpenter in addition to being employed for some time as an auto repair mechanic at a garage in Ellendale, Minnesota.

An outdoorsman, Mr. Steele loved fishing and began constructing spear fishing decoys sometime after his marriage in 1925. He continued making them for himself and to sell to others until his death in December 25, 1971.

Mr. Steel made decoys imitating northern pike, sunfish and perch, while others had no discernible species. He made his fins from aluminum or copper and his line ties were holes punched into the dorsal fin of the decoys. His fish were well made as there are no broken or missing fins found even today. They were also nicely painted.

*Information courtesy of Mrs. Nadine Steele.

JEROME C. STEELE*

Jerome C. Steele was born on November 11, 1909 in Park Rapids, Minnesota. He worked as a box factory employee. Later, he was self employed as a carpenter, and subsequently founded Jerome Steele Sash Door & Cabinet. Mr. Steele was married and had nine children. He died December 24, 1987.

Mr. Steele enjoyed spear fishing, especially on Lake Plantanganet. In 1933 he began making decoys for himself and for sale. From 1933 to 1976, when he stopped making them, it is estimated that he produced 350 to 500 decoys. He sold them from 50¢ to $1.00 to Fullers Tackle Shop in Park Rapids. His decoys were constructed from white pine because it was easy to whittle. Steele's earliest decoys had tin tails, but his later ones had wooden tails. Acquainted with Pearl and Cyril Bethel, Mr. Steele's decoys resemble the Bethel fish. Steele's decoys all had carved open mouths. They had a pronounced dorsal fin while the pectoral fins had a different shape than those of the Bethels. Both Pearl and Cyril Bethel painted small dashes around the outer edge of the pectoral fins. Mr. Steele did not use this painting technique. Moreover, Mr. Steele painted his decoys' eyes with a black iris surrounded with a yellow circle. Cyril Bethel painted the eyes of his decoys on the top of the head, but Mr. Steele painted the eyes in their natural position.

Mr. Steele also carved one German trout plaque.

*Information supplied by Mike Meyers.

LEON "ED" STEIN*

Leon Stein was born in Bemidji, Minnesota on March 7, 1927. He was employed as a barber in Bemidji and retired from that business in 1989. Mr. Stein is married and has three grown boys. He now resides on the Woman Lake Chain near Hackensack, Minnesota.

Discouraged by the poor swimming quality of available decoys, Leon began making decoys in 1953. He made two decoys for his own use and constructed others for sale. Over the three years that he made decoys, he produced more than 2,000 of them. His decoys were constructed from basswood. He made the fins from Prince Albert tobacco cans at first, and later made them from aluminum. Fins were cut by hand at his barber shop while waiting for customers. There were two pectoral fins on each side, anal and dorsal fins, and a tail fin. A slot was cut in the body of the decoy into which the rear pectoral fins were inserted and then tacked into place.

Mr. Stein soaked his decoys in linseed oil to make his paint more water resistant, sprayed them with white enamel, and painted the edges of the fins with black or black and red in what he termed his "lightning" design. The head of the decoy was painted red with black trim. He painted the eyes white with black iris. The nose of the decoy was cut straight, while leaving a protrusion of wood as a lower lip. Some Stein decoys were painted black on the decoy's back, followed by a bar of grey paint which blended into a white painted body. Thus, decoys that have been pictured as orange, black, brown or red were overpaints as Mr. Stein painted the bodies of his decoys white.

Leon attributes the excellent swimming characteristics of his decoys to the great amount of lead weighting that he used.

He sold his decoys for $2.50 each to sporting goods and bait shops. The lack of profit in his endeavor prompted him to cease making decoys in 1956.

Mr. Stein was an avid spear fisherman and enjoyed spearing on Lake Bemidji.

*Information provided in an interview with Mr. Stein. The Kimballs, op. cit., have erroneously referred to his (Stein's) decoys as having been made by "John Linblom" (see Kimball, Vol. II, p. 106, and Vol. III, p. 100).

HOMER STINAR*

Homer Stinar was born in October of 1923 in Casper, Wyoming. He later moved to Verndale, Minnesota where he worked for the railroad. Mr. Stinar is now retired.

Homer spans the gap between the old time carvers and the contemporary ones. His earliest decoys, made in the 1950's, were strictly limited to northern pike and were realistically painted. Mr. Stinar retains essentially the same style today but has added frog decoys to his repertoire. Stinar's northern decoys have a noticeable curve to the belly. Another characteristic is the carved mouth which was open and normally painted red. For his line tie attachment, he used a screw eye. Stinar used two pectoral fins on either side of his fish which were made of metal, along with a metal dorsal and anal fin. The metal tail fins on his decoys were large, sweeping and graceful. The eyes on his early fish were made of glass and either glued or pushed into the decoy's head. His contemporary northern pikes are often painted black and white.

RAYMOND STOTZ*

Raymond Stotz was born in 1897 in LeSueur County, near Savage Lake, west of Cleveland, Minnesota. As a small boy he was interested in hunting and fishing. He made his own baits in the early years. Fly fishing was his main hobby. Ray tied and made all types of baits for fly fishing. His special popper fly was a great fish attractor and was widely received.

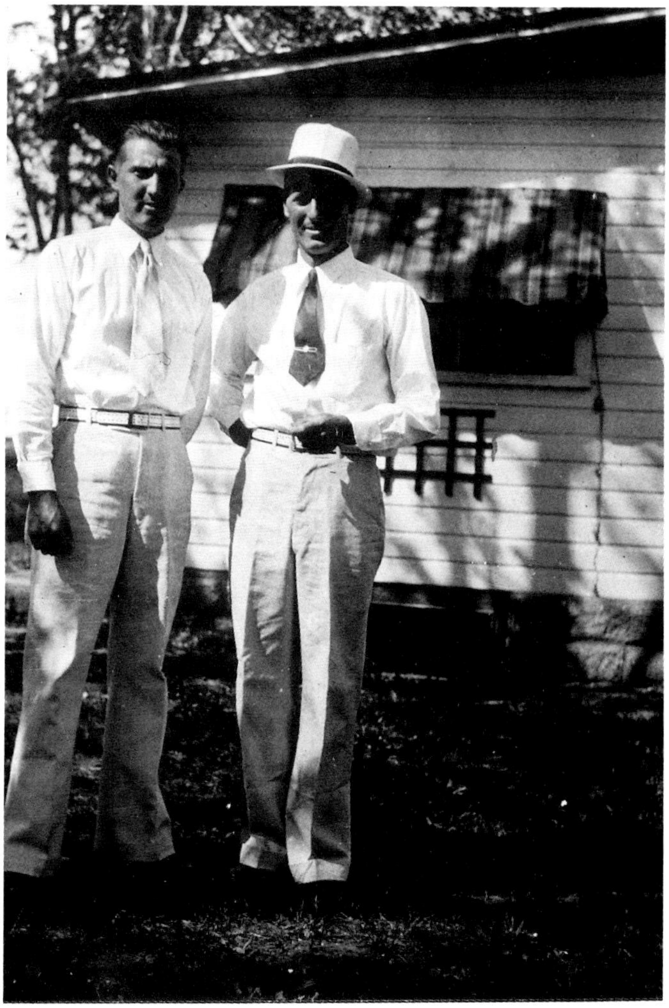

Raymond Stotz [in hat] with his brother, Clarence. Photo courtesy of Jerry Wintheiser.

In about 1943, Ray moved near Scotch Lake, Minnesota. At that time, Scotch Lake was a wonderful duck hunting lake. Ray also loved to hunt ducks and geese. His ability to place the decoys at the proper location in the proper order allowed him many close shots.

It was at this Scotch Lake location that Ray made most of his fishing plugs and spearing decoys. During the summer months he acted as a guide on Jefferson and Washington Lakes, and also painted houses as a sideline. In the winter evenings, he made spearing decoys. He had many requests for his decoys because they performed well in the water and were beautifully painted. Ray also carved some decorative decoys for his close friends.

He was a noted hunter of small and large game. He guided hunters in northern Minnesota for deer and bear. Small game trapping was his delight. He was a professional mink trapper. Ray was also effective trapping fox because he developed scents that would lure them into the traps that he put in the fields.

In later years, Ray would spend the winter months in California where his brother lived. His brother also did some decoy carving. Mr. Stotz died in 1976.

*Information courtesy John Banholzer and Peter Meyers.

CLIFFORD JASON STUBBS*

Clifford Stubbs was born in 1892 at Stubbs Bay on Lake Minnetonka. Stubbs Bay was named for his great grandfather. Clifford's nick-name was "Horns" because he made deer horn plaques. A large man, Clifford was six feet three inches tall and weighed 300 pounds. He held many jobs and was involved in many activities. In the 1940's he performed dock installations and removals. From 1945 to 1955, he invented and used a weed cutter and cut weeds on Lake Minnetonka. He also farmed near Princeton, Minnesota and served as a bouncer at Long Siding Bar and Dance Hall. In addition, Clifford was a constable for ten years.

He carved fish decoys from 1954 to 1965 and made approximately 300 to 500 during this time. He would carve his decoys at the kitchen table or in an upstairs work room.

Stubbs' decoys are readily identifiable because of the sloped nose, tack eyes and wooden tails. He used a single pectoral fin on either side that was long and flowing. His later fish utilized a large dorsal fin into which his line tie holes were punched. He used a variety of painting schemes.

*Information courtesy of Ron Adamson.

JOHN F. TAX*

John Franklin Tax was born in Osakis, Minnesota on September 11, 1894, and he lived there his entire life. He served in the U.S. Navy during World War I, and returned to Osakis to work in his father's harness making and shoe repair business. John took over the business in 1928, making important improvements. Tax was married and had three children. He died on July 15, 1967 from cancer.

In addition to being a harness maker, John has been described as an inventor of tools, a tinkerer and a person who was constantly whittling. He frequently carved in his back yard on Lake Osakis where he would take his ideas and quickly produce a final carving of whatever idea he had in mind. He was known to be a very friendly, personable man who liked everyone and consequently, in turn, was liked by everyone. He also was a practical joker. Tax began carving in the 1920's but ultimately was forced to quit due to calcium deposits in his joints. John never became a wealthy man but his love of hunting and fishing was more important than monetary gain.

In addition to producing fish decoys, Tax made wooden Canadian and snow geese was well as canvas Canadian geese, wood and canvas ducks (mallards, bluebills, canvasbacks, redheads and coots), pheasants, bird houses, door knockers, souvenir wall plaques and Masonic ritual items.

He made pike, sunfish, sucker, perch and frog fish decoys. These had a set of pointed pectoral fins [two on each side] and a wooden tail. Frequently, his fish decoys had rectangularly shaped dorsal and anal fins [although occasionally these were rounded]. The line ties on his decoys were of the band type. Some of his fish decoys were marked on the underside with a circular or rectangular stamp bearing his name. Tax fish decoys sold for $1.00.

*Information courtesy of Carter Stenberg. See also Donna Tonelli, "John Tax A Minnesota Whittler from the Shores of Lake Osakis," *Decoy Magazine,* March/April 1992, pp. 8-11.

CLARENCE THOMAS*

Clarence Thomas was born in Minneapolis in 1917. He later moved to Foley, Minnesota. Mr. Thomas served in the Navy for three years during World War II. Subsequently, he went to work for Benton County as a heavy equipment operator, and later became a foreman over mechanics. In all, he worked 43 years for the County. Mr. Thomas was married to Bernice and had six children. He died in January of 1989.

In addition to making spears [see Chapter 7], Mr. Thomas also fashioned fish decoys. His decoys had wooden tails and two pectoral fins on each side of the decoy. He made decoys imitating northern pike, suckers and a kind of generic fish. The painting was usually crude — or at least plain.

*Information supplied by Bernice Thomas.

BURT E. THOMPSON*

Burt E. Thompson was born in 1913 in Floodwood, Minnesota. He has worked as a lumberjack, a farmer, and for the highway department. Burt served in the Merchant Marines during World War II. Since 1939, he has resided near Big Sandy Lake in McGregor, Minnesota.

In 1948, he made fishing decoys which he used on Big Sandy, Turtle and Glacier Lakes. His frog decoy, made from a rubber tire, is pictured. In some cases, his other decoys (also made from rubber) were covered with felt. Another example was painted.

*Information from an interview with Mr. Thompson.

RAYMOND ALBERT THOMPSON*

Ray Thompson, better known as "Hair Lip" Thompson, because of a deformity in his upper lip, was born August 8, 1887, and died March 7, 1966, at the age of 78. He lived his entire life in Park Rapids, Minnesota, where he was a barber. Considered as a character around town, he is said to have been a poacher, moonshiner, and an alcoholic. Whether or not these apocryphal tales are true, he has to be considered the finest decoy maker in Minnesota. During a stay in jail, Thompson produced his best know eight decoys. All were made to imitate trout and it is unlikely that these decoys were ever placed in the water. Not only were these decoys beautifully carved and painted, but he even made teeth in the open mouths of his fish. Thompson also made beautifully carved fishing sticks and other outdoors related carvings.

*See also Donna Tonelli, "Ray Thompson Maker of Quality Fishing Tackle and Fish Decoys," *Decoy Magazine*, September/October 1992, pp. 32-35.

GEORGE TOMBARGE*

George Tombarge was born February 12, 1907 in Zumbro Falls, Minnesota. He lived in Frontenak, Minnesota where he was a carpenter making cupboards, as well as a maintenance man at the Oak Center Creamery in Oak Center, Minnesota. George never married. He died in 1987.

Mr. Tombarge loved fishing and hunting. He made fish decoys from pine and basswood in the 1930's. Mr. Tombarge made northern pike, suckers, sunfish, and walleye-like decoys. These decoys were relatively small, in the Mississippi River tradition of spear decoy makers. Fins on the decoys were fashioned from copper and some had small white glass bead eyes.

George's decoys were sold at an auction in 1982.

*Information courtesy of Mrs. Karl Tombarge. It has been reported that George Tombarge was part Indian. The author was told that he was 100 percent German descent.

JOHN VAVRA*

John Vavra was born in 1883 in a log cabin in LeSueur County, Minnesota. He was one of five children. He was also a self-taught machinist and owned his own shop in LeCenter, Minnesota. Mr. Vavra was married to Anna and they had no children. He died in 1965.

Mr. Vavra began to craft spearing decoys in the 1930's. His earliest decoys were made of metal and formed in molds. The two halves were then soldered together. He apparently made two sizes of metal decoys—a 5 3/4 inch fish and a nine to ten inch decoy. These metal decoys had copper heads which overlapped [were slightly higher than] the chrome bodies. The decoys had a dorsal, anal and tail fin, and two small pectoral fins which were inserted into each side. The finished decoy was then varnished to help retain its sheen. It is estimated that Mr. Vavra may have made 50 to 100 of these metal decoys, some of which were sold to bait and liquor stores in the LeCenter area. Sometimes these decoys were used as "hanging" decoys in a spear fishing hole. The string holding them would be twisted and the decoy would slowly turn in the water, creating added interest for nearby fish.

Subsequently, in the 1950's or 1960's, Mr. Vavra was involved in an automobile accident. He suffered broken ribs and could not work for an entire winter. It was during this time that he began to fashion decoys made from wood, presumably to help pass the time of convalescence. He made a perch, sunfish, bass and a bullhead. On each decoy he would carefully mark scales in pencil and then paint the decoy with oil based paint. Over the finished decoy, he would apply a light coat of varnish, under which the pencil-marked scales would still remain visible. For his bullhead decoys, he attached small strings to simulate whiskers. He may have made as many as 100 wooden decoys over the years, most of them during his convalescence from the automobile accident. Some of the wooden decoys were sold in liquor stores for $5.00 to $20.00—a very high price in those years. Unfortunately, none of Vavra's wooden decoys were available to be photographed for this book.

John Vavra, a spear fishing enthusiast, speared on lakes in the LeCenter area, such as Clear, German, Jefferson, Gorman and Greenleaf. Mr. Vavra also enjoyed deer hunting.

*Information courtesy of Mr. Milo Vavra.

RAYMOND N. "PIKE" WEIS*

Raymond Nicholas Weis was born in 1907. His family moved to Minnesota from Brighton, Wisconsin in 1911,

Steve Jarnot

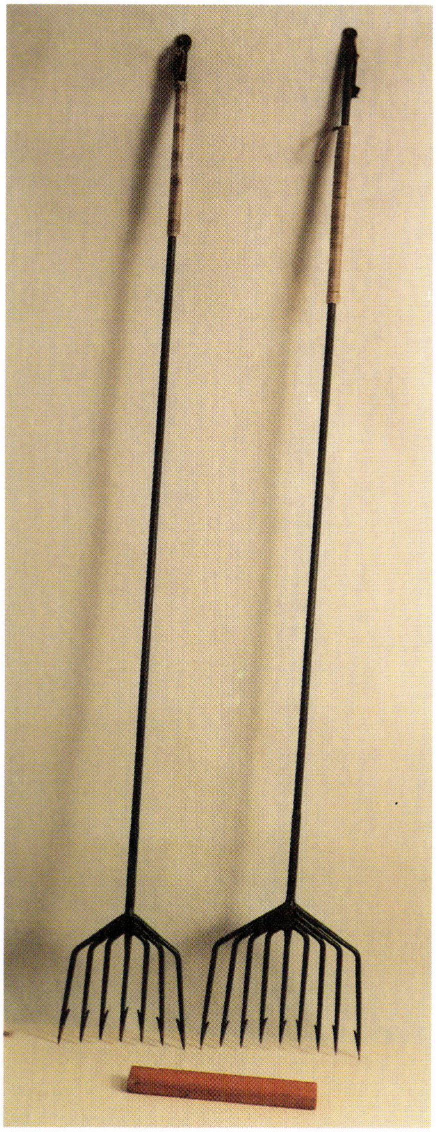

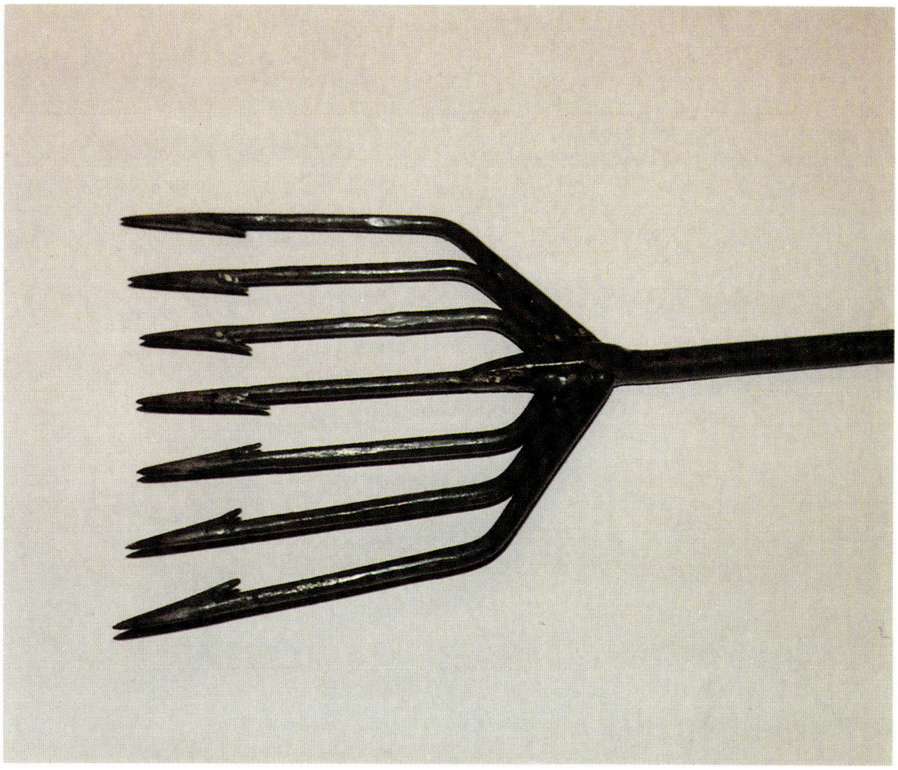

Closeup of a Steve Jarnot spear, painted green. Tines are 8 1/2 inches long, and the spear head is 7 1/2 inches wide at its widest point. Collection of Larry Hochmayr.

Two Steve Jarnot spears, 7 and 9 tines [Mr. Jarnot made only 7 and 9 tine spears]. Left: a 7 tine spear, 62 inches long, 9/16 inch rod; tines 8 inches long and 8 1/4 inches wide. Right: a 9 tine Jarnot spear, 63 3/4 inches long, 9/16 inch rod; tines 9 inches long and 10 1/2 inches wide. Larry Hochmayr collection.

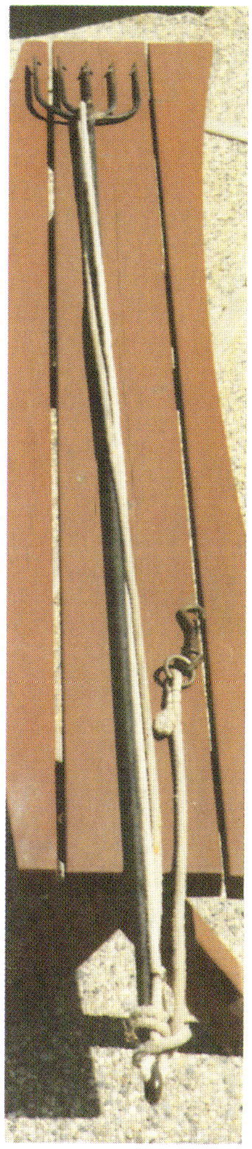

Gideon Hjalmer Kauppi

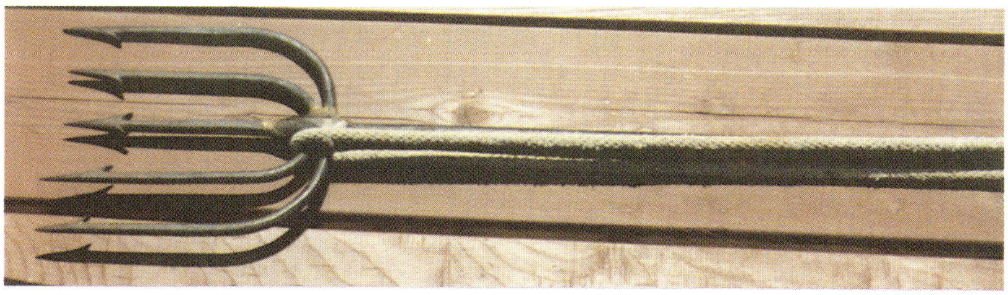

Closeup of a 5 tine Kauppi spear. Collection of Clarence Koehler.

Kauppi spear. Collection Clarence Koehler.

Henry "Heinie" Louis

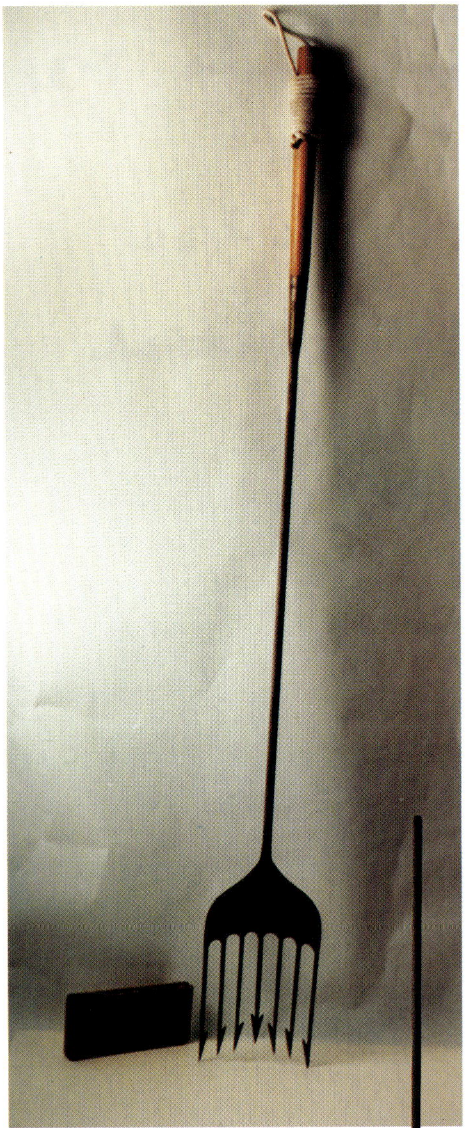

Heinie Louis spear, 58 1/2 inches long, 1/2 inch stock; tines 6 3/4 inches wide and 11 inches long.

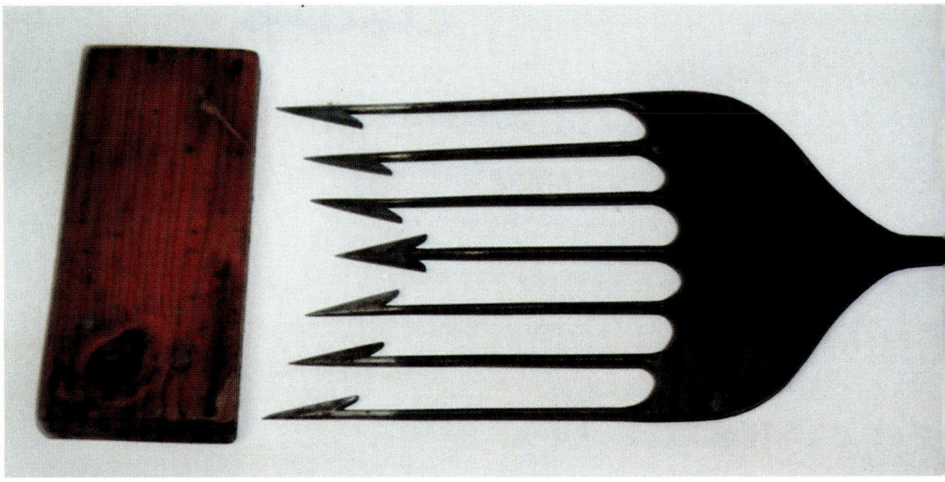

Closeup of spear tines.

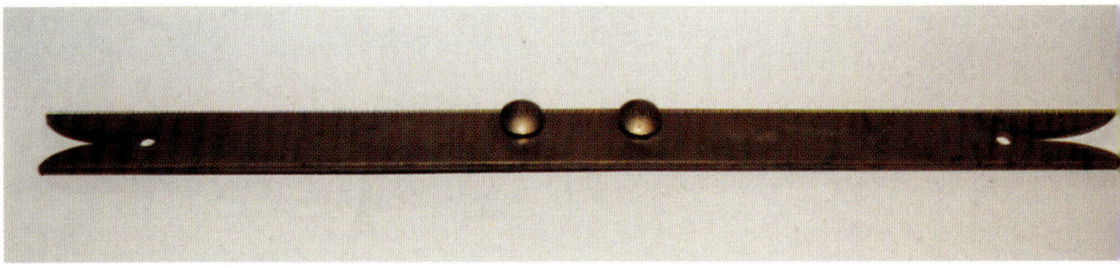

Henry Louis holder for a spear.

John Maki

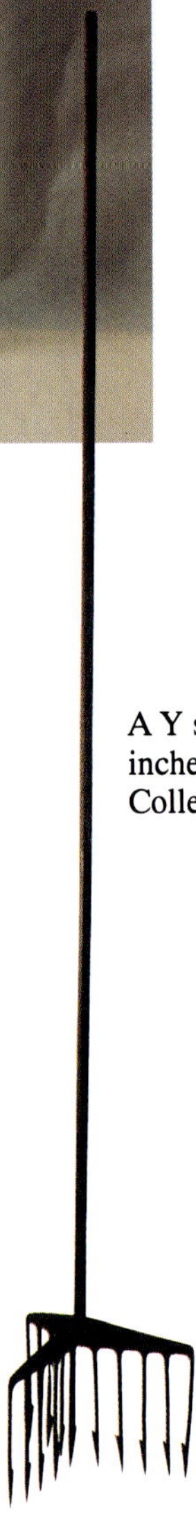

A Y shaped [triple headed] Maki spear with 15 tines. It is 61 1/4 inches long, with a metal shaft measuring 9/16 inches in diameter. Collection of K. David Hirschey.

Closeup of 10 tine Maki spear. Collection of K. David Hirschey.

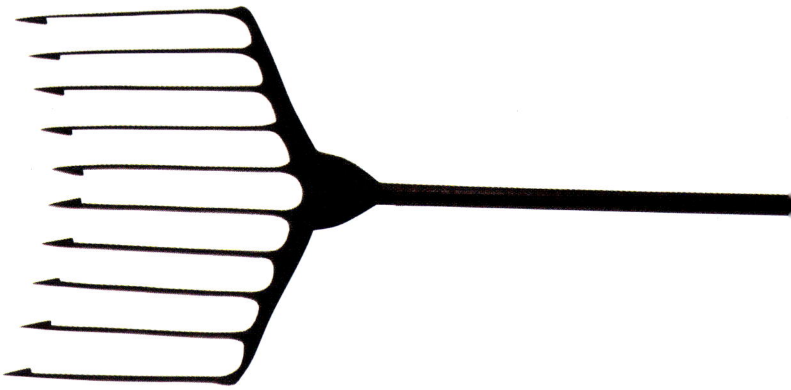

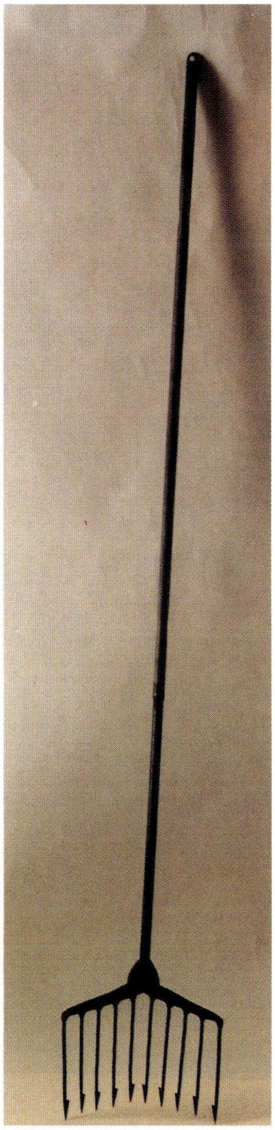

Conventional John Maki spear, measuring 63 1/2 inches long, tines are 10 inches long and 9 1/2 inches wide, with a 5/8 inch steel rod. Collection of K. David Hirschey.

Michael P. Meyer

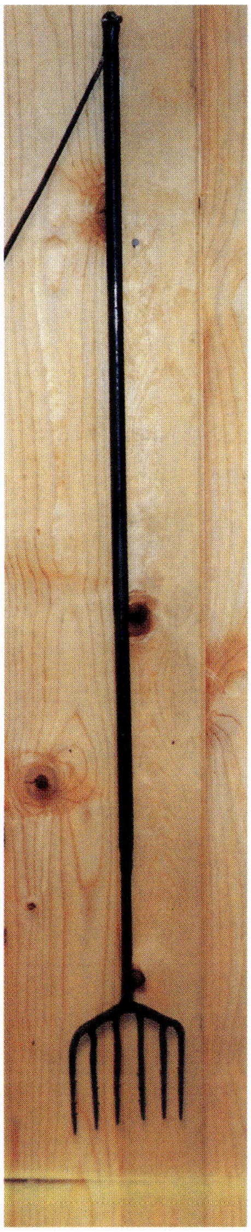

A "Mickel Meyer" spear.

Closeup of a Michael Meyer spear.

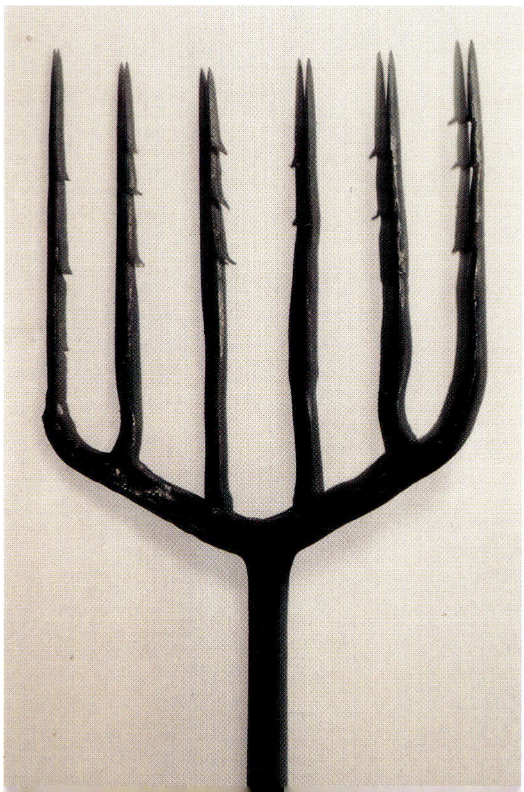

Wendlin "Charlie" Pimpl

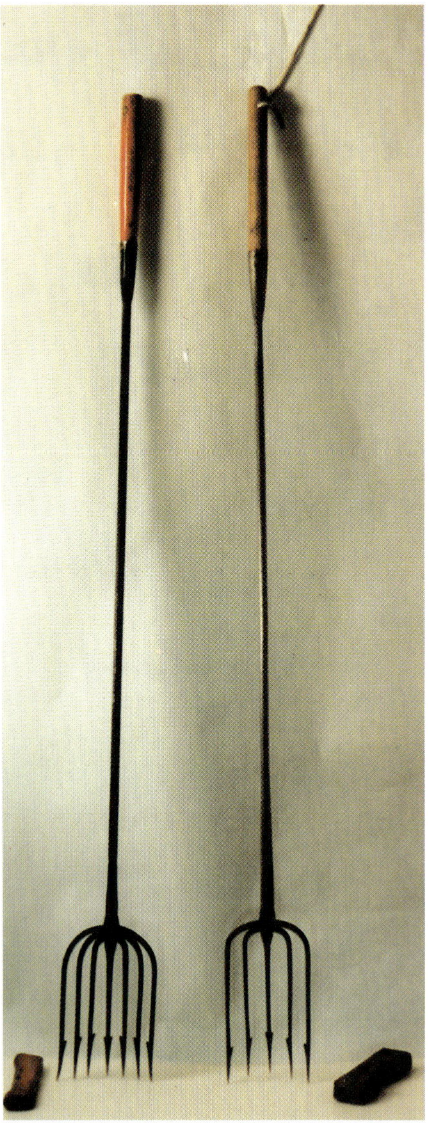

Two 5 tine Pimpl spears, one with a red painted handle and the other a natural wood handle. Left: 7 tine, 55 1/2 inches long, 1/2 inch stock; tines 5 1/2 inches wide, 8 3/4 inches long. Right: 5 tine, 56 1/8 inches long, 1/2 inch stock; tines 5 inches wide, 9 1/2 inches long.

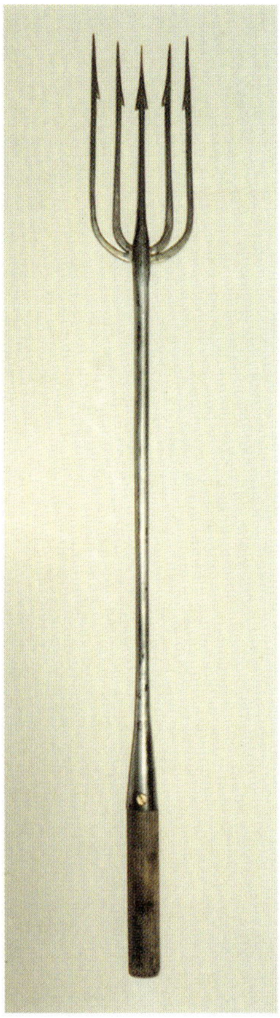

"Salesman's" sample Pimpl spear. Collection of Ron Adamson.

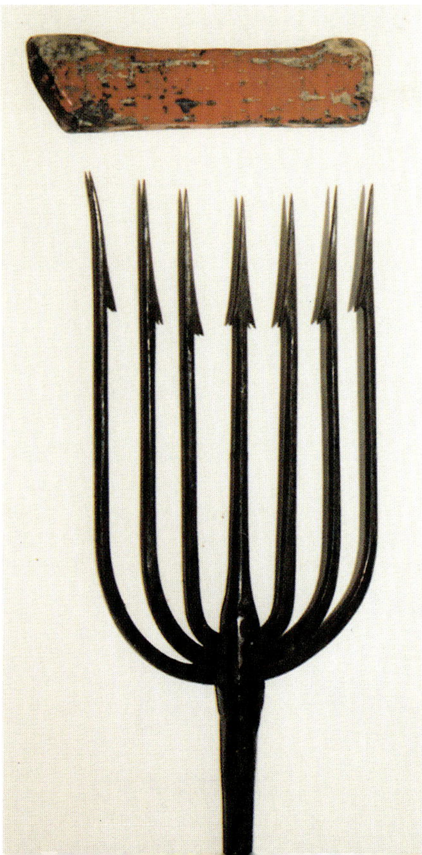

Closeup of 7 tine Pimpl spear.

John Plackner

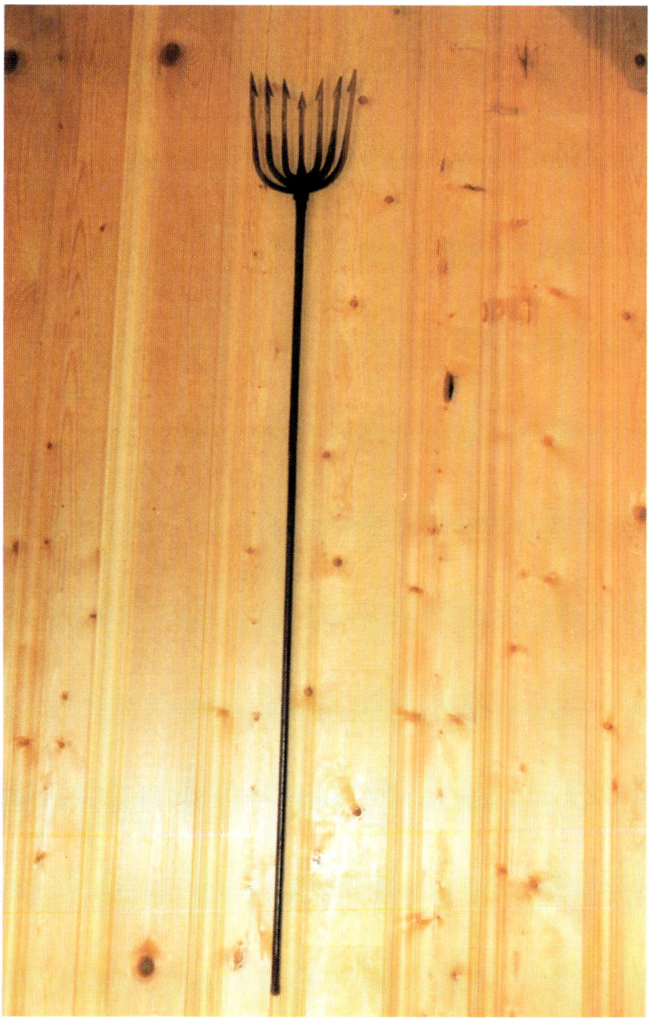

John Plackner spear, overall length 56 1/4 inches, all steel construction, 1/2 inch shaft width. Longest tine length 8 inches, and widest width of head of spear, 6 7/8 inches.

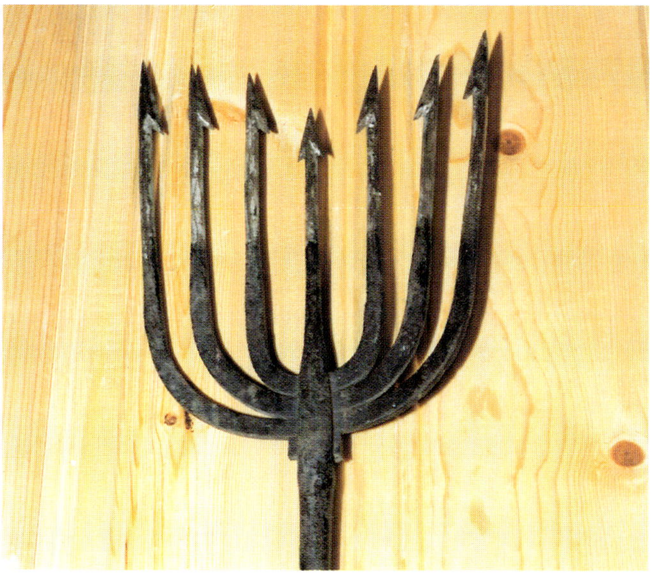

Closeup of head of John Plackner spear.

Joseph E. Portner, Jr.

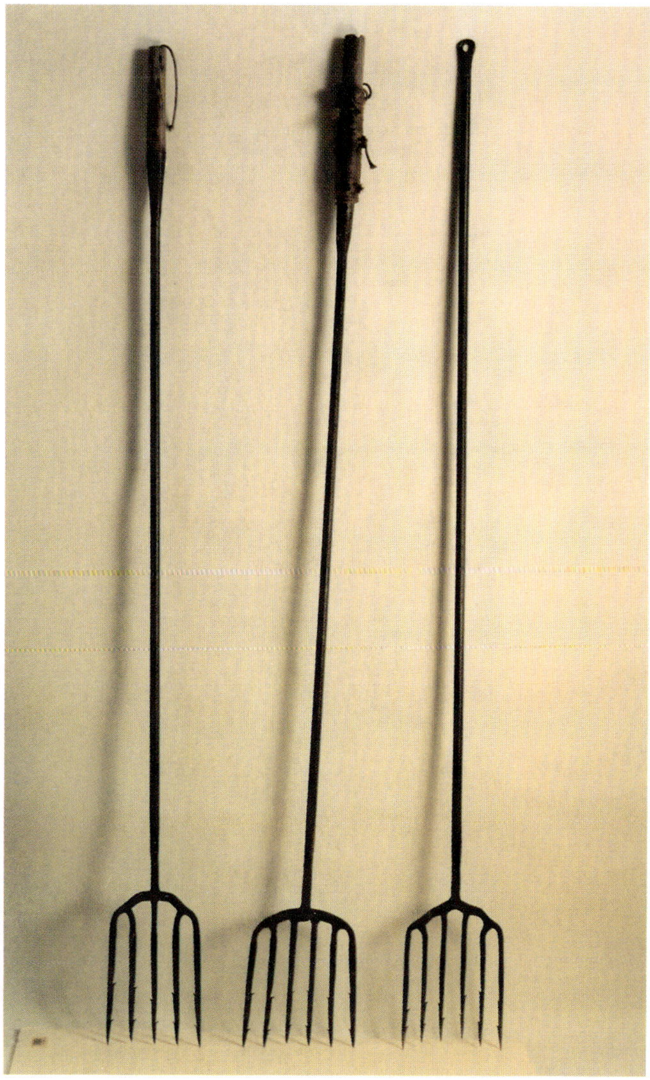

Three Portner spears. Left: a 5 tine spear with a wooden handle, 55 inches long, 9/16 inch rod; tines 5 3/8 inches wide, 8 1/2 inches in length. Middle: wood handle 6 tine spear, 56 inches long, 9/16 inch rod; tines 6 1/2 inches wide, 7 1/4 inches in length, 9/16 inch rod; tines 6 inches wide, 7 3/4 inches in length. Larry Hochmayr collection.

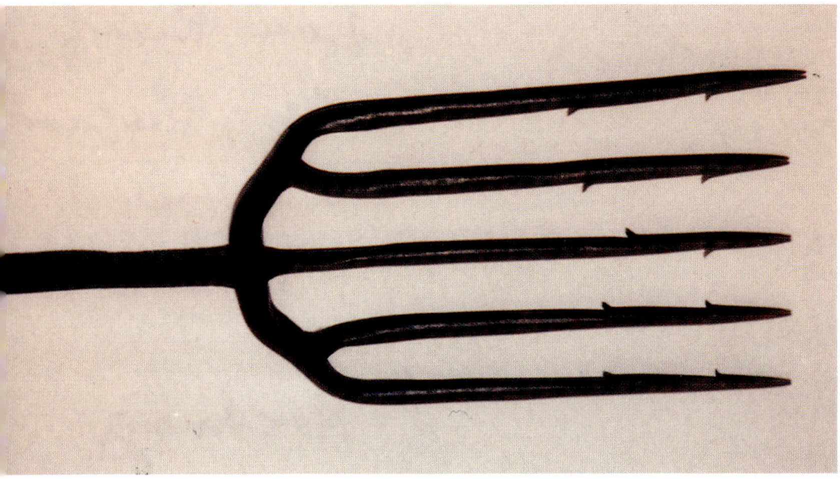

Closeup of Portner 5 tine spear. Larry Hochmayr collection.

George Randall

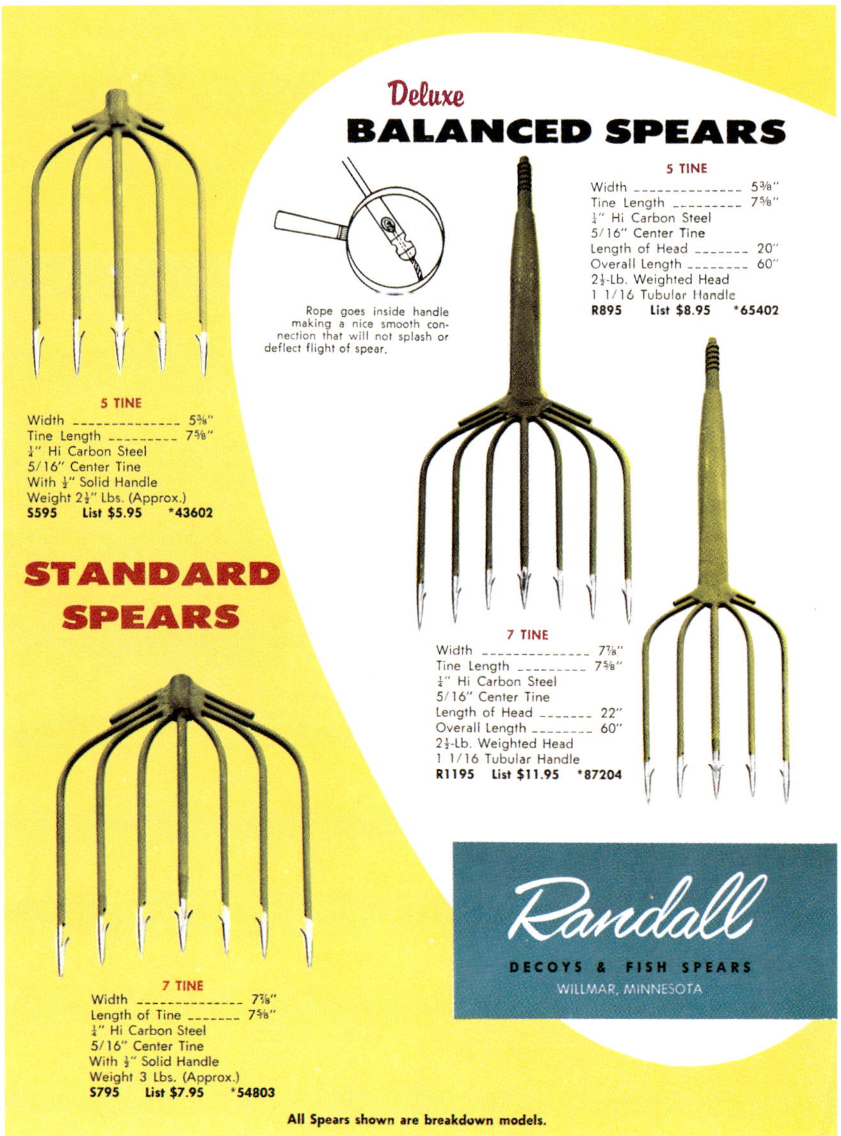

Randall advertisement showing details of his spears and their dimensions.

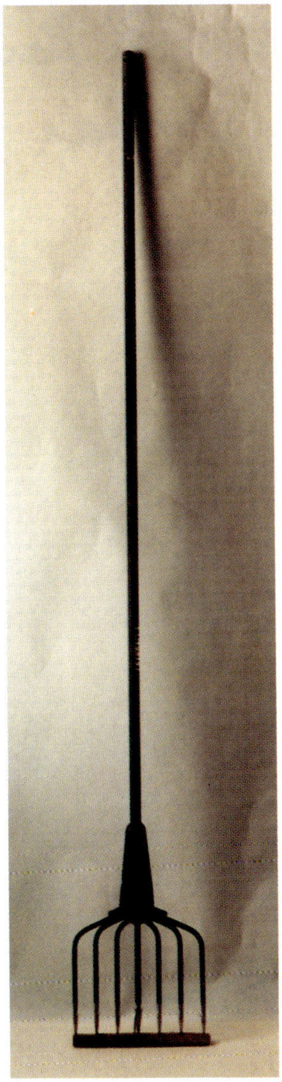

A 7 tine "standard" Randall spear.

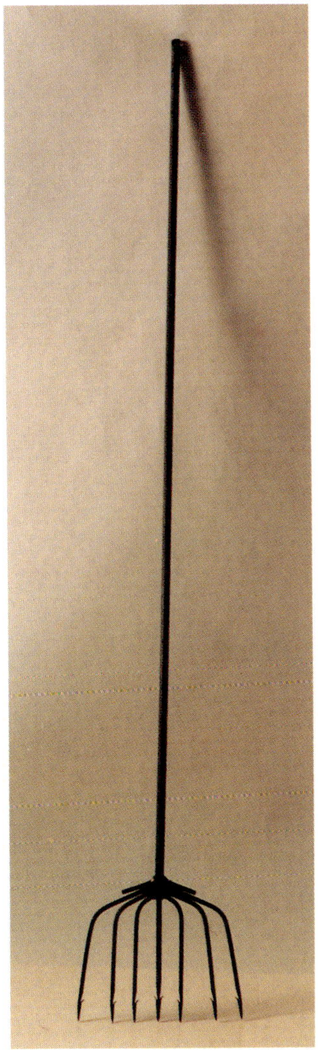

A 7 tine "deluxe" Randall spear. K. David Hirschey collection.

Edward and Joe Skiple

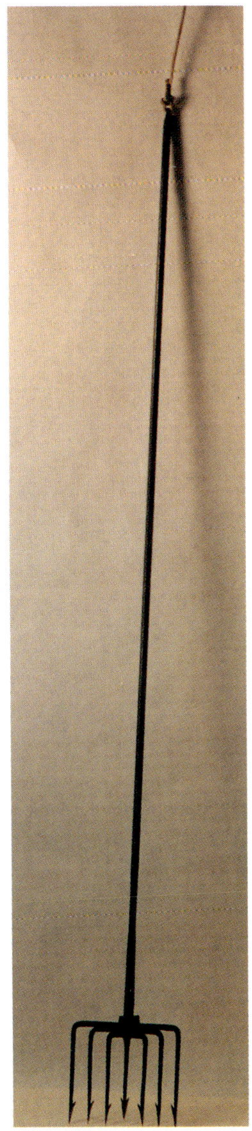

Skiple spear. Length 61 1/2 inches, width of tines 7 inches, tine length 6 1/2 inches, and rod 1/2 inch. Collection of Mike Meyers.

Clarence Thomas

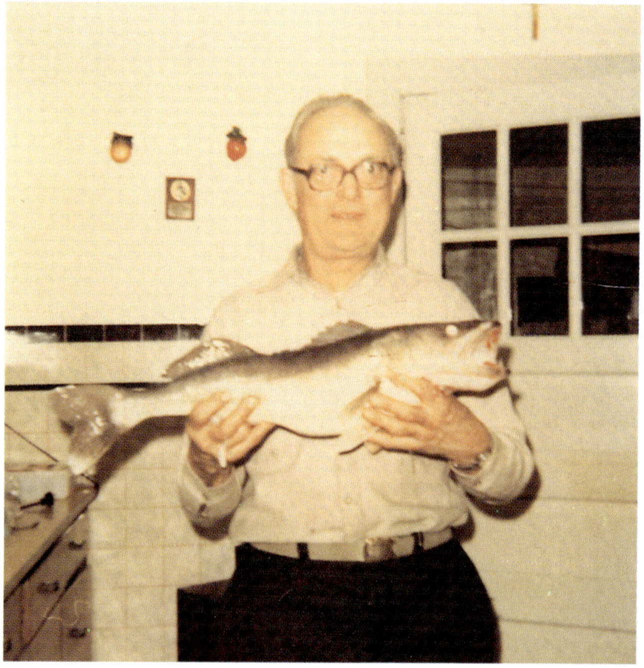

Clarence Thomas holding a prize walleye.

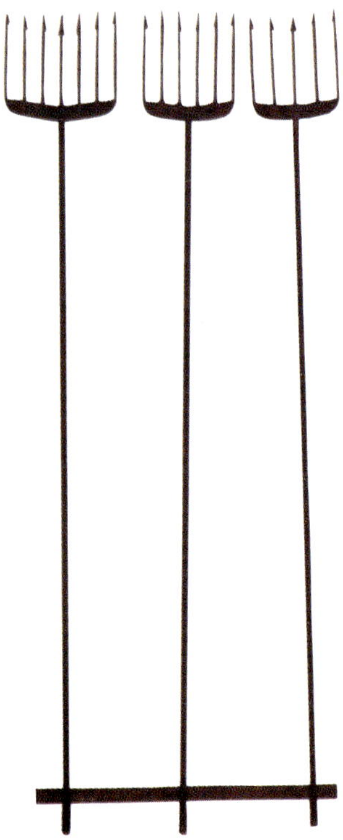

Examples of 5, 6 and 7 tine "Foley Spears" by Clarence Thomas. While Thomas' spear head is similar to that of Gustis, the former abandoned the U shaped line tie at the top of the spear that was a characteristic of the "Brainerd Spear." The Thomas' spear is rather flat on the end, with a hole through the shaft. Overall, the spears measure 54 3/4 inches in length with a 1/2 inch stock.

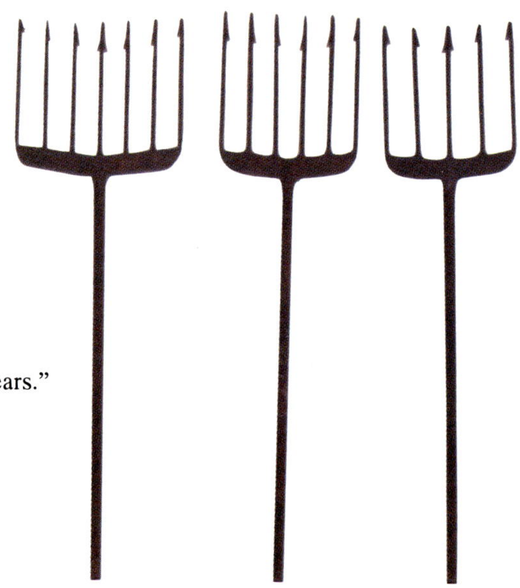

Closeup of 5, 6, and 7 tine "Foley Spears."

Paul Zitzloff

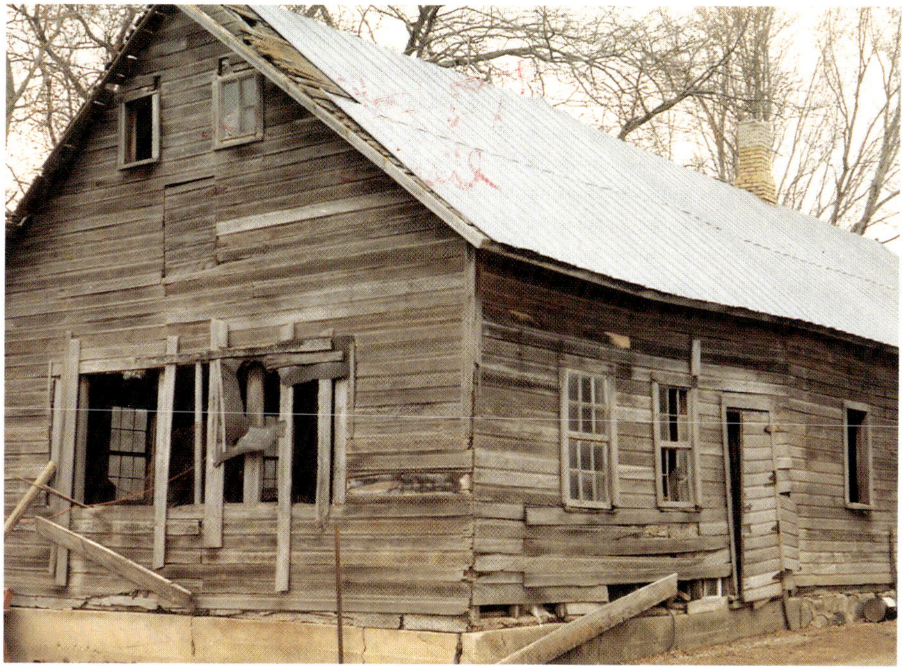

Blacksmithing and woodworking building on the [former] Zitzloff farm, near Buffalo.

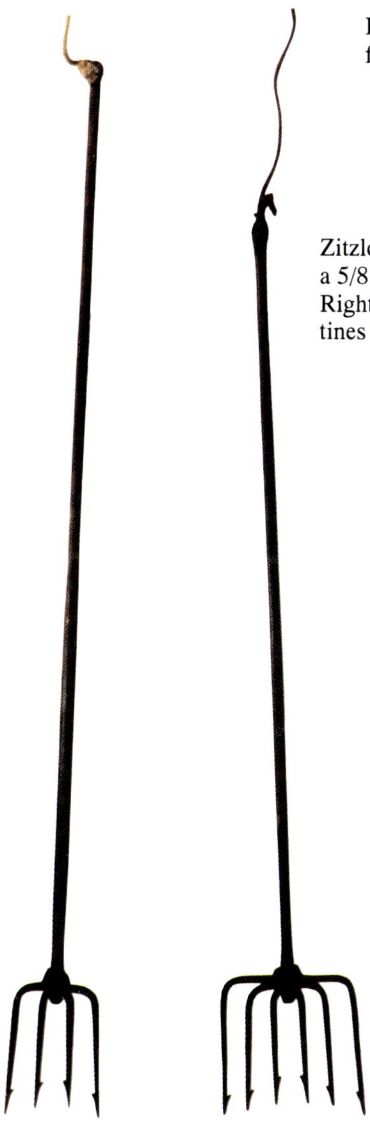

Zitzloff spears. Left is a 4 tine spear, 55 1/2 inches in length, with a 5/8 inch shaft; tines are 4 7/8 inches wide and 7 1/2 inches long. Right: a 6 tine spear, 48 inches long, with a 5/8 inch diameter stock; tines 7 1/2 inches wide and 7 3/4 inches long.

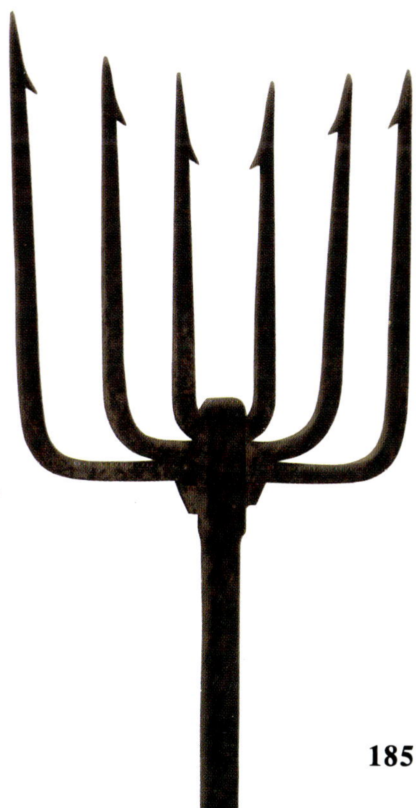

Closeup of a 6 tine Zitzloff spear.

Jigging Sticks

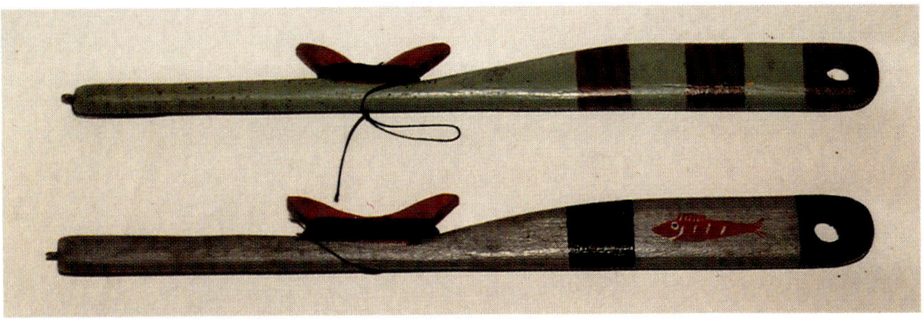

Two jigging sticks, made by Chester Buss, 12 3/4 inches long.

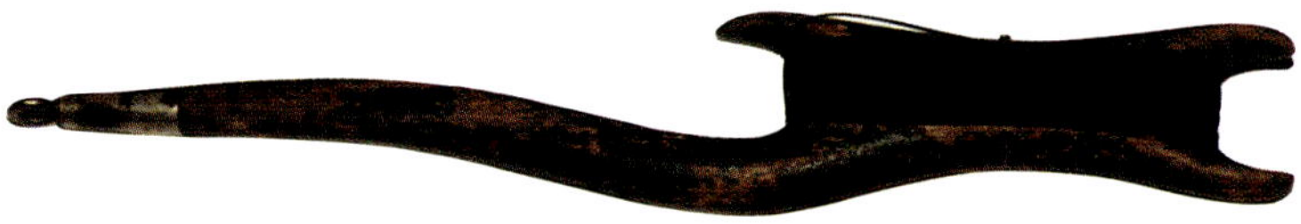

Green painted jigging stick made from a single carved stick, 8 1/2 inches long.

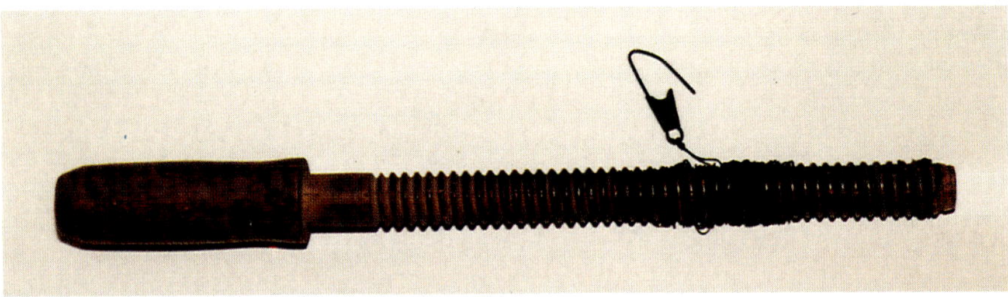

A wooden vice lock used as a jigging stick, 10 1/2 inches long.

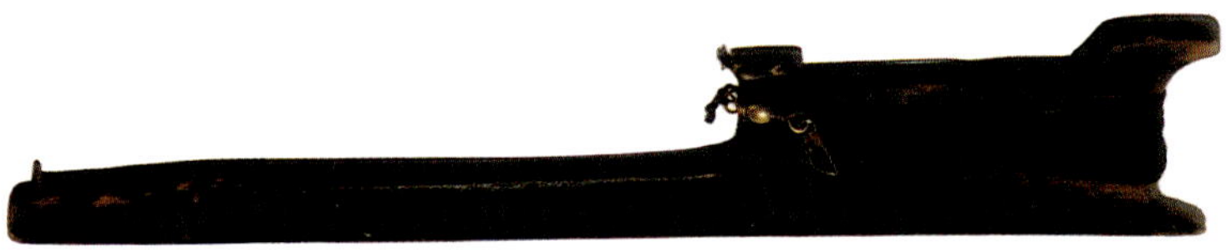

Black painted jigging stick with attached line wrap, 11 1/2 inches long.

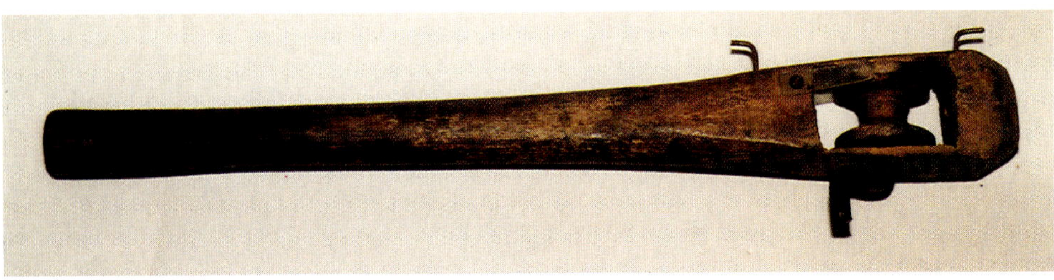

Home made jigging stick with a tine guard decorated with fish incised, featuring a built in wooden reel, and a line wrap painted on its side, 13 inches long.

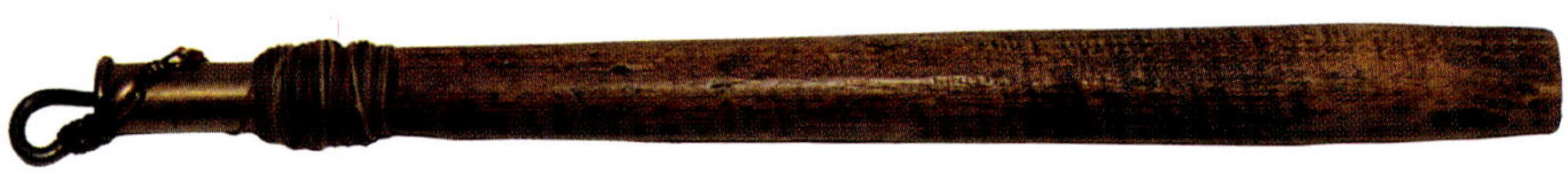

Short jigging stick with bullet casing for end piece, 9 1/2 inches long.

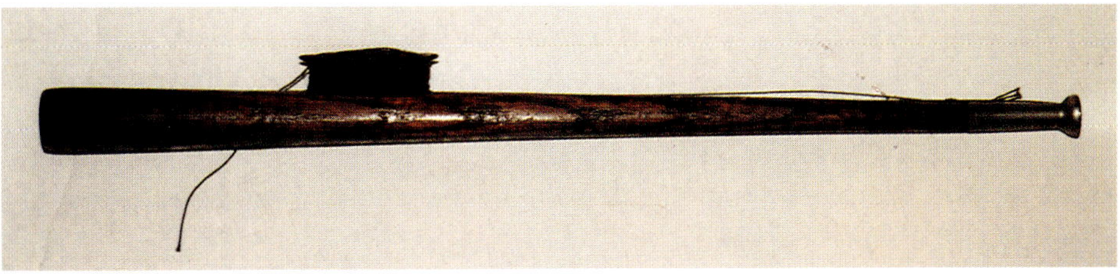

Metal tipped jigging stick, 14 inches long.

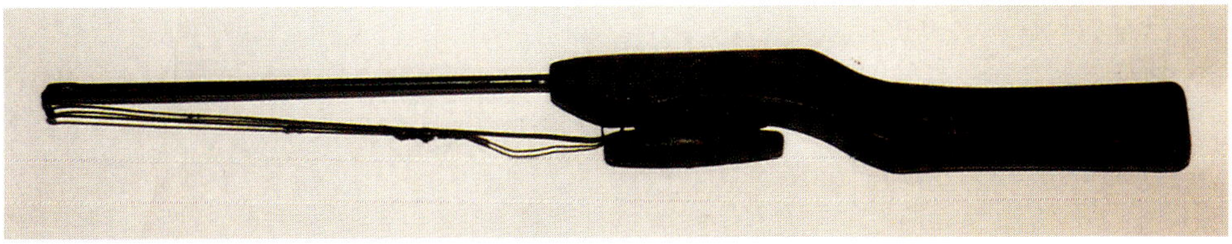

Green painted wooden handle with a metal fishing rod tip inserted into the handle, used as a jigging stick, 16 inches long.

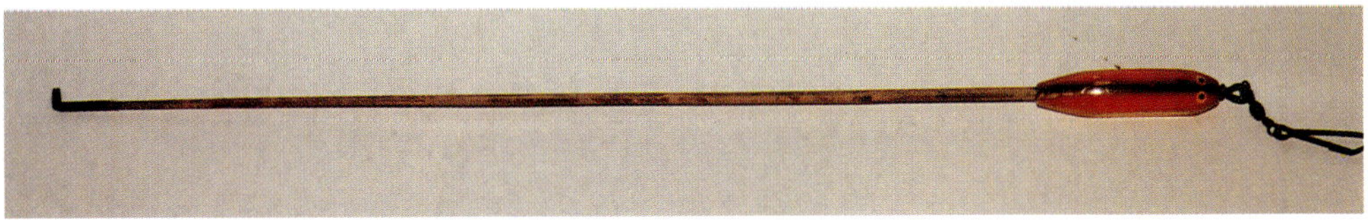

Bamboo rod inserted into a fishing lure for a handle, 19 1/2 inches long.

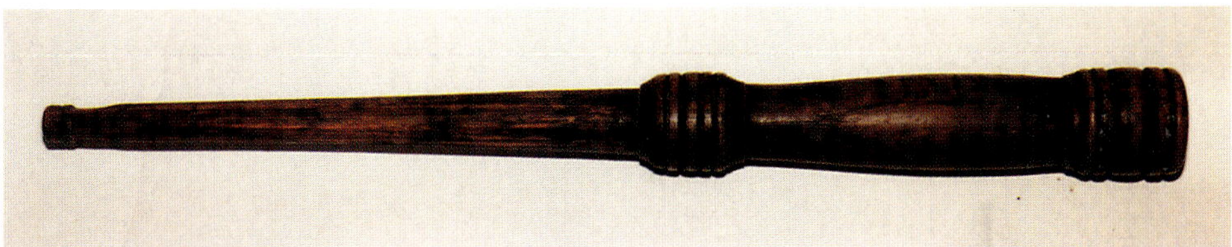

Carved wooden jigging stick, 14 inches long.

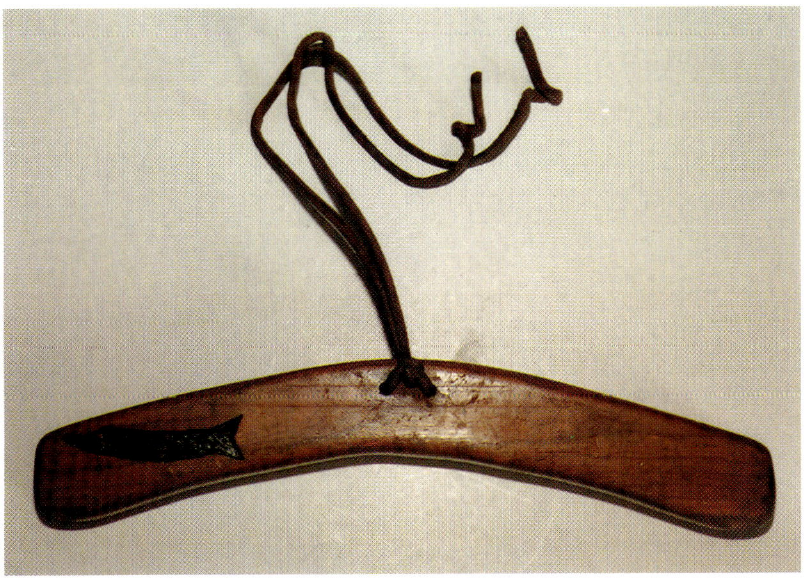

Tine guard with fish incised and painted on it.

Decoy Boxes

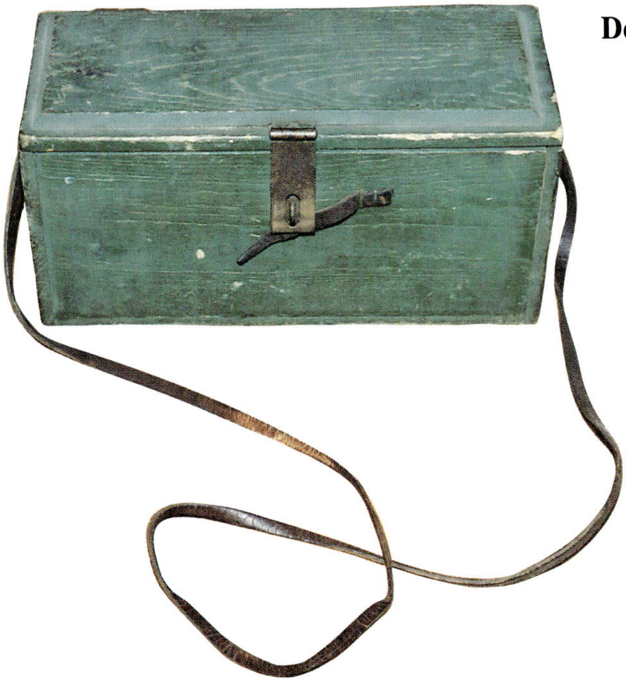

Green painted decoy box with long leather strap for carrying it over the shoulder. Larry Hochmayr collection.

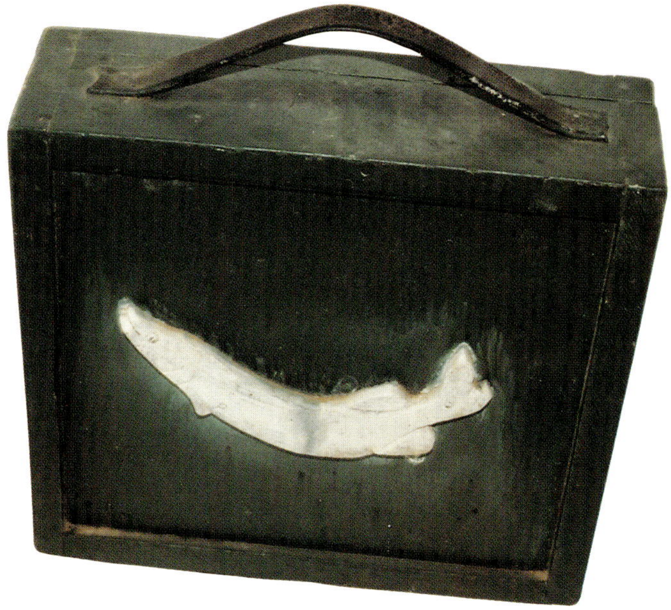

Green painted decoy box with upraised northern pike which is painted white, on one side of the box (walleye pike on other side).

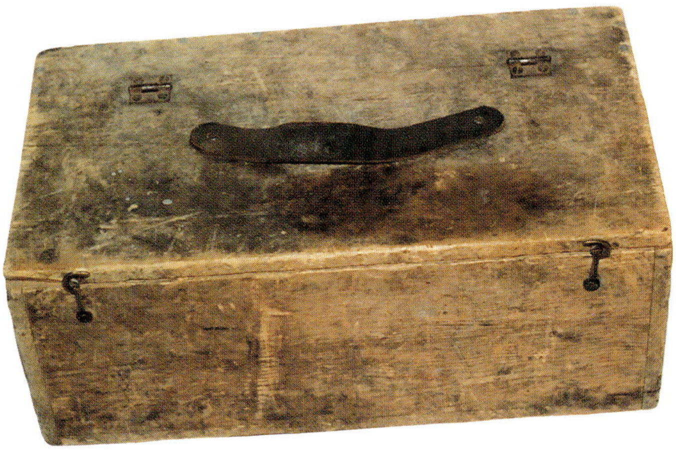

Undecorated decoy box.

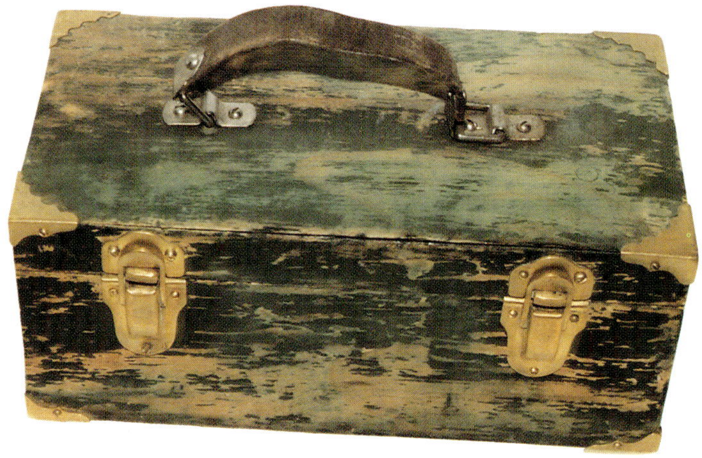

Green painted box said to be owned by Steven Oates of Crosby, Minnesota.

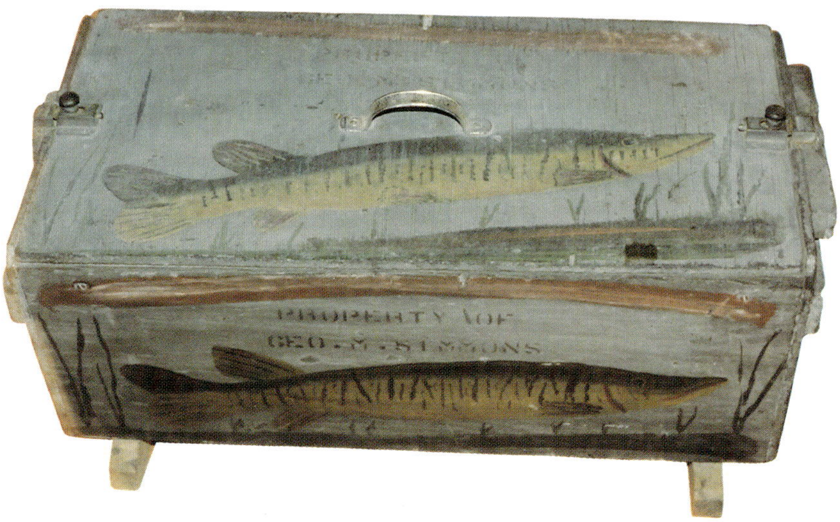

Large grey painted box with muskellunge painted on top and sides.

following a decision by his father, Peter, and uncle, Henry, to seek better farm land. They took the train west and exited in Renville County, Minnesota because "the land looked good there." There they remained.

Ray enjoyed working with wood as a boy, constructing boxes, etc. He continued his love of basic carpentry as a farmer, living near Bird Island, Minnesota. Friends and neighbors referred to him as "Pike."

"Pike" began carving fish decoys in the 1940's and he continued this endeavor until his death. There were three distinct periods which reflect the evolution of his decoys. His earliest decoys were made from a thin peach crate side board, only 1/4 inch wide, and painted simply, but nicely. The second period decoys were constructed from one inch pine or basswood. These second period decoys were painted with the "Christmas Tree" style of vertical markings. Ray referred to them as his "Tiger" fish. Decoys of this period also may show a "Raccoon" eye patch. Third period decoys were constructed in a manner similar to that of Ernest Newman [see this chapter]. Pike painted dots and had glass eyes on these later fish. He was adept at pleasing color combinations such as green with yellow or black with red and white.

Ray suffered a fatal heart attack on December 8, 1975 as he, Tom Elfing and Wenzel Frank were chopping holes in the ice on Lake Kabetogema, preparatory to spearing fish. "Pike Weis enjoyed spear fishing and left us from his favorite place."

*Information courtesy of Jerry Wintheiser.

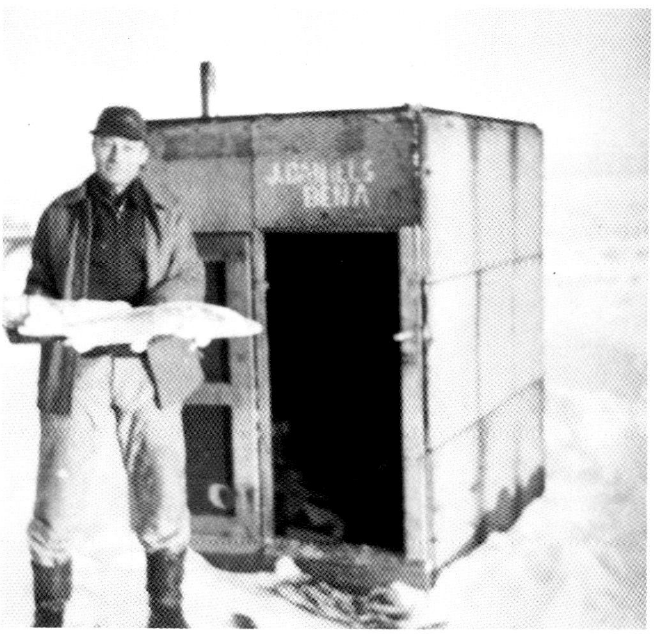

"Pike" Weis in 1957, standing before a dark house with his name sake.

CARL WOREN

Carl Woren was born in 1880 in Smoland, Sweden. When he was 16, his family settled in White Rock, Minnesota. They built a small house on a farm. At the age of 18, he bought farm land in Rosholt, South Dakota. Carl built the house, barn, and other buildings. His first construction project was a granary in which they lived until the house was completed. He married Emma Pearson in 1909. Mr. Woren met her when she was visiting South Dakota from the Twin Cities.

In 1926, they moved to a small farm by Green Lake, Minnesota. Carl wanted to take life easy. However, when they did not prosper, he sold the lake shore land and began building boats. His first shop was a small shed on the farm. He steamed his boards for the boats in a boiler used to heat laundry water. Later, a boat house was built on a piece of land that he had retained on the north shore of Green Lake. Mr. Woren made boats and carved fish decoys and some duck decoys in that building until his death in 1943.

Woren decoys had notched wooden tails and two pectoral fins on each side. They had carved wooden mouths and a screw-eye for a line tie. Most were crudely painted.

FRANCIS C. "FRANK" WOTRING*

Frank Wotring was born May 11, 1917 in Hibbing, Minnesota. Thereafter, his family homesteaded on Big Sandy Lake near McGregor, Minnesota. He entered the Navy in 1936, and when he retired in 1957, he had attained the rank of Machinist's Mate with a specialization in refrigeration. Frank returned to his home town of McGregor and began a refrigeration business. It was during the years 1957 to 1968 that Frank spear fished, mainly on Big Sandy Lake.

In 1966, Frank took a position with the Minnesota State Park Service. Wotring first served at Savannah State Park, then at Caledonia State Park, but was asked to move to Splitrock, where he helped establish that former coast guard station as a park.

He was transferred from Splitrock to Gooseberry Falls State Park in 1973, and worked at the latter for a total of eight years, six as a manager, before taking retirement from the Minnesota State Park Service in 1981.

Since retirement, he has devoted more time to his various hobbies which include wood carving, photography, and travel. He now resides in Two Harbors, Minnesota. Frank is married and has four grown children.

As previously noted, Frank speared only while he lived on Big Sandy Lake (1957-1968). It was during this time that he made his decoys, only four of which have survived. Of these four, one was a northern pike, realistically painted with pectoral fins fastened to the bottom of the decoy, plus a metal dorsal and anal fin. He used a screw head for the decoy's eye (see picture). Frank used a large piece of plastic for his decoy's tail (except in one case where he utilized a metal tail). He claimed that the plastic tail was very effective for manipulating the decoy to move in circles around the ice hole. His other three decoys had carved gills, tack or nail eyes, and in two cases, a dorsal fin carved right from the wood body of the fish. Except for the northern pike, Frank placed glitter on the painted surface of his decoys.

*Information from an interview with Mr. Wotring.

JOSEPH A. ZURN*

Joseph A. Zurn was born on March 14, 1905 in Callaway, Minnesota. In his earliest years, he farmed with his father and brothers. Later he worked as a garage mechanic and then he was involved in trucking cattle to St. Paul and taking freight back to Callaway. Subsequently, he bought a filling station, but then went back to working as a mechanic at a garage. Mr. Zurn then purchased a grocery store. Finally, he worked with Burton Ness, a contractor, until he retired in 1972.

Joe began spear fishing in the 1930's. He made mostly sunfish and crappie decoys. His primary material was white pine and he constructed his decoys' fins from sheet aluminum. Occasionally, he would burn the sides of his decoys to represent scales. After his fish were painted, he would varnish them and sometimes sprinkled them with glitter for greater attraction. Zurn claims that he has made between 200 to 300 decoys during his lifetime. Some he made for himself, others he sold or gave away.

Mr. Zurn also states that he has made about 20 fishing spears out of old pitch forks.

His favorite spearing lakes were Mille Lacs, Buffalo, Strawberry, and Shell.

*Information from an interview with Mr. Zurn.

RUDOLPH ZWIEG*

Rudolph "Rudy" Zwieg was born on October 17, 1919 north of Alexandria, Minnesota. He currently resides in Alexandria. Rudy has farmed for a living, but retired from Alexandria Light and Power, where he worked in maintenance. Following retirement, he has kept a small farm. Mr. Zwieg is married and has three grown children.

He began making spear fishing decoys in 1945, but in 1949 he was constructing them for sale. He charged $2.00 each and sold mainly to friends. Mr. Zwieg made a sunfish, pickerel and perch. His ordinary decoy had a red head and white body. Rudy's older decoys were tastefully painted in green and yellow tones. His tie line fastener was of the band type, but he also used a screw eye. The most important distinguishing feature of a Zwieg decoy is the painted "star eye."

Mr. Zwieg is still making fish decoys, but mostly as a hobby. Today he charges $8.00 and $10.00 for a decoy. While the price of a Zwieg decoy has increased with the years, the use of the "star eyes" still remains a characteristic of his fish.

*Information from an interview with Mr. Zwieg.

UNKNOWN MAKERS

A number of decoys of unknown origin have been included in this book. While this list could have been multiplied exponentially, it has been limited to those decoys which appear in private collections with some frequency, but whose makers remain a mystery. In some cases, names of these makers have been offered, but there is limited or no support for the identification. It is hoped that the readers of this book will be able to shed some light on these unknowns.

CHAPTER V

CONTEMPORARY DECOY MAKERS

As previously discussed, there sometimes exists a fine line between those carvers of fish decoys who may be described as "contemporary" versus those referred to as the "old-time" decoy makers. Age of the maker, of course, has some bearing on the dichotomy, as younger men and women (below the age of 50) appear to dominate the field. Some of these carvers began making decoys only within the last ten years, and then, only for the purpose of selling the decoys as pieces of folk art, and not necessarily for spear fishing. Indeed, the prices of some decoys make it prohibitive for a fisherman of average means to use them for fishing purposes.

On the other hand, there are carvers who are now in their sixties of seventies who have literally made decoys all of their lives. Some made them while actively spear fishing, then after ceasing to spear, made no further decoys for some time, until renewing this pursuit in recent years.

In some cases, the design, painting and overall quality of decoys changed for those individuals who have carved in the past and still continue to make decoys. Sometimes this change has been for the better, and in other instances, quality has declined.

On the whole, it is fair to say that contemporary carvers have produced very high quality decoys. Collectors of fish decoys may be faced with the question of whether or not to purchase the work of contemporary carvers.[1] Some collectors have no difficulty accepting both new and old decoys together on a shelf. Others prefer old-time decoys solely. A few collectors approach contemporary carvers' decoys as an investment. Today's relatively unknown carver may become tomorrow's Picasso of decoy carving.

In any event, contemporary decoy makers are a part of the Minnesota folk art tradition and deserve consideration for their fine work.

MEL ASSERUDE*

Mel Asserude was born on April 11, 1941 in Grand Forks, North Dakota. He presently resides in Cass Lake, Minnesota. Prior to beginning fish decoy carving in 1984, Mel was a driver and a mail and shipping clerk. He holds a college degree in elementary education.

For the past ten years, he has spent his summers at flea markets, buying and selling, as well as carving decoys. An avid spear fisherman, Mel began to carve decoys well after taking up the sport of spearing. At present, he makes 15 to 20 decoys a year. His preferred medium is cedar because it resists water damage and produces a nice finish for sanding and painting. He makes crappies, northern pike, walleye, muskies, bluegills, bullheads, suckers, tullipees, turtles and frogs. In his earlier days of carving, he also made a fine crawdad. Another specialty of Mel's is fashioning and painting fishing sticks.

*Information courtesy of Mr. Asserude.

LAWRENCE BETHEL*

Lawrence Bethel was born in January of 1930 in Park Rapids. His father was Pearl Bethel, the famous Minnesota decoy carver. Lawrence lived in Park Rapids until 1948 when he joined the Navy. Mr. Bethel was in the Navy for 20 years and retired from it in June of 1968. He then worked in Washington State for nine years in a sawmill, but returned to Park Rapids in 1977. Bethel began making decoys commercially after 1980, when his uncle Cyril Bethel died. He waited until after Cyril's death because he did not wish to be in competition with him. Since 1980, Lawrence has produced well over 3,000 decoys.

Mr. Bethel makes his decoys from basswood. He claims that it is light wood and does not "gum up" his sandpaper. Fins for his decoys are made from aluminum. Since 1983 he has stamped a "B" on the bottom of his decoys. All of his decoys are painted white until orders come in for various colors. His wife, Margaret, does all of his painting.

Bethel sold his decoys to the Fuller Tackle Shop in Park Rapids. His best seller is his red and white color combination.

Mr. Bethel left Minnesota for the state of Washington in the 1990's and still continues to produce decoys.

*Information from an interview with Mr. Bethel.

VERN "BUB" COSS*

"Bub" Coss was born on July 2, 1941 in Willmar, Minnesota. He served in the U.S. Navy for four years. Mr.

Coss has also been engaged in construction work. In 1987, he opened "Bub's Guns," a gun store located in Spicer, Minnesota.

In his early years, he was an avid spear fisherman, but has not spear fished in years. In 1992, he began making decoys for resale. His decoys are fashioned from cedar, black walnut (gun stock scrap), or oak. He makes a walleye, brook trout, sunfish, northern pike and chad. Copper fins are used, but glass eyes are found in many, but not all of his fish decoys. Normally, he stamps "Coss" on the bottom on his decoys or on the bottom of the fin.

"Bub" is married and has three children, all of whom are grown.

His decoys all have wooden tails and he paints them himself.

*Information from an interview with Mr. Coss.

BRUCE DIXON*

Bruce Dixon was born on October 30, 1952 and resides in Backus, Minnesota. He grew up at "Sandy Beach Resort" on Ponto Lake. His grandfather had started this resort in 1919. Bruce's father took over the operation of the Resort after he returned from World War II in 1946. The Resort was sold in 1969.

Bruce was in the air force for four years and has also worked for the United States' Post Office.

He began making decoys for resale in 1993. His "fish" are realistically painted. Bruce makes a tullibee, sturgeon, sunfish and a blue bill duck decoy. He airbrushes his colors and hand paints details.

Bruce is married and has one child, a son.

*Information from an interview with Mr. Dixon.

WILLARD LEROY "KING" HENSON*

Willard Henson was born in 1930 in Buffalo, Minnesota and still resides there. He was employed primarily as a digger of sewer, water and septic tanks. Mr. Henson enjoyed spearing, but has not speared since 1979. When he speared, he did not make his own decoys, but rather used those he bought from Henry Ramthun (see Chapter 4), who also lived in Buffalo.

Willard began carving decoys for resale in 1973, when his back became so bad that it was difficult to engage in his regular occupation. He uses basswood because it is easy to carve. Fish species that he imitates with his decoys include crappies and sunfish, but he also makes special orders for northern pike, perch, walleye pike, and frogs.

Willard paints his fish with acrylic paints. Mr. Henson stated he had to learn painting in order to craft his decoys [he is apparently a quick study]. Decoys were made only during the winter months. Tendinitis has halted his construction of decoys since 1992.

Mr. Henson is married and has three grown children.

*Erroneously referred to as "Willard King Hanson" in Kimball, op. cit. Volume II, p. 97, Information provided by Mr. Henson.

BURT HYATT*

Mr. Hyatt was born in 1917 in Iowa. He came to Minnesota in 1939 and now resides in Waubun. Burt was postmaster in Waubun for 32 years until his retirement.

He began carving decoys and spear fishing within a year of arriving in Minnesota. However, in the early years his decoys were for his own use. In 1980, Burt began making decoys for resale. His decoys are realistic and have carved scales. He makes northern pike, sunfish, crappies, walleye pike, suckers and tullipees. These decoys range in size from the twelve inch northern to the six inch sunfish.

Mr. Hyatt is married but had no children.

*Information provided by Mr. Hyatt.

JOHN JENSEN*

John Jensen was born November 21, 1929 in Minneapolis. For a time, he and his wife moved to Arizona where he was employed as a gardener. A serious back problem forced his early retirement. They moved from Arizona to Frazee, Minnesota in 1971. Mr. Jensen had previously carved decoys for his own use for spear fishing. The decoys he presently carves are much more elaborate in design and painting than his earlier models.

After a long hiatus, Mr. Jensen began making decorative fish decoys in 1986. His decoys are fashioned from basswood, white pine and cedar. He corrugates his own metal for fins, but purchases eyes for his decoys from a taxidermist. It is possible for him to carve two small decoys in a day, but it takes about five days for the paint to dry. John's decoys range in length from 2 1/2 inches to 48 inches in length. He makes all of the trout species of fish, sunfish, sturgeons, walleye pike, white fish, short nosed gars, catfish, bullheads, crayfish, salamanders, turtles, frogs, dog fish, perch and eel pouts. In addition, he has made a duck spearing decoy. Shorebirds and duck decoys complete his repertoire.

An adjunct to his fish decoys are jigging sticks, ice fishing sticks, and canes.

Mr. Jensen's work has been recognize by the Minnesota state Arts Board and he is listed in the Minnesota Artisan Directory. He has played his carvings at the Minnesota State Fair in St. Paul.

Mr. Jensen is married and has six grown children.

*Information from an interview with Mr. Jensen.

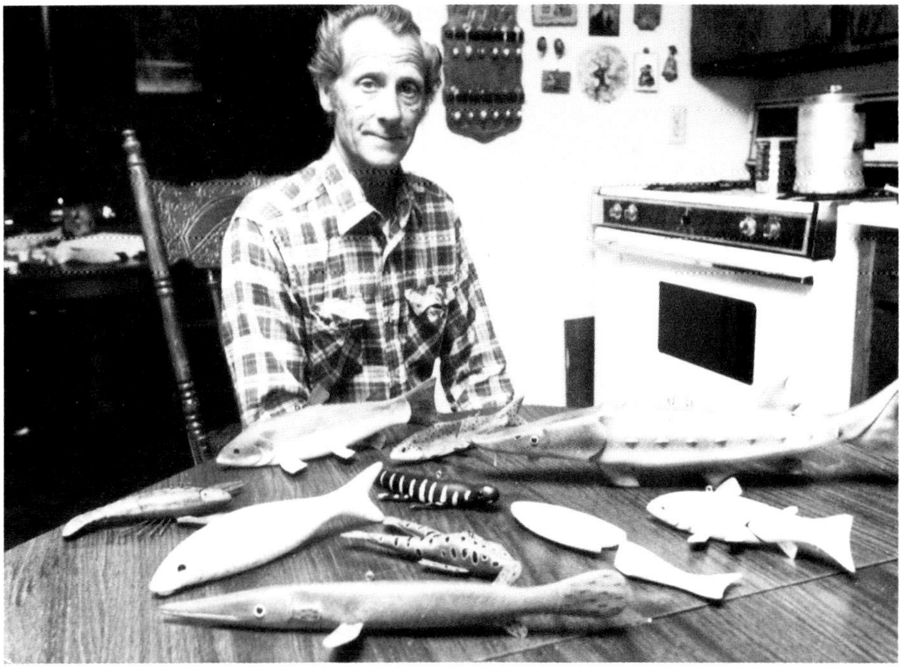

John Jensen relaxing in his kitchen with some of his decoys.

LAURENCE KASPER*

Laurence Kasper was born on October 18, 1919 in Cobb County, Minnesota. In 1937, his family moved to Nashwauk, Minnesota, as his father found work in the iron mines located in that region. Later, Laurence also worked in the mines as an electrician. He was also an auctioneer for 50 years, retiring in 1981. Mr. Kasper is married and has grown children.

In 1935, Laurence began making spear fishing decoys. As paint was not affordable during the Depression years, he utilized burned designs. By 1940, he was making decoys to sell—mainly to bait stores, some at Brainerd and Walker. Decoys were also sold to individuals desiring them. He fashioned his decoys from basswood because it whittled easily.

His early decoys are scarce. However, their basic design has changed little over the years. Currently, he carves a large bass or sunfish, northern pike, sucker and frogs. Laurence's more fanciful decoys include an alligator and tadpole. Fins are constructed from aluminum and include two pectoral fins on each side, a dorsal, anal and tail fin (although his sucker decoy has a wooden tail). His earlier decoys had fins made from brass. Paint patterns are a pleasing jumble of colors and his decoys are clear varnished after painting.

Over the years, Mr. Kasper estimates he has made over 10,000 decoys. He still spear fishes, and prefers Sucker Lake, Winninbigoshish Lake, and the Jay Gould park area.

*Information provided courtesy of Mr. Kasper.

RICHARD LARSEN*

Richard Larsen was born in 1915 in Little Falls, Minnesota. He currently resides in Isle, Minnesota. Mr. Larsen's description of himself is a "jack of all trades" [but he is certainly a master of decoy making]. He was a quarry foreman for 38 years. Mr. Larsen also owned a resort on Mille Lacs Lake.

When he retired in 1975, Richard began to produce spear fishing decoys to pass the time. He crafted them mostly from pine and basswood. Sunfish, suckers, bullheads, and perch are in his repertoire of fish species imitated by his decoys. His wife, Mary, paints the fish.

Mr. Larsen has also carved birds and duck decoys. However, failing eyesight recently has caused Richard to cease crafting fish decoys. He has only made about 50 decoys. It is a pity, because his work is excellent.

*Information from an interview with Mr. Larsen.

CLIFFORD LARSON*

Clifford Larson was born on April 7, 1922 in Virginia, Minnesota. His place of residence is currently Minneapolis. Cliff has done wood carving his entire life. At the age of twelve, he began whittling floats or bobbers which he sold to the Grandy Hardware Store in Virginia for 75¢ a dozen. Though he spear fished in his younger days, Mr. Larson did not make spearing decoys.

As an adult he worked as a sales representative for the Tandy Leather Company. He also participated in Leathercraft demonstrations at trade shows. Later, he became a teacher for home-bound handicapped children. Cliff was one of the early occupational therapists, teaching leather crafting, wood carving, etc. He was employed in this profession for twelve years.

Subsequently, in 1983, while he was residing in Minneapolis, Mr. Larson was approached by a local collector of spearing decoys, Frank Pasiewicz, who requested that Cliff do some restoration on some fish decoys. Apparently, the job was so well done that Frank urged Larson to carve and paint decoys of his own. The results were encouraging and Cliff estimates that he has carved more than 2,000 fish from 1983 to 1993. An illness suffered in 1993 has all but curtailed his fish decoy carving activities.

Mr. Larson has mainly constructed fish decoys based on the species of fish commonly found in Minnesota lakes, such as northern pike, walleye pike, sunfish, crappies, muskies, and even some gar fish. On occasion, he has also carved decoys imitating species found outside Minnesota.

The popularity of his decoys is demonstrated by the fact that he has sold fish to dealers and individual collectors throughout the United States and even as far away as Australia. Examples of Larson fish may also be found in the Museum of Folk Art in New York, another testimony in the high regard in which his fish decoys are held.

*Information from an interview with Mr. Larson.

ROGER LASHUA[2]

Mr. Lashua was born in 1947 in Duluth. He presently resides just outside Akeley, Minnesota. His primary occupation is as an antique dealer.

Although he has always been a spear fishing devotee, Mr. Lashua did not begin to make decoys until 1985. He makes two styles (pictured) and sells them out of his house and to other dealers. Sometimes he tries to make his decoys appear old by painting them in earth tone colors.

A nice adjunct to his decoys is a folk art spear fishing shanty with a man inside spear fishing (pictured).

Mr. Lashua is married and has three children.

JOE LEACH*

Mr. Leach was born on October 17, 1933 in Sauk Centre, Minnesota. He resides, at present, in Melrose, Minnesota. For 33 years, Mr. Leach was an art teacher. He is now retired. In his retirement, Mr. Leach both owns a pottery business and is engaged in crafting spear decoys.

Joe began making decoys in 1955 when his parents owned a resort on Leach Lake in northern Minnesota. These decoys he made mainly for himself, but he did sell a few of them. In 1991, he began to seriously carve decoys for sale. He describes his decoys as "working fish." His preferred medium is basswood or yellow cedar. Mr. Leach makes northerns, suckers, perch, a salmon style, and "critters" such as frogs. Most of his fish are left in the natural wood color, but a few are painted. He states that his decoys have become more "sculptural" over the years.

Mr. Leach is married and has five children.

*Information from an interview with Mr. Leach.

MURRAY J. MARLETTE*

Murray Marlette was born on August 6, 1947 in Slayton, Minnesota. He now resides in Little Falls, Minnesota where he works as a painter at Camp Ripley.

Mr. Marlette began making decoys in shop classes when he was twelve years old. However, he began fashioning decoys for resale in 1990. Murray has made about 175 decoys to date and charges between $45 and $50 for a decoy. His decoys are crafted from basswood, sugar pine, arbor vitae, walnut or any recycled wood from the base. Murray makes northern pikes, suckers, crappies, sunfish, and a frog. He also makes what he calls his "generic" fish (pictured). Many of his decoys are painted realistically.

He also makes fish to order, and will fashion copies of old decoys. Murray has also made a few duck decoys.

Mr. Marlette still enjoys spearing and states his favorite spearing lake is Swan Lake. He is married and has five children.

*Information provided by Mr. Marlette.

DAVID E. PERKINS*

David Perkins was born November 9, 1934 in Nimrod, Minnesota. He currently resides in Duluth. He has been a merchant seaman, a barber, a hard rock miner, a worker in the Alaskan oil fields, and a welder. David began making decoys for his own use in the late 1940's.

At the present time (1994), he has made over 200 decoys. He fashions them from white pine because it is sturdy, easy to carve and does not have much grain. His best known decoys are his northern pike. However, Dave also carves perch, trout, and crappies. Critters that he carves include a mouse, dragon fly, turtles and frogs. He also fashions duck decoys, diamond willow canes and chairs. His fish decoys are marked with "D.F.D." (Duluth Fish Decoy). He insists that his latest decoys are becoming more "folky" and have a one-of-a-kind finish.

Mr. Perkins has sold his work to the Museum of Folk Art in New York, other wildlife art galleries, and to collectors.

He is married and has two grown children.

*Information from an interview with Mr. Perkins.

LARRY PETERSON*

Larry Peterson was born in 1931 in Inver Grove, Minnesota. He worked for Swift & Company from 1950 to 1969. Larry finished his career with the Senex Corporation, retiring in 1989. Thereafter, he moved to Nisswa, Minnesota.

Mr. Peterson began crafting decoys in the 1940's. His decoys may appear to be familiar to you—they should be. His uncles were Walter and Herbert Peterson of Osakis, Minnesota. Larry copied his decoys from his uncles.

*Information provided by Larry Peterson.

CARL L. SILVER

Carl Silver was born March 12, 1936 in Tennessee. He passed away in Coon Rapids, Minnesota on August 25, 1993. Mr. Silver was self-employed. To help supplement his income, he was an antique dealer.

He was also a gifted carver and painter. He crafted fish decoys, birds, and ducks. Although he fished, he did not spear.

Mr. Silver was divorced and had two daughters and a son.

JOHN & EVELYN SWENSON*

John and Evelyn Swenson were married in 1953. He was born on April 17, 1935, and she was born January 19, 1935. They have six children and 20 grandchildren.

Though John has carved all of his life, his full-time career of carving and selling decoys began in 1984 while he was recuperating from an accident. Evelyn also carved during her childhood. Much of their carving is done as they travel in a motor home, towing a van that has a sign painted on the rear doors, "Do you have a Swenson Decoy?"

They make bass, northerns, walleyes, trout, perch, crappies, bullheads and frogs. Evelyn paints the decoys, but John's are mostly stained. They use glass and tack eyes for their fish. Basswood and white cedar are preferred woods for the decoy bodies, although their earlier decoys were fashioned from redwood. These early decoys were also oil painted and unsigned. More recent fish bear their initials within the outline of a fish. Oil paints have been replaced with a special stain wash.

The Swensons also make attractive ice fishing and jig sticks, rustic signs and a few duck decoys. Their material is offered through a mail order catalog, through a west coast dealer and by friends.

Although neither John or Evelyn received formal art training, their carvings have been widely acclaimed. Twelve Swenson decoys reside in the State Arts Museum collection in Tempe, Arizona. Their carvings have also been featured in *USA Today* and the *New England Antique Journal.*

*This information is based on an article by K. David Hirschey, "Do you have a Swenson Decoy?" in *Decoy Magazine,* March-April 1993; pp. 44-45, and a telephone interview with Evelyn.

JOHN UNGER*

John Unger was born in the Grand Rapids, Minnesota on April 22, 1916. He began working in a barber shop in Bovey, Minnesota at age eleven doing odd jobs and clean-up. John later began shining shoes, for which he was paid 15¢ (while other shoe shine boys were only earning a dime, he explained). Fred Lexow, who owned a sweet shop across the street, and who is also a well known Minnesota decoy maker [see Chapter 4], used to pay John 25¢ for a shine. At age 14, Mr. Unger was already a barber and remained in that occupation until his retirement in 1984.

He learned the art of decoy making from his father, who was a carpenter. John was also influenced by Fred Lexow. He began making decoys when only eight or nine years old. His earliest decoys were made from cedar, but later he changed his medium to pine. He has made golden shiners, herring and smelt decoys, all of which have wooden tails. His contemporary decoys are realistically painted. He also has made crawdads, but does not do so anymore.

*Information from an interview with Mr. Unger.

CHAPTER VI
COMMERCIAL DECOY MAKERS

Some spear fishermen in Minnesota lack the skill, time or patience to craft their own decoys. At the present time, about 60 percent of the spearing population uses artificial decoys more than half the time and only one-third use live decoys more than half the time.[1] Commercial decoy manufacturers serve (and have served) an important need, therefore, supplying decoys to those spear fishermen who do not make their own, or to those who wish to supplement their decoy rig. It is difficult to draw a meaningful line as to who should be included as a "commercial decoy maker." On the one hand, there were people such as the Faue brothers, Frank Mizera, Leroy Howell, etc. who produced vast quantities of decoys to sell. Were they commercial decoy makers? In the sense that they made decoys to sell, they qualified. However, many decoy makers produced extra decoys which they gave away to friends and/or sold. On the other hand, there were those who also produced large quantities of decoys, but under a brand name such as "Fisheretto," "Cy's," etc. These latter individuals may have marketed their decoys through national retailers, developed boxes or other packaging for their decoys bearing the brand name, advertised locally or in a wide area, and so on. It is the makers in this category that I have chosen to include in this chapter. While the distinction is admittedly artificial, it may represent a more accurate picture of the truly "commercial decoy makers" than those who sold decoys, but lacked the other accoutrements described above.

Collectors have something of a love-hate relationship with commercially made decoys. Those who admire the folk art of fish decoys tend to prefer the more homemade ones, while those who primarily collect fishing lures tend to enjoy commercial decoys, sometimes even to the exclusion of the folk art variety. Naturally, there are also those collectors who seem to be comfortable with both.

This chapter reviews the known Minnesota commercial fish decoy makers, providing a history of the business development as well as examples of their decoys and related products.

BRAINERD BAIT COMPANY*

Very little is known regarding the Brainerd Bait Company. The *Minnesota Manufacturers Directory* first listed it in 1941 (although it may have been in business before this date), located at 2470 University Avenue in St. Paul. By 1952, it had moved to 385 Prior Avenue North and was called the National Export Company, selling fishing tackle, baits, and supplies. In 1963-64, the company was located at 1564 Englewood Avenue, selling fishing lures, spinners, hooks, spoons, weedless hooks and frog harnesses. Its final list in the *Directory* was 1967-68, and reference to it is absent in 1970-71.

There is no indication that the company either made, or did not make, spear fishing decoys. It marketed its products through catalogs.

*Information courtesy of the Minnesota Historical Society.

BROWN BROTHERS' "FISHERETTO"[2]

In 1865, Mr. and Mrs. John B. Brown left their native Ireland to come to the United States. They settled first in Chicago. Later, they moved to a farm near Sauk Centre, Minnesota, with their two children, Neil and Sam. Eight more children would be born to them including Tom, Ann, Hannah, John, Bill, Mike, Ed, and Kathryn ("Kit").

In 1900, three of the sons, Tom, Bill and John, came to Osakis, Minnesota where they opened the Brown Brothers General Merchandise Store. In 1904, following the death of their father, the rest of the children moved to Osakis. The Store became a family operation. Also in 1904, Bill, John and Tom opened a farm implement business in Osakis. Another farm implement business in Alexandria, Minnesota was acquired in 1914.

In 1910, the Brown family purchased a spacious corner home located across the street from the Osakis Creamery. Sam Brown began making and selling fishing lures in the basement of the house as well as in a rear shop that same year [i.e., 1910]. By October 30, 1918, Sam had filed a patent for a "Fish Bate or Lure."

After Sam died in 1925, Mike and Ed carried on the lure manufacturing business. The General Store was sold in 1932, but the lure business continued until 1945. Probably few lures were made or sold during World War II because of material shortages. Mike subsequently died in 1953 and Ed passed away in 1962. Both men were avid fishermen.

The Brown brothers made fish decoys called "Dark House Fish Decoys." They were hand painted and no two were exactly alike. Most of the decoys were painted in vivid colors. The Browns' had an assembly line process for making their lures and decoys. Decoys had the same basic body form or shape as their lures, but, of course, without hooks.

BRU-ELL DECOYS*

Bru-ell decoys are named for Bruce [the "Bru"] and Helen [the "ell"] Wakefield of Watkins, Minnesota. Both were born in 1915, she in southern Iowa, and he in Minneapolis. They have two sons and have been married for over 60 years.

Their decoy-making enterprise was formed out of necessity in 1949 when Mr. Wakefield's back was broken by a falling tree. No longer able to farm and raise minks and cattle, Bruce decided to begin making spear fishing decoys to sell. Over the years, there have been thousands of Bru-ell decoys produced. Mr. Wakefield makes his decoys from 3 to 14 inches in length. All of the decoys are made by hand with the aid of jigs that Mr. Wakefield has developed. The decoys are fashioned from cedar and are primed and painted with enamel paint. Their predominant color combination is red and white, but they have also painted their decoys blue, orange, yellow, black, etc. More recent [1990's] colors include chartreuse, pink and white, and green and chartreuse.

The Wakefields also have provided boxes for some of their decoys marked "One Genuine Bru-ell Decoy" [see photograph]. Their decoys were distributed through manufacturer's representatives as well as marketed directly to bait and hardware stores.

Over the years, Bru-ell decoys have demonstrated some pronounced changes in form and construction. The earlier models had taxidermy eyes, multiple line ties, and a more distinct and sharper indentation in the metal tail fin. More recent decoys have painted tack eyes, one line tie, and a more rounded indentation on the tail fin. In addition, the earlier models only had one set of pectoral fins fashioned in a different shape from their later versions. These fins were bent up and nailed to the body of the decoys [see photograph] while more recent decoys have the fins inserted into the decoy.

Moreover, the nose of the earlier Bru-ell decoys was more blunt-shaped than the sharply pointed ones prominent in the more recent decoys.

The Wakefields enjoyed spear fishing until Bruce's disabling accident. Helen was an interior decorator for many years.

*Information courtesy of Helen Wakefield.

CY'S DECOYS[3]

Cyrus D. "Cy" Halvorson was born on May 16, 1905 in Willmar, Minnesota. He was married to Ruth Land, who died in 1969. Their marriage produced a son and a daughter.

Mr. Halvorson was a sporting goods distributor, an operator of White House Hamburger in Willmar, and was also employed by the Great Northern Railroad. By 1954, he owned a sporting goods store, called "Cy's Tackle Box," located at 332 W. Benson in Willmar. Telephone directories in Willmar from 1961 through 1971 list a "Cy's Sporting Goods" at 304 E. Becker Ave.

For many years, Mr. Halvorson made decoys in his home. He employed an assembly line system, making the wood bodies, inserting the fins, pouring the lead and nailing the metal fins and tail into place. He made both a six and eight inch minnow and a few larger ones (twelve to sixteen inches). Painting was accomplished with an air gun through mesh screens. His predominant color schemes were red and white, red and yellow, black and white, etc. The boxes for his decoys referred to them as "Cy's Fish Decoy," "Made by a Fisherman — for a Fisherman." Production of his decoys ended somewhere between 1962 and 1964.

Cyrus Halvorson passed away on December 31, 1971.

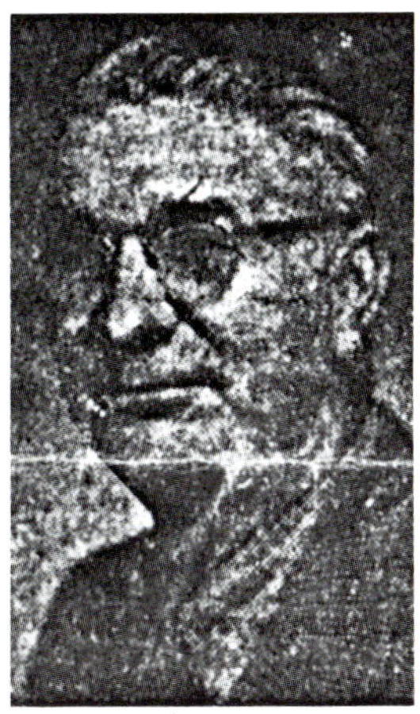

Cyrus D. Halvorson, 1905-1971.

FISH BUST'R

A red and white decoy, covered in part by glitter, was produced by a company called P & F Products of Crosby, Minnesota. It sold the decoys under the name "Fish Bust'r." The "Fish Bust'r" was apparently sold in a cellophane bag with a paper label sealer.

HERTER'S, INC.*

A Herter's letterhead describes the business as being founded in 1893 by George L. Herter. The business began as a fly tying and fishing lure business in some rooms above his father's Bee Hive Dry Goods Store. It later grew to carry thousands of items. When the Bee Hive Store burned down, Mr. Herter moved the business to Waseca.

After World War II, George Herter built a warehouse on Highway 13, just south of Waseca, and subsequently added a second distribution center in Mitchell, South Dakota. Herter's was a retail catalog and sporting goods supplier. The Hunting Equipment Division was located in Waseca, Minnesota.

While spear fishing decoys were only sold in catalogs for two years, 1964 and 1965, other such decoys were sold from its distribution centers. The catalog decoys featured an eight inch and ten inch decoy which resembled a northern pike. They came in color combinations including a red head and white body, orange body, black spotted, tiger, and perch. The eight inch decoy sold for $1.02 while the ten inch sold for $1.20. Fins were produced from a die cast alloy which could be easily bent. The decoys sold from the retail outlets were fancier in design and painting than catalog models.

*See also Charles W. Frank, "Affordable Decoys Alternatives for Collectors," *Decoy Magazine,* May-June 1994, pp. 17-18.

LEE'S DECOYS[4]

Lee's Decoys was founded by LeRoy Carlson, who was born in Dassel, Minnesota on June 18, 1936. He now resides in Coon Rapids, Minnesota. Mr. Carlson is a quality engineer with Honeywell Corporation.

In 1966, he began making the Lee's decoy. Spear fishermen were said to have good success with it.

His decoys sold for between $2.00 to $2.25 to bait shops in the area. In 1988, Mr. Carlson went out of business after making approximately 300 "Lee's" decoys. Ironically, Mr. Carlson was not a spear fisherman himself.

RANDALL DECOYS*

George Randall, the founder of the Randall Decoy business, was born on August 19, 1921 in Morris, Minnesota. During his high school days, George made decoys and spears for himself and friends, and also made boats as a hobby. Graduating in 1940 from Willmar Senior High School, he went to work for the Burlington Northern Railroad as a machinist and inspector. In 1941, he entered the service during World War II as a member of the Navy Seabees.

After his return from active duty in 1946, he again worked for the Railroad until the Yards closed in Willmar in the late 1950's. Prior to his retirement from the Railroad, Mr. Randall had begun manufacturing spearing decoys and spears which he sold to local hardware stores and to some larger sporting goods stores. He produced his decoys and spears in a "garage-type" operation at his home in Eagle Lake near Willmar, Minnesota.

In 1960, he moved to Spicer, Minnesota, purchasing the Hultgren Cafe there in 1963. Mr. Randall used the basement of the cafe for his fish decoy and spear business. The upstairs was Randall's Cafe.

In 1969 or 1970, Mr. Randall sold the Cafe and purchased the old blacksmith shop in Spicer and moved the fishing business to that location. There, he employed as many as seven assemblers at his factory. At the height of his operations, George Randall made fish decoys in ten colors and designs in four sizes—six, eight, ten and twelve inches. He also produced a crappie and bluegill decoy which came in a five inch size. His "Golden Sucker" was manufactured in the six inch to twelve inch size range. Pickerels of 16 inch length were made in a "natural" and red and white finish.

Randall decoys had a wood body with lead weights in the form of fins attached to the bottom. The prices varied with the length of the decoy, a six inch decoy selling for $1.25 and a twelve inch for $2.00. The 16 inch pickerels listed for $4.95, while the bluegills and crappies sold for $1.35.

Mr. Randall would take samples of his products with him on the road and sold them to local hardware and sporting goods stores. His wares were also marketed in Michigan and North Dakota.

Mr. Randall was married to Millie, and they had one son and two daughters. He worked full time until his untimely death on February 12, 1979 from a heart attack. The factory in Spicer was sold seven or eight months after his death.

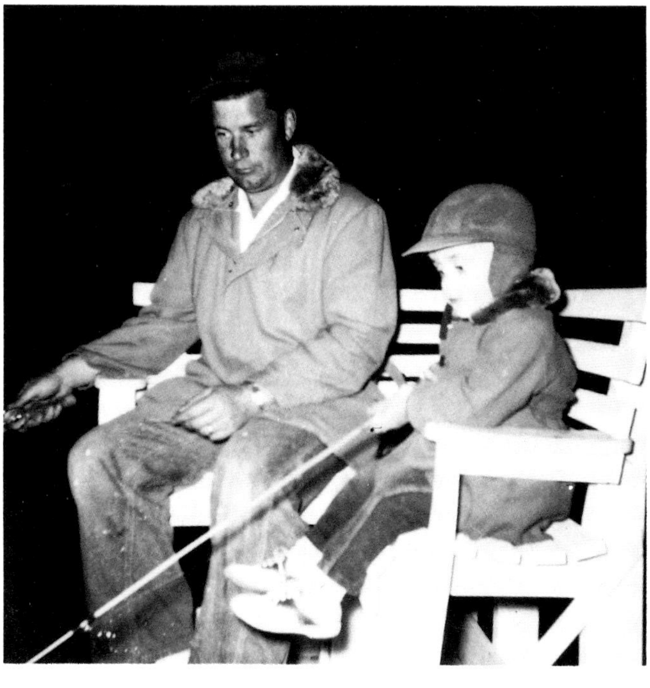

George Randall fishing with his son, Grayson (age 3), off the dock at his home on Eagle Lake near Willmar, Minnesota.

*Information courtesy of Mrs. Mildred Randall, Leah Randall Stanek, and Carter Stenberg.

PHONE: BE 5-4584

ROUTE I WILLMAR, MINN.

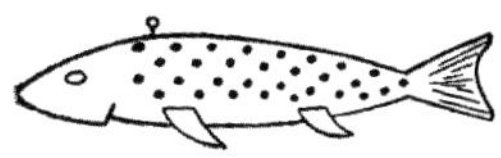

GEORGE L. RANDALL

DECOYS and FISH SPEARS

George Randall's business card.

REIGSTAD DECOYS*

Oliver (b. September 28, 1910) and Olga Reigstad were a husband and wife team of decoy makers, who lived in Duluth, Minnesota. Mr. Reigstad worked for the Erie Mining Company from 1957 until 1963. It was during this time that all of their decoys were produced (a total of about 650 finished decoys were made). Each work day, Olga would give her husband six blanks of pine or basswood. Oliver worked on a barge in the Duluth Harbor and his main responsibility was to monitor a warning light. This job allowed him time to whittle the blanks into the proper form. The finished decoys were brought home and metal fins made from tobacco cans were inserted into the decoys. Lead would then be poured into the body cavity. Olga would paint the decoys. Red and white, black and white, and green and white were the predominant color schemes, but there were 22 other color variations. Most of the decoys had glitter added while the paint was wet. Thumb tacks were used for the eyes. Some finished decoys were put in boxes and hand stamped "Reigstad Decoy."

Decoys were sold in Duluth and other places for $1.00 each. However, the decoys did not sell well. Oliver Reigstad experienced health problems in 1964, and with the onset of his illness, production of the decoys ended.

Mr. Reigstad passed away on January 20, 1979. Olga still resides in Minnesota. Their unsold decoys were stored in her attic until she sold the remainder to a collector in 1990.

*Thanks are extended to Mrs. Olga Reigstad and Carter Stenberg for the information provided.

RIPLEY'S "DECOY MINNOW"*

Horace E. "Slim" Ripley was born in Riceville, Iowa on November 21, 1891. He married Lucy Hendricks in 1911. In 1920, they moved to Alexandria, Minnesota. Mr. Ripley was a house painter by profession. Because of the strong odor of paint in those days, few people wanted to have their houses painted in the winter when the windows were shut and the paint smell would be retained. Therefore, he began to produce spear fishing decoys in about 1927 to help supplement his income. Slim would whittle the decoys and one of his daughters (Dawn) would help paint them while another daughter (Mary) was assigned the task of folding boxes. The boxes were stamped "Ripley's Decoy Minnow, Alexandria, Minnesota." A number of his decoys were marked with a red or black "RP" on the lead weight. He would produce one to two thousand decoys in a year's time.

The decoys were sold to Our Own Hardware in Alexandria. Later, Mr. Ripley took orders for his fish from Hall Hardware in Minneapolis.

The Ripley decoy was fairly standard in length and form, but with numerous color combinations due to his utilization of left over house paints. Frequently, his fish had spots or dashes in addition to blends of two colors.

In 1954, Slim Ripley retired to Florida. That move effectively ended his decoy making business. He passed away on August 30, 1976 at the age of 84.

*Thanks are extended to Bill Stoetzel and Mrs. Mary Hibbard for the information provided regarding Slim Ripley.

SLETTEN MFG. COMPANY*

Kermit Sletten was born on February 13, 1911 in Willmar, Minnesota. He served in World War II in the radar services. After the War, in 1946, he converted his home garage in Willmar, located at 720 W. Third St., into a plant to manufacturer spear fishing decoys. Later, he moved his operation to a rental building at the fairgrounds. His decoys were made of aluminum and had a single aluminum fin. He made six types of decoys representing pickerel, perch, pike, chub, crappie, and sunfish. These ranged in size from 3 to 7 1/2 inches in length. His production in 1946 was 1,000 decoys per day.

He also produced a lure called the "Water Bug."

Mr. Sletten designed all of his own decoy making equipment and the firm of Lobnitz and Swanson of Willmar permitted him the use of their shop to build it. There was a crucible for melting the aluminum by bottled gas, stacks of aluminum in ingot form, 22 molds into which the molten metal was poured, specially constructed ladles, cooling vats, special sawing adjustments, grinding machines, a tumbler of crushed rock to remove the film remaining on the aluminum after casting, a line tie drill, slot saw and a stenciling machine.

Air brushes applied a base paint color to the decoys. Trim and eyes were placed by spotting brushes. Finished decoys were packed 25 to 500 in a case. Each decoy was placed in a cardboard and cellophane bag. Mr. Sletten was assisted by two to four assemblers. He was married and had one daughter. Mr. Sletten was killed in an automobile accident on September 15, 1959 in Shevlin, Minnesota.

*Information courtesy of Carter Stenberg and the *Willmar Tribune,* October 28, 1946.

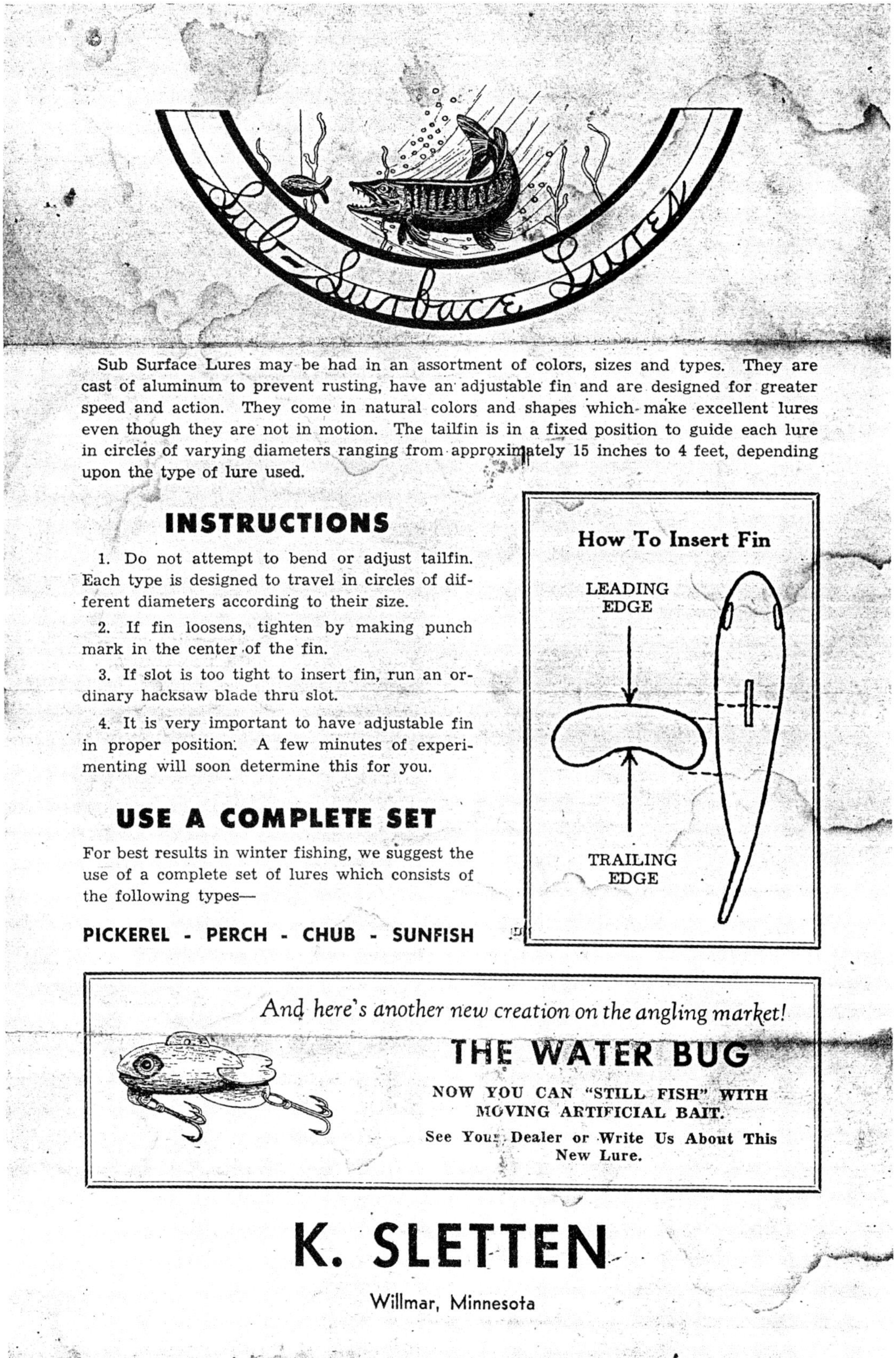

Sletten advertisement for his decoys including the "Water Bug."

TITLOE HEIGHTS BAIT MFG.*

W. C. Oldenburg, "Ole" as he was known to his friends, was county auditor for Sibley County from 1935 to 1962. In the mid-1930's, Mr. Oldenburg received a patent for his "Ole 3-way fish lure" (U.S. Patent Office number 762989). The decoy, made of metal, could be converted to a fishing lure by attaching treble hooks to a hole drilled into the lower part of the metal tail and/or one drilled into the decoy's mouth. His earliest decoys had six line tie holes and featured glass eyes. The later version had only three line tie holes and had bulging rivet eyes. Mr. Oldenburg's earlier decoys were hand painted, but later he began spray painting them. His major color scheme was red and white, but he also featured other color combinations such as blue and white, black and white, and green and white.

His decoys were apparently advertised and he packaged and sent them through the mail. In the 1940's his decoys sold for $1.50 each which included two detachable treble hooks. The decoys were 4 3/4 inches in length and weighed two ounces. He sold them under the name of the Titloe Heights Bait Manufacture, Gaylord, Minnesota.[5]

Mr. Oldenburg also built martin houses, portable fishing houses, and bird and squirrel feeders.

He was a World War I veteran and was married. Both his wife and son preceded him in death. Mr. Oldenburg died in 1963 and is buried at Fort Snelling National Cemetery.

*Information provided by the Sibley County Historical Society and Mr. George Anderson.

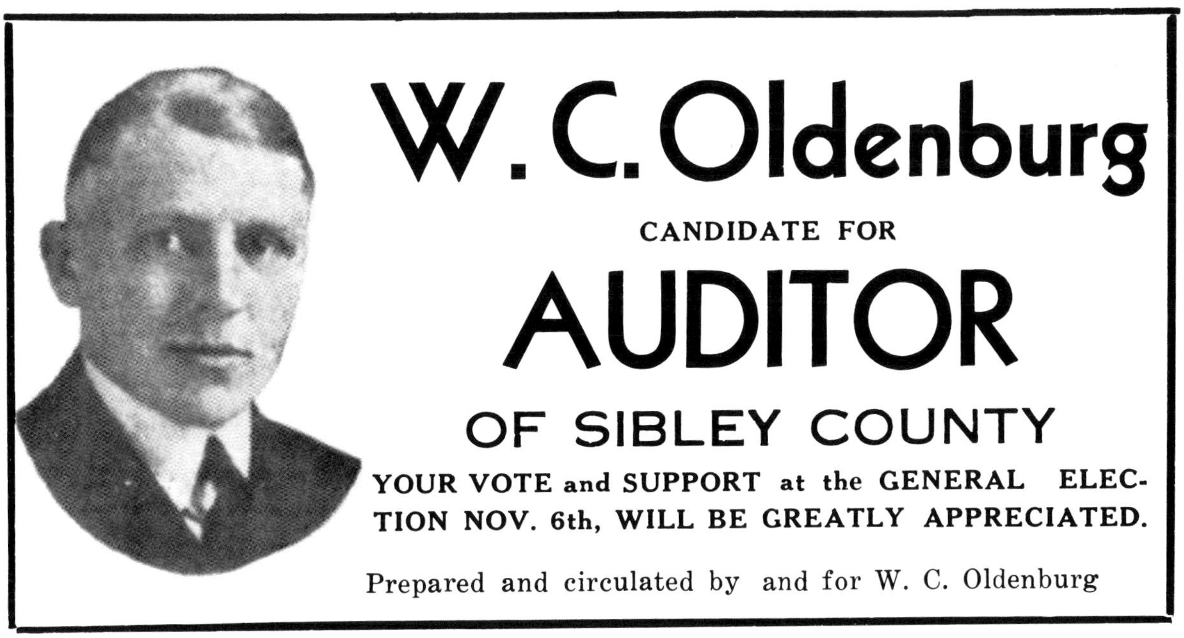

Political advertisement with a picture of W. C. Oldenburg.

The "OLE" 3-WAY FISH LURE

A Tried and Tested Fish Lure Which Is a Proven Success

Manufactured Under U. S. Patent Office Serial Number 762989, Series of 1935, By the "Titloe Heights" Bait Manufacturer, Gaylord, Minnesota.

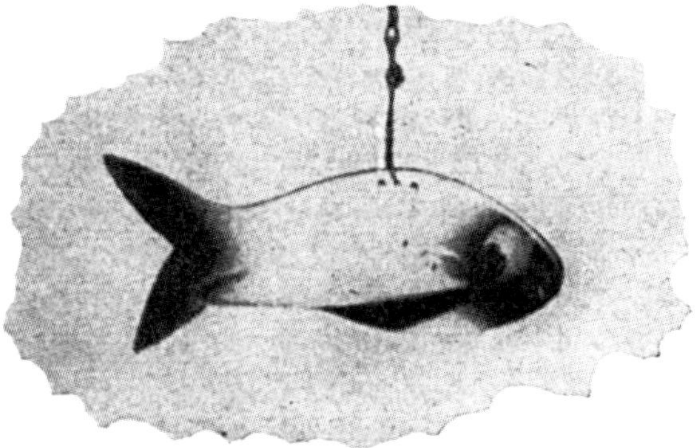

Feature Number "1"

Feature Number "1"

The Lure serves as an excellent Decoy for spearing fish through the ice in a dark house. When used for this purpose, detach the treble hooks from the body by way of the slip on rings and attach your decoy line to one of the three holes in the top of the body of the Lure, suitable to your adjustment, as illustrated in the picture to the left. Sink the Lure in the water to a suitable depth, then by gently raising and lowering the line the Lure will maintain a continuous circular movement in the water, within a radius of several feet. This is the action demanded by skilled fishermen and always gives the best results.

Feature Number "2"

For your fishing through the ice in a shelter or out in the open, the Lure will serve just as well as when spearing in a dark house. For this type of fishing, attach the treble hooks in the two large holes in the mouth and tail of the Lure by way of the slip on rings and attach your line in one of the three holes in the top of the body of the Lure, suitable to your adjustment, as illustrated in the picture to the right. When adjusted in this manner the same action and results will be obtained as described in Feature Number "1."

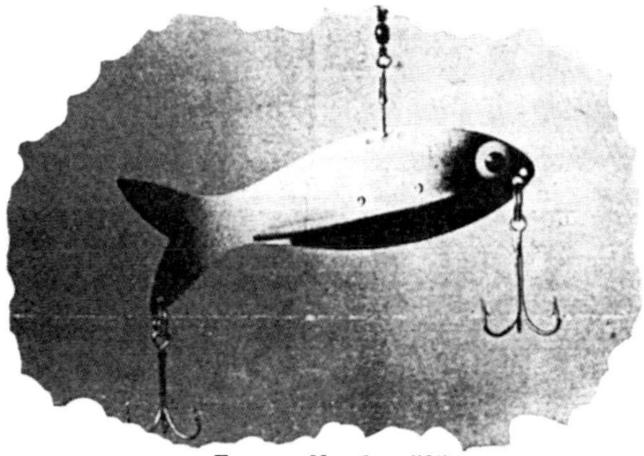

Feature Number "2"

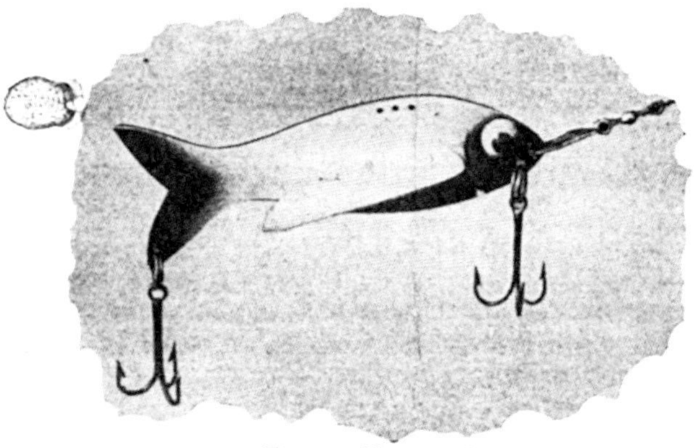

Feature Number "3"

Feature Number "3"

For summer fishing, the Lure also serves as an excellent bait when trolling or casting. To use the Lure for this purpose, fasten your line in the hole in the mouth of the Lure and attach the treble hooks if they have been detached. The wings of the Lure are flexible and can be adjusted to produce the various actions which you may desire. Try tilting the right wing downward and the left wing upward to obtain best results. See illustration in the picture to the left. The Lure also serves well in the summer for drop fishing. When drop fishing the line should be attached at the top of the body of the Lure as shown in Feature Number "2" and should be operated in the same manner.

The "3-Way" Feature has made this Lure famous. The Lure is constructed of metal material, and is approximately 4¾ inches in length, weighing approximately 2 ounces. It is beautifully decorated in colors and is equipped with two treble hooks which are attachable and detachable from the main body of the Lure by way of slip on rings.

The colors and prices of the Lure are as follows:

NUMBER	COLOR	PRICE
No. 501	Red and White	**$1.50**
No. 502	Blue and White	**1.50**
No. 503	Black and White	**1.50**
No. 504	Green and White	**1.50**

This Lure is sold direct by the Manufacturer only. To be assured that your Lure will reach you in time for your winter fishing this year, place your order now. All orders will be filled in the order in which they are received. Enjoy a successful season of fishing with the "Ole" 3-Way Fish Lure.

Titloe Heights Bait Manufacturer,
Gaylord, Minn.

...., 194........

Enclosed, herewith, please find currency, draft, money order, in the amount of $............................, for which please send me........................"Ole" 3-Way Fish Lures, in the following colors:..

....

Name..

Address..

TONKA BAITS-SCHIPPER BROS.*

Ithel Schipper was born in 1919 and founded the Minnetonka Bait Company along with his brother, Darel, in 1944. Darel Schipper (b. 1926) purchased the business in 1947-48 from Ithel and changed the name of the firm to Schipper Brothers. Although the Company was located in Wayzata, Minnesota, the decoys were actually produced in Stillwater. The Schipper decoys came in two sizes—small: 5 1/2 inches in length, and large: 8 inches in length. Early decoys were hand-dipped and sold locally. Later, the decoys came in four color combinations including a red-head and white body, yellow with dark green back and face, a perch color, and orange with black back and black face. The three loop line tie device was patented in 1945. Schipper decoys were marked "Schipper Mfg." on the bottom of them. Schipper employed four assemblers at the peak of their production, and about 10,000 decoys had been made by the late 1940's.

Decoys were sold to Sears in Boston, Chicago, Philadelphia, and Minneapolis; Coast-to-Coast Hardware Stores; and to Farwell, Osmond and Kirk in St. Paul. Schipper Manufacturing also sold decoys to local hardware and sporting goods stores. The large decoy sold for about 80¢ while the small one sold for about 60¢.

Schipper Mfg. went out of business in 1976-77 when demand for fish decoys was waning. Ithel Schipper died in 1986 and Darel still resides in Minnesota.

*Information courtesy of Darel Schipper.

CHAPTER VII
SPEAR MAKERS OF MINNESOTA AND ICE FISHING ACCOUTREMENTS

Minnesota at one time was a state dotted with blacksmiths. These men worked long hours for very little pay. Those who were located in an agricultural area would, of course, spend the preponderance of their time engaged in the repair of agricultural equipment, shoeing horses, etc. If they were located in a mining area, the work would be oriented toward tool and mining equipment repair, etc. Welding also played a major role in the typical blacksmithing business, especially in later years, replacing forging as the preferred method of construction and repair.

As the growing season is primarily in the spring and summer months in Minnesota, blacksmiths would be at their busiest during this time. A similar situation existed for the smithies located in mining regions. Winters were times of idleness in the mines, while during summer months they were hotbeds of activity.

With the onset of cold weather, a blacksmith's business would usually drop to almost nothing. It was usually in the late fall and winter months that he would entertain orders for spears, ice chisels, etc. from spear fishermen. Some blacksmiths made such highly regarded spears that they attracted a regional, and not just a local, reputation. In many cases, these spears have remained in families for many years.

Of course, where a blacksmith was not available, or when an individual could not afford a blacksmith-made spear, local people would perform their own smithy work. According to Borge and Leitch, homemade spears account for 23 percent of those used in Minnesota, while local blacksmiths made 26 percent of the in-use spears.[1] Factory-made spears make up the remainder. It is difficult to discern attribution of the homemade spears as they were made for an individual's use only; their origins have been lost in most cases.

Spears were made from a variety of metals including wrought iron, saw blades, plow shares, brass, and stainless steel. They were forged, forged and welded, or brazed. Spears that have been sand mold casted are not typically found.[2]

Obtaining information concerning old-time spear makers was more difficult than researching for similar data regarding fish decoy makers. A number of problems explain this dilemma. One is that some of the famous blacksmiths died in the 1940's or earlier and their families have long since moved from the town or area where the smiths originally worked. In addition, there seemed to be fewer blacksmiths making spears than individuals making decoys. After all, a decoy may be assembled with a piece of wood, some lead, and tin for fins. On the other hand, to craft a spear requires forging or other metal working skills.

Interest in collecting old spears seems to be growing. The spear is to the spear fisherman what the shotgun is to the duck hunter.[3] Spears run the gamut from the most crude to the elegant, with the majority falling somewhere in between. It is the purpose of this chapter to present a number of well-known blacksmiths from Minnesota and their spears. It concludes with a review of spear fishing accoutrements such as decoy boxes and jigging sticks.

MILTON BETTS*

Milton Betts was born in 1880 in New Brunswick, Canada. He came to Minnesota in 1894, and worked in a lumber camp near Marcell, Minnesota owned by someone on his mother's side of the family. During his tenure in the lumber camp, Mr. Betts learned some blacksmithing skills.

Mr. Betts married in 1910 and came to live in Grand Rapids, Minnesota in 1911. After working for another blacksmith for approximately one year, he began his own blacksmith business in 1912, located on 4th Street. Mr. Betts shoed horses and performed other heavy iron work. He sold his business in 1945 to Clarence Bunnell and retired [almost].

Being something of a work-a-holic, Mr. Betts did not respond well to a life of retirement. Accordingly, he converted a garage he owned located at the west end of Ice Lake in Grand Rapids in 1945 into another blacksmithing business. Unable or unwilling to continue with heavy work, his main work at his new business was to sharpen picks for the Blandin Paper Mills [located in Grand Rapids] and to produce custom-made spears for spear fishermen. Spears sold for about $10.00—a princely sum considering the times. He continued working at his garage-blacksmithing business until just days before he died in 1965.

Although his spears today are highly prized by collectors, it is ironic that Mr. Betts did not spear fish or even angle. He simply was too occupied with his work or gardening—another labor of love for him.

Mr. Betts' spears were forged and welded. Two surviving examples have six and nine tines respectively. They are approximately 61 inches in overall length with a metal, tapered shaft, measuring 5/8 of an inch at the narrowest diameter, and the tines are nine inches in length.

*Information courtesy of Ray Betts, Joyce Hein, and an article by Walter Eldot, "Rapids Blacksmith Still Sinewy at 80," *Duluth News-Tribune*, April 16, 1961, p. 3.

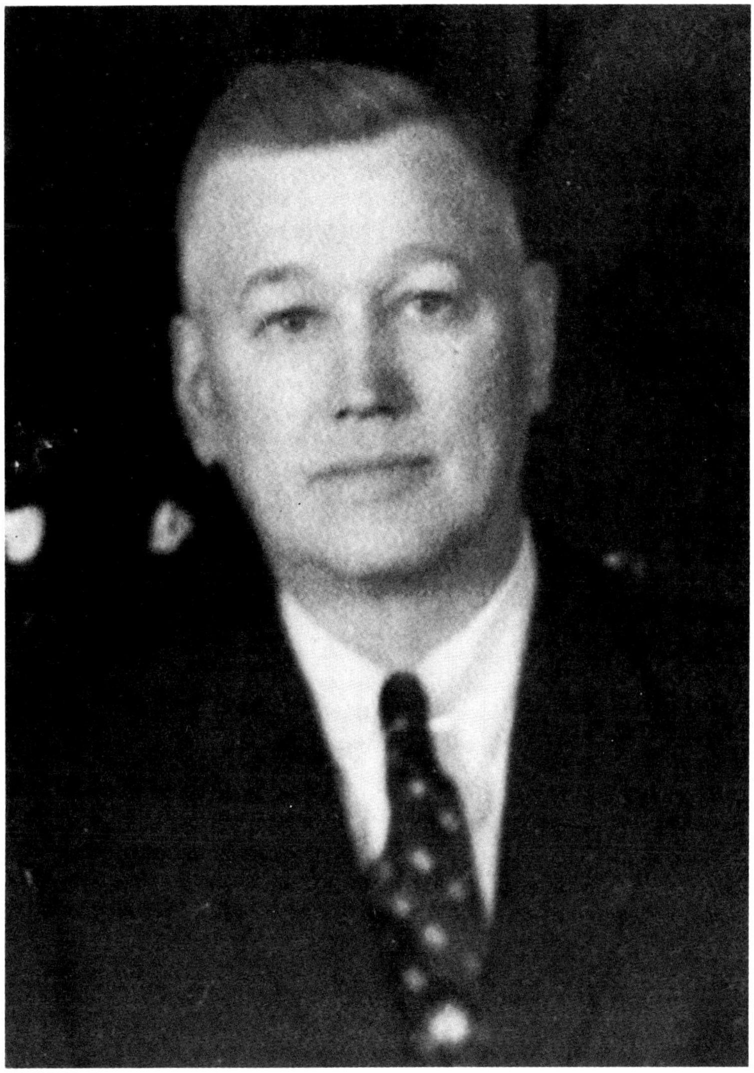

Milton Betts.

FRANK CLARK*

Frank Clark was born in 1880 and died in 1972. He was a man of many talents and was an adept machinist, wood worker, blacksmith and farmer. Mr. Clark made spinning wheels and little chairs. Frank was married and had eleven children.

Frank's spear making activities began around the early 1900's. Mr. Clark made spears with long wooden handles for spearing suckers in rivers. However, the spears for which he was most noted were constructed from both common and stainless steel. The later were prized for spear fishing in the Eden Valley, Minnesota area.

Mr. Clark also made spear fishing decoys.

*Information courtesy of Mrs. Shirley Rud.

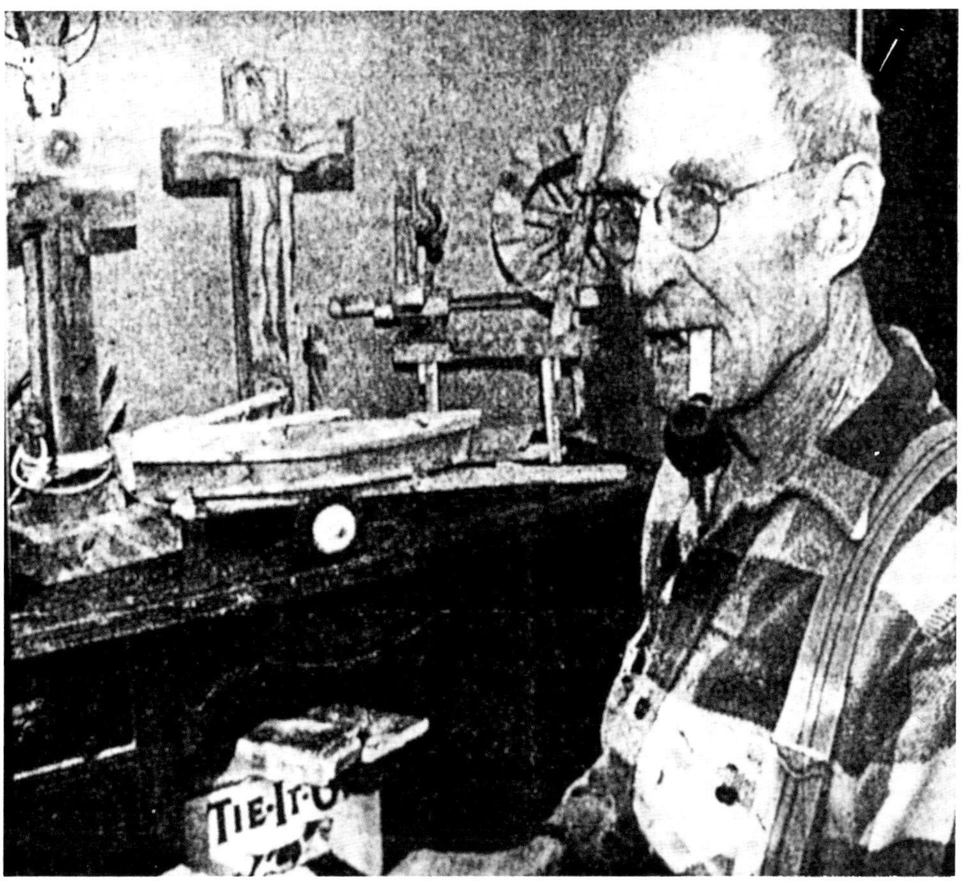

Frank Clark at 88. Photo courtesy of Mrs. Shirley Rud.

FRED DREXLER

Fred Drexler was born in Antwerp, Ohio on February 13, 1866. He subsequently moved out west for three years and was working on a farm in Kansas where he met his wife-to-be. They married in 1890, and shortly thereafter moved to Brainerd, Minnesota in an ox-cart. Drexler worked in the railroad shops for about a year and a half. Then, he sawed lumber until he went into business for himself — opening a blacksmith shop on 6th Street in Brainerd. He remained in this business for about 34 years, retiring in the late 1920's or early 1930's.

Mr. Drexler was active in politics, serving as an alderman in Brainard for six years, a charter commissioner for six years, school board member for twelve years and a county commissioner for four years.

In his retirement years until his death on December 27, 1945, he lived on a 160 acre farm seven miles south of Bemidji, Minnesota.

Precious few of Mr. Drexler's spears remain. Two pictured spears are five tine spears, measuring about four feet in length. Another spear head, marked "F. Drexler," is also shown.

WILLIAM ELMOR

William Elmor was born in 1875 in Williamsport, Pennsylvania and died in 1956. He came to Deerwood, Minnesota in 1902 or 1903 where he became a blacksmith.

Mr. Elmor made spears of almost incomparable quality. He also made lures and spear fishing decoys, but unfortunately, none of the latter have been positively identified.

LLOYD FREDERICKS

Lloyd Fredericks was born in 1914. He worked for the Northern Pacific Railroad in their shops in Brainerd, Minnesota. A few spears were constructed by Mr. Fredericks while he was employed there, one of which is shown in this book. Mr. Fredericks died on May 18, 1985.

PETER J. FUCHS*

An exceptional maker of spears resides in Avon, Minnesota. Peter J. Fuchs [pronounced "Fooks"], or "Pete" as his friends call him, was born in 1918 in a log house in Albany, Minnesota. His father, Chris, was a blacksmith, and Pete learned the trade from him. Peter moved to Avon, Minnesota [a short distance from Albany] to establish a blacksmith business there in competition with his father in 1939. He made some spears during this time, fashioned from hay rake tines.

Pete went into the service in 1942 and saw action in several theaters of the war in the South Pacific. When he returned to Avon in 1946, he had contracted malaria. He decided to go into the bait business, but built a blacksmithing shop across the road from his bait shop.[4] It was during this time [1946-1948] that he perfected his art as a spear maker [also, the greatest demand for his spears was between the 1940's and 1950's]. Abandoning the notion of forging spears from hay rake tines, he learned that a new high carbon spring steel made a very desirable spear. Pete began making spears from this metal. His post-war spears are distinguishable from others because of the diamond-shaped holding piece for the times. Fuch's spears have tines that are square and not rounded. They have a knurled handle at the top of the spear for a good grip, and a second knurled handle farther down on the metal shaft [he did not use wood handles for his spears, contending that they made the spear somewhat buoyant and thus threw off the fisherman's aim]. At the very top of the spear handle, he inserted parachute cord over which he screwed a pipe plug to hold it in place. Another unique feature to his spears is that the bottom of the barb on the spear points is dull rather than sharp. This, he claims, makes it more difficult for a harpooned fish to wiggle free. There is one further "dead give away" to identify a Fuch's spear—he sometimes stamped "P.J. Fuchs, Avon, Mn." into the side of the diamond-shaped tine holding piece.

Pete has not made a spear since 1991, but is currently working on forging knives from the chains on chain saws and from steel cable.

Mr. Fuchs has been married over 50 years and had two grown sons and a daughter.

*Information from an interview with Mr. Fuchs.

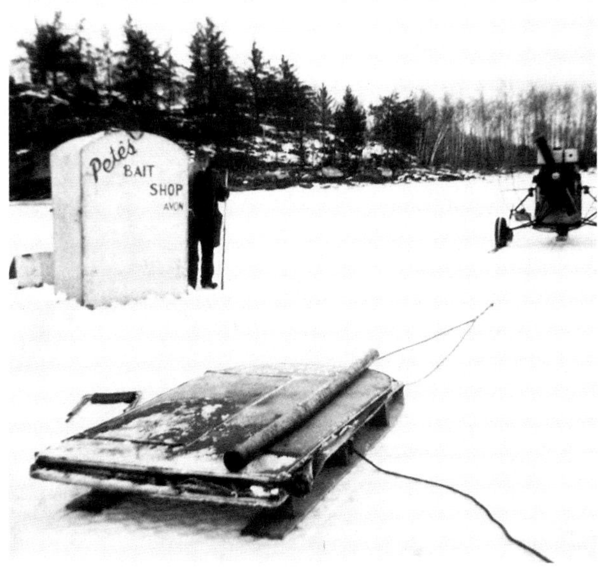

Pete Fuchs standing along side of his dark house. The latter advertises "Pete's Bait Shop."

BEN GEORGE*

Ben George was born in 1904. For a time, Mr. George worked as a stone cutter. In 1940, he went to work as machinist for the Dezurik Corporation in Sartell, Minnesota (near St. Cloud). Around 1950, he began producing spears, mostly for friends. Tines were constructed from spring steel and were joined to a diamond-shaped holder by brazing. The shaft of his spears were made from stainless steel. A wooden handle, made of hickory, completed his spears. Most of the George spears had seven tines.

Mr. George was himself an avid spear fisherman and made his own decoys. He was married and had six children. Mr. George died in 1990.

*Information courtesy of Milon George.

LOUIS A. GUSTIS

Precious little is known of the famous "Brainerd Spear Maker." He was born in 1887 and his wife's name was Lydia. A search of the *Brainerd City* [Telephone] *Directories* revealed the first reference to him in the 1931-32 *Directory*, listing him as working in "blacksmithing." In the 1939-40 *Directory*, he is shown as is being occupied as a blacksmith and working for the Highway Department in Crow Wing County. The 1951 *Directory* indicated that he was working as an auto mechanic and still employed with the State Highway Department. After 1961 he is not listed as working and it may be presumed that he was retired [he would have been 74 years old in 1961]. He died in 1974.

Mr. Gustis' Brainerd spears were forged and he made five, six and seven tine versions.[5] A characteristic of the Brainerd spear is the U shaped cord holder at the top of the spear, under which is a hole for tying the cord.

WILLIAM O. "BILL" HEIN*

Bill Hein was born November 15, 1895. His father, Fred, established a blacksmith shop in 1888. When Bill was a small boy, he worked in the shop. In his early years, he would get up early and walk to his father's farm to milk the cows. The farm was located a mile and a half from town, and he would walk that distance every day.

During World War I, Bill served in the armed forces and fought in Germany. When he returned, he went into the blacksmithing business with his father until the latter died in 1939. Thereafter, Bill ran the shop on his own until he retired in 1972. He would begin work at 4:30 a.m. and work until 6:00 p.m., six days a week. Then he would eat dinner and work on his rose garden until dark. A devout Christian, Bill would read his Bible every night before bedtime.

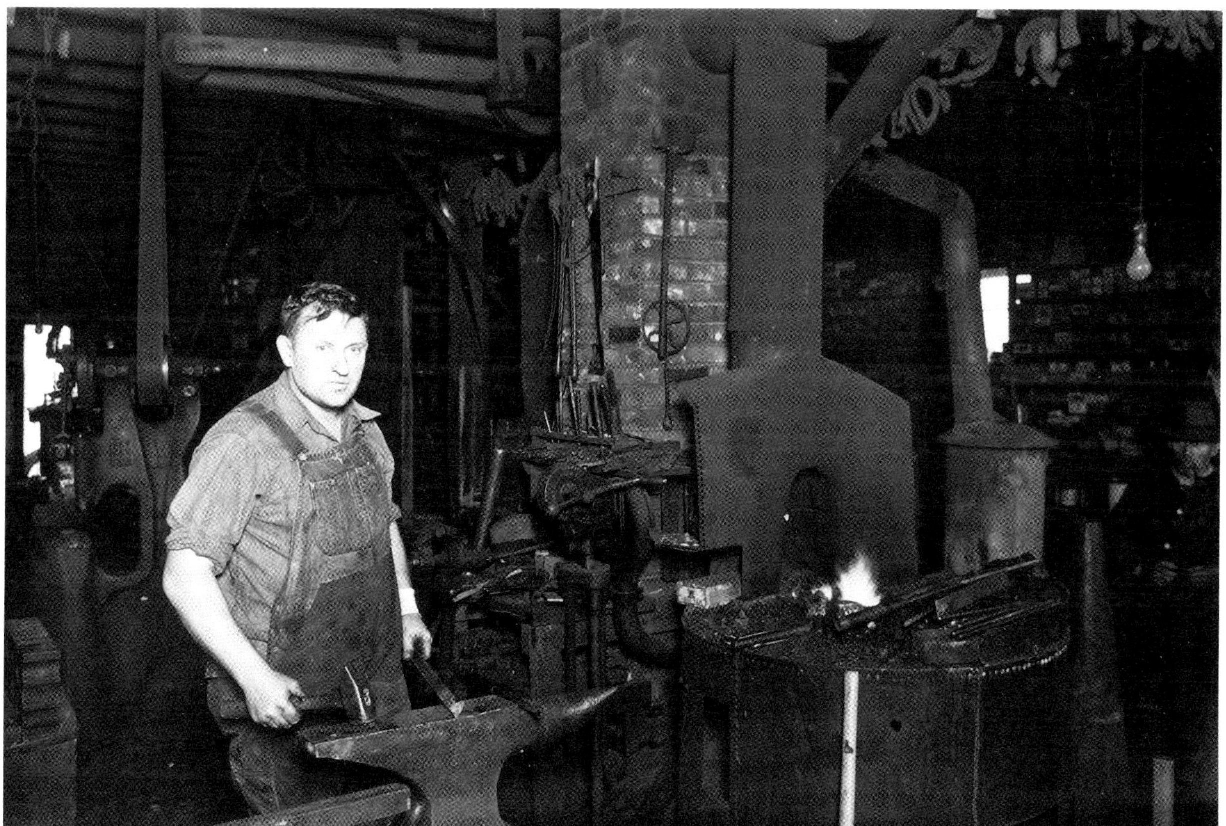

Bill Hein in his blacksmith shop. At the far right of the picture, his father is visible. Photo courtesy of Leonard Hein.

Summer was the busiest season. He would have as many as 600 plow shares in the shop at one time. Bill could sharpen up to 40 per day as long as he did not have to forge or weld new points on them.

During the winter, when work slowed down, he would make spears and ice chisels. The tines for the spears were made of spring steel which came from discarded farm equipment. The chisels were constructed from old car axles. Bill would always draw a pattern before he began work or would take measurements from one still on hand. He had a wood turning lathe for making the wooden handles on his spears. Mr. Hein sold his spears and chisels to people in many areas of Minnesota, as it was his only income during the winter. Bill received about $10 for a chisel and from $14 to $20 for a spear. This was not a great sum of money considering that it took several days for him to make one.

After Bill's wife died in 1972, he retired and lived with his son, Leonard, until his death on February 3, 1983.

*Thanks is extended to Leonard Hein who kindly supplied the information for this write up and some of the pictures.

DILLO HINNENKAMP*

Dillo Hinnenkamp was born on a farm just south of Melrose in Stearns County, Minnesota, on April 4, 1905. At the age of 20 he began working for Charlie Pimpl, who owned a blacksmith shop in Melrose [see write up in this chapter]. When World War II occurred, Dillo moved to Milwaukee, Wisconsin, and there worked for an ammunition factory as a welder. He became the foreman of a crew that welded gun turrets on tanks. His prior blacksmithing experience helped him secure the job, and because he was working in essential industry, he was deferred from active service.

After the war, Dillo returned to Melrose and bought Pimpl's blacksmith shop in 1945. With encouragement from his friend and fishing partner, Soup Zirbes, he worked toward making the perfect spear. Using 30-60 manganese steel forged points, and possessing an artist's eye, he was able to create a spear which was highly effective [as well as beautiful].

Dillo sold his shop in 1982 to make room for the expansion of a turkey processing plant. His eyesight was failing, so the sale of his shop meant the end of his spear making endeavors. Prior to this time, Dillo had made hundreds of spears and sold them out of his shop.

Dillo still resides in Melrose with his wife, Della. They have three grown children, a girl and two boys.

*Thanks to Joe Leach who secured the above information.

STEVE JARNOT*

Mr. Jarnot was born in 1904 in Holdingford, Minnesota. He worked in factories in his younger days, and also operated a blacksmith's shop in Annandale, Minnesota. In 1955, Steve and his wife moved to Brainerd, Minnesota and opened a blacksmith shop on a hobby farm of about 80 acres. Mr. Jarnot produced spears of seven and nine tines, as well as making ice chisels. Tines were made from coil springs from railroad cars. He would then straighten them in his forge. He also made spear fishing decoys [see Chapter 4]. Mr. Jarnot passed away in 1991.

*Information provided by Mrs. Steve (Gertrude) Jarnot.

GIDEON HJALMER KAUPPI

Mr. Kauppi was born in Vassa, Finland on either March 25 or April 1, 1878. He left his homestead to come to the United States and went to work for the logging and lumber camps in the state of Washington. Kauppi was married on August 7, 1909.

In 1914, Mr. Kauppi and his wife had plans to follow friends to Cuba. On their way east, they arrived in Aitkin, Minnesota. There they were persuaded to remain. Mr. Kauppi did blacksmithing work in Aitkin until 1931. Then he moved to New York Mills, Minnesota, where he operated a blacksmith shop at the site of the Keskitalo Brothers Garage.

A very diligent worker, Mr Kauppi never took a vacation. Ironically, he died on October 16, 1944, on the eve of a planned pleasure trip to the state of Washington.

HENRY "HEINIE" LOUIS[6]

Mr. Louis was born December 22, 1907, at Waconia Township, Carver County, Minnesota. He came to Cologne, Minnesota in 1932, where he began his blacksmithing business with his uncle Frank. Mr. Louis was married on June 16, 1936 to Florence Zrust. His blacksmithing business included shoeing and trimming horse hooves. Another source of income was plow lay sharpening.

Mr. Louis, in an autobiography,[7] first mentions making spears and ice chisels during the winter of 1934-35. He and his uncle Frank made eleven fish spears and six ice chisels during that time. The spears sold for $5.00 each in 1936. Prices were increased to $16.50 for spears and $5.00 for chisels. His first spear was made for Herb Dols and was engraved.

In 1941, Mr. Louis built a new shop which provided him room to expand. World War II brought much business and he was welding twelve to fourteen hours a day. By the end of the War, he had enough time to make a spear for himself and his uncle, and they spear fished together.

In 1949, Mr. Louis lost the sight in his left eye due to a hot babbitt accident. Though his doctor warned him not to weld, he continued for another 31 years.

The next year [1950], Heinie bought out his uncle Frank's share of the business [the business to that point was called "Louis and Louis"]. Heinie then took a partner, Robert Fritz, and ten years later [1960], Fritz retired. Mr. Louis celebrated 50 years as a blacksmith on April 1, 1981. He died on January 27, 1992.

Apparently, all of Mr. Louis' spears were seven tines.[8] The tines were made from spring steel, the rod was cold rolled, and the blade was of mild steel. He fashioned the handle from apple wood, turned on a wood lathe, and treated it with linseed oil to waterproof it and give it a smooth finish. The number of grooves on the spear indicate what year it was made.

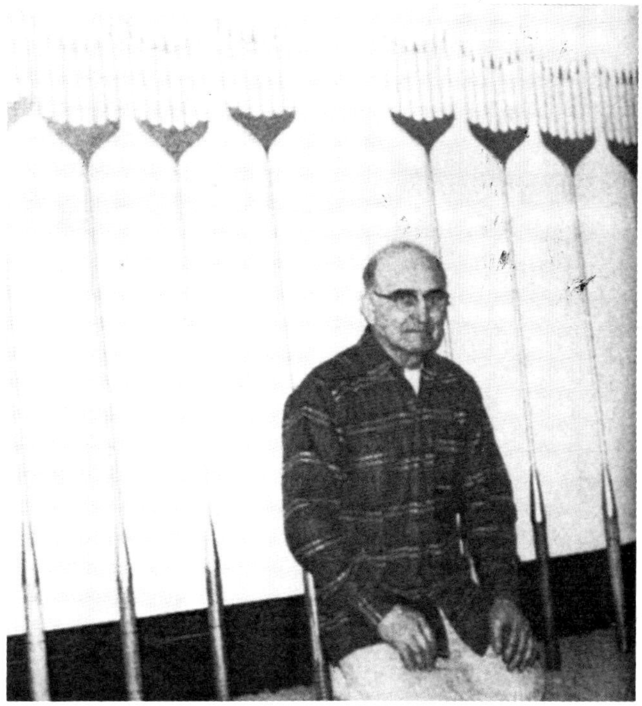

"Heinie" Louis seated, with a number of his 7 tine spears behind him. Photo courtesy *Cologne: The First 100 Years 1881-1981*, p. 96.

MARCEL KITOWSKI*

Marcel Kitowski was born in St. Cloud, Minnesota on January 30, 1904. His father, Fred, worked as a blacksmith and had his own shop in Courthouse Square in St. Cloud, which opened in April of 1909.

Marcel spent much of his time in the blacksmith shop as a child. He attended State Teacher's College and completed a course at Dunwoody Institute. He joined his father in the family business in about 1925. The Kitowski Shop moved from its Courthouse location to 14th Avenue north. This property was then acquired by the City of St. Cloud for parking purposes and the Shop was relocated to 5th Avenue and 2nd Street north.

In the early 1900's, their work consisted chiefly of wagon and buggy repair, sleigh and bobsled repair in the winter months, and horseshoeing. The Kitowski Blacksmith Shop cared for the St. Cloud Fire Department horses. The department had two sets of teams—two ladder wagons and two pump wagons. With the advent of motor cars, the need for draft and delivery horses gradually died out. The Kitowski Blacksmith Shop changed its services to vehicle and machine equipment repair, gas welding, and manufacture of automobile and truck springs.

The manufacture of auto springs required certain tools that were unavailable on the market. Fred Kitowski devised and patented a machine to form "eyes" on the ends of springs. There was such a demand for such a machine in other spring shops that Mr. Kitowski manufactured them for sale to other shops. These machines are still being manufactured and are found throughout the United States, Canada and in some foreign countries.

Marcel Kitowski spear, late 1930's, in the Sterns County Historical Society. Photo courtesy of the Stearns County Historical Society.

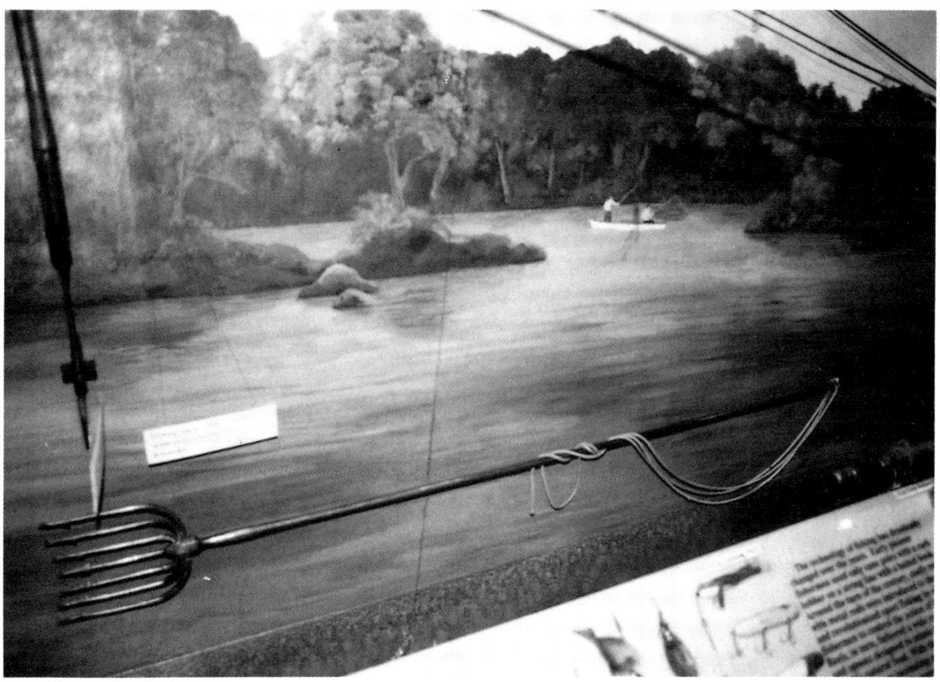

Marcel Kitowski also produced spears during the slower winter months.

After the Kitowski Blacksmith Shop property at 5th Avenue and 2nd Street North was acquired by H.R.A. for a dwelling site, Marcel Kitowski retired in about 1975. The business, however, continues at Lincoln Avenue N.E. and has expanded to many types of industrial repair, welding and fabrication.

Marcel Kitowski passed away on December 20, 1989 at the age of 85.

*Information courtesy of Stearns County Historical Society.

JOHN MAKI*

John Maki was born on December 23, 1916 and lived in New York Mills, Minnesota. His parents were from Finland. John was in the service in World War II. He is said to have thrown himself on a live hand grenade in order to save his comrades. Miraculously, Mr. Maki survived.

He took up residence outside New York Mill on a 40 acre farm. Never marrying, he lived a somewhat reclusive life. Mr. Maki died on March 18, 1993.

While a blacksmith in New York Mills, John produced some very fine spears including a Y shaped spear and more conventional spears.

*Information courtesy of K. David Hirschey.

MICHAEL P. MEYER*

Michael P. Meyer was born on November 20, 1910 in Pierz, Minnesota. Known to local people as "Mickel Meyer," he lived in Pierz all of his life. His major occupation was a blacksmith and he made spears for dark house fishing.[9] Undoubtedly influenced by the Portners — Joseph Sr. and Jr. — who were also blacksmiths in the Pierz area [see Joseph Portner later in this chapter], Mr. Meyer made his tines with numerous barbs on each tine. Thus, it may be difficult to distinguish a "Mickel Meyer" spear from that of a Portner.

Besides his duties as a smithy, Mr. Meyer served as an officer in several law enforcement agencies, in such positions as deputy sheriff, chief of police in Pierz, Pierz fire chief, deputy game warden, and chief of firearms safety instructors. He was the past president of the Pierz Commercial Club, past president of the Sportsmen's Club and the Minnesota Blacksmiths Club. Mr. Meyer also was a captain in the Salvation Army and was president and cofounder of the Eastern Morrison County Dark House Fishing Association.

"Mickel Meyer" was married and had three sons and a daughter. He retired from blacksmithing in 1975 due to declining health, and died on July 28, 1979.

*Information courtesy of the Morrison County Historical Society, the *Little Falls Daily Transcript,* July 30, 1979; and the *Morrison County Record,* August 6, 1979.

WENDLIN "CHARLIE" PIMPL*

Wendlin Pimpl,[10] [pronounced "pimple"] one of the premier spear makers in Minnesota, was born in 1884 in Austria. In 1888, his family immigrated to the United States, settling near Albany, Minnesota. He had an eighth grade education and became a farmer. Wendlin married a woman from Minnesota and their union produced a daughter. After the daughter married in 1935, her new husband largely took over the operation of the farm while Pimpl began to spend more and more time in his blacksmith shop. The shop was located on the farm premises but blacksmithing was really only a sideline for Pimpl. He sharpened plow lags and threshing knives. He even made knives for household use.

However, Pimpl also made spears—perhaps hundreds over the years. These are now highly prized by collectors. His spears were made from hay rake tines. Most are either five or seven tines, but some extra tine spears were made as special orders. Pimpl spears normally had a long metal shaft and a relatively short wooden handle, ten to twelve inches long. A work-a-holic, Mr. Pimpl never went spear fishing himself, but occasionally angled during the summer. He died in 1961 after a brief bout with cancer.

*Information provided by Pimpl's daughter.

JOHN PLACKNER

See biographical information in Chapter 4.

JOSEPH E. PORTNER, JR.*

Joseph E. Portner, Jr. was born December 26 1916 in Lastrup, Minnesota. He died August 24, 1987 and is buried in Fort Snelling National Cemetery. His father, Joseph Sr. (born in 1876 and died February 9, 1963), was employed as a farmer and carpenter. Apparently, Joseph Sr. made spears from broken pitch forks donated by neighbors. He owned his own forge and his children would take turns running it. Spears were sold to Indians in the Mille Lacs Lake area.[11] Joseph Sr. retired in 1942.

Joseph Portner, Jr. opened a blacksmith shop in 1947 in Buckman, Minnesota after returning from service as an Army engineer during World War II. Joseph Jr. never married. He retired in 1982.

The Portner spear is very distinctive with hooks on the side of the tines for better purchase when spearing a northern. Most had five and six tines, and some were made with wooden handles and some without them.

*Information courtesy of the Morrison County Historical Society.

GEORGE RANDALL

The history of the George Randall Company is presented in Chapter 6.

In addition to manufacturing spear fishing decoys, Mr. Randall also produced four, five, seven and nine tine spears. The latter were made from high carbon steel, and he manufactured both standard and deluxe models. Deluxe models were heavier than their standard counterparts and permitted the fisherman to detach the tine-heads from the handle. An advertisement for his spears presents their dimensions. His spears were distributed by direct sales as well as through Herter's catalogs.

Mr. Randall also produced ice chisels in two models—a one piece solid construction and a two piece telescoping model. He also manufactured sucker harnesses for live bait spearing.

EDWARD AND JOE SKIPLE*

Edward Skiple was born in 1892 in Fosston, Minnesota. His brother, Joe, was born in 1890. They were not married and lived on a farm in McIntosh, Minnesota. The brothers also did welding and other blacksmith work. They began making spears in the 1920's and developed a regional reputation for the quality of their work. Initially, they charged $1.50 to $2.00 for a spear, but toward the end of their spear making activities, the price had increased to $35 for one. They made between 20 and 50 spears a year. Both brothers spear fished on Maple Lake.

Edward passed away in 1970 and Joe died in 1973.

*Information courtesy of Mike Meyers.

CLARENCE THOMAS*

Clarence Thomas was born in Minneapolis in 1917. He later moved to Foley, Minnesota. Mr. Thomas served in the Navy for three years during World War II. Subsequently, he went to work for Benton County as a heavy equipment operator, and later became a foreman over mechanics. In all, he worked 43 years for the County.

In the late 1950's or early 1960's Mr. Thomas traveled to Brainerd, Minnesota to study spear making with a master blacksmith, Louis Gustis. Gustis' spears were referred to as "Brainerd Spears."

After returning to Foley, Mr. Thomas built a shop behind his house, where he crafted his own spears. He made five and seven tine spears. His advertisements indicated that his tines were constructed from spring steel, with steel handles, knurled for a better grip. Mr.Thomas' spears have come to be called "The Foley Spear."

He also made an ice hole cleaner, ice chisels and fishing stoves for dark houses. In addition, Mr. Thomas was a woodcrafter, and even constructed dark houses.

He was married to Bernice and had six children. Mr. Thomas died in January of 1989.

*Information provided by Mrs. Thomas.

PAUL ZITZLOFF*

Paul Zitzloff was born in Germany on February 24, 1878. He moved to the United States before the start of World War I. Following that War, he became a U.S. citizen. Locating in the Buffalo, Minnesota area, he farmed, did woodworking and blacksmithing. There was a long wooden building located on his farm. At the north end of the building he had his blacksmith shop and at the south end was his woodworking area. In the blacksmith shop he made livestock truck tracks and bobsleds. He repaired wagons and wagon wheels.

Apparently, Mr. Zitzloff began forging spears in the 1920's. His earlier spears were for open water spearing (sucker spearing) and had long wooden handles. His spear fishing spears were forged from wrought iron, including the handle. He made four, five, six and eight tine spears.

The Skiple clan. Edward is on the far right and his brother, Joe, is next to him.

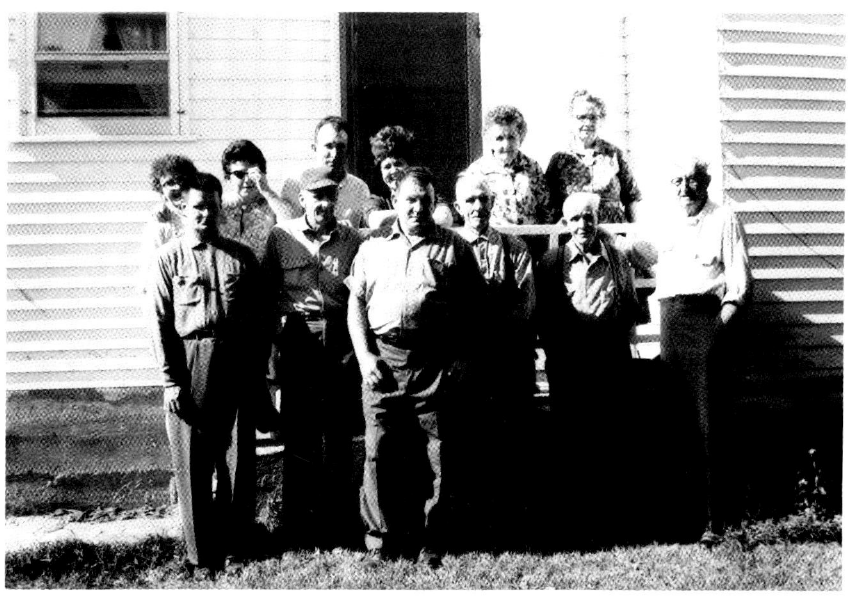

The length of the tine was 7 1/4 inches and the overall length of his spear was relatively short, measuring just under four feet in length. He made the tines from dump rake teeth.

Mr. Zitzloff was married to Selma and they had one child. He died on October 17, 1961.

*Information provided by August Bruska and Peter Meyers, both of Buffalo, Minnesota.

JIGGING STICKS

An indispensable accoutrement to spear fishing was the jigging stick. These sticks varied in length from less than one foot to two or more feet. Some jigging sticks were literally that—a stick from a tree left undecorated. In other cases jigging sticks were carved and decorated with a varnish or painted finish. Some were tipped with a used metal shell casing. All sticks had a device for wrapping and unwrapping line to which the decoy was attached, as well as a circular line guide at the tip of the stick. Frequently, these took the form of two nails punched into the stick several inches apart. A few spear fishermen even attached a reel to the jigging stick to pay out or retract line. Deft handling of the jigging stick permitted an up and down movement to the decoy, or created a circular, swimming motion. Variations in jigging sticks are demonstrated in the pictures.

DECOY BOXES

Decoys have been known to be stored in a variety of containers when not is use. They have been found sitting on shelves in garages or basements in cigar boxes, in pails, tackle boxes, lunch buckets, etc. However, sometimes the decoy maker was so dedicated to the sport that he made a special container for his decoys. These homemade boxes were sometimes adorned with paintings of outdoor scenes or fish, not to mention the maker's name or initials. On the other hand, the wooden boxes were also left undecorated. Beside serving as containers for decoys, the boxes were frequently used in dark houses as seats for the spear fishermen. Some examples of interesting decoy boxes are shown.

FOOTNOTES

Chapter 1

[1] Jay A. Leitch, *Darkhouse Spearing Across North America,* Fargo, N.D.: Tri-College University, Center for Environmental Studies, 1992, p. 5.

[2] See for example R. Stephen Irwin, "Spearing Decoys," *Great Lakes Fisherman,* January 1986; "Old Fish Decoys now Hooking Collectors," *Chicago Tribune,* April 20, 1986, Section 15, p. 20; Larry M. Smith, "Fish Decoys," *Antique Angler,* May-June 1985, p. 1, 5; Seth Rosenbaum, "American Fishing Lures and Fish Decoys," *Country Living,* July 1985, p. 26; William C. Ketchum, Jr., "Delightful Deceptions," *Country Home,* February 1986, pp. 83-87; Anita Gold, "Carved and painted fish decoys are bait for collectors," *Chicago Tribune,* March 16, 1990, Section 7, p. 83; Tobin Morrison, "Hooked on Decoys," *The Saturday Evening Post,* March 1991, pp. 64-67, 110-111; Anonymous, "The Allure of Fish Decoys," *Country Living,* September 1992, p. 59. In addition, there have been a number of exhibits dedicated to displaying fish decoys. Probably the most famous of these was "Beneath the Ice," a show organized by the Museum of American Folk Art, which visited various cities throughout the United States. It was at the John G. Shedd Aquarium in Chicago from February to April 1992. "Fish or Fowl: the Art of the Decoy," featured about 150 fish decoys at the Carl Hammer Gallery in Chicago in 1993. An interesting display of American Indian fish decoys was gathered for a show called "Objibwa Hunting and Fishing Exhibit," held at the Mitchell Indian Museum at Kendall College in Evanston, Illinois, during July through December of 1991. An early recognition of the beauty of fish decoys was a display entitled "Fish decoys: Artful Dodge of the Ice Fisherman," exhibiting the decoys of Joe and Donna Tonelli, in January of 1983, at the John G. Shedd Aquarium in Chicago, Illinois.

[3] An auction held at the Richard A. Bourne Co., on June 20, 1986, in Hyannis, Massachusetts, sold 26 fish decoys. Single fish, i.e., those not sold in multiple lots, brought from $90 to $375 each (Richard A. Bourne Co., *Fishing and Sporting Auction Catalog,* June 20, 1986). Smith, *op. cit.*, writing in June of 1985, stated that the fishing decoys range in value from an average of $15 to $25 to the middle range of $50 to $75. The first known auction where 42 lots of fish decoys were put up for sale was held March 8, 9, 1983 (The Ray Bull Decoy Collection) conducted by the Richard A. Bourne Company. Prices range from a low of $35 to $140 for a single decoy. At a July 1992 auction by Guyette and Schmidt, a Ray Thompson trout was estimated to sell in the $8,000 to $10,000 range, but did not make the minimum and was withdrawn. Frank Baron's 1990 catalog of fish decoys for sale offered a Frank Mizera at $50, while in 1993, a similar Mizera was priced at $100. A Louie Anderson decoy was listed at $125, a Fred Lexow trout for $475 and a Slim Ripley minnow at $75 in Frank Baron's summer, 1990, list.

[4] *Minneapolis Star & Tribune, Sunday Magazine,* July 20, 1986, p. 20; Mary Daniels, "Americana, c. 1986—A Sampler of Our Country Treasures," *Chicago Tribune,* Sunday, June 29, 1986, Section 15, p. 1.

[5] See also Marcel L. Salive, "Determining the Age of Ice-Fishing Decoys," *Maine Antique Digest,* February 1994, pp. 36-B to 38-B, for an excellent discussion of techniques for identifying fake decoys; and Wad Miller, "Phony Fish," *Fish Decoy,* No. 1, undated, p. 6.

Chapter 2

[1] William Radcliffe, *Fishing from the Earliest Times,* Chicago: Ares Publishing, Inc., 1921, p. 308.

[2] *Ibid,* p. 309. Radcliffe's observation notwithstanding, regulation of spearing as a sport as well as a developing business was noted on Lake Chautauqua in New York State as early as 1856 (see Gene and Linda Kangas, "Chautauqua Fish Decoys," *Decoy Magazine,* September 1988, p. 40).

[3] Radcliffe, *op. cit,* p. 307.

[4] *Ibid,* p. 307.

[5] *Ibid,* p. 459.

[6] Leitch, *op. cit.* p. 10.

[7] Duane Esarey, "The Ancient Art of Decoy Fishing," *The Living Museum,* Vol. 55, No. 1, 1993.

[8] The exact date of the discovery of lead has been lost in antiquity. However, it is known that Egyptians used lead in glazing pottery, in making solder, and for ornamental objects. The Hanging Gardens of Babylon (605-562 B.C.) were floored with lead sheets soldered together to retain moisture. In Spain, the Rio Tinto deposits were worked by the Phoenicians about 2,000 B.C., and also by the Romans in the third century B.C. *Collier's Encyclopedia,* New York: Macmillan Educational Company, Vol. 14, 1991, pp. 409-410

[9] Robert L. Frankenberger, "On the Origins of the Fish Decoy," *Fish Decoy,* No. 16, undated, p. 4.

[10] William W. Fitzhugh and Aron Crowell, editors, *Crossroads of Continents,* Washington, D.C., Smithsonian Institution Press, 1988, p. 9.

[11] *Ibid,* p. 152.

[12] Charles Miles, *Indian and Eskimo Artifacts of North America,* Chicago, Henry Regnery Company, 1963, p. 11.

[13] Three early Eskimo fish decoys are in the collection of the Lowie Museum of Anthropology, University of California, Berkley. These are pre-1900, carved from bone and were probably designed to attract either pickerel or large white-fish. Each has inlaid eyes, carved gills and scale patterns; see Gene Kangas, "Underwater Decoys: Fish," *North American Decoy Magazine,* Spring 1978.

[14] Austin S. Hogan, "The Origins of Fishing," *The American Fly Fisher,* Winter, 1976, p. 20.

[15] *The American Heritage Book of Indians,* American Heritage Publishing Company, Inc., 1961, p. 270.

[16] *Ibid.*

[17] Hogan, *op. cit.*

[18] Leitch, *op. cit.*, referencing Erhard Rostlund, *Freshwater Fish and Fishing in Native North America,* Publications in Geography, Vol. 9, Berkeley, University of California Press.

[19] Seth Rosenbaum, "American Fishing Lures and Fish Decoys," *Country Living,* July 1985, p. 137.

[20] Alexander Henry, *Travels and Adventures in Canada and the Indian Territories Between the Years 1760 and 1776,* Rutland, Vermont, Charles E. Tuttle Company, 1969, pp. 66-67.

[21] There is evidence that while settlers began using dark houses in Michigan in the 1850's and in Wisconsin by the 1870's at the latest. By the turn of the 20th century, it was widely used by white spear fishermen. Art, Brad and Scott Kimball, *The Fish Decoy,* Boulder Junction, Wisconsin Aardvark Publications, Inc., 1986, pp. 58-59.

[22] Charles M. Gates, ed., *Five Fur Traders of the Northwest,* St. Paul, Minnesota, Minnesota Historical Society, 1965, p. 82.

[23] *Autobiography of Gurdon Saltonstall Hubbard* (1863), quoted in Harold Dickert, "Ice Spearing Decoys — Circa 1811," *The N.F.L.C.C. Gazette,* March 1986, p. 6.

[24] George W. Featherstonhaugh, *A Canoe Voyage up the Minnay Sotor,* Vol. I, St. Paul, Minnesota, Minnesota Historical Society Press, 1970, p. 145.

[25] Henry R. Schoolcraft, *Schoolcrafts' Narrative Journal of Travels* (ed. by Mentor L. Williams), East Lansing, Michigan, Michigan State University Press, 1992.

[26] *Ibid,* p. 270.

[27] Leslie A. White, editor, *Lewis Henry Morgan The Indian Journals 1859-62,* Ann Arbor, Michigan, The University of Michigan Press, 1959, p. 109.

[28] *Ibid.*

[29] Kangas and Kangas, *op. cit.*, p. 41.

[30] Milo Quaife, editor, *John Long's Voyages and Travels in the Years 1768-1788,* Chicago, The Lakeside Press, 1922, p. 75.

[31] Letter to the author, dated October 14, 1986, from Lloyd Hustvedt, Secretary, *The Norwegian-American Historical Association,* St. Olaf College, Northfield, Minnesota 55057.

[32] See for example: Morten Edlund, ed., *Fiske Historier fran pol till pol,* Stockholm, Folket i Bilds Forlag, 1961; and Bertil Haglund, ed., *Det Nappar,* Stockholm, Norstedt & Sons, 1951.

Chapter 3

[1] Of course, American Indians living in Minnesota had spear fished during the winter from at least the eighteenth century.

[2] Lila J. Borge and Jay A. Leitch, *Winter Darkhouse Spearing in Minnesota: Characteristics of Participants,* Fargo, N.D. Tri-College University, Center for Environmental Studies, September 1988, p. 1, quoting D.H. Schupp, *A Review of the Status of Northern Pike in Minnesota,* Staff Report. Minnesota Department of Natural Resources, Division of Fish and Wildlife, Section of Fisheries, St. Paul, 1981. Only Minnesota residents can purchase spear fishing licenses.

[3] Telephone conversation with Minnesota Department of Natural Resources, License Bureau, February 1994.

[4] Today, snowmobiles and pickup trucks are frequently used to drag dark houses to their desired location.

[5] A dark house with two holes permitted more than one fisherman to spear at the same time. It also facilitated the social nature of spear fishing.

[6] Borge and Leitch, *op. cit.* p. 7

[7] Ibid.

[8] Borge and Leitch, *op. cit.*, report that the preferred depth of water for spearing today in Minnesota is eight to ten feet, p. 9.

[9] Contemporary Minnesota spear fisherman use an ice chisel, chain saw, auger, axe, and other means (in that order) as the preferred ways for cutting the hole in the ice (Borge and Leitch, *op. cit.*, p. 6).

[10] Floater decoys appear to be less popular in Minnesota as in other spear fishing states, judging from the paucity of surviving, old, examples.

[11] Borge and Leitch, op. cit., report that only one-third of contemporary sample spear fishermen use live bait more than half the time, p. 4.

[12] As previously noted, there are a number of present day individuals who are still carving fishing decoys. Some of them, however, are up in years but carve and paint decoys in the old manner. Their work is presently collectible and will undoubtedly increase in value when they are gone. In addition, there are contemporary carvers whose work is quite good (see Chapter 5).

[13] A good picture account of present day spearing by a Chippewa Indian, Ben Chosa, appeared in an article in the June 25, 1986, "Focus" section of the *Chicago Tribune,* Section 4, p. 4. See also, Catherine Whipple, "Nin Akwawa (I Fish with a Spear)," *Lac Du Flambeau News,* February 1994, pp. 12-13.

[14] Frances Densmore, *Chippewa Customs,* St. Paul, Minnesota: Minnesota Historical Society Press, 1979, p. 126. Densmore's description, notwithstanding, numerous examples of surviving American Indian decoys from the 1920's onward, reveal that they have metal tails and fins, not ones made of birch bark.

[15] See also Donna Torelli, "Copper Fish Decoys Casting Variety and Form," *Decoy Magazine,* Nov.-Dec. 1993.

[16] Simon Otto, "First 'fish story' was the painful truth," *The Record-Eagle,* Monday, January 31, 1983, p. 27.

Chapter 4

[1] In some cases, attribution of certain decoys is known, but no, or little, biographical information was able to be obtained.

[2] This is a similar error to that made by early ethnologists collecting American Indian material from the various tribes. During the reservation days, members of different tribes, formerly at war with one another, would visit and bring presents of their own tribal material. These presents would be the first to be sold to the collector/ethnologists, and the pieces obtained were consequently attributed, in error, to the tribe from which they were purchased.

[3] One of Mr. Berens' daughters, Clara Taft, is still making decoys and painting them in the Berens' design.

[4] Craig McEwen, "Park Rapids guide reels in fishermen," *Sunday Forum-Fargo Moorhead,* January 20, 1980, Section c, p. c-1.

[5] See Kimball, *op. cit.*, Volumes II and III.

[6] Gerald S. Beskin, "The Lucky Stick," *Sports Afield,* May 1951.

[7] Mr. Hesjedal has been erroneously identified by some sources as being named "Hespedahl."

[8] Donna Tonelli, "Fred Lexow: One of Minnesota's Fine Folk Articles," *Decoy Magazine,* July/August 1989, p. 34.

Chapter 5

[1] See for example, Kent Frank, "Fancy Fish. Six Contemporary Decoy Carvers of Minnesota," *NFLCC Gazette,* Vol. 18, No. 60, March 1994, pp. 13-14.

[2] Erroneously referred to as "Roger Lasha" in Kimball, *op. cit.*, Volume II, p. 103.

Chapter 6

[1] Lila J. Borge and Jay A. Leitch, *Winter Darkhouse Spearing in Minnesota: Characteristics of Participants,* Fargo, N.D., Center for Environmental Studies, 1988, p. 4.

[2] Thanks are extended to Terry Jacobson of Eden Prairie, Minnesota for some of the above information. Also consulted was the *Osakis Review* of March 18, 1967 and Brian J. McGrath, "Brown's Fisheretto Folk Art at its Finest," *Lure Collector.*

[3] Thanks are extended to the Kandiyohi County Historical Society and Carter Stenberg for the information regarding Cy Halvorson.

[4] Information courtesy of Frank Baron.

[5] Gaylord, Minnesota is located on the southwest shore of Lake Titloe.

Chapter 7

[1] Lila J. Borge and Jay A. Leitch, *Winter Darkhouse Spearing in Minnesota: Characteristics of Participants, op. cit.*, p. 4.

[2] For a detailed description of spear assembly, see Marcel Salive, *Ice Fishing Spears,* Marjac Publishers, 1993.

[3] See Harold Dickert, "The Spear," *NFLCC Gazette,* Vol. 15, No. 52, March 1992, pp. 10-11.

[4] He operated the bait shop for 27 years.

[5] Salive claims that Gustis made three different tine variations. He erroneously lists his [Gustis'] name was "Lewis Gustis," see Marcel Salive, *Ice Fishing Spears, op. cit.*, p. 225.

[6] Mr. Louis is erroneously referred to as "Hine Lewis," by Marcel Salive, *Ice Fishing Spears, op. cit.*

[7] *Cologne: The First 100 Years 1881-1981* and Rosie Fahey, *Colonge — I Remember When and 50 Years In The Life of The Village Blacksmith* [Cologne, 1981].

[8] Mr. Louis is shown sitting with seven tine spears of his construction behind him. A seven tine spear is shown in Salive's book, *op. cit.*, on page 214.

[9] Mr. Meyer's father, Peter, was in partnership with his [Peter's] brother, Valentine, for four years, after moving to Pierz. Valentine continued to run the shop.

[10] Salive erroneously refers to him as "W. Pipple." See Marcel Salive, *Ice Fishing Spears, op. cit.*, p. 215.

[11] According to one of Joseph Portner Sr.'s daughters, Leola, the former made more spears than Joseph Jr. It is uncertain whether or not the spears may have differed in design or construction.

BIBLIOGRAPHY

Books:

American Heritage Publishing Company, Inc., *The American Heritage Book of Indians,* 1961.

Apfelbaum, Ben, Eli Gottlieb, and Steven J. Michaan, *Beneath the Ice. The Art of the Spearfishing Decoy,* New York: E.P. Dutton Co., 1990.

Bishop, Robert and Judith Weissman, *Knopf Collectors' Guide to Folk Art,* New York: Knopf, 1983.

Borge, Lila J. and Jay A. Leitch, *Winter Darkhouse Spearing in Minnesota: Characteristics of Participants,* Fargo, North Dakota: Tri-College University, Center for Environmental Studies, September 1988.

Colio, Quintina. *American Decoys,* Ephrata, Pennsylvania: Science Press, 1972.

Densmore, Frances, *Chippewa Customs,* St. Paul, Minnesota: Minnesota Historical Society Press, 1979.

Dolan, Tom, *Know Your Fish,* New York: Hearst Corporation, 1960.

Edlund, Morten, ed., *Fiske Historier fran pol till pol,* Stockholm, Sweden: Folket i Bilds Forlag, 1961.

Featherstonhaugh, George W., *A Canoe Voyage up the Minnay Sotor,* Vol. I, St. Paul, Minnesota: Minnesota Historical Society Press, 1970.

Fitzhugh, William W. and Aron Crowell, editors, *Crossroads of Continents,* Washington, DC: Smithsonian Institution Press, 1988.

Forester, Frank. *The Complete Manual for Young Sportsmen,* New York: W.A. Townsend, Publishers, 1866.

Fritz, Ronald J., *Michigan's Master Carver Oscar W. Peterson 1887-1951,* Boulder Junction, Wisconsin: Aardvark Publications, Inc., 1987.

Gates, Charles M., ed., *Five Fur Traders of the Northwest,* St. Paul, Minnesota: Minnesota Historical Society Press, 1965.

Gilman, Carolyn, *Where Two Worlds Meet,* St. Paul: Minnesota Historical Society Press, 1982.

Haglund, Bertil, ed., *Det Nappar,* Stockholm, Sweden: Norstedt & Sons, 1951.

Henry, Alexander, *Travels and Adventures in Canada and the Indian Territories Between the Years 1760 and 1776,* Rutland, Vermont: Charles E. Tuttle Company, 1969.

Hubbs, Carl L. and Karl F. Lagler, *Fishes of the Great Lakes Region,* Bloomfield Hills, Mich.: The Cranbrook Press, 1947.

Kangas, Gene and Linda Kangas, *Decoys. A North American Survey,* Spanish Fork, Utah: Hillcrest Publications, Inc., 1983.

Kimball, Art and Scott. *Collecting Old Fishing Tackle.* Boulder Junction, Wis.: Aardvark Publications, Inc., 1980 (see Chapter 5, "Ice Spearing Decoys").

Kimball, Art, Brad and Scott, *The Fish Decoy,* Boulder Junction, Wisconsin: Aardvark Publications, Inc., Vol. I, 1986.

Kimball, Art, Brad and Scott, *The Fish Decoy,* Boulder Junction, Wisconsin: Aardvark Publications, Inc. Vol. II, 1987.

Kimball, Art, Brad and Scott, *The Fish Decoy,* Boulder Junction, Wisconsin: Aardvark Publications, Vol. III, 1993.

Leitch, Jay A., *Darkhouse Spearing Across North America,* Fargo, N.D.: Tri-College University, Center for Environmental Studies, 1992.

Little, Gene, *Ice Fishing,* Chicago: Henry Regnery Company, 1975.

McDonald, John. *The Origins of Angling.* Garden City, New York: Doubleday and Company, Inc., 1963.

Miles, Charles, *Indian and Eskimo Artifacts of North America,* Chicago: Henry Regnery Company, 1963.

Olson, Sigurd F., *Sigurd F. Olson's Wilderness Days,* New York: Alfred A. Knopf Co., 1973.

Pfaff, Tim, *Paths of the People the Ojibwe in the Chippewa Valley,* Eau Claire, Wisconsin: Chippewa Valley Museum Press, 1993.

Quaife, Milo, ed., *John Long's Voyages and Travels in the Years 1768-1788,* Chicago: The Lakeside Press, 1922.

Radcliffe, William, *Fishing from the Earliest Times,* Chicago: Ares Publishers, Inc., 1921.

Salive, Marcel, *Ice Fishing Spears,* MarJac Publishers, 1993.

Stark, Larry and Magnus Berglund, *Hook, Line and Shelter,* Cambridge, Minnesota: Adventure Publications, Inc., 1990.

Starr, Robin, "Fish Decoys," in *The American Sporting Collector's Handbook,* ed. by Allan J. Liu, New York: Winchester Press, 1982.

Walton, Izaak. *The Compleat* [sic] *Angler.* New York: The Heritage Press, 1948.

White, Leslie A., ed., *Lewis Henry Morgan The Indian Journals 1859-62,* Ann Arbor, Michigan: The University of Michigan Press, 1959.

Wilcox, Alvin H., *A Pioneer History of Becker County, Minnesota.* St. Paul, Minnesota: Pioneer Press Company, 1907.
Williams, Mentor L., ed., *Schoolcrafts' Narrative Journal of Travels,* East Lansing, Michigan: Michigan State University Press, 1992.
Zumbro, Jim, *Icefishing East and West,* New York: David McKay Company, Inc., 1978.

Magazines

Apfelbaum, Ben, "Fish Decoys A Native American Craft," *The Clarion,* Winter 1990, pp. 46-49.
Baron, Frank, "The Fish Decoy," *The Decoy Hunter,* March/April 1985, pp. 5-9, 16.
Baron, Frank, "Collecting Ice Decoys," *Tackle Trader,* Spring 1988, pp. 7, 14-15.
Bauer, Erwin A., "Gadget World of Ice Anglers," *Sports Afield,* Vol. 151, No. 1, January 1964, pp. 42-45.
Beskin, Gerald S., "The Lucky Stick," *Sports Afield,* May 1951.
Carmichael, Hoagy B., "Crafty Catches," *Arts and Antiques,* Summer 1987, pp. 75-76, 126.
Clark, Edie, "Hooked on Fish Decoys," *Yankee,* Vol. 51, No. 3, March 1987, pp. 94-99.
Clark, Malcolm, "Ice Hole Angler," *Sporting Classics,* Sept./Oct. 1984, pp. 69-70.
Dana, Gordon K., "The Joys of Ice Fishing," *Sportsman's Digest,* Vol. 2, No. 2, February 1923, pp. 53-55.
Dewhurst, C. Kurt and Marsha MacDowell, "Fine Fooler of Fish," *Michigan,* September/October 1987, pp. 39-43.
Dickert, Harold, "Ice Spearing Decoys—Circa 1811," *The N.F.L.C.C. Gazette,* March 1986, p. 6.
Dickert, Harold, "The Spear," *N.F.L.C.C. Gazette,* Vol. 15, No. 52, March 1992, pp. 10-11.
Esarey, Duane, "The Ancient Art of Decoy Fishing," *The Living Museum,* Vol. 55, No. 1, 1993.
Fashingbauer, Bernard S., "Spearing," *Fur-Fish-Game,* Vol. 81, No. 1, January 1987, pp. 12-13.
Foshee, Rufus, "Fishing in Foul Waters," *Antique Journal,* April 1990, p. 6.
Frank, Charles W., "Affordable Decoys Alternatives for Collectors," *Decoy Magazine,* May-June 1994, pp. 17-18.
Frank, Kent, "Fancy Fish Six Contemporary Decoy Carvers of Minnesota," *N.F.L.C.C. Gazette,* Vol. 18, No. 60, March 1994, pp. 13-14.
Frankenberger, Robert L., "On the Origins of the Fish Decoy," *Fish Decoy,* No. 16, undated, p. 4.
Gilbert, James C., "Fishing Thru The Ice," *Game Stories,* Vol. 1, No. 1, January 1932, pp. 24-27.
Guthrie, Gregg, "John Snow Expressing Native American Heritage Through Spear Fishing Decoys." *Decoy Magazine,* January/February 1996, pp. 32-33.
Hirschey, K. David, "Do you have a Swenson Decoy?" *Decoy Magazine,* March/April 1993, pp. 44-45.
Hogan, Austin S., "The Origins of Angling," *The American Fly Fisher,* Winter 1976, Vol. 3, No. 1, pp. 18-21.
Kangas, Gene and Linda Kangas, "Chautauqua Fish Decoys," *Decoy Magazine,* Sept./Oct. 1988, pp. 38-45.
Kangas, Gene, "Underwater Decoys: Fish," *North American Decoy Magazine,* Spring 1978, pp. 14-23.
Ketchum, William C., Jr., "Delightful Deceptions," *Country Home,* Vol. VIII, No. 1, February 1986, pp. 83-87.
Kimball, Art and Scott, "The Jay Rhodes Fish Decoy," *The N.F.L.C.C. Gazette,* June 1991, p. 14.
Kranstover, Steve, "John Jensen Carving Realistic Fish Decoys," *Decoy Magazine,* January/February 1995, pp. 40-41.
McGrath, Brian J., "Brown's Fisheretto Folk Art at its Finest," *Lure Collector,* Spring 1987, pp. 8-9, 29.
Miller, Gary L., "Fish Decoys-Hottest New Sporting Collectible," *Lure Collector,* No. 5, Fall 1986, pp. 20-23.
Miller, Wad, "Phoney Fish," *Fish Decoy,* No. 1, undated, p. 6.
Morrison, Tobin, "Hooked on Decoys," *The Saturday Evening Post,* March 1991, pp. 64-67, 110-111.
Pennington, William, "Fish Story," *North American Decoys,* Fall 1973, pp. 30-33.
Reno, Dawn E., "Fishing Collectibles," *The Antique Trader Weekly,* October 2, 1991, pp. 98-99.
Rosenbaum, Seth, "American Fishing Lures and Fish Decoys," *Country Living,* July 1985, Vol. 8, No. 7, pp. 26, 137.
Rucker, Laurence, "Minnesota Memories, an Interview with John Tax, Jr.," *Decoy Magazine,* January/February 1995, pp. 28-30.
Salive, Marcel L., "Collecting Wrought-Iron Eel Spears: Their Value," *Maine Antique Digest,* March 1996, pp. 28-c-29-c.
Salive, Marcel L., "Determining the Age of Ice-Fishing Decoys," *Maine Antique Digest,* February 1994, pp. 36-B to 38-B.
Salive, Marcel L., "Why Collect Contemporary Ice Fishing Decoys?," *Fish Decoy, AFDA Forum,* No. 11, undated, pp. 4-5.
Smith, Larry M., "Fish Decoys," *Antique Angler,* May-June 1988, pp. 1, 5.
Smith, Larry, "Getting Hooked on Fish Decoys," *Antique Angler,* May/June 1983, pp. 1, 4.
Stephen, Irwin R., "Fish Decoys," *Sports Afield,* February 1981, pp. 56-58.
Stephen, Irwin R., "Spearing Decoys," *Great Lakes Fisherman,* January 1986, Vol. 15, No. 1, pp. 20-21.
Stoetzel, William, "Minnesota Style: The Decoys of Dave Lahti," *The N.F.L.C.C. Gazette,* Vol. 12, No. 39, December 1988, p. 10.
Thaler, Frederic I., "Discover Fish Decoys: Folky, Fun and Unique," *Antique Monthly,* October 1984, p. 16A.
Tonelli, Donna, "Fred Lexow: One of Minnesota's Fine Folk Artists," *Decoy Magazine,* July/August 1989, pp. 32-35.

Tonelli, Donna, "One of Minnesota's Finest Leroy Howell," *Decoy Magazine,* November/December 1990, pp. 32-34.
Tonelli, Donna, "Ernest Newman Minnesota's Master Tackle Maker," *Decoy Magazine,* March/April 1991, pp. 16-18.
Tonelli, Donna, "Frank Mizera Minnesota Fish Decoy Maker," *Decoy Magazine,* July/August 1991, pp. 33-35.
Tonelli, Donna, "William 'Slow' Batters Minnesota's Real Harry Blancherd," *Decoy Magazine,* September/October 1991, pp. 33-35.
Tonelli, Donna, "Chet Sawyer Folk Artist of the North Woods," *Decoy Magazine,* July/August 1992, pp. 32-34.
Tonelli, Donna, "John Tax A Minnesota Whittler from the Shores of Lake Osakis," *Decoy Magazine,* March/April 1992, pp. 8-11.
Tonelli, Donna, "Ray Thompson Maker of Quality Fishing Tackle and Fish Decoys," *Decoy Magazine,* September/October 1992, pp. 32-35.
Tonelli, Donna, "Chuck Hall Carving Out the Good Life," *Decoy Magazine,* January/February 1993, pp. 36-38.
Tonelli, Donna, "Copper Fish Decoys Casting Variety and Form," *Decoy Magazine,* November/December 1993.
Tonelli, Donna, "Heddon Breaks the ice with spearfishing decoys," *Decoy Magazine,* January/February 1994.
Unsigned, "These Fish are Keepers," *Time,* February 26, 1990, p. 55.
Unsigned, "The Allure of Fish Decoys," *Country Living,* September 1992, p. 59.
Walcheck, Ken, "Ice Fishing: 'Hot' Pastime for a Cold Day," *Montana Outdoors,* Vol. 5, No. 1, 1974, pp. 19-26.
Zabar, Lori S., "A Collector's Guide to Fish Decoys," *The Clarion,* Vol. II, No. 4, Fall 1986, pp. 25-29.

Newspaper Articles

Barry, Ann, "Fish Decoys aren't fooling collectors," *The New York Times,* August 13, 1989, p. 34.
Blaubaugh, Jim, "Whittling Fish Lures a Delicate Procedure," *Duluth News-Tribune,* February 4, 1973.
Boyd, Bentley, "Handmade lures show how fish respond to beauty—and eccentricity," *Chicago Tribune,* Nov. 26, 1989, Sec. 15, p. 3.
Daniels, Mary, "Americana, c. 1986—A Sampler of Our Country Treasures," *Chicago Tribune,* Sunday, June 29, 1986, Section 15, p. 1.
Eldot, Walter, "Rapids Blacksmith Still Sinewy At 80," Duluth News-Tribune, Cosmopolitan Section, April 16, 1961, p. 3.
Gold, Anita, "Carved and painted fish decoys are bait for collectors," *Chicago Tribune,* March 16, 1990, Section 7, p. 83.
Hart, Hugh, "Collectors are hooked on vintage ice fishing decoys with their intricate detailing," *Chicago Tribune,* May 8, 1994, Section 15, p. 10.
Husar, John, "Gimme Shelter: Fishing on Ice," *Chicago Tribune,* Section 4, pp. 1 and 4.
Kreh, Lefty, "Fish are there, even in winter," *Chicago Tribune,* December 27, 1985, p. 87.
McCracken, David, "Something Fishy," *Chicago Tribune,* February 27, 1992, Sect. 5, p. 3.
McEwen, Craig, "Park Rapids Guide Reels in Fishermen," *Sunday Forum-Fargo Moorhead,* January 20, 1980, Section 3, p. c-1.
Otto, Simon, "First 'fish story' was the painful truth," *The Record-Eagle,* Monday, January 31, 1983, p. 27.
Spehn, John, "Good anglers don't walk on thin ice," *Chicago Sun-Times,* November 27, 1985, p. 99.
Unsigned, "Fish Decoy Manufacturer Talks a Cold Language," *St. Cloud Daily Times,* 1984.
Unsigned article, "Old Fish Decoys now Hooking Collectors," *Chicago Tribune,* April 20, 1986, Section 15, p. 20.
Unsigned, "Rising tide of interest in fish decoys," *Chicago Tribune,* January 19, 1986.
Unsigned, "Tradition on the tips of a spear," *Chicago Tribune,* June 25, 1986, Sec. 4, p. 8.
Vogel, Don, "Musician strums fishing tune," *The Oakland Press,* Sunday, July 20, 1986, p. E-6.
Whipple, Catherine, "Nin Akwawa (I Fish with a Spear)," *Lac Du Flambeau News,* February 1994, pp. 12-13.

PRICE GUIDE

The asking prices shown below were compiled from dealers and/or collectors and from auctions. They assume that the decoys were in good condition (i.e., little paint flaking, no fins missing, etc.). Fish decoys are folk art and are often one-of-a-kind items. They are not standardized so they do not permit the type of exact pricing which might exist for antiques such as tin wind-up toys. Even a desirable decoy maker may have had his "bad day" and decorated a decoy in a less than pleasing fashion. Moreover, a decoy may be repaired (or restored) which may further depress its value. I have attempted to provide a range of prices (in U.S. dollars) for the production of each decoy maker, assuming good condition, but allowing for such things as decoy size, pleasing paint patterns, rarity of imitated species (e.g., I have only seen one Willie Peterson sucker decoy), age of the decoy, and the number of a particular maker's decoys available (e.g., contrast the relatively large number of Chester Buss' or Henry Max's decoys with the paucity of "Hair Lip" Thompson's).

Complicating the pricing scene are market fluctuations. Ebbs and flows of prices are partially dependent on market demand for decoys. However, as the primary source for decoys, i.e., the number of decoys still in the hands of spear fishermen and/ or their families, is declining, it is likely that prices will be driven upward over time.

Part I - "Old Time" Decoy Makers

Ernest Aamodt	$500-$1500
Arvid Alho	$100-$150
Lewis Anderson	$100-$125
Thomas J. Annis	$75-$100
William Batters	$150-$350
Gerhart Berens	$350-$450 (decoys before 1960)
Pearl Bethel	$125-$450
Cyril Bethel	$75-$150
Otto Bishop, Sr.	$250-$350 (decoys before 1960)
Cecii Blank	$75-$150
Art Boelter	$200-$350
Merrill Booth	$200-$300
Leo Borash	$50-$100
Slim Brinkman	$100-$350
Chester Buss	$25-$100
Marion Butcher	$750-$1250
Harvey Case	$10-$50
Willis Clark	$75-$150
Jack Cooper	$150-$350
George Dahl	$50-$75
Al Dincau	$50-$75
Otis Doty	$200-$250
Carl "Gus" Dornquast	$30-$50
Milton Ebinger	$40-$60
Charles Engel	$150-$350
Leo Eppel	$100-$200
Nels Fairbanks	$100-$150
Otto Faue	$300-$1500
William Faue	$500-$2000
Frank Filipek	$100-$200
William Flanagan	$200-$300
Peter J. Fuchs	$50-$200
"Tarz" Geiselhart	$25-$50
Bill Green	$350-$450 (decoys before 1960)
Joe Gustin	$75-$450
Arnold Hafstad	$125-$200
Charles"Chuck" Hall	$200-$1500
William Harrison	$100-$350
John Hesjedal	$75-$200
Leroy Howell	$100-$3500
Andrew Huse	$75-$250
Steve Jarnot	$75-$150
R.E. Johnson	$100-$200
Dr. Lester Johnson	$500-$3500
Sheldon Johnson	$75-$350
Albert Jokela	$150-$350
Vince Kampmann	$100-$350
Emil Keck	$75-$150
John Kent	$1200-$1500
Earl Kielmeyer	$25-$50
Russell C. Kolb	$150-$250
Nick Knaus	$75-$175
Clarence Koehler	$150-$200 (sunfish decoys only)
Lambert Kolodji	$100-$200
Toivo "Dave" Lahti	$250-$350
Leonard LaPlante	$100-$200
Gus Larson	$100-$150
Louis Leach	$50-$200 (depending on size and painting)
Fred Max Lexow	$250-$600
Norman Lien	$75-$150
Emil Liers	$300-$400 (frog decoys only)
Harry Lillis	$200-$300
Gust Lind	$50-$125
Emil J. Loe	$50-$150
Charles Lundgren	$350-$500
John McGillis	$50-$150
Henry G. Max	$30-$60
Mike Meholensky	$125-$300
John Melquist	$50-$75
Dave Mertens	$125-$250 (before 1960 only)
Albert Meyer	$50-$75
Leo Miller	$30-$60
Frank Mizera	$100-$350
Nick Moes	$150-$175
E.W. Mooers	$125-$150
Math Mueilner	$30-$60
Melvin Nesset	$100-$125
Ernie Newman	$200-$300
James Newman	$275-$300
Albert Niehaus	$35-$75
Francis Northburg	$50-$100
Northern Pump decoys	$150-$200
John Novak	$100-$200
Reino Nurmi	$100-$150
Harold Nygaard	$125-$200
Oliver Olmschenk	$50-$75
Elmer Oxley	$125-$150
Willie Peterson	$125-$500 (top end for Peterson frogs)
Clemen Place	$125-$200
John Plackner	$125-$250
Henry J. Ramthun	$50-$100
George Randall	$300-$500 (decoys from personal rig)
Myron Roberts	$125-$175
George Robideau	$100-$150
Ray Rosengren	$150-$300
Harry Sandell	$175-$250
Chet Sawyer	$125-$450
Edward Schulk	$100-$150
William Schultz	$150-$175
Art Seguin	$150 $350
Louis and Ed Setka	$350-$500
Silhouette decoys	$75-$150
Harry Simonsen	$75-$150
Charlie Slechta	$250-$1800

	(multiple head copper decoys)
Ted Snell	$125-$200
Hember Steele	$50-$125
Jerome Steele	$125-$250
Leon Stein	$85-$125
Homer Stinar	$100-$150 (before 1960)
Raymond Stotz	$350-$2500
Clifford Stubbs	$250-$400
John Tax	$350-$600
Clarence Thomas	$50-$75
Burt Thompson	$75-$250
Ray Thompson	$250 (working fish) -$8000 (special decoys)
George Tombarge	$200-$300
John Vavra	$250-$300 (copper decoys only)
Ray "Pike" Weis	$200-$400
Carl Woren	$75-$125
Frank Wotring	$150-$300
Joseph Zum	$150-$250
Rudy Zwieg	$200-$350 (before 1960)

Part II- Contemporary Makers

Mel Asserude	$200 and up
Laurence Bethel	$50 and up
Vem Coss	$40 and up
Bruce Dixon	$100 and up
Willard Henson	$100 and up
Burt Hyatt	$40 and up
John Jensen	$200 and up
Laurence Kasper	$20 and up
Richard Larsen	$100 and up
Clifford Larson	$50 and up
Roger Lashua	$75 (decoys) to $300 (dark house)
Joe Leach	$50 and up
Murray Marlette	$50 and up
David Perkins	$50 and up
Larry Peterson	$40 and up
Carl Silver	$250 and up
John and Evelyn Swenson	$50 and up
John Unger	$75 and up

*Some contemporary decoy makers have established a single price for all of their decoys; others have a price range; and some have "special" prices for custom orders. The stated prices above should not be considered a guaranteed price from the maker.

Part III Commercial Fish Decoys

Brown Brothers' Fisheretto	$35-$60
Bru-ell	$35-$75
Cy's Decoys	$35-$50
Fish Bust'r	$50 (in bag)
Herter's	$125 (catalog decoys) - $250 (non-catalog decoys)
Lee's Decoys	$50
Randall "Commercial" decoys	$35-$200
Reigstad Decoys	$35-$50 (with box)
Ripley's"Decoy Minnow"	$100-$150
Sletten	$40-$150 (Water Bug)
Titloe Heights	$50-$75 (in box)
Tonka Baits-Schipper Bros.	$30-$50

Part IV - Spear Makers

Milton Betts	$100-$150
Frank Clark	$200-$250
Fred Drexler	$150-$200
William Elmor	$150-$250
Lloyd Fredericks	$75-$125
Peter Fuchs	$150-$200
Ben George	$150-$200
Louis Gustis	$75-$150
William Hein	$100-$150
Dillo Hinnenkamp	$150-$200
Steve Jarnot	$75-$125
Gideon Kauppi	$75-$100
Henry Louis	$300-$400
John Maki	$75-$200
Michael P. Meyer	$75-$125
Charlie Pimpl	$200-$300
John Plackner	$125-$175
Joseph E. Portner, Jr.	$75-$125
George Randall	$75-$100
Edward and Joe Skiple	$150-$200
Clarence Thomas	$75-$125
Paul Zitzloff	$125-$150

Jigging sticks*	$15-$75
Decoy boxes	$50-$200

*Chester Buss jigging sticks $100-$150

INDEX

N

O

P

R

S

T

U

V

W

Z

ACKNOWLEDGMENTS

Obviously, in any book of this scope, an author will rely on the help of others. Special thanks are extended to the following individuals: John Banholzer, Frank Baron, John Cook, Bruce Dixon, Jerome Erickson, K. David Hirschey, Larry Hochmayr, Ron Holloway, Roger Lashua, Joe Leach, Mike Meyers, Peter Meyers, Bill Nikoley, Rich Oxley, Frank Pasiewicz, Carter Stenberg, Doug Sutton, Tom Swentufske, and Jerry Wintheiser. I also wish to thank the decoy and spear makers, their families, and the historical societies of Minnesota for their help and support. Any errors in this book are the responsibility of the author.

Donald J. Petersen
Loyola University Chicago